OPPOSITION TO SOVIET RULE
IN LITHUANIA
1945-1980

THOMAS REMEIKIS

OPPOSITION TO SOVIET RULE IN LITHUANIA 1945-1980

INSTITUTE OF LITHUANIAN STUDIES PRESS

CHICAGO, ILLINOIS

The Institute of Lithuanian Studies, Inc. gratefully acknowledges the grant from the Lithuanian American Community, Inc., which made this publication possible.

Manufactured in the United States of America.

Institute of Lithuanian Studies Press
2422 W. Marquette Road, Chicago, Ill. 60629 USA

Library of Congress Catalog Card Number 76-028275

To NIJOLE
and GINTA, AUDRIUS, and PETRAS

For any oppressed group the primary task is to overcome the moral authority of the sources of their suffering and to create a politically effective identity... The second aspect of the process is cultural rather than social: the creation of standards of condemnation for explaining and judging current suffering.

Barrington Moore, Jr.,
Injustice: The Social Bases of
Obedience and Revolt (*New York, 1978*), p. 87

ACKNOWLEDGMENTS

This study and collection of documents was a result of a gentle prodding by and material support from the Lithuanian American Community, especially its former President and current Chairman of the Public Affairs Committee Algimantas Gečys.

Access to original sources was made possible by the generosity of many individuals, who shared their private collections of archival materials. In particular, appreciation is due to Bronys Raila, Col. Antanas Šova, Karolis Drunga, Bronius Kviklys, Algirdas Vokietaitis, and Marija Žymantienė for providing copies of valuable materials on the partisan war. Rev. Pranas Garšva and Bronius Kviklys, editors of the Lithuanian daily newspaper *Draugas* in Chicago, and Rev. Casimir Pugevičius, Director of the Lithuanian Information Service in New York, provided copies of most of the latest *samizdat* publications.

Last, but not least, a number of people assisted me in various technical and editorial capacities. A special thanks is due to Aldona Zailskas, Ginta Remeikis, and Algis Lukas.

LITHUANIA

SCALE

0   50   100   150 km

- ◉ National capital
- ● ○ District (raion) centers over and under 100,000 inhabitants respectively
- • ○ Towns and small towns and villages
- ▬▬▬▬ International boundaries between (1) Latvia and Soviet Russia in 1920; (2) Latvia and Lithuania in 1921; (3) Germany and Lithuania in 1928; (4) Poland and the Soviet Union in 1945
- ▭▭▭▭ Boundary according to the 1920 Peace Treaty between Lithuania and Soviet Russia with sections of the 1569 Lithuanian-Polish border and the 1919 frontier of Germany in East Prussia
- ▬ ▬ ▬ Present actual boundaries: (1) between Byelorussia and Lithuania established in 1940 under the Soviet occupation; (2) Potsdam line of 1945 dividing East Prussia between Poland and the Soviet Union; (3) Curzon line between Lithuania and Poland proposed in 1919, established in 1945
- ·············· Former boundary of Germany in East Prussia 1919-1939

The United States of America and certain other countries do not recognize the forcible annexation of Lithuania, Latvia and Estonia by the Soviet Union.

CONTENTS

Part Two

DOCUMENTS ON NATIONAL AND POLITICAL OPPOSITION

Part Three

DOCUMENTS ON RELIGIOUS DISSENT

Epilogue

THE DEMAND FOR FREEDOM AND INDEPENDENCE

APPENDICES

LIST OF TABLES

ILLUSTRATIONS

INTRODUCTION

Among the outstanding characteristics of the Soviet scene in the 1970s is the growing dissent movement, understood here in the broad sense of opposition to the established order, involving not only passive and moral refusal of assent to, but also violent, even revolutionary efforts to change or overthrow the system. A broad struggle for political, national, and religious rights in the Soviet Union has gained attention and sympathy world-wide and a determined attempt to suppress it by the Soviet regime. A stream of materials documenting this struggle is reaching the West. Unfortunately, these materials tend to be selective, and as such distort the scope and nature of dissent in Soviet society by focusing, for example, on the capital of the Soviet state, to the relative neglect of the periphery, where dissent is often more intense and explosive. This volume is in part an attempt to restore the balance and to provide a more systematic coverage of dissent on the periphery of the Soviet state.

The relative openness and publicity of recent opposition also tends to obscure the fact that it was always a part of life under the Soviet regime. The police apparatus and the Gulag Archipelago are lasting reminders of this. The secrecy, in which the Stalinist terror—and later coercion—were shrouded, prevented a full comprehension of the struggle for basic human rights. Opposition and counterterror are coterminous with the history of the Soviet regime, in the creation of which all the principal Soviet leaders, from Lenin to Brezhnev, had a hand. On the one hand, coercion and terror was a matter of survival for the new class; on the other hand, it was a consequence of the efforts to create a different society. Whether one views that society as a communist utopia or simply a new modernized Russian imperial state, the policies of the party regime sought to negate certain basic attributes of human nature as means toward its goal. Yet even after sixty years of rule, the Soviet regime has been unable to eradicate at least three "vestiges of the past"—national identity, theistic world view, and individualism. These basic ethnic, religious, and individualistic attributes of human nature have constituted a major source of opposition to any system which attempted to negate them. Terror is an indispensable instrument in maintaining such an unnatural order, as the experience of the Soviet state so dramatically suggests.

— — —

Dissent has been especially intense in Lithuania. It emanates from the above-mentioned psychological roots of national identity, religious orientation, and individualism—traits that have been strongly developed through the ages of Lithuanian history. A long tradition of statehood, a pervasive Catholicism, and a strong peasant attachment to land and individualism militate today as in the past against the antinational, atheistic, and collectivist policies of the regime.

The opposition to occupation regimes began with the Soviet occupation of Lithuania in June of 1940 and the simultaneous imposition of the Soviet system. Since then, three distinct periods of opposition, each influencing the nature of the subsequent, may be identified: (1) opposition during the first Soviet occupation of Lithuania, 1940—1941, which culminated in a national uprising against the Soviet rule at the start of the German attack on Russia; (2) opposition to the German occupation, 1941—1945; and (3) postwar anti-Soviet opposition. Each period is sufficiently distinct to justify a separate treatment. This volume is devoted exclusively to the postwar period, which in turn can be subdivided into three distinct periods.

In compiling this anthology of documents on dissent, several serious problems had to be dealt with. First of all, the comprehensiveness of this anthology was affected by the availability of authentic materials concerning the opposition. Documentation is uneven in part because the changing circumstances in the Soviet state. In some years dissent was quite overt and well known, in others it was extremely subtle and indirect. Furthermore, gaps in the knowledge of any closed society are inevitable. Only access to KGB files could reveal the full story of opposition, an unlikely possibility in the foreseeable future. Consequently, to supply at least some of the missing pieces a number of documents from official Soviet sources and testimony of emigrés were included in this collection. Similarly, the introductory study of dissent is intended not only to provide a historical and theoretical context for the various items of this anthology, but also to fill in some of the lacunae of documentation.

Fairly well documented by both Soviet and non-Soviet sources is the partisan war, which lasted from 1945 to approximately the death of Stalin. Soviet journalists have published a number of monographs dealing directly or indirectly with what is ideologically called "bandits" or "class war" (these publications are cited throughout this volume). Perhaps the most important Soviet source on the partisan struggle is a series of "documentaries" under the general title "Faktai kaltina" (Facts Accuse), consisting mostly of transcripts of police interrogations. Despite their obvious ideological bias, these Soviet sources are valuable because they contain factual data not available elsewhere.

The non-Soviet sources of the partisan war so far have not been published extensively. Most of the materials are in the private collections of individuals living in the West, who are either avid collectors or were involved in the postwar Lithuanian resistance movement. These private collections include materials brought out of Lithuania by special partisan couriers or through other clandestine channels and extensive materials resulting from emigré political activity. Access to a number of such private holdings has contributed immensely to a more objective documentation of the partisan struggle.

Documents about religious dissent during the immediate postwar years are extremely scanty and are not adequately represented in this volume. Nevertheless, enough factual data is available to enable a fairly accurate reconstruction of church and state relations during this violent period.

Very little direct testimony on national and religious dissent is available for the period between Stalin's death and the invasion of Czechoslovakia. Dissent was relatively subdued and not productive of dramatic events or underground publications. National values were increasingly safeguarded and advanced through the established institutions and cultural activity in an extraordinarily subtle manner which can be described and analyzed in spite of the fact that very few documents are available.

In the 1970s active opposition surfaced again and is most extensively documented by samizdat publications. Consequently, the bulk of the materials in this volume deals with the latest dissent and is derived mainly from samizdat periodicals. Unfortunately, many known samizdat publications are not available, and those that have reached the West are mostly associated with the religious rights movement. Consequently, the available sources over-emphasize the Catholic national and religious dissent and create a somewhat distorted picture of the opposition movement.

A second problem in dealing with underground materials involves their authenticity. It is well known that the KGB itself on occasion has created "underground" organizations and "samizdat" publications as a means of flushing out "anti-Soviet" elements and disorientation of these individuals. The authenticity of materials from the underground cannot be easily confirmed, and they should be treated with a modicum of skepticism. For most documents of this anthology a high degree of reliability can be established through the sources of the documents, secondary or indirect references to them, occasionally through direct confirmation of their authenticity, and by the nature of the document itself. Those documents for which a substantial question of reliability remains are so identified in source references.

A third problem involves determining the significance of the various dissent materials. For many documents neither the authorship nor the extent of their dissemination is known. Circulation of *samizdat* publications is extremely limited and in many cases reports about them by Western radio are probably a partial substitute for mass circulation. There is no way of directly and systematically checking the extent to which *samizdat* publications express the views of the masses or particular strata of the population. Consequently, the determination of their significance remains a highly speculative and subjective task.

Dissent in Lithuania, as elsewhere in the Soviet Union, involves the gamut of human concerns—political, economic, social, and religious. The materials in this volume in one sense distort the nature and scope of dissent by their thematic limitations. In part because national and religious dissent is the most intense and dramatic in the Lithuanian context, in part because most of the available materials deal with nationalism and religion, this volume is organized around those two categories of dissent. However, there is another, perhaps more important, reason for focusing on national and religious dissent in the same anthology. Religious dissent in Lithuania cannot be strictly separated from national dissent. The Catholic Church is a *national* as well as religious institution, and an attack on it is also an attack on national values. It is, therefore, not unusual that even those who consider themselves nonreligious support the Catholic struggle for rights, motivated by national interests. In the Lithuanian context, the struggle for religious rights is also a struggle for national rights.

— — —

The significance of opposition as a factor in the evolution of the Soviet system cannot be precisely evaluated. Only in historical perspective will we be able to judge its relevance with some certainty. For the present, dissent in the Soviet Union, and especially in Lithuania, is suggestive of profound repressed grievances involving basic issues of national and political rights, which could erupt into a full-fledged revolution in a crisis situation. This possibility was demonstrated time and again in the Eastern European space (the Hungarian, Czech, German, and Polish revolts), as well as in Lithuania in 1972, when a minor regime miscalculation brought thousands into the streets demanding freedom and independence for Lithuania. While the balance of forces so far has favored the party regime, recent events underscore the fact that the Soviet system still largely rests on force rather than on legitimacy. The materials of this volume constitute a modest testimony of the existing contradictions between the Soviet regime and the people.

PART ONE

ANALYTICAL AND HISTORICAL PERSPECTIVES

Chapter I

ANALYTICAL PERSPECTIVES

1. ON OPPOSITION

The popular term "dissent" is used here in the broad sense of opposition to a regime, although some scholars restrict it to "within-system" or reformist forms of opposition. Rudolf L. Tökés, for example, distinguishes between "within-system" and "system-rejective" opposition: "Reformist change implies attempts at influencing or manipulating political power, and revolutionary change means its forcible acquisition and exclusive possession. Political activity leading to change of the system does, therefore, entail an unconditional commitment to overthrowing a political regime and establishing a new one in its stead."[1] Tökés prefers to view dissent in terms of this basic dichotomy, restricting it essentially to the reformist position.

While such a dichotomized conception of opposition may be useful in analyzing certain political regimes, especially pluralistic ones, it is not readily applicable to hegemonial regimes. In a hegemonial or even a near-hegemonial regime, interest articulation is so restricted that even "reformist" opposition may be essentially subversive. For example, Sakharov's proposals for reforms are revolutionary in terms of the likely consequences to party dictatorship. Thus, in the case of the Soviet Union, with a hegemonial regime, very little can be considered within-system dissent; this "reformist" dissent is mostly restricted to the power struggle at the apex of the ruling elite, or to what Barghoorn calls factional opposition.[2] For the purposes of analysis of dissent in Lithuania, we shall use the continuum preferred by Dahl,

---

1. Rudolf Tökés, ed., **Dissent in the USSR: Politics, Ideology, and People** (Baltimore, 1975), introduction by the editor, p. 18.
2. Frederick C. Barghoorn, "Factional, Sectoral, and Subversive Opposition in Soviet Politics", in Robert A. Dahl, ed., **Regimes and Opposition** (New Haven, 1973), pp. 27—87.

which ranges from within-system reforms to system-rejective revolutionary efforts.[3] (Table 1 classifies dissent in Lithuania along these lines.) The unique feature of Lithuanian dissent as compared to that of the Moscow intelligentsia is that the former is largely system-rejective and has considerable mass support.

Opposition to an essentially hegemonial regime obviously varies in form, intensity, and sources of dissent. There is a strong tendency in scholarly literature to ascribe dissent in contemporary Soviet society largely to modernization. One such interpretation emphasizes the mode of integration of an increasingly complex society. Modernization, according to this theory, differentiates society into numerous interest groups that in the Soviet Union are coordinated through command by the Party apparatus (rather than by contract with the people). This denies autonomy to the different interest groups. While it is possible for associational interests to be represented in the institutional party, there are limitations (for example, the rule against factional activity) and, inevitably, interests begin to be articulated outside the established institutional order.[4]

Yet essential societal changes brought about by modernization do not adequately explain dissent in the Soviet Union. Dissent in the broad sense used here has always been a prominent part of Soviet life. Dissent by the Lithuanian Catholic clergy and nationalists did not begin only in the 1970s. It has always been there. Priests and believers were tried and convicted, thousands opposed the regime from the first day of its imposition, but little was heard of this dissent. Only now are we beginning to realize the scope of the repression, which was preventive, as well as punitive, against potential and actual dissidents. Aleksander Solzhenitsyn's *Gulag Archipelago* and Roy Medvedev's *Let History Judge* are just two of many first-hand accounts of the scope of the opposition to the Soviet regime and its reaction to the dissent.

While modernization creates socioeconomic rifts in society, this is not the only source of conflict. Religious, ethnic, tribal, and linguistic distinctions, often cutting across socioeconomic lines,

---

3. See Dahl's introduction and the studies of Barghoorn and Skilling in **Regimes and Opposition, op. cit.,** for development of perspectives used here.

4. For one such perspective, see Walter D. Connor, "Differentiation, Integration, and Political Dissent in the USSR", in Tökés, **op. cit.,** pp. 139-157.

TABLE 1. THE NATURE OF OPPOSITION IN THE 1970s

COMPONENTS OF OPPOSITION	Within-system "LOYAL OPPOSITION"		System-rejective "SUBVERSION"	
PREDOMINANT TACTIC	Institutional interest articulation	Civil disobedience Cultural assertiveness	Passive opposition—ideological struggle	Revolutionary course, overthrow of regime
REPRESENTATIVE PUBLICATION	OFFICIAL PRESS (to some extent)*	LKB Kronika	Aušra Alma Mater Perspektyvos	Partisan press (up to 1952) Laisvės Šauklys (?) Bulletins of the National People's Front
REPRESENTATIVE STRUCTURES	Certain official organs of gov't and public organizations*	Helsinki monitors Catholic Committee Ethnographic clubs	Ad hoc groups, informal circles (literary, historical, gen. discussion)	Partisan units (up to 1952) National People's Front Baltic Committee Freedom League Spontaneous groups (demonstrations, riots)
PRINCIPAL POLICY OUTPUTS	Republic oriented policies in economic, cultural, political, cadre, educational spheres. Lobbying in the Kremlin.	Peaceful demonstrations of protest. Reports of violations of law by regime. Disobedience to laws considered unjust. Legal expression of grievances	Private discussions of political and cultural issues. Production and dissemination of samizdat Fundamental critique of the system Opinion formation Maintenance of national consciousness	Armed struggle (up to 1952). Clandestine action groups. Violent mass demonstrations. Self immolations.
REPRESENTATIVE PARTICIPANTS, GROUPS	Nationalist party, economic, cultural intelligentsia*	Rev. Zdebskis Rev. Garuckas Tomas Venclova	Editors, publishers of samizdat Student circles	Leaders of clandestine organizations* Partisans (up to 1952)

* Not specified for obvious reasons

have been more important sources of conflict in many societies. For this reason Marxist economic determinism fails to explain politics for many societies—it ignores the noneconomic sources of conflict, which are not restricted to the preindustrial society; in fact, they are present in both the industrial and even in the postindustrial state.

A multiplicity of interests exists in any society, although in a modern industrial society the configuration of conflict is vastly more complex than in an agrarian or developing one. The ability to at least partially satisfy the predominant interests in a society is obviously an important determinant of the viability of any regime. A hegemonial regime that limits interest articulation and allocates scarce values according to its own restrictive criteria can survive by implementing widely distributive policies, by imposing repression, or by a combination of both approaches. Dissent in a hegemonial system can be viewed as a function of the degree of societal dissatisfactions and the level of repression. Dissent may be intense as a result of a combined extreme deprivation and repression, or as a result of low deprivation and low repression. In any case, dissent in the hegemonial system tends to be system-rejective. The appearance of a within-system dissent in the Soviet Union may simply indicate a modification of the hegemonial regime, which is in part a result of modernization and in part may be an outcome of the power struggle after Stalin. In polyarchical systems a significant number of interests are taken into account in the allocation of material and nonmaterial values, the legitimacy of interest articulation is recognized, and therefore, the opposition that tends to predominate in such regimes is within-system.

The concept of opposition involves a sense of relative deprivation. Only when an individual feels that he has been unjustly deprived of something—a symbolic, ideological, or material value—is he likely to take some action to change the system partly or entirely. For various reasons in Soviet society there are increasing manifestations of a sense of relative deprivation. Since a regime is immune from the reactions of its society, a major problem of methodology is measuring the power that the people hold.[5] While the Soviet regime has so far been able to preserve the essentials of its rule through a combination of repression and value allocation, its ability to wipe out potential and actual challenges to the monopoly of power has become problematical. On the one hand, there are limits to the

---

5. For a preliminary consideration of this question, see the article by Jerry F. Hough, "The Soviet Experience and the Measurement of Power", *Journal of Politics*, Vol. 37, No. 3 (August, 1975), pp. 685-710.

use of instruments of coercion, both for political and economic reasons. Coercion is counterproductive in a complex industrial economy and is dangerous even to the ruling elite. On the other hand, dissatifaction among the nationalities, religious denominations, and the population at large (with respect to democratic or economic values) cannot be simply resolved without at the same time modifying the political role of the party-technocratic elite and the structure of the state. Thus, while we are unable to measure the power of the people with any accuracy, it is possible to say that the population has more voice today than ever before. The unilateral policy outputs of the Soviet regime are increasingly challenged by various sectors of society. The balance of power so far has remained with the ruling elite, but its long-term ability to overcome the challenges has become at least problematical.

2. NATIONAL CONSCIOUSNESS AND NATIONALISM

Opposition to the Soviet regime in Lithuania stems mainly from national and religious collectivities. The focus of this work is on nationalism, since religious dissent, though having autonomous religious ends, is very closely intertwined with the national movement.

For the purposes of this study, the following definition of nationalism will be used: "Nationalism consists of organizationally heightened and articulated group demands directed toward securing control of the distributive system in society."[6] Nationalism emerges as a consequence of a degree of social mobilization accompanied by a widely held perception that the allocation of scarce values in a society, especially those relevant to the ethnic group, is in some way unjust, which leads to attempts to acquire either a greater or total control over policy-making institutions. Such a concept of nationalism involves two interrelated elements: national consciousness or identity and a sense of relative deprivation. Without national consciousness there can be no demands for control over governmental institutions. On the other hand, even with national consciousness, nationalism does not automatically follow.

---

6. Chong-Do Hah and Jeffrey Martin, "Toward a Synthesis of Conflict and Integration Theories of Nationalism", **World Politics**, Vol. 27, No. 3. (April, 1975), p. 362.

NATIONAL IDENTITY

A number of objective differences distinguish one nation from another—language, racial characteristics, religion, and culture. But a nation cannot be said to exist until its members become aware of these distinctive characteristics. This requires a degree of social mobilization and communication among the members of an ethnic group. A nation is really a collective consciousness consisting of symbols, memories of historical experiences, and shared values.[7] "National awakening" refers to the emergence of such a consciousness, usually as a result of social mobilization and communication, appearance of a leadership group, and/or a relationship with "outsiders."

National consciousness in Lithuania, despite Lithuania's long history of statehood, began to emerge at the end of the eighteenth century, but its development was arrested by the disintegration of the Lithuanian-Polish Commonwealth and the imposition of czarist rule. Only in the last three decades of the nineteenth century did a truly national intelligentsia emerge, beginning to articulate the interests of Lithuanians as Lithuanians. The first Lithuanian-language newspaper, *Aušra* (The Dawn), was published only in 1883. But by 1905 the national movement had become politically differentiated, proposing a widely accepted program for Lithuania's autonomy or independence. The course of separation from the Russian empire was definitely set at the first major gathering of representatives of the Lithuanian nation. Gathering in December of 1905, it became known as the Great Vilnius Assembly. When the opportunity for independence materialized in the course of World War I, only the extreme left had any doubts about its desirability. Two decades of independence with great progress in all spheres of life could not help but strengthen national consciousness and the conviction that national independence is desirable.[8] National

---

7. This is Durkheim's formulation. For an elaboration and application of the concept of conscience collective to Scottish nationalism, see Michael Hechter, **Internal Colonialism: The Celtic Fringe in British National Development 1536—1966** (Berkeley, 1975), particularly the Introduction.

8. The national movement and the establishment of the Lithuanian state has been extensively studied by Lithuanian historians. The latest attempt at synthesis is that of Pranas Čepėnas, **Naujųjų laikų Lietuvos istorija** (History of Modern Lithuania) (Chicago, 1977), Vol. 1. Competent English language studies of the national movement are

identity and nationalism in the 1970s are in large measure sustained by developments during these two decades of national independence.

However, the emergence of a national identity is not necessarily inconsistent with a multinational state. A nation could be satisfied with a minimal cultural autonomy in a multinational framework. Nationalist demands may range from minor adjustments in status to complete national self-determination and independence. In the case of Lithuania, as we have seen, demands for at least national autonomy emerged very rapidly with the emergence of national consciousness. While social, economic, and political factors were involved, the early appearance of Lithuanian nationalism was largely the result of national consciousness. The Rousseauean idea of popular sovereignty and its transformation by romanticism led legitimacy to be associated with national will. According to this ideology, a nation had an inherent right to self-determination.[9] When one adds the long tradition of Lithuanian statehood to the ideology of self-government of nations, it is easy to understand why Lithuanian nationalism was almost coextensive with the emergence of national consciousness. Thus, while national consciousness need not lead to nationalism, it is a prerequisite, and under certain circumstances it is itself a cause of nationalism. When the contemporary concept of national self-determination, enshrined even in international law as a fundamental human right, combines with national identity, it becomes transformed into a revolutionary force.

In the context of the Soviet state, the solution of what is called the nationality question is essentially based on the policy of eradication of national identity. National identity is tolerated only

---

lacking. However, for a good summary the reader is directed to the work of Alfred Erich Senn, **The Emergence of Modern Lithuania** (New York, 1959), ch. I. The rest of Senn's book is devoted to the study of the establishment of the Lithuanian state. A very useful theoretical and empirical study of the national movement in Lithuania is that of Miroslav Hroch, **Die Vorkämpfer der Nationalen Bevegung bei den Kleinen Volker Europas** (Universita Karlova-Praha, 1968), which includes a section on the Lithuanian intelligentsia in the national movement.

9. A historical perspective on the development of the idea of self-determination is presented by Walker Connor, "The Politics of Ethnonationalism", **Journal of International Affairs**, Vol. 27, No. 1 (1973), pp. 1—21.

as a tactical policy. The long-term merger of nationalities and transformation of their loyalties remains the goal of Soviet policy. Basically. this policy amounts to russification of the non-Russian nationalities. Surprisingly, however, Soviet nationality policy seems to have reenforced national identity rather than eroded it.

Why has this occurred? In discussing the policy of ultimate assimilation of the nations under the conditions of Communism, it is useful to distinguish between "russianization" and "russification." Russianization refers to the processes of diffusion of Russian culture among the nationalities of the Soviet Union, while russification refers to the "process whereby non-Russians are transformed objectively and psychologically into Russians."[10] The distinction is necessary because the diffusion of Rusian language does not thereby signify the decline of non-Russian cultures and languages and the change in national identity. Even linguistic assimilation may not eliminate distinct ethnic consciousness.[11] Thus, although russianization may be necessary for change in the national identity, such change does not necessarily follow. At the same time it follows as a corollary that the vitality of non-Russian culture, its capacity to resist the intrusion of alien elements, can be correlated with the persistence of ethnic identity.

National identity is a psychological phenomenon that can be defined and measured through direct socio-psychological testing. Unfortunately, no such direct study of national identity in the Soviet Union is possible. We have to rely on indirect objective indicators, such as the census data on language, ethnic composition of the population, ethnic intermarriage, migration patterns, etc. In addition, the absence of nationalism does not indicate the erosion of national identity, for loyalty to the system is quite compatible with national consciousness. On the other hand, intense nationalistic manifestation is an indicator of national consciousness. Let us consider the objective indicators of national identity (including both russianization and russification measures) to see what changes have recently occurred in Lithuania, as this is reflected in Table 2.

---

10. This distinction is that of Vernon V. Aspaturian, "The Non-Russian Nationalities", in Allen Kassof, ed., **Prospects for Soviet Society** (New York, 1968), pp. 159-160.

11. The Basques of Spain is one of numerous examples of this. See Milton M. da Silva, "Modernization and Ethnic Conflict: The Case of the Basques", **Comparative Politics,** Vol. 7, No. 2 (January, 1975), pp. 227-251.

Table 2: Selected Objective Indicators
of National Identity

Indicator	Year/Year
1. Ethnic composition of republic population	1959/1970
a. % of population Lithuanians	79/80
b. % of urban population Lithuanians	69/73
c. % of rural population Lithuanians	86/87
d. % of Lithuanians living in the republic	92/94
2. Population in-migration	
a. In-migration as % of total population increase, 1959—70 and 1970—79	12/24
3. Language of Lithuanians in the republic	1959/1970
a. % consider Lithuanian as native	99/99
b. % fluent in Russian	1970 34
c. % of all Lithuanians consider Lithuanian as native language	98/98
4. Language in schools	1960/1975
a % of primary and secondary students attending Lithuanian language schools	84/85
5. Publications in the Lithuanian language	1960/1977
a. % of books published	80/78
b. % of copies of books	82/85
c. % of periodicals	85/79
d. % of copies of periodicals	91/96
6. Ethnic intermarriage	1970
a. % of individual Lithuanians intermarrying	7
b. % of mixed couples	13

Sources: For indicators #1 and #3—Itogi vsesoyuznoi perepisi naseleniya 1959 goda: Litovskaya SSR (Vilnius, 1973); Itogi vsesoyusnoi perepisi naseleniya 1970 goda (Moskva, 1973-1974, Vols. 4 and 7. For indicator # 2—Soviet census data and preliminary results of the 1979 census, Tiesa, April 28, 1979. For indicators # 4 and # 5—the statistical annual Lietuvos TSR ekonomika ir kultūra 1977 metais (Vilnius, 1978). For indicator # 6—Wesley A. Fisher, "Ethnic Consciousness and Intermarriage: Correlates of Endogamy Among the Major Soviet Nationalities", Soviet Studies, Vol. 29, No. 3 (July, 1977), p. 398.

Relative ethnic homogeneity is an important variable since it influences the degree of internationalization of the cultural and social life of a republic and, consequently, also affects national identity. The census data for 1959 and 1970 indicate some gains for Lithuanians, their proportion increasing from 79.3% to 80.1%. This was a result of several factors: a) the birth rate among Lithuanians is slightly higher than among the other nationalities in the republic; b) there evidently is some assimilation of non-Lithuanians, particularly the Poles; c) the children of ethnically mixed families tend to opt for the nationality of the republic; d) the immigration of other nationals was relatively very small. As the experience of Latvians and Estonians indicates, immigration can quickly change ethnic balance in the republic. In the case of Lithuania, immigration so far has been limited despite the attraction of a high standard of living. Among the reasons for this are the greater availability of labor reserves, the slowing pace of industrialization, and tight labor markets in the neighboring republics. Republic planners, in prospective long-range development plans, have called for slower development and optimal utilization of republic resources. Although a labor shortage is already felt in some branches of the Lithuanian economy, there appears to be no immediate economic pressure for a massive influx of workers from other republics. For the time being, even with falling birth rates, the favorable national demography is likely to persist unless a ruthless political upheaval brings about a deliberate political colonization.

Native language is considered one of the best indicators of national identity by both Western and Soviet scholars. In the case of Lithuania, linguistic assimilation has been negligible; in fact, the percentage of Lithuanians not considering Lithuanian as the mother tongue has slightly declined—from 0.8% in 1959 to 0.5% in 1970. Linguistic assimilation, however, is pronounced among Lithuanians living outside of Lithuania, among whom the percentage considering Lithuanian as their mother tongue has been dropping from about 70% in 1959 to about 60% in 1970. This suggests that linguistic assimilation rates are in part determined by the degree of ethnic intermixture. Within the republic, the native language is holding more than its own because of the nationally homogeneous population and schooling in the native language.

Bilingualism is a different matter. There is no question that it is spreading rapidly, especially among the younger generation. For example, we find that in the 20—39 age category, over 60%

of all Lithuanians in the Soviet Union are fluent in Russian. This means that the conditions for the diffusion of Russian culture and the justification of the use of Russian in official functions are in the making. How this will affect national identity and the functionality of the native language remains to be seen.

The possible acculturation impact of bilingualism is undoubtedly being counteracted to some extent by schooling in the native language. A possibly disproportionate number of students are attending basic schools with Lithuanian language and, moreover, the proceedings in higher schools are also conducted mostly in Lithuanian. In addition, Lithuania has an eleven-year secondary education, the additional year being helpful not only for learning Russian but also for mastering the native subjects as well.

Data are limited to published materials concerning the use of native language in mass communications. Here the "national form" dominates disproportionately if we look at the percentage of copies (books and periodicals) printed in Lithuanian. It is apparent that the Lithuanian language remains functional not only in the domestic but also in the scientific and technological spheres.

The social distance between nationalities in Lithuania remains unbridged, as can be judged from the very limited statistics on ethnic intermarriage. There is no intensive social interaction between members of different nationalities except in formal occupational situations. For the most part, different national groups have their own separate cultural life, press, and involvement in social affairs.

It seems reasonable to conclude that to the extent that the cited objective indicators reflect national consciousness, the national identity of the Lithuanian people has not been affected in any significant way. At the same time, a good deal of acculturation, specifically russianization, is going on, the long-term impact of which on the vitality of national identity cannot be measured.

One can draw similar conclusions in regard to most of the major nationalities of the USSR. An analysis of linguistic assimilation has led one scholar to conclude that

> despite enormous social, economic, and cultural change, distinctive ethnic identities are not about to be eliminated in the Soviet Union... For now, it should be noted that the preservation of ethnic consciousness need not signify a lack of loyalty to the Soviet regime; much less support for nationalist activities.... But the maintenance of national

identities does provide an enduring potential focus of
nationalist activity, especially because of the strong
emotional content of ethnic symbols.[12]

The evidence is quite substantial that national consciousness,
at least among the major nationalities of the Soviet Union, has
not been significantly transformed, negating the efficacy of the
social theory behind the Soviet nationality policy. Marxism views
the nation as an exclusively historical phenomenon that is a
function of economic development. The Marxist view of history
suggests that smaller ethnic groups progressively integrate into
larger ones. This process allegedly continues under modern
conditions, leading to the development of larger national
communities until, under the conditions of Communism, the
nations will merge to form one socialist nation of the world.
Furthermore, the theory goes on, there is no guarantee that
historical laws will be realized spontaneously. The Leninist
version of Marxism thus required deliberate intervention by the
state to promote this historically inevitable merging of nations.
The Party's nationality policy consists of a number of specific
programs (e.g., conglomeration of ethnic groups, linguistic
acculturation, ideological unity, proscription of nationalism, etc.)
designed to achieve the heralded merger of nations. It has been
stated that a new historical entity, "the Soviet people," has
emerged, which is characterized by a common socioeconomic
structure, common language of communication (Russian), and
common ideology (Marxism-Leninism).[13]

The Marxist concept of nation, as proceeding from the
modernization process, is similar to Western theories. As society
modernizes, status groups are eroded and associational groups
emerge as the primary claimants in the political arena. Furthermore, modernization, particularly because of the improved social
communication that results from it, leads to cultural diffusion.
Thus, both the social structure diffusion model and the cultural

---

12. Brian Silver, "Social Mobilization and Russification of Soviet
Nationalities", **The American Political Science Review,** Vol. 68, No. 1
(January, 1974), p. 66.

13. For a sampling of this theory, see G. Zimanas, **Per suklestėjimą į
vienybę** (Toward Unity Through Development) (Vilnius, 1968); Y.
Modrzhinskaia, **The Problem of the Nation** (Moscow, n.d.); the 1961
Program of the CPSU. See also the summary of this theory in Thomas
Remeikis "The Evolving Status of Nationalities in the Soviet Union",
Canadian Slavic Studies, Vol. 1, No. 3 (Fall, 1967), pp. 404—423.

diffusion model predict the gradual weakening and elimination of separate ethnic identities.[14]

Both the Western and the Marxist-Leninist versions of the modernization model have failed to predict the survivability of status groups. In part, modernization reenforces status (ethnic) solidarity through the communication process (i. e., knowledge of national history and schooling in the native language) or through cultural diffusion (i.e., familiarity also breeds contempt—the hate of colonists). Michael Hechter attempts to explain the persistence of Scottish identity and nationalism by what he calls "internal colonial model." This is also applicable to the Soviet state. The likelihood of political integration of a multinational state, according to Hechter, varies as follows:

> 1. The greater the economic inequalities between collectivities, the greater the probability that the less advantaged collectivity will be status-solidarity and, hence, will resist political integration.
>
> 2. The greater the frequency of intra-collectivity communication, the greater the status solidarity of the peripheral collectivity.
>
> 3. The greater the intergroup differences of culture, particularly insofar as identifiability is concerned, the greater the probability that the culturally distinct peripheral collectivity will be status-solidary. Identifiable cultural differences include language (accent), distinctive religious practices, and life-style.[15]

In Hechter's theory, then, ethnic identity is maintained by the relations among the ethnic collectivities and by a colonial relationship, by processes of communication and interaction within a particular nationality, and by the cultural distinctiveness of a particular national group from other. All of these factors are obviously at work withing the Soviet state and go a long way to account for the fact that ethnic identity has not been significantly eroded among the major nationalities despite the modernization of society and regime efforts at acculturation and assimilation.

RELATIVE DEPRIVATION

A sense of relative deprivation consists of subjective feelings and cognitions that an individual has about his status and life chances. Ted Gurr defines it "as perceived discrepancy between

---

14. For a critical evaluation of Western theories of ethnic change, see Hechter, **op. cit.**, ch. 2.

15. Hechter, **op. cit.**, p. 43.

value expectations and value capabilities."[16] A sense of relative deprivation can be said   to exist when what an individual considers his just desert is not or cannot be met by the polity. It applies to both material and non-material values. Gurr classifies these values into three categories: (1) welfare values, which include economic goods, (2) power values, which pertain to the allocation of scarce values in society (such as participation in decision-making), (3) interpersonal values, such as status.

The sense of relative deprivation may be very generalized, leading to the rejection of the entire political arrangement, or quite specific, producing only efforts to reform the political system. "Consequently, one can infer a likely increase in RD [relative deprivation] as a result of social process and patterns systematically associated either with rising expectations or declining capabilities."[17] Gurr derives three distinct models of relative deprivation: (1) decremental deprivation, when value capabilities decline in relation to value expectations, which remain stable, (2) aspirational deprivation, when value expectations rise in relation to value capabilities, which remain constant, and (3) progressive deprivation, when there is an upward curve of value expectations but a stabilization or decline in value capabilities after a steady improvement (J-curve).

Ted Gurr's models of relative deprivation are useful in explaining and classifying dissent in the Soviet Union, including nationalism. We have defined nationalism as an ethnic group's effort to control in part or entirely the distributive system of society. Its manifestation is a result of a perceived injustice in allocation of values relevant to the ethnic group. Nationalism

---

16. Ted Robert Gurr, **Why Men Rebel** (Princeton, 1970), p. 37. Among the earliest formulations of this theory of political violence is that of James C. Davis, "Toward a Theory of Revolution", **American Sociological Review,** Vol. 27, No. 1 (February, 1962), pp. 5-19. Gurr's work represents the most ambitious formulation of the theory and is relied on in this work. The concept of relative deprivation has been applied to explain nationalism by a number of scholars, including Hechter, **op. cit.** (for Scottish nationalism); Gary K. Bertsch, "The Revival of Nationalism", **Problems of Communism,** November-December, 1973, pp. 1-15, (nationalism among the nationalities in Yugoslavia). A systematic application of the theory to dissent and nationalist opposition in the Soviet Union is still lacking, in part because the empirical data to test the theory are deficient, particularly in respect to the attitudinal data on popular expectations.

17. Gurr, **op. cit.,** p. 92.

thus involves political values, although it may be produced by a sense of relative deprivation of any or all the categories of values specified by Gurr. Thus, economic dissatisfaction may lead to nationalistic demands if that dissatisfaction is connected with the absence of self-determination for an ethnic group. In other words, it is easy to "blame the Russians" for any inadequacy.

It must be emphasized, however, that sense of relative deprivation does not automatically lead to assertive behavior such as nationalism. Many factors and circumstances affect the chances of aggressive behavior as a result of relative deprivation. As Gurr has expressed it,

> deprivation-induced discontent is a general spur to action. Psychological theory and group conflict theory both suggest that the greater the intensity of discontent, the more likely is violence. The specificity of this impulse to action is determined by man's beliefs about the sources of deprivation, and about the normative and utilitarian justifiability of violent action directed at the agents responsible for it.[18]

Dissent in any society, including a democratic one, involves risks and costs, ranging from danger to life and liberty to subtle social ostracism. The manifestations of a sense of relative deprivation, therefore, are only partially explained by the presence of it. The calculation of costs inevitably enters into considerations of dissident behavior, as do estimates of the efficacy of such behavior in changing the allocation of values. However, an individual with an extreme sense of alienation or ideological commitment may ignore both the cost and the efficacy considerations in dissent. The behavior of masses and elites may depend on the availability or nonavailability of legitimate arrangements for redress of grievances, the perceived effectiveness of using the established institutions, and the perceived capability of the regime to oppose demands (this also includes the belief about the extent of support for a particular policy among the people internally or internationally).[19] Finally, even a severe deprivation may be tolerated if it is perceived as being just or

---

18. **Ibid,** p. 13.

19. One empirical consideration of the conditions under which relative deprivation may lead to action is that of Edward N. Miller, "Relative Deprivation and Aggressive Political Behavior", a paper delivered at the 1975 annual meeting of the American Political Science Association, San Francisco, 1975.

beyond. anyone's control.[20] Thus a sense of relative deprivation
with respect to national values may or may not lead to overt or
covert nationalistic behavior and could be expressed in a variety
of actions and intensity.

Many factors affect value expectations and value capabilities.
One of the tasks in explaining relative deprivation is to
enumerate and evaluate the relative significance of a range of
factors accounting for a particular level of value expectations,
value capabilities, or both.

Allworth and his students basically employ the concept of
relative deprivation in attempting to explain nationalistic
behavior among Soviet nationalities.[21] He describes nationality
behavior in terms of satisfaction/dissatisfaction balance: dissatisfaction with respect to national identity values triggers a
number of defensive or offensive reactions. Allworth explains
this as follows:

> Dissatisfaction among modern nationalities does not
> arise merely because of their ethnic awareness. Until a
> background of corporate disability or discrimination has been
> well established and fastened upon that ethnic identity,
> simple consciousness of group identity alone should not
> provoke nationality dissatisfaction.[22]

Allworth focuses on the defensive reactions rather than on
sources of dissatisfaction, which obviously vary among the
various nationalities and in time. Allworth enumerates three
categories of factors that may be functional or dysfunctional for
the maintenance of group identity: identifying and physical
factors (i.e., language, race, religion), relativity factors (i.e.,
dependence/autonomy of the ethnic group), and regulatory
factors (i.e., policies of the regime). When dissatisfaction with the
status arises with respect to any of the factors, the nationality
group shifts deliberately or even spontaneously to other identity
support factors to counteract the perceived threat. Thus, for

---

20. For a lucid consideration why people are capable of accepting
even the most severe injustice (including death), see Barrington Moore,
Jr., **Injustice: The Social Bases of Obedience and Revolt** (White Plains,
N.Y., 1978).

21. Edward Allworth, ed., **Nationality Group Survival in Multi-
Ethnic States: Shifting Support Patterns in the Soviet Baltic Region**
(New York, 1977).

22. **Ibid.**, pp. 2-3.

example, the policies of the regime of linguistic acculturation may lead to intensified efforts to develop the native language.

Allworth considers that a slight dissatisfaction is most functional for the survival of the nationality:

> With its false sense of security, prolonged satisfaction nearly always undermines a group's set of supports or creates gaps among them.... Extreme dissatisfaction converts itself into self-destructive rage or immobilizing apathy... A point on the satisfaction/dissatisfaction scale close to the exact balance, but slightly on the side of dissatisfaction, offers reasonable stability, with moderate but continuing change consistent with ordinary times.[23]

For some reason Allworth avoids the term nationalism, although his defensive reactions are clearly within the accepted definition of nationalism. Efforts to preserve nationality identity may not directly involve an effort to control the distributive system of society, but they certainly do in the long run and may merely be a tactic to preserve group identity until circumstances permit overt assertions of political goals. Allworth seems to counsel against system-rejective (revolutionary) nationalism in favor of manipulating institutions and political conditions of society to maintain ethnic identity.

Nationalities react to perceived threats to their identity in a covert and overt manner, although in different ways, in differing intensity, and varying scope (the solidarity of an ethnic group may be a factor affecting the intensity and direction of its defensive or even offensive reactions). What are the specific conditions that lead to dissatisfaction, or a sense of relative deprivation? Although in the cited passage Allworth specifies "corporate disability or discrimination," the objective factors and their perception leading to a sense of discrimination are not systematically elucidated.

The idea of internal colonialism, developed by Hechter, focuses on the sources of dissatisfaction. Part of the internal colonial relationship is what Hechter calls "cultural division of labor"—a system of stratification based on ethnic groups rather than social class and on economic inequality.[24] The major sources of a sense of relative deprivation in the Soviet Union with respect to nationality-relevant values can be specified from this perspective of internal colonialism. First, there is a clearly

---

23. **Ibid.**, p. 9.

24. Hechter, **po. cit.**, p. 38.

established hierarchy of nations. The glorification of the Russian nation, the primacy of the Russian language, and the primacy ascribed to the Russian people in the socialist revolution are among the manifestations of this hierarchy. Second, although there is some co-optation of elites from the various nationalities, the top positions in the power structure (the party apparatus, military command, top economic managerial positions) are disproportionately assigned to Russians. Third, the allocation of economic values among the nationalities is not necessarily fair from an objective or subjective point of view. The propagandists emphasize the mutual fraternal aid and economic interdependence of Soviet nationalities, but nowhere are the inflow and outflow accounts published. Thus, there exists the possibility, at least in case of some republics, that the economic relationship may in fact be exploitative. Even in an obviously prosperous republic, the local perception may be that the economic status is unsatisfactory—since the economy is developed from the union point of view, the standard of living is depressed by obligations to the center; local allocation and control over economic forces would result in even greater productivity and greater prosperity, which the current system excludes. Whether such perceptions are objectively true or not is immaterial to elite and mass behavior. The fact is that such perceptions do exist. Finally, the denial of self-determination should be considered as an aspect of internal colonialism. As long as integration of different nationalities into the Soviet state is achieved by coercion, the legitimacy of the regime, especially in light of the worldwide understanding of self-determination, is likely to be extensively questioned. In the case of Lithuania and the other Baltic states, which had managed to establish independent states despite Red intervention following the October Revolution, the forcibly imposed status of a Soviet republic is the most obvious sign of a colonial relationship and a serious problem for developing a sense of the legitimacy of a Soviet rule among the Lithuanian people.

When such a colonial relationship is superimposed upon a culturally distinct group which possesses self-consciousness and intense internal communication, "the chances for successful political integration of the peripheral collectivity into the national society are minimized." [25] Under these circumstances a system of coercion becomes the essential ingredient for stability and survival of a multi-national state.

---

25. **Ibid.**, p. 43.

3. PERIODIZATION OF POSTWAR OPPOSITION

Applying Gurr's models of relative deprivation to postwar Lithuanian nationalism, three distinct periods of nationalist opposition are readily apparent.

The severe nationalist opposition during 1945—1953 took the form of an extensive armed partisan war against the Soviet regime. It is best explained by the decremental deprivation model: there was a very severe deprivation of political, economic, and personal values—essentially a foreign regime, supported by a foreign army and security force, was imposed and self-determination was completely eliminated. Personal security was in constant jeopardy as Stalin's police dealt not only with actual enemies but also with potential, vaguely defined "enemies of the people." In addition, the severe deprivation of property rights, especially for the peasantry, first through a radical land reform, later through collectivization (1948), disrupted the economic life of the country, plunging it to an unheard of low.

Given such radical redistribution of scarce values, opposition would be severe under any regime. Opposition in an ultimate form of armed struggle, however, was in part inevitable because of the absence of alternatives under a Stalinist regime. The ruthlessness of the Soviet forces in dealing with opposition left clandestine struggle as the only option for a very large part of the nation. Armed struggle was also abetted by the widespread expectation of an inevitable clash between the East and the West. Given the hegemonial system, opposition could be only system-rejective. Although the nationalist opposition was crushed by the superior armed forces of the Soviet Union, it did leave an indelible mark on national consciousness and had other important consequences for national identity and nationalism in the 1970s.

The second period corresponded roughly with Khrushchev's rule. During this period a degree of calm and normalcy was achieved. Nationalist expectations were significantly lowered as a result of the crushing of partisan forces, and the defeat of the Hungarian freedom fighters in the absence of Western aid. At the same time, value capabilities improved significantly. Some national aspirations could now be satisfied as a result of fewer restrictions on the cultivation of national culture, native control over the institutions of the regime, the increased local control over the economy through the *Sovnarkhoz* arrangements, and finally, the rapid growth and significant improvement in personal security as a result of destalinization. As value expectations and value capabilities were brought into an acceptable balance, a degree of acquiescence to the regime became evident. A significant shift away from a hegemonial system created opportunities for achievement of national values within the existing institutional framework and for cultural assertiveness. Opposition shifted markedly from system-rejective to within-system activity. The situation is best described as a mild decremental deprivation with opportunities to express nationalist and other aspirations through the institutional order.

The third period corresponds to the Brezhnev rule. The overthrow of Khrushchev brought about changes in a number of policies, leading to intensified, extrainstitutional dissent. Because of the time lag for various policies to produce their effects throughout the society and the polity, reaction to Brezhnev's rule in Lithuania appeared somewhat later than in Moscow—in the early 1970s. The model of relative deprivation that most closely corresponds to the dynamics of this situation is that of progressive deprivation except that the J-curve is not clearly evident; there is no sudden decline in value capabilties. The appropriate model in this case is a variation—called accelerated deprivation: both expectations and value capabilities increase, but the gap also increases, leading to dissent and instability.[26]

Value capabilities have increased at a slower rate or even decreased in the post-Khrushchev years. The economy is growing at a declining rate, consumer goods and the standard of living have shown a very slow growth, in part as a consequence of very high military expenditures. With respect to personal freedom, a degree of restalinization has occurred while participatory (political) values have not increased at all. At the same time, collective expectations of values have, if anything, increased. While the gap has not become destabilizing and it is not wide enough to produce a mass movement, it is sufficient to embolden dissent by individuals and small groups, occassionally resulting in spontaneous or organized mass pressures among the nationalities, religious groups, or the workers.

The dissent of the seventies is thus a complex mixture of within-system and system-rejective assertions. Manipulation of regime institutions for national purposes is accompanied by continued (though somewhat more repressed) cultural assertiveness and clandestine political activity, a prolific samizdat, and occasional mass eruptions of protest.

---

26. As defined by Mark N. Hagopian, **The Phenomenon of Revolution** (New York, 1974), pp. 174-75.

Chapter II

THE PARTISAN WAR
1944-1952

As the Red Army reoccupied Lithuania in late 1944 and early 1945, there already existed numerous underground organizations and armed groups ready to oppose the invader. The opposition movement, which emerged even before Soviet power could be reestablished, was a rather comprehensive reaction to Soviet rule, involving various social, economic, and occupational groups of society. The opposition was not equivalent to a "class war", as the Soviet historians claim, but rather a nationalistic reaction to a foreign invader by a cross-section of the Lithuanian population. It was an opposition that derived in large measure from the expectations of deprivation of personal, political, and economic values, which was already experienced during the 1940-41 Soviet occupation, as well as from the widely held view that Soviet rule would be of short duration as a result of the implementation of the principles of the Atlantic Charter by Western democracies.

Although opposition to Soviet rule involved the entire range of actions (from intellectual, passive, moral resistance to violent reactions), its principal manifestation was the armed anti-Soviet partisan struggle, lasting until about 1952. The focus of this chapter is on this armed struggle. Of course, such emphasis leads to some distortion of the complex postwar reality. A complete study of opposition during the Stalin years, however, would require the writing of a comprehensive history of the period and, therefore, some limitation of the subject is in order here.

1. MAGNITUDE OF ARMED OPPOSITION

The magnitude of the armed resistance movement is suggested by a number of indices. According to Soviet sources, "between July of 1944 and December of 1945, 1,067 anti-Soviet underground organizations and groupings, 839 armed groups of

bandits,   11,870   counter-revolutionaries   were   liquidated." [1]
Another Soviet source claims that 13,000 new settlers, collective
farmers, party and government workers were killed by the
partisans. [2] George Weller, an American journalist, has reported
that in a conversation with the Director of Party History
Institute of the CPL, R. Šarmaitis, it was revealed that about
20,000 partisans and a similar number on the Soviet side
perished in the struggle. [3] Such figures are plausible and probably
on the conservative side. It is almost impossible to determine
with any precision partisan casualties, many of which have never
been reported; many partisans died in Soviet camps. A list of
casualties on the Soviet side has been published for eight raions
(out of the approximately 44). The list of 3,281 casualties of
partisan action since 1944 involves mostly local Soviet personnel,
collective farm workers and organizers, and the so-called people's
defenders (istrebiteli). [4] Projecting these figures for the entire
territory of Lithuania, a casualty figure of about twenty
thousand is possible. There is no way to estimate property losses,
such as burned farms, destroyed bridges and public buildings, or
slaughtered herds.

The number of partisans varied throughout the period and
can only be guessed at. One partisan report estimates that
initially there were about 30,000 men ir partisan ranks,
decreasing to about 5,000 by the 1950s. [5] In one report partisan
emissary in the West claims that in 1945 partisan formations of up
to 800 men openly operated and controlled the countryside and only
in district centers and larger cities did Soviet power prevail. [6]

Indicative of the intensity of partisan activity during this

1. As cited by the political prisoner Liudvikas Simutis, in his
statement to the Presidium of the Supreme Soviet of the USSR, July 20,
1970. For a copy of the statement, see **Arkhiv samizdata**, No. 691.

2. **Tiesa,** November 14, 1973.

3. **Chicago Daily News,** August 17, 1961.

4. Lists of casualties are provided in the following volumes of the
Soviet documentary series on the partisan war under the general title
"Faktai Kaltina" (Facts Accuse): **Kruvinos žudikų pėdos** ("Faktai kaltina",
IX) (Vilnius, 1968), pp. 235-330; **Buržuazinių nacionalistų gaujų siau-
tėjimas Dzūkijoje** ("Faktai kaltina", VI) (Vilnius, 1964), pp. 171-230.

5. These figures are cited in a report on the partisan movement by a
representative of the underground, dated November 2, 1950; copy of the
report obtained from personal papers of Mr. Bronys Raila.

6. From a letter of the resistance leader Jonas Deksnys, not dated,
but written sometime in May of 1948; copy of the letter obtained from
the personal archives of Mr. Bronys Raila.

period are the data on Soviet casualties in the eight raions mentioned above. Of the 2,328 instances of reported partisan action in which one or more casualties occurred, 2.4% were in 1944, 14.0% in 1945, 22.1% in 1946, 16.2% in 1947, 18.3% in 1948, 14.1% in 1949, 7.0% in 1950, 3.8% in 1951, 2.0% in 1952 and later. While the data for about a fifth of the Lithuanian territory may be distorting reality to some extent, it does appear to reflect the general course of the partisan war. Partisan actions reached a high point in 1946 and 1947, declining slowly but maintaining a high intensity until 1950, when they drop sharply to insignificance. When the alleged order to disband in 1952 was given, it is unlikely that more than a thousand partisans were still in the hidden bunkers.[7]

A special Bureau of the Central Committee of the A-UCP(b) for the Lithuanian republic was established in December of 1944 to deal with the partisan war and the reestablishment of Soviet rule.[8] For a year and a half, this Bureau, headed by M. Suslov, in fact was the authority in Lithuania. Suslov's policies were enforced by massive security forces. Two NKVD divisions and a number of Border Guard regiments, and other security-military detachments were thrown into the fight.[9] During 1944-45 special NKVD detachments, under the command of Gen. Kruglov, the deputy of Beria, swept the forests. Again in 1950-1951 Gen. Kruglov used two special MVD divisions in a final sweep against the partisans.[10]

In order to break the massive resistance, the Soviet regime

---

7. This claim is made in **Lietuvių enciklopedija** (Boston, 1969), Vol. XXXVI, p. 463. This is plausible, for after 1952 partisan activities became very sporadic and rare.

8. The existence of the Bureau was publicly revealed very late; the first known mention of it is some fifteen years later in the publication **Tarybų Lietuvos valstybės ir teisės dvidešimtmetis** (Vilnius, 1960), p. 161. See also the selected works of M. Suslov—**Rinktiniai raštai** (Vilnius, 1973), p. 3.

9. A **samizdat** article on Suslov's role in Lithuania enumerates specifically the military-security formations used in the pacification. The article circulated separately as a **samizdat** publication, which is the basis for the translation in Doc. No. 15.

10. See the testimony of the Soviet Border Guard officer Lt. Col. Burlitski, who participated in Gen. Kruglov's campaign, in US Congress, House of Representatives, Select Committee to Investigate Communist Aggression and Forced Incorporation of the Baltic States into the USSR, 83rd Cong., 2nd Sees., **Hearings, Fourth Interim Report** (Washington, 1954), pp. 1368-1374; reprinted here as Doc. No. 14.

carried out mass deportations, at least one such campaign every year between 1945 and 1951, and used terror and intimidation against the population. Between 1945 and 1950 Lithuania's population declined from about 2,630,000 to about 2,570,000.[11] Taking into account natural birth rate, migration, casualties in the partisan war, it is probable that about 300,000 people were deported to the cold and uninhabitable northern areas of the USSR. The prewar population was attained only in the 1960s. Overall, during World War II Lithuania lost about 850,000 people, one of the severest war-related population losses in the world.

2. CAUSAL FACTORS

Serious deprivations or expectations of deprivations of political, economic, personal security, religious, and national values undergirded the opposition movement. The intensity of individual sense of relative deprivation, combined with certain broad societal forces and conditions, erupted in the widespread violent reaction. On the level of the individual, opposition to Soviet rule may have been a result of various factors— deprivation of economic values through a radical land reform and eventually collectivization of agriculture, deprivation of liberty or even life because of one's social class or former occupation, conscription into a foreign army (mobilization of men into the Red Army was defined as illegal), deprivation of national self-government and religious liberty, and so on.[12] But what translated these underlying motives into a particularly violent reaction to Soviet rule were a number of societal period or historical forces, which affected more or less the entire nation and propelled the opposition movement upon a course of violence. Among the sweeping period forces, foremost is the definition of the international situation, the inputs from the international environment, and the extremely coercive and radical nature of the Stalinist regime. While the impact of these forces was

---

11. Z. V. Rekašius, "Population Changes in Lithuania, 1940—1970," in Thomas Remeikis ed., **Proceedings of the Institute of Lithuanian Studies** (Chicago, 1971), pp. 177-187.

12. Specific motives for joining the partisans are treated in some detail by V. Stanely Vardys, "The Partisan Movement in Postwar Lithuania", in V. Stanley Vardys, ed., **Lithuania Under the Soviets** (New York, 1965), pp. 86-93; see also Thomas Remeikis, "The Armed Struggle Against Sovietization of Lithuania After 1944", **Lituanus,** No. 1-2 (VIII), 1962, p. 31.

differential on various social, economic, or occupational groups, none of them completely escaped it.

DEFINITION OF THE INTERNATIONAL SITUATION

The choice of armed struggle, as opposed to other forms of opposition, first of all was a result of a widely shared interpretation of the international situation and a particular vision of postwar political settlement. Political as well as military leaders of Lithuania perceived that the victors of World War II will be the Western democracies, which will dictate peace terms. To leaders and masses alike it was inconceivable that Western democracies would tolerate communist totalitarianism, which they had so painfully experienced in 1940-41. They chose to believe in the declarations of the Atlantic Charter and the promised reestablishment of independence and democracy.[13]

During the war Lithuanian anti-German resistance leaders, including the underground political center—the Supreme Committee for Liberation of Lithuania—formulated the following scenarios of the outcome of the war: 1) Germany will make a compromise peace with Western democracies, which will force Germany to grant Lithuania independence; 2) Germany will lose the war to Western democracies and will be forced to grant independence and if necessary defend Lithuania by force of arms from Soviet designs; 3) Germany will also lose the war to Russia, which in all probability will mean the destruction of Lithuania. In the first two cases, cooperation with Germany would be possible in the event that independence was restored. Short of that, cooperation with Germany must be minimal, sufficient to avoid massive German repression and severe losses.

In case the Red Army threatened to occupy the Baltic States as a result of the collapse of the German armies, there was a strong resolve to defend the frontiers by all means to the "last drop of blood."[14] As the Red Army approached Lithuania, in

13. Such views are quite apparent in the anti-German underground press and pronouncements of resistance organizations. See, for example, the "Appeal of the Supreme Committee for the Liberation of Lithuania to the Governments of Great Britain and the United States," September 30, 1944; text of the appeal in Bronis J. Kaslas, **The USSR-German Aggression Against Lithuania** (New York, 1973), pp. 388-391. Also see the diaries of one of the Lithuanian Counsellors to the German Zivilverwaltung in Lithuania, Jonas Matulaitis, **Neramios dienos** (Toronto, 1975), **passim.**, for similar viewpoint.

14. This, in fact, is a paraphrase of the theses of one of the major

February of 1944 an agreement was reached with the German authorities to set up a Home Guard (Vietinė Rinktinė), or *Sonderverbande* in German, for the purpose of defending the homeland from red partisan menace and the Red Army. The Lithuanian force was to be under Lithuanian command and to be used in Lithuania only. When the Germans broke this agreement in May of 1944, the Lithuanian command ordered the dissolution of the force. Many of the recruits of the Home Army with some weapons took off to the woods and eventually constituted one of the sources of armed resistance to the Soviets.[15] Thus even before the reoccupation of Lithuania by the Red Army, the resistance groups had committed themselves to an armed struggle, providing the initial impetus for a guerilla-type war. Again, it must be emphasized that the policy rested on the assumption of Western victory and the implementation of the pledges in the Atlantic Charter.

The third possibility, i.e. Soviet victory over Germany, which in fact occurred, had to be redefined after the war. Armed struggle against the Soviet regime now was justified by the expectation of conflict between the East and the West. As early as January of 1944, the representatives of Lithuanian and Latvian resistance organizations, meeting secretly in Riga, expressed the view "that the Allies sooner or later will not be able to avoid a collision with the Bolsheviks."[16] This viewpoint was especially strongly expressed by the armed partisans, as is evident from their underground press.[17] It was also evident in the

---

resistance organizations by the German Security Police (SP) in Kaunas. See the report on the Lithuanian anti-German resistance organizations by the Sicherheitspolizei and the Sicherheitsdienst (SD) in Kaunas, dated May 31, 1944; copy of the report in the archives of Reich Ministry for Occupied Eastern Territories, US National Archives, Microfilm series T-454, Roll 100.

15. The story of the Home Guard is well documented by two Lithuanian officers who were involved in its organization: V. O. Urbonas, "The Home Guard in 1944", **Karys,** May 1951—September 1952; Stasys Raštikis, **Kovose dėl Lietuvos** (Los Angeles, 1957), Vol. II, pp. 343-351.

16. See the copy of the report of the meeting of representatives of Lithuanian and Latvian resistance groups in Riga, Jan 8-9, 1944, in the archives of the Reich Ministry for the Occupied Eastern Territories, US National Archives, Microfilm series T-454, Roll 100.

17. All the available copies of partisan press in 1946-1947 express a strong belief in the inevitability of conflict. See Doc. No. 5, 7, for a sampling of underground opinion.

thinking of the Catholic hierarchy and clergy, who also viewed Soviet regime as temporary and gave aid and comfort to the partisans. Most of the bishops and ordinaries refused to condemn the partisan underground and one bishop was even executed by the Soviets for alleged participation in the movement.[18] The emerging Cold War fueled unjustified hopes for liberation. The American atomic bomb, the Iron Curtain speech of Churchill, the Truman Doctrine, the Berlin blockade, the Korean conflict could not help but sustain dogged determination to resist sovietization. The partisans in their bunkers, listening to Western broadcasts, were encouraged if not incited to persevere. The armed partisans in particular rejected any suggestion that immediate war is not at all certain. Even after the armed struggle subsided, this viewpoint to some extent survived until 1956. After all, Dulles and Eisenhower did proclaim the policy of liberation. It took the crushing of the Hungarian and Polish revolutions by Russian tanks and the inconsequential verbal response from the West to dash the hopes of liberation. But until that time, in the perspective of the armed underground, it made sense to engage in an all-out struggle, to prevent sovietization and economic transformation of society, to be ready militarily and politically to reestablish an independent state during the expected East-West conflict.

The misinterpretation of the policy of containment as a policy of liberation was not corrected even by special emissaries of the resistance movement, who on several occasions breached the Iron Curtain in order to inform themselves about the international situation, to inform the West about their struggle, and to solicit moral and material aid from the Western democracies. It is known that a number of realistic appraisals of the international situation by Western observers did reach partisan leadership. One such realistic report was brought to Lithuania in 1946 by an emissary from the West, Jonas

---

18. See **Žudikai bažnyčios prieglobsty** ("Faktai kaltina", Vilnius, 1963), **passim.**, which contains Soviet evidence on the alleged participation of the bishops and lower clergy in the partisan movement and their expectations of a new world conflict. Also see the Soviet study by J. Aničas on the Catholic Church reaction to the Soviet order: **Socialinis politinis Katalikų bažnyčios vaidmuo Lietuvoje 1945-1952 metais** (Vilnius, 1971), esp. chapters III and IV. Aničas reveals that as late as March of 1949 the administrator of the Diocese of Vilkaviškis expressed the belief in a new world conflict which "the Soviet Union will lose." (p. 112).

Deksnys.[19] Also the communication by the Chief of Diplomacy
Stasys Lozoraitis, dated April 15, 1947, reached the partisan
leadership.[20] Lozoraitis wrote:

> It is not certain that the tension arising out of the
> territorial and political expansion of the Soviet Union must
> necessarily and immediately lead to war. As long as the
> internal situation of the Soviet Union remains unimproved,
> they have no interest to attack America and England. As to
> the latter, at this moment they are not prepared for war
> materially or morally, especially for war on behalf of the
> freedom of states which found themselves in the Soviet
> sphere. From this it follows that in Lithuania it is necessary
> to save resources, avoiding sacrifice in the armed struggle,
> avoiding additional reasons for the bolsheviks for depor-
> tations and so on. From abroad I cannot judge how much the
> activities of our partisans protect the people from the terror
> of the occupational regime and whether it is necessary for
> the preservation of national consciousness of the masses.
> However, as far as the impact of the armed struggle on the

19. Jonas Deksnys, a participant in the anti-German resistance
during the war and former inmate of a Nazi concentration camp, was
among the founders of the first leading resistance center—The United
Democratic Resistance Movement. On several occasions he traveled to
Lithuania and to the West. Probably around 1950 he ended up in the
hands of the Soviet secret police and apparently he was forced to
cooperate as a price for survival. There is no evidence that Deksnys
might have been a double-agent and his confessions in Soviet press do
not reveal anything that was not known. Deksnys' account of his role
was published in **Tiesa,** February 20, 1960, and in a series of articles in
Švyturys, 1962, Nos. 9 through 12. Deksnys himself claims that he
provided the more realistic briefing on the international situation to
partisan leaders; see **Švyturys,** 1962, No. 12, pp. 10-11. Deksnys'
colleagues in the West have also testified to that effect and the story
seems to be confirmed by Juozas Lukša, another partisan leader, whose
reliability is beyond question.
20. Stasys Lozoraitis, former Minister of Foreign Affairs and
Minister in Italy, was appointed by President A. Smetona before the
Soviet occupation of Lithuania to act as chief among the Lithuanian
representatives abroad. Copy of the telegram of appointment, dated May
31, 1940, in files of the author, obtained from the personal archives of
Mr. Lozoraitis. Mr. Lozoraitis continues to function as Chief of the
remaining Lithuanian diplomats to this day from his residence in Rome.
Complete text of Lozoraitis' communication to the underground was not
available. Excerpts cited here are from an article by Stasys Žymantas in
Dirva (Cleveland), March 21, 1950.

evolution of present-day international politics, pertaining to the Lithuanian question, is concerned, I feel I can confirm that the death of our best men will not accelerate development of events and its political effect, influence on the propaganda for Lithuanian freedom, will be painfully disproprotionate to the sacrifices and national losses.

The partisans, however, responded to such communications with bitterness or did not want to believe them. The partisan leader Juozas Lukša, in his account of the partisan movement, has described the reaction of one partisan leader to an unidentified pessimistic assessment of the international situation as viewed from the West in the following words:

> They condemned us to death at Yalta, Potsdam... They continue to repeat the mistakes, not daring to raise a voice of protest against the annihilation of our nation, not even wishing to know that we are not yet disappointed with them, that we are continuing the struggle with their "ally" not knowing defeat... [21]

International tensions contradicted the sobering voices from the West. And, as will be suggested below, the bulk of communications from the West during the 1949—1952 period tended to reenforce the partisan definition of the world as verging on the precipice of war.

---

21. Juozas Daumantas (pseudonym of Juozas Lukša), **Partizanai už Geležinės Uždangos** (Chicago, 1950), pp. 305-6. Juozas Lukša, known as Skirmantas, Daumantas, Skrajūnas in the underground, a relatively young man (born in 1921), played quite a prominent role in the partisan movement, which is discussed in some detail here. At the end of 1947 he was sent to the West by the Presidium of the United Democratic Resistance Movement with a mission to establish contact with Western powers and Lithuanian political centers abroad. He reached Sweden in the beginning of 1948, bringing along documents on the situation in Lithuania and the status of the resistance movement. While in the West he wrote a somewhat romanticized account of the partisan movement under the title cited above. A second edition, with appendices of some documents brought out by Lukša, was published in 1962. It is also now available in an abbreviated English translation: Juozas Daumantas, **Fighters for Freedom: Lithuanian Partisans Versus the USSR** (New York, 1975). In the fall of 1950 Lukša returned to Lithuania by way of a parachute drop from a CIA plane. He was killed in an encounter with the MGB in October of 1951.

INTERNATIONAL INPUTS

The pleas of partisan emisaries for Western assistance failed to elicit anything approaching a decisive involvement by Western states in destabilizing Soviet power. Whatever assistance the partisans received, it was from the American, British, French, and Swedish intelligence services, which were primarily interested in information and the resistance movement as a source for it. At the same time, however, the Western intelligence services were in fact encouraging resistance beyond the necessities of information gathering. Two groups of parachutists were dropped in Lithuania in 1950 and 1951. It is quite clear that their operations went well beyond mere intelligence collection, or at least the fact that Western powers were sending such missions could easily be interpreted by the partisans as a signal of Western support for their cause and the imminence of liberation.[22]

The two missions of Lithuanian partisans sponsored by the CIA were part of the policy of "positive intervention" in communist countries that was attempted by the US and Britain through their secret agencies during the height of the Cold War and the raging Korean fighting. The following is a British account of this policy:

> Britain's Foreign Secretary, Ernst Bevin, was adamantly opposed to the idea. But the Foreign Office contained a vocal militant faction in favour of establishing resistance movements in virtually every country in Eastern Europe and which, in turn, was enthusiastically supported by SIS... The issue was swung by the hawks in the American State Department who saw this as a chance to remould the face of Europe in a more sympathetic image.[23]

---

22. For the Soviet version of these missions, see M. Chienas, K. Smigelskis, E. Uldukis, **Vanagai iš anapus** (Vilnius, 1960); for the non-Soviet version and biographies of the principal participants in these missions, see the appendices to J. Daumantas, **Partizanai** (Chicago, 1962), 2nd ed., pp. 409-419, 470-495. Both missions included three men each, the first was led by Juozas Lukša, the second by Julijonas Butėnas. J. Butėnas, born in 1915, was a journalist, active participant in the anti-Nazi underground. His mission was particularly short-lived: he was parachuted in Lithuania on April 19, 1951, and committed suicide under a siege of Soviet security forces sometime in early May of 1951. Lukša's expedition lasted about a year, from early fall of 1950 to October of 1951, when he was killed by Soviet security forces.

23. Bruce Page, David Leitch, and Phillip Knightely, **The Philbv Conspiracy** (New York, 1968), p. 199.

One of the CIA executives involved has confirmed the policy of covert intervention. The CIA was assigned the mission "to carry out covert actions designed to weaken Soviet control over its own population and the peoples of Eastern Europe; to weaken pro-Soviet regimes and Communist parties throughout Eurasia."[24] Part of this policy was the support of resistance movements in the Ukraine, the Baltic States, Poland, and Albania. The covert operations within communist countries were to be supported by propaganda campaigns through radio and other means and support of emigrés abroad in their anti-communist activities. The Albanian project particularly was viewed as important. It was believed that a guerilla force could start a revolt in Albania, which could easily spread to the rest of Eastern Europe and the Soviet Union itself. "The whole basis of the Russian satellite empire could be shattered by an uprising that had had its birth in one small guerilla operation."[25]

The Albanian operation was a total disaster, in part because of the treachery of Kim Philby, who was a co-director of the project and a Soviet agent at the same time. The Lithuanian operation, though on a much smaller scale, was an equal disaster and fatal to the Lithuanian partisans parachuted in 1950 and 1951. Eventually the two groups of Lithuanian partisans were annihilated, very likely with some assistance from Kim Philby.[26] But before that happened, the partisans from the West managed to add fuel to the smouldering partisan struggle. Their input was reenforced by the now fully operating VOA and CIA's Radio Liberty and Radio Free Europe, as well as the hot war in Korea, which could easily be interpreted as the beginning of the anticipated East-West showdown.

Juozas Lukša-Daumantas, who headed the first group of

---

24. Harry Rozitzke, **The CIA's Secret Operations** (New York, 1977), p. 17; see also Rozitske's article "America's Secret Operations: A Perspective", **Foreign Affairs,** January, 1975, pp. 334-342.

25. For details about the Albanian operation, see Page, et. al., **op. cit.,** chapter 14.

26. Soviet version of the missions in **Vanagai iš anapus, op. cit.,** suggests that MGB organs expected parachute drops and it is quite possible that Kim Philby, who knew about the CIA operations at least in a general way, may have played a role in alerting Soviet security. It is very likely that Jonas Deksnys, who worked with the British intelligence, was also a victim of Philby's treachery. All the partisan couriers had contacts with British intelligence agents when Kim Philby was in charge of the counter-Soviet department in the British Secret Intelligence Service (from 1944 on) and served with the CIA in Washington.

partisans dropped in 1950, in his report to the partisan leadership
clearly implied Western interest and aid to the partisan
underground as going beyond mere information gathering. The
Soviets have published a few brief excerpts from his report,
including the following:

> Again at the end of summer of 1948 I had an informative
> conversation with high military intelligence people of one of
> the great powers. Besides the economic, social, cultural,
> religious situation, they were especially interested in the
> situation of the resistance. Such a report was made together
> with Audronis upon the arrival in Sweden to the Swedish
> intelligence.
>
> In the fall of 1949 I made a very thorough report to the
> intelligence service of another great power. In this case I had
> to answer systematically three hundred questions, making
> the report clearer with a number of drawings. This report,
> covering the situation of our underground, was the basis for
> a concrete commitment of this power to supply to our
> resistance material aid.
>
> ... With such relations established, the question of
> material aid to the country was solved. I find it necessary to
> communicate verbally the details about the provisions of
> material aid to the country. [27]

More details of what Lukša reported to the underground are
found in the bulletin of partisan command of the Southern
Region of the Movement of the Freedom Struggle of Lithuania,
the principal formation at that time, where Lukša was active upon
his return. The bulletin, dated July 7, 1951, claimed that armed
struggle, as opposed to passive resistance, was approved by a
powerful Western state (obviously the US) and the Lithuanian
political organizations and individual leaders abroad. It further
suggested that moral and material aid had been assured by this
powerful state and that support had even been promised by the
Holy See. This item, verly likely composed by Lukša himself, was
clearly encouraging total armed struggle.[28] The same bulletin in
fact calls for an intensification of the struggle, because liberation
is imminent:

> Dark and great storm clouds are gathering in the West. They
> shall smash with thunder and lightning, they shall sweep from the

27. **Kruvinos žudikų pėdos** ("Faktai kaltina", IX), p. 9.

28. Copy of the bulletin obtained from the private papers of Mr.
Bronys Raila; see Doc. No. 11 for complete text of the bulletin.

holy land of Lithuania all foreigners and crush all the Lithuanian traitors and fawners. But you, Lithuanian, should not await the liberating storm by sitting on your hands. You must join this holy struggle against Bolshevism with weapon in hand.

Such uncompromising armed struggle was also encouraged by the communication of the principal political organization abroad, the Supreme Committee for Liberation of Lithuania, which was cooperating with the CIA in arranging Lukša's mission. In a leaflet for massive distribution in Lithuania, taken along by Lukša, the Supreme Committee explained the Korean conflict as the beginning of the final East-West confrontation, and, at least by implication, encouraged armed opposition. The leaflet said in part:

> 1. To most people in the West it is clear that in Korea the conflict is not between the interests of South and North Korea, but between the interests of East and West.
> 2. These interests are too contradictory for accommodation... All efforts to find peaceful means of resolution (of the conflict) cannot satisfy the East or the West. Even if at this moment a peaceful accommodation could be achieved, it would be only temporary. The spark of fire shall explode in another place, for the interests are no longer reconcilable, and compromises are impossible.
> 3. The United States has sufficiently understood its mission to be the vanguard of the West, fighting no longer for the liberty of an individual nation, but for all of mankind... [29]

The leaflet concludes that "The rush of political events of today is approaching the moment... when the independence of Lithuania will manifest itself again."

Whether the CIA agreed with such an assessment of the situation and to what extent it encouraged the guerilla tactic remain secrets burried in CIA files. One available source does indicate that the CIA was much more restrained, advising to avoid casualties and terroristic tactics on the part of the partisans. But the final instruction to Lukša's group that the US "associates the liberation of all occupied countries and therefore of Lithuania with the resolution of the entire complex (problem of communist rule), and not separately" could be interpreted as

---

29. "Freedom is Coming From the West" is the title of the 8 page message; copy of the leaflet obtained from the private archives of Col. Antanas Šova.

an affirmation of the policy of liberation, which, given the circumstances, could be perceived as imminent.[30]

The Soviets have claimed that the missions of infiltrated guerillas were not only to collect information, but also to destabilize the Soviet regime, "to form a united center and to undertake active terrorist and diversionary work in the Baltic countries." [31]

The result of Lukša's mission and other factors in the international environment (e.g., radio propaganda from the West) revived violent activity for a brief time. This is indicated by the cited bulletin of partisan command and confirmed by a report of a passive resistance center which reached the West. [32] The last combing action against the partisans by Soviet forces under Gen. Kruglov's command is associated with the revived armed activity.

STALINISM

Stalinist terror was both a causal factor and a consequence of armed opposition. The definition of the "enemies of the people" and "Hitlerite collaborators" was so broad as to include entire social strata (the "kulaks" or well-to-do farmers, for example) or parts of most social and occupational groups. To a large extent, Stalinist terror was directed at categories of people, rather than at individuals. Thus, as the experience of 1940-41 indicated, repressions could be expected by categories, regardless of individual guilt, by former political leaders, bureaucrats, army officers, businessmen, and the bulk of the Lithuanian

---

30. Two personal memoranda of Col. A. Šova, dated August 17, 1950, and July 31, 1950, outline the final instructions of a CIA agent to the Lukša group pertaining to their mission. Col. Šova was the principal Lithuanian functionary in organizing the missions and therefore he sat in on the final briefings of the Lukša group. Copies of the memoranda obtained from Col. Šova.

31. J. Jakaitis, **Išdavystės keliu** (Vilnius, 1976), p. 202. This Soviet exposé of Western subversion, also contains an account of the training of Lithuanian, Ukrainian, Polish operatives in Western Germany, France, and England in 1949-1952 (see pp. 201-225). The Soviets also claim that Latvian and Estonian operatives were also trained in the West and sent back for diversionary purposes. See the "non-fiction" novel **Gintaro jūra** (Vilnius, 1966) by N. Asamovas and J. Sturytis.

32. Copy of the report, dated April 23, 1952, from Supreme Leadership of the Fighting Lithuanian Nation, obtained from the private archives of Mr. Bronys Raila; see Doc. No. 13 for complete text of the report.

population—the relatively prosperous farmers. To thousands of individuals the choice was between a Soviet prison, concentration camp, execution, or possible survival in the underground. One repressed young partisan of very modest social background gave the following reasons for joining the resistance:

> I found myself under the flag of anti-Soviet underground, the Movement for the Freedom Struggle of Lithuania, not because I did not like the idea of socialism—I was then too young to orient myself sufficiently in theory—but because the Soviet government, brought to Lithuania by the Red Army, dealt with the people who did not accept the incomprehensible new order with excessive and criminal cruelty. [33]

Later on, after destalinization even the Lithuanian communist leaders admitted that Stalinist terror was in part responsible for the violence. The First Secretary of the CPL Antanas Sniečkus, in a speech before the Twenty-Second Congress of the CPSU in 1961, made these revealing admissions:

> In the period of the personality cult great difficulties used to materialize in our republic since the Soviet government has been established relatively recently. During the class war in those years, when the Lithuanian nation had to break the resistance of bourgeois nationalist bands formed and aided by Hitlerite occupants and intelligence services of America and England, the violations of socialist legality produced considerable harm. The adventurers of Beria's type, unjustly treating innocent people, tried to discredit the policy of the Soviet government, made the struggle against traitors more difficult, and sometimes enabled the true enemies of the people and socialism to evade responsibility. Violations of legality created grave difficulties in our work to rally the masses of working people around the Party and the Soviet government. [34]

It is therefore understandable why the partisan ranks were constantly renewed by recruits, why the population at large gave aid and sympathized with them, why very few partisans were willing to avail themselves of amnesty, proclaimed by Soviet authorities in 1946, 1951, 1955, and allegedly as late as 1959, and why only in 1952, after decimation and exhaustion, the

33. From the appeal of Liudvikas Simutis to the Presidium of the Supreme Soviet of the USSR, July 20, 1970, **Arkhiv samizdata,** No. 691.
34. **Tiesa,** October 24, 1961.

remaining partisan leadership called for the abandonment of armed struggle. [35]

3. ORGANIZATION AND TACTICS OF THE OPPOSITION

The development of central leadership and organization of the entire resistance movement were slow, intermittent, and never complete due to the incessant actions of Soviet security organs and casualties among the leading members of the underground. Upon the second Soviet occupation in 1944-45 the principal political leaders and resistance centers ended up in the Western occupation zones of Germany. In Lithuania the few remaining political leaders were quickly isolated. One consequence of this was the dominance of the underground by former army officers up to the colonel level. This fact, perhaps, explains in part the strong tendency to favor military tactics in the struggle for national independence. A number of new political groups emerged along the vestiges of the older resistance organizations and the more or less spontaneously formed partisan units.

There was no policy setting and coordinating resistance center until June of 1946 when the United Democratic Resistance Movement (Bendras Demokratinis Pasipriešinimo Sąjūdis) was founded. The UDRM united the vestiges of resistance groups which functioned during the German occupation (such as the Association of Lithuanian Freedom Fighters, the Lithuanian Freedom Army), the newly organized resistance groups (such as the Unity Committee), and the armed partisan formations. At the apex was the Committee (later the Presidium) of the UDRM, which was composed of representatives from the various constituent units mentioned. There is very little data on its precise composition. The UDRM in effect was an organization of the political and military parts of the resistance movement.[36] The armed partisans refused to subordinate themselves to a purely

---

35. A photostatic copy of the 1946 amnesty order has been published in **Lithuanian Bulletin** (New York), Vol. 4, No. 4 (November, 1946); see Doc. No. 2 for complete text. Other offers of amnesties have been cited, on basis of some reference in Soviet press, by J. Brazaitis, in **Lietuvių enciklopedija** (Boston, 1960), Vol. XXII, p. 49. See also the references to amnesties by Aničas, **op. cit.,** pp. 78-79, 84-85.

36. The formation of the UDRM is described in J. Daumantas, **Partizanai už Geležinės Uždangos, op. cit.,** p. 211ff.; for statement of principles of the UDRM, see Doc. No. 3.

political organ and insisted on an equal voice in it.[37] The Supreme
Staff of Armed Partisans, supposedly subordinate to the UDRM,
was formed to direct the military program.

The armed partisans were somewhat skeptical participants in
the UDRM. From the very beginning there was disagreement
over tactics of the movement.[38] The majority on the Committee
of the UDRM was in favor of shifting emphasis from "active" or
armed to "passive" or political resistance on the grounds that war
was not imminent and, therefore, casualties should be avoided.
The armed partisans, on the other hand, were in favor of total
military struggle since, in their view, war was imminent. The
advocacy of the less violent course was derived from a more
realistic assessment of the world situation, which at least partly
came from the West (especially J. Deksnys, the partisan leader
who had returned from the West, and the Chief of Lithuanian
Diplomats abroad Stasys Lozoraitis).

The armed partisans, however, were reluctant to follow the
UDRM directives. As is evident from the available documents,
partisan leaders responded to the suggestion of passive resistance
with notable vehemence, calling the advocates of passive
resistance "bolshevik agents."[39] In part this may have been a
reflection of "the military mind" and the absence of noted
political leaders in the ranks of the resistance movement,
including the UDRM itself.

The conflict over tactics also stemmed from the somewhat
different existential situation of passive and armed resistance.
Members of passive resistance were to some extent in a position
to legalize themselves and adapt to the new order, while the men
under arms had no reasonable alternative to active struggle.
Soviet amnesties, repeatedly proclaimed, were neither trusted
nor truthfully implemented by the authorities. Thus, despite the
warning from the West that war was not imminent, the armed
partisans clung to their only hope of liberation from the West to
the very last. They could not help but interpret the Cold War
dialogue as a prologue to war rather than as a substitute for one.
To the men in the woods containment sounded like a promise of
liberation. Western propaganda and Stalinist terror assured such
misperception of reality.

---

37. **Ibid.,** p. 239.

38. This is evident from Lukša-Daumantas' account, as well as from
the available partisan press; cf. particularly Doc. No. 6 and Doc. No. 7.

39. See this point made in the assessment of world situation by the
partisan newspaper **Laisvės Varpas,** October 15, 1947; Doc. No. 7.

Besides opposition to its tactics by many partisan leaders, the UDRM was beset by security problems. There is ample evidence that Soviet security agents had inflitrated the apex of the UDRM, producing some losses and declined effectiveness in directing the underground.[40] By 1948 UDRM leadership was barely functioning. It is at this time that the partisan leaders began moving to set-up an exclusively partisan resistance organization and leadership. There are reports that the remaining leaders of the UDRM sought accommodation with the partisans, but agreement was not reached.[41] In February of 1949 a new resistance center—the Movement for the Freedom Struggle of Lithuania (Lietuvos Laisvės Kovų Sąjūdis) came into being.[42] It survived as a rather loose partisan center until approximately the middle of 1952.

The MFSL took the course of an exclusively armed struggle. The movement sought to prevent sovietization and especially collectivization of agriculture, the initiation of which corresponded roughly with the formation of the MFSL. The movement issued orders to liquidate collective farm organizers and conduct propaganda against collectivization. The entire organization took the form of an army, including ranks up to a general. The total and uncompromising struggle against the Soviet regime is evident in the Penal Code promulgated by the MFSL. The first article states:

> During the present time of red occupation every individual, a citizen of Lithuania or a foreign state, or a

---

40. For Soviet admission of infiltration, see Jakaitis, **op. cit.,** p. 233; for non-Soviet evidence—Daumantas, **op. cit.** 2nd ed., p. 480; Sometime in 1949 while in the West, Lukša wrote a long memorandum on the role of one of the Soviet agents—Dr. Juozas Markulis, who was a member of the UDRM Committee. Copy of the memorandum in the files of the author. Although there is no question that Markulis was a Soviet agent, his precise role in contributing to the disorganization and decimation of the UDRM leadership remains very vague.

41. This is the claim of Stasys Žymantas, who was an intermediary between the UDRM and British intelligence and Lithuanian political groups abroad, thus in a position to know about the politics of the opposition movement. See his article in **Dirva** (Cleveland), September 1, 1965.

42. Some of the circumstances leading to the formation of the MFSL are revealed in the Soviet protocols of interrogation of the leader of the MFSL Jonas Žemaitis, published in **Kruvinos žudikų pėdos** ("Faktai kaltina", IX), pp. 203-231; excerpts in Doc. No. 1.

member of the MFSL, who through his actions impairs the Lithuanian nation and the MFSL to defend Lithuanian interests and to struggle with the enemies of the Lithuanian nation for the reestablishment of independent Lithuania, is punished by the courts of the MFSL... A person who commits an offense by not carrying out the public directives of the movement or the rightful demands of individual partisans, is punished, according to the severity of consequences, up to the death penalty.[43]

Such a policy of total armed struggle led to excesses on both the partisan and the Soviet sides. The inhabitants were placed in an untenable position between two opposing forces.

Documentary evidence on the thinking of the partisans about how the total armed struggle would lead to liberation is scanty. One observer-participant, who had access to a good deal of information about the movement, has summarized the MFSL thinking as follows:

Having categorically, uncompromisingly rejected the Soviet occupation as illegal, forcible, and imposed, having refused not only to recognize but also to acknowledge the very fact of occupation, the partisans prohibited the inhabitants of Lithuania to carry out the decrees or laws of Soviet occupational regime and its administration, to vote in the announced elections to Soviet organs and in general to assist the occupants or to cooperate with them.

The partisans were hoping in this way to force the Soviets, in view of the total and strict resistance and boycott of Soviet administration, to withdraw from Lithuania, especially, since they thought and strongly believed that sooner or later there will be war or that the Western states will find some effective means to intervene on behalf of Lithuania and force the Soviets to restore the seized freedom and independence.[44]

The Lithuanian national underground tended to overemphasize ideological conflict in their expectations of future events, neglecting a realistic analysis of the balance of power and the national interests of the adversaries, factors which did not necessarily portend an all-out conflict. The tactics of the opposition movement rested on the assumption of a short

---

43. Excerpts from the penal code published in the partisan newspaper **Partizanas,** July 20, 1951; see Doc. No. 12.

44. This is Prof. Žymantas' interpretation in an article in **Dirva,** August 25, 1965.

struggle and quick reestablishment of an independent state. For this reason a centralization of the resistance movement was sought, including the establishment of incipient future institutions of an independent state. The underground thus acted in many respects as a counter-government, and in rural areas it often was in fact the government. Over the long haul, however, centralization played into the hands of Soviet security and was dysfunctional for survival. The balance of forces was extremely disadvantageous to the partisans, and in the absence of sanctuaries and aid from abroad, survival was problematical from the start. Indeed, it is amazing that the partisans remained active as long as they did.

4. OFFICIAL AND POPULAR INTERPRETATIONS OF THE CONFLICT

The official Soviet interpretation of the partisan war is that it was, first of all, a class struggle, an effort of the bourgeoisie to reestablish the ancient regime, a counter-revolution and, secondly, that it was a movement of fascist and criminal elements in the service of German and later Western intelligence services.[45] Although there is an element of truth in such allegations, the over-all reality of the partisan movement is quite different from the stereotyped and ideological Soviet view. Basically it was an opposition to a foreign invader and the regime it imposed, in other words, a nationalistic opposition movement. Let us consider some facts.

The anti-Soviet resistance movement rested on a rather broad social and occupational base. Although systematic evidence is not available on the social and occupational composition of the partisan ranks, the published materials on various partisan groups indicate a good deal of diversity in their composition, including representatives from the upper and the lower classes, the intelligentsia, former army officers and members of the bureaucracy, the smaller and the larger farmers, and even the Catholic clergy.[46] The broad Soviet definition of the "enemies of

---

45. The documentary series "Faktai kaltina," containing mostly testimony of witnesss and protocols of interrogation of partisans, expresses both versions of Soviet interpretation of the partisan war. See also the monograph of A. Rakūnas, **Klasių kova Lietuvoje 1940-1951 metais** (Vilnius, 1976), for a systematic statement of the official line.

46. For example, in June of 1945 the following people constituted the staff of a partisan unit in Skardupiai: Rev. Ylius, pastor of Skardupiai

the people" cut across class and occupational lines. Even the economic reforms were to at least some extent detrimental to the middle and even lower classes. For example, a rather broad land reform had been carried out in the 1920s. Consequently collectivization deprived of land not only the so-called "kulaks" (who were, in the first place, owners of medium-sized farms, 30 ha. of land or more), but also the numerous class of small-holders, who had become self-sufficient farmers with very close attachment to their land. Similarly, nationalization of business establishments and limitations on trades affected people of various means. And last but not least, Lithuanian nationalism was not restricted only to the so-called bourgeoisie. While the Soviet policies obviously affected the upper social classes more drastically than the lower strata, the resistance movement had too heterogeneous a socio-economic base to be defined simply as a class movement.

As to the program of the resistance movement, it certainly did not endorse the capitalist-authoritarian system of the pre-Soviet period. The principal aim of the opposition was the reestablishement of an independent state. Available evidence is vague as to what kind of social and economic order was desired. A commitment to a democratic system does come through, but neither the political, nor the socio-economic agenda was worked out in detail. The intense underground struggle did not permit long-term projections and of necessity was focused on the achievement of the primary goal—an independent state. It is, nevertheless, clear that the opposition envisioned neither socialism nor capitalism, but rather something akin to the Western conception of a democratic welfare state, an independent state, but within a commonwealth of nations. [47]

The Soviet charge that the partisan movement was merely an instrument of foreign intelligence agencies shifts the view from the real motives of the resistance. The Germans did train several groups for intelligence and diversion (probably not more

---

parish; Pileckis—former policeman; Lasevičius—farm manager; Januškaitis—cleric, student in a teachers' college; Urbonas—guard of the Skardupiai church; Gudelevičius—a carpenter; Bukaveckas—draft avoider to the Red Army. See **Žudikai bažnyčios prieglobstyje** ("Faktai kaltina", II) (Vilnius, 1963), p. 196, as well as the other volumes in the series "Faktai kaltina".

47. See the outline of such a political, economic, social, and international program in the statement announcing the formation of the United Democratic Resistance Movement, Doc. No. 3.

than 200 people were involved), and parachuted them behind the front line when it was cutting accross Lithuania late in 1944. Their activity was of short duration; most of the groups were out of commission within a year. The German-trained operatives were communications specialists and demolition experts and had no appreciable impact on the evolution of the partisan movement or its leadership.[48]

The partisan groups, which were formed in Northern and Northwestern Lithuania (collectively known as the Lithuanian Freedom Army or later the Legion of Samogitia) while the German authorities were still in Lithuania, did have a tacit German approval and received limited arms aid. The Soviet effort to present the LFA as an instrument of German military is non-sensical in view of the fact that this military-type organization was formed in 1942 for anti-German purposes. As the Red Army again approached Lithuania, the LFA reoriented itself for an anti-Soviet struggle. Despite the limited German aid and cooperation, the LFA was not under German military command and cooperated with the Germans to the extent that this was vital for its own national mission.[49]

As we have seen, later on the Western intelligence services also sent back partisan emissaries for information gathering purposes, and the partisan command did order the collection of information for transmission to the West. But the projected image of the partisans as mere spies in the pay of foreign countries ignores the political and ideological aims and even the personal motives of the partisans, who were fighting for personal survival as well as their own country's liberty.

The charge that the partisans were Nazi collaborators and war criminals attempting to avoid justice is so broadly applied as to be meaningless. Included among the "collaborators" are those who participated in the uprising against the Soviet regime in 1941, who served in any civilian capacity during the German occupation, men and officers of the ill-fated Home Army, and members of the various guard and police batallions under German control.[50] The Soviets have failed to provide systematic data to

---

48. Such conclusions are justified by the evidence offered in the Soviet documentary booklet **Hitleriniai parašiutininkai** ("Faktai kaltina," VIII) (Vilnius, 1966); see also **Archyviniai dokumentai apie nacionalistų antiliaudinę veiklą** (Faktai kaltina", III) (Vilnius, 1961).

49. For Soviet evidence on the activities of the LFA, see **Hitleriniai parašiutininkai, op. cit.,** p. 63ff.

50. The Germans failed to form an SS unit in Lithuania and all

substantiate this charge. An examination of Soviet documents on the partisan movement has revealed only a few partisans who may have committed criminal acts in the service of Nazi organs.[51] In most instances of alleged war crimes committed by an individual, on basis of Soviet sources it is impossible to establish with any certainty the extent of real individual guilt or to what extent this is a result of the individual's association or service in some capacity in the German occupation regime. Mere service in a certain position is often defined as a crime without regard to whether the individual committed anything contrary to law. In effect, too often we are dealing here with "political crimes" as they are defined by the victors. Thus, for example, those who participated in the uprising against the Soviet regime in 1941 are usually accused of "war crimes", even though the uprising was an insurrection against an occupying power, during which casualties occurred on all sides.

To the extent that can be judged from impressionistic evidence, the popular view of the partisans rejects the Soviet interpretations but at the same time is ambiguous. On the one hand, the partisan struggle is viewed as a genuinely patriotic one, but, on the other hand, there is a strong sense that it was a futile

---

efforts of mobilization were sabotaged. They did manage to form a number of guard and police batallions. In August of 1942 there were 20 such batallions, with 341 officers and a total man power of 8388. Eleven of the 20 batallions served in German-occupied Polish and Belorussian areas. These batallions guarded various installations and often were used in punitive actions against Soviet partisans and hostile populations. Some of the units in these batallions were involved in anti-Jewish campaigns, including executions. According to Soviet sources attrition of these units was high as a result of casualties and desertions. By the end of the war these units were practically out of commission. Some of the surviving members of these units eventually ended up in the West and some, no doubt, became partisans. Statistics on their fate are not available, but their number among the partisans clearly could not be great. See the Soviet collection of documents on mass exterminations in Lithuania during the war: B. Baranauskas, E. Rozauskas, **Masinės žudynės Lietuvoje (1941-1944)** (Vilnius, 1965), Part I, pp. 322, 334.

51. A number of officers, who served in various military and police capacities during the German occupation and who may have committed war crimes, as defined in the Nuremberg process, are mentioned in **Hitleriniai parašiutininkai** ("Faktai kaltina", VIII), **passim.** In the other volumes of "Faktai kaltina" it was possible to identify not more than a handful of individual partisans who might have been guilty of war crimes.

struggle (it turned out), unnecessarily extracting a prohibitive suffering and loss of life and placing the people in a crucible of clashing forces.[52] The latter view assumes that a lower level of violence would have significantly decreased Stalinist repressions against "class enemies" and saved many lives. Such a popular interpretation and evaluation of the partisan movement as a genuine manifestation of a national will, which, however, was perhaps too costly, seem to be the predominant view. As time heals the postwar wounds, the popular evaluation of the partisan movement is likely to change and take the form of a more objective balance sheet of costs versus consequences of the opposition movement. There are, in fact, indications in the *samizdat* press that opinion may be shifting toward a more favorable interpretation of the postwar conflict.

5. SOME LONG-TERM CONSEQUENCES OF THE PARTISAN WAR

Whatever the evaluation, the partisan movement left an indelible mark on the national consciousness and continues to impress and motivate the younger generation. Although the costs were very high and the aims were not achieved, in magnitude and intensity the partisan war ranks among the other major struggles for self-government: the 1863 revolt against czarist rule, the war of independence of 1918-19, the revolt of 1941 against the Soviet regime. Such a national historical experience can neither be forgotten nor ignored.

The official regime reaction to the partisan movement is indicative of its lasting impression. Until about the 1960s the Soviet regime tried to ignore it, only occasionally referring to what it called "bandit bands." After years of relative neglect, the Soviet regime finally went on an offensive to discredit the partisans as remnants of the capitalist class, Nazi collaborators, and Western spies. Beginning with the early 1960s a series and separate monographs and articles, including documents, testimony of witnesses, and interrogations of caught partisans, began to appear and continued to appear as late as 1976 [53] At the

---

52. Systematic public opinion data on the partisans is not available. These generalizations are based on random interviews with tourists from Lithuania and information obtained by tourists in Lithuania.

53. Between 1960 and 1973 18 documentary volumes were prepared by the Editorial Board for Publication of Archival Documents of the Institute of History, Academy of Sciences of the Lithuanian SSR. Included

same time efforts were made to publicize the communist partisan exploits against the Germans. This rather late and incessant campaign to discredit the partisans suggests that the Soviet authorities felt a need to counter popular evaluations and interpretations of the resistance movement.

In the popular mind the partisan war reenforces the fact that the Soviet regime was brought to Lithuania by an alien force. It helps to create a chasm between the Lithuanian nation and its rulers in Moscow, a chasm which today is evident not only in everyday anti-Russian behavior of the average individual and even the leading cadres, but also in dramatic manifestations of nationalism. The partisan war remains a symbol of national honor and self-respect, a sign of a subdued but unconquered people. As a current underground publication put it, "if the Lithuanians had met the Red Army with flowers, as is written in the official Soviet press... the name of Lithuania today would be completely forgotten." [54] The postwar struggles are viewed as productive of the latest national martyrs, such as Romas Kalanta and Mindaugas Tomonis.

Besides the impact on national consciousness, the partisan war also had important consequences for Lithuania's socio-economic development, which indirectly contributed to the maintenance of national identity and relative ethnic homogeneity of the country. For example, per capita capital investment in Lithuania during the fourth five-year plan was among the smallest, amounting to about 650 rubles; only Moldavia received a smaller allocation. Per capita capital investment was almost three times higher in the RSFSR, almost four times higher in Estonia, and more than twice in Latvia. [55] The rate of growth of industrial production was also much slower in Lithuania than in the sister republics of Latvia and Estonia. Only in the late 1950s an above-average economic growth rate was prescribed for Lithuania. [56] Of course, it is imposible to judge precisely to what extent the slower pace of economic development was due to the

in this series are the "Faktai kaltina" volumes cited throughout this study. For a bibliography, see **Lietuvos istorijos metraštis, 1974** (Vilnius, 1976), pp. 167-186, which is a yearbook of the Institute of History.

54. **Aušra,** No. 2 (February 16, 1976).

55. Calculated from **Narodnoe khoziaistvo SSSR 1958 godu** (Moskva, 1959), pp. 626-27.

56. Thomas Remeikis, "Modernization and National Identity in the Baltic Republics: Uneven and Multi-Directional Change in the Components of Modernization", in Ihor Kamenetsky, ed., **Nationalism and**

partisan war or to other considerations. However, rapid economic development was less likely under conditions of wide-spread opposition of the population. The imperatives of pacification—the repression of opposition and the creation of state apparatus—made rapid economic development at least an inefficient policy.

The partisan war had an even greater impact on the agrarian sector of economy. Due to an intense partisan action against land reform and collectivization, agricultural production was seriously impaired and socialist reconstruction of the countryside was accomplished through massive repression and deportations of the peasantry. By 1951 agricultural production was below 60% of the prewar level. Soviet historians have admitted that partisan and peasant opposition was partly responsible for the deterioration of agricultural production and some delay in implementation of the policy of collectivization.[57]

The delayed industrial and agrarian revolution meant that the republic leaders under Khrushchev's decentralization and the *sovnarkhoz* system would be able to shape to a degree the economic future of the republic. National cadres were developed for the economic take-off in the late 1950s and the 1960s. Economic plans took into account republic resources. National control over economic and political institutions and containment of immigration were among the consequences of delayed industrial revolution. Thus, one can argue that in time the partisan war indirectly contributed to some national control over the distributive system and helped to preserve national consciousness and the determination to survive as a nation. The opposition in the 1970s owes a good deal to the partisan movement. It reenforces the popular perception of Soviet rule as illegitimate and provides many of the cadres of national and religious dissent.

Human Rights: Processes of Modernization in the USSR (Littleton, Colo., 1977), pp. 116-119.

57. M. Gregorauskas, **Tarybų Lietuvos žemės ūkis, 1940-1960** (Vilnius, 1960), pp. 206, 212.

Chapter III

INSTITUTIONAL AND CULTURAL NATIONALISM 1953-1970

The hope of liberation by the West did not disappear with the end of the partisan war, which roughly coincided with the end of the Stalin era. The release of many political prisoners from concentration camps and exile, the uncertainties of the succession struggle, and the continuing cold war (as well as the Eisenhower-Dulles policy of liberation) continued to fuel hopes of emancipation, creating a sensitive political atmosphere. There is some evidence that a new political underground came into being (the National People's Front claims to have been founded in 1955, for example), arousing new political expectations. The Hungarian events were followed by significant nationalist demonstrations in Vilnius and Kaunas. However, the sudden violent crushing of the Hungarian freedom fighters also finally dashed the hopes for a national liberation achieved by popular action and/or intervention by the West. A long struggle was clearly to be the only path to national emancipation.

The post-Stalin dissent took the form of a movement that sought to maintain national identity and values through national control of regime institutions and through a program of cultural development within and outside the legal framework of the system. Clandestine nationalist activity continued but was mainly passive in nature, with only sporadic nationalist outbursts. The most important national work, however, proceeded within the framework of the regime. At this point, let us briefly consider the extra-legal nationalist activity.

1. COVERT NATIONALISM AFTER STALIN

The very fact that demonstrations occurred in Vilnius and Kaunas during the Hungarian events indicates that the period of massive repression was over.[1] A recent anonymous account from

---

1. For two eyewitness reports of these demonstrations, see Doc. No. 16.

Lithuania, which appears to be genuine, describes the reaction of the Soviet regime to the demonstrations:

> MVD soldiers and Russians, their bayonets poised, would surround the peaceful demonstrations, but would not fire at the demonstrators. When the Lithuanian SSR security checked with Moscow about opening fire on the demonstrators, Moscow categorically forbade any shooting. The demonstrators were dispersed by militia employing nightsticks, truncheons, and even rifle-butts against the students. The KGB was acting rather tactfully at that time; although it kept the students under very close observation, it arrested only about a dozen individuals after one of the demonstrations. Only a few days later did the security arrest several dozen activists, yet under pressure of a new wave of rebels, it released most of them. When the student unrest subsided, the security quietly arrested many demonstrators in Kaunas and Vilnius. Members of several nationalist groups were arrested on that occasion. In Vilnius, security men arrested members of the *Nacionalinis Liaudies Frontas* (The National People's Front) which, according to a KGB estimate, had a relatively more widespread underground organization that was active in all the institutions of higher learning in Vilnius by using the conspiratorial pattern of the Russian revolutionary democrats—small separate units unknown to and independent from each other. The names of the legal and illegal groups and organizations frequently changed but their goal was the same: to raise the nation's consciousness, to fight against the intruders, to seek social equality and political freedom for Lithuania, to collaborate with all the Baltic nations, and, taking to task Lenin's theses about the right to national self-determination, to protest to the government in Moscow the curtailment of freedom for non-Russian nations, who are seeking to restore or to create their national independent states.[2]

The same account also outlines the national movement, especially during the 1960s. This account deserves special attention in view of the scarcity of documents for this period:

---

2. This account was published in the Canadian Lithuanian newspaper **Tėviškės Žiburiai,** July 31, 1975. According to the editorial note the author was a participant in some of the events described. The account was written while the author was on a trip to the West. This report is the most significant corroborative evidence that a National People's Front did in fact exist. Some of the statements of the NPF are published in this anthology in Doc. Nos. 26, 34, 36.

The university students of the Lithuanian SSR, influenced by the members of intelligentsia who had returned from
their forced exile in Russia, joined a new kind of nationalist
movement, manifesting itself in many forms, legal and
illegal. Only a small percentage of the young sold out by
assisting the KGB, the Party, and the Communist Youth
Organization and by acting against the Lithuanian rebirth
movement that manifested itself during the so-called Soviet
renaissance.

Students developed a more active interest in Lithuania's
history. They criticized the officially promulgated history
textbook by J. Žiugžda, calling it falsification of Lithuania's
history and looking instead for the forbidden book on
Lithuania's history written by Antanas Šapoka.[3] They
demanded that the curriculum of literature, taught in the
departments of philology, be enlarged to include the
Lithuanian writers and poets who had fled to the West, such
as Bernardas Brazdžionis, Vincas Krėvė-Mickevičius, and
others.[4]

To honor the rehabilitated poets who had returned from
the distant areas of the USSR, such as Kazys Inčiūra and
others, the students organized semi-legal literary evenings.
The members of the intelligentsia who had returned from
Russia joined the student movement not without risk. V.
Paulaitis, for instance, who was subsequently arrested again
by the KGB, was active in Kaunas, and Kazys Inčiūra in
Vilnius.[5] Inčiūra's poetry written during the years of
deportation was read by the students in private soirees and
within small illegal groups.

3. Juozas Žiugžda directed the writing of history to fit the Soviet
and Marxist model. **Lietuvos TSR istorija** (Vilnius, 1958) is the summary
of a four volume history issued by the Institute of History of the
Lithuanian SSR Academy of Sciences. The history is notable for its
distortion of Russian-Lithuanian relations and emphasis on class
struggle as the basis of Lithuania's historical development. A. Šapoka
(1906—1961) was the editor and author of **Lietuvos istorija** (Kaunas,
1936 and later editions), still among the most objective histories of
Lithuania.

4. Bernardas Brazdžionis, now residing in the US, is known for his
fervent patriotic, religious, and humanistic verse. Vincas Krėvė-
Mickevičius (1882—1954), a noted dramatist and literary scholar, served
for a while in the People's Government of Lithuania (June—July, 1940),
but broke with the Soviets and left the country. He died in Philadelphia.
Some of the works of Krėvė have been published in Lithuania, but
practically nothing of Brazdžionis' poetry.

5. Paulaitis (first name Petras, rather than V. as in the text) was a

Thus, the student body of the Lithuanian SSR began to
grasp the situation and to form, first in a spontaneous and
then in a planned manner, both legal and illegal groups and
underground organizations. The student movement spread
even to the rural areas and had its effect on factory workers as
well as soldiers.

Small secret groups working to raise the national
consciousness were organized at the V. Kapsukas State
University in Vilnius, alongside the officially permitted
circles of history, philology, ethnography, tourism, and
others.

In order to oppose an atheist circle active in one
institution of higher education, an illegal Catholic group was
organized. This group grew and subsequently became the
Lietuvos Katalikų Sąjunga (Lithuanian Catholic Association).[6] A
group was formed inside the official ethnography circle.
Taking advantage of the statutes of the circle, that group
started visiting Lithuanians living in Belorussia.[7] The
Lithuanian SSR KGB became interested in academicians and
historians, even in Lithuanian Communist Party members
who, instead of paying homage to the monuments of Lenin,
Dzerzhinski, Vincas Mickevičius-Kapsukas, and other
revolutionaries, "sank into the morass of venerating national
antiquities," according to a Marxist expression.

As if that were not enough, during the decade of the
"Soviet renaissance," students of the Kaunas Polytechnical
Institute, the Vilnius Academy of Art, and the Vilnius State
University wrote letters to Justas Paleckis on the subject of
building a monument to Gediminas at the foot of the castle-
hill.[8] They sent anonymous letters to individual citizens,

---

leader of the anti-Nazi and anti-Soviet underground, has spent over 30
years in the Gulag Archipelago. For a brief biography, see **Aušra,** No. 11
(May, 1978). Kazys Inčiūra (1906—1974) was an actor, playwright, and
poet. He continued to act until 1951 when apparently he was deported.
Destalinization permitted Inčiūra to return home. His precise role in the
national activity here described is obscure.

6. This organization is mentioned as one of the constituent units of
the National People's Front. No further information on this organization
is available. See Doc. No. 26.

7. A lengthy two-part report "On the Situation of the Lithuanians in
the Belorussian Republic" has been issued in the **samizdat.** For excerpts
from this report, see Doc. No. 21.

8. At that time Justas Paleckis was the Chairman of the Presidium of
the Lithuanian SSR Supreme Soviet. Gediminas (ca 1275—1341) was a
great ruler of the medieval Lithuanian state, a founder of a long line of
Lithuanian-Polish kings.

enclosing the testaments of Salomėja Nėris and Antanas Žukauskas (Vienuolis), who are considered anti-Soviet by the KGB.[9]

Several patriotic groups, calling themselves *frontininkai* (frontliners), were active in the academic milieu. They established connections with Latvian and Estonian students in Riga and Talinn and formed a semi-legal organization—the Baltic Students' Association, which was later abolished by Moscow for its too intensive brotherly friendship among the three nations. Yet links among Lithuanians, Latvians, and Estonians, especially between the Lithuanians and Estonians, were developing without official governmental control.

Several of the noteworthy activities mentioned in this account deserve special attention. The efforts of students and intellectuals to assist Lithuanians in Belorussia have been documented in a lengthy *samizdat* document, dated 1972, excerpts from which are published in the documents section (Doc. No. 21). The activity goes back to the late 1950s and resembles the legal protests of the 1970s: writing of statements and petitions to Soviet leaders, demanding the respect of national rights guaranteed by Soviet law.

Judging from the security and party organ crackdown on ethnographic clubs in 1972 and later, some of these clubs had become centers of nationalist activity.[10] The legally functioning ethnographic society provided a means of contact and nationalistic activity not only among the young intelligentsia and students but also with their counterparts in other republics. Evidently the ethnographic clubs focused attention on the non-Soviet past or even on the anti-Soviet ethnography (such as the collection of songs of the postwar partisan movement). In 1973 the head of the party's Agitation and Propaganda Department, J. Kuolelis, acknowledged that "in recent years not only great achievements of enthusiasts of ethnography, but also essential errors and shortcomings became evident in the work of

---

9. Salomėja Neris (1904—1945), an oustanding poetess of Lithuania, joined the communist cause in 1940. Allegedly before her death she became disenchanted with the Soviet regime and wrote a statement to that effect. Antanas Vienuolis-Žukauskas (1882—1957), a noted writer of occasional leftist leanings. Texts of the alleged testaments are not available in the West.

10. A lengthy survey of ethnographic activities is provided by **Aušra,** No. 9 (January, 1978). For excerpts and reports of repressions of ethnographic club members, see Doc. No. 24.

ethnographic associations."[11] The security began a campaign of harassment, interrogation, and even arrests of ethnographers, continuing as late as 1976, while the party and Komsomol organizations were directed to shift the attention of such groups to the study of the Soviet period.

Finally, the cited report on the national movement suggests that *samizdat* materials began circulating in the country, such as the alleged testaments of the writers Neris and Vienuolis, practically nothing of which has reached the West. An example of an early attempt to publish literature in *samizdat* is provided by Tomas Venclova, a poet and scholar of literature, who has recently chosen emigration.[12] According to Venclova, the optimism born of Khrushchevian reforms quickly developed into what he calls "cultural and partly technological opposition." "For a long time," writes Venclova, "people sought to work within the limits of the system, do something or other.... At that time also in Lithuania there appeared a certain cultural revival... There appeared people who were doing something within the framework of the system—in literature, art, music, science, and many other spheres—they did what has not been done and could not be done during the Stalin years." In Venclova's view, this opposition was divided into two currents: one working within the framework of the system, remaining loyal to it; the second tending to move in the direction of a more open confrontation and *samizdat* activity. At the end of 1960 Alexander Ginzburg went to Vilnius to arrange for a special issue of his unofficial journal *Syntax* to be devoted to Lithuanian literature. Venclova and a number of others began preparing the issue, but the KGB discovered and seized the materials upon the search and arrest of Ginzburg. The Lithuanian collaborators were interrogated, but no charges or punishment resulted. The only outcome was an anti-intellectual book by J. Marcinkevičius, based on the materials of the case, under the title *Pušis, kuri juokėsi* (The Pine That Laughed). It was obviously politically motivated work to warn as well as ridicule those who dissent from official ideology. This case was among the first known attempts of collaboration between Moscow and Vilnius dissidents.

The national movement in the 1960s produced no spec-

---

11. **Komunistas,** 1973, No. 3 (March), p. 12.

12. See Venclova's account of the dissident movement in the Soviet Union and Lithuania in **Į Laisvę** (Los Angeles), 1977, No. 71 (December), pp. 24—35.

tacular achievements, but it clearly contributed to a more militant confrontation with the Soviet regime in the 1970s. It also began forging ties between the Moscow and the Vilnius dissidents, which stimulated dissent in Lithuania and made it known throughout the world.

2. INSTITUTIONAL NATIONALISM

REPUBLIC-ORIENTED POLICIES

Until the 1970s Western scholars tended to dismiss nationalist deviations as insignificant aspects of Soviet politics, in part because of the extreme centralization of the system and because of the pervasiveness of political and police controls. Yet the frequent Soviet references to "localism," "bourgeois nationalism," "national exclusiveness," "nationalistic cadre policies," and "autarchy," suggest that significant decentralist tendencies have been and remain part and parcel of Soviet political development.

Of course, not all deviations from centralism are nationalistic. Some may be defined as nationalistic in that they deliberately seek to maintain or enhance national identity and separateness and to control at least in part the distributive system of society. Other decentralist tendencies may be defined as bureaucratic, i.e., they are the efforts of provincial elites to expand their sphere of competence and to enhance their role in decision-making. Such bureaucratic tendencies may nevertheless be supportive of national interests to the extent that they contribute to local control over the distributive system. In reality, behind every decentralist policy there are nationalistic and bureaucratic motives. Thus, the decentralist policies of republic elites could be defined as "republic-oriented" and, whatever the motivation, they tend to be nationalistic in their effect.

A number of circumstances have enabled the republic elites to promote policies that favorably affect republic autonomy and national distinctiveness. First, there has always been some—and occasionally much—ambiguity in the formula for nationality policy. Both the assimilationist and the developmental ("the flowering") position could be derived from statements by the authorities of Marxism-Leninism. Especially in periods of doctrinal uncertainty, it is much easier to articulate republic or national demands and to implement them. In addition, leadership crises have created policy vacuums and opportunities for advancing republic interests. Finally, the federal principle and the formal recognition of "republic sovereignty" do give some authority to republic organs in decision-making and especially in policy implementation.

Besides the general conditions for deviation within the system, a number of Khrushchev's moves offered unprecedented opportunities for advancing republic interests. Of overwhelming significance was destalinization. As a result of loosened police and ideological controls, the possibilities for national creative expression were vastly expanded. Khrushchev also moved to expand the role of the republics. In part this expansion was symbolic (for example, the persmission to have republic flags, anthems, republic penal codes), but more significantly, the new republic role offered opportunities for promotion of national cadres. The decentralization of economic management and the creation of republic-based Economic Councils (the *Sovnarkhoz*) gave the republic responsibility over most of the economy within the republic. The *Sovnarkhoz* raised the republic managers and economic planners to new heights of power and required the expansion of republics' administrative and political bureaucracies. All in all, the republic ruling elites, at least for some time under Khrushchev, found themselves within significantly wider political parameters that could be exploited to national or bureaucratic advantage.

Of course, mere existence of opportunities is not sufficient to produce republic-oriented policies. However, in the case of the Lithuanian Communist Party leadership, for whatever motive, these opportunities were effectively utilized. In particular, the First Secretary of the Communist Party of Lithuania (CPL) Antanas Sniečkus was able and willing to maximize the promotion of republic interests and he was generally seconded by the intelligentsia to the extent that his policies appeared to be nationally advantageous. Sniečkus was among the most astute and influential provincial functionaries of the CPSU. He was one of the oldest first secretaries, having remained in the position since the imposition of Soviet rule in Lithuania in 1940. He had powerful friends and sponsors in the Kremlin (among them certainly M. Suslov, and very likely A. Kosygin) and in the central party-government bureaucracy. Since the early 1950s his policies, to the extent that he and his colleagues could influence or determine them, became increasingly republic-oriented. On the occasion of his death in 1974, an intimate of Sniečkus defined these policies as follows:

> This policy was multi-faceted: cultivation and utilization

of strong connections in Moscow (in this respect especially important were his old personal ties of friendship with M. Suslov, who in 1945-46 directed the Bureau for Lithuania of the All Union Communist Party (b) and lived in Vilnius); the establishment of his influence over the second secretaries sent in from Russia (this was very successful in the cases of Isachenko and Trofimov, completely unsuccessful with Sharkov, who, however, had to leave Lithuania); the appropriate selection of cadres in the apparatus, who were obedient and personally committed to him; the sabotage of certain directives of Moscow, proceeding as though they were being most thoroughly implemented (for example, the campaign for corn cultivation and the expansion of area for grain production at the expense of pastureland); the exaction of various additional privileges for Lithuania (one of the perennial arguments for this—the mass Lithuanian emigration, the need to prove that Lithuania is flourishing in the family of fraternal republics); the procuring of special privileges of all kinds (as, for example, the right for the peasants to use personally 1 ha. of land in return for the feeding of one pig and the delivery to the state); and so on... And if today Lithuania has remained ethnically one of the most compact republics (over 80% of the inhabitants are of Lithuanian nationality), if the development of industry in Lithuania proceeded more or less smoothly, without damage to the beauty of our nature and without pollution of the environment, if agriculture has remained productive and the provisioning of the inhabitants is maintained at higher levels than in other republics, if not only Donelaitis, but also Basanavičius and Maironis are being taught in schools—all this is a consequence of such a policy of Sniečkus. However difficult and sad life may be in contemporary Lithuania, in the Soviet Union the latter is considered as the republic having the best preserved traditions and at the same time having advanced farthest on the road of modernization.[13]

Of course, such policies, which in their consequences though not necessarily in motivation contributed to the national identity of Lithuania, were not consistently or evenly pursued. Their extent and success depended on many factors, not the least of which was the political situation in the Kremlin. Sniečkus apparently began to turn away from Stalinism when his Jewish colleagues in the party and old revolutionary accomplices came under attack in

13. T. Ženklys (pseudonym), in **Akiračiai** (Chicago), March, 1974, p. 7. The article is an excellent first-hand survey of politics on the republic level, especially the role of Sniečkus.

the wake of the last excesses of Stalin. He was obviously relieved by the death of Stalin. Again his fortunes were at their lowest when Khrushchev began to rescind his nationality policy in the early 1960s. There was an obvious friction with Khrushchev, who had publicly criticized Snieckus on several occasions (for the reconstruction of the historic castle in Trakai and for resistance to his agricultural policies). Allegedly one of the reasons why Khrushchev refused to visit Lithuania was its nationalism. Snieckus was in favor of the coup against Khrushchev and with great enthusiasm related the events in Moscow to his republic party leaders.[14] Under the Brezhnev-Kosygin regime, Snieckus' tenure was relatively secure, for he apparently had the support of Suslov and Kosygin; at the same time, the collective leadership in the Kremlin was not in a position to engage in personnel changes. Nevertheless, as will be suggested later, the rising nationalist and religious dissent in the 1970s was making his position precarious. Snieckus' death in 1974 probably relieved the Kremlin of a politically difficult task.

Destalinization and decentralization of economic management, combined with a republic-oriented elite, created the conditions for an institutional nationalism that was always on the verge of becoming openly known. Snieckus knew the limits and managed to contain the nationalistic tendencies through a combination of threats, bargaining in the Kremlin for concessions for the republic, and safeguarding his cadres. Thus, for example, in 1958 in the Tenth Congress of the CPL, Snieckus delivered this blunt warning: "Either we go with the Russian nation, with all the Soviet nations on the road of national development, or with imperialist slavery, the possibility of annihilation of the Lithuanian nation. There is no third road."[15] Snieckus managed to avoid extensive purges (as in Latvia, for example[16]), and an occasional scapegoat sufficed to prevent Kremlin intervention.

---

14. Private communication.

15. **Tiesa,** February 13, 1958.

16. A major purge of the Latvian party leadership was carried out in 1959 under the supervision of Khrushchev himself, who traveled to Riga for the occasion. The reason for the purge—a strong bid for autonomy in economic policy and efforts to curtail denationalization of Latvia through massive immigration of Russians. See the study by Gundar Julian King, **Economic Policies in Occupied Latvia: A Manpower Management Study** (Tocoma, Wash., 1965); also the study by Thomas Remeikis, "Modernization and National Identity in the Baltic Republics: Uneven and Multi-Directional Change in the Components of Moder-

With some justification Sniečkus was popularly referred to as "šeimininkas," which can be translated as "master of the household." His death in 1974 was marked by a genuine concern and anxiety regarding the future of the republic.

How the Lithuanian intelligentsia and the populace at large perceive and utilize opportunities for the advancement of national interests is described in a recent *samizdat* report by Eitan Finkelstein, Jewish dissident in Lithuania:

> During the past twenty years the bulk of the Lithuanian inhabitants has put its hope in the gradual and unswerving Lithuanianization of the country. This process proceeds in three directions: the appointment of Lithuanians to leading and administrative apparatus, the development of national culture, and the education of the younger generation in the national tradition. From a formal point of view achievements in all these areas have been impressive.[17]

It should be added that in the economic sphere as well the republic elite has sought to maximize republic interests and to preserve ethnic distinctiveness and a degree of economic autonomy. A brief survey of these achievements with respect to cadre policy, culture, and the economy suggests why the intelligentsia has been so confident in its ability to preserve national values and why it has viewed open dissent with considerable skepticism.

THE NATURE OF PARTY ELITE

Among the significant factors contributing to decentralist tendencies is the ethnic composition of the republic party organization and the intelligentsia in general. The responsiveness of the local regime to popular sentiments depends in part on the ethnic background of the leadership group. Thus, recruitment and promotion of national cadres may be viewed as an indicator of an attempt to safeguard republic interests through control over political, economic, social, and cultural institutions of the regime.

The postwar period began with seriously depleted Lithuanian cadres. As a result of war and Stalinism, most of the prewar elite

---

nization", in Ihor Kemenetsky, ed., **Nationalism and Human Rights: Processes of Modernization in the USSR** (Littleton, Colo., 1977), pp. 115—138.

17. First published in **Akiračiai**, June, 1977.

either fled to the West or were repressed. The CPL came out of the war with 3,536 members, of whom only 1,127 were Lithuanians.[18] As a result, cadres from other republics, mostly Russians, were commandeered to Lithuania. By 1947 communists of Slavic nationality constituted over 70% of the CPL membership. Non-Lithuanian functionaries dominated in the top party and government bureaucracies—an alien regime was indeed imposed upon the Lithuanian people.

After Stalin's death an intense nationalization of leading cadres began. The succession struggle offered opportunities for change. The liquidation of Beria was followed by a series of changes in the top personnel in the Lithuanian Soviet regime, especially affecting non-Lithuanian functionaries. Involved in the shakeup were Ministries of Internal Affairs and State Security, a number of deputy ministers, and even the second secretary of the CPL, the Kremlin's watchdog in the republic. Briefly that position, normally reserved for an outsider, was occupied by a Lithuanian.[19]

Following Beria's liquidation a green light for a more intense promotion of national cadres was given. The signal was given in the Fifth Plenum of the CPL Central Committee on June 11-13, 1953, when the main item on the agenda was "Concerning serious shortcomings in the political work and leadership for economic and cultural development in the Lithuanian SSR." The plenum pointed out a number of distortions in the nationality policy in the republic. "These distortions are especially manifested in the weak development of Lithuanian national cadres and their advancement to leading party, government, and economic work."[20] The subsequent vigorous promotion of national cadres is reflected in the growing proportion of Lithuanians on the CPL Central Committee, the Council of Ministers, and other institutions of the Soviet regime. Similar tendencies are apparent with respect to the membership of the CPL. The membership of the CPL grew by about 7,000 between 1953 and 1956, while the number of communists of Slavic

---

18. Statistics on CPL membership derived from Partijos Istorijos Institutas prie LKP CK, Lietuvos Komunistų Partija skaičiais, 1918-1975 (Vilnius, 1976).

19. See reports of personnel changes in Tiesa, March—June, 1953; also Thomas Remeikis, Communist Party of Lithuania: A Historical and Political Study (Ph. D. Dissertation, University of Illinois, 1963), chap. XVII.

20. Editorial in Tiesa, July 2, 1953.

Table 3. Ethnic Composition of the
Leading Cadres in Lithuania

Cadre Group		% Lithuanians
1. Membership of the Communist Party of Lithuania	1945	32
	1953	38
	1956	47
	1964	63
	1975	68
2. a) Central Committee members & candidates	1949	54
	1952	56
	1960	75
	1976	77
b) Politbureau and Secretariat	1971	87
	1976	93
3. Council of Ministers	1947	55
	1959	77
	1967	87
	1975	93
4. Scientific workers	1960	84
	1973	86
5. Specialists with higher education	1960	78
	1973	81
6. Students in higher education	1960	89
	1973	84

Sources: 1) Ethnic composition of CPL membership is provided in the statistical collection **Lietuvos Komunistų Partija skaičiais 1918-1975** (Vilnius, 1976), pp. 120-123, compiled by the Party History Institute of the CPL. 2) Biographical data for most Central Committee and Council of Ministers members are readily available; ethnic identification is made on the basis of a biographical file compiled by the author; in cases where biographies are not available, the ethnic identification is made on basis of surnames, consequently involving some inaccuracies in percentages given. 3) Ethnic composition of specialists and students is derived from the annual of statistics **Lietuvos TSR ekonomika ir kultūra 1973 metais** (Vilnius, 1974), pp. 58, 304, 397, 398.

nationalities even declined. In fact, membership figures indicate that several thousand non-Lithuanian communists left the republic during this period.

The second round of promotions of national cadres occurred between the destalinization speech and 1959. All in all, the number of Lithuanians in the CPL increased from 17,761 to 36,129 between 1956 and 1961, while the number of communists of Slavic background reached 19,784, slightly more than in 1952. By 1959 Lithuanians were dominant, even disproportionately so in a number of instances, in the leading positions of the party, government, industry, and cultural institutions.

Several conditions favored the rapid advancement of national personnel. First of all, by 1956 the Soviet regime in Lithuania developed its own cadres, which had not been available after the war. Secondly, a period of intense socioeconomic development began, requiring expansion of various bureaucracies. The decentralization of industrial management and the creation of the Economic Councils further increased republic control and opportunities for cadre selection and promotion. Finally, the advancement of the newly trained cultural and technical intelligentsia to high positions was favored by the central leadership, which was concerned with increasing the effectiveness of cadres in all areas of activity. Thus the Lithuanian regime pushed young specialists into top posts replacing the relatively uneducated and incompetent old Lithuanian communists and the non-Lithuanian cadres in general that had been sent into Lithuania by Stalin.[21]

The non-Lithuanian cadres were pushed out for two reasons: incompetence and language. The centrally sanctioned requirement that various functionaries and administrators in a republic must know the language of the population gave a chance to local leaders. to appoint cadres strictly on the basis of their knowledge of Lithuanian, applying this policy sometimes even to hiring of ordinary laborers. A number of non-Lithuanian communists were, in effect, forced to leave the republic for lack of knowledge of the Lithuanian language or of competence.

The ascendancy of native communists was marked by friction between communists of different nationalities and forced the leadership to take steps to safeguard from discrimina-

---

21. The rapid promotion of young cadres is reflected in the 1959 census data, according to which the overwhelming majority in leading government and party posts were people under 40 years of age. **Lietuvos TSR gyventojai** (Vilnius, 1963), p. 103.

tion non-Lithuanian communists and cadres in general. The matter reached a showdown by 1959, when in May of that year the Central Committee of the CPSU discussed the issue and issued a decision, "Concerning the work with cadres of the Central Committee of the CPL." The decision was subsequently reviewed in a Plenum of the Central Committee of the CPL, which met on July 17, 1959. Fragmentary disclosures of the discussions during the session confirm the above interpretation.[22] Among the scapegoats for nationalistic cadre policies was the Rector of the University of Vilnius and a number of other educators. The First Secretary of the CPL Antanas Sniečkus stated in the meeting that:

> Not all heads of organizations and offices, however, paid attention to the fact that our republic is multinational and that this circumstance must be reflected in the work with cadres. There were even such leaders who took a nationalist road. This road was taken by the former rector of Vilnius State University Juozas Bulavas.[23]

In another speech, to the Vilnius Party organization, Sniečkus further added that "it is not permissible in the future that valuable workers must leave the republic just because they do not know the (Lithuanian) language." However, at the same time he continued to emphasize that appointment of personnel should be on basis of merit and that incompetents should be weeded out, no matter what their nationality. In effect, competence still could be used by local functionaries to discriminate against nonnatives. However, by 1959 national intelligentsia assumed key positions of influence within the republic and have managed to maintain their role ever since.

TENDENCIES OF ECONOMIC AUTARCHY

Republic orientation was also evident in the economic sphere. It was manifested in a number of areas, including the shaping of the economic future of the republic consistent with its labor and resource profile. Two circumstances favored republic-

---

22. Apparently neither the decision of the Central Committee of the CPSU nor the decision of the CPL Central Committee Plenum was published in full. An indirect account is found in an article by P. Kanopa, "Internationalist Upbringing of Collectives in Factories in Vilnius (1956-1961)," in **LKP istorijos klausimai** (Vilnius, 1964), Vol. IV, pp. 97-114.

23. **Komunistas**, 1959, No. 8 (August), p. 2.

oriented policies. First of all, industrial development of Lithuania was at a low level after World War II and for various reasons was pushed at a much slower rate than in the rest of the Soviet Union. This meant that the pattern of economic development was finally set in the late 1950s and early 1960s when opportunities for republic input into economic planning were most numerous. In addition, the *sovnarkhoz* system provided the framework for a greater role of the republic in the determination of its economic future.

The decentralization of economic management led to serious nationalist and autarchic tendencies, requiring a statement of "containment" from Sniečkus:

> Every development of the creative initiative must be attuned to the centralized elements.... Separate tendencies toward localism, attempts to solve economic problems on the basis of limited local tasks may become evident. Such tendencies must be combatted from the very beginning.... One should not forget that our enemies may try to exploit tendencies of this kind in order to inflict harm on us or to undermine our forces. Nobody will ever succeed in weakening the unbreakable force of friendship among the nations of the USSR or in separating the Lithuanian nation from the great Russian nation and from other nations of the Soviet Union.[24]

In general, the republic economic managers were relatively satisfied with the *sovnarkhoz* system, which increased their role in administrative management, gave greater control over personnel and the development of the republic's economy, and provided some funds that could be used at the discretion of the republic. Even though in the early sixties Khrushchev again took a centralist course, republic managers continued to play key roles, and this was still preferable to branch management of industry from Moscow. The decision of the September 1965 Plenum of the Central Committee of the CPSU to return to branch management meant a power shift to Moscow and was received by republic economic managers with reluctance. The implications of the post-Khrushchev reforms to republic interests were clear: if under the *sovnarkhoz* arrangement localist tendencies were more likely, then under the new system, ministry-oriented deviation, with neglect or insufficient attention to republic interests, was a likely consequence. Typical was the reaction of A.

---

24. **Tiesa**, June 8, 1967.

Drobnys, Chairman of the Lithuanian SSR State Plan Commission:

> Under the new conditions for leadership in production planning, it is especially important to correctly reconcile the planning from the center for development of separate branches of industry with the tasks of comprehensive development of production forces according to territory, considering local economic and natural conditions and the general direction of development of the republic economy. In other words, the main task of the planning organs of our republic—to assure comprehensive development of the national economy, to form the most rational structure of the entire industry, independently of the jurisdiction over separate branches of industry, maintaining economically sound directions and tendencies of development of our industry, blocking the road for possible manifestations of branch orientations and localism. [25]

The concern of the republic planners was quite evident: would the center pay sufficient attention to republic interests— comprehensive development of republic economy consistent with natural and human resources? Drobnys especially singled out the machine tool industry and metal-working industries, which are under union jurisdiction and at the same time key industries in the economic development of Lithuania.

> Therefore, despite the changed nature of jurisdiction over the industry, it is necessary to continue devoting no less attention to the development of this branch of industry. It is especially important to maintain the principal direction of specialization of republic machine production, consistent with available labor resources as well as with the perspective development of cities.[26]

Thus the question is whether Moscow or Vilnius will decide where and what kind of industrial plant would be built or expanded. Despite Moscow's jurisdiction over the machine industry or any other industry, the republic planners hoped that their "suggestions" as to location and specialization of industry would be heeded by planners. In the minds of the Lithuanian intelligentsia the kind and location of industry are of utmost economic and national significance, for the type of industry developed will determine the degree of integration of Lithuanian economy into the

25. **Tiesa,** November 3, 1965.
26. **Ibid.**

union and the location of it will affect the ethnic demography of the country.

Whatever the fears of republic elites, by the time the *sovnarkhoz* system was abandoned, the pattern of economic development of Lithuania was pretty much set, and the reorganization of economic management does not appear to have upset the determined direction of development. The economic development in the 1970s essentially followed the lines projected in perspective development plans during the 1960s. [27]

Among the specific economic policies for which the republic elite lobbied and to a significant extent achieved their objectives, the following may be indicated. First, specialization of industrial production, especially the machine tool and metal-working industry and the industry for processing agricultural production—in general, the development of labor-intensive industries in resource-poor Lithuania—prevailed. Such development was not only rational and economically advantageous to the republic, but also, one might add, most autarchic.

Second, industrial development was designed to utilize locally available labor reserves and specialized personnel. One of the devices used was a master-plan for a decentralized urbanization through dispersal of industry.[28] Still under the *sovnarkhoz* system, the republic planners set up a development of several medium provincial cities where rural labor surplus could easily and cheaply be absorbed by industry. An additional, though formally unspecified, advantage of industrial dispersal would be containment of immigration from other republics, for studies have shown that new plants in large metropolitan areas such as Kaunas and Vilnius were more likely to attract a very large proportion of labor from other republics.[29] In the more industrialized Latvian republic, Russian immigration had reached

---

27. For a description of the perspective economic development plan up to the 1980s, see K. Meškauskas, V. Januškevičius, "Problems of Long-run Development and Distribution of the Productive Forces of the Lithuanian SSR", **Lietuvos TSR Mokslų akademijos darbai,** Serija A, 2(30), 1969, pp. 3-19; also **Liaudies Ūkis,** 1968, No. 7 (July), p. 203.

28. For details of the regional urbanization plan, see Thomas Remeikis, "Preliminary Results and Prospects of Controlled Urbanization in Lithuania", in **Proceedings of the Institute of Lithuanian Studies, 1971** (Chicago, 1971), pp. 191—226.

29. See, for example, the study by R. Blažys and V. Januškevičius on the sources of labor for new factories, published in **Liaudies Ūkis,** 1966, No. 4 (April).

alarming proportions, largely due to labor shortage, threatening the ethnic identity of the republic. Lithuanian planners learned from this situation and sought to evade the Latvian fate through eventual moderation of the republic's industrialization and through maximal utilization of local labor reserves.

Third, in the agricultural policies, republic planners sought to specialize agriculture in the direction of meat and milk production, a direction most consistent with the natural environment of the Lithuanian countryside. This effort involved defiance and sabotage of, for example, Khrushchev's corn campaign.[30] In the end, the policies of the Lithuanian agriculturalists prevailed.

The massive development of the chemical industry can be considered one of the failures of republic planners. There was a notable disagreement concerning the desirability of developing that industry in the republic.[31] Many prominent members of the economic, scientific, and cultural intelligentsia opposed the industry on economic, environmental, and even national grounds. While a fertilizer plant might be necessary for Lithuania's agriculture, an oil refinery, on the other hand, seemed to many to be neither necessary nor desirable. Thus, when in 1966 Moscow's proposal of constructing a large oil refinery at Jurbarkas on the Nemunas river became known, impassioned debate and behind-the-scenes lobbying to scrap the project ensued.[32] The debate indicates the motivations of the republic intelligentsia and perhaps even of the political elite. One source close to First Secretary of the CPL Antanas Sniečkus has suggested that the effort might have been inspired by Sniečkus to provide him with arguments in Moscow.[33] In the relatively open debate over the merits of the project printed in *Tiesa* in March 1966, the following arguments against the refinery emerged: the dislocation of national economy due to overconcentration on the project; a disproportionate and one-sided development of the economy; influx of a large number of specialists from other republics; pollution of water, air, and the countryside, with considerable harm to the beauty of the country, fishing industry, tourism, and

30. According to the testimony of T. Ženklys, **op. cit.**, and other private communications.

31. This is reflected, for example, in an empirical evaluation of the relative value or rationality in developing various branches of industry: V. Januškevičius and A. Skupeika, "Which Industry Should We Develop in Lithuania?," **Mokslas ir Technika**, 1967, No. 6, pp. 8-10.

32. See **Tiesa**, March 16, 1966 and March 19, 1966.

33. According to T. Ženklys, **op. cit.**

even to the health of the population; diversion of funds needed for alleviation of housing shortage; creation of industry without a base of human and natural resources, hence a closer economic integration of the republic into the Soviet Union; and doubtful economic returns to the republic. While not all the arguments are valid, the republic orientation behind them is quite obvious.

Opposition to the refinery was not confined to open discussion in *Tiesa*. There were actual efforts to pressure authorities to abandon the project. This is evident in a lengthy letter by prominent scientists, professors, and intellectuals submitted to the Lithuanian authorities in March 1966, arguing against the project specifically and against tendencies of overindustrialization and the ensuing environmental ravages.[34] The letter was deliberately leaked to the West, with intimations that the emigré circles raise a cry of Soviet colonialism. Although the pressure did not result in abandonment of the project, it did result in significant modifications of the original proposal. The site for the refinery was shifted to Mažeikiai, near the Latvian border and the Baltic Sea, where the environmental impact was likely to be less critical. Furthermore, assurances were given that most modern techniques of pollution control would be implemented.

The development of industry in the absence of a natural base or of one that is not designed to serve essentially the republic is viewed as a form of colonialism motivated by political and military considerations. This viewpoint, obviously shared by many, was recently expressed in an article in the *Chronicle*, which summarized the 1966 memorandum of the intelligentsia and added its own critique of the construction of a nuclear power station in Northeastern Lithuania:

> Moscow sees only utility in our natural environment. The oil refinery and the nuclear power station are being constructed primarily for military and political reasons: (1) In case of war, Lithuania would become a fuel depot and transfer station for electrical power, (2) Lithuania would be

---

34. Most of the text of the letter was published in the West in **The Baltic Review**, 1967, No. 33, pp. 23—24. Excerpts from the letter published here in Doc. No. 17. For an obvious response to the letter, see the interview with A. Žukauskas, Vice-President of the Lithuanian SSR Academy of Sciences, in **Tiesa**, January 4, 1967. In the interview Žukauskas promised that the major objections to the project would be considered and resolved.

more closely bound to Russia's economy, (3) the northwestern (where the oil refinery is under construction— ed.) and the northeastern parts of Lithuania would become areas of Russian influx.[35]

All in all, the republic elites had a conception of republic distinct from the all-union economic interest and actively sought its realization. The economic well-being, prosperity, and ethnic identity of the republic are in part a consequence of these efforts.

CULTURAL ASSERTIVENESS

The "national in form, socialist in content" formula for cultural development is not ethnically neutral and inter- nationalizing, as the theory behind the formula assumes. For even the form, i.e., language, constitutes a principal element of identity and loyalty, the strongest correlate of nationality.[36] Likewise, the content of culture cannot be so purified as to exclude all elements of ethnic distinctiveness and world view. The extent to which the content of culture has a national orientation depends on the political context. This defines the parameters of creative activity and the willingness and capability of the intelligentsia to obtain maximal national benefits. The situation in Lithuania is well described by the noted Jewish dissident Eitan Finkelstein, a resident of Lithuania:

> The position of the intelligentsia in present-day Lithuania is in many respects different from the position of the intelligentsia in Moscow, Leningrad, and other major cultural centers. This is because the Lithuanian intelligentsia won much more in the process of destalinization than their Russian or Ukrainian counterparts. Among other things, destalinization provided the opportunity for the Lithuanian creative intelligentsia to create in the native language and, utilizing national themes, to immerse themselves in the studies of national culture and history; that is, to do things that were, a few years earlier, denounceable or criticizable as manifestations of nationalism. This up-to-then unheard of opportunity became a source of unique euphoria for a large part of the intelligentsia and its intensity was raised to a high degree by the rapid expansion of cultural and scientific

---

35. **Chronicle,** No. 20 (December 8, 1975).

36. This is a consensus among Western and Soviet scholars. See, for example, Brian Silver, "Social Mobilization and the Russification of Soviet Nationalities", **The American Political Science Review,** Vol. 68, No. 1 (January, 1974), pp. 45—68.

centers in which Lithuanians   occupied the principal
positions.

It is exactly due to this tempestuous creative activity of
the Lithuanian intelligentsia, erupting to the surface in the
late 1950s, that Lithuania saw great achievements in
architecture and decorative art, and book publishing and
applied art. During the first decade after Stalin's death,
interesting and, for that time, bold works appeared in
graphics and painting, unique theatrical productions, elegant
films, talented poetry, and promising prose.[37]

The impressive cultural reconstruction lasted longer in
Lithuania than it did elsewhere. Serious constraints on creative
and national activity appeared only after 1972 in the wake of the
dramatic nationalistic outbursts and the appearance of religious
dissent. Consequently, at this time, many intellectuals did not
perceive the threat of russification as very serious, as they had
during the years of Stalinist rule. Even though there were
limitations on the propagation of national culture, the limits were
broad enough for creative and scientific work to proceed on a
high level of competence and objectivity. According to Eitan
Finkelstein, even in 1976, "A large part of the creative Lithuanian
intelligentsia is still in the clutches of the illusion of 'freed
national culture'." To some extent this illusion explains why the
intellectual circles, with only a few exceptions, have been
reluctant to join the open dissent movement. A number of
impressive achievements in the cultural sphere have sustained
and continue to sustain an optimism that national culture can be
fruitfully   cultivated   within   the   existing   institutional
arrangements.

Of course, such optimism is not shared by the entire
intelligentsia. Some of the intelligentsia (and it is impossible to
estimate how many) obviously care nothing about the national
future and are concerned exclusively with their personal careers.
There are also those who view the national question with
foreboding and see russification as a serious threat to national
identity. However, this group of what may be called national
pessimists sees, at the same time, no alternative but to extract as
much as possible under the circumstances. For the time being,
they see no advantage in open dissent either, no matter how
sympathetic they might be to the goals of the dissenters.

Whatever the division of the intelligentsia among oppor-

---

37. Finkelstein in **Akiračiai**, June, 1977.

tunists, national pessimists, and national optimists, the latter can point to several obvious facts that have contributed to the maintenance of national identity and consciousness. For purposes of illustrations we shall consider three areas of achievement in this respect.

A fundamental concern, especially in view of Stalin's genocidal tendencies, has been the perservation of the ethnic homogeneity of the republic. In part because of the higher birth rate among the Lithuanians than among other nationalities, the repatriation of at least 200,000 exiles from Siberia and other parts of the Soviet Union, but also as a result of formal and informal policies followed by republic leaders, the percentage of Lithuanians in the republic increased from 79.3 in 1959 to 80.1 in 1970.[38] Among the policies of the republic elites that contributed to this are the following: cadre policies emphasizing the development and promotion of Lithuanians; economic planning and dispersal of industry to minimize immigration from other republics; some assimilation of non-Lithuanian minorities; and a generally hostile atmosphere toward the Russians. Last but not least, First Secretary of the CPL Antanas Snieckus reportedly successfully opposed the proposed merger of the Kaliningrad Oblast with Lithuania, which would have added over half a million people of non-Lithuanian nationality, thus significantly altering the ethnic balance and cultural atmosphere in the republic.[39]

The educational system, despite its goal of socializing the new internationalist Soviet man, has contributed to the national upbringing of the younger generation. As can be judged from the numerous spontaneous reactions of youth reported in the Soviet as well as the *samizdat* press, the effectiveness of Soviet socialization has been limited. Education from grade school to the university is in the Lithuanian language. In 1973, 85% of the primary and secondary students were attending Lithuanian-language schools.[40] The percentage suggests that some non-Lithuanian students attend the Lithuanian-language schools. Precise data are not available on the language in higher schools; however, private information indicates that there are very few

---

38. Data from the 1970 Soviet census. For analysis, see Benediktas Maciuika, "Auswertung der Volkszahlungsergebnisse von 1970 in Sovjetlitauen", **Acta Baltica** (Königstein in Taunus, W. Germany), 1972, Vol. XI, pp. 87-116.

39. According to the testimony of T. Zenklys, **op. cit.**, and other private communications.

40. See Table 2 and sources, p. 27.

specialties that can be acquired in the Russian language. A Jewish journalist who has since emigrated from Lithuania suggests that Lithuanian authorities deliberately eliminated most of the parallel Lithuanian and Russian courses at the University of Vilnius and other institutions of higher learning, forcing many Russian professors to leave their positions. The requirement that all prospective students pass entrance examinations in the Lithuanian language in effect excluded Russians from the universities. According to this source, one consequence of these nationalistic tendencies was the removal of the Chairman of the Council of Ministers M. Gedvilas and his deputy J. Grigalavičius from office (in 1956 and probably 1959, respectively).[41] The leadership of the University of Vilnius and the Pedagogical Institute of Vilnius were also later purged in 1959.

The republic educators managed to keep the general education schools teaching in other languages separate, despite efforts during the Khrushchev years to integrate all schools. Only a few schools are ethnically integrated; they provide parallel classes in Lithuanian and either Russian or Polish. Such nationally segregated educational facilities contribute to the maintenance of social distance between ethnic groups in Lithuania.

In Lithuania there is an eleven-year primary and secondary education (ten years in the rest of the Soviet Union outside the Baltic republics). The additional year of schooling may have been justified as necessary to teach competence in Russian, but at the same time it has provided additional time for native subjects. The privilege was about to be swept away by Khrushchev's educational reforms in 1964, but his fall from power intervened.[42] One private account of the situation claims that the educational commission from Moscow sent to deal with the question was dispatched by republic authorities back to Moscow upon the change of command in the Kremlin.

With respect to the content of education, there is no question that the presentation of Lithuanian culture and history suffers seriously from distortions or omissions. Nevertheless, the student is exposed to or has access to the principal primary sources on the history and culture of his nation and studies of his heritage which are remarkably competent despite the ideological

41. According to an article by Bar-Amas in **Tėviškės Žiburiai,** October 12, 1978.

42. It was already announced that Lithuanian schools will follow the ten-year pattern. See **Tarybinis Mokytojas,** August 1, 1964.

constraints. All in all, the schools as instruments of acculturation and assimilation (or russianization or russification) have
been largely ineffective and perhaps even counterproductive.

In the creative sphere a remarkable renaissance occurred as a
new generation of artists, writers, critics, and cultural scholars
began producing works in the freer post-Stalin context. The
ferment in arts involved modernistic trends and estheticism,
expanding or going beyond the constraints of socialist realism
and also the modern utilization of national motifs and a more
objective and fuller treatment of cultural heritage. For example,
in literature, experimentation in modern techniques such as
stream-of-consciousness in the novel, was undertaken by several
writers. Soviet life began to be depicted in a more honest manner
(warts and all!). The Soviet system itself and the cult of
personality became objects of critical writing. Even the postwar
partisan struggle received an even-handed treatment, sometimes
verging on a positive evaluation of the partisan movement.
Finally, cultural values—from works of the principal writers to
archeological artifacts—received scholarly attention and were
made available to the public.

The containment of these modernistic, nationalistic, and
liberal trends began in Lithuania in 1969, on the occasion of the
First Congress of Cultural Workers meeting in Vilnius. The most
vehement attack on these trends came from Bielinis, at that time
a still obscure ideological functionary, but later the Minister of
Culture. Some of his remarks are indicative of the real
achievements of the creative intelligentsia:

> The party demands that the creators be teachers of
> socialist society, its spiritual leaders, the heralds of and
> fighters for the most progressive humanist ideas.... However,
> individual writers and critics do not always correctly
> comprehend the criticism of occasional shortcomings in our
> life. Sometimes, present shortcomings are painted too darkly
> and, most importantly, they are criticized from very abstract
> and ideologically clearly undefined positions.... It must be
> noted that a serious concern is raised by the insignificance
> of the subject matter, purposeless rummaging in the
> labyrinths of subconscious byways, the shallowness of
> content, the superficiality of external effect, the fascination
> with separate details of form, and the avoidance of depicting
> integral and willful personalities—traits that have recently
> appeared in the works of individual writers and artists. To
> write novels, short stories, poems, to create paintings, to
> stage spectacles as elaborately, incomprehensively, and as

abstractly as possible has become an outright fad among individual artists... Modern Western art cannot be an example to be emulated nor the future for our literature and art because it is essentially antihumanistic... In scientific articles and major studies on literature and art it is sometimes written that the creative individuality of the artist had been smothered formerly. The entire responsibility for this is placed only on the vestiges of subjective dogmatism. However, if we accepted this as the whole truth, we would simplify and vulgarize the complexity and antagonisms of life at that time... [43]

The First Secretary of the CPL Antanas Sniečkus in his remarks to the meeting of the cultural workers, called attention to another perennial deviation: "We cannot tolerate attempts to revive again the idea of 'united current.' In the recent past, such attempts are notable in history as well as in history of literature." [44] The criticism refers to the idea that national culture and history are products of an organic nation and should be treated as organic and single entities. Sniečkus was denouncing tendencies in literary and historical scholarship that ignored or minimized the theoretically postulated class conflict in society and its relevance to the historical and cultural development of a people. In literary scholarship, for example, a writer must be interpreted and evaluated in terms of his function in the class struggle; in other words, his "progressive" or "reactionary" role must be indicated. The "united current" theory thus negates the Marxist-Lenininst view that in every society there ar two cultures—one of the exploiters and another of the exploited. In historical scholarship the "united current" theory tends to minimize the role of class conflict in national history. Indeed, national past and culture were being presented and evaluated principally from scientific and esthetic points of view rather than strictly according to the precepts of Marxism-Leninism. Many works could be cited as examplifying scientific competence and only nominally paying homage to the authorities of official ideology.

---

43. Cited here from a mimeographed working paper distributed at the First Congress of Cultural Workers, copy in possession of the author. A collection of reports to the Congress is available: **Pirmasis Lietuvos TSR kultūros darbuotojų suvažiavimas** (Vilnius, 1971). The official report contains a notably "sanitized" version of Bielinis' speech.

44. **Ibid.**, p. 162.

Such criticism of the cultural intelligentsia has always been a part of Soviet life and the only significant thing about this is perhaps its intensity and timing. It suggests the difficult position of a creative worker. Even at the height of "the thaw," the creative individual had to make compromises; his art was inevitably at least partly deformed by ideological dogmas and the intervention of the censor. Whether the Lithuanian artist, writer, or scholar had a wider latitude than his counterparts in other republics of the USSR is subject to debate. He was, however, convinced that he is indispensable to national survival and that indeed his political superiors sought to and did provide him with the optimal conditions for the realization of the mission. The situation of the creative worker is well described by Marija Jurašienė, a writer-scholar and recent emigrant from Lithuania:

> For Lithuanians—as compared with the large nations that have never so sharply experienced dependence, occupation, and the complex of their own inferiority—culture has an additional meaning. For us it means the preservation of national life and a spiritual support against oppression.... For a country as small as ours it is so easy... to melt in the clutches of a large empire, and this constant danger in a way stimulates the consciousness and makes it more active...
>
> Who are they, those chiefs of culture, those benefactors before whom many of our artists humble themselves with fear and compulsory gratitude for the right to at least partly fulfill their cultural mission? In a sense, they are also our brethren, but they are treating us like potential criminals. Even when they promise a carrot for our merits, they hold a whip in the other hand. They punish and they sometimes forgive, but they never forget our sins. They teach us how to serve "god" and Caesar alike and they dispose meaning: dipense? the magic formula "that's how it must be," which tames the living and contradicting mind and inculcates resignation. They bless cultural enterprise officially, while rejecting any responsibility for the ruined souls. All that is redolent of the inquisition is attributed to Moscow's supreme power. And so they wash their hands—blame yourselves, trespassers; we wanted nothing but good for you. And we ourselves are inclined to believe our "good chiefs" because they have arisen from our midst, they are our own people, Lithuanians, and they know how to keep Moscow from getting angry. And those who succeed them may be even worse...
>
> We never cease hoping for better times; we cling to the illusion of new "thaws" that is receding ever further from us.

And we patiently carry our cross, with our heads bowed, following our "good chiefs," not daring to entertain any doubts, to resist, or to stop, with the sole purpose of preserving our nation's life and the process of our culture. Therein lies the historical meaning and the sacred mission of many artists. But if the iron hand of the totalitarian system will one day push our faces to the ground, will that universal submissiveness be justified then?[45]

Indeed, many creative individuals must have asked themselves that last question—is the compromise of creative integrity and one's self tolerable and, in the end, justified by national need? A few have answered in the negative and opted for withdrawal into a private world or emigration. For the time being, however, most do not see open defiance of regime norms as a sensible alternative. Such an attitude has been openly expressed even by establishment intelligentsia. After severe restrictions on creative freedom led a number of prominent artists to seek emigration, Eduardas Mieželaitis, a Lenin Prize laureate in literature, in an opening speech before the Congress of the Lithuanian Writers Union on January 14, 1976, appealed to the intelligentsia to remain and to exploit in his view the still unexploited areas within the socialist realism, to serve one's country—the highest ideal of a creator. With emotion he added: "To be without one's nation is the same as to be without a mother. Together with her always..."[46]

3. NATIONAL ORIENTATION AND OPPORTUNISM

A final note on the political, economic, and cultural elites as bastions of national strength is in order. A number of dissidents and critics of the Soviet system have defined the new class as parasitic and totally opportunistic. As the Jewish dissident Eitan Finkelstein has expressed:

One would have to say that the leadership in Lithuania is in Lithuanian hands. But indeed, the real power of these "nationals" is very limited. This is true even though they do enjoy all the privileges of high rank in the Soviet Union. Although the number of this privileged elite is very small, its destructive influence is out of proportion to its size. This influence is most readily felt in cultural life and education; but probably the most destructive influence of this privileged

45. **Draugas,** February 22, 1975.
46. **Literatūra ir Menas,** January 17, 1976, p. 3.

elite is that by the fact that they occupy many governmental
and administrative positions, the rest of the Lithuanians get
a false sense of security that their country is governed by
Lithuanians.[47]

Similar views are expressed by Tomas Venclova, a noted poet
and scholar who recently chose emigration:

> This elite is very often absolutely cynical, concerned with
> personal well-being and essentially lacking a political opinion;
> it does not deliberate about national matters, it lacks a vision
> of national future. Their vision of the future is only personal
> and for their children. To them, it is important that nothing
> would actually change because for them and their children it
> will no doubt be better in the present situation. There were
> idealists, but they are dead now.[48]

Venclova adds that the new generation of leading cadres may be
more cynical: "If the new generation will sense that support for
(national) culture threatens their position, it will cease such
activity at a moment's notice."

Unfortunately, reality is not that simple. The intelligentsia is
differiantiable in terms of its basic motivation (opportunistic,
bureaucratic, nationalistic), as well as in terms of its viewpoint
concerning the present situation and future prospects for
national life. Unfortunately, without direct study of the attitudes
of the intelligentsia, it is impossible to judge precisely the relative
importance of various groups. All that can be said is that a
significant part of the leading elites, including top political
functionaries, have displayed republic orientation, resulting in at
least some control over the distributive system of the republic.
This republic orientation helped to create the conditions and the
atmosphere for the cultivation of national values that cannot be
ignored as a background for the open dissent in the 1970s.

---

47. Finkelstein in **Akiračiai**, June, 1977.
48. Venclova, in **Į Laisvę**, 1977, No. 71, p. 50.

Chapter IV

OPPOSITION IN THE 1970s

1. SOURCES OF OPPOSITION

The 1970s witnessed the emergence of open, within-system opposition and the revival of system-rejective opposition. This was due to a number of developments in the Soviet polity and society and in the international environment that tended to increase the gap between the expectations of the people and the performance of the system. What follows is an attempt to identify the factors that can be considered as contributing to the sense of relative deprivation and the consequent opposition in Lithuania; to some extent they are also present throughout the Soviet state. In the absence of survey research data, these generalizations have been inferred from a variety of indirect evidence, such as the economic performance of the regime, specific nationality policies, contents of *samizdat* materials, the nature and scope of internal and external communications, and the nature and scope of political controls.[1] Empirical indices of a

---

1. The observations which follow have been made in one way or another by numerous scholars of the Soviet system. The following are representative studies on the conditions in Soviet society. For a general survey of developments during the Brezhnev period, see the following works: Archie Brown and Michael Kaser, **The Soviet Union Since the Fall of Khrushchev** (New York, 1975); John W. Strong, ed., **The Soviet Union Under Brezhnev and Kosygin** (New York, 1971); Mark Field, ed., **Social Consequences of Modernization in Communist Societies** (Baltimore, 1976); Teresa Rakowska-Harmstone, ed., **Perspectives for Change in Communist Societies** (Boulder, Colo., 1979). For analysis of economic development and prospects, see the following: CIA, **Soviet Economic Problems and Prospects** (Washington, 1977); Keith Bush, "Soviet Economic Growth: Past, Present, and Projected", **Survey,** 23:2 (Spring, 1977-78), pp. 1-15; NATO-Directorate of Economic Affairs, **The USSR in the 1980s** (Colloquium) (Brussels, 1978). On nationalities and nationalism: E. Allworth, **Nationality Group Survival in Multi-Ethnic States: Shifting Support Patterns in the Soviet Baltic** (New York, 1977); Ralph S. Clem, **The Soviet West** (New York, 1975); Helene Carrere d'Encausse, **Decline of an Empire** (New York, 1979); Ihor

sense of relative deprivation could also be developed, but that is a complex and difficult task, worthy of a separate study.

The sources of opposition to the system are either internal or external. With respect to the internal factors, there are a number of structural features of the system that at least facilitate, create opportunities, or reduce costs for opposition behavior. The increasing complexity of social, economic, and cultural processes that has been brought about by modernization limits the effectiveness of the regime in uniformly enforcing its policies; it also creates opportunities for increasing subsystem autonomy. This socioeconomic complexity makes the command mode of integration counterproductive and inefficient. Even cybernetics do not seem to provide adequate functional alternative to centralized controls. As a result we are witnessing an ongoing modification of what began as a near hegemonial system. Within this mature industrial society there are strong impulses ("seeds of self-destruction") toward pluralism. And the current hegemonial system is now grappling with them. In the long run, it has been seriously argued, a "bourgeois" revolution is still in store for the Soviet Union. While today we may argue about the extent to which the Soviet system has moved away from pure hegemony, there is no question that to some extent it already has.

Among the other internal features facilitating opposition is the revolution in communications. The tape recorder, the copying machine, the telephone, and the automobile are the primary technological means of communication that are increasingly difficult for the regime to control and that provide the means of autonomous channels of communication. The Soviet dissident today is able to communicate within and outside the Soviet state. He can mobilize support, create networks of information, form organizations, and communicate his actions and views to large audiences. No such capabilities existed under Stalin.

Kamenetsky, ed., **Nationalism and Human Rights: Processes of Modernization in the USSR** (Littleton, Colo., 1977); George W. Simmonds, **Nationalism in the USSR and Eastern Europe in the Era of Brezhnev and Kosygin** (Detroit, 1977). On religion: David E. Powell, **Anti-religious Propaganda in the Soviet Union: A Study in Mass Persuasion** (Cambridge, Mass., 1975); Gerhard Simon, **Church, State and Opposition in the USSR** (London, 1974); Dennis J. Dunn, ed., **Religion and Modernization in the Soviet Union** (Boulder, Colo., 1977); Richard H. Marshall, Jr., ed., **Aspects of Religion in the Soviet Union, 1917—1967** (Chicago, 1971).

The internal coercive controls have also undergone significant change. The costs of opposition are no longer as prohibitive as they were even under Khrushchev, when an undesirable individual could still disappear without the world finding out about it. The restraints placed on police organs and a degree of institutionalization of the legal process have mitigated the coercive process and made it more predictable. Political trials can no longer be secret; now they involve tremendous costs to the regime—to the point that a degree of reluctance to prosecute has emerged. As one example, since the early 1970s, trials of Lithuanian priests for religious activities have ceased, probably because of the uproar that the trials had caused and because they undermined the credibility of the Soviet profession of religious liberty.

Several possibilities are apparent regarding the internal factors contributing to a sense of relative deprivation with respect to national values. The legal status of the ethnic group is an issue. The incorporation of Lithuania into the Soviet Union has not been accepted as legitimate or desirable despite great efforts by the regime to disparage the period of independence ("appendage of world capitalism"). As can be judged from voluminous evidence (including *samizdat* publications and official attacks in the press), independence remains the ideal of the overwhelming majority of the nation. It is part of the national consciousness and the vision of the future and it has not been erased by Soviet indoctrination even among the Soviet-educated generation. The forcibly imposed status remains a basic component of a colonial relationship and an obstacle to the legitimacy of Soviet rule.

The various theoretical and practical ramifications of the Soviet nationality policy also contribute to nationalistic reactions. The Marxist-Leninist conception of the nation is historical and basically antagonistic to cultural pluralism. The posited merger of nations under Communism represents a threat to national survival; it is clearly perceived as such and it cannot be hidden by dialectical logic or terminology. The so-called eventual merger or nations is perceived as out-and-out russification.

The practical implementation of the nationality policy, of course, has varied. During the Khrushchev thaw, nationalism died down somewhat because of the tremendous expansion of limits for cultivating national values. But toward the end of his rule Khrushchev began to backtrack and his 1961 Party Program definitely set the course for assimilation. As a result, his overthrow was quite enthusiastically supported by republic leaders such as Antanas Sniečkus. And so, national renaissance in Lithuania gained a lease on life—at least until the early 1970s. The new Kremlin leadership vacillated on the national question until 1973, when Brezhnev once again enunciated a hard line on the occasion of the fiftieth anniversary of the USSR. The consequent tightening of ideological screws and restrictions on the development of national culture, accompanied by new efforts of cultural and political integration thus contributed to the nationalist reaction.

Among the specific features of the nationality policy that have been noted in the underground press and that have contributed to defensive nationalist reactions, the following are outstanding: the slightly increased immigration rate from other republics (mostly Russians); the apparent or real privileges of nonnatives; the new linguistic policy of more widespread use of Russian; Russian chauvinism, specifically manifested in the obligatory glorification of everything Russian and the deprecation of national culture and history; and the further erosion of the rights of the republic through the centralizing tendencies of the new Soviet Constitution.

The tightening of ideological controls also limited the opportunities to cultivate national values within the existing institutional order and raised doubts about the possibility of creative activity under the circumstances. One result of such a policy was an open break with the regime by a number of prominent intellectuals and artists.[2]

Soviet religious policy also had effects on nationalism. The policy on religion has been counterproductive in two ways: The close interrelationship between Catholicism and Lithuanian national identity means that the attack on religion and the Church is also an assault on national identity. In addition, the Catholic dissidents have not hesitated to appeal to national identity to mobilize support for religious rights. Some Catholic militants even identify the struggle for the faith with the struggle for national survival. In the Lithuanian context, the national and religious movements overlap and possess a mass basis.

Soviet anti-religious militancy comes from three sources. First, the materialist philosophy of Marxism is antithetical to religious orientation. Secondly the Marxist view of religion as an opiate of the people, masking class contradictions and class

---

2. Two most prominent cases—of Jonas Jurašas and Tomas Venclova—are presented in this anthology in Doc. No. 22 and 29.

consciousness, leads to branding of religion as an anti-revolutionary and reactionary force. Thirdly, Leninist abhorrence of pluralism leads to intolerance of any independent viewpoint. No other communist system has gone so far in seeking to realize these dogmas in life as the Soviet Union. Its policies toward religion have prevented the emergence of an accommodationist church, except, perhaps, the state church of the Orthodoxy. But the international and autonomous Catholic Church has not submitted easily to Soviet control. The confrontation of Church and state and the ruthlessness of the secular power have resulted in a deep sense of deprivation of religious values not only among the clergy, but also among the masses of believers.

Nationalist frustrations are widely felt and occasionally manifested in spontaneous outbursts of protest and, more frequently, by small groups and individuals. However, without upheavals in other parts of the Soviet Union or without further intensification of a sense of relative deprivation among the Soviet masses, for the time being nationalist and religious dissent does not threaten to erupt as a mass phenomenon. Although the elite may be moved by power values, the masses are more likely to be aroused to a mass movement with deprivation of material values.[3] The Soviet regime so far has been careful not to reduce the standard of living. Economic growth, although slowing down, has kept the Russian masses in particular relatively quiescent. More spontaneous activity is evident in Lithuania, but here progressive deprivation may be involved. The Baltic republics are referred to in Moscow as "our foreign countries" in part because of their higher standard of living. The greater contacts with the outside world (through Poland and relatives abroad) and the higher standard of living are possibly raising expectations to a greater extent than is the case in Russia. The greater degree of economic dissatisfaction, combined with national and religious frustrations, create a potentially more explosive environment and generate oppositionist behavior not only among the upper Lithuanian society, but also among the masses.

Among the external factors abetting opposition is the reactionary direction of the Brezhnev regime. Relaxation of controls raises expectations.[4] As a consequence, the institution of a freeze leads to an intensified sense of deprivation. The partial restalinization and ideological reaction in the mid-1960s led to the appearance of open dissent among the Moscow intelligentsia. The

---

3. Ted Robert Gurr, **Why Men Rebel** (Princeton, 1970), p. 148.
4. **Ibid.**, p. 119.

tightening of ideological controls in Lithuania after the events of 1972 (self-immolations and mass demonstrations, the appearance of *samizdat*) also had the same impact, with dissent growing rather than declining.

The appearance of dissent in Lithuania is partially due to the "demonstration effect." The open challenge to the regime by Moscow intelligentsia and some success of Jews to emigrate were models for the Lithuanian dissidents. The tactics of the Catholic movement, for example, are a carbon copy of the Moscow-based movement for the defense of human rights and the *Chronicle of Current Events*. The Lithuanian dissidents not only modeled their activities on those of the Moscow dissidents, but through close contacts with them were able to achieve some of the same objectives—to publicize outside the Soviet state the violations of human rights in Lithuania and to communicate with their countrymen through the international media.

Several factors in the international environment have had an obvious impact on the development of an alternative view of the Soviet system and have stimulated efforts to change it. In the 1970s, the ideology of human rights began receiving increasing global recognition. The human rights provisions of the Helsinki accords, for example, unexpectedly emerged as the most significant political consequences of the agreement, providing an ideology for the opposition and stimulating human rights activity. Soviet efforts to counteract the subversive effects of human rights were to some extent counterproductive. The presentation of the case of Angela Davis, for example, had the effect of spotlighting the violations of rights under the Soviet regime. The Lithuanian underground press was quick to point out the contrasting treatment of Angela Davis in the United States and the dissidents in Lithuania.

Human rights in effect constitute "the new moral standard of condemnation" for a system of oppression.[5] To be sure, these standards are as old as Western civilization, but their recent global recognition demonstrated their urgent relevance to the situation in the USSR and provided a universally recognized standard for judging the behavior of any government toward its people. Furthermore, the global legitimacy of human rights concerns facilitated the mobilization of international support for human rights campaigns in the Soviet Union. The principle of noninterference in the internal affairs of other states, which until

---

5. Barrington Moore, Jr., **Injustice: The Social Bases of Obedience and Revolt** (White Plains, N.Y., 1978), p. 88.

recently protected repressive regimes from international scrutiny and sanctions, no longer enjoys an unqualified legitimacy or legality.

The idea of human rights includes the rights of collectivities. The right to self-determination of nations, which in the contemporary world is also a principle of international law, justifies and encourages nationalist demands throughout the world. The process of decolonization is not complete. Every emergence of a new nation-state raises the issue of self-determination for the nations in the Soviet state, which is a traditional multinational empire, created by force and hegemony and not by consent and equality of all its constituent nations. While Western and Third-World diplomats and intellectuals are, for various reasons, reluctant to conceive the Soviet Union as an empire that should be dismembered, there is no doubt about its imperialistic nature among Soviet dissidents, including the Russian nationalists. This is still an age of nationalism, inevitably raising the question of legitimacy of any multinational state.

(Among the Lithuanian dissidents, civil rights and liberties are secondary to national rights. For example, in its initial statement the Lithuanian Helsinki group pointed out that the situation in Lithuania is a consequence of foreign occupation. Because of this, there is a tendency to consider national rights as primary in the contemporary struggle.)

All in all, the ideology of human rights and self-determination has sustained and encouraged democratic opposition to the Soviet system and nationalist opposition to its imperial structure.

Finally, the changing nature of international communications and contacts is also affecting dissent in Lithuania. International radio serves not only as a source of alternative information, but also as a means of communication between the leaders of dissent and the masses of their countrymen. It takes only one copy of an underground journal smuggled abroad to reach thousands, even millions, at home through reports of the contents of the publications on Vatican Radio, Radio Liberty, or occasionally even the Voice of America.

Tourism and visiting relatives in both directions have enormously increased since the Khrushchev era. Communication with countrymen abroad has been very active for some time now, as there are few Lithuanians without relatives abroad. In Lithuania, the intense cultural and political activity of the Lithuanian emigrés is widely known and represents an alternative vision of the future. Their political and material supports of the dissidents in Lithuania are important resources for otherwise powerless individuals. It is impossible to measure the extent to which the Lithuanian diaspora has had an impact on dissent, but the Soviet regime has repeatedly pointed its finger at "bourgeois nationalists" abroad as the primary culprits in stimulating nationalism. This is patently an exaggeration, probably motivated in part by the need of the local officials to protect themselves from charges of nationalist deviation. (This can also be used in reverse—to extract from the Kremlin nationally desirable objectives.) A foreign enemy is a convenient excuse or mask for the real domestic sources of opposition.

International inputs help shape the perceptions of reality and, under certain circumstances, influence expectations and the intensity of a sense of deprivation. At the same time, the international environment supplies some of the resources necessary for dissident activity. International factors in opposition behavior are, however, most likely of secondary importance in relation to domestic stimuli. The Soviet system itself is its own greatest enemy.

Obviously, this is not an exhaustive list of factors leading to contemporary opposition in Lithuania and the Soviet Union. It is also "impressionistic," although empirical evidence could be developed to support these generalizations. Without access to the minds of the people, however, it is impossible to ascertain with any precision the relative significance of various factors. Nevertheless, however impressionistic, such a list of factors not only suggests an explanation for the opposition but also indicates the range of policies that could reduce or contain it. A different allocation of values could contain opposition within manageable bounds for some time. Note, for example, the careful efforts of the regime not to commit the Polish mistake. A sense of relative deprivation is not irreversible, as the postwar history of opposition in Lithuania indicates.

In view of this, the opinion of many Soviet dissidents concerning the imminent demise of the Soviet system should be taken with caution. The regime possesses a number of resources for dealing with challenges against it. The question is whether the regime will choose policies consistent with its survival. For example, how is it going to deal with the economy, which is beginning to show ossification and a course toward stagnation? Will it be willing to shift the allocation of resources away from the military sector toward the consumer to meet the increasing demands of the masses? The answer to these and similar questions will determine the future of the regime and the role of opposition. The victory of justice and morality is by no means assured in the foreseeable future.

2. THE EMERGENCE OF PUBLIC AND COVERT OPPOSITION

In Lithuania, public within-system dissent emerged somewhat later than in Moscow. Significantly, the within-system dissent in Lithuania was also accompanied by renewed efforts in system-rejective opposition.

The later appearance of public dissent in Lithuania was due to several circumstances. What has been called "the demonstration effect" took some time to penetrate to Lithuania. Contacts with the Moscow democratic and human rights movements were in the making for some years. For example, in 1960 Aleksandr Ginzburg was in touch with Lithuanian intellectuals in connection with the publication of *Syntax.*[6] Acquaintances between Lithuanian and Moscow dissidents were struck later on, in prisons and camps.[7] But a more or less regular channel of communication was not established until 1970.

The first report on events in Lithuania appeared only in the 17th issue (Dec. 31, 1970) of the *Chronicle of Current Events,* considerably later than similar reports on the Ukraine and the other Baltic republics.[8] Since then, practically every issue of the *Chronicle of Current Events* has contained reports on "Events in Lithuania." From reports about trials and interrogations of dissidents, we know that close contacts were established between the Lithuanian dissidents and the principal figures of dissent in Moscow—Sakharov, Kovalev, Tverdokhlebov, Ginzburg, and others. There is no doubt that these ties profoundly shaped the

6. See the testimony of Tomas Venclova in **J Laisvę** (Los Angeles), No. 71 (December, 1977), pp. 24-35.

7. For example, in 1969 the prominent Lithuanian dissident Balys Gajauskas was in a Mordovian camp with Ginzburg, Daniel, Galanskov, and others.

8. There were several earlier reports in the **Chronicle of Current Events** on Lithuanian political prisoners (Gajauskas, for example). Issue No. 15 contained the first report of a **samizdat** publication from Lithuania by V. L. Sevruk. The direct coverage of events, however, begins only with issue No. 17.

nature of dissent in Lithuania, to a notable extent directing it toward legality and openness.

The Jewish emigration movement in response to the rising anti-Semitism after the Seven-Day War may have provided a model for some dissident activities. Among the first to push for the right to exit were Lithuania's Jews. On February 15, 1968, twenty-six members of the Jewish intelligentsia wrote a letter to the First Secretary of the CPL Antanas Sniečkus.[9] Conceding that they received better treatment in Lithuania than elsewhere in the USSR, the Vilnius Jews complained about the growing anti-Semitism and discrimination and requested the Secretary's intervention on behalf of their emigration. The two hijackings by Lithuanians, to be described here, bear a strong resemblance to the earlier case of the Leningrad twelve, who were arrested on June 15, 1970, for planning to leave the Soviet Union by commandeering an airplane.

The political situation in Lithuania was less compelling for expressing grievances publicly than it was in Moscow. Khrushchev's later attack on religions and their institutions was less devastating in Lithuania than it was in Russia. The emerging contacts with the Vatican on the part of the Brezhnev regime and some concessions to the Lithuanian Catholic Church were hopeful signs.[10] Khrushchev's overthrow postponed the implementation of hard-line nationality policy and a degree of restalinization and tightening of ideological controls did not really occur until after 1970. A rather vigorous cultural life and broad limits for creativity lasted in Lithuania until 1969, when a restrictive course (but for the time being with little effect) was undertaken.[11] The regime of First Secretary Antanas Sniečkus, who had considerable clout in the Kremlin, provided some of the necessary local support for a national renaissance and reduced the potential for dissent.

---

9. Summary of the letter in **Jews in Eastern Europe,** Vol IV, No. 2 (July, 1979), pp. 51-55.

10. On April 27, 1966, Andrei Gromyko visited Pope Paul VI, while on January 30, 1967, Nikolai Podgorny called on the Pope. On November 21, 1965, while in Rome, Rev. Juozas Matulaitis-Labukas was consecrated bishop and appointed Administrator of the Kaunas Archdiocese.

11. The hard line in cultural life was enunciated in the First Congress of Cultural Workers, which met in June of 1969. See the proceedings of the Congress: **Pirmasis Lietuvos TSR kultūros darbuotojų suvažiavimas** (Vilnius, 1971).

THE RISE OF RELIGIOUS DISSENT

The first public salvo of dissent emanated from the Catholic clergy. By the end of the 1960s it became all too evident that the regime's religious policies were threatening the survival of institutional religion. The perceived crisis of the Church was due to years of restrictions, repressions, and atheistic indoctrination. The following outline of Church-state relations since the war will provide a background of the religious dissent.[12]

From the very first day, the Soviet regime in Lithuania has sought to bring the Catholic Church under state control, a policy that was bound to be vigorously opposed by a church that in the past has maintained independence from the state or has even dominated the state. Deep roots in the history and culture of the people, the tradition of the Universal Church, and ties with the Vatican have sustained Catholicism in Lithuania despite the comprehensive attack on it by the state.

In the immediate postwar period opposition to the Soviet religious policies also stemmed from the hierarchy's and clergy's perception of the political situation as temporary. The expectation of an East-West conflict affected the behavior of the Catholic clergy as it did the rest of the nation. In those circumstances resistance to the occupying power at any cost seemed justifiable. Accomodation was largely excluded as a tactic because of the uncompromising nature of the regime. Thus, the clergy opposed with unusual unity not only the religious policies of the regime but also gave aid and comfort to the partisans.

The relationship of Church and state during the years of Stalin's rule involved three major issues: the attitude of the Church toward the partisan movement, the introduction of

---

12. For a comprehensive treatment of the situation of the Lithuanian Catholic Church under Soviet rule, see the study of V. Stanley Vardys, **The Catholic Church, Dissent and Nationality in Soviet Lithuania** (Boulder, Colo., 1978). Also extremely useful for important factual information is the **samizdat** monograph **Arkivyskupas Mečis-lovas Reinys,** published in Chicago, 1977, a story of Archbishop Reinys. The Soviet church historian Jonas Aničas has written a useful booklet **The Establishment of Socialism in Lithuania and the Catholic Church** (Vilnius, 1975), which is a slightly revised version of his Lithuanian language book—**Socialinis politinis katalikų bažnyčios vaidmuo Lietuvoje 1945—1952 metais** (Vilnius, 1971). The outline of church-state relations relies heavily on these sources.

secular controls over church activities, and the attempt to set up a national church, independent of the Vatican.[13]

As early as June 1945, the Chairman of the Council of People's Commissars M. Gedvilas summoned the diocesan administrators and demanded that they condemn partisan activities.[14] The only one to do so was the Administrator of the Kaunas Archdiocese S. Jokubauskas. In February 1946, the bishops and administrators agreed to issue a general statement condemning killing. Of course, the commandment "Thou shalt not kill" was applicable to both sides of the conflict. The hierarchy was reluctant to issue an unconditional condemnation of the partisans primarily because they did not trust the Soviet regime to honor its pledges of amnesty. In addition, the hierarchy tried to stay out of "politics," as Bishop T. Matulionis put it[15], and, as was pointed out, the hierarchy and the clergy hoped for a quick end to Soviet rule. Finally, the resistance to sovietization was so widespread that by suddenly siding with the Soviet authorities, the clergy might easily have lost credibility and influence with the masses. And so, as a result, the Church, on the whole, resolved the issue in favor of nationalism.

The introduction of secular controls over church activities through parish committees evoked the most vigorous opposition. The Soviet regime sought to transfer control of the parishes from the pastor and ultimately the bishop to elected committees of religious associations registered with and subservient to the local Soviets. The opposition to this arrangement was virtually unanimous. In July 1948, Bishop Paltarokas presented a counterproposal that would preserve essential hierarchical control over the church, but this compromise was rejected by the Soviet regime.[16] The controversy continued until the second half of 1948, when the hierarchy, after devastating repressions, finally capitulated, agreeing to set up parish committees.

---

13. To be sure, there were other controversies, such as the teaching of catechism to children in schools, the number of seminarians and seminaries, the closing of the convents and monestaries, etc. Those interested in greater detail should consult the study of Prof. Vardys, **op. cit.**

14. Report on this meeting in Aničas, **Socialinis politinis katalikų bažnyčios vaidmuo, op. cit.,** ch. 3; **Arkivyskupas Mečislovas Reinys, op. cit.,** pp. 200-201.

15. Aničas, **Socialinis..., op. cit.,** p. 83.

16. Text of the proposal in **Arkivyskupas Mečislovas Reinys, op. cit.,** pp. 207—214.

Contrary to expectations, however, this was not the severe blow to religion and its institutions that it might have been. As it turned out, the parish committees amounted to a formality and the parishes remained under the actual control of the pastor rather than of the local authorities. The failure of this policy was recognized only in the 1970s, when a new effort to transform the parish committees into instruments of secular power was undertaken.

The effort to form a national church began as early as 1944 but failed because of the virtually united opposition by the clergy. One report claims that a priest under a 25-year sentence was offered freedom, the church of St. John's in Vilnius, and a 100,00-ruble bribe to take the initiative.[17] He did not accept the generous offer. Another attempt to breach ties with the Vatican was made in 1949—1950. This was occasioned by the decree of Pope Pius XII excommunicating Catholics who became communists. A petition to condemn the Pope was started by B. Pušinis, the Representative for Religious Cults in Lithuania. Again there was no cooperation; only 19 priests of about 800 still present in Lithuania signed it.[18] The regime did not attempt to set up a national church again.

The method of dealing with the resisting church was wholesale repression. By the end of 1947, only Bishop Paltarokas remained free. Bishop Borisevičius was executed in 1947 for alleged participation in the partisan movement. Bishops M. Reinys, P. Ramanauskas, and T. Matulionis were in prisons or camps. Meanwhile, two older bishops—A. Karosas and P. Karevičius—had died in 1947 and 1945, respectively. Diocesan administrators had been changed several times. In effect, the organizational head of the Church had been severed. The Church was completely isolated from the Vatican.

Under these circumstances, attempts were made to contact the Vatican. In 1947, Rev. P. Račiūnas sought to communicate with the Vatican by way of the Catholic chaplain in Moscow Rev. Laberge, to ask the Pope permission to consecrate new bishops. Rev. Račiūnas was arrested, charged with spying, and sent to a concentration camp.[19] The same year a desperate attempt to reach the Pope through partisan couriers succeeded. The letter to

---

17. Reported in **Arkivyskupas Mečislovas Reinys,** p. 201; **Chronicle,** No. 10 (1974); see also Doc. No. 60 in the anthology.

18. **Chronicle,** No. 15 (1975) contains the text of the petition.

19. This effort is described by Rev. Račiūnas himself in an open letter, published in **Chronicle,** No. 10 (1974).

the Pope by Lithuania's faithful summarized the tragic situation
of the Church and appealed for help.[20] For as yet unexplained
reasons, the Pope did not respond to the letter, did not extend
even moral support to the persecuted Church.

The heaviest persecution of the clergy occurred somewhat
later. There is indirect evidence that by the time Stalin died, of
about 1,000 priests remaining in Lithuania, 300—350 had been
deported or imprisoned. In 1954 Bishop Paltarokas revealed that
741 clergymen served in 688 churches.[21] The *Chronicle* has
supplied lists of repressed priests in the dioceses of Panevėžys,
Telšiai, and Kaišiadorys.[22] Out of approximately 500 priests in
those dioceses, 137 were deported or imprisoned; 22 of these died
and 115 were eventually allowed to return to Lithuania. Most of
the arrests occurred in 1948—1950. These repressions were in
part connected with the regime's effort to finally break national
resistance to sovietization, which was again inflamed by the
collectivization of agriculture. The regime viewed the clergy as
politically disloyal and sympathetic to their peasant congregations
and thus an obstacle to the aims of sovietization. Their refusal to
cooperate in condemning the Pope was no doubt contributory to
such a political assessment of the clergy.

A number of other serious blows against the Church should
be mentioned at least briefly. The number of seminarians was
cut immediately from the prewar 425 to 150 and to about 80
during the 1950s. The latter number was still close to what was
necessary to provide for the attrition of clergy due to natural
causes. While only about 20 churches were closed, all chapels
were. Most important, all 85 convents and 37 monasteries were
closed and their residents dispersed. This policy backfired, for the
scattered religious were forced into a catacomb existence, where
they developed new forms of monastic life. In particular, the
illegal nuns, whose ranks have apparently been supplemented by
new secret recruits, have been a tremendous resource for
pastoral work, especially for the catechization of children.

When Stalin died, the Catholic Church was subdued but not
conquered. Destalinization permitted a partial recovery. The
Church began to adjust to life under the new conditions and to
develop a style of pastoral work that combined permissible
activities with catacomb tactics. Certainly, those who were

---

20. See Doc. No. 49 for excerpts from the letter.
21. Cited in Vardys, **op. cit.**, p. 82.
22. See **Chronicle**, No. 28 (June 29, 1977), No. 30 (November 1,
1977), and No. 32 (March 26, 1978).

repressed learned the meaning of the catacombs well and upon their return from camps and prisons appplied the lessons to pastoral work.

The shift away from persecution to a more tolerant attitude toward the religious and the clergy came in 1954. On November 11, 1954, the Central Committee of the CPSU declared that the struggle against religion must be viewed as a conflict between scientific-materialist and anti-scientific-religious viewpoints, that the feelings of the believers and the clergy must be respected, and that coercion is contrary to the aims of the party and is counterproductive.[23] The policy was echoed by the party organ in Lithuania, *Tiesa:*

> There are many collective farmers and workers in our republic who, while engaged in productive work and conscientiously performing their duties of citizenship, are still influenced by religious beliefs. Our party teaches us to be more considerate in our dealings with these people. It would be foolish and harmful to treat them with suspicion solely because of their religious beliefs, which are merely a residue of the past. Our struggle with religious superstitions must now be viewed as a struggle of the ideological, scientific, materialistic concept against the unscientific and religious point of view.[24]

Besides the more tolerant attitude toward believers, who were no longer defined as enemies of the people, the new policy also permitted some gains for the institutional church. The amnesties of 1954 and 1955 allowed most of the repressed priests to return to Lithuania. Judging by the available evidence, about 250 priests returned to pastoral duties. The enrollment in the seminary was roughly sufficient to replace the priests who died. By 1960, there were 929 clergymen, close to the number in 1945. The episcopate was also partially reconstituted. On September 11, 1955, Bishop K. Paltarokas, with the consent of (or at least in the absence of objection from) the Soviet regime, consecrated two new bishops—Julijonas Steponavičius for the Vilnius Archdiocese and Petras Maželis for the Telšiai Diocese. On September 25, 1957, Bishop T. Matulionis, having returned from exile but not being permitted to administer his see of Kaišiadorys, consecrated his successor, Vincentas Sladkevičius. This, apparent-

---

23. As cited in Hansjakob Stehle, **Die Ostpolitik des Vatikans, 1917-1975** (München, 1975), p. 317.

24. As cited in Dr. J. Savasis, **The War Against God in Lithuania** (New York, 1966), p. 28.

ly, had not been explicitly cleared with the Soviet authorities and after a year and a half Bishop Sladkevičius was barred from exercising his duties and exiled to a small town in Northern Lithuania. The two still living repressed bishops, T. Matulionis and P. Ramanauskas, were allowed to return from exile in 1956 but were barred from their sees.[25]

There is an indication that Bishop Paltarokas had reached an understanding with the Council for Religious Cults in Moscow concerning the catechization of children in small groups.[26] The bishops were finally allowed to visit parishes and administer the sacraments. A prayer book and a religious calendar were published, the first religious publications since the war.

These gains, however, were short-lived. They were made possible in part by the succession struggle in the Kremlin and the loosening of controls in the wake of destalinization. As soon as Khrushchev attained control over the party and the state, a new antireligious campaign, involving both psychological pressure and physical persecution began to emerge. Its inception is evident in the proceedings of the Twenty-first Congress of the CPSU in 1959.[27]

While the new policy was more devastating to the Russian Orthodox Church, it also had serious repercussions in Lithuania. The case of Bishop J. Steponavičius reflected the hard-line policy. Bishop Steponavičius succeeded Bishop Paltarokas, who died in 1958, as Apostolic Administrator of the Vilnius Archdiocese and of the Panevėžys Diocese. In 1961, by a decision of the Lithuanian SSR Council of Ministers, Bishop Steponavičius was banned and exiled to the small town of Žagarė. In a 1975 statement, Bishop Steponavičius revealed the issues of his conflict with secular authorities.[28] He refused to ban his priests from teaching religion to children in small groups, he opposed the attempts of the Representative for Religious Cults to direct the

---

25. Statistical data on the clergy and changes in the hierarchy in Matas Raišupis, **Dabarties kankiniai** (Chicago, 1972), ch. V.

26. See a claim to that effect made by Bishop Steponavičius in his statement, published in **Chronicle,** No. 20 (December 8, 1975), reprinted here as Doc. No. 67.

27. For analysis of Khrushchev's policies, see Donald A. Lowrie and William C. Fletcher, "Khrushchev's Religious Policy, 1959—1964", in Richard H. Marshall, Jr., ed., **Aspects of Religion in the Soviet Union, 1917-1967,** ch. 7.

28. Text of the statement in **Chronicle,** No. 20 (Dec. 8, 1975); Doc. No. 67.

appointment and transfer of priests, and he objected to the interference of the state in the admissions to the seminary and the consecration of new priests. The bishop was ordered to forbid the participation of children in liturgical ceremonies, group retreats for priests, and traditional Christmas visitations of the faithful. These are among the issues in the conflict that led to the open Catholic rights struggle at the end of the 1960s and that remained largely unresolved at the end of the 1970s. Bishop Steponavičius became the symbol and the suspected leader of resistance to the all-out campaign against religion and its institutional life.

While the change of the leadership in the Kremlin in 1964 meant no lessening of attack on religion, a movement toward a relationship with the Vatican, already evident under Khrushchev, did occur.

The Vatican's Ostpolitik found a response among Soviet leaders, because in many points it coincided with the interests of the Soviet state. The Vatican sought a dialogue and a *modus vivendi* with communist regimes as a way to preserve Catholicism. Dennis J. Dunn, a scholar of Soviet religious policy, has summarized Soviet motives for entering into a dialogue with the Vatican as follows:

> First and foremost among Soviet motives is Moscow's apparent belief that the Church can help in maintaining order in the Soviet Union and the Soviet empire in Eastern Europe... A second reason... is that Catholicism, as a major religion in Spain, Ireland, Italy, West Germany, Belgium, France, Luxembourg, and Portugal can help win Western European acceptance of Soviet security goals on the USSR's western border... Another Soviet ambition for affiliation is related to the fact that the Catholic Church is an authority in the Third World... An additional reason... for a concord is that the Vatican can be manipulated as Russian Orthodoxy has been exploited, to belie the charge that the Communists persecute religion and suppress dissent and minority groups.[29]

One might add to this array of motives that a concord with the Vatican could be manipulated to elevate subservient clerics to the episcopate and through them to divide and demoralize the Church from within. This is one of the fears of the Lithuanian

---

29. Dennis J. Dunn, "Papal-Communist Detente: Motivation", **Survey,** Vol. 22, No. 2 (Spring, 1976) pp. 148-153.

Catholic dissidents and one of the reasons for opposing the Vatican's Ostpolitik.

Among the results of the Vatican's Ostpolitik was the reestablishment of ties between the Church in Lithuania and the Vatican and the elevation of new bishops (though not the reinstatement of the banished bishops Steponavičius and Sladkevičius). Still under Khrushchev, a Lithuanian delegation was permitted to attend the Second Vatican Council and subsequent meetings. While in Rome at the fifth session of the Council, Juozas Matulaitis-Labukas was appointed administrator of the Kaunas Archdiocese and consecrated bishop on December 5, 1965. Rev. Juozas Pletkus was consecrated bishop on February 25, 1968, and appointed administrator of the Telšiai Diocese. On December 21, 1969, two additional bishops were elevated: Bishop Liudvikas Povilonis as Coadjutor to the Apostolic Administrator of the Archdiocese of Kaunas and of the Diocese of Vilkaviškis, and Bishop Romualdas Krikščiūnas as the Apostolic Administrator for the Diocese of Panevėžys. A Council of Ordinaries, headed by Bishop Matulaitis-Labukas, began to function as the religious governing authority in Lithuania. Finally, several publications in limited editions were issued, including a translation of the New Testament, the decisions of the Vatican Council, a book of Psalms, and a book of ritual; but there was no catechism or prayer books so needed by the faithful.

On the pastoral level, the Vatican's Ostpolitik had no impact. It soon became obvious that the Kremlin's overtures to the Vatican had nothing to do with the internal religious policy of the regime. Ostpolitik was nonproductive and perhaps counter-productive, for it offered nothing to the faithful and possible demoralization and impotence of the Church as a result of possible appointments of subservient bishops and administrators. Many of the prohibitions of religious activities, verbally communicated to Bishop Steponavičius, were enacted into law in May of 1966 by the Presidium of the Supreme Soviet of the Lithuanian SSR, explaining in some detail the application of Article 143 of the Lithuanian SSR Penal Code (separation of Church and state and school and Church). The enforcement of restrictions on pastoral work, especially the catechization of children, and the alarming attrition of the ranks of the clergy led to the open Catholic opposition movement.

Among the most threatening policies to the survival of the Church was the reduction of seminarians from 80 in 1958 to 28 in 1964. This was insufficient to replace the priests who died.

Between 1960 and 1970, 198 priests died and only 92 candidates were admitted to priesthood. As a result, by 1975 the number of priests dropped to 765, to about the same number as in 1954.[30] This rapid attrition of the clergy, resulting from restrictions on the seminary, was among the first concerns of the emerging dissent movement in the late 1960s.

Initially the response was in the form of petitions. On August 7, 1978, Rev. V. Šlevas wrote to Kosygin requesting intervention to increase the number of seminarians, to abolish discriminatory fees for the electricity used by churches, and to publish a prayer book.[31] By the end of 1970, seven known petitions to Kosygin, Brezhnev, and republic and Church authorities were generated, involving signatures of about a fourth of the priests in Lithuania.[32] Their complaints— restrictions on seminary admissions; restrictions on pastoral work, including the internal banishment of two bishops; the lack of basic religious literature; restrictions on the teaching activity of the Church. At first, the petitions were not circulated publicly and reached the West after 1970, following a generally hostile reaction by the regime, especially by the republic authorities.

The breaking point came with the trials of three priests for teaching children religion.[33] Rev. Antanas Šeškevičius was tried, convicted, and sentenced to a year in prison on September 8-9, 1970. His eloquent and legalistic defense speech was smuggled out of the country and reported in Moscow's *Chronicle of Current Events* (No. 17). Rev. Juozas Zdebskis was arrested on August 26, 1971, and tried on November 11, 1971. That trial was accompanied by demonstrations and public disturbances. Rev. Prosperas Bubnys was arrested on July 25, 1971, tried, and convicted on November 12, 1971, also receiving a one-year sentence. The latter two cases received considerable publicity in the world press and involved demonstrations and petitions by several thousand of their parishioners.[34]

---

30. Statistics from Vardys, **op. cit.,** p. 86, and Raišupis, **op. cit.,** p. 394.

31. Text of Rev. Šlevas letter in **Chronicle,** No. 9 (1974), reprinted here as Doc. No. 50.

32. Texts of these petitions and letters: **Arkhiv samizdata,** No. 768 (signed by 63 priests); **AS** 769; **AS** 631; **AS** 766 (signed by 40 priests); **AS** 632 (signed by 61 priests); **AS** 692 (signed by 49 priests); **AS** 655 (signed by 104 priests).

33. These cases are presented in Doc. No. 52, 53, 54.

34. See, for example, the reports on these cases in the **New York Times,** November 27, 1971, and the **Baltimore Sun,** November 27, 1971.

The trials of Revs. Šeškevičius, Zdebskis, and Bubnys apparently led to the decision to go public. The first major public act of the dissidents was a petition to the Secretary General L. Brezhnev, to be transmitted by way of the UN Secretary General Kurt Waldheim. A petition of some 17,000 signatures, a fantastic number under the existing circumstances, was organized and transmitted to the UN at the beginning of 1972. By this time the dissidents found ways to communicate their grievances to the world at large—copies of their statements began reaching the West, and the events were regularly recorded in the *Chronicle of Current Events*. At the same time the Catholic dissidents launched their own information bulletin—*Lietuvos Katalikų Bažnyčios Kronika* (Chronicle of the Catholic Church in Lithuania). The first issue appeared on March 19, 1972.

Thus launched, the religious rights movement continued to gather momentum throughout the decade. It spawned a prolific *samizdat* literature, reached world opinion and the Holy See itself. It had an obvious impact on the morale of believers, reenforcing faith and its practice among the masses. To some extent it has provided a rallying point for nonreligious grievances and has closely identified itself with Lithuanian nationality. And, finally, it stimulated opposition on many fronts.

RESURGENCE OF NATIONALISM

Parallel to and partly in conjunction with the Catholic rights movement, a national movement also came into being. Nationalist activity did not cease after the Soviet takeover of Lithuania; there were numerous small underground groups and individuals articulating nationalist demands.[35] As was pointed out, a national movement within the framework of the regime emerged in the 1960s, but it crystallized into an open nationalist reaction only in the 1970s.

Besides the demonstration effect of the Moscow dissidents and stimulation by the Lithuanian Catholic movement, a number of events within a brief span of time contributed to the emergence of nationalist opposition. Four unconnected events in 1970 evidenced the existence of deep political grievances.

---

35. **Chronicle of Current Events,** No. 33 (December 10, 1974) lists a number of Lithuanian political prisoners convicted in the 1950s. The political repressions of the 1960s are virtually unknown because at that time channels of communication with the outside world were still very limited. See also **Chronicle of Current Events,** No. 17 (December 31, 1970) for other reports of political repressions.

On October 15, 1970, two Lithuanians—Pranas Brazinskas, 46, and his 15-year-old son, Algirdas—forcibly diverted an Aeroflot airliner from Soviet Georgia across the Black Sea to Trebizond, Turkey. In the course of the hijacking, the pilot took evasive action and a stewardess was killed. In Turkey the two hijackers asked for political asylum. Pranas Brazinskas claimed that he was imprisoned for nationalist activities on several occasions and was discriminated against, while the Soviet authorities presented the hijackers as simple speculators and thrill-seekers. The case received worldwide publicity, even in the Soviet press.[36] Whatever the truth about the past of the hijackers, the event was symptomatic of underlying grievances.

A second hijacking attempt, this one unsuccessful, occurred on November 16, 1970. On that day Vytautas Simokaitis, 31, a construction worker and former administrative director of the famous "Lietuva" ensemble, and his pregnant wife, Gražina, 21, attempted to force an Aeroflot plane from Palanga in Lithuania across the Baltic Sea to Sweden.[37] Although Simokaitis was reportedly armed, he was overpowered by a navigator, while his wife was prevented "from setting fire to an inflammable fluid". Simokaitis was tried for treason (Art. 62 of the Penal Code) on January 14, 1971, and was sentenced to death. On appeal, his sentence was commuted to 15 years of hard labor. The commutation was parallel to the Leningrad trial and sentence of Jews for planning a hijacking. World protest in both instances was probably an important factor in the eventual commutation of the death penalties. The motivation of Simokaitis and his wife is unknown to this day. It probably involved a host of grievances—political, national, and personal. This act of desperation could not be perceived by their countrymen as other than an understandable revulsion against the Soviet way of life.

The third event involved the unexplained disappearance and death of the noted linguist, Prof. Jonas Kazlauskas.[38] He

---

36. See the reports about the hijacking in **New York Times,** October 18, 1970, and October 21, 1970; also **Izvestia,** October 20, 1970, among the numerous world and Soviet press reports. The two hijackers were kept in Turkish jails for several years, but eventually were permitted to leave Turkey. Their latest known residence is in the US.

37. The Simokaitis case is reported in **New York Times,** January 20, 1971, and February 11, 1971; see also **Chronicle of Current Events,** Nos. 18 and 19.

38. Information is mostly from private communications. See also Doc. No. 28, note 6, for further information.

disappeared on October 7, 1970, and his body was discovered in the Neris River in Vilnius some six weeks later. While the authorities attempted to explain the death as a suicide, the underground has charged that Prof. Kazlauskas was a victim of foul play on the part of the KGB. Prof. Kazlauskas was a party member, "a progressive and active scholar who had incurred the displeasure of the authorities with his brave theories in Baltic studies."[39] Apparently, he had confrontations with the regime on a number of issues, including travel to Pennsylvania State University for lectures, which was denied by the authorities, and possibly a disagreement over the contents of an article on Baltic linguistics commissioned by the *Encyclopedia Britannica*. More important, party functionaries were absent from his funeral, signalling the party's displeasure. Whether Prof. Kazlauskas was a victim of the KGB, as the dissident sources claim, or committed suicide, as the Soviet authorities intimate, will probably never be known for sure. The fact remains that the authorities were using Kazlauskas' death to create an atmosphere of uncertainty and terror among the intelligentsia. By its actions in the case, the regime was signalling to the intellectuals that dissent or a critical attitude might be dealt with by secret police methods. The Kazlauskas case heightened political sensitivities and anxieties, especially among the intelligentsia.

While these cases had only indirect nationalist connotations, that of Simas Kudirka turned into a nationalist manifestation.[40] Simas Kudirka, a sailor on the mothership of the Soviet fishing fleet in the Atlantic, *Sovetskaya Litva*, attempted to defect to the United States by jumping onto the US Coast Guard cutter *Vigilant*, which was moored alongside the Soviet ship while a conference on fishing rights was taking place in US territorial waters off Martha's Vineyard, Mass. The November 27, 1970, jump to freedom turned into a tragedy for Simas Kudirka, whom the Coast Guard, ignoring American traditions of political asylum and procedure for similar cases, permitted the forcible return of Kudirka to the Soviet ship. The actions of the Coast

---

39. **Chronicle,** No. 21 (January 25, 1976), also Doc. No. 28.

40. For his own story, see Simas Kudirka and Larry Eichel, **For Those Still at Sea** (New York, 1978). For further documentation, see the introductory note of Doc. No. 18, which presents the court proceedings and Kudirka's self-defense. The trial is covered in **Chronicle of Current Events,** No. 20 (July 2, 1971). Simas Kudirka was released in 1975, after serving almost four years, upon the discovery of a valid claim to US citizenship.

Guard outraged the American people, including President Nixon. The negation of American ideals received worldwide publicity.

Kudirka was tried in Vilnius on May 18-19, 1971, for treason (Article 62 of the Penal Code). He was given a ten-year sentence in a strict regime labor camp. Kudirka's defense speech and exchanges during the trial were smuggled out of the country and received international publicity. In his speech, Kudirka denounced the court as a court of an alien ruler and therefore illegal. In conclusion, he demanded the granting of independence to Lithuania. Whatever his personal motives may have been, he turned his own defense into a defense of freedom and Lithuania. His speech was reprinted in major newspapers, including the *Washington Post*, the *Boston Globe*, and the *Chicago Sun-Times*, which on August 7, 1971, carried the headline: "Tell Defector's Stirring Plea for Free Lithuania." As a result of Kudirka's actions, Lithuania's case received the greatest world attention in many years, certainly since 1945. Perhaps, more important, from the standpoint of the people in Lithuania, where the speech was widely known and available among dissidents, Kudirka once again questioned the legitimacy of the status of Lithuania and no doubt reflected the sentiments of a great number of people.

The Kazlauskas and Kudirka cases raised the political fever and created anxieties about repression. Psychological terror was actually used in the Kazlauskas case, while Kudirka narrowly escaped "psychiatric treatment." On November 20, 1971, Dean Mills of the Moscow Bureau of the *Baltimore Sun* reported that "a group of Lithuanian intellectuals" addressed a letter to the Fifth World Psychiatric Congress, in which they "demanded an international investigation of Soviet psychiatric practices." The letter is notable for two reasons. First of all, it calls attention to psychiatric practices directed wholesale against national opposition. Secondly, the letter indicates that the Lithuanian dissidents were quickly learning— especially from the Soviet Jews—how to appeal to Western public opinion, or, to put it differently, how to mobilize outside support for their cause. Unfortunately, the original text of the letter is not available, and we have to rely on Mills' report, which makes the following points:

> But the authors also take the opportunity to propagandize about the 10-year guerrilla war by Lithuanian nationalists "against the occupation of Lithuania by Soviet Russia" following the tiny republic's liberation from Germany.

From 1944 to 1953, the letter says, 100,000 Lithuanians died in the unsuccessful anti-Soviet uprising.

Half of that number died in active battle, according to the letter and the others died "in prisons and exile in Siberia, where about 350,000 Lithuanians were sent—every sixth Lithuanian."

"And this is a conservative estimate," the letter maintained, "although the Soviet press has said nothing about this, as if very cruel and hypocritical violence had not been inflicted upon the will of a peace-loving people."

The mentally ill among the prisoners were rarely treated, the letter continued. "Often, they were in the position of a mad dog, struck down by a bullet for any deviation from the regime."

An especially large number went mad in 1956, the letter charged, when, after a few years of freedom granted in a post-Stalin amnesty, 1,000 Lithuanians were sent back to Siberia. The new punishment followed demonstrations in the cities of Vilnius and Kaunas in support of the Hungarian uprising.[41]

These events were symptomatic of deep frustations that finally burst into a mass antiregime riot in the spring of 1972. On May 14, 1972, around noon, a worker-student Romas Kalanta, 19, deliberately set himself on fire in a park in Kaunas, in front of the theater where the Soviet system in Lithuania had been proclaimed in 1940.[42] Kalanta died several hours later. The political nature of the suicide became evident at his funeral. Apparently, a large number of youths were planning to attend the funeral. To prevent a mass demonstration, the police hastily buried the victim secretly. This act set off widespread disorders on May 18 and 19, involving several thousand participants, extensive property damage, numerous injuries and possibly the death of a policeman, arrests of hundreds of persons, and the intervention of internal security troops to quell the riots. The demonstrations were clearly nationalistic, under the slogan of "Freedom for Lithuania."

---

41. **The Sun,** November 20, 1971.

42. The May events were reported in **Chronicle of Current Events,** No. 26 (July 5, 1972) and in major newspapers around the world. On May 22, 1972, front page articles on self-immolations appeared in the **London Times, Washington Post, Wall Street Journal,** and also in **New York Times, Chicago Tribune, Los Angeles Times,** and numerous other newspapers. It should be mentioned here that three other self-immolation attempts were reported, indicating either some planning or an imitation effect.

Self-immolation as a method of protest was widely known at that time. The South Vietnamese Buddhist monks had provided the most dramatic models. This method had been used by Jan Pallach in 1968 to protest Soviet intervention in Czechoslovakia. A number of protest suicides have also been reported in the Soviet Union. It does not seem that Kalanta carried out the act alone or without forethouht. There is evidence of planning. The self-sacrifice was timed to coincide with Nixon's visit to Moscow. The intended participation at his funeral by a large number of youths suggests that some group must have been involved. One source claims that it involved a group of rebellious youths who drew lots for the protest suicide.[43] Another source has suggested that the planned suicide by Kalanta was to be joined by a Latvian and an Estonian, who, however, were detained while on a train to Kaunas.[44]

The participants of the demonstrations were a cross section of Kaunas youths. It is significant that the rioters were not only students, who have been traditionally politically active and rebellious, but also young workers of Kaunas factories. Among the eight participants who were later convicted, there was a stagehand, three students from a trade school, a packer, a construction worker, and an apprentice in a printing plant.[45] It is therefore understandable that the First Secretary of the CPL Antanas Sniečkus rushed to the factories of Kaunas rather than to the schools or Komsomol cells to argue the merits of the Soviet system. The theme of his speech was not "proletarian internationalism" or "internationalist education of workers," but the economic achievements during the Soviet rule as compared to the alleged backwardness of the "bourgeois period." Sniečkus was arguing against Lithuania's independence on economic grounds. But he may also have been responding to the dissatisfactions with economic life in general, which burst into a nationalist reaction. In effect Sniečkus said: "Forget about independence, for economically you never had it as well as under the Soviets."

Whatever the personal motivations, thousands in the streets confirmed what Kudirka was saying in the court. The riots in Kaunas, "possibly timed to gain publicity during the Nixon visit, are the sharpest public expression of minority nationalist

---

43. This claim is found in Vardys, **op. cit.,** p. 173. Prof. Vardys does not indicate his source.

44. As reported by Jonas Jurašas in the underground journal **Aušra,** No. 1 (October, 1975).

45. See the report on the trial in **Tiesa,** October 5, 1972.

sentiment in the Soviet Union since riots erupted in Armenia in 1965."[46] Together with the petition of the 17,000, the demonstrations in Kaunas indicated the potential for mobilizing the masses around religious and national issues.

3. THE GROWTH OF OPPOSITION

After 1972, the opposition movement grew steadily and became differentiated and diversified. It acquired a degree of organizational structure and was served by a prolific underground press. Despite trials, harassment by the KGB, extralegal persecution, and ideological pressure, the movement has not only survived, but has gained momentum and depth.

An empirical study of public protest by David Kowalewski provides some indications of the scope and character of the movement.[47] Kowalewski examined 51 cases of public protest reported mainly in the underground press. Such a data base, however, is obviously limited in several ways. The sample of public protest events is rather small and most likely overrepresents Catholic protest. Futhermore, the data are on public protest only and thus exclude the bulk of opposition activity from the analysis. Finally, it tends to overemphasize within-system dissent. Kowalewski's study is thus only suggestive of the nature and scope of the opposition activity in Lithuania.

According to Kowalewski, the 51 cases of public protest he examined represent 10.3% of such demonstrations in the USSR in 1965-1978. This suggests the relative intensity of the opposition movement in Lithuania compared to that in other areas of the Soviet Union. Of the 51 cases, 66.7% were for religious rights and 33.3% for national rights. The number of demonstrations has generally increased every year. The annual breakdown of demonstrations is as follows (year and percent of demonstrations): 1970—2.0; 1971—9.8; 1972—17.6; 1973—11.8; 1974—11.8; 1975—15.7; 1976—19.6; 1977—11.8 (incomplete data). The locale of demonstrations suggests their nationwide character: 31.4% occurred in villages, 25.5% in towns under 40,000 (1970 census), and 43.1% in cities over 40,000 in population. While most of the demonstrations involved a few

---

46. Hendrick Smith, "Some Cracks in the Kremlin Wall," **New York Times,** May 28, 1972.

47. David Kowalewski, "Lithuanian Protest for Human Rights in the 1970s: Characteristics and Consequences", **Lituanus,** Vol. 25, No. 2 (Summer, 1979), pp. 43-57.

Table 4: Underground Periodicals, 1972-1979

Year	No. of Titles	No. of Issues	Est. No. of Pages
1972	1	4	170
1973	1	3	130
1974	1	6	250
1975	3	10	360
1976	5	18	870
1977	6	24	1300
1978	8	31	1500
1979	6	14	900
Total	31	110	5,480

The data are derived from copies of *samizdat* periodicals available in the West (see Note on Sources in the Appendix for listing) and from reports-reviews of other underground publications in the available periodicals. The number of pages is a rough estimate, based on the average number of pages per issue of the particular periodical available for examination. The data for 1979 is probably incomplete because it includes periodicals which have appeared up to September of that year. The periodicals are all type-written, single spaced, usually on about 6" by 8" paper.

people, a significant mass participation is evident: 39.2% of demonstrations involved up to 49 people; 35.2% 50 to 999 people, and 25.5% over a thousand people. Because of the within-system character of most demonstrations, they were largely passive and peaceful. According to Kowalewski, in only 7.8% of the cases did an attack on property or officials of the regime occur. The data indicate a multi-generational participation, although there is a heavy representation of the younger, Soviet-educated group. Kowalewski found that in over a fifth of the demonstrations, people under thirty years of age were in the majority.

The growth and diversification of the opposition movement is also suggested by the data on the underground publications, presented here in Table 4. Between 1972 and 1978 the number of underground periodicals increased from 1 to 8, the total number of issues from 4 to 31, and the number of pages from 170 to about 1,500. Most of the output is associated with the Catholic movement. Three periodicals are essentially religious in presentation *(LKB Kronika, Tiesos Kelias, Dievas ir Tėvynė)*, and two are national-cultural journals *(Aušra, Rūpintojėlis). Varpas,*

Laisvės Šauklys, and *Perspektyvos* are associated with a non-Catholic liberal and leftist viewpoint. *Alma Mater* appears to be a Vilnius University journal, probably associated with the Catholic movement, *Kultūros Archyvas* is a collection of source materials on recent cultural history.

The intellectual level and content of articles suggest that the contributors represent mostly the middle-level intelligentsia. There is obvious input by the Catholic clergy and former political prisoners. The latest publications, in particular *Alma Mater, Perspektyvos,* and *Kultūros Archyvas,* indicate that dissent has spread to the upper levels of cultural and political intelligentsia.

The opposition movement has become differentiated in terms of tactics of opposition and ideology. With respect to the former, opposition ranges from within-system reformism to a system-rejective revolutionary course (this is represented in Table 1. Two distinct positions within "loyal opposition" are evident. Least opposed are what are here called national communists, who seek limited national and political goals through the institutions of the regime and who accept the basic political arrangements but would like to have greater autonomy in developing the culture and economy of the country. Next are those who publicly articulate grievances and seek legal reforms of the regime or who openly assert themselves in the cultural sphere. Included here would be the human rights advocates, who, at least formally, do not question the legitimacy of the regime and who attempt to operate within the legal framework of the Soviet state. Among the two subversive positions on the system-rejective side, passive opposition fundamentally rejects the system but for the time being does not advocate the immediate or forcible overthrow of the system. Finally, the revolutionaries not only reject the system, but are ready to take concrete actions to overthrow it (involving, among other activities, formation of clandestine organizations).

It is noteworthy that in the 1970s opposition has shifted noticeably from within-system to system-rejective positions. What has been called here passive opposition is the most prominent approach.

To some extent the various positions on the opposition continuum correspond to the political-ideological differentiation of the opposition movement. The following major currents of opposition can be identified: national communists, the human rights movement (especially religious rights), Catholic nationalists, liberal nationalists, and the nationalist left ("new left" and Eurocommunists). There is a degree of overlap among these currents of opposition, and they cannot be defined precisely either structurally or ideologically. Best known and documentable are the human rights activities and Catholic nationalism because of the availability of extensive underground literature associated with them. Other positions are known in the most general outline form only. National oppression and survival are the principal concerns. To some extent the strategy and tactics for liberation are discussed, but there is very little about the preferred social and political order, the relationship of church and state, and foreign policy. There is an obvious general commitment to democracy, but very little about its ways and means. To describe the currents of opposition and their specific organizational structures and viewpoints is therefore risky, with many possibilities for error and distortion. Nevertheless, at least a preliminary sorting out of a rather complex movement is in order.

4. PRINCIPAL CURRENTS OF OPPOSITION

THE HUMAN RIGHTS MOVEMENT

THE CATHOLIC RIGHTS MOVEMENT

Opposition to the Soviet regime emanating from the Catholic Church, its clergy, and laity is by far the most prominent, best organized, and well-financed element of dissent. To a great extent, the prominence of the Catholic movement is due to the superior resources of the Catholic Church, which remains the only relatively autonomous institution in a politically penetrated society. It maintains contact with the Vatican, the Catholic clergy and hierarchy of other countries (in particular Poland), and the Lithuanian Catholics abroad. The movement has sufficient resources to finance, produce, and disseminate voluminous underground literature. Unlike the non-Catholic samizdat press, most of the Catholic publications have been reaching the West on an almost regular basis. For this reason, the available samizdat materials from Lithuania tend to inflate the role of the religious movement in the overall opposition to the regime. The Church provides an effective framework for autonomous communication. The clergy is assisted by over a thousand nuns and brothers, organized for pastoral work in catacomb fashion, by lay activists numbering in the thousands.

Finally, the deep roots of Catholicism in the social structure and consciousness of the masses enable large-scale mobilization of the laity.

The Catholic movement is two-pronged—religious and nationalist. The two directions reinforce each other and are intertwined. However, for purposes of analysis, it is useful to study each of these facets separately. The movement for religious rights is a within-system opposition, proceeding from the legal basis of the Soviet state. The nationalist direction is clearly one of passive subversion. The former is best represented by the *Chronicle of the Catholic Church in Lithuania;* the latter by the underground journal *Aušra* (The Dawn).

The religious rights movement was a response to the regime's policies directed at the Church and its pastoral activities as well as at the masses of believers (who were subjected to atheistic indoctrination and sanctions for being religious). The ongoing secularization of society due to modernization was no less alarming than the decimation of the clergy or the restrictions on pastoral work. It is thus necessary to keep in mind the strong tendencies of secularization in order to understand the Catholic dissent movement.

Soviet statistics on religious beliefs and practices are both scarce and problematical, while independent statistics are not available. The few sociological studies that have been conducted indicate a primitive sociological method and their results are ambiguous. In addition, the reliability of the data is uncertain: the political environment and official disapproval of religious life are not conducive to truthful responses. Unfortunately, there are no systematic Church data on the believers with which to check Soviet sociological findings. What is available in the way of statistical data must thus be taken with a grain of salt and considered as a rather impressionistic indication of trends.

Recently Soviet sociologists have claimed that the parents in about half of the families are "more or less" religious.[48] It is claimed that this is one of a number of circumstances accounting for the survival of religious beliefs among many youths. A Soviet survey of religious attitudes among 2,727 students of upper grades of secondary schools, conducted in 1968, found that about one fourth of the youths identified themselves as firm or wavering believers, about another fourth as atheists or militant atheists, and the rest as nonbelievers or indifferent to both religion and atheism. The nonbeliever category supposedly includes those who have not

---

48. J. Jaselskis, **Jaunimas ir religija** (Vilnius, 1977), p. 44.

internalized their atheistic-materialistic orientation to the point of permanence and thus remain susceptible to religious appeals.[49] It is very likely that this category of youths includes a significant number of secret believers. At the same time, it is very likely that the vast majority of these "nonbelievers" deliberately or spontaneously avoid church-centered religious practices. The overall situation could be described as one in which religious orientations are most likely present in a substantial majority of such youths, but at the same time, to the vast majority, religion has become a personally and privately experienced matter, rather than institutionally expressed.

Similar conclusions could be reached concerning the adult population. Among adults, as among youths, religious orientation is more evident in rural areas. One Soviet study claimed that in 1975 about 52% of the rural population was classified as religious and only about 30% of the urban population.[50] Another study claims that 43.91% of workers in factories and 66% in rural areas "in various ways were associated with the church and religion."[51] Religion thus is far from dead, but the role of the Church has declined precipitously.

Reflecting the declining role of the Church are the data on religious practices. One Soviet study has provided data on the percentage of christenings, weddings, and funerals conducted with religious ceremonies. According to the author, the statistics on religious ceremonies were derived from registers maintained by the Church. It is impossible to judge the accuracy of statistics supplied by the Church. There may be some distortions, for even in the official press it is acknowledged that a number of religious ceremonies are performed in secret. Thus again we should consider general trends rather than specifics. According to this study, 79% of the funerals in 1958 were conducted with religious ceremonies; by 1977, the percentage dropped to 43.9%. These are probably the least distorted data because it is relatively easy for

---

49. This is an interpretation of data from the survey conducted by the Soviet sociologist Rimantas Tidikis, **Moksleivių mokslinių ateistinių įsitikinimų formavimas** (Kaunas, 1974), pp. 12-21, as cited by Kęstutis Girnius, "Some Soviet Statistics on the Number of Catholics in Lithuania," **Radio Liberty Research,** 312/79 (October 18, 1979). Girnius reaches a somewhat more optimistic appraisal about the survival of religious orientations and behavior than this author.

50. J. Aničas, J. Mačiulis, **Katalikybės evoliucija** (Vilnius, 1979), p. 62.

51. Claimed by A. Balsys in B. Kuzmickas, comp., **Katalikybė ir šiuolaikinė ideologinė kova** (Vilnius, 1978), pp. 171-72.

the authorities to determine whether or not funeral services were held in church and whether or not a priest officiated at any phase of the funeral. The percentage of children baptized dropped from 81% to 44% between 1958 and 1977, while religious marriages declined from 69.6% to 25.2% during the same period.[52]

These data suggest that the majority of the population do not avail themselves of religious ceremonies even for the major milestones of life. They also suggest that to the extent that the population possesses a basically theistic orientation, it is not one that relies on the Church or is expressed in religious behavior. Thus, it is not unusual that Catholic teachings on everyday matters such as birth control, divorce, and abortion are not internalized, and so the Church no longer performs the role of internal moral guide for the vast majority of the population. For example, the divorce rate has jumped from 0.2 per 1,000 population in 1950 to 2.7 in 1975, when there were 29,609 marriages and 8,987 divorces.[53] Widespread birth control practice is evident in the statistics on birth rate, which plummeted from 23 per 1,000 population in 1940 to 15.7 in 1975.[54] Clearly contributing to this trend is the availability of abortion on demand. Official abortion statistics have never been published, but at least one dissident source has claimed 60,000 abortions annually, or about three times the natural increase of the population.[55] Although this figure may be somewhat distorted, it is plausible that for every live birth one is aborted.

The issue has been raised whether the perceived decline of religion as regulator of social behavior and morality is due to modernization *per se* or to the enforced secularization of society by the Soviet regime through the isolation of the Church from society and through state regulation of religious institutions. Soviet sociologists and ideologues have generally argued that secularization is a natural consequence of modernization.[56] They

---

52. Pranas Mišutis, **Religija, bažnyčia, ateizmas** (Vilnius, 1978), p. 90.

53. **Lietuvos TSR ekonomika ir kultūra 1975 metais** (Vilnius, 1976), p. 17.

54. **Ibid.**, p. 16.

55. These data are cited by Rev. Karolis Garuckas in a letter to P. Griškevičius, the First Secretary of the Lithuanian Communist Party, in which anti-religious policy is blamed for various social ills. Text of the letter in **Aušra**, No. 16 (May, 1979).

56. This is the standard view of Soviet ideologues and sociologists,

view science and technology as incompatible with religious viewpoint and that as societies modernize (through the application of science and technology for control over nature), religion naturally withers away, is simply "a vestige of the past" that is condemned to extinction. Deliberate atheistic policies merely help implement that which is ordained by the laws of history.

A contrary argument has been presented by a leading specialist of Lithuanian Catholicism, Prof. V. Stanley Vardys: "If it (the Latin Church) has lost ground, it was not because it did not adapt itself to the age of technology and science but largely because it has been forbidden to employ technology and science in its service." [57]

Prof. Vardys' viewpoint is shared by the Catholic dissidents. Secularization is perceived as a consequence of the atheistic policy of the regime both toward the masses and toward the Church. At least the available *samizdat* press has not considered modernization to be the culprit in declining religiosity and amorality or immorality in much of contemporary behavior. On the contrary, it has indicated the regime's limitations of pastoral activity and its atheistic-materialistic worldview as responsible for most of the social ills, such as alcoholism, sexual degeneracy, family instability, and crime. [58]

Available sociological data and the experience of other modernizing societies do indicate a major impact of modernization on the secularization of society. Nevertheless, it is also clear that the magnitude of secularization in Lithuania is a result of intense state intervention in the pastoral activities of the Church and ideological pressure upon the masses, with sanctions to conform. Some of the limitations on pastoral activities, enacted into law in 1966, have already been discussed. Particularly serious was the prohibition of the catechization of children in groups and the limitation on the number of candidates to the priesthood. The regime allowed limited religious publication, mainly for clerical use, and at the same time excluded the use of all communications media for religious purposes. The pulpit remained the only officially sanctioned means of communication with the faithful.

such as Aničas, Mišutis, Balsys, Jaselskis, and others, some of whose works have been cited above.

57. V. Stanley Vardys, "Modernization and Latin Rite Catholics in the Soviet Union", in Dennis J. Dunn, ed., **Religion and Modernization in the Soviet Union** (Boulder, Colo., 1977), p. 376.

58. See, for example, the cited letter of Rev. Garuckas, in **Aušra**, No. 16 (May, 1979).

The Representative of the Council for Religious Affairs in practice directed the appointment of priests to pastoral work and in general tolerated those diocesan administrators who followed state's directives, which often were contrary to both the spirit and the letter of the Canon Law. As a result of constant state interference and pressure upon the Church, many clergymen became pastorally complacent or sought to adjust to the situation by cooperating with the civil authorities against the interests of the Church.

The Church also faces one additional serious problem. The present parishes and churches were established to serve a rural population (77% rural in 1939). By 1975, the country became urbanized, with over 56% of the people living in cities. As the population shifted to the cities, no corresponding shift in the organization of the Church was permitted. Thus, it came to pass that in 1974 thirteen percent of the clergy served in the ten largest cities with 39% of the country's population.[59] New churches were not allowed in the suburbs around the largest cities; in fact, not a single church anywhere has been built since the war. To the contrary, the *Chronicle* has listed 23 churches in Vilnius and 14 churches in Kaunas as closed by the regime.[60] One Soviet writer has claimed that Easter morning Masses in Kaunas are attended by some 20,000—25,000 faithful or 6%—7% of the population of the city.[61] Probably, the number represents the near capacity of existing churches in Kaunas, built before the war, when that city's population was half of that in 1975. All in all, then, the special distribution of the churches and the clergy is inconsistent with the distribution of the population to provide optimal opportunities for the faithful to avail themselves of religious services or for the clergy to engage in pastoral work.

Many of the existing parishes lacked pastors or were served by a rapidly aging clergy. One Western survey found that in 1974 twelve percent of the parishes were served by a neighboring pastor.[62] The same survey indicated that 49% of the priests were over 60 years old.[63] Given the age structure, it was predicted that in 20 years half of the priests living in 1974 will have died, and given the 1974 ordination rate, perhaps only half

59. Data from Rev. Casimir Pugevičius, ed., **World Lithuanian Roman Catholic Directory** (Brooklyn, N.Y., 1975), p. 102.

60. **Chronicle**, No. 18 (1975).

61. Jaselskis, **op. cit.**, p. 25.

62. Pugevičius, **op. cit.**, p. 100.

63. **Ibid.**, pp. 56-72.

would be replaced by new priests. Thus, at the turn of the second millenium, the Catholic Church in Lithuania would have about half the number of clergymen in 1940. Given such projections, attrition of priests was among the first concerns of the dissident movement.

As we have seen, initially the Catholic rights movement addressed itself to select problems, such as the number of candidates admitted to the seminary. Very quickly, however, it went beyond petitions and protests, and by 1972 it evolved into a comprehensive campaign against secularization. The religious rights campaign consists of several components.[64] First of all, the movement involves a deliberate confrontation with civil authorities concerning the respect of freedom of conscience and worship. The confrontation is conducted within the legal framework of the Soviet state and involves civil disobedience to laws and administrative decrees that, in the interpretation of the dissidents, are contrary to the international conventions signed by the Soviet Union and the liberties guaranteed by the Soviet Constitution itself, and those contrary to the conscience of the dissidents. Besides protests to civil authorities, the campaign involves open defiance of discriminatory decrees or civil proscriptions contrary to the conscience of the clergy and the Canon Law. Examples range from the teaching of religion to groups of children (Revs. Šeškevičius, Zdebskis, Bubnys, and other) to unauthorized processions to the cemetery or visitations by priests to neighboring parishes.

Secondly, the rights campaign involves the mobilization of internal supports of the laity, as well as the international supports, such as the Holy See, the Catholics and clergy around the world, and the Lithuanian Catholics abroad. The extent to which the clergy supports the rights campaign can be judged from the number of priests signing various petitions and protests. Although there are differences among the clergy and the activist laity on how to proceed with the rights struggle (this is discussed later), there is widespread consensus on the need to oppose the most blatant discrimination against believers. For example, the Decree on Religious Societies of 1976 has been protested by about 70% of the clergy.[65] All the administrators of

---

64. The various facets of the religious rights campaign described here are documented extensively by the authentic underground materials on religious conditions presented in Part III of this work. Additional documentation will be provided only when necessary.

65. At the beginning of 1979 priests in each of the six dioceses

dioceses and bishops of Lithuania criticized the new Soviet Constitution for making believers second-class citizens. The extent of support for the campaign among the laity can be gauged from the thousands of signers of various petitions and protests. The 1972 petition to L. Brezhnev, signed by 17,000 believers and transmitted to the addressee through United Nations Secretary General Kurt Waldheim, is the best known example of several such massive actions by religious persons. The Lithuanian Catholics have received moral support from the bishops of the United States and Germany, the Catholics of Ireland, and even an occasional word of sympathy from the Pope. Lithuanian Catholics abroad have provided some of the material means for dissidents and have also facilitated the communication of the dissidents' views to the world.[66] As a result, Catholic dissent became one of the best known components of Soviet dissent, to the point of creating a somewhat distorted perception in the West that dissent in Lithuania involves only religious rights. The ability to mobilize supports has given the movement a momentum that could neither be ignored by the regime nor dealt with by ordinary police methods.

The third component of the Catholic rights movement is the development of unofficial means of communication. This involves the self-publishing of periodical literature as well as books for religious needs. Several hundred books have been issued in *samizdat;* thousands of copies of prayer books have been produced illegally.[67] However, the periodical press has played the most significant role for the sustenance of the movement.

The *Chronicle of the Catholic Church in Lithuania* is the voice of the rights movement. From its inception in March 1972 until the end of 1979, thirty-nine issues, averaging about 50 typed single-spaced pages each, have been produced and transmitted to the West. This continuous record of publication is amazing in light of the KGB efforts to silence the *Chronicle,* efforts involving at least

---

submitted protest statements to church and state authorities. 522 priests signed the statements. Texts of statements and names of priests signing in **Chronicle,** No. 38 (May 1, 1978).

66. Among the Lithuanian organizations especially involved in aid activities to the dissidents are: Lithuanian Roman Catholic Religious Aid and United Lithuanian American Relief Fund—for general material aid; Lithuanian Roman Catholic Priests' League of America and Society for the Publication of the Chronicles of the Catholic Church in Lithuania—for publication, translation, and dissemination of Catholic **samizdat.**

67. Private communication.

four major trials for alleged participation in the publication activity.[68] The record of publications in spite of repressions attests to the superior resources of the publishers and the widespread support for the activity among the clergy and the activist laity.

The *Chronicle* is modeled on the *Chronicle of Current Events*, providing confirmable data on violations of religious rights. In scope it is almost exclusively devoted to Catholic rights, and only occasionally has it published information on other human rights, national-political questions, or religious rights of other denominations. The *Chronicle* has regularly included essays and even polemics on the present status and problems of the Catholic Church; it has criticized the clergy, the hierarchy, and even the Pope for subservience to the Soviet authorities. In addition, it has published the texts of petitions and protests to civil authorities and reported the news from the dioceses. Finally, a large portion of the *Chronicle* is devoted to reporting violations of freedom of conscience, especially atheistic indoctrination and persecution of religious youths in schools.

Three other specialized religious journals published in the underground should be mentioned. *Tiesos Kelias* (The Way of Truth), whose publication began in 1977, is a pastoral journal for the clergy. *Dievas ir Tėvynė* (God and Motherland), published since 1976, is a religious journal devoted heavily to polemics against the atheist worldview and in defense of religion. The third journal, *Rūpintojėlis* (The Sorrowing One), serves the religious and cultural needs of the faithful.

The fourth component of the Catholic rights movement involves a development of a style of pastoral work appropriate for catacomb conditions. The effort here is directed at the institutional Church rather than at the regime. Among the concerns in this area is the leadership of the Church (who shall be appointed as bishops), the pastoral and personal behavior of clergymen, the admission of candidates to the priesthood, and consecration of only worthy seminarians. The dissidents are seeking the approval of the Holy See for the Catacomb Church and for the clandestine pastoral work. An underground seminary

---

68. Three trials—of Petras Plumpa and others, Nijolė Sadūnaitė, and Vladas Lapienis and Ona Pranckūnaitė—are presented in Doc. No. 63, 64, 65, and 72. The fourth trial, that of the Russian rights activist Sergei Kovalev, is covered extensively in **Chronicle,** No. 21 (January 25, 1976). For a complete record of the trial of Kovalev, see the Russian-language publication **The Case of Kovalev** (New York: Khronika Press, 1976).

for priests is said to exist. Also convents, which were disbanded by the authorities, continue to function in the underground. The nuns especially, who may number over a thousand, constitute a core of activists and provide a good deal of the catechization of children. There are indications that a lay movement, called Friends of the Eucharist, is in existence, but the precise nature of this activity is unknown.[69] The dissidents see the survival of the Church as possible only through the development of an active pastorate that is not controlled by the state. The existence of what the dissidents themselves call the Catacomb Church alongside the official Church recognized by the state and the Vatican raises the difficult issues of unity and discipline in the Church and complicates the relationship between Moscow and the Vatican, in effect challenging the so-called *Ostpolitik* of the Vatican.

The Catholic rights movement has avoided setting-up formal organizations on the model of legal dissent groups, such as the Helsinki monitor groups or Amnesty International chapters. The *Chronicle,* edited and published by unknown people (the four trials in connection with the *Chronicle* involved charges of production and dissemination rather than editing), is the main manifestation of some kind of an organizational network. Apparently, the leaders of the Lithuanian rights movement had no faith in the formal Soviet constitutional guarantees for activities they considered legal otherwise.

The break with the pattern occurred on November 13, 1978, when the Catholic Committee for Defense of the Rights of Believers was announced, with five known activist priests signing as members.[70] The Catholic Committee is modeled on Moscow's Christian Committee for Defense of the Rights of Believers in the USSR. The Catholic Committee intends to cooperate with the Christian Committee in Moscow. In fact, the two committees have issued joint statements.[71] The Catholic Committee has issued

---

69. **Chronicle,** No. 39 (July 22, 1979) carries a greeting to the organization on its tenth anniversary and describes a July 7, 1979, meeting of its representatives in Žemaičių Kalvarija, a small parish with a famous sanctuary. No further details are provided about its activities.

70. The announcement of the formation of the Catholic Committee in **Chronicle,** No. 36 (January 6, 1979). Subsequently the **Chronicle** has published only Documents No. 5, 12, 15, 16, and summaries of several other documents. All of the documents of the Catholic Committee, however, have reached the West separately.

71. A letter to world church leaders and statesmen, dated November

documents on violations of religious rights following the documentary style of other rights groups. By September of 1979 the Catholic
Committee issued 23 numbered documents with supporting
materials. Sometime in the spring of 1979 the Catholic Committee
began issuing a compilation entitled *Documents of the Catholic
Committee for Defense of the Rights of Believers.* It is not clear why this
became necessary as long as the *Chronicle* continued publication.
Among the possibilities is the divergence on tactics among the
dissidents. One feature of the Catholic Committee in particular
should be mentioned. It has promised to defend the rights of all
believers, not just Catholics, something which the *Chronicle* has
avoided completely. Also, for still unexplained reasons, the *Chronicle*
has published the texts of only four documents.

The specific issues between the Soviet authorities and
Catholic dissidents are presented in detail in various documents
and articles published in the *Chronicle,* the more important of
which are included in this anthology. The issues can be grouped
into four major areas of conflict: 1) the teaching authority of the
Church, especially the catechization of children; 2) the degree of
secular control over the Church; 3) the freedom of conscience
and worship; 4) the publication of religious literature. What have
been the results of the last decade of conflict over these issues?

Catechization of children remains among the most serious
problems of the Church. Through its legal rules on separation of
school and Church, the Soviet regime has sought maximum
isolation of children from the influence of the Church.
Particularly relevant are the decrees of 1966, which bar teaching
of religion to groups of children, as well as the participation of
children in religious services. In effect, legally, though not
necessarily factually, only the parents are permitted to transmit
religion to their offspring. Prison terms and administrative
penalties have been imposed on priests who taught religion to
groups of children. In fact, the regime has sought to discourage
parental influence through ostracism and informal sanctions
against believing students and their parents. Open practice of
religion may mean that the youth will not get the proper
character attestations for admission to higher education. The
regime has dismissed religious teachers and reprimanded those
schools where religious students are prominent. Publication of

---

22, 1978, asking for the ecanctment in the UN of an international
convention to prevent discrimination in the sphere of religion. A copy is
available in the West.

any literature for teaching religion has been prohibited and only *samizdat* catechisms have been produced.

Limitations on catechization have reduced the number of children receiving basic sacraments. According to Soviet statistics, if in 1957 about two thirds of the children were still confirmed, the proportion dropped to about a third by 1977 [72] The *Chronicle* has claimed that in 1979 about 40,000 children will receive the First Communion.[73] The number, if true, would represent about two thirds of the children in the appropriate age group. Also according to the dissidents, in 1972 at least 44,000 children were preparing for the First Communion, while at the same time a Soviet ideologue P. Mišutis claimed that only about 20,000 received the First Communion that year.[74] In view of such a divergent numbers, no firm conclusion can be arrived at. The most optimistic estimate would be that not many more than half of the children in appropriate age categories receive the First Communion or the Confirmation. This would be an alarming situation from the point of view of the Church, forecasting increasing losses to the Church. On the other hand, given the restrictions on catechization, such statistics testify to an amazing effectiveness of religious teaching. Underground nuns, lay teachers, and the clergy have largely ignored or circumvented the prohibitions on religious education. For example, recently the Representative of the Council for Religious Affairs has complained that many priests circumvent the legal rules by using their sermons during religious services to transmit religious teachings.[75]

Soviet authorities have reduced some of the overt pressure on the Church in respect to catechization. Trials for catechization have ceased since 1972 and administrative penalties have been reported with decreasing frequency. In 1979 the administrators of dioceses were negotiating the first printing of a catechism.[76] At the same time, however, the regime has sought to strengthen atheistic indoctrination in schools, including institutions of

---

72. Mišutis, **op. cit.,** p. 90.

73. **Chronicle,** No. 39 (July 22, 1979). In an earlier issue, No. 36, the claim was made that about 70% of the children are prepared for the First Communion by priests and parents in catacomb fashion.

74. **Chronicle,** No. 9 (1974).

75. **Chronicle,** No. 39 (July 22, 1979).

76. Document No. 15 of the Catholic Committee reveals that the ordinaries were requesting from the government a printing of 500,000 copies of a catechism. Text of the document in **Chronicle,** No. 39.

higher learning.[77] The shift in policy involves reduction of overt persecution of the clergy and religious activists engaged in religious education and an increased indoctrination and continued use of coercion through the educational process. As the *Chronicle* reports, the school continues to be used in a coercive manner against believing students and their parents, thus violating the freedom of conscience and worship. While the lessened persecution of the Church for its teaching activities may have permitted some stabilization of the trend toward secularization (for, example, the proportion of children confirmed remained relatively stable throughout the 1970s, according to data supplied by the Soviets[78]), the problem is nevertheless far from resolved from the point of view of the Church and particularly the dissidents, for freedom of conscience continues to be grossly violated in the schools and too many children are not reached by the Church.

Several issues in the relationship of the Church as an institution and the state deserve attention. Foremost among the unresolved problems is the appointment of bishops. At the end of 1979 Bishop L. Povilonis was the Apostolic Administrator of the Archdiocese of Kaunas and the Diocese of Vilkaviškis (succeeding Bishop Matulaitis-Labukas, who died in 1979); Bishop R. Krikš-čiūnas was the Apostolic Administrator of the Diocese of Panevėžys; Bishop J. Steponavičius was still under internal exile and ban from his see in the Archdiocese of Vilnius, which was run by the Administrator Rev. A. Gutauskas (who replaced Msgr. Č. Krivaitis in January of 1979); Bishop V. Sladkevičius was also banned from the Diocese of Kaišiadorys, which was administered by Canon J. Andrikonis; and the Diocese of Telšiai was run by Rev. A. Vaičius. In effect, all the dioceses were led by administrators, most of whom, in the view of the dissidents, were too cooperative with the civil authorities for the good of the Church.

The dissidents were particularly critical of Msgr. Krivaitis, both for his alleged total cooperation with the civil authorities and his moral laxity. Even his successor, Rev. Gutauskas, was considered unacceptable as bishop. Similarly criticism was launched against the Rector of the Kaunas Interdiocesan Seminary Rev. Butkus. Canon Andrikonis and Bishop Krikščiū-

---

77. Text of a decree of the Ministry of Education, dated May 27, 1977, fulfilling the decisions of a Central Committee Plenum in 1976, is published in **Chronicle**, No. 34 (August 15, 1978).

78. This is apparent in the statistics supplied by Mišutis, **op. cit.**, p. 90.

nas were treated as allies of the atheists. Even Bishop Matulaitis-Labukas, who served as the Chairman of the College of
Ordinaries of Lithuania, came under dissident censure.[79] In a
letter to Bishop Matulaitis-Labukas (dated Feb. 2, 1978), the
priests of the Kaunas and Vilkaviškis dioceses criticized the
bishop for not providing leadership and proper upbringing of the
candidates for priesthood in the seminary, for not overseeing the
discipline and pastoral work of the clergy, for imposing
limitations on catacomb pastoral activity, and last but not least,
for general concessions to the Soviet authorities, detrimental to
religion and the Church.

In a statement intended for Pope John Paul II, the dissidents
have expressed the dissatisfaction with the hierarchy in no
uncertain terms:

> Lithuania's religious life suffers greatly from the
> appointment of bishops who utterly submit to the atheists.
> In our situation the bishop must be a strong backbone for the
> priests and laity in defending religious freedom and the
> Church's rights. An especially unfortunate occurrence befalls
> us if a bravely struggling nation's and clergy's leader—a
> bishop—by utterly submitting to the atheists, destroys the
> militancy of believers. This makes the faithful and clergy
> pessimistic and causes them to lose hope to the point of
> anger at those, who, out of ignorance or lack of sympathy for
> us, recommend such weak-willed people for the bishop's seat.
> They also become angry at those who appoint the bishops.
> (...) The atheists will approve only those candidates for
> bishop that they expect will be obedient helpers in the
> destruction of religion.[80]

Thus the dissidents have consistently implored the Pope not to
appoint new bishops who would be Trojan horses—agents of the
atheists—within the Church. They were especially apprehensive
about the possible appointment of Msgr. Krivaitis and Rev. Butkus, who, in their view, were favored by the government. They
consider Bishop Steponavičius as their spiritual leader and an
example of a principled hierarch, ready to fight for the interests
of the Church. They insist that no bishops be appointed until the
two exiled ones are reinstated in their sees.

The hierarchy question remained unresolved upon the

---

79. The text of the letter was not printed in the **Chronicle,** but
separately transmitted to the West by the editors of the **Chronicle.** Copy
in possession of the author.

80. **Chronicle,** No. 36 (January 6, 1979).

election of Pope John Paul II. The Soviet government refused to reconsider the case of Bishop Steponavičius, although there were indications that Bishop Sladkevičius could be permitted to assume his duties. The Vatican refused to appoint new bishops, possibly because of the failure to find candidates acceptable to all parties, including the dissidents. The dissidents rejoiced "that finally our voice has reached the Apostolic See and that the atheists of the Soviet Union could not push through their candidates. Even happier news has reached us: the new Holy Father is not preparing to appoint new public bishops until the exiled bishops—H. E. Julijonas Steponavičius and Vincentas Sladkevičius—are allowed to resume their duties."[81] So far, then, Vatican's position has corresponded with that of the dissidents. It remains to be seen if the Polish Pope will manage to unravel the existing impasse with Moscow and the dissidents over the appointment of new leaders. Meanwhile, however, in the absence of respected authority a number of problems—discipline, unity, pastoral work—are bound to plague the Church.

Another issue involving the Church as an institution is the preparation of new clergy. The number of seminarians permitted to enroll annually in the Kaunas Interdiocesan Seminary has been increased from 10 in 1970 to 21 in 1979, when there were 72 seminarians. The Representative of the Council for Religious Affairs Anilionis indicated that within two years 100 or more seminarians may be permitted.[82] For the time being the number admitted is still insufficient to replace those dying. Thus, for example, 19 priests died in 1978, but only only 9 candidates were admitted to priesthood. As a consequence about 100 parishes are without a pastor.

The dissidents see an additional problem with the seminary. According to them, while the number of seminarians admitted has been increased, at the same time the KGB increased its pressure on the seminarians and sought to place its own candidates. Furthermore, the secular authorities still have a final say about who will be admitted to the seminary. According to the dissidents, the government sponsors those who are of questionable health, ability, or are willing to cooperate with the security police. As a result a number of unfit candidates were admitted and a number of undeserving seminarians were consecrated as priests.

The legal rules pertaining to the Church, particularly the

---

81. **Ibid.**
82. **Chronicle,** No. 39 (July 22, 1979).

Decree on Religious Societies of 1976, represent a threat to the integrity of the Church as an institution. The legal rules have sought to place all power over the Church in church committees and local authorities. The role of the clergy is merely to perform as servants of the cult. This is contrary to the long-held authority of bishops and pastors to direct the organizational and economic activities of churches, in addition to providing spiritual guidance. One pastor expressed this to the Representative of the Council for Religious Affairs as follows:

> In respect to the relations between the pastor and the church committee, it must be remembered that every priest, when he is appointed to perform the duties of a pastor, he is appointed not just for liturgical matters, but also as administrator of all the church properties. He even gives an oath to perform all these duties well. This is pointed out and required by Church canons. The church committee is merely an advisory body to the pastor. [83]

As a result of the conflict between secular and Church laws, only reluctantly did the hierarchy agree in 1948 to the formation of church or parish committees and the registration of religious societies. The Church managed to adjust to the new order formally, while in fact the pastor ran most of the affairs of the parish. The issue was raised again after the enactment of the 1976 Decree on Religious Societies and the push to conclude new contracts between local authorities and the religious societies. [84] In the view of the dissidents, the legal rules even further subjected the Church to civil authorities, which, under the current provisions, could refuse to register a religious society, could close the church, and could paralyze the work of the pastor. On top of that, the Church lacked the character of a juridical person and, therefore, had no recourse to the courts to contest arbitrary implementation of existing legal rules. The *Chronicle* advocated the resistance to the signing of the new contracts. It even pointed out several cases in which the secular authorities meddled in the election of church committees, claiming that the new rules permit the atheists to put their agents in charge of the church committees. [85] But by 1979, according to Representative

---

83. **Ibid.**

84. Text of the new contract is published in **Chronicle,** No. 26 (March 19, 1977).

85. See **Chronicle,** No. 39 (July 22, 1979); Document No. 21, September 12, 1979, with attachments, of the Catholic Committee presents one case of meddling in the election of a church committee.

Anilionis, there were only 36 parishes (out of about 630) holding out.[86]

The strengthened secular control over parish activities was one of the steps taken to control dissent. Upon his appointment to the post as Representative of the Council for Religious Affairs at the end of 1978, Anilionis reportedly threatened a thorough implementation of the Decree on Religious Societies. The upshot of this was a wave of protests from the clergy, demanding the abrogation of the law. Protests were signed by 522 priests, about 70% of the clergy. Such unexpectedly wide opposition led to some backtracking by the government in respect to the implementation of the decree. Unofficial sources have reported that a representative of the Council for Religious Affairs in Moscow intervened to cool the emerging confrontation. So far the church committees remain factually under the control of the pastor and have not served as instruments of government control. It remains to be seen whether the regime will seek to exclude people unacceptable to them from the executive organs of religious societies. It also remains to be seen to what extent the laws on religion will be implemented. In practice the relationship of the pastor and the executive organs of religious societies on the one hand, and the local authorities (specifically, the Deputy Chairman of the Executive Committee of a raion) on the other hand, has varied from total confrontation to a live and let live attitude. In other words, it depends to a great extent upon the personalities involved. Nevertheless, the existing law represents a Democlean sword, which could be utilized with devasting ruthlessness at any time.

There is no notable change in the treatment of believers. The *Chronicle* has continued to document numerous violations of religious rights and discrimination and punishment of believers, such as dismissal from work for religious practices (particularly teachers are subject to such punishment), punishment for observing religious holidays, ostracism and sanctions against religious students and their parents, prohibition of religious services for those institutionalized or in hospitals, etc. The regime considers religious beliefs as incompatible not only with Communist Party membership, but also generally with positions of responsibility in social, cultural, economic, and administrative spheres. The predominance of older people among churchgoers is not necessarily an indication that religion is mostly professed by "backward" older generation, but rather it reflects the fact that sanctions are applied upon those in productive years who practice

---

86. **Chronicle**, No. 39 (July 22, 1979).

religion. The higher the position in the system, the higher the
costs for religious practices. This is certainly the impression that
comes through in private conversations with members of Soviet
intelligentsia.

It is difficult to judge whether there has been any shift in
government policy toward the believers. On the theoretical and
formal level there is nothing that could be pointed to indicating
substantive change. But in real life, private sources do suggest, a
minor religious revival seems to be in progress, a new openness
in expressing religious beliefs is evident, even among students of
the universities. This is confirmed indirectly by Soviet sources as
well. For example, recently an article in the party's theoretical
journal *Komunistas* acknowledged that "modernization" of
Catholicism "assists for some time to revive interest in religion
among certain people."[87] It is also confirmed by impressions of
Western correspondents.[88] The revival of religious life is a result
of several factors. No doubt, the rights movement has helped to
revitalize the pastoral work of the Church, has contributed to
self-renewal and modernization in the spirit of the Vatican
Council decisions, and imbued confidence among the believers to
resist regime sanctions. The election of the Polish Pope,
particularly his visit to Poland, also has had a salutory effect. An
American correspondent quotes the Deputy Representative of
the Council for Religious Affairs Juozėnas that "The influence of
religion is gradually decreasing, but what happens here next will
depend on the leadership in the Vatican."[89] And last, but not
least, several private sources have suggested that in general there
is an increasing disregard of the Soviet order among the masses
as well as unwillingness or impotence of the authorities to
enforce officially sanctioned behavior.

Finally, the solution to the needs of religious literature has
not been satisfactory resolved. In thirty-five years since the war
only six officially approved books have been published: *Catholic
Prayer Book* (1957), *Roman Catholic Ritual* (1966), *Resolutions of the
Second Vatican Council* (1968), *Liturgical Prayer Book* (1968), *The New
Testament* (1972), and *The Book of Psalms* (1973). None of these
publications contains information on the number of copies
printed, as is the normal practice in Soviet publications, but the

87. **Komunistas**, No. 8, 1979, p. 32.

88. See, for example, a report by Jim Gallagher in **Chicago Tribune**,
June 4, 1979.

89. See Craig R. Whitney, "In Lithuania, Too, Catholics Look
Hopefully to New Pope", **New York Times**, July 26, 1979.

dissidents have claimed that the needs of the believers could not be satisfied. For example, one source claims that only 10,000 copies of *The New Testament* were issued.[90] Furthermore, as the list of publications indicates, the issued religious works were intended mainly for the use by the clergy in performance of the cult, in effect denying the masses of believers essential religious works. Neither a catechism nor any philosophical-theological works have been published and, therefore, had to be produced in the underground. Finally, there is no periodical for internal communication within the Church, let alone for interaction with the masses of believers.

During 1979 government attitude was undergoing a change. The ordinaries were negotiating for a number of publications, for which a favorable government response was indicated.[91] The ordinaries were asking for a publications of 500,000 catechisms, expansion of liturgical calendars to include materials for sermons, issuance of a regular illustrated journal on the activities of the Church, a new edition of a prayer book, and a preparation of a missal. It remains to be seen to what extent these requests will be met. The dissidents, however, appeared to remain skeptical, charging that the proposed journal is likely to serve only propaganda interests of the regime and will not be able to report the true situation in the Church.

These issues and the limited regime concessions on some questions have led to a disagreement among the hierarchy, the clergy, and the laity whether the tactics of confrontation with the regime and catacomb pastorate are productive and whether a tolerable *modus vivendi* between the Church and the state is possible. At one extreme is the Catacomb Church, represented by the Committee for the Defense of Rights of the Believers, those associated with the *Chronicle,* and certainly the two exiled bishops.[92] This pole is supported by the majority of the clergy, as can be judged from the number of priests signing petitions. The dissidents remain convinced that the faith among the masses can

90. **Chronicle,** No. 6 (1973).

91. See the reports of the meetings of the Representative of the Council for Religious Affairs Anilionis with the ordinaries and Doc. No. 15 (May 5, 1979) of the Catholic Committee, addressed to the bishops and administrators of dioceses. Both items published in **Chronicle,** No. 39 (July 22, 1979).

92. A detailed presentation of their views is found in a survey on the situation of the Catholic Church in Lithuania and the Soviet Union, addressed to Pope John Paul II. See **Chronicle,** No. 28 (June 29, 1977).

be maintained only through vigorous evangelization by the underground Church. They appeal to the Vatican for recognition. They explicitly reject Vatican's *Ostpolitik*—the normalization of Church-state relations on the hierarchal level, without extracting significant concessions for the rights of believers. At the same time they pledge loyalty to the Holy Father. They believe that Vatican's *Ostpolitik* will lead to regime control over the Church, its destruction from inside, while the pastoral work among the people will be neglected. For this reason they oppose the appointment of new bishops until the exiled ones are reinstated and criticize the hierarchy and the clergy who compromise with the government and are less than zealous in spreading the word of God.

At the other extreme is what may be called the official Church, represented by a number of priests identified as "loyal" to the government, including members of Church leadership, such as Msgr. Krivaitis, the former Administrator of the Vilnius Archdiocese. The non-dissident clergy, which is convinced that a *modus vivendi* with the regime is possible, has countered with its own accusations that the dissidents are dividing the Church internally and are exacerbating the already difficult relationship between the Church and the state. Their views were given limited exposure in the *Chronicle* in 1974, but with a lengthy rebuttal.[93] In 1977 there appeared apparently another *samizdat* publication, entitled *The Church and the Chronicle*, representing the views of the non-dissident clergy and, according to the *Chronicle*, the KGB.[94] Whether the publication, dubbed "Anti-Chronicle", was inspired by the KGB to split the clergy is impossible to ascertain. The views expressed there, however, appear to represent some of the genuine thinking of the non-dissident clergy. The "Anti-Chronicle" maintains that the *Chronicle* was initially welcomed, but when its tone began to change, the *Chronicle* began to "indulge in a pernicious criticism and splintering tactics directed against the Church in our country... The atheist government is using the *Chronicle* for its own interests." There is also a very emotional response of unnamed seminarians to the charges of the *Chronicle*, which include not only intimations of KGB presence in the seminary, but also suggest that those recruited to the seminary are physically weak

---

93. See **Chronicle** No. 12 (1974) and No. 14 (1975); also Doc. No. 62 in this work.

94. **Bažnyčia ir "LKB Kronika"** (Lithuania, 1977), 30 pages, with six articles.

or mentally deficient. The "Anti-Chronicle" maintains that the *Chronicle* distorts reality and that religious life is possible under the circumstances. "In Lithuania the Church has no privileges, but it is possible to work." An article suggests that the negativism of the *Chronicle* is due to the need to justify the work of the dissidents, who receive material and moral support from abroad, and that it is encouraged by the guilty conscience of those priests who left their flocks and escaped to the West.

The "Anti-Chronicle" is an understandable reaction to some of the more extreme statements and inevitable distortions which have appeared in the *Chronicle*. The frequently absolute rejection of non-dissidents and intimations about their alleged collaboration with the regime to the detriment of the Church neglect the considerable contributions of the official Church to religious life. However, it is significant that the tactic of the Catacomb Church is not totally rejected by the "Anti-Chronicle" and a basic consensus that the Church is persecuted and discriminated remains. Even the bishops and administrators of dioceses, who have been criticized in the *Chronicle*, have not openly denounced the dissidents. Despite the arguments, the schism is not unbridgeable. Both sides recognize that under the circumstances both the public and the underground churches are necessary for the survival of faith. Dissent has contributed to the emergence of a more confident Church, a more open expression of religion by the masses, and led to some concessions to religious life on the part of the government.

It is problematical whether an agreement between Moscow and the Vatican can be consummated. The Kremlin has viewed religion as only tolerable and occasionally useful for world peace campaigns. Marxist-Leninist dogma on religion and intolerance of pluralism by the Communist Party remain essential obsacles to a tolerable arrangement of relations between the Church and the state. However, as in everything, changes are inevitable, a model of relationship between a communist state and Catholicism does exist. A change in Kremlin leadership and/or attitude toward religion is in the realm of possibilities. In the past the Kremlin has shown willingness to make concessions even to organized religion when its interests are served. And a greater toleration of religion could be in the interest of the Soviet state, for it could reduce significantly, if not eliminate completely, religious dissent and at the same time reduce nationalistic pressures, which in Lithuania partly stem from the association of Catholicism and nationality.

THE LITHUANIAN HELSINKI GROUP

The Final Act of the Conference on Security and Cooperation in Europe, signed in Helsinki on August 1, 1975, was received by the dissidents with notable skepticism. The *Chronicle* wrote that "This game of the powerful of the world produces bitterness and disappointment in the hearts of millions. What can this glorified Helsinki Conference give us when we in Lithuania are not even provided with the full text of the Final Act".[95] Tomas Venclova, a member of the Lithuanian Public Group to Support the Implementation of the Helsinki Agreements, (hereafter referred to as the Lithuanian Helsinki Group), testified before the US Commission on Security and Cooperation in Europe to the same effect: "At first it seemed that it would only confirm the European status quo, and that the humanitarian articles would be, even under the best of circumstances, no more than good intentions."[96] Certainly, the Soviet leaders hoped that the outcome of the Conference on Security and Cooperation in Europe would serve as a substitute for a peace treaty ending World War II and legitimize Soviet gains in Eastern Europe. Strong arguments were made to dissuade President Ford from signing the Final Act for exactly these reasons. None suspected that the humanitarian articles would become the most significant part of the accords, stimulating dissent in the Soviet sphere.

Within a year after the signing of the Final Act, opinion about its relevance to the dissent movement changed. In its evaluation of the Final Act a year after its conclusion, the Public Group to Promote Observance of the Helsinki Agreements in the USSR (hereafter referred as the Moscow Helsinki Group) explained the changing perspective as follows:

> Relying on past experience, Soviet dissidents were skeptical of the possible results of the European Conference, not without justification fearing that the authorities would use it for the consolidation of their own power. The first months after the Conference, it appeared, confirmed these fears. But with time, it came to light that ever more frequently people being oppressed for ideological, political,

---

95. **Chronicle,** No. 18 (August 31, 1975). **Tiesa,** August 2, 1975, published only the first part of the Final Act dealing with general principles, "guiding relations between participating states."

96. Text of Venclova's testimony in: Commission on Security and Cooperation in Europe, **Hearings on Implementation of the Helsinki Accords** (Washington, D.C., 1977), Vol. I, p. 54.

national, or other such reasons began to refer, in their complaints to authorities, to the humanitarian articles of the Final Act. To be sure, the authorities in the best of cases ignored such references. But protests of world public opinion with reference to the Final Act showed that it could serve as a legal point of departure. [97]

Thus convinced that pressure can be brought to bear on the Soviet regime with respect to its human rights policies, the dissidents, first in Moscow, set up the public groups to monitor Soviet compliance with the humanitarian articles of the Final Act. Following the example set by the Moscow Helsinki Group, on November 25, 1976, five individuals in Lithuania formed the Lithuanian Helsinki Group. The announcement of its formation was made on December 1, 1976, in Moscow, with the assistance of the Moscow Helsinki Group. This was done to maximize exposure of the act to Western correspondents, who rarely have the opportunity to visit Vilnius. Yuri Orlov's apartment served as the locus of the press conference where Viktoras Petkus made the announcement.[98]

The Lithuanian Helsinki Group represented a coalition of the principal currents of dissent in Lithuania. Although obviously no formal organizations were represented in the Group, its members were associated with or active in the religious, democratic, nationalist, and minority dissent. The biographies of the Group members are indicative of its broad basis.

The leading member of the Group and perhaps the most prominent personality of the recent dissent was Viktoras Petkus.[99] He was born in a poor peasant family in 1929, in the Raseiniai raion. As a youth, he was active in the Catholic youth organization *Ateitis*. In 1947 he was arrested for leading the illegal Catholic organization in the Raseiniai gymnasium and received a ten-year sentence. Another ten years were added for escaping from camp. Because he was a minor at the time of conviction, he

97. Text of this document in **Arkhiv samizdata,** No. 2605, dated July 22, 1976.

98. See the testimony of Tomas Venclova, **op. cit.,** for details on the announcement of the Lithuanian group.

99. The biography here is a composite of many sources. It is mostly derived from references to him in the underground press. See particularly **Aušra,** No. 4 (October 20, 1976), No. 7 (August, 1977), No. 8 (October, 1977); **Chronicle,** No. 30 (November 1, 1977); **Keleivis** (Boston), September 30, 1975, **Tiesa,** February 6, 1972. The information provided by Tomas Venclova has also been useful.

was released after six years (ca. 1953). Thereupon he completed middle school and enrolled at the university (probably Vilnius University) for the study of Lithuanian language and literature.

At the university Petkus was apparently involved in some kind of unauthorized group activity. On Christmas Day of 1957 he was arrested again in the "Case of Eleven Intellectuals" and sentenced eight years for the possession and dissemination of anti-Soviet literature. This literature in fact consisted of literary works of Lithuanian authors who were censored at that time. Among them were the works of the symbolist poet Jurgis Baltru-šaitis, the national oracle Vaižgantas, and the poetry of a number of authors who had emigrated to the West.

Given the time frame, it is not likely that Petkus completed formal university studies. However, those who have known him testify that he is extremely knowledgeable about Lithuanian literature, possesses one of the best private collections of poetry, and is a competent scholar of Lithuanian history. Apparently he shared his literary and historical knowledge with others, especially the younger generation, whose knowledge of their national past had been distorted by Soviet education and indoctrination.

Upon fully serving the second term (ca. 1965), he was unable to find stable employment in line with his training. In 1972 he was working as an accountant in the Vilnius chapter of the Folk Art Society, which, among other things, manufactured various art objects created by folk artists. He and a number of others were critized in a newspaper satire for exploiting the position for vague personal gain, but no legal charges were made. It is not clear how long he worked at the Folk Art Society, but he was probably dismissed soon after the appearance of that article (after February of 1972). Subsequently he became a sacristan at St. Michael's church in Vilnius.

Details on Petkus' possible involvement in dissident activity after his second return from incarceration are not available. It is likely that he was among a number of Lithuanians who established contacts with the emerging Moscow dissident movement. In 1972 he was among those interrogated in Lithuania by the security police in connection with the celebrated Case 24, involving the publication of the *Chronicle of Current Events.* It is known that he assisted the family of Simas Kudirka. In 1975 he observed the trial of Sergei Kovalev in Vilnius, although the KGB tried to isolate him. He has signed a number of petitions on behalf of Soviet dissidents, including Aleksandr Ginzburg and

Sergei Kovalev. There is some indication that he may have again organized a Catholic youth group in the Vienuolis Middle School in Vilnius. From his prison days, Petkus had close contacts with Latvian and Estonian dissidents and, as a result, was instrumental in forming the Supreme Committee of the National Movement of Estonia, Latvia, Lithuania.

His nationalist activities and work in the Helsinki Group and with Catholic youths led to his arrest on August 3, 1977. He was tried and convicted on July 10-13, 1978, and received a ten-year sentence in a labor camp and five years of internal exile.[100]

The Rev. Karolis Garuckas (b. 1908), a Jesuit priest, was among the leaders of the Catholic rights movement until his death in April of 1979.[101] After theological studies in Germany and the Netherlands, he was ordained in 1940. During the war he worked as a chaplain in a gymnasium. He continued his pastoral work especially among the youth throughout the Soviet years. In a statement to Secretary General Leonid Brezhnev, dated December 26, 1975, he revealed that he had been in confrontation with the Soviet authorities at least since 1960 but was never tried in courts.[102] He had been denied work permits on several occasions and transferred to other parishes upon the insistence of Soviet authorities. The specific reasons for the administrative action against him are only implied. His pastoral work among children and a vigorous reaction to discriminatory and suppressive religious policies of the regime were at the root of the ongoing conflict. In the same statement he indicated that his case was one of the reasons why the Soviet authorities removed Bishop J. Steponavičius from the Archdiocese of Vilnius. One of the reasons for Bishop Steponavičius' conflict with the regime was the resistance of the Bishop to civil authority's attempts to control the assignment of priests. From about 1961 he served in a small parish of Ceikiniai in the raion of Ignalina. The Ceikiniai parish is frequently mentioned in *samizdat* publications, no doubt reflecting the influence of Rev. Garuckas. One document indicates that a conflict between parishioners and their church committee and local and republic

---

100. Details about his trial are provided in **Aušra,** No. 12 (August, 1978); **Chronicle,** No. 34 (August 15, 1978); **Chronicle of Current Events,** No. 50. The **Aušra** account is presented here as Doc. No. 47.

101. A biographical and political profile is presented in **Aidai,** No. 6 (1979), pp. 268-273.

102. See **Chronicle,** No. 23 (June 13, 1976) for the text of this biographically revealing statement.

authorities had raged at least since 1964.[103] His name appears on many petitions to Soviet authorities. The KGB had interrogated him for alleged participation in the publication of the *Chronicle*, but failed to charge him. He was also interrogated at length in the Petkus case, acknowledged participation in the Helsinki Group, and refused to take part in the court proceedings.

Ona Lukauskaitė-Poškienė, born in 1900, is a poet.[104] She received a degree in natural sciences at the University of Kaunas and did some postgraduate work at the University of Vienna. During the years of independence she worked as a teacher and a librarian. She made her literary debut in the leftist periodical *Darbas* (Labor) in 1932 and published two collections of poetry— *Brangiausios pėdos* (The Most Precious Footsteps) in 1933 and *Eilėraščių kraitis* (A Treasury of Poems) in 1938. As far as is known, she has not published anything since the war, either in the official or the underground press. In her writings she gives a prominent place to themes of social justice and reform. After the Soviet Union reoccupied Lithuania in 1944, she became involved with a number of other leftist intellectuals in the national underground, joining the Council of the Lithuanian Nation, the composition and activity of which remain nebulous. For her part in this organ of national leadership, she was sentenced (probably in 1946) to a long term in Archangelsk and Vorkuta camps. She was released in 1955 and returned to her long-time residence in Šiauliai. As a prominent intellectual of the left, she has contributed to the representativeness and prestige of the Lithuanian Helsinki Group. She appears to have taken the initiative in the group after the conviction of Petkus.

Tomas Venclova was born in 1937 in the family of the prominent leftist intellectual and writer, Antanas Venclova (1906-1971).[105] His father had already joined the communist regime in 1940 and eventually became the elder statesman of Soviet Lithuanian letters. As a consequence, Tomas was in a position to absorb a good deal of Western cultural heritage. In 1960 he graduated from the University of Vilnius with a specialty in Lithuanian language and literature. He had subsequently

---

103. See **Chronicle**, No. 5 (1972).

104. For a brief biography, see **Lietuvių enciklopedija** (Boston, 1958), Vol. XVI, p. 507; also **Aušra**, No. 7, (August, 1977).

105. A brief biography is supplied by **Mažoji lietuviškoji tarybinė enciklopedija** (Vilnius, 1971), Vol. III, p. 712.

taught at his alma mater, lectured at the University of Tartu (Estonia), and worked in the Lithuanian SSR Academy of Sciences. He has translated into Lithuanian many important works of Western literature, including James Joyce's "Ulysses." He has published a collection of poems, *Kalbos ženklas* (The Sign of Language), but his poetry has been received with reserve because of its abstract, metaphorical, and philosophical bent.

As early as 1960 Tomas Venclova displayed nonconformist attitudes when he became involved in a *samizdat* project of A. Ginzburg to publish an anthology of Lithuanian poetry. The KGB uncovered the plan but no charges were brought, possibly because of his father's high status. The final break with the regime came in 1975. In a letter to the Central Committee of the CPL he requested permission to emigrate on the grounds that the "opportunities of broader and public literary, scientific, and cultural activities are barred to me."[106] Subsequently he joined the Lithuanian Helsinki Group as a founding member, which must have been shocking to the party establishment in view of the prominence of his father. In 1977 Tomas Venclova was allowed to leave the country with a visa for five years but on June 14, 1977, he was stripped of Soviet citizenship "for behavior, smearing the name of a Soviet citizen."[107]

Eitan Finkelstein represents the Jewish emigration movement.[108] He was born in 1942 in a Lithuanian Jewish family. He has been seeking emigration since 1971 but because as a doctor of science in physics he allegedly possesses classified information, his request for emigration has been denied. Finkelstein contributes articles to the *samizdat* journal *Jews in the USSR* and has written a perceptive essay on the contemporary political and social situation in Lithuania. In 1976 he hosted A. Sakharov during the latter's visit to Vilnius to observe the trial of Sergei Kovalev. Like other members of the Lithuanian Helsinki Group, he has been interrogated and threatened by the KGB, but so far punitive action has not been taken. He, like the other members, refused to take part in the proceedings against Petkus.

---

106. Text of his letter in **Chronicle,** No. 20 (December 6, 1975).

107. Photostatic copy of the notification of the action by the Soviet Consulate in San Francisco in **Draugas** (Chicago), September 8, 1977.

108. Biography derived from information in **Profiles: The Helsinki Monitors,** compiled and prepared by the staff of the US Commission on Security and Cooperation in Europe, Wahington, D.C., June 6, 1978. This source also includes basic biographical data on the other members of the Lithuanian Helsinki Group.

The aims of the Lithuanian Helsinki Group expressed in its announcement were somewhat broader than those of their Moscow counterpart. The Lithuanian Group intended "to concentrate on those articles (of the Final Act) that relate to human rights and basic freedoms, including freedom of thought, conscience, religion and belief, and also contacts between people..." But in addition, the group found it necessary to remind the Helsinki signatories "that the contemporary status of Lithuania was established as a result of the entrance of Soviet troops onto her territory on June 15, 1940."[109] In effect, Lithuania, as an occupied country, which has never assented to the forcible incorporation into the Soviet Union, is a special case in which national rights are of critical importance. Tomas Venclova explained this before the US Commission on Security and Cooperation in Europe:

> We must note that Lithuania has its own very serious problems which are very different from the problems of Russia. We have the problem of maintaining our nation. We have the problem of maintaining our culture and enriching our culture and we have a religious problem, since most of the Lithuanians are Catholics and that is a big difference from the religious problem in Russia.[110]

Such broader concerns of the Lithuanian Helsinki Group were reflected in its output. Before the review of implementation of the Final Act in Belgrade in November of 1977, the Lithuanian Helsinki Group produced two memoranda of a general nature, one dealing with the general political situation and cultural policy in Lithuania and the other with the policies and legal aspects of the persecution of religion and its institutions.[111] In addition, the group produced twelve numbered reports, one unnumbered

---

109. The announcement and other documents of the Lithuanian Helsinki Group in English translation are found in **Reports of the Helsinki Accords Monitors in the Soviet Union,** issued by the US Commission on Security and Cooperation in Europe. Vol. I (February 24, 1977), p. 120, contains the announcement and the first three documents of the Lithuanian Helsinki Group. The other documents are published in Vol. II (June 3, 1977). The announcement is repeated here as Doc. No. 41.

110. US CSCE, **Hearings, op. cit.,** Vol. I, p. 60.

111. These two memoranda are published here as Documents No. 45 and 71. The memorandum on the national question was published in **Aušra,** No. 8 (October 1977), and the memorandum on the status of religion in **Chronicle,** No. 29 (August 26, 1977).

document, and one jointly with the Moscow Helsinki Group on specific violations of human rights.[112] Among the subjects of their reports are the exile of two Catholic bishops, the text of the Decree on Religious Societies, the persecution of a Russian Pentecostal, the discrimination against former political prisoners and persecution for political beliefs, the harassment of two Estonian dissidents, the discrimination against Volga Germans living in Lithuania, and the psychiatric mistreatment of nonconformists.

In 1979 the Lithuanian Helsinki Group was still active, but decimated and with a different cast. Petkus was in prison, Garuckas was dead, and Venclova in effect was exiled. Among the later available documents, No. 14, dated January 1979, is signed by Ona Lukauskaite-Poškienė, Rev. Karolis Garuckas, and Rev. Bronius Laurinavičius.[113] The latter was probably co-opted in place of Petkus. Rev. Laurinavičius is one of the Catholic activist dissidents, born in 1913, ordained in 1944. Presently he serves as pastor of Adutiškis.

The latest available document, No. 18, November 2, 1979, protesting the arrest of the leading dissident A. Terleckas, is signed by Ona Lukauskaite-Poškienė, Eitan Finkelstein, Rev. B. Laurinavičius, and two new members—Mečislovas Jurevičius and Algirdas Statkevičius.[114] The new members have been active in dissident circles but are not well-known. According to biographical information published in the West, Jurevičius was a partisan after the war.[115] He was arrested on May 29, 1950, and sentenced to twenty-five years. For ten years he was employed in a teaching factory for the blind in Šiauliai, but was dismissed from work in 1975 apparently for religious dissent. Statkevičius was born in 1937. He was arrested and confined to a psychiatric hospital, released in 1970.

Although the Helsinki Final Act remains "a legal point of departure," it is doubtful whether it can continue to remain a forceful basis for dissent. The results of the Belgrade review conference were disappointing as far as the human rights issues were concerned, and Soviet repression of the Helsinki monitors

---

112. The original texts of documents 4 to 12 were reproduced in **Aušra,** No. 8 (October, 1977).

113. Text in **Aušra,** No. 15 (February, 1979).

114. Copy of Document No. 18 in possession of the author.

115. The biographical information is supplied by an anonymous source in **Draugas,** October 31, 1979.

was swift and ruthless.[116] Although the Lithuanian Helsinki Group has been reconstituted, its original level of authority, representativeness, and activism has not been attained.

CATHOLIC NATIONALISM

Catholicism has become an integral part of Lithuanian history and culture and nationality in general, to the extent that some Catholic historians and intellectuals have equated Catholicism with Lithuanian nationality or at least strongly emphasized the contribution of religion to national culture and consciousness. It is not within the scope of this study to analyze critically Catholic historiography. It must be pointed out, however, that historically, national and religious interests have not always coincided, and specific religious motifs in ethnic consciousness and its cultural manifestations constitute only a part of the Lithuanian psyche. A measured appraisal of the role of the Catholic Church in national political development and the contribution of religion to national character and consciousness remains among the unfinished tasks of historical scholarship.

As can be expected, Catholic nationalism in contemporary Lithuania tends to emphasize the importance of the Church and religion in national life. Religion is given an inordinate emphasis, almost making the ascertaining of religious rights a condition for the survival of Lithuanian nationality. From that point of view, the struggle for religious rights, which is justified by itself, is also viewed as a struggle for national rights. And, conversely, atheists are considered not only implacable enemies of Catholicism, but also of nationality. There is even talk about the convergence of Catholicism and nationality in contemporary Lithuania.[117]

The idea of convergence is problematical, for it can be argued that national and religious interests are distinct and may or may not be consistent with each other. The idea of convergence excludes the diversity of viewpoints that is evident in the underground press. The Catholic movement is not an umbrella under which all kinds of opponents of the Soviet regime are

116. Summary of the proceedings in Belgrade in the report of the US Commission on Security and Cooperation in Europe, **The Belgrade Follow-up Meeting to the Conference on Security and Cooperation in Europe: A Report and Appraisal** (Washington, DC, 1978).

117. See, for example, the study of V. S. Vardys, **The Catholic Church, Dissent and Nationality,** pp. 17, 168.

united. So far the Catholic Church has not attempted to play the role of the Ayatollah Khomeini. However, this does not suggest that various strands of opposition cannot coalesce and cooperate. While the Catholic opposition is certainly the most prominent, it is neither the only opposition nor is it the unifier of all.

The underground journal *Aušra* can be considered the organ of Catholic nationalism.[118] *Aušra* considers itselfs a successor of the first Lithuanian periodical, published under the same name in 1883-1886. The contemporary *Aušra* even continues the numeration of its predecessor. It thus attempts to be an organ of national rebirth, as was its nineteenth century counterpart. This suggests the view of the editors of *Aušra*, that national consciousness and sensitivity have been dulled by Soviet oppression and indoctrination and that the primary task today is to work toward the regeneration of national spirit and morality. This task, expressed in the editorial of the first issue, has been systematically carried out in the contents of the journal.[119] While national independence is the long-term goal, *Aušra* rejects revolutionary activity and concentrates on preserving a nationally conscious and morally strong people—a precondition for independent statehood. "The Lithuanian nation, seeking independence, must prepare for a long and difficult struggle."[120] Moral, rather than physical, opposition is prescribed, reflecting the influence of the Catholic clergy and the Moscow democratic movement.

The tactics of the struggle were inspired by the policies of Bishop Motiejus Valančius (1801-1875), who opposed the czarist policies of introducing Orthodoxy in Lithuania through a program of russification after the suppression of the 1863 revolt. Although his aim was to preserve Catholicism and not to create a national state, Valančius did see through the czarist strategy, which assumed that with the elimination of Polish influence in Lithuania and the replacement of it with Russian, Lithuania would become Orthodox and Russian, just as it was Catholic and Polish because of the polonized Church and leading elites. In his efforts to preserve Catholicism, Valančius opposed the policies of russification and engaged in an intense pastoral work to maintain a morally strong and conscientious people. In the course of his work Valančius contributed significantly to the preservation of

118. The discussion which follows is based on an analysis of the contents of the sixteen available issues of **Aušra.**

119. **Aušra,** No. 1 (October, 1975); Doc. No. 31.

120. **Aušra,** No. 4 (October 20, 1976); Doc. No. 32.

national character and the creation of a Lithuanian Church that eventually would become reconciled with the idea of a national state.[121]

The contemporary dissidents, however, tend to reinterpret and reverse Valančius' tactics. Valančius saw ethnicity as a precondition for the survival of Catholicism; the contemporary Catholic dissident tends to view the survival of Catholicism as a precondition for the survival of the nation. An essay on Valančius in *Aušra* concludes: "As long as the Lithuanian's spiritual world, religion, world view, and morality, urging the love of Motherland, is different from the materialistic world view, it will not be compatible with the denationalized, atheistic, morally depraved mass of the oppressors."[122] Similar views are expressed in an editorial of *Aušra*, "What Must We Do?" It sees a dual threat to national survival: linguistic russification and destruction of the faith. "The history of mankind affirms the truth that religion, particularly Christianity, is a source of national spiritual life... Therefore, it is necessary today: to preserve the faith as a source of national life; to study the truths of the Christian faith so that we could prove the unfounded nature of atheistic propaganda; to celebrate religious holy days; to maintain religious customs; to attend in church."[123]

Aušra is certainly not as one-sided as the above passage suggests. It is concerned with ethnic character, history, culture, and language as the foundations of national distinctiveness. Its viewpoint is more balanced and moderate compared to the views expressed in *Aušrelė*, which equates the survival of the Catholic Church with the survival of nationality.[124] Nevertheless, its emphasis of religion as fundamental for national existence is unmistakable.

Although *Aušra* does not call for revolutionary action, it has found it necessary to argue the case for independence. It considers that the younger generation lacks a knowledge of the past that is necessary to make correct judgments for the present and the future. It has systematically included essays on recent

---

121. The best monograph on Valančius remains that of Antanas Alekna, **Žemaičių vyskupas Motiejus Valančius** (Kaunas, 1922; 2nd ed.—Chicago, 1975). Especially valuable is the introduction to the second edition by Vincas Trumpa, whose interpretation of Valančius is followed here.

122. **Aušra,** No. 1 (October, 1975); Doc. No. 32.

123. **Aušra,** No. 8 (October, 1977).

124. See the editorial in **Aušrelė,** February 16, 1978; Doc. No. 48.

history and has countered apparently existing opinion that independence for a small nation is not a viable proposition because of economic and security problems. It views the moral degeneration in society as a serious threat to national survival and considers its duty to fight this moral decline, which was brought about by atheism and addiction to alcohol. *Aušra* has also documented cases of repression against individuals and regime policies of denationalization.

Aušra has gone beyond the concerns of national survival and has attempted to express a vision of the future. In one issue it has published a lengthy essay on the desirable socioeconomic and political system in an independent state. The author of the essay believes that although some may laugh at such hopes for the future, they are necessary. "These visions move us, awaken the thirst for freedom, do not permit us, especially the youth, to drown in the puddle of careerism and accommodationism; they remind that we as a nation have one goal and that we shall seek it without concern for any difficulties or obstacles."[125]

Politically, according to this author, only democracy is a viable and acceptable way or rule. All parties are equal and all voters must choose their representatives in a secret ballot. But these political rights do not automatically extend to all the people in Lithuania. All Russians and their children who came to Lithuania after 1944, in effect as colonists, should be repatriated. Other nationalities will be treated according to their disposition toward the Lithuanian nation. The Lithuanian emigrés are to be invited to return and to contribute to the development of the country. Strict neutrality is to be the foreign policy, shunning all military blocs or alignment with some powerful country. Defense forces are necessary, but they would be modeled after the Swiss. The territory of Lithuania should include all areas where Lithuanians predominate; in other words, the author seeks a state basically within ethnographic boundaries. Eventually, perhaps, it would be a good idea to form a Baltic federation, consisting of Lithuania, Latvia, and Estonia.

The relationship between the Church and the state is foreseen as follows:

> The Church will have to be separated from the state. After World War I the greater part of Lithuania's inhabitants were religious. The influence of the Church in national life

---

125. See the article by J. Medvegalis (pseudonym), "A View of Future Lithuania", **Aušra**, No. 14 (December, 1978).

was enormous. Meanwhile, after several decades of Soviet life, when a strong atheist propaganda affected the nation, not a small number of Lithuanians became atheists or indifferent religiously; therefore the demand to require baptism of children and to make religious instruction in school mandatory, to marry in church, will be contrary to democratic principles. The state must cooperate very closely with the Catholic Church as an institution educating, perfecting, and making the nation more cultured. It is necessary to support the Catholic press in every way, and the Church must be given opportunities to utilize radio, television, and other means of communication because only with the aid of the Church will we be able to overcome that negative Soviet influence which took root over all the years of slavery. [126]

In the economic sphere emphasis should be on agriculture because Lithuania lacks natural resources. The organization of agriculture should be mixed, including medium-sized family farms, cooperation with others to provide the material basis for industrial farming, and large state farms. Industrial development should be geared first of all to the agricultural sector. Labor-intensive industries, requiring few natural resources, should be also developed. Large industry should be state-owned, but it should be governed by workers' councils on the Yugoslav model. Small industrial establishments could be privately owned. Free trade unions with the rights to demonstrate and to strike must be permitted.

In the cultural and social sphere the most important task will be the elimination of what the author considers negative Russian influences: bureaucratic red tape, bribery, formalism and dogmatism in decision-making, and alcoholism. Among the positive things brought by the Russian rule and which should be maintained are free education and medical care. At the same time the author warns about a possible negative influence from the West: pornography, drugs, and guns.

In general, the essay presents a vision of life not much different from the one held by most people in the democratic West. It is a combination of capitalist and socialist economics, democratic politics, and a Christian view of man.

Catholic nationalism in contemporary Lithuania reflects in a moderate way the great division in Lithuanian politics between the clerical and secular ideologies. The division emerged at the

126. **Ibid.**

end of the nineteenth century, rather early in the political differentiation of the national movement. There was a good deal of cooperation and agreement among most of the political parties of the clerical right and secular left in reestablishing an independent national state in 1918 and during the initial years of independence. Since about 1922 the two currents, represented mainly by the Christian Democrats on the one hand and the Peasant Populist and Socialist parties on the other hand, tore the nation apart, resulting in a coup d'etat and the installation of the Nationalist regime at the end of 1926. The Nationalist regime to some extent bridged and transcended the political divide between the left and the right, producing about fifteen years of relative political calm.

This ideological division apparently has not been completely eroded by more than three decades of Soviet rule. The Catholic Church fought separation of state and Church during the years of independence, seeking something approaching a church state. Ironically, the Soviet policy, if implemented completely, would merge the state and Church, actually creating state church, despite the formal acceptance of the principle of separation of Church and state. The Catholic Church today, fighting to survive the takeover attempts of the state, has now accepted the principle of separation of Church and state, but with certain reservations. It still sees an integral role for itself in society and expects state cooperation in carrying out its pastoral functions. Judging from the contents of the *Chronicle*, the Catholic Church has not made explicit the acceptance of the principle of freedom of conscience and so far has not shown concern for the plight of other religious denominations under the Soviet heel.

LIBERAL NATIONALISM

Liberal nationalism is not as well defined as Catholic nationalism. It is represented by a number of activities, publications, and organizations. Essentially it is a democratic nationalist movement without the underpinnings of Catholic ideology. Politically it is centrist, it emphasizes nationality, and it advocates a somewhat more aggressive opposition to the Soviet regime than the Catholic movement does.

So far liberal nationalism has lacked the resources, central focus, or internal and external communications for a sustained opposition effort. Its publication output is much smaller than that of the Catholic movement, and most publications that have been issued have not found their way to the West. As a consequence, liberal nationalism is difficult to define structurally and ideologically. Among the manifestations of liberal nationalism should be included the activities of ethnographic clubs, the underground publications *Varpas* (The Bell) and *Laisvės Šauklys* (The Herald of Freedom), and the clandestine organization, the Lithuanian Revolutionary Liberation Front.

As is evident from reports about the activities of ethnographic clubs and the attack on them by the party and the KGB, they were engaged in a broad program of rediscovering and preserving the pre-Soviet past of the nation, its history, and culture.[127] While such a cultural movement has no direct connection with nationalism, its consequences inevitably lead to assertions of national exclusiveness, uniqueness, and independence. The widespread movement of youths, students, and the intelligentsia utilized the state-sanctioned public organizations—the amateur ethnographic clubs—to carry out national education and even attempted to preserve the national character of the threatened Lithuanian communities in the Belorussian SSR.[128] These clubs also provided a convenient cover for contacts with ethnographers in other republics. It is known that Lithuanian ethnographers had contacts with Latvians, Armenians, and Georgians and that they organized excursions to Lithuanian-inhabited or historical areas outside Lithuania— Eastern Prussia, Belorussia, and Siberia. By 1973 the KGB caught up with these groups and carried out a devastating attack against individuals involved in the movement. The Party ordered a redirection of the ethnographers' focus to the Soviet period and to the history of the "revolution."

The cultural movement spawned attempts to form underground political organizations. In 1974, five individuals, apparently led by Š. Žukauskas, were tried for attempting to form a political organization.[129] Their liberal orientation (in terms of Lithuanian history) is suggested by the title of a planned underground publication—*Naujasis Varpas* (The New Bell), thus

---

127. The activities of the ethnographic clubs have been described in some detail in **Aušra**, No. 5 (February 16, 1977), No. 9 (January, 1978); **Chronicle**, No. 6 (May, 1973), No. 11 (1974); see also Doc. No. 24.

128. An underground report in two parts "On the Situation of Lithuanians in the Belorussian SSR" (first part dated 1972, second — 1978) is available in the West. Excerpts from this 97 page report are presented in Doc. No. 21.

129. The trial is reported in **Chronicle**, No. 10 (1974); Doc. No. 25.

associating them with the *Varpas* of Vincas Kudirka, which began publication in 1889 and which marked the beginning of the liberal tradition in Lithuanian politics.

After the Žukauskas group was liquidated and the ethnographic movement was curbed, a Lithuanian Revolutionary Liberation Front (LRLF) appeared. Its liberal orientation is again indicated by its title and the contents of its underground organ *Varpas* (The Bell).[130] The LRLF appeared sometime in 1975 and structurally it is similar to the National People's Front (discussed below). It allegedly included a number of organizations— Lithuanian National Revolutionary Council, Human Rights Committee, the Lithuanian chapter of Amnesty International, the Lithuanian Freedom Fighters Movement, and the Free Communist Party of Lithuania. These were obviously fictional organizations, and the front itself was a creation of a small group whose only activity was the publication of four issues of *Varpas*.

Each issue of *Varpas* was devoted to a particular topic. The first three issues included a statement on Soviet nuclear arms in Lithuania, an appeal for joining the front, a demand for the reestablishment of Lithuania's independence, and an appeal for amnesty for political prisoners. The fourth issue contained a lengthy article on the role of M. Suslov in the pacification of Lithuania, an article that had previously circulated as a separate *samizdat* publication.

For some reason the LRLF disappeared sometime in 1976. There is no available evidence on KGB repression of it. In its place a liberal-nationalist journal *Laisvės Šauklys* (The Harold of Freedom) appeared in the spring of 1976. Eight issues of the journal appeared before the end of 1977, when the journal was allegedly liquidated by the KGB. Unfortunately, not a single issue has reached the West, and we can judge about its orientation only from indirect sources. Knowledge about *Laisvės Šauklys* is mostly derived from a collection of some of its articles republished by Catholic circles in a special publication *Aušrelė* (The Little Dawn, an offshoot of *Aušra?*).[131] *Aušrelė* contains two editorials and several historical essays from *Laisvės Šauklys*. Most importantly, the

---

130. Four issues of **Varpas** have reached the West. They were published in 1975-1976. The contents of three issues are reproduced here in Doc. No. 15, 38, and 39.

131. **Aušrelė,** Feb. 16, 1978, is available in the West. There is no indication that subsequent issues would be produced. It is an interesting question why the Catholic dissidents decided to reprint a collection of articles from **Laisvės Šauklys** and disseminate them in their own

editors of *Aušrelė* itself include their own editorial, which is a polemic against vague charges made in *Laisvės Šauklys* with respect to the policies and underground publications of the Catholic national movement. A sense of the orientation of *Laisvės Šauklys* is obtainable from this polemic.

Laisvės Šauklys undertakes to document "the lasting national yearning for liberty, the efforts of those people, who under the most impossible circumstances continue the tradition of free Lithuanians."[132] In pursuit of this task, the journal has sought to provide an objective record of the nation's response to Soviet rule. Among the historical essays in *Aušrelė* we find a different interpretation of the execution of four Lithuanian communists after the 1926 coupt d'etat in Lithuania, implying the complicity of Moscow. There is also a detailed account of the international machinations of Stalin and Hitler, leading to the destruction of independent Lithuania. The revolt against the Soviets at the beginning of the war in 1941 is presented as a genuine manifestation of the national will for independence. Included also is the cited article on the role of Suslov in Lithuania after 1944.

The second major task undertaken by *Laisvės Šauklys* is "to fight bolshevik disinformation wherever it manifests."[133] Evidence of how this task is accomplished is lacking. It probably involves rebuttal and polemics against Soviet propaganda.

The third and most important task it set for itself is to bridge the gap between those who consider religion as fundamental for nationality (i.e., the Catholic nationalists as described above) and those who "affirm that primacy should be given to stimulation of national conscientiousness."[134] The journal attacks cosmopolitanism, propagated by both the regime and "some of the clergy" and criticizes those who negate the role of the Catholic Church (i.e., anticlerical liberals or integral nationalists), thus attempting to take a position between extreme clericalism and secular nationalism.[135] Although *Laisvės Šauklys* seeks unity between the two camps, it tends toward secular nationalism. This is evident from the *Aušrelė* editors' polemic against the secular nationalists.[136] Unfortunately, the editors of *Aušrelė* did not

---

publication instead of facilitating the dissemination of **Laisvės Šauklys** itself at home and abroad.

132. As reported in **Aušrelė**.
133. From an article "Our Tasks" in **Aušrelė**; see Doc. No. 40.
134. **Ibid.**
135. **Ibid.**
136. See the lead article in **Aušrelė**.

publish the article from *Laisvės Šauklys*, which attacked the policies
of those associated with *Aušra* and other Catholic publications.
Nevertheless, the polemic does suggest the basic issues between
Catholic and liberal nationalists and by contrast illuminates the
viewpoint of one strand of non-Catholic opposition. The
following points emerge in reading the Catholic response to the
charges in *Laisvės Šauklys*.

1. The publishers and editors of the Catholic press allegedly
lack "political judgment." It is unclear what is meant here. Among
the possible charges may be that at least part of the clergy are
cooperating with the regime, that the clergy exhibit clericalist
tendencies, that they have not sufficiently supported the partisan
struggle. Obviously, these are not quite fair charges. The
majority of the clergy have been involved in the struggle for
religious rights, although they may not have been as avid
supporters of other human rights, including national rights, as
the critics would like to see.

2. It is quite clear that the Catholic movement is criticized for
overemphasizing religious freedom as the goal. The Catholic
response to the criticism is an extreme assertion that the survival
of nationality depends upon the survival of the Catholic Church.

3. There is a reproach that the well-financed Catholic
movement has not been willing to aid others and there is an
implication that Catholic underground publications, especially the
Chronicle, have not been willing to publish unspecified articles (i.e.,
a charge of Catholic censorship), instead suggesting the founding
of another underground publication.

4. The critics object to the Catholic treatment of atheists as
both anti-Church and anti-national. This is an issue of toleration
of different beliefs and the reconcilability of atheism and
nationality. On the whole, Catholics have considered atheists as
the instruments of russification as well as secularization, while
the liberals have not been willing to categorically posit such a
contradiction between atheism and nationality.

As a consequence of such perceptions, the critics of Catholic
opposition claim that there is no "common language of
Lithuanians."

Echoing these implied complaints against Catholic
nationalism are statements of a number of dissidents reported in
the liberal-socialist underground journal *Perspektyvos* (Perspectives), which began appearing in 1978.[137] In No. 9 (1979) issue,

137. More about this interesting journal in the section, "Reflections
of Eurocommunism" below. The journal was received in the West too late

the journal reports on a "press conference" of Lithuanian dissidents with three Western journalists, who were in Vilnius as official guests of the republic government. The report on this informal press conference with Western newsmen provides the most explicit definition of the attitudes of liberal (or secular, even anticlerical) nationalists.

First of all, some of the participants in the press conference display a rather aggressive brand of nationalism. They seem to proceed from an assumption that nationality is an absolute and primary value of man. This leads not only to an almost chauvinistic attitude toward other nationalities, but also to a deprecation of other human rights and values. As one of the participants in the conference put it, "our struggle first of all is a struggle for the freedom and independence of Lithuania. Even the human rights movement here has a purely national hue."

The Lithuanian dissidents expressed a strong criticism of the Russian dissidents. Although some of the Russian democrats are helpful and acknowledge the rights of the Lithuanian nation (Academician Sakharov would obviously be included among them), in the views of the Lithuanian nationalists Russian dissidents on the whole have not been able to shed imperialistic tendencies. The Lithuanian nationalists demand from their Russian colleagues unequivocal and complete endorsement of freedom and independence for Lithuania as a condition for a common front against tyranny. Even the principle of self-determination seems to be subordinated to national freedom: self-determination is meaningful only under conditions of statehood. The issue is not one of self-determination but of the occupation of Lithuania by an imperial power, which is Russia (and not the Soviet Union or some kind of an international communist regime).

Such perspectives are bluntly expressed by one of the participants in the press conference:

> One cannot liberate man and leave nations in slavery. Russian imperialism is incompatible with democracy. To some Russian dissidents it seems that it would be sufficient to implement human rights in the empire and there would be no need for the enslaved nations to create their own states. But we do not want voluntary slavery. And our goals will not coincide until the Russian dissidents will not come out for

---

to include excerpts from it in this anthology. What follows is a summary of the views expressed in the press conference, as reported in **Perspektyvos**, No. 9 (1979).

complete freedom for the colonies. The right of national self-determination is now recognized by separate individuals, but this does not change the general outlook of the dissidents. For us there is no common road with the Russians.

Thus, in the minds of these nationalists (and all the evidence suggests, also in the minds of the vast majority of the Lithuanian people) Russian imperialism (and not human rights) constitutes the principal problem. They look skeptically at the feasibility of a coalition between the national movements at the periphery and the Russian dissident intelligentsia as well as the Russian masses in overthrowing the current regime. In a crisis situation the relationship between the Lithuanians and the Russians threatens to be negatively extreme. There seems to be a perception that the regime could easily utilize the nationalism of the Russian masses to keep the national periphery under control.

Nevertheless, in the view of the Lithuanian dissidents, the balance of power is shifting. The Vilnius dissidents see a challenge to Russian imperialism in the growing national movements. Their advice to the West in the containment of "Russian imperialism"—"to support and encourage the struggle of the enslaved nations in Russia for independence. Exactly here is the weak spot of the empire."

The attitude of Catholic nationalists is only somewhat more moderate in that they do, for the time being, emphasize the human rights struggle, especially for religious liberties, and advocate the tactic of passive resistance. This difference in emphasis and tactics of opposition has led to the divergence of views evident in the polemic discussed above and articulated in the press conference.

The secular nationalists tend to view religion as merely a stabilizing factor, which plays no decisive role in national emancipation. "No doubt, religion defends our nation and increases its resistance; however, it is incapable of attack, it does not play an offensive role. And in order to overcome or at least to defend ourselves, an active offensive power is necessary." According to them, religion is only one, and not the most important value to be preserved. They express their viewpoint as follows:

> The Catholic opposition thinks that only religion can save our nation from decline. For this reason all of its attention is concentrated on religious freedom. According to our understanding, the most important problems of Lithuania are of national character. Even the granting of full

religious freedom will not resolve these problems significantly.

After the Western correspondents left the conference, the *Chronicle* was sharply attacked because it did not report the situation in Lithuania comprehensively, thus creating a false perception of the opposition movement among Western peoples. In other words, the non-Catholic nationalists would like to see the *Chronicle* shed its purely religious orientation and, like the Moscow *Chronicle of Current Events,* cover the entire range of human rights concerns. The criticism is not entirely fair because the Catholic nationalists do that in their other underground journals, particularly in *Aušra.* On the other hand, the criticism has some merit, for the *Chronicle* has received the bulk of attention in the West, while the other publications, especially those not connected with the Catholic movement, have received no corresponding exposure in the West. From this fact stem the reproaches of non-Catholic dissidents against the Catholic press.

THE NATIONALIST LEFT

REFLECTIONS OF EUROCOMMUNISM

A national and/or republic orientation among the party elite and the intelligentsia has been noted in the previous chapter. There is a category of party functionaries and intellectuals who could be called national communists, who seek to manipulate existing institutions and opportunities for national development without rejecting the republic status of Lithuania or party monopoly of power. Since such tendencies, which are, of course, proscribed by the central authorities and therefore could be viewed as within-system factional opposition, have been discussed at length, no further analysis is necessary. There is, however, a different strand of Communism, which could be called nationalist Communism, that needs elucidation.

A new underground journal, *Perspektyvos* (Perspectives), appeared in the spring of 1978. In its first editorial, it stated in part:

> *Perspektyvos* will raise the most topical problems of daily life, will indicate the possible ways of solving them, will provide the readers with an opportunity to express their views and opinions... *Perspektyvos* wants to help find ways out of the present dead end to a renovation, founded on the principles of true democracy and on the basis of international

agreements... *Perspektyvos* will not close its pages to sharper critical articles, which, however, shall not contradict Article 49 of the USSR Constitution and Article 47 of the Lithuanian SSR Constitution, allowing the presentation of suggestions in any form for the improvement of state organs (including the very highest ones) and the criticism of shortcomings. All articles in *Perspektyvos* will be published in order of debate, according to the principle that the opinion of others must be respected even if one disagrees with them.[138]

In a later issue the editors reminded the readers that" *Perspektyvos* is not a press organ of some one organization, association, group, committee, or some kind of movement." [139]

The known contents of this journal indicate that it is a journal of opinion associated with the liberal and/or socialist left.[140] While it may not be an organ of nationalist communists, it has certainly articulated their viewpoint. It contains a fundamental critique of the Soviet system from democratic and classical Marxist points of view and, therefore, despite its invocation of Article 49 of the Soviet Constitution [141] (which probably is done more for political than for legal reasons), places the journal among the system-rejective activities.

Indicative of the liberal-socialist and nationalist orientation of *Perspektyvos* is the content of its No. 11 (1979). It includes A. Sakharov's article "On the Struggle of the Movement for Defense of Human Rights in the Soviet Union and Eastern Europe"; details about the increased efforts of linguistic russification; a polemic with a Soviet ideologue concerning the

---

138. Every issue of **Perspektyvos** reprints this editorial. It is cited here from issue No. 2 (1978).

139. **Perspektyvos,** No. 11 (1979).

140. Only three issues—2nd, 9th, and 11th—of the known eleven published have reached the West and were available for examination. Other underground journals have reviewed briefly the contents of various issues of **Perspektyvos.** Up to the 5th issues, each number is devoted to a single topic. **Chronicle,** No. 35 (November 16, 1978), has reported the following articles in **Perspektyvos:** No. 1—K. Kuraitis, "Socialism, Communism, and Democracy"; No. 2— A. Sakharov, "My Country and the World"; No. 3—M. Baskas, "The Rubicon"; No. 4— "Thanks to You, Party!" With issue No. 5 **Perspektyvos** became a multi-article journal of opinion.

141. According to the new Soviet Constitution, every citizen has the right to present suggestions to state and public organs and to point out shortcomings. This article also prohibits persecution for suggestions or criticism.

significance of emigré cultural contribution; an essay on personal response to oppression; an essay on existing and true socialism; and the speech of Mikhail Mikhailovich before the national convention of American social democrats.

Leftist ideology of *Perspektyvos* is evident in its 5th and 6th issues, published in 1978. The 5th issue contains materials (up to the 36th page), received from the "Association of Lithuanian Communists (for the Secession of Lithuanian from the USSR)". The 6th issue contains an article," To All Concerned With the Future," that "analyzes the contemporary situation in Lithuanian and points out the possible alternatives." This article is also presented by the "Organizational Central Committee of the Movement for Secession of Lithuania from the USSR" of the Association of Lithuanian Communists.[142] And the 11th issue (1979) contains an article by Marius Baskas (obviously a pseudonym) "Concerning the Existing and True Socialism," also supplied by this organization. This article is indicative of the orientation of the Association of Lithuanian Communists. The gist of this essay is expressed in the first and last paragraph as follows.

> Among the most important accusations against Eurocommunists is that they allegedly are inciting an anti-Soviet mood when they contend that socialism created in Eastern European countries is not yet true socialism, i.e., it is not the same as that about which mankind has dreamt and is still dreaming. In other words, the real, existing socialism does not correspond to the image, which was created, on the basis of historical development, by the brightest minds of the world and which is the realization of liberty and justice. It is a distorted socialism that lacks political liberty, and if this is absent, then there is neither democracy, justice, nor truth itself. Western social democrats go even further. They contend that without liberty in general socialism does not and cannot exist. But this is not quite true because just as capitalism can exist without freedom and democracy, so can socialism. Life confirms this truth: socialism as an economic system exists in the USSR as well as in other countries of Eastern Europe. The matter is this: that the superstructure of this economic formation (and not the whole superstructure but only the method of governing) does not correspond to the principles of socialism. This is why such a socialism cannot be true socialism (...) It thus follows that socialism, divorced from freedom, is not and cannot be true because it

---

142. These topics in **Perspektyvos** are reported in the underground journal **Alma Mater,** No. 1 (January-March, 1979).

does not correspond to the concept of socialism and at the same time to the truth. Such is the socialism created in the Soviet Union and which the Kremlin wishes to present the truest of all. Reflecting only a part of the concept, this socialism is incomplete, distorted, and not something completely different, as the social democrats like to contend.

This latter circumstance enables us to draw an important conclusion. Because the really existing socialism is incomplete, it could have the greatest possibility in the future to become the truest (socialism). It is only necessary to change the method of governing which contradicts the concept of socialism. As long as the governing method negates political liberties, so long will socialism be freedom without freedom, democracy without democracy, i.e., it will not be true socialism. A truthful viewpoint requires this alleged paradox to be recognized as reality. And not only to recognize that which exists, but also to internalize this factuality, to consider why the created reality is not the same as was desired and which must be desired. Without the fulfillment of this condition—truthfully and openly—the transformation of (existing) socialism into a true socialism is impossible.[143]

Clearly, the short-lived Czechoslovak experiment with a socialism that had a human face and the Eurocommunist viewpoint are reflected here. The creation of a democratic socialism is the goal. Since this article was supplied by the Association of Lithuanian Communists, there is a strong presumption that it represents their viewpoint. In addition, the program of these "communists" includes secession of Lithuania from the USSR. The arguments for secession by this alleged organization or a group of individuals are not known. The goal of a national state could be derived from the principle of democracy (national self-determination is an integral part of political liberty) and from the provisions for secession in the Soviet Constitution.

Whether there is an organization of such nationalist communists is neither certain nor important. There is no question, however, that a Eurocommunist viewpoint exists and may be increasingly manifested, especially if Eurocommunism does not dissipate. Furthermore, as long as national independence and political liberties are espoused, the viewpoint of the Lithuanian Eurocommunists is not incompatible with the ideology and aims of other currents of opposition.

---

143. From **Perspektyvos**, No. 11 (1979).

NATIONAL PEOPLE'S FRONT (NPF)

The Lithuanian National People's Front (NPF) claims to be an umbrella organization, founded in 1955 and uniting several underground organizations (the Association of Free Democratic Youth of Lithuania, the Lithuanian Catholic Association, the Association of Lithuanian Patriots, and others). It obviously is modeled on the national liberation movements of the third world and uses some of their terminology and interpretation of the international balance of power. Its rather detailed program was allegedly formulated in June 1974 and reached the West a year later. Since then, the NPF has issued about two proclamations or appeals annually.[144]

The unusual structure of the NPF and its somewhat radical program have raised questions about the front's real nature. The available underground press has not mentioned the NPF nor any of its constituent organizations, although there are vague references about the existence of some kind of "fronts" in the 1950s and the 1960s.[145] However, one source from Lithuania tends to confirm its existence.[146] It seems unlikely that it is a front of the KGB, for the NPF has not sought contacts with other opposition groups (this would be one reason to set up a police front to flush out other dissidents). Most likely the NPF is an instrument of a small conspiratorial group or even several small groups, using the national liberation front model and its fictional constituent organizations to propagate a certain viewpoint. Whatever the nature of the NPF, the viewpoint articulated appears to be genuine and deserves some attention.

The NPF's analysis of the world balance of power to some extent resembles the viewpoint of China. The NPF defines the

---

144. The analysis of NPF position which follows is based on the following available materials: The program of the NFL, dated June 9-14, 1974, as published in **Tėviškės Žiburiai** (Toronto), June 12, 1975, also published here as Doc. No. 26; proclamation, December 25, 1975, published in **Draugas** (Chicago), February 20, 1976, also Doc. No. 34; declaration, June (?) 30, 1976, as published in **Nepriklausoma Lietuva** (Montreal), August 25, 1976, also Doc. No. 36; an appeal, January 1, 1977, unpublished copy in possession of the author; a declaration, April 30, 1978, as published in **Europos Lietuvis** (London), May 8, 1979.

145. See references to "fronts" by the dissident A. Terleckas in his letter to KGB chief J. V. Andropov, in **Chronicle,** No. 21 (January 25, 1976); Doc. No. 33.

146. As reported in **Tėviškės Žiburiai,** July 31, 1975.

Soviet Union as an expansionist imperialist state. It also views the West as primarily concerned with the maintenance of monopolistic capitalism. The NPF dismisses the West and particularly the US as supporters of national emancipation. In its 1976 declaration the NPF said: "We fully perceive the imperialistic goals of these countries (political, military, economic). Neither the USSR nor the US defended, are defending, or will defend our national interests. They are concerned about other matters—such as dividing up the world into their spheres of influence." The NPF thus is in favor of dismantling of military blocs, reunifying divided nations, and eliminating foreign bases. It visualizes a Europe of free nations in a loose alliance stretching from the Atlantic to the Urals.

Since the two hegemonial powers are not interested in the freedom of small nations, only the Lithuanians' own efforts can bring about emancipation. The NPF emphasizes internal factors, the joint efforts of the national movements in the Baltic, the Ukraine, and the Caucasus to bring about the dismemberment of the Soviet empire. The NPF sees the strength of national movements in the Soviet Union as growing and calls on various sectors of society, including the communists and Komsomols, to take action, presumably to overthrow the Soviet regime.

The minimum program of the NPF demands the realization of basic political and civil rights, including the right of self-determination. Its maximum program calls for the reestablishment of an independent national state under the supervision of the United Nations.

The NPF materials use the expression "People's Lithuania." The meaning of the expression is apparent in a passage of the 1976 declaration:

> We are for a secession from the framework of the USSR (this is guaranteed by the USSR Constitution) and for the status of People's Republic in a bloc of socialist states... The accusations of the KGB that we are nationalists are unfounded and do not stand up to critical examination. We, the Younger Generation of Lithuania, born and matured in a socialist society, support a free and independent People's Lithuania, and not a restoration of a moribund capitalism. We are for amity among all nations, socialism, democracy, and peace.

In the 1977 declaration, the NPF disassociates itself from both the bourgeois past and the Stalinist present:

Let us not go down the path of national betrayal, as has been done in the past in former Lithuania by the intelligentsia, poets, and writers, "activists" of varied shades and vague national orientations, carreerists who committed treason against our homeland in a difficult time, relinquishing it to the Soviets without firing a shot in 1940, and others who collaborated with the Nazis. This was not the Lithuanian nation, not its people, not the true Lithuanian intelligentsia born of the people, but the Lithuanian bourgeoisie, narrow-minded and egotistical, which brought us to the precipice of national tragedy and which, with the aid of alien bayonets, with the help of Lithuanian-Jewish communists and other dregs of society, established the puppet government of the Lithuanian SSR. Not having any of the rights of a state, it assists Moscow in dissolving us in the sea of nations in the USSR.

The NPF thus appears to represent the radical-socialist wing of opposition. It appears to be a voice of the younger generation, whose goals are national and universal at the same time—national independence, democracy, social justice, peace, internationalism, and commonwealth of nations.

5. CONCLUDING PERSPECTIVES

On August 23, 1979, the fortieth anniversary of the signing of the Nazi-Soviet Pact, 45 Baltic citizens released a statement in Moscow demanding that the consequences of the secret protocols of the pact, which doomed the independence of the Baltic States, be abrogated by the signatory powers.[147] The statement of the Balts was supported by the leaders of the Russian democratic movement, including Academician A. Sakharov. The evidence presented in this anthology supports the conclusion that the Lithuanian people are in agreement with the demands for independence. Legitimacy of Soviet rule in Lithuania is obviously questioned by the vast majority of the population, some of which have expressed this in open protest and defiance of Soviet order.

It is also quite evident that nationalist and religious grievances are reluctantly and sporadically articulated openly, perhaps because of the painful lessons of the partisan war and the fate of the revolutions in Hungary and Czechoslovakia. Internal movements

---

147. See Doc. No. 74 for text of the statement.

are still weak in most of the Soviet republics, while the Russian masses are not only immune from the appeals of the Moscow democratic intelligentsia, but also could be mobilized on the basis of Russian nationalism to counter the national movements on the periphery. Thus, for the time being, a total confrontation with the regime by its opponents would be futile and very costly. Although in Lithuania there is a wing of opposition which advocates direct confrontation with the regime, for the time being the opposition prefers indirect passive subversion tactics, maintenance of national consciousness, and exploitation of opportunities to advance national interests within the established order.

Thus, as the 1970s came to an end, opposition in Lithuania and other areas within the Soviet Union was still manageable. In the absence of a union-wide crisis, stemming from economic, political, or international conditions, the Soviet regime was able to control opposition by selective repression and ideological pressure. The sense of relative deprivation was moderated by policies of gradually increasing the standard of living for the masses. Nationalism remained a potential threat, religious dissent was spotty and to a great extent localized, while the democratic movement was restricted mostly to a small stratum of Moscow intelligentsia.

The opposition movement so far seems to have had a minimal impact on the Soviet system. But as the 1980s opened, the Soviet state faced a number of difficult problems. The failure to address them effectively could lead to serious nationalist and democratic challenges to the regime. Included among the problems is the declining rate of economic growth, which if unchecked, could revolutionize the masses, including the Russian people. Leadership succession offers both, the dangers of continued stagnation and decay and the opportunities for constructive change. In both cases the regime faces a no-win situation: continuation of the *status quo* would exacerbate nationalist and democratic pressures, while a more favorable nationality policy and a move toward pluralism would merely reenforce and raise nationalist and democratic expectations. Last, but not least, the demographic situation, both in respect to the patterns of population growth and the changing balance of nationalities, has serious implications for the possibilities of improved economic performance and the allocation of powers between the center and the republics and their elites. It is in the context of these broad systemic conditions that the still manageable opposition movement assumes great significance for the further development of the Soviet polity, including the possibility of its total transformation.

The historical survivability of national distinctions and identity and the reenforcement of nationalism by modernization suggest that the nationality question is likely to remain problematical even under the most favorable economic and political circumstances and is not likely to be definitively resolved without some basic changes in the territorial makeup and the internal political system of the Soviet Union. Even a significant change toward pluralism is not a sure prescription for dealing with nationalism. In an age of nationalism, self-determination, and decolonization a stable consensual multi-national state is an unlikely possibility. Liberty and democracy for the peoples in the Soviet Union depend upon the implementation of the principle of self-determination. Without it a system of coercion is essential to maintain an imperial state. Certainly as far as the Lithuanian people are concerned, the only thing that keeps them within the Soviet state is superior force controlled by the rulers in the Kremlin, and there is nothing to indicate that their attitude is likely to change in the foreseeable future.

One final note is in order. In a recent study of nationalism in the Soviet Union, Hélene Carrere d'Encausse has made some rather startling prognoses concerning the fate of Lithuanian nationalism. She believes that "the balance of international relations must inevitably doom Lithuanian nationalism.' [148] In the conclusion she goes even further, adding that the Baltic nations, especially the Estonians and Latvians, are doomed not to cultural assimilation, but to physical extinction as a result of ethnic conglomeration. "Despite the strength of their national feeling, despite everything distinguishing them historically and culturally from the other peoples of the USSR, these nationalities are headed not toward assimilation, but toward physical extinction." [149]

While such apocalyptic prognoses may have some validity if we assume the survival of the multi-national Soviet state for a century or more and its rule by an integrationist elite, the present evidence contradicts such a perspective, at least in the case of Lithuania. The opposition in Lithuania has maintained a degree of tension between the regime and society, conducive to the maintenance of national consciousness. The demographic situation in Lithuania has been quite stable, with the Lithuanian nationality more than holding its own in numbers and culturally. There is no immediate danger of either significant acculturation/assimilation (i.e. russianization

---

148. Hélene Carrere d'Encausse, **Decline of an Empire: The Soviet Socialist Republics in Revolt** (New York, 1979), p. 248.
    149. **Ibid.**, p. 267.

and russification) or physical extinction as a result of ethnic intermixture. Whether Lithuanian nationalism can attain its goal of national self-government depends upon a host of factors, internal and external to the Soviet state, which cannot be precisely anticipated or defined and which cannot be assumed to be exclusively unfavorable for an independent Lithuania, or Estonia, or Ukraine, or any other republic of the Soviet Union. What is significant today, as the scope and intensity of opposition in Lithuania indicates, is that the demands for self-determination and independent statehood have not decreased over the 35 years of Soviet rule, but, on the contrary, have been sustained and even intensified lately. This is a necessary condition for any hope of independence, for the overthrow of a system of coercion and its replacement with politics of consent.

PART TWO

DOCUMENTS ON NATIONAL
AND POLITICAL OPPOSITION

AN EXPLANATORY NOTE

Unless otherwise indicated, documents were translated from the Lithuanian language. The translation is essentially literal, reflecting the style, vocabulary, and the intellectual level of the various materials.

All footnotes have been added by the editor. The first note, marked by a document no., provides the source, explanation, and commentary on the document. Cross-references to various items published here are by document number only. All titles of documents, except those in quotation marks, were supplied by the editor.

Biographical data have been supplied for the more important living and historical persons referred to. Unless otherwise indicated, basic biographical information was derived from the following references: **Lietuvių enciklopedija** (Boston, 1953-1969), 36 volumes; **Encyclopedia Lituanica** (Boston, 1970-1978), six volumes; **Mažoji lietuviškoji tarybinė enciklopedija** (Vilnius, 1966-1971), three volumes; **Prominent Personalities in the USSR** (Metucken, N. J., 1968), a biographical directory compiled by the now defunct Institute for the Study of the USSR.

Copies of the Lithuanian **samizdat** publications were obtained from various private sources. The most systematic public collection of **samizdat** materials, including those from Lithuania, is in the Arkhiv Samizdata, Munich (a Radio Liberty activity). Arkhiv Samizdata is issuing copies of its holdings in the series **Sobranie Dokumentov Samizdata**. Volume 17 of the series contains the most important (but not all) the dissent materials from Lithuania for the period 1969-1976. Each item registered in the Arkhiv Samizdata is assigned an AS number, which is also given (whenever available) in the references of this anthology.

The most extensive Lithuanian **samizdat** publication is **Lietuvos Katalikų bažnyčios kronika (Chronicle of the Catholic Church in Lithuania)**, a major source for materials in this volume. In the footnotes it is briefly referred as **Chronicle**. It should not be confused with the Moscow **Chronicle of Current Events (Khronika tekushchikh sobitii)**.

Wherever possible, quotations from Lenin are not translated from the Lithuanian, but rather cited from the English translation of the fourth edition of **Collected Works** (Moscow, 1964-1965). Quotations from various human rights conventions are cited from official English texts, as compiled in **Human Rights: A Compilation of International Instruments of the United Nations** (United Nations publication, Sales No.: E. 73. XIV. 2, New York, 1973). Texts of various penal code articles are translations from the official compilation **Lietuvos Tarybų Socialistinės Respublikos Baudžiamasis Kodeksas** (Vilnius, 1970).

1. FROM THE INTERROGATION OF PARTISAN LEADER J. ŽEMAITIS

July 2, 1953

In 1941 after fascist Germany's attack on the Soviet Union, I, as the head of the school of the 617th regiment, received an order to withdraw eastward with the staff of the regiment. I did not obey the command, but of my own free will went over to the German side.

It happened in this way. About two kilometers before Valkininkai, I, with a group of 12 to 15 soldiers, purposely lagged behind, wishing to go over to the Germans.

On arriving in Valkininkai, at the command of the German *Feldfebel*, we surrendered our weapons. With other prisoners we were herded into a small clearing not far from the station.

On June 29, 1941, we were marched to Vilnius to a prisoner-of-war camp. On the following day they transferred the Lithuanians to separate barracks not far from the market of Kalvarija, where we were all released. While the prisoners were being released, it was announced that an order for the formation of Lithuanian units was awaited—units to be sent to the front against the Red Army, and we were ordered to remain until we received separate orders.

No. 1. From Archyviniams dokumentams skelbti redakcija, **Kruvinos žudikų pėdos** ("Faktai kaltina," Vilnius, 1968), pp. 203-207, 211-216, 226-230. The source is part of the Soviet documentary series on the partisan movement "Facts Accuse." Since this document is a result of the interrogation of J. Žemaitis by the Soviet security organs, its terminology (i.e., "bandits", "bourgeois," etc.) and some of its interpretive passages reflect the Soviet view of the partisan movement. Nevertheless, the basic story of the nationalist guerilla movement as told by Žemaitis appears to be quite accurate, confirmed by other Soviet and non-Soviet sources. The partisans used code names for security reasons, and some of them cannot be identified by their real names. The various partisan formations identified themselves by symbolic and patriotic designations, which are given in the text untranslated. Jonas Žemaitis (1909-1954) was a captain in the Lithuanian army, with training in French military schools. He was the top commander of armed partisans between 1949 and 1951, when, because of illness, he gave up his duties. Žemaitis was caught by Soviet security organs apparently in the spring of 1953 and, according to the testimony of former Soviet prisoners, was executed on November 23, 1954. The story of Žemaitis' execution is given in Elena Juciūtė, **Pėdos mirties zonoje** (New York, 1974), p. 299.

I agreed and settled in the city, waiting to be enrolled in the soon to be formed Lithuanian national units.

Colonel Špokevičius and Dabulevičius commanded the Lithuanians assembled in the barracks. The staff headquarters had been established in a house near the cathedral. Here they told us that the Lithuanian unit will not be formed and invited us to enlist as volunters in local defense units to fight against the Soviet partisans.

I refused to enlist and went home to my wife in Lentvaris, where I lived until August of 1941. Later I moved to Kaunas, where I worked at a technician for peat production in the energy agency.

In June 1942 I travelled to the village of Kiaulininkai, in the county of Šiluva, district of Raseiniai. From the fall of 1942 until March of 1944, I worked as the director of the Šiluva Agricltural Cooperative

The LFA (the Lithuanian Freedom Army) was the largest military political organization of Lithuanian nationalists, which was composed mostly of former officers and soldiers of the Lithuanian bourgeois army.[1] Its formation was begun nn January 1943. Its purpose was to prepare an armed resistance and prevent the reestablishment of the Soviet government in Lithuania if the Soviet Army conquered Germany, or to seek help for the Lithuanian nationalists from the hands of Hitlerite Germany, in the event it conquered the Soviet Union.

I joined the LFA in March 1945.

In actuality, the task of the organization was to establish anti-Soviet groups on a military basis—sections, groups, divisions, regional formations; to form command staffs; to appoint

---

1. Lietuvos Laisvės Armija—the Lithuanian Freedom Army (LFA) —was organized at the end of 1941 for the purpose of armed struggle against the German occupation. During most of the German occupation it was dormant, engaged in organizational and training activity. As the war turned against Germany and the occupation of Lithuania by the Soviet army became imminent, the organization shifted its efforts toward armed struggle with the Soviet regime and undertook military action. Its various armed units were led by the officers of the Lithuanian army. When the Soviet army occupied Lithuania, the LFA constituted one of the several sources of ormed resistance, playing an important role in the initial stages of the partisan war. See the introductory study for a critical discussion of Soviet efforts to associate the LFA with the German military and intelligence.

leaders and acquire weapons and to distribute them to the members of the organization.

This organization contributed substantially to the beginning of armed banditry in Lithuania. Its members lived illegally and belonged to armed bands.

I know that in 1944 there was a consultative meeting between a group of high officers of the former bourgeois army of Lithuania and the leadership of the underground nationalist LFA organization. It had a dual purpose: first, to strengthen the leadership of the LFA organization with officers and, second, in cooperation with the Germans, to organize Lithuanian military units to fight against the Soviet Army.

After the discussions General Pečiulionis[2] of the bourgeois Lithuanian army was appointed commander of the LFA armed forces. In the fall of 1944, Pečiulionis, with one of the LFA leaders, K. Veverskis,[3] crossed the front into the territory of Lithuania liberated by the Soviet Army in order to lead the armed struggle against the Soviet government.

Moreover, I know that the members of the nationalist underground, Antanas and Bronius Lesys, in the spring of 1945, after completing training in an intelligence school in Germany, were parachuted behind the lines of the Soviet Army in the area of the town of Baisogala. They were required to join the leadership of the Lithuanian nationalist underground and maintain ties with the leadership of the German army. With them there was a third person, a radio operator, also trained in a German school, but he immediately surrendered to the workers of Soviet security organs.

The negotiations of the Lithuanian generals Raštikis,[4] Plechavičius[5] and the delegates of the Supreme Committee for

---

2. Motiejus Pečiulionis (1888-1960), a volunteer in the struggle for Lithuania's independence, a graduate of French artillery school, a general, was the highest ranking officer in the resistance movement. He was caught sometime in 1946, spent ten years in Vorkuta, and returned to Lithuania in 1956.

3. Kazys Veverskis (1912-1944?) was the founder and leader of the LFA until he disappeared, probably at the end of 1944. For Soviet data on Veverskis and the LFA see Hitleriniai parašiutininkai ("Faktai kaltina", Vol. 8) (Vilnius, 1966) pp. 12-32, passim.

4. Stasys Raštikis (1896-), a capable soldier of the wars of independence, Commander in Chief of the Lithuanian army (1934-1939),

the Liberation of Lithuania[6] with the German military command resulted in the formation of the Home Army[7] in February 1944. Its purpose—to fight against the Soviet partisans in Lithuania and to participate in combat against the Red Army in the event it approached the borders of the Lithuanian SSR.

In February 1944 the chief of the Rase'niai district Captain Gužaitis invited me to a meeting of former officers of the Lithuanian bourgeois army. I was assigned the task of organizing volunteers to the Home Army of Plechavičius in the counties of Šiluva and Tytuvėnai. As a result of my work, about 150 people from these counties enrolled in the Home Army of Plechavičius.

---

an important political person of independent Lithuania. Apparently, Gen. Raštikis supported the idea of the Home Army and was consulted about it but did not participate directly in negotiations with the Germans. He also refused to serve in any formal capacity in the new military force. See his memoirs, **Kovose dėl Lietuvos** (Los Angeles, 1957), Vol. 2, pp. 332-351.

5. Povilas Plechavičius (1890-1973), a general of the Lithuanian army, was noted for his exploits against bolshevik forces in Lithuania in 1918-1919. He was a staunch nationalist (but not a fascist), a rather popular and legendary figure in Lithuania. During the war the Germans accepted him as commander of the so-called Home Army. For not following German orders, he was arrested and briefly sent to a concentration camp. After the war he emigrated to the United States, where he died.

6. The Supreme Committee for Liberation of Lithuania—Vyriausias Lietuvos Išlaisvinimo Komitetas—was founded in 1943 by the principal political parties and resistance organizations to provide direction and leadership in the struggle for national independence. The Committee was as much an anti-German as anti-Soviet resistance organization. In fact, the Germans sent a number of its members to the concentration camps for aiding in the sabotage of German plans in Lithuania. There is no documentary evidence that the Committee, an underground organization, engaged in negotiations with the German authorities concerning the formation of the Home Army, although it was obviously consulted informally by those involved in the negotiations and gave its sanction to the idea. The Committee continues to function to this day, with headquarters in New York. For an outline history of the Committee see Juozas Audėnas (ed.), **Twenty Years' Struggle for Freedom of Lithuania** (New York, 1963).

7. The Home Army was born out of the desperation resulting from the real prospects of another Soviet occupation of Lithuania. Throughout the war the Germans failed to persuade or force the Lithuanians to form military units or an SS legion within the German military framework. As the German front began collapsing and com-

On March 15, 1944, I was invited to the headquarters of the Home Army of Plechavičius and appointed commander of the 310th battalion. The 310th battalion was based in the town of Seredžius. I served there until May 1, 1944, and later, after transferring the battalion to Captain Gintautas, I took a leave of absence with my family.

On my return, I came to Kaunas and learned that the Germans had arrested the entire staff of Plechavičius' Army for refusing to send it to combat beyond the borders of Lithuania; and that part of the soldiers of the Home Army deserted for home, part were disarmed and sent under guard to Germany. I did not return to my place of service, and, dressed in civilian clothes, travelled to Šiluva and hid there, fearing that the German police would arrest me for deserting from the Plechavičius Home Army.

Living illegally in Šiluva, I maintained contact with the members of the underground national guard organization.[8] Captain Guža'tis, Žukauskas, Taučius, Mockus, Stasiulaitis. We periodically had discussions on how to organize the fight against

---

munist partisan activity in Lithuania began to rise alarmingly, both the German authorities and leading Lithuanian figures sought to find a formula for a Lithuanian military force. On February 13, 1944, an agreement was signed by SS and Police Chief for the Ostland Gen. Jeckeln and SS and Police Chief for Lithuania Gen. Harm on the one side and General Plechavičius on the other side. The agreement called for the formation of a Home Army (**Litauische Soderverbande** in German) under the command of Lithuanian officers for the purpose of antipartisan action and defense within the territory of Lithuania. The initial goal was 13 batallions (about 12,000 men). The call for volunteers was immediately successful. Thereupon the German authorities saw this as an opportunity to finally acquire a Lithuanian force. Various German demands and direct orders led to a conflict with the command of the Home Army. Finally, on May 15, 1944, the staff of the Home Army was arrested and sent to a concentration camp, a number of units were forcibly dispersed among German military formation, a number of soldiers were executed, while those who escaped German vengeance took to the forests with their weapons. Ultimately, these vestiges of the Home Army constituted another source of manpower and arms for the partisan war. O. Urbonas, "Lietuvos vietinė rinktinė 1944 metais", Karys 1941, No. 8-14; 1952, No. 1-6. See also Raštikis, op. cit., II, pp. 343-353.

8. Reference to the volunter auxiliary military organization, Šaulių Sajunga, of independent Lithuania, which functioned illegally during the German occupation.

the Soviet authorities if the German army withdrew.

In the summer of 1944 Captain Gužaitis visited me and commanded me to select two volunteers from our county organization for an intelligence school in East Prussia.

According to Gužaitis, the Germans were supposed to give us weapons and ammunition and well-trained communications people. I discussed this matter with the members of our organization, Lušas and Žukauskas, but they refused to travel to Germany. Since other suitable candidates were not available, I informed Gužaitis accordingly. Gužaitis did not demand additional candidates. Thus, no one from our organization was sent to Germany.

We also discussed with Gužaitis how in the future we will have to organize underground activities behind the lines of the Red Army, since the Germans were retreating and it was obvious that Germany will be defeated. We thought that I would remain here, live illegally, and continue the fight against the Soviet government. To identify the members of the national guard organization, Gužaitis gave me about 20 cards with the seal of the Vytautas Division, which were to be used as a secret sign for recognition of our people.

At the end of July 1944 a unit of about 200 people, commanded by the captain of the bourgeois Lithuanian army, Švilpa, was withdrawing westward from Panevėžys. He settled in the village of Pyragiai, not far from Šiluva. They called themselves "partisans." Rev. Kazlauskas and I met Captain Švilpa. We found out that Švilpa was retreating westward but intended to return and begin an underground fight against the Soviet government. Kazlauskas agreed with Švilpa and recommended that he actively join in the disruptive underground activities.

At the direction of Gužaitis I did not withdraw with the Germans, but remained in place to organize the underground work against the Soviet government.

After the arrival of the Red Army units I began to hide. In September 1944 the state security organs began to take an interest in me, some captain questioned the neighbors about me. This forced me to be careful and I finally decided to live illegally. At first I hid at the house of my cousin Marijona Blužienė in the village of Meiliškiai in the area of Dotnuva. Near her house in the bushes there was a bunker, built even before the retreat of the Germans.

It was not safe to hide for long on Blužienė's farm, so in November 1944 I returned to my farm in the village of Kiaulininkai. I built a bunker and hid in it.

In December 1944 Captain Gužaitis visited me in Kiaulininkai. He tried to persuade me that in 2-3 weeks the Germans would push the Red Army units from Lithuania and that he would contact me then. He said that contact with me will be maintained through our acquaintance, the peasant Pranckevičius, who lived in the village of Obelkalnis. Gužaitis left Lieutenant Urbutis as his deputy. The latter was also hiding near Raseiniai. I never met Gužaitis again and had not yet joined in the disruptive activities.

In January 1945 an armed group of LFA members—Bartkus, Juodis, and Petryla—came to the farmstead where I was hiding. I had met the latter earlier. They asked me to join the LFA and lead this armed organization. They said that many underground members were hiding in the forests and farmsteads, but there was no one to lead them; experienced officers were lacking. I accepted and a little later joined the armed gang. From then on I participated continuously in the disruptive activities of the nationalist underground.

July 6, 1953

In January 1946 preparations were under way everywhere for the elections to the USSR Supreme Soviet. Čeponis and I, in a meeting with Bartkus, decided to organize a boycott of the elections.[9] In the newspaper Bartkus wrote slanderous articles directed against the elections, he urged the people to boycott the elections: not to go to the meetings, not to listen to the agitators, not to go to the polling places, not to vote for the candidates. We issued several special leaflets before the elections. The members of bands subject to our authority distributed these leaflets and newspapers among the people on our command and also conducted verbal propaganda against the elections.

In an effort to frighten the people and the activists, in the leaflets and verbally we warned that we would shoot all who voted for the Communist and Non-Party Bloc,[10] we also

9. See Doc. No. 4 for the partisan account of the elections.

10. This was the official name for the sole list of candidates compiled under Communist Party supervision.

threatened to shoot the members of the electoral commissions. We behaved in this way to allow persons of anti-Soviet disposition and those unwilling to participate in the electoral commissions to have an excuse for not participating in the election campaign.

Moreover, we gave orders to the members of the bands to organize attacks on the polling places on the night before the elections, to destroy the ballot boxes and other election materials, to punish those members of the electoral commissions who will fight against our propaganda. I and Čeponis ordered my Venclauskas group to shoot up the polling place of the village of Ginčaičiai in the district of Raseiniai. We ourselves, with other members of this group, attacked the polling place of the village of Rimkiškės in the county of Viduklė. After cutting the telephone lines to Viduklė, from a distance of 100-150 meters we shot up the polling place. In the shooting we killed a soldier and an officer who were in the ranks of defenders for the area.

In the winter of 1945-46 the members of the "Žebenkštis" division, led by Čeponis and myself, killed about 10 local inhabitants who worked against the bandits and their supporters.

In March 1946 Bartkus came to our hideout because a fire had broken out in his bunker. After the arrival of Bartkus, we discussed a plan of action for 1946. According to the plan, we were to form a regional unit and create a staff to lead the armed nationalist organizations, which would make up the regional formation.[11]

We decided that Čeponis will remain in the same place in the district of Raseiniai, where about half of the bandits under our leadership were, and will continue to lead them. He also had to take steps to establish ties with the Tauragė division and with its delegates agree to form a single region.

Bartkus and I were to transfer to the county of Šiluva, to the Morkūnas group, and from there lead the practical activities of the Morkūnas and Vareikis groups, and also to establish

---

11. Generally, the partisans operated in assigned territory. The country was divided into regions. The regional partisan command was in charge of several divisions (rinktinės), which in turn were subdivided into small partisan groups.

ties with the division of Šiauliai and Kėdainiai. In May 1946 we moved to the camp of the Morkūnas group in the forest of Pyragiai.

Here we became well acquainted with the bandits of the Morkūnas and Lazdauskas gangs, strengthened them organizationally, and took steps to forge ties with the divisions of Šiauliai and Kėdainiai.

In order to establish ties with the Šiauliai division, we used the bandit "Jurgis" who belonged to the "Nemunas" gang, a part of the Šiauliai division.

He was wounded and accidentally ended up in the Morkūnas gang. In the beginning of June 1946 Bartkus learned from "Jurgis" the places of contact with "Nemunas" and went to the district of Tytuvėnai. He found "Nemunas," presented our opinions about the question of centralizing the underground, and suggested that he organize a meeting with the commander of the division Beloglovas.

While they were discussing, soldiers stumbled upon the groups of "Nemunas" and Bartkus in the forest. One bandit was killed, the others managed to escape. The meeting was disrupted. Another meeting with Beloglovas was set for July 1946.

In June of that year in the Žaiginis forest I accidentally met a gang of three bandits. It was led by "Jurgis" who worked independently. We agreed that he will set up a meeting for me with the leader of the Kėdainiai division. "Jurgis" set up the meeting at the end of July 1946 in the forest of Žaiginis. I had not been acquainted with the leader of the Kėdainiai division earlier, but I knew that he had been a reserve lieutenant in the bourgeois Lithuanian army. By the end of the year he acquired legal status, using falsified documents, but the MVD organs arrested him. During the meeting he agreed with my arguments for the organization of a regional staff but postponed the next meeting and did not appoint a representative for the staff. Later it became clear that he did not intend to join in establishing the staff, since his division was falling apart and in the fall its members began to acquire legal status with falsified documents and to obtain work in various cities of the republic.

In the Morkūnas gang we organized the publication of the newspaper "Alio." In the newspaper we published directives on questions of underground activity, news about the international situation, and other anti-Soviet materials. We typed 20-25 copies and sent them to the Morkūnas, Lazdauskas, Venclauskas, and Vareikis gangs.

In July 1946 MVD organs discovered our place of residence. On July 5 Bartkus with a group went to the forest of Bedančiai to meet Čeponis, but I remained behind. On the morning of July 6 a group of soldiers unexpectedly attacked the Lazdauskas gang. While withdrawing with his people, Lazdauskas came to our camp. Hearing the shooting, we took up our defense positions in previously prepared trenches. When the battle began, the Lazdauskas people, discarding their equipment and ammunition, escaped from the camp and forced us once again to distribute the available ammunition among ourselves. We could not resist, so we broke through the encirclement and escaped.

Only one of us was killed. I do not know how many soldiers died in the battle, but I heard from people that there were 5 or 7. On the following day Bartkus returned to the camp, but not finding us and discovering signs of battle, went to Čeponis.

After the fight in the forest of Pyragiai I moved to the forest of Žaiginis where I lived for about a week in the camp of the "Jurgis" group, and from there I went into hiding in a camp in the forest near the village of Akmenė, in the county of Šiluva.

Knowing that a meeting between Bartkus and Beloglovas was to take place, I went to the vicinity of Tytuvėnai and met with them in a "Nemunas" unit at a farmstead near the Tyruliai swamps. We did not decide anything with Beloglovas since he did not have anyone suitable for work in the regional staff.

The only result of the discussions was this: we exchanged information about the situation in the region of our activities, and we established exact boundaries and communication points. I placed the responsibility of maintaining contact with the Šiauliai division on Morkūnas.

In the camp Morkūnas told me that he was planning to meet Father Kazlauskas. He also invited me to the meeting which took place in the woods near the Tyruliai swamps. Kazlauskas came with the organist Stankaitis. Morkūnas and I exchanged information with him. I got the impression that

Kazlauskas was withdrawing from our organization, so I did not decide anything with him.

Stankaitis was only a guide who brought Kazlauskas to the meeting place.

I traveled from the Tyruliai swamps to Raseiniai district looking for Čeponis and the others. In the Bedančiai forest I found only Bartkus in the Venclauskas gang. After talking with him it became clear that the situation of our organization had essentially changed. Čeponis had an argument with Bartkus and was expelled from the division. He, along with junior lieutenant Vareikis, moved to the Birbiliškė forest in the county of Girkalnis and by his own initiative formed a new "Vaidotas" division, which he commanded together with Vareikis, whom he appointed chief of staff. The gangs, which were active in the counties of Girkalnis, Seredžius, Veliuona, and partly in the county of Šimkaitis, were subject to Čeponis. He worked actively, formed nationalist organizations from persons living legally, and gave special attention to the formation of such organizations in Kaunas.

While I tried to establish ties with the Šiauliai and Kėdainiai divisions, Bartkus and Čeponis contacted the leader of the Tauragė division Danilevičius and called a meeting in which, in addition to them, "Giedrys" (a teacher from Kaunas) and Kasperavičius participated.

At this meeting they decided to unite the Tauragė and Raseiniai divisions and the "Vaidotas" group into one region, which they agreed to call the "Kęstutis" region, and formed its staff, which included the regional commander, Kasperavičius, the chief of the supply and information section, "Giedrys," and the chief of the organizational section, Bartkus. Soon Paulaitis also joined the regional staff as chief of the information section.

Learning this, I began to command the Raseiniai division and tried to understand its situation better, so that I could decide upon the means to strengthen it. Together with Bartkus, I met Lieutenant Vareikis and Captain Čeponis. At the meeting Čeponis gave me the documentation of the staff and informed us of the situation.

With the assistance of Bartkus I chose two people for the staff—the Pakarklis brothers. One of them had been a teacher, the other an accountant in a cooperative. I appointed one of them to head the supply section, the other—the propaganda section. Soon Čeponis and Vareikis returned to the region of their gangs. Bartkus travelled to the Tauragė district to work on the staff of the "Kęstutis" region. I remained to command the division.

The division under my command was part of the "Kęstutis" region. I maintained contact with the regional staff and was subject to it.

In the fall of 1946 the leader of the "Kęstutis" region Kasperavičius ordered me in writing to take measures to join my division with the Urbutis division. This had to be done since in the small territory of the Raseiniai district three divisions were active. I tried to contact Urbutis but was unsucessful for a long time. Only in January 1947 I accidentally met him, his wife, and another bandit in the Didvėjas village, where he was staying. In the conversation with Urbutis it became clear that he was not interested in the problems of the underground organization and had lost contact with his division. The bandit who was with him told me that the bandits under his command expelled him from the division for his inactivity and because his wife tried to command, forcing the bandits to supply her with food, clothes, and other things. Later I learned that Urbutis had obtained falsified documents, withdrew from the gang, and settled in Šiauliai or Panevėžys.

In the summer of 1947 I travelled with my gang to the former Urbutis region and joined his groups there to the staff of the "Žebenkštis" division. There were four groups with about 20 bandits. Therefore, organizationally the Urbutis divisions ceased to exist in the winter of 1946-1947.

The bandits subject to the "Kęstutis" region murdered Soviet citizens. The regional staff issued directives to take terroristic measures against everyone who works against the bandits and actively participates in the activities of the Soviet authorities.

I remember that before my taking over the leadership of the division, the bandits "L6putė," Juodis, and "Paukštis" killed 13 Soviet citizens in the Šiluva county. I learned about this later.

In April 1947 I met Bartkus and received instructions from him to go immediately with him to a meeting with representatives of the "Tauras" region. Bartkus and I first tried to reach the vicinity of Girkalnis to meet Captain Čeponis. However, already during the first night Bartkus was accidentally injured. I left him to recover with the contact Grigalavičiūtė. Kasperavičius was supposed to catch up with us, but for unknown reasons he never came. After discussing the possibilities of meeting with the delegation of the "Tauras" region, we decided to forego the meeting and returned home.

I returned to Raseiniai district. On the way I visited the ailing Bartkus and learned from him that in the beginning of April 1947 the state security organs found the hideout of the "Kęstutis" regional staff in the Batakiai forest, where they killed the regional commander Kasperavičius, while the chief of the information section Paulauskas disappeared without a trace. It became clear later that he had been arrested. In the same hideout one of the technical workers of the regional staff was also killed.

On May 20-25, 1947, Bartkus called a meeting of the "Kęstutis" regional leaders to discuss the leadership. The discussions took place in the forest near the village of Gėgė in the Raseiniai district. The chief of the supply section "Giedrys," Bartkus, the leader of the Tauragė division, Danilevičius, and I, —Žemaitis participated. At the meeting it was decided to reconstruct the regional staff and I was elected chief. Then we wrote a letter to the leader of the "Tauras" region Baltūsis— "Žvejys," in which we informed him about the changes in the personnel of our regional staff and suggested that we maintain regular contacts between the regions.

July 14, 1953

Wishing to establish a supreme nationalistic underground leadership as quickly as possible, after consultations with the staff leaders of the armed organization of the "Jūra" district Milaševičius, Gužas, Antanas Lesys and Ivanauskas, I issued Order No. 1 on the organization of the United Freedom Struggle Movement[12] around July 10-15, 1948. In the order I announced myself as the leader of all underground forces and

12. This apparently was a preliminary name given to the exclusively partisan central resistance organ, later to be named the Movement of the Freedom Struggle of Lithuania (MFSL). Žemaitis was instrumental in founding the new organization. It represented a split from the United Democratic Resistance Movement, established in 1946, which included both the passive and the armed resistance organizations. See Part I, Chapter 2 for details.

appointed as my assistants the leaders of the Southern, Eastern, and Western regions of Lithuania, not giving their pseudonyms, since I did not know the pseudonym of the leader of the Southern Lithuania region. In the same order I demanded that the leaders of all regions furnish me monthly information about the activities of their organizations. The first time I signed the order under the pseudonym "Vytautas." This order was the beginning of my activities in the post of leader of the Lithuanian nationalist underground.

We lived in bunkers until February 1, 1949, i.e., until the arrival of the leader of the Southern Lithuania region Ramanauskas, the leader of the "Tauras" region "Faustas," and the chief of staff of the Western Lithuania region "Jūra."

After their arrival, we organized a meeting in which the following participated:

1. Ramanauskas—"Vanagas," the leader of the Southern Lithuania region.[13]

2. Šibaila — "Merainis," the chief of the public section of the Presidium of the United Democratic Resistance Movement.

3. Bartkus—"Žadgaila," the secretary of the Presidium, UDRM.

4. Gužas — "Kardas," the chief of staff of the Western Lithuania region.

5. Grigonis — "Užpalis," the leader of the "Prisikėlimas" region.

6. "Faustas," the leader of the "Tauras" region.

7. Bronius Lesys—"Naktis," the chief of staff of the "Prisikėlimas" region.

---

13. Besides Žemaitis, Adolfas Ramanauskas is best known among the participants of this conference. He was born in the United States in 1918, but grew up in Lithuania, where he graduated from the military school and a teachers' institute. During the war he was an instructor in a teachers' institute and an organizer of the Lithuanian Freedom Army. He became active in the partisan struggle from the beginning and rose to be the last commander of the partisans. When Žemaitis became ill in 1951, Ramanauskas took over as the Chairman of the Presidium of the Movement of the Freedom Struggle of Lithuania and commander of the partisans. In 1952 he allegedly ordered the demobilization of the partisans, thus formally ending the armed struggle. He was apprehended and executed by the Soviet security organs in 1956.

8. I, Žemaitis—"Vytautas," the supreme commander of the armed forces of the UDRM, temporarily fulfilling the duties of the Chairman of UDRM Presidium.[14]

Besides the mentioned persons, a chief of one of the sections of the "Prisikėlimas" regional staff participated in the discussions as an assistant.

The meeting occurred in the bunker of the "Prisikėlimas" regional staff in a village between Baisogala and Radviliškis. I presided over the meeting.

The consultations lasted 20 days. The following decisions were made:

1. Since the old name, the UDRM, had, in our opinion, become outdated, we decided to change the name to the Movement of the Freedom Struggle of Lithuania—MFSL *(Lietuvos laisvės kovos sąjūdis)*. I suggested this name and those present at the meeting accepted it.

2. To assign the leadership of the Lithuanian nationalistic underground to the Presidium of the Council of the MFSL, considering it to be the supreme executive organ.

3. To elect me—Žemaitis, as chairman of the MFSL Council and supreme commander of the Lithuanian underground armed forces, Šibaila as the chief of the public (political) section of the MFSL Presidium, Bronius Lesys as chief of the public section, and Bartkus as secretary of the Presidium of the MFSL Council. The four of us made up the Presidium.

4. To assign me the task of preparing the final MFSL statutes, and to the member of the Presidium Šibaila — the program.

We stated the decisions in the minutes. The consultations were called a meeting of the MFSL Council, which was the supreme leading center of the underground.

We agreed to continue the anti-Soviet activities, to struggle against the Soviet government in Lithuania with weapons and with other methods, believing that the Western states would

---

14. While it is quite plausible that Žemaitis was a member of the Presidium of the UDRM (as commander of the "Kęstutis" region), in all probability the positions of Supreme Commander and Chairman of the UDRM Presidium were arbitrarily assumed. Other resistance sources indicate that the UDRM Presidium disagreed with the hard-line armed struggle tactics of Žemaitis. The MFSL did not replace the UDRM, which continued to function at least until 1952.

attack the Soviet Union, and then the underground would establish a bourgeois regime in Lithuania. We also agreed to add immediately two representatives from the nationalist underground of Southern Lithuania to the Presidium of the MFSL Council.

We discussed the question of communications of the armed nationalist underground with the outside world. Ramanauskas and "Faustas" furnished the information. They announced that from the letters received from abroad, specifically from "Skrajūnas," "Mažytis," and "Audronis," it is known that emigré centers are actively working abroad.[15]

Ramanauskas and "Faustas" said that "Skrajūnas" and others wished to come to Lithuania, but circumstances did not allow this wish to be fulfilled. The Council, therefore, decided to maintain the outside contacts and inform them about the state of the nationalist underground in Lithuania, and also to furnish information about the economic, political, and military condition of the Soviet Union.

The organization of foreign contacts was assigned to Ramanauskas who, while heading the armed underground in Southern Lithuania, already maintained such contacts through special representatives of the UDRM Presidium.

In discussing the question of the collection of intelligence data on the economic, political, and military conditions of the Soviet Union, the Council stated that this work of the underground was not being done satisfactorily. The information sections of the unit staffs do not perform the underground tasks in the area of intelligence, the people who gather the spy data are not sufficiently instructed. The Council, therefore, decided to strengthen the work of the intelligence sections, to select qualified people for this task, and to instruct them thoroughly.

We adopted the decision to strengthen the terroristic acts against the Soviet government in Eastern Lithuania since the active groups there, in our opinion, were poorly organized

---

15. Reference to partisan couriers who were sent abroad at the end of 1947. "Skrajūnas" was Juozas Lukša. His role is discussed in some detail in the introductory study. "Mažytis" and "Audronis" are the code names of Kazimieras Piplys (1923-1949). He was killed in a bunker of the staff of "Dainava" region (in Southern Lithuania) soon after his return to Lithuania.

and were insufficiently active. Moreover, it was proposed to form armed organizations in the regions of Klaipėda, Priekulė, Šilutė, and Pagėgiai, since, according to our information, they did not exist there.

At the meeting we decided to strengthen the anti-Soviet propaganda against collectivization in Soviet Lithuania. Special attention was given to the fight against the construction of communal buildings on collective farms and the transfer of individual farmsteads to collective centers since with the liquidation of the farmsteads the armed nationalist underground would lose its material base and the assistance of the people.

The meeting adopted the directive to the nationalist underground of Lithuania not to allow the socialization of the farms into collective farms and the transfer of individual farmsteads to collective centers. The Council decided to burn down the communal buildings and centers under construction to which the farmers from the individual farmsteads were to be transferred. To broaden the struggle against the organizers of the collective farms and people actively supporting the construction of collective farms, we warned them in the name of the underground that if they do not cease their active work in the organization of the collective farms, they will be shot by the members of the armed underground.

After the end of the meeting of the MFSL Council all the leaders of the armed underground departed to their areas and began to fulfill the decisions adopted by the Council.

In June 1949 I received a letter from Ramanauskas and from the special representative abroad of the UDRM Presidium "Audronis." I also received the minutes of the meeting of the delegates of the Supreme Committee for Liberation of Lithuania which was attended by the special representatives of the UDRM Presidium "Skrajūnas" and the delegate abroad of the Lithuanian nationalist underground "Prapuolenis," and information about the activities of SCLL.[16]

---

16. "Prapuolenis" is the code name of Jonas Deksnys, who was a member of the Presidium of the UDRM, at the time active abroad. The meeting of Juozas Lukša and Jonas Deksnys on the one hand and the representatives of the Supreme Committee for Liberation of Lithuania, which functioned at that time in West Germany, on the other hand, took place in Baden-Baden (West Germany) July 7-9. The

In his letter Ramanauskas informed me that in April 1949 he successfully returned to the headquarters of the Southern Lithuania region. While he was gone, the MVD organs had discovered his bunker and that of one the division leaders (pseudonym "Žaibas"). The acting leader of the Southern Lithuania region "Kariūnas," the leader of the division "Žaibas," and three or four bandits were killed in the bunkers.

Ramanauskas listed all the documents I mentioned which were enclosed with the letter.

In this letter "Audronis" informed me that on May 1, 1949, he arrived from abroad, is in the territory of the "Tauras" region, and must meet me as soon as possible since he has news that he can relate only verbally. "Audronis" also informed me that the two Estonians who came with him, in his opinion, were arrested by the MVD organs, and that the Latvian went to Latvia.

In the minutes of the meeting of the delegates of the Supreme Committee for Liberation of Lithuania, which was also attended by the special representative of the UDRM Presidium "Skrajūnas" and the delegate abroad of the nationalist underground "Prapuolenis," it was stated that there is a nationalist center abroad, called the Supreme Committee for the Liberation of Lithuania and that on the territory of Lithuania a leading center of the underground is in operation.[17]

After becoming familiar with the materials received from the SCLL, I sent a letter addressed to it in West Germany, which I signed as the Chairman of the MFSL Presidium. In the letter I confirmed that the MFSL Presidium received the sent documents and in the name of the Lithuanian underground I asked for material and moral support.

---

purpose of the meeting was to discuss the relationship between resistance organizations in Lithuania and the SCLL, which functioned in West Germany. A copy of the minutes of the meeting is available in the private collection of Mr. Bronys Raila.

17. The Baden-Baden agreement stipulated that the liberation struggle abroad will be conducted by the SCLL, which eventually will act as government-in-exile. The liberation struggle at home will be directed by its own resistance center. The agreement established procedures for a close cooperation between the two centers. The agreement has been a controversial matter in emigré politics. It was confirmed by the newly founded MFSL but rejected by the UDRM. Copies of the communications from Lithuania are available in the collections of Mr. Bronys Raila and Mr. Karolis Drunga.

Material support to us should have included the supply of funds, weapons, ammunition, means of communication, equipment, medicines, and so on.

I know that my letter, which I sent through Ramanauskas, never went abroad, since I never received any news from Ramanauskas that he had sent it.

It was the duty of my first assistant Ramanauskas to select people and send them abroad, and he independently decided all questions dealing with foreign contacts. I thought that Ramanauskas had opportunities to maintain constant contacts with the outside, since "Audronis," who had come from the other side, was visiting him, so I therefore sent him the letter destined for abroad, believing that he would forward it.

In December 1947 the leader of the "Tauras" region Baltūsis sent abroad "Skrajūnas" and "Mažytis" with a group of bandits.

At the request of Baltūsis, a stronger leader of the nationalist underground than I carried out the task of gathering intelligence information about Soviet Lithuania. I gathered information in the western part of Lithuania and passed it on to Baltūsis. In 1950 "Skrajūnas," after his return from abroad, later informed me that he gave all the information gathered in Lithuania, including mine, to the delegate abroad of the nationalist underground "Prapuolenis."[18]

In January 1951 through "Skrajūnas," who had returned from abroad, the Supreme Committee for the Liberation of Lithuania sent the Lithuanian nationalist underground symbolic support—1,000 American dollars, of which I received 500, the other 500 I never received, since the bandit who was to give them to me was killed. We received no other material assistance from abroad.

I know that "Skrajūnas" received about 100 Swiss wrist watches, which he was to distribute among the armed members of the underground. I received one of these watches as a gift from "Skrajūnas" himself. Besides the watches, "Skrajūnas" was also supplied abroad with radio equipment.

"Sakalas," who arrived with "Skrajūnas" from abroad,

---

18. Juozas Lukša, together with two companions—Benediktas Trumpys and Klemensas Širvys — was parachuted into Lithuania by Western intelligence in October 1950. For details of his mission, see Part I, ch. 2 of this study. The pseudonym "Sakalas" is probably that of B. Trumpys.

said that he also brought ammunition for the Lithuanian nationalist underground, but it did not reach the bandits since the
MVD organs seized it.

"Sakalas" told me that before being parachuted into Lithuania he finished a special course at an intelligence school.
This school is in West Germany.

He accompanied "Skrajūnas" to Lithuania and, as a specially trained radio operator, he had to maintain communications between the Lithuanian nationalist underground center
under my leadership and the SCLL, which was functioning
in West Germany.

"Sakalas" was not a deputy of the SCLL, but through him
I maintained contact with the committee.

2. NKVD AMNESTY FOR SURRENDERING PARTISANS

ORDER OF THE PEOPLE'S COMMISSARIAT OF THE INTERIOR

VILNIUS, FEBRUARY 15, 1946

The Red Army, having heroically liberated the Lithuanian SSR from the German fascist invaders, the organs and the army of the People's Commissar of the Interior, supported by the citizens and the defenders of the people, accomplished a great feat in crushing the Lithuanian-German nationalist bands.

Almost all of these bands and the illegal and anti-Soviet bourgeois nationalist organizations have been destroyed in most of the districts.

The leaders of the Lithuanian-German nationalists, with a few exceptions, have been captured and exterminated. Those members who had been forced into the gangs by deceit, threat, or terrorizing surrendered to the organs of the Soviet government and returned to peaceful work. Many of them redeemed their sin against the Motherland by conscientious effort and work.

It is known, however, that some bandits surrendered to the organs of the Soviet government not of their own voli-

No. 2. A photostatic copy of the amnesty order was first published in the **Lithuanian Bulletin**, November, 1946 (Vol. 4, No. 4), p. 14. The leaflet indicates that 150,000 copies were printed. The identification of the anti-Soviet underground as "Lithuanian-German nationalist bands" reflects the current Soviet interpretation, which has very little to do with historical fact. See the introductory study for an evaluation of such Soviet interpretation. Amnesty was first proclaimed on February 9, 1945, reconfirmed on June 3, 1945, and in 1947, according to Soviet historian A. Rakūnas in **Klasių kova Lietuvoje 1940-1951 metais** (Vilnius, 1976), p. 191. There is evidence that the amnesty was again announced as late as 1956. See J. Brazaitis: "Partizanai," **Lietuvių enciklopedija**, Vol. 22, p. 47. No reliable evidence exist on the number of people availing themselves of the 1946 amnesty. The samizdat journal **Aušra**, February 16, 1976 (No. 2-42), citing **Vestnik Leningradskoga universiteta**, 1966, No. 2, claims that in April 1946 over 40,000 left the forests and surrendered to the authorities. The partisan command did not oppose the amnesty because it felt that too many people were involved in the partisan movement. See J. Daumantas, **Partizanai už Geležinės Uždangos** (Chicago, 1950), p. 117.

tion, but on the instructions of their leaders; moreover, it is also known that they did not give up their arms, that they still maintain contact with their leaders, and that they help the Lithuanian-German nationalists execute their inhuman crimes against peaceful citizens.

Giving due consideration to the fact that some remnants of the Lithuanian-German nationalists still survive and hinder the peaceful life of the citizens by their acts of banditry, and striving to finally liquidate these Lithuanian-German remnants,

I ORDER

1. That the heads of the districts and counties of the People's Commissariat of the Interior, the army of the People's Commissariat of the Interior, and the groups of defenders of the people immediately take stern measures to wipe out the remnants of the Lithuanian-German nationalists in all of the districts of the Lithuanian SSR.

2. That no repressions be aimed at those bandits who surrender freely, even the leaders among them, or at the members of the Lithuanian Freedom Army and other bourgeois nationalist organizations after they surrender and give up their arms, that they be allowed to return to their homes, and that passes be issued to them.

3. That members of the gangs who are forbidden to surrender at their own wish to the organs of the Soviet government destroy those leaders and prepare to come with their weapons to the offices of the People's Commissariat of the Interior. No person who has killed a leader of a bandit gang or a bandit preventing him from surrendering will be prosecuted.

4. That bandits who surrendered earlier but who have not as yet given up their arms, and all other individuals holding arms, return them without delay to the offices of the People's Commissariat of the Interior.

5. That the families of the bandits and members of the bourgeois nationalist organizations who have not surrendered to the offices of the People's Commissariat of the Interior be taken into custody and sent into exile.

6. That inhabitants whose homes and farms house bunkers or other hiding places for bandits and others hiding from the organs of government inform without delay the offices of the

People's Commissariat of the Interior concerning this.

Individuals who have not surrendered concealed arms and who have not reported bunkers or hiding places on their property will be captured and tried as bandits.

7. That individuals who know the locations of bunkers and hiding places, regardless of where these places might be, report this without delay to the offices of the People's Commissariat of the Interior.

All who, knowing the location of bunkers and hiding places, do not report them to the offices of the People's Commissariat of the Interior will be captured and tried as accomplices of the bandits.

People's Commissariat of the Interior
of the Lithuanian SSR
Major General Bartašiūnas

3. FORMATION OF THE UNITED DEMOCRATIC RESISTANCE MOVEMENT

In seeking more appropriate and productive results in the struggle for the reconstruction of Lithuanian Independence and the realization of the great ideals of democracy upon the restoration of the Lithuanian state, we, the undersigned deputies of fighting and resistance organizations, the representatives, who are actively fighting and seeking the same goals, do hereby establish the United Democratic Resistance Movement (UDRM).

The UDRM is a political movement of struggle, which has matured during the long years of struggle with the occupants of Lithuania and the enemies of the entire mankind — Fascism and Bolshevism.

The UDRM, unrelated to any of the hitherto functioning movements and parties, expresses the will of the struggling Lithuanian Nation. It will guide itself by a unique ideological, political, economic, and social program which will be proclaimed later, a program whose principal features already have become evident in the various militant movements and organizations during the long and ruthless time of struggle.

No. 3. A copy of this document obtained from the private collection of Mr. A. Vokietaitis. The signers of the document can now be identified. Alg. Žaliukas — partisan leader Varkala (first name or biography not available); Alfonsas Hektoras — Jonas Deksnys; Juozas Vytis — Juozas Lukša; Juozas Erelis — Juozas Markulis; Andrius Meškis — Vytautas Staneika. Varkala signed for the partisans in general. Deksnys was the long-time leader of the Lithuanian Freedom Fighters Association — an underground organization established in 1940 and especially active during the German occupation, composed of younger political activists of national-liberal orientation. The Lithuanian Front was a Catholic-oriented resistance organization, tracing its origins to the revolt of June, 1941, against the Soviet regime. The Lithuanian Freedom Army was founded at the end of 1941 (for details, see note 1 of Doc. No. 1). The Lithunian Youth Unity Movement "Atžalynas" was a small resistance organization active during the German occupation. The UDRM thus united the principal resistance organizations which functioned during the war and the newly emerging partisan formations. One of the signers of the statement—Juozas Markulis—turned out to have been a Soviet plant, raising the question of the authenticity of the statement. Whatever his role may have been, other underground materials and testimony of at least two of the signers (Lukša and Staneika) do clearly suggest that the statement was a genuine reflection of views held by the leading personalities of the resistance movement.

During the period of the Nationalist regime, as during the years of German and bolshevik occupation, the Lithuanian farmer, worker, intellectual, the old and the young, men and women, fought and died for the liberation of themselves and their descendants, felt and perhaps in many instances expressed in a spontaneous manner the principal characteristics of their aims, for which it was worthwhile to fight and to die. The UDRM, in determining its line of action and the program of work, will be guided by the thoughts, ideas, and aspirations of those who have died and who are fighting.

The UDRM understands well that under the current development of world civilization and technology and the pulsation of lately manifesting ideas, a strictly independent, national, and isolated movement is impossible. Therefore, the UDRM, in seeking to realize its ideals, to improve the welfare of its members and the entire country, will consider the welfare and rationality of life not only of the neighboring nations, but also of the people of the entire world.

In foreign policy the UDRM will support the efforts to form a common world government as the best means to permanent peace.

In respect to the internal policy of its country, the UDRM will adhere to the principles of Western Democracies and will seek the practical realization of the Four Great Freedoms. In developing intensely the economy of its country and its most rational exploitation, the UDRM will immediately contribute toward the realization of a World Economic System as the most appropriate means for the allocation of natural resources, industrial goods, labor, and capital.

In the solution of social problems, which will be especially difficult after these wars, the UDRM will maintain the outlook that social welfare is not a concern of the individual citizen or organizations, but one of the primary tasks of the state. The rational resolution of social problems is inherently related to agricultural and industrial reforms, which the UDRM intends to carry out at the very beginning of independent life.

In the relations among popular organizations and social groupings, the UDRM will strictly adhere to the principles of Christian morality, the principles of Western Democracies. Love of one's fellows, humanism, the freedom of conscience, speech and thought, justice, toleration are necessary conditions for an orderly social life. The only norm for human behavior and inter-individual relations is the law, based on the principles of Christian morality. Physical coercion can be used, as an inevitable necessity, in the execution of decisions of the organs of justice.

One of the most important causes, pushing mankind toward wars and other gigantic misfortunes, is the relatively slow cultural progress, weak individual self-enlightenment. The general elevation of the cultural level among the wide masses is a necessary condition for the wider dispersal of new humanistic ideas.

The UDRM believes in the endless creativity of the Lithuanian nation and the strength of moral and physical abilities; it believes in the truth of its ideas, the power of the world's people of good will, the goodness and blessing of the Lord of the Universe. It believes in and is determined to continue the struggle, which was commenced by separate individuals, groups and organizations, with united and well organized forces until the ultimate victory is achieved.

The UDRM invites the members of fighting organizations, all the Lithuanians of good will, wherever they may live and whatever work they may do, to join this struggle; it invites all those who are struggling for the liberties and rights of the people of the world to support this difficult struggle of our nation, to support the realization of the ideas of the UDRM.

Lithuania, June 6, 1946

4. A RESISTANCE REPORT ON THE 1947 ELECTIONS

ACT NO. 4

Suvalkija, February 14, 1947.

I, Budrys, the Prosecutor of the Tauras Region, assigned to investigate and prosecute the crimes which the bolsheviks have committed and are continuing to commit in Lithuania, on the evidence of the testimony of witnesses, of my own observations, and of other sources, draw this document about the violation of the Lithuanian nation's freedom of will by the Bolshevik government, Bolshevik party, and Bolshevik activists in conducting the forced and illicit elections to the Supreme Soviet of the Lithuanian Soviet Socialist Republic.

1. The armed forces and local Red Army troops, consisting of approximately 50,000 MVD (formerly NKVD), already present in Lithuania were not sufficient to conduct these elections in Lithuania. About 60,000 soldiers of the regular army, therefore, were called in for this purpose. The army arrived a few days before the elections. Part of the army, in groups of 25-50 men, was distributed among the buildings of the districts in which the elections were being held. Besides this, motorized forces stood by in the centers of the counties and districts. The army was armed with submachine guns, semi-automatic rifles, and automatic pistols. It was learned from the soldiers that they came to Lithuania from Poland, where they had participated in the elections and had taken part in open and fairly severe clashes with the local underground forces. A small part of the army had been brought in from East Prussia, having had to come by foot all the way. The army guarded those

---

No. 4. From J. Daumantas, **Partizanai už Geležinės Uždangos** (Chicago, 1950), pp. 250-257. Daumantas—pseudonym of Juozas Lukša— was one of partisan couriers who reached the West in 1948. The book is his account of the partisan movement, including a number of documents. This report on the 1947 elections to the Supreme Soviet of the Lithuanian SSR was compiled by the partisan command of the "Tauras" region in Suvalkija, the Southwestern part of Lithuania. The partisans sought to operate as an alternative government, hence the author's title of "Prosecutor." This and other similar reports evidently were intended to serve as evidence against the collaborators with the Soviet regime after the reestablishment of an independent state.

districts in particular which had large forest areas, while the MVD patrolled the districts which in their opinion were less susceptible to attack.

2. A few days before the elections, bolshevik agents spread the rumor that those who did not vote would be deported to Siberia.

3. During the last week before the elections, the entire Bolshevik apparatus, the clerks and officials of the central agencies, the cooperatives, and other employees were sent into the villages for the purpose of mobilized agitation and other work connected with the elections. It was noticed that, in comparison with previous elections, bolshevik activity and scrupulousness had increased greatly in preparing for these elections. Meetings were organized in the villages, but the villagers did not attend. There are known instances where there were more agitators at these meetings than listeners in the audience. News has been received to the effect that in one district the chief prosecutor arrived and called together village representatives for investigation and questioning. He explained the electoral procedure to them and made them responsible for persuading the villagers to vote. The representatives were told to march all of their villagers to the polls early on election day. If they did not comply, they were threatened with severe punishment.

4. Written invitations to vote were sent out to everyone eligible.

5. Fifteen to twenty farm wagons were driven into the election areas in the villages. Lists of the sick and disabled, unable to come to the polls, were drawn up. Specially appointed Bolshevik officials were to come to their homes and collect their votes.

6. An MVD or MGB (secret police) officer was appointed to each of the election districts, of which there were 2,277 in Lithuania. This officer was responsible for conducting the election and was in reality and fact the president of the election committee. Moreover, according to the secret instructions pertaining to the elections and to the method by which they were to be conducted, the militia, in addition to other officials, was to keep close watch on the "anti-Soviet" and "lawless" attitudes of the people.

7. Companies, factories, and all other agencies were ordered to come to the elections with all of their employees. The

administration was made responsible for carrying out this order. Thus, the employees felt a double pressure, not only from the government organs but also from their supervisors and were forced to vote in order not to harm their management.

8. Those who were to arrive first at the polls were promised two bottles of pure alcohol and a piece of sausage.

9. The elections were to be held on February 9, 1947, from 6:00 to 24:00 (Moscow time). At 6 A.M. the bolsheviks and all of their servants and guards began to vote. The workers and employees of the various agencies and factories also came, compelled by force. However, the situation was different in the farms and villages. Here, apart from the bolsheviks themselves, only one or two of the more easily frightened citizens came to vote. There were areas in which only 0.40 per cent of the 500 registered voters had voted by noon.

10. In spite of the arrival of the Bolsheviks and the impending danger, the Lithuanians ignored these elections much more than they had ignored previous ones. On that day the inhabitants did not leave their homes for any reason at all; they did not even go, as ordinarily, to church. I observed the elections in the Suvalkija villages. These villages seemed like ghost towns except for the bolshevik agents on foot or on horseback. Confirmed reports from villages having 30-50 families indicate that only 2-3 people went to the election districts.

11. When the bolsheviks saw how few people came to vote, they tried a new line of attack. Around 12:00 (Moscow time) groups of 10-15 armed men were sent out from the polls with portable ballot boxes to collect votes from the villagers. But they encountered resistance from the people. In some cases the people locked themselves in their rooms and refused to let the vote collectors come in. In other cases adults were hiding while the children told the collectors that their parents had gone to vote. The bolsheviks searched some homes looking for voters. Lithuanians found at home refused to vote, giving all sorts of excuses. Some explained that they were satisfied with the present government and did not want a better one. Others said that they had never participated in any election and did not wish to do so now. There were also individuals who categorically refused to vote. These were threatened by the militia in various ways. They were accused of banditism, their names were taken down, and they were

told to come to the militia offices for questioning. Some, frightened by this, did vote. But there were also others who told
the militia that they realized that they could be shot or deported
for this, but that they still would not vote. When threats failed,
the bolsheviks placed as many votes into the box as there
were adults in that home. A case has been registered where a
bolshevik forced a ballot into a woman's hand and then
forced her hand into the box. The farmers who were forced
to drive the bolsheviks around reported that in some instances
the bolsheviks did not even bother to enter the homes but
counted the number of voters, placed an equal number of votes
into the box, and returned to their office. It is also known
that in some cases an individual came to the polls to vote and
found that someone had already voted for him. He was often
forced to vote again, even though he explained that he had
already voted.

It was noticed in one district that weeping women came to
vote at the polls. Upon questioning, they explained that they
had refused to vote despite the threats. At this, the bolsheviks
had forced them to kneel, half-naked, in the snow at —25°C
until they would vote. The party official of the Pilviškiai
district, Juozas Petrauskas, especially distinguished himself in
this type of work. He not only forced the women to kneel,
but beat them as well.

12. Some Lithuanians, fearing Bolshevik terrorism, came to
vote but tried to get a certificate of voting without placing
their ballot in the box.

13. The official newspaper *Tiesa*, No. 35, February 10,
1947, prints the report of the central election commission: "The
elections took place with unusual enthusiasm among the voters.
Great activity and organization on the part of the voters were
noticed in all the election districts. At midnight of February 9
the elections officially ended throughout the land... no less
than 96 per cent of the voters participated..."

As is evident from the above facts, the elections took place
under conditions of extremely great resistance; terrorization of
unheard of proportions was employed, but the majority of the
nation did not succumb.

It is also not true that the election ended on February
9th at 12 o'clock midnight. Many cases are known in which
the bolsheviks collected votes among the villagers until noon

of the following day. The final report from the Vilkaviškis district, the electoral district of Oželiai, states that the collection of votes continued until noon of February 10th, since on election day, despite threats and surveillance, only 10 people had voted out of 500 registered. The election commission sent for help. A truck filled with soldiers, MVD officials, and a representative of the Central Committee of the Communist Party was sent to Oželiai. This representative formed groups for collecting votes and sent them out again to collect votes in the villages at 6 A.M. on February 10th. The groups were told not to return without 100 per cent of the votes. However, it was impossible to collect 100 per cent of the votes anyway. The missing votes, therefore, were cast by the Bolsheviks themselves upon their return to the polls.

In that same Oželiai district, early in the morning on February 10th, six armed people's defenders went with the ballot box to see every inhabitant and forced him to vote. They did not visit those who lived near the forest since they feared guerrilla reprisal. Having finished this "free" voting in one farm, they left and disappeared. The farmer, fearing that they would steal something, hurried outside. There, in back of the outhouse, he found the armed men stuffing the ballot box with the votes supposedly gathered from those living closer to the forest. The farmer laughed out loud at the sight. The men, however, ignored him and went on with their task.

Reliable evidence shows that even before the elections each electoral district had received a preset plan indicating how many votes each district was to collect. Each commission was bluntly told that if they did not execute this plan, they would be severely punished. For example, in the Paežeriai electoral district, 114 votes were still missing after all the threats and collections. The commission itself placed these 114 ballots into the box on February 10th in full view of many outsiders.

14. Act No. 3 contained a description of the fraud perpetrated during preparation for the election. It was shown that in the 180 electoral districts in Lithuania, 180 candidates were presented for election, one for each district. Thus, there was one "block," one candidate, one ballot with the one name of the sole candidate from that district, and the Lithuanian had to place this ballot into the box so that by this act the Bolshevik fraud would be justified. But the Lithuanian nation

refused to participate in this hoax and the Bolsheviks themselves had to place 85 per cent of the ballots into the boxes.
Only 5 per cent voted freely, while 10 per cent were made to
vote by force. The remaining votes were cast by the Bolsheviks
themselves. *Tiesa*, No. 38, February 13, 1947, published the
names of 180 "newly-elected" deputies — names which had
been known long before the elections. This same issue reports that 97.91 per cent of the electorate voted. "24,138 voters
cast votes against the candidates... 4,699 ballots were found
invalid." It is obvious that there could have been invalid
ballots and that there were many more than the reported
number. Yet how could it be possible to vote against the
candidates if there was only one ballot? This is incomprehensible to everyone and even the election rules did not foresee
such a possibility. This is an obvious Bolshevik trick.

Tiesa, No. 36, February 11, 1947, writes: "This is the
victory of the Communist and Non-Party Bloc — a new glorious triumph of the Bolshevik party." History will one day
evaluate this triumph against a small, enslaved nation through
deception and terrorization.

15. The army, having helped to conduct the elections
in Lithuania, immediately left the country. It is suspected that
it went to conduct elections in other republics.

16. A full report of the murders committed by the bolsheviks during the elections has not yet been received. The latest
word reveals that on February 9, 1947, in the district of Vilkaviškis, the laborer Jonas Jašinskas was killed by MVD officials.
Jašinskas, being deaf, was unable to answer the questions of
the MVD. His skull was cracked open with guns and his brain
was seen splattered. His corpse was desecrated by being thrown
on a dung heap in the militia yard and left there for three
days following the murder.

17. In this manner were the elections conducted in Lithuania — elections which the bolsheviks crown as the most
democratic in the world. And in the opinion of the American
friend of the bolsheviks, Wallace, this bolshevik democracy is
of a better quality.

18. According to news received today, an order has been
given to make up lists of those who did not vote.

These rigged elections, from the initial organization of the
election commissions until the conduct of the elections with

the help of armed forces and terror, were conducted in Lithuania by the Lithuanian party and non-party bolsheviks, by the officials of the local administrative apparatus, by the members of the bolshevik activists, by the members of all the electoral commissions, by the "deputies," and MVD and MGB officials according to the government and politburo in Moscow. All of the party officials, officials of the above-named institutions, and all others who actively participated in the execution of this hoax are hereby accused of this crime and will be prosecuted by the court of independent Lithuania. Their individual responsibility will be determined after questioning.

One copy of the *Election Rules, The Constitution of the Lithuanian SSR*, other election literature, and the issues of the official newspaper *Tiesa* pertaining to the election are appended to this document as *corpus delecti*.

We, the undersigned, witnesses, have read this document and testify that the facts contained herein are true.

Witnesses:	(———)	Žvejys
	(———)	Grafas
Prosecutor of the Region:	(———)	Budrys

A copy of this act is correct.

The Adjutant of Tauras Region

5. PARTISAN PRESS ON WORLD EVENTS

IN THE DEVELOPMENT OF WORLD EVENTS

The latest political developments attracted the attention of the whole world. Last week everyone's center of attention was the mutual assistance pact signed by England and France. The press of the entire world, as well as the radio, appreciated this as a grouping of the Western Powers against the Eastern Powers. Immediately after the signing of the pact between these countries, a mutual assistance pact was signed between Belgium and France. The signing of these pacts attracted everyone's attention especially because they were signed just before the Moscow Conference, and that clearly showed that the Western states will be of one mind during the Conference as well. On the other, that is the Eastern, side, a grouping of powers also began. A mutual assistance pact was signed between Poland and Czechoslovakia. In the treaty of France and England, as well as in that of Poland and Czechoslovakia it is stated that the pacts are being made because of a possible attack from the German side; however, that is only a subterfuge concealing the true purposes of these pacts.

Having begun, the Moscow conference showed from its first days that there will be no unified accord between the East and the West. The Russians, as they had in previous conferences, continue blowing their own propaganda horn about their achievements in Germany and elsewhere. The Western states exposed the true works of the Russians. Especially Molotov compromised himself when, after he attacked the Western states for their poor government of their zones in Western Europe, England's Minister of Foreign Affairs Bevin asked him how much armaments and how much various industrial equipment they shipped out of Germany, why the Russians did not destroy the German battleships but refurbished them, why the Russians do not release German prisoners of war but "retrain" them and form new platoons from them. All the Western states were unified at the Moscow Conference.

No. 5. From the partisan bulletin **Laisvės rytas**, March 15, 1947 (No. 5). The onset of the Cold War, specifically the failure of the Moscow Conference and the announcement of the Truman doctrine, fueled partisan hopes of quick liberation and sustained the course of armed struggle.

However, all these events paled last Wednesday, that is, March 12, before the speech of the President of the US, delivered at a session of both Houses of the Senate (read "Congress" — Ed.). In his speech President Truman stated that the US will not be involved in the politics of isolation and that it will finally take action so that peace would be put into practice in the world. In his speech, Truman noted the difficult and troubled present situation of the nations in the Near East, which the US cannot regard complacently. At the same time Truman promised support for the nations fighting for their freedom.

In addition, Truman announced that he has earmarked $4 million in aid to Greece and Turkey for the agricultural development of these countries. This aid is to be provided as soon as possible. These states are also being given military and civilian personnel who will supervise the use of the aid.

The press of the entire world considers Truman's speech a great historical event and as a new direction for US foreign policy. The world's press also hails this speech, for it gives all nations fighting for their freedom the hope of being liberated. The communist press attacks Truman rather severely for this speech and considers the new direction of US foreign policy as imperialistic aspirations and a desire to dominate the world. The press of Yugoslavia and Russia are especially strongly agitated. However, the communist press also shows its fear, for it sees a rapidly approaching end to Communism.

The granting of aid to Greece and Turkey is also considered an important political event. The material support of these countries and their acceptance by the US under its guardianship means very much strategically because for Greece this is a bridge to Turkey and from there to Iraq. All this is nothing else but the installation of US military bases.

All these latest events show that at this time the final stage of preparation for war is under way.

6. DIRECTIVES OF THE UNITED DEMOCRATIC RESISTANCE MOVEMENT

Top Secret

The Committee of the United Democratic Resistance Movement of Lithuania

INSTRUCTIONAL BULLETIN

March 16, 1947

A. Concerning:
  1. Our struggle.
  2. Our battles — the ways, methods, and means of our resistance.
  3. Urgent matters in our day-to-day struggles.

B. For the information and guidance of:

  1. All units and affiliates of the UDRM
  2. The Supreme Staff of the Armed Forces
  3. The regional leaders of the Lithuanian Freedom Fighters
  4. The more important features for every participant of our struggle — our Movement.

1. *Our Struggle.*—Seven years ago the dismal and confining night of slavery closed in over the day of the Freedom of our Lithuania and relentlessly weighs upon our chests until now. In that night of slavery, one tyrant was changed by another, and the second was again replaced by the first, who, once again having returned to our roads and our fields, with the cinders of battle still smoldering, resumed oppressing us with

---

No. 6. Copy of the directive obtained from the private collection of Mr. Bronius Kviklys. The available copy of the directive is illegible in several places. The last part of the directive, dealing with the political bickering among emigré politicians and between resistance leadership in the country and in the political centers abroad, is omitted here. The directive represents the policy of reducing armed struggle as a means of preserving capabilities for the decisive moment—the war between the East and the West — which was not viewed as imminent by the UDRM. For opposition to this policy, cf. Doc. No. 7.

his dreadful plague, destroying and smothering, leaving in peace neither the living nor the dead. That is the awful, raging night of slavery. In the history of Lithuania there has not been such a night. It is a night forcibly imposed, veiled by falsifications, satiated by puppets and pushovers; trampling underfoot every form of honesty, justice, and decency, it systematically lulls all to a lethargic sleep, and—we weep in that dismal misfortune. But so what if our eyes have run dry of tears; so what if our cheeks are now moistened by drops of blood; so what if our hearts are rent with pain, and suffering strangles our hope? So what if all of Lithuania, cowering at the feet of a wayside Sorrowing Christ overgrown with moss, weaves her wailings into prayers, and her ranks grow thinner and thinner. The blood in the veins of the Lithuanian has not frozen in that harsh, freezing winter, and Lithuania is still alive and will be alive because *"only those ideals die for which no one dies."* Like pelicans, we give drink to Lithuania by the blood of our breasts, we wash away the dust of her troubles by the sweat of our battles and the tears of our orphans, and we believe that "nevertheless, Lithuania will arise sometime; could she suffer so much in vain?"

Our struggle, which began seven years ago,[1] has gone on uninterrupted and goes on to this day, and will go on until the shackles of slavery break, until the Morning of Freedom dawns or the blood of the last Lithuanian freedom fighter grows cold and the last Lithuanian falls.

Our struggle today is the organic continuation of the battles for freedom. Our struggle today is the very cruelest, the most agonizing stage in the Calvary of our battles. That this is true is known by everyone who is personally experiencing the loss of his parents, brothers, or friends; who has seen with his own eyes the desecrated bodies of his brothers; who is himself living the days of an eternal wanderer—persecuted, pursued—of a hunted animal; who has lost everything, except life in a nightmare of slavery.

Our battle ranks have spontaneously begun to swell; of itself, one fighting breast drew toward another; of itself, one foot began to march next to another across the battlefields; one hand grasped a weapon, the other the hand of a comrade, and so, slowly, step by step *rose up a fighting Lithuania,* com-

---

1. Reference to the occupation of Lithuania in June of 1940.

posed of the Lithuanian Freedom Army, the Freedom Fighters, and various armed battle groups and units of partisans; our *United Democratic Resistance Movement, fighting for the restoration of Lithuania, was also born.* Every decent, noble, and unselfish Lithuanian understood it and valued it, and so our battle ranks began to increase, our battle movement began to flow as a refreshing stream, directing all those fighting to the ways shown by wisdom; they began to share accurate analyses of the situation, began to rely on accurate data and a firm basis—the information sent by our Foreign Delegation and our Information Center,[2] our senseless sacrifices became fewer, and the current phase of our struggle began, enabling us to continue the battle with the least loss of blood, permitting the greatest number of battle participants to hold out, to survive, to live to see the Dawn of Freedom and Lithuania's Resurrection.

Yes, Lithuania is already fighting, and, with tiny exceptions (cf., sec. 3, 4) she is fighting resolutely, circumspectly, and wisely, marching in the appropriate paths of battle. But what is Lithuania fighting for? For what did the Lithuanians rise up and why is the majority of Lithuanians marching in the battle ranks of the Democratic Resistance Movement? *What is the essence of our struggle?*

The answer to those questions is written in the blood of the heroes and martyrs fallen over seven years in the field of an uneven battle, it is made clear by the groanings and wailings of exiles, it is amplified by the silent and wordless sighs of prisoners, the answer is concluded by the immeasurable sufferings and hardships borne by all Lithuanians. What is that answer?

We are fighting because:

1) having been born in freedom, having grown up in freedom, we treasure freedom, and *in freedom we wish to live and die.*

2) *We long to live only in a free, independent, demo-*

---

2. Reference to an information and liaison center (Užsienio Delegatūra), established in the West by the special representative of the UDRM abroad, Jonas Deksnys. Some of the papers of this activity are available in the private collection of Mr. Bronys Raila and especially among the papers of Prof. Stasys Žymantas, who served as the director of the activity for a long time.

cratic, united Lithuania, in which life is based on the principles of Christian morality; in which there are no slaves-serfs and dictatorial satraps-tyrants; in which the various manifestations of cultural life and creative progress flourish and thrive; in which one can expect justice in the laws, a respect for rights, protection, and safety.

3) We are fighting because *we are obligated to carry on and fulfill* the legacy of those who perished for freedom, the writing of which is scribed in their lifeblood and their immeasurable pain and suffering.

4) We are fighting because *we want to show the world that there are ideals that inspire* and enable a dwarf to become a giant, that give so much courage and strength that the powerful tyrant no longer knows how to suppress it, if he is still ashamed of publicly hanging everyone.

5) We are fighting because we believe that we are fighting not only for our own freedom and well-being, but that we are fighting for the ideals, justice, and rights of all our brothers, our Motherland, our Lithuania, which the Great Western Democratic Powers ceremoniously proclaimed to the world, founding their value in the blood and lives of millions of their finest sons shed in battle, strengthened by the massive joining of forces and the triumph of victory, and showed the value and sublimity of those ideals, created by cultural values and progress of a scale until now unimaginable.

6) We are fighting because *we are unable, we no longer have the strength to see the columns of agonizing prisoners,* the ranks of exiles, the Russian infiltration of all areas of life and their forcing themselves into even the tiniest crack; we cannot calmly look on at the economic dissipation, exploitation, at the cunning stifling and poisoning of the spirit, making of a living man a man-wolf, who wants to live only for the present day, whose ideal is a crust of bread, who is unfeeling for his brothers' tears, who becomes a robot to whom nothing is precious, who has no knowledge of spiritual values, to whom Christian morality is an object of spite, and for whom at the center of everything is unlimited fear, the uncertainty of tomorrow, and trembling and slavish flattery.

7) We are fighting because *we think and believe that one day the hour will come,* and the world's patience will run out, and it will tear off the mask of the rapacious tyrant, it

will rally all its forces and will help free the enslaved millions, the martyrs, the exiles, the prisoners and slaves, and in that battle the movement of our struggle will enable our united ranks to break the chains of bondage and to rise up after the night of terror to a new life of reconstruction.

8) We are fighting because the Supreme Ruler of the World commanded us to fight with the kingdom of evil and, to those fallen in this battle, promised the crown of eternal happiness and glory.

9) We are fighting because we have not yet gone mad from terror and are still alive. *Can we not but fight?*

That is why we are fighting, that is why we are not afraid to perish, that is why we are dying. That is why he is a liar and does not know the essence of our battle, who wants to explain our fighting as a liking of risk, a search for personal safety, a vengeance, a nappropriation of land, as motivated by factional objectives, or as a direct pursuit of glory, a martyr's crown, a desire to entrench ourselves and then, in the future Lithuania, like porpoises to swim around in the sea of arrogant parasitism. Such a person is not only a liar, but also blind and deaf; such an individual is not even a human being, for even an upstanding enemy speaks the truth of his foe.

Brothers, we know why we are fighting. Even our fields, homesteads, and a handful of our forest soil knows it; ask and it will answer. It will answer that we are fighting because we feel the voice from under the sod forcing us to fight and that the battle is essential. It will tell all and discredit those who shout that we are trying to ride into the New Dawn on the political factions as if they were a wooden horse, that we want to be ministers, rulers. Brothers, we are fighting and we know that "today you and tomorrow I" will lie down in the soil of our motherland, but that our children will enjoy the happiness of freedom, that the coming new generation will continue the work of reconstruction, will push forward the progress of culture. *We are fighting not for our own posts or positions, but for the life of others, for the freedom of our motherland, and for the immortal ideals of mankind.* That is why this struggle is our life, and our life is the life of our motherland. That is why our struggle is a continuation of that struggle with the minions of evil that was begun by the handful of fishermen of Genesareth inspired by His Ideas, the banner of which has been borne by the martyrs of the Colisseum and all times into these days of ours. Those banners are now flying in many places; they are waving in our land as well, and as long as those ancient banners of battle were waving in our free motherland, the Lithuanian was quiet and peacefully went about his work, but when they began to defile those banners, when the tyrant threatened to trample them underfoot, then the quiet Lithuanian was moved. Having been silent like the rivers of our fields, like the rustling of our silent birch-woods, his blood grew restless and the Lithuanian rose up to battle. Can a Lithuanian not fight? This is what kind of a battle ours is; this is the essence of our struggle. But how must we fight?

2. *Our battles—the ways, methods, and means of our resistance.*

In the summer of last year (Aug. 21, 1946), in an instructional bulletin,[3] we analyzed, among others, these two questions:

1) *Shall we continue following the path we have been,* or shall we look for new ways? and

2) *Which path shall we follow,* which way shall we choose?

Since we do not foresee new possibilities in our struggle, our suggestions of new forms of warfare are based on:

a) the need to *reduce needless sacrifice* and bloodshed without clear benefit,

b) the need to help *the greatest number of Lithuanians* to stay in their motherland, to avoid the hardships of exile, and not to drag needlessly hundreds of our peaceful countrymen into suffering and ruin,

c) the need *not to give the enemy justification before the world* in claiming that those fighting are those who have trampled on human decency, the scum, the murderers of innocent people, and former flunkeys or collaborators of the Germans who wish to obstruct government and the raising of the standard of living, that they are rapacious, treacherous murderers,

d) on the fulfillment of the legacy of our fallen brothers,

e) on the current world political situation—on the fact that it has become known that *there is no basis to expect a war soon,*

---

3. The cited bulletin was not available in the private archives examined.

f) *on the essence of the struggle we are waging:* we are fighting for freedom, justice, humanism, democracy, Christian morality, and inborn rights and not for: political domination, the hegemony of some political faction, the supremacy of some clique, the egotistical advantages of personal interests or the need to simply kindle the fires of vengeance, and not to avenge wrongs, killing everyone in sequence, accusing them and killing more, repaying with the same actions as those of the enemy, not being any different in his bestial cruelty, at the lowest depths of immorality. We, however, affirm that we are civilized people, loving ideals, understanding the principles of Christian morality and living by them, and fighting as befits a true soldier, fighter, defender of freedom, and Lithuanian, and that we do not measure by the same bloody measure as the enemy.

After that, to the question, *Which way shall we choose,* we gave the answer that:

1) The selected way should be one that would enable Lithuanians following it not to lose hope, to preserve the longing of freedom of the motherland, to preserve themselves and their loved ones from meaningless suffering and hardships (besides those that now oppress them), that the chosen path would enable them to stay alive and survive as long as possible and that our struggle would require smaller sacrifices, to enable larger groups and more numerous ranks to rise up at the hour of the critical battle for the freedom of Lithuania, and to enable them to heal the wounds and reconstruct a free Lithuania more quickly.

2) The only path that would satisfy all the requirements of our struggle and the goals of our struggle—is the path of a *strict conspiracy, of a more passive underground resistance—the path of democratic opposition, the path shown by the United Democratic Resistance Movement*—a conscientious thinking, fighting Lithuania, realistically interpreting the situation.

We are not simply coming up with assertions, but we are taking them from life, from true sources, from the heart and mind of the Lithuanian. Those who have consciously taken that path, circumspectly and in an orderly manner, those know the value and usefulness of that path; in their ranks there is less bloodshed, in the vicinities of those battles the people do not fear the freedom fighters but love them and care for them because they know that they wish no harm and for their sake are bearing the greater share of the burden of hardship, suffering, and concern. Those who think that that path shows cowardice, that it necessitates relinquishing the goals of our struggle, and for that reason have taken the course of active armed resistance, coining slogans about an imminent war between the East and the West (a matter of days), they have brought entire countrysides to senseless hardship, have forced hundreds into the claws of the enemy needlessly—into prisons, exile; they have sacrificed too early... (copy illegible—Ed.)... Lithuanian blood and lives; they have revealed headquarters of the struggle, they have lost the material goods necessary to continue the struggle, they caused the battle ranks to grow thin, and have engendered a harmful ambivalence and mistrust of statements, they have forced... (copy illegible—Ed.)... and to rescue only from fear, quietly asking, "are there no more intelligent people left?" Could it be pleasant to bait, incite people, and then, having stepped aside in helplessness, to look on at our troubles hopelessly? Why do you fling about deceptive trinkets? Why don't you take the path of a thoughtful struggle? No— enough of that. *That stilted wave of activity provoked a backlash from the enemy, has enabled them to find justification for their loathsome deeds of destruction,* and many a vicinity, packed with the military-militia forces of the enemy-occupant *create greater hardship; more tears of our people are streaming, even more heartbreak and pointless suffering is born.* The question arises: *Who forces us to continue this?* Can it be that they can no longer think coolly and analyze the situation, the provided information? Could it be that a desire to show one's pride, an unwillingness to accept information based on facts and wise tactics, provided by others, is playing a role here? It seems that that is the case. That is why it becomes so sad and frightening because in some places recent days have brought great losses to our struggle and caused pointless suffering. Will this go on much longer? Won't the hearts of those tremble, who are taking leading their brothers to ruin by spreading unfounded rumors, who are taking false paths thereby unwittingly aiding the enemy and his evil intentions? Isn't it time to come to our senses, to stop arrogantly demonstrating our cleverness, and *isn't it time to admit our error and start moving on the true path of our struggle? It seems that it is time. But does everyone feel it?...*

7. PARTISAN PRESS ON THE IMMINENCE OF WAR

EVENTS ARE TAKING THEIR COURSE.

Our struggling nation—from the youngest person to the oldest—lives with but one yearning, to become free of Bolshevism. But liberation is not dependent solely on our wishes —Lithuania is only a minor participant in the world struggle. We must admit that the hour of deliverance has been delayed, which has raised, and continues to raise, anxious thoughts in the minds of many. This is so because the sufferings of our nation are so great that it is beginning to appear to some that those events can weaken, or even destroy, the resistance of our nation. However, in reality, our resistance is not decreasing, but increasing. Only bolshevik agents and weak-willed persons influenced by public bolshevik propaganda begin to convince themselves and others that the events, i.e. an armed conflict, will not come soon. Such an opinion, as disseminated, is totally erroneous. To say nothing of the ideological differences of two worlds, economic confrontations hasten events. Recently, for example, the Russian press rejoiced over the English "dollar crisis" that had developed. But that is only one facet of English-American economic relations, which does not determine, and cannot determine, the general development of world events. Suffice it to mention several facts.

Having become even richer during the war, today America has in its hands 90 per cent of the industry of the entire world. The Soviet Union and the countries it controls interfere with the basic circulation of commodities, regardless of the fact that because of this, millions of people are condemned to starvation. Millions of workers in America and elsewhere have work only because of the extraordinary arming that is going on. But the world cannot long continue being a forge for arms; production of arms in the long run usurps all material resources. All this inevitably leads to breaking.

No. 7. From the partisan newspaper **Laisvės varpas**, October 15, 1947 (No. 123). The paper was the organ of the Kęstutis region (mainly Tauragė and Raseiniai districts), which at that time was commanded by Jonas Žemaitis, a hardliner in respect to resistance tactics (cf. Doc. No. 1).

A well-founded question arises: why has the delay lasted until now? We cannot forget that at this time the concern is not for the liberty or interests of any one particular country, but for a truly democratic ordering of the entire world. And for this, of course, time is needed both for the battle preparations and for the formation of public opinion in various countries. Preparations involving arms, are of course, kept secret. But it is not difficult to imagine what could be done, at American speeds, in the more than two years after the war, including the atomic bomb and new, as yet unknown weapons. As for the winning of public opinion, data are fully adequate. All the countries on the American continent, Turkey, Greece, China, etc., have standardized not only their weapons, but their opinions. The unceasing bolshevik propaganda fools the people of lower intelligence. The above-mentioned facts clearly show that an armed conflict is a matter of the near future, not of several years. In recent weeks, American-Soviet Union relations, as can be seen from international reviews, have become very strained. As always, unity, patience, and caution are essential to us, but there may be facts which do not always become public but which significantly hasten the course of events. The Russians have concentrated great forces in the Balkans and are awaiting a convenient moment to catch new victims. America is not dozing either. Because of these and a whole array of similar circumstances, we can confirm that events are taking their course.

8. A RESISTANCE MEMORANDUM TO THE UNITED NATIONS

I. SEIZURE OF THE STATE OF LITHUANIA

Disregarding the Peace Treaty of July 12, 1920, the Nonaggression Treaty of 1926, renewed in 1936, and pending its entry into the war, the U.S.S.R. in the fall of 1939 compelled Lithuania and the other Baltic States to accept mutual assistance pacts and its military garrisons and bases.[1]

It was clear that this meant the introduction of a Trojan horse into the Baltic States. Nevertheless, failing to obtain support from other states, Lithuania was forced to bow to this demand.

Eight months later, taking advantage of the temporary defeat of the Western powers at the hands of Germany, on the eve of the fall of Paris, the U.S.S.R. occupied Lithuania with huge forces (June 15, 1940). This occupation was prepared for in advance by loud and false propaganda charges to the effect that Lithuania was allegedly not complying with the pact made in 1939 and was preparing acts of violence against the Red. Army.[2]

Immediately after the occupation Molotov solemnly declared that the U.S.S.R. did not intend to change either the political or social system of the state of Lithuania and demanded that the government, administration, and armed forces

---

No. 8. The memorandum was first published by the **Lithuanian Bulletin**, Nov.-Dec., 1948 (Vol. 4, No. 11-12), pp. 8-12. According to the editorial note, it was transmitted to the United Nations and representatives of the Foreign Ministers Council in Paris by the Supreme Committee for Liberation of Lithuania. The memorandum was brought to the West by partisan courier Juozas Lukša. The signatories of the memorandum have not been identified.

1. English-language texts of the various treaties referred to are found in the League of Nations **Treaty Series**. A convenient collection of documents, including the texts of treaties, is that of Bronis J. Kaslas, **The USSR-German Aggression Against Lithuania** (New York, 1973) Nos. 3, 8, 49.

2. The aggression of the Soviet Union against Lithuania and the illegal process of annexation is well documented in the following collections of diplomatic papers: US Department of State, **Documents on German Foreign Policy 1918-1945**, Series D, Vols. V, VIII, IX (Wash-

of Lithuania refrain from any action and remain at their posts. This was a temporary maneuver intended to pacify external and internal public opinion; it was designed to mitigate the brutal aggression during the first days of its operation. Nevertheless, events immediately following the occupation exposed the blatant deceit of those maneuvers.

Even though today the Soviet Union proclaims that the Lithuanian state had voluntarily joined the U.S.S.R., the farce of the merger was not well rehearsed during the first weeks in 1940, although some justification of the military Soviet occupation had to be shown. Therefore, in their speeches, Soviet Russia's leaders and agents justified the occupation as a "realistic policy."

In the summer of 1940 a representative of the Foreign Office of Lithuania inquired why Russia, disregarding the non-aggression treaty, occupied Lithuania. Mr. Ivanov, at that time the *charge d'affaires* of the U.S.S.R. in Paris, frankly declared: "If we had left Lithuania on the other side of the fence, Germany would have seized her; therefore, we moved the fence to the Lithuanian-German frontier."

Later Russia fabricated her justification of the aggression by broadcasting the fiction of the allegedly voluntary merger of Lithuania with the U.S.S.R.

In this connection we may cite the speech made in the so-called People's Diet on July 21, 1940, by Justas Paleckis, at the time a Moscow-imposed Prime Minister and now Chair-

---

ington, 1953-1954); US Department of State, **Foreign Relations of the United States: Diplomatic Papers. The Soviet Union, 1933-1939,** Washington, 1952); US Department of State, **Foreign Relations of the United States: Diplomatic Papers,** 1939, Vol. I (Washington, 1956) and 1940, Vol. I (Washington, 1959). An important source on Soviet aggression against the Baltic States is the massive collection of testimony and documentary materials by US Congress, Select Committee on Communist Aggression and the Forced Incorporation of the Baltic States into the USSR, **Third Interim Report,** 83rd Congress, 2nd Session (Washington, D.C., 1954); and the preceding **Hearings** of this Committee. The subject is treated by a number of historical studies: Boris Meissner, **Die Sowjetunion, die Baltischen Staaten und das Voelkerrecht** (Koeln, 1956); Albert N. Tarulis, **Soviet Policy Toward the Baltic Sates, 1918-1940** (Notre Dame, Ind., 1959); V. Stanley Vardys (ed.), **Lithuania Under the Soviets: A Portrait of a Nation,** 1945-1965 (New York, 1965); Leonas Sabaliūnas, **Lithuania in Crisis: Nationalism to Communism, 1939-1940** (Bloomington, 1972).

man of the Presidium of the Supreme Soviet (of Lithuania). He said, without any evasion:

> "The struggle of Lithuania's common people is tied to the struggle of liberation of the international proletariat, whose vanguard was always represented by the proletariat of the Soviet Union. These struggles and sacrifices had been fruitless for a long time, and would long have remained fruitless had it not been for the fraternal aid provided us by the ever fraternal and friendly peoples of the great Soviet Union and brought to us by the liberating Red Army." (*Liaudies Seimo Stenogramos* — The Verbatim Record of the People's Diet — 1940, page 34.)

That is why Paleckis, in the name of the expansion of Communism and the red imperialism of Russia, declared:

> "In the People's Republic of Lithuania, the Soviet soldier is greeted as the good and sincere comrade liberator and the carrier of culture."

He continued:

> "I emphasize once more our gratitude to the Soviet Union and to the Red Army, thanks to whom our common folk's ultimatum to the old plutocratic order was, at last, accepted and executed." (*Liaudies Seimo Stenogramos, supra,* p. 80.)

Realizing that the communists could not win and hold out in Lithuania without the support of the armed forces of the Soviet Union, Moscow's agents, and among them Sniečkus,[4] secretary of the Communist Party, proposed to incorporate

---

3. Justas Paleckis (1899—1980), a leftist journalist before World War II, was chosen to head the puppet People's Government by G. V. Dekanozov, Deputy Foreign Commissar of the USSR, who was sent to Lithuania to oversee the Soviet takeover. Paleckis' power was very circumscribed; he served mainly as a figurehead—first as a Prime Minister, later as Chairman of the Presidium, Supreme Soviet of the Lithuanian SSR. He remained a rather moderate communist, was even respected by many for his relatively national political orientation. He retired from active service in 1967. His memoirs in Russian: **V dvukh mirakh** (Moskow, 1974).

4. Antanas Sniečkus (1903-1974) was the most powerful individual in the Lithuanian Soviet regime. The son of a prosperous farmer, he

Lithuania into the U.S.S.R. In the People's Diet he stated:

> "Introduction of the Soviets or Councils in Lithuania could not of itself provide a firm guarantee of survival of a socialistic Lithuania. The common folk in Lithuania realize that such guarantee of survival can be provided only by their entrance into the family of the fraternal peoples of the Soviet Union. Having liberated our country, the glorious and invincible Red Army will guarantee the integrity of our frontiers." (*Liaudies Seimo Stenogramos, supra*, p. 25.)

The legal government of Lithuania (whose majority was deported to Siberia) was forced to resign and was supplanted by a provisional "people's government," with Paleckis, an agent of Moscow, at its head. This "government" was ordered to effect the political and social changes which the government of Moscow deemed timely and ripe.

Oddly enough, the "people's government" initially utilized the former constitution of an independent Lithuania, even though the latter's spirit was diametrically opposed to a communistic regime. But the end justified the means. According to Paleckis:

> "We are applying the selfsame instrument (the constitution) in behalf of the working people, against the people's enemies. The common people picked up the same stick, only by the other end." (*Ibid.*, p. 9)

"The vanguard of the proletariat," in whose name Moscow and the army of occupation operated in Lithuania, was in reality composed of 400 political and criminal prisoners, convicted of subversive activities against the Republic of Lithuania. The "people's government" discharged these prisoners as communists immediately after the Russian army of occupation entered. Most of them "at once enthusiastically united in the task of realizing the people's liberation and to guarantee it" (*Liaudies Seimo Stenogramos*, p. 13). These same poli-

---

became a member of the Communist Party in 1920. He was appointed to the secretariat in 1926 and served as the party's First Secretary from 1940 until his death. A fanatical communist, he nevertheless followed policies that could be defined as "republic-oriented." For an evaluation of Sniečkus' political role, see Part A, ch. 3 of this study.

tical prisoners composed the majority of the People's Diet, where, by Moscow's orders, they hastened to bury the independence of Lithuania and to incorporate her into the U.S.S.R.

According to Sniečkus, at that time Director of the Security Department and Chairman of the Credentials Committee of the People's Diet, who later became secretary of the Central Committee of the Communist Party-Bolshevik of Lithuania, 49 persons of a total of 78 deputies of the People's Diet, or 62.2 per cent of the entire membership of it, were formerly imprisoned in penitentiaries and detention places (for subversive communist activities) (*Liaudies Seimo Stenogramos*, p. 105). Nevertheless, it is of interest to note that such candidates were named and, moreover, elected in a country where, it may be said, there were no communists.[5]

Disregarding the opposition of the entire nation to the occupation and the boycott of the elections, the Communist Party alone drafted the slates of deputies and forced the people, by moral and physical coercion, to vote for such slates. One of the coercive threats was the stamping of the passports with "VOTED" or "DID NOT VOTE." Repressions were applied against those lacking the voting stamp — they were either driven to the polls or were discharged from work. When the majority refrained from voting, forgery was employed: election boards themselves stuffed the ballot boxes.[6]

It is well known that these methods, first tested in the Baltic States, were later employed in Central European states. Present events in Greece, China, and other countries show how a political minority, supported by external power of arms, manages to terrorize the majority. Fortunately, in those countries the external force faces the other force, which does not allow the violence to establish itself. But Lithuania at that time in 1940, or even now, could not avail itself of such a privilege or of moral and material assistance, as Greece or Turkey could,

---

5. According to official count, just prior to the Soviet occupation of Lithuania on June 15, 1940, there were 1,690 members in the Communist Party of Lithuania. See the statistical work of Party History Institute of the Central Committee of the Communist Party of Lithuania, **Lietuvos Komunistų Partija skaičiais** (Vilnius, 1976), pp. 41-2.

6. The election fraud is well documented by testimony of people involved in various phases of the proceedings in **Lietuvių archyvas: Bolševizmo metai** (Kaunas, 1942), Vol. 3, pp. 2-71.

in order to successfully resist Soviet violence and restore its most sacred rights.

The above-mentioned People's Diet, pressed by the occupational organs of Moscow, against the will of the Lithuanian people, adopted "the Stalin Constitution of the best model" (*Liaudies Seimo Stenogramos*, p. 10), which authorized the ultimate destruction of the political and social order of Lithuania by allegedly legal means. This was done on the sad days of July 21-23, 1940.

Consequently, within one month and one week of the Soviet occupation, a series of declarations was enacted pertaining to the state system, Lithuania's incorporation into the U.S.S.R., the nationalization of lands, industries, banks, and private real estate.[7] As a consequence of these cumulative measures, the inhabitants were impoverished — even their savings were confiscated.

Bearing in mind that about 80 per cent of the inhabitants of Lithuania earn their livelihood by farming, the nationalization of lands affected the largest segment of the population. Even though the agrarian reform enacted by independent Lithuania in 1922 left only 82 hectares of land as the largest norm of land holdings, which was small indeed, the Soviet government left a maximum of 30 hectares to an individual farmer. Since the second occupation in 1944 this norm is being gradually decreased. In preparation for the collectivization of land, propaganda and terror are directed against the so-called kulaks. The property of the farmers who had formerly owned in excess of 30 hectares of land (presently — in excess of 20 hectares) is confiscated and their families are evicted.

This Soviet type of "agrarian reform" is difficult for a civilized person to comprehend. This is not a simple statutory nationalization. It is an attempt to destroy the farmer and his family morally and physically, by taking away from him the right to any sort of livelihood. Namely, he can obtain no employment, no living quarters, no food, no ration cards, and

---

7. The most extensive documentation of Soviet rule in 1940-1941 is **Lietuvių archyvas: Bolševizmo metai** (Kaunas, 1942-1943), 5 vols. Although published during the German occupation of Lithuania and, therefore, biased in some respects, the series does contain basic factual data on the period.

his children are barred from secondary and upper schools. His road leads to the concentration camps in Siberia.

Privately owned homes of the city dwellers in excess of a 180-square-meter area were nationalized. The socialistic housing administration is notorious for its negligence. Many homes became unlivable for lack of repairs. For this reason there is a great housing shortage in the cities, as there is no incentive to build new homes.

Nevertheless, all these measures of socialization are nothing in comparison with the terror employed against practically the entire Lithuanian population.

In order to break down the morale and resistance of the Lithuanian people, the occupant soon conducted arrests and, on June 15, 1941, began mass deportations to Siberian labor and concentration camps.[8]   More than 40,000 people were deported in the period of 1940-41. Families were split up, husbands were separated from their wives and children. It was verified later that nearly all of the deported male exiles have died because of the unbearable treatment. To mask this crime before world public opinion, the organs of the NKVD compelled the exiles, during the war years, to sign statements that they had evacuated themselves for labor of their own will.

If the German atrocities are being prosecuted by the Allied Powers, — the atrocities being committed on a greater scope at this time by a member of the United Nations, the Soviet Union, should not be forgotten.

II. SOVIET OCCUPATION OF JULY 1944

After more than three years of a severe German occupation (1941-1944), the exhausted Lithuanian people, together with the entire world, believed in an Allied victory and expected a reconstitution of its independent state after the victory. How-

---

8. The deportation orders were written in such broad terms that up to 700,000 people, about 25 per cent of the population, could be defined as "enemies of the people." The start of World War II interrupted the planned purge and, according to Red Cross count, 34,260 persons were deported within less than a week. The 40,000 figure used in the memorandum probably includes persons deported earlier. See Lietuvių archyvas: **Bolševizmo metai**, Vols. 1-3, passim.

ever, our people were to fall under a second, harsher and more cruel Soviet occupation.

Having experienced the cruelties of the first Soviet occupation, masses of the Lithuanian population fled from their country before the approaching Red Army and repressions, hoping to be able to return soon to their own homes. However, more than three years have elapsed — and they are still unable to return to a free homeland.

Meanwhile, the people who remained in Lithuania are suffering a vengeance by the Soviet occupant and repressions which could only be invented by the experienced NKVD executioners.

Invading the territory of Lithuania for the second time in the summer of 1944, the Soviet occupant did not consider Lithuania an independent country and treated her as Soviet territory legalized by the first occupation. Furthermore, encouraged by their victory over the Germans, the Soviets began to rule without entertaining any international accountability for their actions. The Soviet counter-espionage, the NKVD and the NKGB, began to probe in a most cruel manner every Lithuanian inhabitant's behavior with respect to the Soviet rule and his behavior during the German occupation. The pretext for all sorts of charges was found under the banal yet convenient labels of a "people's enemy" or "war criminal."

Included among such war criminals were township employees and farmers who, under coercion by the occupant, had delivered requisitioned grain. Terror struck the entire country and all strata of the population with full force. During the first Soviet occupation the Soviets eliminated and exiled to Siberia mainly the people formerly active in the independent state, the state employees, and people known in political life. Presently, these measures are applied against all "people's enemies and war criminals." It is now convenient to apply the chapter on "counter-revolution" of the Penal Code and to mete out sentences of 10 to 25 years at hard labor in Siberia.

In this manner the mass deportations of 1940-1941 were replaced during the present occupation by the procedure of Military Tribunals. This procedure gradually fills the prisons and cellars of private homes with prisoners. These are deported in groups to Siberia, always making room for new parties of prisoners. This method of destroying a people is no less effective than mass deportations.

Is the United Nations Trusteeship Council intended for the protection only of the colonial areas and can it give no relief to an occupied country entitled to membership in the United Nations?

The war which raged in Lithuania cost her about one third of her inhabitants, and the alleged "vacuum" is deliberately filled in with Russian soldiers, civilian employees, and agriculturists. Diverse experts, instructors, and propagandists swarmed in. The Poles evacuated from the Vilnius district are supplanted by Russians.[9] Especially the counties of Vilnius, Trakai, and Švenčionys became objects of serious Russian colonization.

The capital city of Vilnius became the center of "Russian culture and progressive democracy" (Communism). Here resides the Soviet Council of Ministers, two thirds of whom are Russians from Moscow. Of the present 29 "Ministers", 15 are Russians; their deputies and counsels are nearly all Russians. It is of no importance ultimately that no Lithuanians are included in this Council of Ministers, inasmuch as all of them receive the same orders from Moscow. Ministries of the Union republics are mere agencies of the U.S.S.R. ministries, and they cannot function without an order from Moscow. The ministries of foreign affairs provided for in the Constitution of 1944 for the Union republics are merely fictional, intended to provide more voting delegates to the United Nations organization.[10]

---

9. Postwar Soviet estimates of population loss are set at 850,000 people (including the loss of natural increase). See A. Stanaitis, P. Adlys, **Lietuvos TSR gyventojai** (Vilnius, 1973), p. 13. According to an agreement between the Lithuanian SSR and the Polish Committee of National Liberation, signed on September 22, 1944, a total of 171,158 Poles transferred from Lithuania to Poland. M. Požarskas, **Tarybų Lietuvos ir Liaudies Lenkijos santykiai** (Vilnius, 1973), pp. 49-50. The Poles were more than replaced by Russians, Belorussians and Ukrainians. By 1959, there was an influx of at least 250,000 Slavs.—**Tarybų Lietuvos dvidešimtmetis** (Vilnius, 1960), p. 78.

10. Stalin sought recognition for the Soviet regime in Lithuania by suggesting that Lithuania be made a member of the United Nations, together with the Ukraine and Belorussia, and that the delegates of the Baltic republics be recognized in the Paris Peace Conference. Stalin's suggestion was turned down by the United States. See the study of the role of union republics in foreign affairs of the USSR by Vernon Aspaturian, **The Union Republics in Soviet Diplomacy** (Geneva, 1960), pp. 75-79.

The world is probably convinced by now that not only Union republics but the allegedly independent countries of Eastern Europe can have no "foreign policies"; only satellites of the Soviet Union are represented in the United Nations.

The situation prevailing in the Council of Ministers is duplicated in Lithuania's Supreme Soviet. Distribution by nationality of the deputies of this Supreme Soviet, "elected" on February 10, 1947, is to be noted.

In 1947, of the total number of 180 deputies of the Supreme Soviet, about 30 are Russians from Moscow. There is nothing surprising in the fact that Stalin, Molotov, Shcherbakov, and assorted Red Army and NKGB garrison commanders and representatives of the Russian administration are deputies to the Supreme Soviet of Lithuania.

The world would have been astounded to hear that Hitler, Ribbentrop, and Goebbels had become parliamentary deputies of, for instance, France. But under the "democratic" Soviet regime, similar facts are called "fraternal people's friendship." What a farce is made of the democracy of the Western World!

One might inquire why, after all, should these Russians of the Supreme Soviet outweigh the majority?

The Supreme Soviet is made up almost exclusively of communists who receive instructions from Moscow. The All-Union Communist Party's Central Committee is represented in the Communist Party of Lithuania by Shcherbakov, who directs the entire political apparatus in Lithuania.[11] Several nonparty deputies are included merely for the sake of public opinion that, besides the Communist Party, there is another party of "nonpartisans." Nevertheless, it is known that with the aid of the NKGB the six million communists of Russia rule over 160 million of the nonparty or anti-Soviet inhabitants of Russia. They even manage to cause trouble in other countries. Well-trained and well-paid agencies of the communists are operating everywhere, aiming to create a world revolution with the Soviet Union's assistance.

---

11. Vladimir Vasilevich Shcherbakov (1909—   ), worker in the Cadres Section of the Central Committee, CPSU, was sent to Lithuania in 1946 for "strengthening party and Soviet organizations of the republic." Apparently, he replaced M. Suslov as the Moscow plenipotentiary in Lithuania. No data are available on his career after 1947, and the Soviet Lithuanian sources are peculiarly silent on his role. Biographical sketch in **Sovietskaya Litva**, January 18, 1947.

After World War II the Soviet Union found a fertile field for communist expansion. This aim is served not only by the purely communistic ideas but by the ideas of Panslavism and even by the Orthodox Church. The Slav world, counterposing itself against the Western Christian world, finds excellent executors in the Balkan and Central European states.

The gains of the Soviet Union in Europe represent but a period of "marking-time" before a longer leap. Its propagandists, without the least reticence, are focusing their attention on disrupting the unity of America and England. It is proclaimed everywhere in the Soviet Union's possessions that, after the destruction of the British empire through liberation struggles, America alone would remain capable of resistance. But there, too, the Soviets expect to rear a fifth communist column to aid them at the proper moment. Strikes are organized in foreign countries and forces are massed for the decisive blow. Soviet Union propagandists brush aside the idea of a forthcoming war by stating that the Western powers would not attack it, as they do not want war; the war will be initiated only at a time chosen by the U.S.S.R. itself. Soviet propagandists boast of the Soviet might in the occupied countries, hoping that the occupied peoples would resign their hopes of liberation and assist in the destruction of the rest of the civilized world.

Time and terror, of course, slowly accomplish their task.

III. THE RESILIENCE OF THE LITHUANIAN PEOPLE

Since the very start of the second Soviet occupation and in spite of all the measures of terror and propaganda, the Lithuanian people have been resisting, morally and physically, Soviet influence and expansion and have remained faithful to the principles of the Western democracies. Even though during the last war Lithuania expected and aided the Allied victory, she nevertheless understood then the dangers threatening her and the rest of the world from the direction of the Soviet Union.

Therefore, after Germany was defeated, Lithuania — unable to defend her rights by legitimate means — engaged in an underground struggle. Inasmuch as the leaders of the underground organization which had struggled against the Germans were dispersed and its activities were disrupted, a new organization was born spontaneously for the struggle against the Soviet occupation and for the reconstitution of a democratic, free state of Lithuania.

This organization, uniting an absolute majority of the population, all freedom-loving Lithuanians of all social strata and convictions (except the communists), is the *Bendras Demokratinio Pasipriešinimo Sąjūdis (B.D.P.S.)* — the United Democratic Resistance Movement, directed by its Presidium This is the only legitimate voice of the will of the entire Lithuanian people. It also commands the underground armed forces which operate throughout the entire country. Lithuanian representatives, authorized by this Presidium, are acting abroad.

The Presidium of the United Democratic Resistance Movement hereby appeals to the United Nations and the Four-Power Foreign Ministers Council to raise openly in an international forum the question of the reconstitution of an independent and democratic Lithuania.

It requests the delegates of the organized and democratic world to answer the plea of the suffering three million Lithuanian people and to demand from the Soviet Union:

1. To withdraw the armed forces and the administration of the Soviet Union from Lithuania.

2. To stop the terror directed against the population of Lithuania.

3. To return the Lithuanian exiles from Siberia.

4. To recompense the damages inflicted through illegal occupation.

5. To conform to the Peace Treaty of 1920 and other treaties concluded between Lithuania and the U.S.S.R.

In order to assure the implementation of these measures, the United Democratic Resistance Movement requests the establishment of an international control agency.

The Lithuanian people will then be enabled to elect their government freely and without external pressure, as was assured in the Atlantic Charter and the United Nations Charter.

The Lithuanian people request of the Foreign Ministers Council that, when the final settlement of Germany and Europe will be under consideration and the frontiers of Germany shall be defined, due consideration be given to the eternal and historic title and interests of the Lithuanians in that

part of East Prussia which had been seized from the state of
Lithuania by the Teutonic Order.[12]

THE SEAL: BDPS PREZIDIUMAS

(Presidium of the UDRM)
Coat of Arms of Lithuania

(Signatures)

Gintautas
Algimantas
Jonas (surname illegible)
Petras Vytis
Vincas Kalvaitis
Žvejys
Kazys (surname illegible)

---

12. The Potsdam Conference placed the area in question under
Soviet control. Presently, it is a part of the RSFSR, called the Kaliningrad Oblast. The permanence of this territorial arrangement remains
in doubt. For details, see Martin Brakas, ed., **Lithuania Minor** ("Studia
Lituanica", Vol. 3) (New York, 1976), particulary the article by A.
Stikliorius, pp. 9-65. Private communications have indicated that Moscow
wanted to merge the area with Lithuania, but the Lithuanian communist
leadership allegedly rejected the offer on several occasions.

9. AN APPEAL TO BOYCOTT THE 1950 ELECTIONS

BROTHERS, SISTERS OF THE FAITH!

The Red demon, the deadly enemy of Christianity, is preparing "elections," thus seeking to strike another blow against the Christian world if everybody votes for him.

Brothers, sisters who have faith, do not vote. Do not trample upon your holy faith, your holy baptism through which you received the honorable name of a Christian and became members of the Church. If you believe, brothers, sisters, you cannot vote. You cannot denounce the Church, because the Movement of the Freedom Struggle of Lithuania informs you that during the previous summer Pope Pius XII has excommunicated, i.e., *separated from the Church,* all those who will vote for communist candidates or will themselves agree to be candidates.[1]

Therefore, brothers, sisters, resolve yourselves. Do not multiply the number of the godless—enemies of Christ, who are separated from the Church. In other words, *do not vote!*

The Movement of the
Freedom Struggle of Lithuania

No. 9. From **Žudikai bažnyčios prieglobstyje** ("Faktai kaltina," II) (Vilnius, 1963), 2nd rev. ed., pp. 243-244. The appeal is directed against the elections to the Supreme Soviet of the USSR, held on March 12, 1950.

1. Probably a reference to the Vatican decree on Communism of July 13, 1949. Text of the Vatican decree in the Royal Institute for International Affairs, **Documents on International Affairs, 1949-1950** (London, 1953), p. 416.

10. FROM A BULLETIN OF A PASSIVE RESISTANCE CENTER

INFORMATIONAL BULLETIN

Publisher: The Supreme Leadership of the Fighting Lithuanian Nation

November-December, 1950, Nos. 20-21

Freedom and Independence Through Unity and Truth

The fate of the Lithuanian nation during the more than ten years past dramatically reflects the crossroads, meanderings, darkness of global politics and that moral morass, from which all the nations of the world today are so painfully searching for a way out. Lithuania's independence, won by the efforts of the nation's best blood and will, was destroyed at the beginning of the last war by the most brutal and cynical means of violence and treachery by the neighboring Soviet Russia, which repeatedly had promised, in treaties and solemn declarations, to respect the sovereignty and territorial integrity of Lithuania. The last war was waged against totalitarian Fascism under the slogans of democracy, freedom, and justice. The Lithuanian people sincerely believed in these ideals and proved their faith by a determined united opposition by the entire nation to the German occupant's attempts to utilize our physical and moral resources for the goals of fascist world domination. To be sure, Fascism was crushed; but freedom and justice were not universally realized. Instead, the war and postwar years saw repression and arbitrariness extend to new areas and nations of Europe and Asia.

At the close of the war Lithuania was for a second time overwhelmed by the bolshevik colossus. Through comprehen-

---

No. 10. Copy of the bulletin obtained from the private collection of Mr. Bronys Raila. The Supreme Leadership of the Fighting Lithuanian Nation emerged around 1950 and adhered to a viewpoint similar to that of the United Democratic Resistance Movement (cf. especially Doc. No. 6). Very little information is available on the organization. Apparently it was a resistance center of several groups of intellectuals. The people associated with it cannot be revealed.

sive dynamic means of coercion, it sought to sweep away the foundations of Lithuanian statehood and the nation's moral existence. The Lithuanian nation could fight back against this mortal threat to their rights and existence only with moral weapons: the intense love of their country, their thirst for freedom and justice, their internal unity and solidarity, their Christian democratic humanism, a firm resolve, and their political flexibility. Open armed resistance, to the extent it was employed, proved to be politically imprudent. Although the nation's morale was raised by a few successes, armed opposition brought about premature and senseless losses to the partisans, severe reprisals of the enemy against wide strata of the population. Certain regrettable actions of the participants of armed resistance, carried out capriciously against their fellow countrymen who often were involved against their wish and will in the bolshevik reforms of land and property undermined the confidence of many decent Lithuanians in the political judgement and moral sensibility of the partisans.

The emancipation of the Lithuanian people from the bolshevik yoke and the reestablishment of independence is possible only during the course of a global armed conflict. Immediately after the war there were no realistic indications of such a conflict. The course of international politics is determined by the clash of interests among the major powers. A long time had to elapse and a long road had to be traveled before the differences between the Soviet Union (and world Communism under its leadership) and the great Western democracies became so great that today it is already possible to boldly assert that a conflict is not only possible, but also inevitable. However, it would be a grave error to rely on the likelihood of a conflict in the coming months. No one at this time can predict the exact date of a war's outbreak. The military preparations of the Western democracies are of a defensive nature, aimed at repulsing any future communist aggression. Due to its internal dynamics, Soviet Russia will be the initiator and aggressor in the coming war. Nevertheless, a realistic appraisal of the present military deployments by Soviet Russia provides no basis for drawing conclusions about the likelihood of a conflict in the immediate future.

Defeating Bolshevism militarily, though an essential precondition for our freedom, is beyond the physical means of the

Lithuanian nation. It is the major global powers that are concentrating their forces for the decisive struggle with Bolshevism. In the face of extreme hardships, the only realistic goal of the Lithuanian nation was and remains the preservation of its physical, moral, and material potential. The physical power of the Lithuanian nation should be utilized, in coordination with political means, only at that decisive moment when, in the course of the development of international politics and the anticipated war, the concrete conditions for the realization of statehood will materialize. A coordinated and united action, with competent leadership, is necessary to prepare for this task and at the same time to carry on the current opposition struggle with minimal losses. The Supreme Leadership of the Fighting Lithuanian Nation, relying on the best forces in the country and on stable ties with the most competent political centers and diplomatic missions functioning in the Western world, is in possession of all the necessary qualifications to carry on and lead this great and difficult struggle.

The Supreme Leadership of the Fighting Lithuanian Nation is convinced that the life of the future independent Lithuania can be ordered only according to the principle of democratic humanism, as it is understood in the Western world. Such a concept means that the Lithuanian nation itself will have the right to determine the political system and sovereignty of Lithuania. True to our democratic convictions, we do not seek partisan ends or the seizure of state power. At the same time we consider as politically incorrect and morally unfounded those ambitions and pretensions to sovereignty that are manifested by the center of political parties abroad.[1] However, the extent to which the activity of this center manifests itself in the defense of the Lithuanian case in the international arena, it is useful and worthy of backing. With great pleasure we note the successful work in the cause of Lithuania by the envoys of independent Lithuania, accredited by Western states.

As we pass into the year 1951, the Supreme Leadership of the Fighting Lithuanian Nation invites all good brothers and

---

1. Reference to the Supreme Committee for Liberation of Lithuania, which, operating in the West, was asserting the right to form a government in exile. In effect, this organization was rejecting the so-called Baden-Baden agreements (Doc. No. 1, note 17).

sisters of Lithuania in whose hearts the flame of the love of nation and the thirst for freedom has not as yet flickered out to a united endeavor in the cause of Lithuania's freedom. The current developments in global politics offer a realistic hope for our expectations and aspirations. Let us join our minds and hearts for the great and honorable march for freedom.

An International Review

In this period the development of international events resembles oceanic turbulence. International tensions seem to be rising and then ebbing, affecting in their turn the mood in the land.

More than once we have expressed the idea that one should not draw inferences from any single event or delivered speech. Political discourses may be more or less firm or ambiguous. The course of international events can be determined and conclusions drawn from it only on the basis of a comprehensive view of the events.

The political life of states cannot be perceived linearly. It twists and turns, deviates from its course, but primarily in accordance with the national interests. Therefore, one ought not to become excited or to ignore a given policy turn of the great powers.

We should observe whether or not the course of international events is proceeding favorably for the liberation of our country. At this time the answer is definitely yes; it is merely a matter of time. This is evident in current developments. How the Korean war of liberation will finally turn out is difficult to foresee, as the fortunes of this conflict are not certain and all kinds of unexpected events may yet come about. Nevertheless, communist China's military intervention furnished the impetus for the Truman-Atlee discussions, which resulted in a complete agreement between the US and England. Efforts by the Russians to drive a wedge between the US and England did not succeed. It was clearly evident to them that Russia is unscrupulously seeking world domination.

Eisenhower's appointment to head a common West European defense arrangement strengthened that area's military power and unity. Military outlays increased among the Anglo-Saxon bloc of states. All of these developments indicate that the world is arming intensively, that any agreement is impossible among such diametrically opposed regimes, that the language of diplomacy has lost its potency, and that peaceful means offer little hope of resolving international disagreements.

This was evident in the past session of the UN General Assembly. There, the Russian representatives delivered propaganda speeches to persuade the masses, and not the diplomats. It can be firmly stated that neither the Anglo-Saxon governments, nor their people desire war. Consequently, the so-called policy of quest for world peace, pushed by the Russians with a stubborn persistence, no doubt has the support of the masses, a factor which must be taken into account by the Anglo-Saxons. Because of their democratic disposition and their respect for individual rights, the Anglo-Saxons cannot prohibit the dissemination of Russian propaganda. One must also not overlook the fact that the Anglo-Saxons must deal with the workers' movement. We live at a time when the solution of the social question has become a primary concern. The United States, a genuine capitalist country that has not carried out social reforms, faces some problems in this respect, which, however, for the time being are well under control. Capitalism as a system will have to make concessions to social problems. There are also other problems, which must be dealt with by the Anglo-Saxon governments.

It is our understanding that only by viewing the course of world events in this manner will it be possible to determine the tactic and directions for our work.

Lietuvos TSR Vidaus Reikalų Liaudies Komisaro
ĮSAKYMAS

1946 m. vasario 15 d.   Vilnius

Didvyriškai Raudonajai Armijai išvadavus Lietuvos TSR nuo vokiškųjų fašistinių grobikų, Vidaus Reikalų Liaudies Komisariato organai ir kariuomenė, gyventojų bei liaudies gynėjų remiami, atliko didelį darbą lietuviškai-vokiškųjų nacionalistų gaujoms sutriuškinti.

Daugumoje apskričių sutriuškintos beveik visos gaujos ir nelegalios antitarybinės buržuazinės nacionalistinės organizacijos.

Lietuviškai-vokiškųjų nacionalistų vadai, bo mažų išimčių, suimti ar sunaikinti, o tie gaujų dalyviai, kurie apgaule arba grasinimų bei teroro verčiami buvo įtraukti į gaujas — pasidavė Tarybų valdžios organams ir sugrįžo prie ramaus darbo. Daugelis jų sąžiningu darbu išpirko savo kaltę Tėvynei.

Tačiau yra žinoma, kad kai kurie banditai pasidavė Tarybų valdžios organams ne savo noru, o gaujų vadų nurodyti; taipogi yra žinoma, kad jie ginklų neatidavė, tebepalaiko ryšius su savo vadais ir padeda lietuviškai-vokiškiesiems nacionalistams vykdyti jų žvėriškus darbus prieš ramius gyventojus.

Atsižvelgdamas į tai, kad kai kur dar tebėra lietuviškai-vokiškųjų nacionalistų likučių, kurie savo banditiškais veiksmais trukdo ramų piliečių gyvenimą, siekdamas galutinai likviduoti tuos lietuviškai-vokiškųjų nacionalistų likučius, —

ĮSAKAU:

1. Vidaus Reikalų Liaudies Komisariato apskričių ir valsčių viršininkams, Vidaus Reikalų Liaudies Komisariato kariuomenei ir liaudies gynėjų būriams tuojau imtis griežtų priemonių apvalyti visoms Lietuvos TSR apskritims nuo lietuviškai-vokiškųjų nacionalistų likučių.

2. Visiems savo noru pasiduodantiems banditams, jų tarpe ir gaujų vadams, LLA ir kitų buržuazinių nacionalistinių organizacijų dalyviams, po to, kai jie pasiduos ir atiduos ginklus, jokių represijų netaikyti, paleisti juos į savo namus ir išdėioti pasus.

3. Gaujų dalyviams, kuriems jų vadai banditai draudžia savo noru pasiduoti Tarybų valdžios organams, įsakau užmušti tokius vadus ir organizuotai atvykti su ginklais į Vidaus Reikalų Liaudies Komisariato įstaigas. Niekas iš asmenų, užmušusių banditų gaujų vadus ar eilinius banditus, trukdančius jiems pasiduoti, nebus traukiamas atsakomybėn.

4. Anksčiau pasidavusieji banditai, bet dar neatidavusieji ginklų, o taip pat kiti asmens, turintieji ginklus, — privalo sedelsdami atiduoti juos Vidaus Reikalų Liaudies Komisariato įstaigoms.

5. Banditų ir buržuazinių nacionalistinių organizacijų dalyvių, nepasidavusių Vidaus Reikalų Liaudies Komisariato įstaigoms, šeimas suimti ir ištremti.

6. Gyventojai, kurių namuose ir sodybose yra bunkerių ar kitokių slėptuvių banditams ir besislapstantiems nuo valdžios organų asmenims, — privalo neldsdami pranešti apie tai Vidaus Reikalų Liaudies Komisariato įstaigoms.

Asmenis, neatidavusius ginklų ir nepranešusius apie jų turimus bunkerius bei slėptuves, suimti ir teisti kaip banditus.

7. Asmens, žinantieji bunkerių ir slėptuvių vietas, nepriklausomai nuo to, kur tos slėptuvės būtų, privalo neldsdami pranešti apie tai Vidaus Reikalų Liaudies Komisariato įstaigoms.

Visus tuos, kurie, žinodami bunkerių bei slėptuvių buvimo vietas, nepranešė apie tai Vidaus Reikalų Liaudies Komisariato įstaigoms, suimti ir teisti kaip banditų pagelbininkus.

LIETUVOS TSR VIDAUS REIKALŲ LIAUDIES KOMISARAS
Generolas majoras BARTAŠIŪNAS

Spausd. „Spindulio" sp. Vilniuje 1946 m. Tiražas 150 000 egz. LV 00187. Užs. Nr. 8444

A photostatic copy of the 1946 NKVD amnesty for surrendering partisans. See Doc No. 2 for translation of this order.

Scenes from partisan life, ca 1947.

Scenes from partisan life, ca 1947.

A sampling of partisan press, 1946-47.

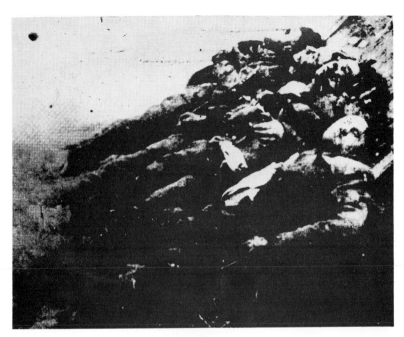

Bodies of fallen partisans displayed in a public square, a frequent deterrent practice of Soviet authorities. The photo is from a small town of Balbieriškis (district of Marijampolė), ca. 1946. Below, partisans at the graveside of their fallen comrades (1947).

Partisan courier Juozas Lukša (kneeling, left), escorted by a partisan unit to the Polish border while on a mission to the West (end of 1947). Lukša (left) with two accomplices while on intelligence training in Paris ca. 1950 before he was parachuted back to Lithuania by the CIA. Soviet display of money and documents allegedly found in the bunker where Lukša perished.

Julijonas Būtėnas, the leader of a second CIA mission to Lithuania in 1951. Soviet photos of weapons allegedly used by Būtėnas and the bunker in which Būtėnas commited suicide while under a siege.

Monuments of the Lithuanian resistance to Soviet rule: a cemetery of Lithuanian exiles somewhere in Siberia (1956 photo) and stone markers of partisan graves in Lithuania's countryside (a contemporary photo).

11. FROM A BULLETIN OF A PARTISAN COMMAND

Movement of the Freedom Struggle of Lithuania

Southern Lithuania Region

July 7, 1951

BULLETIN

The Question of Resistance

Every noble-hearted Lithuanian patriot, determined to fight to the end for the freedom and independence of his nation, is no doubt very much interested in the problem of our resistance. How is the heroic struggle of the Lithuanian nation viewed by the West? What have our political workers done in this area? What are the prospects and what finally is the direction of our resistance within our country as well as abroad?

What is the opinion of the Lithuanians abroad concerning the heroic partisan struggle?

In our opinion, these and similar questions have arisen repeatedly in the thoughts of every virtuous Lithuanian who has been bearing the yoke of the occupation for almost eight years. These questions are even more relevant to those, who with no thought for their strength and health and constantly surrounded by mortal danger, fearlessly and persistently battle the barbaric, ideologically bankrupt Asiatic occupant.

No. 11. Copy of the bulletin obtained from the private collection of Mr. Bronys Raila. A number of sensitive passages have been omitted. The Southern Lithuania region was commanded by A. Ramanauskas, who at that time was probably already serving as the leader of the Movement of the Freedom Struggle of Lithuania (Doc. No. 1, note 13). The partisan courier Lukša, who had returned to Lithuania in October of 1950, was active in that region. The bulletin represents a rather sharp attack on the proponents of passive resistance tactics, it is especially directed against the United Democratic Resistance Movement and its leader Jonas Deksnys. The militant course advocated by the MFSL was at least in part a consequence of US efforts to stimulate resistance behind the Iron Curtain. For a detailed discussion of this policy, see the introductory study.

We shall attempt to answer briefly these questions.

The problem of resistance in Lithuania became salient to our politicians abroad from the first days of the bolshevik occupation. However, it must be pointed out with regret and disappointment that for a long time this problem was being diversely treated because of local party and personal intrigues and also becasue an alien element intruded among the emigrés and in the Supreme Committee for the Liberation of Lithuania. Two opinions predominated: one proposed the tactic of passive resistance, limited to political propaganda and the supply of information abroad; the second, contrariwise, proposed a well-thought-out and organized active struggle against the occupant, of course without omitting information and systematic liaison with the outside. The proponents of the former opinion justified their line on the grounds that, allegedly, any active program evokes unnecessary sacrifices, repressions, and such. For this reason it is supposedly better to quietly await with ears pinned down "better weather from the sea", i.e., to cold-bloodedly watch the occupant devastate the country, deport the people, and rot thousands of decent Lithuanians in prisons. The second opinion, contrariwise, understanding full well that this is all the bolsheviks need—for the Lithuanians themselves to stick their heads into the yoke and to proceed, like the Jews to the ghetto, directed by executioners—completely correctly considered such passive tactics as detrimental to our national as well as state interests. It is not difficult to understand that the proponents of the passive line, who constitute a small group, were guided more by personal interests than by patriotism. Almost all of them, being paid, active intelligence agents of foreign states, engaged in a quiet speculation with the blood of Lithuanian partisans, receiving from them necessary information and selling it to foreign intelligence agencies, obviously not for nothing. And at the same time, without risking anything, they played the roles of "political workers," "Lithuanian patriots," and so on. Thus, for a long time, the conflict of these contradictory lines did not permit the Supreme Committee for the Liberation of Lithuania to function constructively. Only the heroic efforts of the Lithuanian partisans succeeded in correcting this abnormal situation.

In December of 1947, after overcoming a whole gamut of mortal dangers, two representatives of the Lithuanian partisans succeeded in breaching the Iron Curtain[1] and, with appropriate authorizations, finally establishing a direct link with the leading persons of the Supreme Committee for the Liberation of Lithuania and the most notable political leaders of Lithuania, Prof. Krupavičius, the ministers Lozoraitis, Balutis, and others.[2] The impression of the Lithuanian partisan representative was very sad: because of the intrigues of the Prapuolenis group,[3] disinformation, apathy, and inactivity were prevalent among the emigrés.

It was necessary to correct the situation. This was demanded by our national and state interests. Despite all the unpleasantness and at times almost police-like surveillance by Prapuolenis and his group, the representatives of the partisans succeeded in overcoming obstacles, in clearing the fog of disinformation...

As a result of these efforts, a consultation was called on July 8, 1948 in Baden-Baden, where an attempt to find a common coordinated line on resistance was made.[4] Unfortunately, even this attempt ended in failure because of the persistent intrigues of Prapuolenis among the Lithuanians in West Germany, Paris, and Stockholm. These intrigues went so far that Prapuolenis attempted to discredit the partisan representatives in the eyes of intelligence and military circles of certain powerful states. Of course, these attempts finally failed. The representatives of powerful states were finally convinced that the policy of passive resistance is wrong; the energetic activity and weighty arguments of Prof. Krupavičius and his unquestioned authority in Lithuanian problems obviously helped to achieve this. After the departure of Prapuolenis for Lithuania in 1949, which he also achieved as a result of intrigues, and it must

1. Reference to the mission of Juozas Lukša and Kazimieras Piplys, who reached the West in January of 1948.

2. Monsignor Mykolas Krupavičius (1885-1970), leader of the Lithuanian Christian Democratic Party, member of the Lithuanian parliament and government (1920-1926), was the Chairman of the Supreme Committee for the Liberation of Lithuania from 1945 to 1956. He was in favor of a militant course and apparently communicated this through Juozas Lukša to the MFSL. The title "Prof." for Krupavičius is an error.

3. Reference to Jonas Deksnys and the liaison center abroad of the United Democratic Resistance Movement. The attack on Deksnys and his associates is not justified by evidence available to this author.

4. See Doc. No. 1, note 17 for an explanation of the B-B agreement.

be stated that he organized this expedition very ineptly, the representatives of the Lithuanian partisans, with various assistance from Prof. Krupavičius and Dr. Aušra,[5] succeeded finally in steering the question of the resistance in Lithuania on the right course. After long vacillations, other noted personages and politicians of Lithuania—Foreign Minister Lozoraitis, the Plenipotentiary Envoys to England and the U.S., Balutis and Žadeikis, and others—also agreed with the new policy of active resistance...[6]

On his own part the representative of the Lithuanian partisans, Mr. Sk.,[7] completely succeeded in arranging an agreement with the military and political representatives of one powerful state to assure material and moral aid to the Lithuanian resistance, whose nucleus is the partisan movement.

Before departing for Lithuania Mr. Sk. could assert with satisfaction the fact that the new political line, emphasizing active resistance, is fully accepted and authorized by the Supreme Committee for the Liberation of Lithuania, which, after long organizational failures, finally evolved into a monolithic and unitary organ, representing the interests of Lithuania abroad and concentrating within its ranks the most noted Lithuanian political workers abroad, such as the Lithuanian Foreign Minister Lozoraitis and Plenipotentiary Envoys Balutis and Žadeikis; besides, he assured for himself comprehensive material and moral aid from one powerful state,[8] as well as the priceless moral support of the Holy See, with whom a close contact has been established...[9]

---

5. Dr. Aušra — Dr. Stasys Bačkis, a member of the Lithuanian diplomatic corps. At that time he served in a diplomatic capacity in Paris; presently he is the **Chargé de affaires a. i.** in the Lithuanian legation in Washington.

6. Stasys Lozoraitis, the Chief of Lithuanian diplomats abroad who were still recognized by a number of Western states, did not have the title of Foreign Minister. Numerous documents in private collections cited reject the contention that Lozoraitis and his colleagues in the diplomatic service favored a militant course. In fact, the opposite course was advocated, at least by Lozoraitis. Lozoraitis' viewpoint is presented in the introductory study.

7. Mr. Sk.—Skrajūnas—Juozas Lukša.

8. Obviously the United States. What the CIA specifically promised Lukša remains a secret.

9. No evidence is available to substantiate the claim of Vatican support for the partisan war.

*To Intensify the Struggle Against the Lithuanian Nation's
Hangmen and Their Fawners*

Brothers and Sisters. The hundred-headed dragon is mercilessly sucking the blood of the Lithuanian nation. For eight years now it is crushing our best sons and daughters with its dirty paw. Neither the gray-haired grandmother, nor the fair daughter of Lithuania, nor the innocent babe escapes its bloodsucking jaws. However, a Lithuanian is not one to be frightened by the bestial Asiatic. We are the descendants of Duke Margiris and Gražina and the great Vytautas, we are the offspring of Algirdas, before whom the bast-shoed Russians bowed low at the gates of Moscow.[10] No! The Lithuanians will not bow to might. The Lithuanian always loved freedom. He rather burned himself on a bonfire than enter into slavery. Awake, Lithuanian. Get rid of your toadyism and fear. The morning of freedom is breaking. Dark and great storm clouds are gathering in the West. They shall smash with thunder and lightning, they shall sweep from the holy land of Lithuania all foreigners and crush all the Lithuanian traitors and fawners. But you, Lithuanian, should not await the liberating storm by sitting on your hands. You must join this holy struggle against Bolshevism with weapon in hand.

Your task is to pursue vigilantly all the traitors of Lithuania and to punish them with utmost severity. The weeds must be uprooted from among the wheat so that they do not contaminate the harvest of the Lithuanian nation, which shall come after the battles for freedom. An eye for an eye, a tooth for a tooth. May the weaklings and straw-men tremble if they attempt to sell out their nation out of fear or treachery.

The partisan in the village is the stern judge of traitors and the protector and defender of all the suffering and oppressed. His accurate bullet must find the traitors everywhere, his strong hand must straighten out the cowardly and the vacillating.

Such a man must the partisan be.

---

10. Vytautas and Algirdas were powerful rulers of the Lithuanian state in the 13th-14th centuries. Margiris is the legendary duke of Pilėnai, who in 1336 refused to surrender to the invading Teutonic Knights and together with his defenders chose to perish in a fire. Gražina is a romantic literary heroine of the medieval struggles against the Teutonic invaders.

Lithuanian partisan, punish mercilessly those who have sold out their country, their nation for a crumb of gold, a spoon of good food. Remember that the blood of a traitor will never fall upon your head because you are fighting a holy war for national freedom and independence...

Remember, the dawn of freedom is near. Not far behind is the wrathful day of judgement for all traitors and weaklings, and the day of joy and happiness for all virtuous Lithuanians...

12. EXCERPTS FROM A PARTISAN PENAL CODE

The purpose of the Movement of the Freedom Struggle of Lithuania is the restoration of a free, independent, and democratic Republic of Lithuania. In pursuing this exalted and sacred goal, the Movement confronts painfully the violations of justice. However, justice is one of the most important means of strengthening its organizational order, defending Lithuanian nation. For this reason the Movement views attentively and sensitively the petitions and litigations of the freedom fighters and local population, which point out legal lapses and infringements, for the elimination of which it maintains the courts and the Penal Code.

Below are excerpts from the Penal Code of the Movement of the Freedom Struggle of Lithuania which pertain to the country's population:

1. General Rules

Par. 1 Any individual, whether a citizen of Lithuania or of a foreign state, or a member of the Movement of the Freedom Struggle of Lithuania, who, during the course of the present red occupation, should by his actions cause harm to the Lithuanian people and to the Movement of the Freedom Struggle of Lithuania in their efforts to defend Lithuanian interests and fight the Lithuanian nation's enemies for the restoration of an independent Lithuania, shall be penalized by the courts of the Movement of the Freedom Struggle of Lithuania.

Par. 3 Individuals who are not members of the Movement shall
be penalized with:
a) confiscation of property,
b) a reprimand and
c) the death penalty.
Note: penalty a) may be accompanied by penalties
b) and c).

No. 12. From the partisan bulletin **Partizanas,** July 20, 1951 (No. 6-20), organ of the Southern Lithuania region of the Movement of the Freedom Struggle of Lithuania.

III. Penal Code for Individuals Outside the Movement
A. Classes of Crimes and Penalties

Par. 55 Anyone guilty of spying against the activities of the MFSL and passing on directly or indirectly the collected information to the organs of the occupational regime, or consciously harming in some way the MFSL, shall be subject to the d e a t h p e n a l t y.

Note: if property is possessed, part of it shall be confiscated.

Par. 56 Anyone guilty of revealing the daytime presence of the partisans to the enemy shall be subject to the d e a t h p e n a l t y.

Note: if property is possessed, part of it shall be confiscated.

Par. 57 Anyone guilty of poisoning, killing, or conspiring to poison partisans shall be subject to the d e a t h p e - n a l t y.

Note: if property is possessed, part of it shall be confiscated.

Par. 58 Anyone guilty of denouncing the populace to the organs of the occupation administration for reasons of revenge or personal gain, if even one inhabitant be under arrest or suffer exile, now or in the past as a result of the denunciation, shall be subject to the d e a t h p e n a l t y.

Note: if property is possessed, part of it shall be confiscated.

Par. 59 Anyone guilty of utilizing his position to consciously uproot national consciousness from a compatriot's heart and inculcate in him the spirit of assimilationism, shall be subject to the d e a t h p e n a l t y.

Note: if property is possessed, part of it shall be confiscated.

Par. 60 Any official of the occupational administration, who cruelly carries out the measures of the occupational administration against the local populace, shall be subject to the d e a t h p e n a l t y.

Note: if property is possessed, part of it shall be confiscated.

Par. 61 Anyone guilty of using force against a freedom fighter in the line of duty, or threatening him with force or death, (fully realizing he is a partisan), shall be subject to the d e a t h p e n a l t y.

Note: if property is possessed, part of it shall be confiscated.

Par. 62 Anyone guilty of banditry, whether armed or not, alone or in a band, shall be subject to the d e a t h p e n a l t y.

Note: if property is possessed, part of it shall be confiscated.

Par. 63 Anyone guilty of unknowingly passing on erroneous information regarding the enemy to the members of the Movement, shall be penalized with a r e p r i - m a n d.

Note: if property is possessed, part of it may be confiscated.

Par. 65 Anyone guilty of not carrying out the Movement's public injunctions or individual partisans' rightful demands shall, taking into account the significance of the consequences, be subject to penalties, maximum being the d e a t h p e n a l t y.

Note: if property is possessed, part of it may be confiscated.

Par. 66 Anyone guilty of revealing to individuals, who have no need to know, any secret that is entrusted to him or fortuitously come upon concerning the Movement's activities, its members' whereabouts and movements, their relatives' or other courageous compatriots', when they are evading the occupying administration's organs or secret police, shall be penalized with a r e p r i m a n d.

Note: if property is possessed, part of it may be confiscated.

Par. 67 Anyone guilty of unknowingly (not comprehending the gravity of his offense) using the Movement's name (impersonating a partisan) for his personal purposes shall be penalized with a r e p r i m a n d.

Note: if property is possessed, part of it may be confiscated.

Par. 68 Anyone guilty of harming the interests of the Lithuanian nation, or by his actions causing exceptional harm to spiritual and material values of the Lithuanian nation, but having already ceased his harmful actions against the Lithuanian nation for at least a year, may be exempt from the penalties of this code, but he is not immune from the responsibility of his actions when Lithuania's independence will be restored.

— — —

Note: Anyone guilty of infringing on par. 63, 66 and 67 of this code by premeditated offenses and, having been penalized with a reprimand, but has repeated the same offence, shall now be subject to the d e a t h p e n a l t y.

13. FROM A REPORT OF A PASSIVE RESISTANCE CENTER

Right from 1946 there were two principal directions regarding the tactics of the resistance struggle in the land: a) radical tactics of open armed opposition and b) passive political resistance. The former gave scant consideration to the laggard development of international political trends favorable to us and disregarded the vital objective interests of the majority of the nation to preserve itself physically and morally. The latter saw its primary task in the conservation of the nation's physical and moral potential, endeavoring to prepare for the decisive work of liberating the nation and restoring its statehood...

Before assuming the leadership of the underground and formally committing ourselves before our country and beyond our borders, we discussed and analyzed the current situation at great length. Only after the political and tactical direction was clarified, and having the endorsement of the principal underground forces and the confidence of both our foreign and emigré officials, was, at the end of 1950, the actual and final structuring of the leading center (which in fact had been in operation for some time) completed.

As previously announced, the work of the leadership is carried out by means of four sections: military, foreign, organizational, and civilian. The leadership enjoys the full confidence or small but authoritative resistance groups, especially among the older intelligentsia in Kaunas, Vilnius, Šiauliai, and elsewhere. Through Mr. X we secured the support of the hierarchy of the Catholic Church. At present the question of appointing a permanent representative of the Church hierarchy is being considered. More difficult is the use of secondary school and university students for organizational purposes. Because they lack experience, the youth fall prey to MGB provo-

No. 13. Copy obtained from the private collection of Mr. Bronys Raila. A number of sensitive passages have been omitted. The report was signed by the Head of the Foreign Section of the Supreme Leadership of the Fighting Lithuanian Nation, whose identity has not been revealed. The report was sent to the liaison center in the West, originally established by the United Democratic Resistance Movement. The reporting organization is apparently distinct from the UDRM, although similar in viewpoint (cf. Doc. No. 10).

cations and are more susceptible to the poison of Soviet propaganda.

For some time the leadership published a triweekly bulletin of directives, but, at present, it has been discontinued. This was done to prevent the MGB from exposing our organization. Now public sentiment is formed and our line is propagated through personal contact, by word of mouth. It is impossible to expand the organizational structure to the periphery of our land on account of the strong and well-developed MGB network and the increasing number of their supporters as a result of the protracted bolshevik occupation. However, the influence and weight of our allied organizations assure that at the appropriate time they will be sufficient to play a decisive role in the leadership of the liberation and the restoration of Lithuania's statehood.

The integration of the partisans and the political resistance movement into one organizational structure and direction is not possible. By their open armed activities, the partisans are exposing themselves, their liaison men and supporters. They no longer represent the aspirations or interests of substantial segments of the population. They denounce the urban population as "Bolshevik lackeys". In the rural areas the farmers who are struggling to survive physically and materially call the partisans the scourge of God. In this situation the partisans can no longer be counted on as present or future political factor. Nevertheless, in order to prevent needless losses and to safeguard national solidarity, we are doing our utmost to assist the partisans with counsel, suggestions, and directives. Occasionally we meet with success here. The arrival of Skrajūnas and his friends poured more oil on the fire. New acts of terrorism occurred throughout the land, followed by MGB search-and-destroy missions, and partisans in the rural areas being killed and their supporters arrested and deported.[1]

Knowing well the situation of our country; the public sentiment, interests, and aspirations; and also following the development of international relationships without excessive optimism, we base our activities on the following premises:

1. The cause of Lithuania's freedom depends completely

1. Reference to Juozas Lukša and the intensified partisan activity after his return to Lithuania. The MGB counteraction is confirmed in Doc. No. 14.

on the consequences of a possible international conflict. To incite the Lithuanian people now or at the beginning of a future war against Bolshevism would be a gross error and crime. The Lithuanian nation cannot by itself undertake the destruction of world Communism. An uprising of the Lithuanian people against the Soviet Union is to be sought only on the condition that the massive action of the Lithuanian nation would lead to the realization of our national aspirations and those for our statehood.

2. An increasing number of individuals are drawn into the process of consolidating the bolshevik regime as a result of the long period of bolshevik occupation and the complex and sophisticated apparatus for propaganda and education at its disposal. We must also concede that, over time, the bolsheviks are succeeding to a certain extent in inculcating their ideology into the spirit of our nation, especially the youth. We must look at this painfully tragic situation with open eyes and hearts. It would be an irreparable mistake if a small part of the nation, e.g., that living under the different conditions of emigration, would try to lay the blame upon the entire nation. That could lead to the greatest mutual antagonization and chaos. Be that as it may, the foundation of Lithuania's freedom remains in the roots of the nation in this land; the entire painful bolshevik legacy will have to be resolved in this land, and we are not free to break away from the nation, regardless of the situation in which it may be.

3. Heeding all the imperatives of conspiracy and caution, we aim at the following objectives: to resist the consolidation of bolshevik rule in Lithuania, to keep alive in the people the longing for freedom and statehood, and, most important, to prepare for the future, when our efforts will bring about decisive results...

Success in the work of the Supreme Leadership depends to a great extent on financial aid. For this reason your support was vitally important. We once again thank you for it. Besides the financial aid, for the orientation of the Supreme Leadership, the preparation for future tasks, and the implementation of the policy of preserving national strength, it is important for us to receive from you evaluations of the international situation, analyses of domestic and foreign problems, and reviews and clippings of the world and Lithuanian press...

April 23, 1952

14. FROM THE TESTIMONY OF A SOVIET BORDER GUARD OFFICER

Mr. McTigue. What was your next assignment, Colonel, after the deportation operation?

Lieutenant Colonel Burlitski. After the deportation operations were finished, my unit as well as many other units were transferred to the territory of the Lithuanian Republic, in order to fight the so-called bandit-movement.

Mr. McTigue. The so-called bandit-movement was the resistance movement against the communists in Lithuania, is that correct?

Lieutenant Colonel Burlitski. Absolutely so.

Mr. McTigue. When were you assigned to Lithuania? When did you come there?

Lieutenant Colonel Burlitski. After the deportation of the Crimean Tartars, either at the end of June or beginning of July of 1944.

Mr. McTigue. Will you tell us something about what happened there?

Lieutenant Colonel Burlitski. After the Red Army had occupied Lithuania and the Germans had left, the Soviet Government started creating a party and administrative apparatus for Lithuania, beginning with the Central Committee of the Communist Party in Lithuania at the top, and going all the way down to the smallest village.

The absolute majority of the Lithuanian people did not want this party and administrative Soviet apparatus. The more advanced part of the population organized itself in what the Soviets called bandit gangs, and these so-called bandit groups disposed of and liquidated the Soviet party and administrative representatives. They killed them. It is characteristic that these so-called bandits liquidated and disposed of the party leaders

No. 14. From US Congress, House of Representatives, Select Committee to Investigate Communist Aggression and the Forced Incorporation of the Baltic States into the USSR, 83rd Cong., 2nd Ses., **Hearings, Fourth Interim Report** (Washington, 1954), pp. 1368-1374. This is a part of the testimony of Lt. Col. Grigori Stepanovich Burlitski, who was in command of the 2nd Batallion, 668th Soviet Border Guard Division of the MVD until his defection to the West in June of 1953. James T. J. McTigue was the Counsel of the Committee; Charles J. Kersten of Wisconsin—the Chairman.

and the administrative leaders, but only those who were actually Lithuanians, because they considered that these people were traitors to their own country. And these resistance groups did not touch, did not molest the representatives of the party and the government who were Russians, Ukrainians, or belonged to other nationalities of the Soviet Union. In order to strengthen the party apparatus and the government apparatus at the various levels in the various command levels of the Lithuanian Republic, the Soviet Government sent a great number of troops into Lithuania.

Within these many units which were transferred to the region of the Lithuanian Republic was also my unit.

From July 1944 to February 1945 I participated in the fight against the so-called bandits. I was in a few counties in my work in Lithuania. I was in the territory of Vilnius County, Tauragė County, Šiauliai County, Kaunas County, Urburg County,[1] and many others.

Mr. Kersten. These so-called bandits were the young men, young Lithuanian patriots trying to fight for the independence of their nation of Lithuania; is that not right?

Lieutenant Colonel Burlitski. Absolutely correct. But these so-called bandits were supported by the other majority of the Lithuanian population. At the very beginning in the territory of the Lithuanian Republic there were a great number of the so-called bandit formations; they were very numerous and consisted of many people. They were armed with light weapons. The weapons were both of Soviet and German manufacture; they also had machine-guns, heavy machine-guns, Soviet machine-guns, type Maxim, and they also had the German machine guns, which were manufactured in Czechoslovakia in the Skoda Works. Some of the Lithuanian guerilla fighters were also armed with light artillery. In some places into the fight against the bandits were thrown not only the NKVD units but also regular Red Army units and aviation. This particularly applies to the region of Kazlų Rūda not far from the city of Kaunas, in the region of the city of Kaunas. Time had passed by, the troops were becoming more and more fatigued, the fight continued, and yet the local Soviet government and

---

1. There is no such county in Lithuania, possibly a reference to Jurbarkas.

the party apparatus had not been established at all echelons. The so-called bandits were very difficult. They were impossible to catch. Knowing very well the territory in which they operated, and having the support of the local population, they knew exactly what we had in mind, what we planned; when we were loading people on trucks to conduct an operation against these bandits, and they also had information in their possession and left the place where they were to get into the forest to join a fight with us only when it was absolutely necessary. However, whenever they had a chance, they of course, tried to win a fight, and that lasted approximately till September 1944. When the Soviet government saw that it was not achieving any results, the Soviet government made the following decision in September 1944 in the Lithuanian city of Panevėžys; with a special assignment and special rights this brought the deputy to Beria, General Kruglov.[2]

Mr. McTigue. Is General Kruglov the individual who has succeeded Beria?

Lieutenant Colonel Burlitski. That is the same one.

Mr. Kersten. As I understand it, Serov and Kruglov have succeeded Beria; is that correct?

Mr. McTigue. Before you proceed, it is true, then, up to this point, that the Lithuanian bandits, or the partisans were fighting the communists and had been very, very effective; is that correct?

Lieutenant Colonel Burlitski. Yes.

Mr. McTigue. They had become so effective, as a matter of fact, that the Kremlin had lost patience with the whole operation in Lithuania; is that correct?

Lieutenant Colonel Burlitski. Absolutely correct.

Mr. McTigue. And in losing its patience, the Kremlin decided to send into Lithuania its top man, Kruglov, to enforce the laws or the operation in its most stern manner; is that correct?

---

2. Gen. S. N. Kruglov was a top operative of "Smersh"—a special political police established during the war to deal with enemies and potential enemies of the regime, especially in reconquered territories. In 1946 Kruglov was appointed chief of the MVD. He served in this capacity until March 1953, when he was demoted to Deputy Minister under Beria. Ronald Hingley, **The Russian Secret Police** (New York, 1970), **passim.**

Lieutenant Colonel Burlitski. Correct.

Mr. McTigue. Proceed, Colonel, please.

Lieutenant Colonel Burlitski. On a very dark September night, in the city of Panevėžys, Kruglov calls in a top-secret operational meeting. At this meeting there are present the commanders of the units of NKVD troops, the deputies of these commmanders for political affairs, for intelligence, and also the chiefs of staff of the units, the responsible top leaders of the territorial units of the NKVD in Lithuania. At this meeting Kruglov summarized the results of the fight against the so-called bandit movement in Lithuania and said that up to the present time the measures which have been undertaken have not proved to be realistic, that the Politburo of the Soviet Union and Stalin and Beria themselves are not satisfied with the result of what has been achieved in Lithuania, and that it is time to change from words to sharp measures; that order must be brought into Lithuania and that the party and the administrative Soviet apparatus must be reestablished in Lithuania. In the name of Stalin and Beria, Kruglov gives a concrete order that the work of intelligence agents must be intensified and activated.

He orders not to spare any efforts and not to spare any money to create an agents' net, to find out the base and the leadership of the so-called bandit movements, also, who helps and assists them, and to liquidate this base of operations, and he said that, and I quote: "Enough of this sentimental approach, of this sentimentality," and to use all necessary measures in order to get all the information and to brook no interference and to use whatever means are necessary in order to get information from the partisans themselves, from their relatives, or from the people whom the partisans use for liaison purposes. He also ordered that the troops become more active in their fight against the so-called bandits. He told them to comb through the forests, through clearings in forests and villages and he also ordered that during this so-called combing-through operation, if somebody tries to make a getaway even though he is not armed, if he tries to run away, this particular person is to be considered a bandit. The kind of person who tries to run, although he is not armed—against these people firearms are to be used and they are to be killed without any further ado. No court is necessary for them. If these people happen to take refuge or run into a house or into a farm or into a village, then this particular house or farm or village is to be considered a bandit farm, a bandit house or a bandit village, and those houses or farms or villages are to be destroyed by fire. Property and domestic animals which happen to be in this particular farm or house or village which is to be considered bandit are to be confiscated, and turned over to the local party apparatus or local Soviet apparatus. At the end of the meeting Kruglov expressed the hope in the name of the Central Committee of the Soviet Union and also in the name of the Commissariat of Internal Affairs, that this noble assignment which was given to the troops and to the operational organs of the NKVD to liquidate the bandits will be fulfilled by everyone concerned, and after Kruglov left, all the measures which he had ordered were introduced, were actually used.

(The committee reconvened at 2:15 p.m.)

Mr. Kersten. Hearings will come to order. I think we left off at the point the witness was speaking of the orders that came from General Kruglov about the stern measures that were to be applied against the Lithuanian partisans. Will you continue, Colonel Burlitski, now, and tell us of the events in Lithuania following these orders or just where you left off in your statement this morning.

Lieutenant Colonel Burlitski. After the meeting at which Kruglov presented his demands and his orders, the Lithuanian government, that is, the Soviet Lithuanian government, military units which were located at that time in the territory of Lithuania and territorial units of the NKVD which were at that time in Lithuania began fulfilling the orders of Kruglov. Besides these measures, the Soviet government undertook some other measures. For instance, at the Central Committee for the Lithuanian Communist Party, the Soviet government had created a bureau, the ORG Bureau, organizational bureau, This ORG Bureau which was established by the Soviet government was headed at that time by a member of the Central Committee of the Communist Party of the Soviet Union and now one of the secretaries of the Communist Party of the Soviet Union, Suslov.[3] This ORG Bureau actually was the

---

3. The Bureau of the Central Committee, All-Union Communist Party (b), was set up on November 11, 1944. The Bureau, under the direction of M. Suslov, operated at least until 1946. Its existence and role, described by Burlitski, is acknowledged by Soviet sources. See, for example, **Lietuvos TSR istorija** (Vilnius, 1975), Vol. 4, p. 146.

supreme party, exercised party leadership, and was superior in its functions and in its rights to the Central Committee of the Communist Party of the Lithuanian Republic. The aim of this organizational bureau, or ORG Bureau, was to exercise actual and factual power in the entire territory of the Lithuanian Soviet Socialist Republic. The chief aim of this organizational bureau was to strengthen and to resurrect the party and the administrative apparatus in the entire territory of the Soviet Socialist Republic of Lithuania.

This ORG Bureau had as its principal aim the liquidation, the securing of the power and liquidation of the so-called bandit movement in the territory of Lithuania. This ORG Bureau in actuality took over the entire political, administrative, and economic life of the republic. Any kind of orders or directives which were issued by this Suslov were a must for the government of Soviet Lithuania. Besides that, the Soviet government undertook another measure. The Central Committee of the Communist Party in Lithuania, together with the Soviet government of Lithuania, issued a joint appeal to the so-called bandits in Lithuania. This appeal contained a statement which said that the so-called Lithuanian bandits should leave their underground lairs and their forests and should report to the territorial organs of the NKVD of Lithuania, with a statement that they repent their sins. Those people who obeyed this appeal were promised a guarantee that they will be independent; that they will have freedom, and that they will receive Soviet documents. These people were told that they were supposed to give up their weapons and to indicate to the territorial organs of the NKVD where the headquarters of the underground movement is located; where depots for arms are located; who leads these underground formations of Lithuanian guerrillas, and so on.[4] Those were the measures, the steps which were undertaken by the Soviet government.

After this the party apparatus from all the way up, from the Central Committee of the Communist Party of Lithuania which is top echelon, all the way down, and the administrative Soviet agencies have started practically to carry out the orders

---

4. Probably a reference to the joint party-government appeal "To the Lithuanian Nation" of February 9, 1945 (see Rakūnas op. cit., p. 191). Also a possible reference to the amnesty order of February 15, 1946, published as Doc. No. 2.

given to them by Kruglov. A wave of executions and torture started. The people who formed the base of this bandit movement were deported to far-away regions of the Soviet Union, the setting on fire of various villages.

The leadership of this so-called bandit movement, seeing what is happening; these people, seeing how the Lithuanian people were being exterminated, how villages were burned, how cattle was destroyed, made a decision to go and leave the underground; to abandon and to give up some of their units, to let them go and temporarily abandon any kind of active operations. All this in order to preserve the people, the leadership, and the population for a future fight.[5] The Soviet government, utilizing this decision of the leadership of the underground, used this opportunity in order to resurrect the party and administrative apparatus all over Lithuania, and this so-called bandit movement was weakened, but never completely liquidated, and as far as I know, up to 1953 it still existed. That is all.

Mr. McTigue. Colonel, did your men, who were highly disciplined soldiers, ever get sickened by the things that they had to do in connection with the reign of terror in Lithuania?

Lieutenant Colonel Burlitski. At that time, that was 1944 and 1945, I had not seen any open signs of revulsion on the part of my soldiers.

Mr. McTigue. Did you see any later?

Lieutenant Colonel Burlitski. In April of 1945 my unit and I were transferred to East Prussia on the border of Poland, and in April of 1949 I was again returned to Lithuania, to the region bordering on Poland. During 1950-51 the entire fight against the so-called bandit movement of Lithuania was entrusted to two MVD divisions, so-called divisions for special tasks—the 2d and 4th Special Tasks Divisions. The headquarters of the 2d Special Task Division was located at Vilnius, and the commander was General Vetrov, and the 4th Division for Special Tasks is located in the city of Šiauliai and the commander of this division is General Piashov. These 2 divisions, under the command of the two generals I just mentioned, are actually doing all the work and all the fighting against the so-called bandit movement in the territory of the

---

5. This is a rather accurate assessment of partisan policies (see Daumantas, op. cit., p. 117).

Soviet Socialist Republic of Lithuania, of course, in connection and cooperation with the local units of the MVD. In 1949-51, from the members of these two divisions which I have just mentioned, there were many occasions when soldiers, sergeants and even officers, in fulfilling these horrible tasks which were given them by the government, deserted as a sign of protest. And the orders to comb through the various forests in order to search for these so-called bandits, these soldiers fulfilled only formally, superficially. These soldiers, in doing it, were holding onto an old soldier's proverb which reads, "One day passed by," which means it is one day nearer to the time when I become civilian again.

Mr. McTigue. Who was the most famous and troublesome Lithuanian, Colonel, in your experience among the partisans?

Lieutenant Colonel Burlitski. The most troublesome and the acknowledged leader of the entire so-called Lithuanian bandit movement was a Lithuanian by the name of Miškinis. The Lithuanian people considered this Miškinis to be a national hero, and he had a tremendous authority among the Lithuanian people. As far as the fight against the Miškinis group is concerned, I know something which happened during the years 1946-50. From 1948 to 1949 and 1950, during these years, according to the information which was supplied by the territorial organs of the MVD, it was said that Miškinis has finished a two-year intelligence course in an American school, and in 1950 came back to Lithuania, was dragged back to Lithuania, and as at that time in the neighborhood of the Prensky forests. In order to liquidate his group and him, a lot of troops were concentrated, brought together. The operations for the capture and liquidation of Miškinis were all led by Kruglov himself. He was in charge of the entire operation. Having been surrounded and having found himself in an absolutely hopeless situation, in accordance with information from territorial organs of the MVD, Miškinis committed suicide.[6]

---

6. "Miškinis"—literally "man of the woods." From this account, it is quite obvious that Burlitski was referring to Juozas Lukša. There is no evidence that Lukša committed suicide. Burlitski may be confusing Lukša with another partisan from the West-Julijonas Butėnas—who did take poison when surrounded by security forces. According to Soviet sources, Lukša was killed (Chienas, et al., **Vanagai iš anapus**, p. 241).

15. SOVIET MEASURES TO BREAK NATIONAL RESISTANCE

MIKHAIL SUSLOV—THE SECOND HANGMAN OF LITHUANIA

On the second day of the German-Russian war (June 23, 1941), almost all of Lithuania was in the hands of Lithuanian insurrectionists. (More than four thousand Lithuanian partisans died.) Because of this the German Army's losses in Lithuania were very insignificant. Yet despite this the Germans considered Lithuania an occupied territory and dismissed the Provisional Goverment.[1] This action evoked the resistance of the Lithuanian populace against the new occupier. On May 13, 1942, the chief of police of Marijampolė, Schwarz, wrote to his superior in Kaunas concerning this resistance. He described the public demonstration of the people of Marijampolė that occurred when the Germans began to draft Lithuanians into auxiliary units of their army: "... between 3,000 and 4,000 people, two-thirds of them women and girls, came and started shouting to those detained: 'We are not Germans, do not go to the front,' and the like. Some of the draftees tore the white armbands from their arms, threw them on the ground, and stamped on

No. 15. This article by an anonymous author first circulated in Lithuania as a samizdat pamphlet. A copy of it reached the West and is translated here. The sources at the end of the article are provided by the anonymous author, indicating that the author had access to classified archives. The article was published in a slightly abbreviated version in the underground publication **Varpas** (The Bell), probably in 1975. It also appeared in another samizdat publication **Aušrelė** (The Little Dawn), dated February 16, 1978, which in turn reprinted the article from another samizdat journal **Laisvės Šauklys** (The Herald of Freedom). The article is the most comprehensive underground statement available on the postwar Soviet efforts, esp. under the leadership of Mikhail Suslov, to establish control over the widely resisting population. The measures taken by the Soviet authorities suggest the intensity and magnitude of the partisan warfare and resistance among the population. The title of the article refers to another analogous pacifier of the Lithuanian nation— Governor General Mikhail Muravyov—who directed the suppression of the 1863 revolt in Lithuania against the czarist rule.

1. The aim of the Lithuanian insurrectionists was to reestablish Lithuania's independence ahead of the advancing German occupiers. The Provisional Government was proclaimed to the nation over the radio on June 23rd. However, the Nazi plans for Lithuania excluded even the

them. At that moment seventy percent of the students from the Marijampolė Teachers' Academy and the high school arrived to support the demonstration. They assembled and sang the Lithuanian National Anthem, Lithuanian folk songs, and massed in the streets to march in a column into the city. They stoned a truck filled with soldiers of the Wehrmacht, which was driving in that direction. At this time the demonstrators unfurled flags and carried them in the column... while the National Anthem was being sung the policemen stood at attention, and two of them wept..."

Regardless of this and other acts of resistance against the occupiers by the Lithuanian nation, all realized that the returning bolsheviks would doubtlessly avenge themselves on the Lithuanian nation for the insurrection of June 23. Therefore, Soviet propaganda spared no efforts to calm our nation, so that, seized by fear, it would not mobilize and, fully armed, stand together with the German occupiers to meet "the liberating army."

On December 2, 1943, Moscow released "An Appeal to the Lithuanian Nation," signed by A. Sniečkus, J. Paleckis, and M. Gedvilas,[2] which began with the following words: "Lithuanian brothers and sisters!" It enumerated the achievements of the Lithuanian nation in the struggle against the German occupiers and then these reassurances followed: "Do not believe the lies of the Germans and the followers Kubiliūnas[3] that

---

possibility of autonomy and by August 5th the Provisional Government dissolved itself without achieving its political aims. Lithuania became a part of the German Ostland. For an account of the revolt, see Algirdas Martin Budreckis, **The Lithuanian National Revolt of 1941 (**Boston, 1968). A very valuable documentation of the revolt, especially on the German attitude toward it, is available in the memoirs of the leader of the insurrection Kazys Škirpa: **Sukilimas Lietuvos suverenumui atstatyti: Dokumentinė apžvalga** (Uprising for the Restoration of Lithuania's Sovereignty: A Documentary Survey) (Washington, D.C., 1973).

2. At that time Antanas Sniečkus was the First Secretary of the Central Committee of the CPL, Justas Paleckis—the Chairman of the Presidium of the Supreme Soviet of the Lithuanian SSR, and Mečislovas Gedvilas acted as the Chairman of the Council of People's Commissars of the Lithuanian SSR.

3. Gen. Petras Kubiliūnas (1894-1945) was the First Counselor General of Lithuania during the German occupation. In effect he was the principal native instrument of the German occupational regime. After the war Soviet agents secretly abducted Gen. Kubiliūnas from the Western zone of Germany, returned him to Lithuania, and secretly excluted him.

Soviet rule will pour its vengeance on the Lithuanians. Lithuanians! You did not bow your heads before the fascist occupiers.. You destroyed the Nazi plans to mobilize the men of Lithuania into the Nazi army. You ruined the Nazi attempts to create a bandit legion of the Lithuanian SS. In this you dealt the Germans a painful blow..." The appeal ended with the slogan: "Long live the glorious Lithuanian nation, heroically struggling against the Nazi occupiers."

Early in 1944, on Stalin's orders, Major Gladkov mas demonstrably removed from his position as the head of the NKGB of the Lithuanian SSR and was succeeded by A. Guzevičius.[4] This was to show the Lithuanian nation that only Lithuanians would serve in the Lithuanian secret police, that the red terror would not be the political instrument it was in 1940-1941.

In April 1944 an appeal of the Lithuanian Supreme Soviet, the Lithuanian Council of Ministers, the CPL, and the Lithuanian Communist Youth League declared: "Our Lithuanian nation cannot bear the responsibility for the deeds of a handful of disgusting butchers..."

On July 5, 1944, the Supreme Soviet, the Council of Ministers, and the Central Committee of the CPL, acting on Stalin's orders of May 1, 1944, issued the appeal "Dear Lithuanian brothers and sisters!" Once again the Lithuanian nation, distrustful of the Communists, was reassured: "We know very well that the Lithuanian nation stood up honorably during these hard historical trials, and that it is not and cannot be held responsible for the treacherous deeds of the renegades Kubiliūnas, Ramanauskas[5] and others... Great is the suffering which our nation bore. But the noble spirit of the Lithuanian nation has not been broken, her honor has not been stained. The Lithuanian nation heroically resists the German pillagers..."

The entire Chekist underground and Moscow radio, which transmitted Lithuanian programs eight times daily for a total of four hours and five minutes, were harnessed to the movement to russify Lithuania.

---

4. Aleksandras Guzevičius (1908-1969), a Lithuanian writer and old communist revolutionary, served as the People's Commissar of Internal Affairs (NKVD) of the Lithuanian SSR in 1940-41 and is known as one of the more ruthless and fanatical Lithuanian communists.

5. Adolfas Ramanauskas was the General Counselor for Agriculture during the German occupation.

However, a very great part of the Lithuanian nation, particularly its intelligentsia, did not let itself be fooled. Only those intellectuals remained in Lithuania who were prevented by circumstances from withdrawing to the West, who had decided to fight in the underground, and those who were convinced that Soviet rule had taken a turn for the better.

Soon the true face was revealed. In 1940 the Red Army in Lithuania was disciplined and correct, but it returned to Lithuania in 1944 full of vengeance. It did as it pleased.

On October 1, 1944, according to the Order No. 1, "Concerning the mobilization of the draftees born between 1909-26," issued by the russified Soblys,[6] the new occupiers, transgressing the 52nd article of the Hague Convention, which prohibits the mobilization of a country's citizens into an occupying army, proclaimed a general mobilization in Lithuania. However, even before the formal declaration of the mobilization, units of the Red Army surrounded entire villages to capture their men, shoot those who tried to flee, transported them to district towns, laid them down in the market and other public places, mocked their bodies, and led mothers and other family members to look at them, demanding that they recognize their sons. In July Lithuania's horizons were lit up by flames that died down only after 10-15 years. In his memoirs, *The Forest Front*, Albertas Barauskas admits that Lithuanian members of Soviet partisan units were disarmed, placed in uniform, and sent to the front.[7] Former members of the 29th Territorial Corps,[8] who had hidden in their homes during the German occupation, were arrested and placed in death brigades. The few who survived were arrested and sent to concentration camps.

Altogether about 40-45 thousand captured Lithuanian youths were clothed in Russian uniforms. No one bothered to count the number that died.

---

6. Jonas Soblys (1898-1959) fought for Soviet power in Lithuania in 1919. He lived in the Soviet Union between 1919 and 1945, when he returned with the Red Army as the Military Commissar for Lithuania.

7. Albertas Barauskas was a leader of Soviet partisans in Lithuania during the latter years of German occupation. His memoirs: Albertas Barauskas, **Miškų frontuose** (Vilnius, 1968).

8. After the Soviet occupation of Lithuania in the summer of 1940, the Lithuanian Army was integrated into the Red Army as the 29th Territorial Corps. At the start of the war most of the Lithuanian soldiers and officers deserted the Corps and remained in Lithuania.

Usually the towns of "liberated Lithuania" were handed over in three or four hours to Major Gen. Isak Kabukov's NKVD troops which made mass arrests and sent "the enemies of the people" to concentration camps. In September these units were replaced by new NKVD detachments under the command of Major Gen. Vasily Kiseliov.[9]

Meanwhile Stalin, who saw that the Germans did not succeed in mobilizing two hundred thousand Lithuanians into their army and that the Western Powers were silently acquiescing to the slavery he was imposing on the nations of Eastern Europe, discarded his disguise. A. Guzevičius was removed from his post and replaced by the Russian Major Gen. Piotr Kapralov. The former Deputy Head of Internal Security, Colonel Balys Baranauskas, was made head of the agricultural section of the Central Committee of the CPL.

At this time the 4th Infantry Division of the NKVD enforced order in Lithuania and was soon reinforced by the 7th Division. Kapralov transported a thousand Chekists into Lithuania. After Lithuania's "liberation," the following NKVD border detachments, all under the command of Major Gen. Bonych, comprised still further reinforcements: the 20th Border Regiment (under the command of Major Yatsenko), operating in the Vilnius sector (the districts of Vilnius, Trakai, and Alytus); the 33rd Koenigsberg Border Regiment (chief of staff Colonel Govorov), also in the Vilnius sector; the 31st Border Regiment (led by Col. Kotov), in the Vilnius sector; the 12th Riga Border Regiment (under Col. Timofeev), in the district of Švenčionys; the 86th Koenigsberg Border Regiment (under Col. Tselikov), in the district of Panevėžys; the 13th Minsk Border Regiment (under Guards Col. Khemieliuk), in the district of Marijampolė; the 217th Border Regiment, operating in the district of Ukmergė.

Besides the aforementioned 4th and 7th NKVD divisions and the border regiments, the Lithuanian border district, equivalent to a whole division, under the command of Major Gen. Bytskovski, fought the Lithuanian partisans. For its "merits" this formation was awarded by Stalin two Orders of Lenin and an Order of the Red Star. "When the need arose" other

---

9. In the original pamphlet Russian names are given in Lithuanian transliteration. They are transliterated here into English from the Lithuanian and, therefore, may be different from the original Russian forms.

units of the NKVD were also ordered into Lithuania. NKVD units were stationed for years in the forests and the Lithuanian villages adjacent to them.

During these decisive years in the struggle for the existence of the Lithuanian nation, the Lithuanian Freedom Army (LFA)[10] was comprised of 100-110 thousand armed men. According to unofficial sources about thirty thousand died in 1944-1945. According to official documents, forty thousand surrendered to the authorities at the conclusion of the war. The rest fought on for seven to eight years in an uneven and hopeless struggle, presenting the occupiers with a "justification" for the physical and spiritual destruction of the Lithuanian nation.

Approximate calculations show that during World War II and the years immediately after, 850,000 Lithuanians were either killed, fled, or were deported from Lithuania. Thus, Lithuania lost a third of its inhabitants. (A. Stanaitis, P. Adlys, *Lietuvos TSR gyventojai*, Vilnius, 1973, p. 13).

We do not know the resolutions of the Third Plenum of the CPL, but it seems that they aroused the Kremlin's dissatisfaction with the Lithuanian communists. As a consequence the All-Union Communist Party's October 30, 1944, resolution "Concerning the deficiencies in the work of the CPL" accused the Lithuanian communists of a lack of zeal in implementing the land reform and of "insufficient determination in uncovering Lithuanian-German bourgeois nationalists."[11] On November 11, 1944, an All-Union Communist Party Central Committee Bureau for Lithuania was organized, and Mikhail Suslov appointed its chairman. He brought with himself a detailed plan for the spiritual and physical destruction of the Lithuanian nation.

Hitler had said: "Were there no Jews, we would have to invent them." Because the hybrid "Lithuanian-German nationalist" did not exist, Suslov invented him. This was a conscious act of Chekist treachery! Of the roughly four million soldiers to serve under the German colors, Soviet historians calculate

---

10. **Lietuvos Laisvės Armija**, a conspiratorial organization, formed already in 1942 ar an anti-Nazi organization, constituted one of the elements of the postwar anti-Soviet partisan movement. See Part I, Ch. 2 for more details.

11. The text of the resolution has never been published.

that only eight thousand Lithuanians were in that number.
However, even to this day Suslov has not once called Vlasov [12]
a Russian-German nationalist. Although about sixty thousand
Belgians, one hundred thousand Frenchmen, and volunteers of
other countries served in SS and other German formations,
Suslov has never accused the Belgians, the French, much less
the Russians, of treason. But the Lithuanians.—Here is another
fact! Only 286 volunteers enlisted in the SS legion that the
Germans were organizing. Thus, on March 17, 1943, the Germans cancelled the formation of the legion, closed all the
higher educational institutions of Lithuania, and deported many
Lithuanian intellectuals to concentration camps. On November
8, 1966, the Soviet journalist L. Steponauskas wrote in an article
in *Tiesa* that 3,250 Lithuanians were imprisoned in Dachau
alone. But the majority of them, to use the expression of M.
Suslov, were "Lithuanian-German nationalists," because according to official documents only thirty-eight communists were
deported from Lithuania to Germany.

Thus, despite their heroic conduct during the German occupation, the Lithuanians, almost all Lithuanians (excluding
the handful of communists who numbered 1,177 on October 1,
1945) were declared German collaborators and were in fact
placed outside the law. Every Russian colonist could now,
without fear of punishment, shoot, imprison, send to concentration camps, or deport Lithuanians to Siberia.

On August 24, 1944, the Soviets began to organize the
so-called "battalions of destruction" (istrebiteli), renamed
"defenders of the people" on December 18, 1945. There were
about six thousand of them at the end of 1946. For more than
a year, fifty percent of the "stribai" [13] received no salary,
and one half of them received food coupons. From August 1,
1945, they received a salary of forty *červonc* per month, when
a loaf of bread cost six or eight *červonc*. This meant that Suslov
actually sanctioned the pillaging of the Lithuanian nation.
Most of the "stribai" were Russian Old-Believers and Russian

---

12. Col. Gen. Andrei A. Vlasov, Red Army commander captured by
the Germans in 1942, set up a Free Russia Committee and eventually
commanded two divisions of Soviet deserters and captives in battles
against Soviet troops. After the war he was surrendered to the Soviets
and executed in Moscow on August 1, 1946.

13. "Stribai" is a shortened and derogatory Lithuanian designation
for the "istrebiteli".

prisoners of war who had been sheltered by Lithuanians. The latter, fearful of Stalin's repressions for having been captured by the Germans, showed particular zeal in robbing and killing Lithuanians.

It is claimed today that the Lithuanian partisans killed about eighteen thousand inhabitants of Lithuania. Understandably some of those killed were decent Lithuanians. Suslov, who controlled the fictitious staff of the Lithuanian partisans that was led by J. Markulis (now Docent in the Faculty of Medicine at the University of Vilnius) and V. Pečiūra,[14] used the partisans to treacherously murder Lithuania's inhabitants.

On Suslov's orders, secret instructions to the NKVD stationed in Lithuania claimed that the Lithuanian "bandits" killed all Russians. The January 14, 1945, letter of the Chief Political Instructor of the 4th NKVD Division, Col. Ivan Gerasimenko, sent to the political units of all USSR NKVD divisions, characteristically states: "One old Russian was burned alive. There have been cases recorded of the bandits slaughtering entire Russian families." At the same time Russian members of the Lithuanian Communist Youth League were publishing their newspaper *Svobodnoje slovo* (The Free Word).

It is noteworthy that until 1957 the occupier's propaganda was almost completely silent about German atrocities and sought to place all the blame on the Lithuanian-German nationalists. Balys Sruoga's memoirs *Forest of the Gods* were not allowed to be published for many years.[15] The Russian-speaking had to be convinced that all Lithuanians collaborated with the Germans. With this aim in mind, reports from the trials of Lithuanian partisans were almost exclusively published in *Sovetskaya Litva*. Thus, one should not be surprised that, unable to find Lithuanian partisans in the forests, the NKVD indiscriminately killed every Lithuanian man and adolescent, frequently placing the blame for these murders on the Lithuanian partisans.

---

14. The extent to which the Soviet agent Juozas Markulis and his associates influenced or affected the partisan movement is still largely shrouded in mystery. No information is available on Pečiūra.

15. Balys Sruoga (1896-1947), a writer and a scholar, was arrested on March 16, 1943, by the Gestapo and sent to the Stutthoff concentration camp as part of the German revenge campaign for sabotaging the formation of the Lithuanian SS legion. His memoirs about the experiences in the concentration camp were published only in 1957.

In a March 8, 1963, meeting with writers and artists, N. Khrushchev admitted that "Stalin aimed to destroy a large part of the creative intelligentsia of the Soviet Ukraine." Obviously Stalin's plans for the Lithuanian intelligentsia did not differ.

In the twenty years of its independence Lithuania did not have time to educate a numerous intelligentsia. During 1922-1940 the University of Vytautas the Great in Kaunas prepared 3,769 specialists, many of whom (particularly lawyers, doctors, and businessmen) were not Lithuanians. Many died in 1940-1941; many were murdered by the Germans. In 1944 most of those surviving withdrew to the West: 90 percent of graduate foresters, about 400 engineers, 300 doctors, 350 lawyers, 230 priests, 2,000 university students, 3,300 high school students, 300 primary grade teachers, 800 high school teachers, and more than 400 of the staff of the institutions of higher education (more than half). Understandably only a very limited number of intellectuals remained. However, Stalin decided to destroy even them. On Suslov's iniative the Fourth Plenum of the CPL was called in order to legalize the genocide of the Lithuanian nation. Suslov made such an address that, even now after twenty-eight years, he did not dare to include it in his selected works.[16]

Remembering Stalin's words that "the border regions do not easily lend themselves to destruction" (a frequent complaint of the Russian czars), Suslov quoted Lenin, who argued that it is better "to capture and incarcerate, sometimes even shoot a hundred traitors than to wait until they themselves start shooting."

Falsifying the historical facts, Suslov asserted that the LFA was formed "according to the directives of the German Gestapo... and in many cases was led by German officers." In the Plenum Suslov unambiguously accused the Lithuanian communists of alleged liberalism in the struggle with the Lithuanian nation's resistance: "... one must be reminded that the Republic's Party organization from the Central Committee to the Party's primary organizational units should demonstrate an uncompromising attitude toward bourgeois nationalists, even with those nation-

---

16. The Plenum of the Central Committee met on December 27-30, 1944. The reference here is to a selection of Suslov's speeches, published in the Lithuanian language: M. Suslovas, **Rinktiniai raštai** (Vilnius, 1973).

alists who carry a Party card in their pockets.." The style of
A. Sniečkus' speech at the Plenum shows that it was translated
from the Russian. He also declared that the Party's chief task
was "the struggle with the politically suspect, foreign, and even
at times hostile elements."

Cognizant of the fact that during the German occupation
the Lithuanian administration sabotaged all the German efforts to economically exploit and colonize Lithuania, Suslov
decided not to russify and destroy Lithuania. After the Fourth
Plenum the "Lithuanian-German nationalists" in Lithuania's
administration began to melt away. They were arrested at
night... even for merely knowing a foreign language, or because they had visited a foreign country during the years of
independence. Even former prisoners of German concentration
camps were jailed because they had become too clever by surviving.

The Lithuanian Writers Union was subjected to particularly severe repressions and lost over forty members; i.e., more
than half. Characteristically— V. Montvila, K. Jakubėnas, and
K. Boruta had been jailed more than once by the Smetona
regime.[17] Montvila was shot by the Germans; Jakubėnas and
Boruta were arrested by the bolsheviks. Finally after returning
from a concentration camp in Kazakhstan and still showing
no desire "to improve," K. Jakubėnas was killed early in 1950.
The following were deported to concentration camps: J. Keliuo-
tis, A. Poška, A. Miškinis, J. Greičiūnas, A. Biliūnas, P. Juodelis,
A. Vengrys, and others.[18] With the aid of sadistic moral
methods—Genrikas Zimanas [19] succeeded in ruining the broken

17. Reference to the authoritarian rule in Lithuania under President
Antanas Smetona. 1926-1940.

18. The application of Zhdanovite cultural policy in Lithuania led
not only to a repression of the remaining writers and artists (those
mentioned in this article are only the most dramatic cases of direct
physical terror), but also to a sterility in creative endeavors. The postwar
attack on writers is evident in a collection of materials from the general
meeting of writers on October 1-2, 1946: Už tarybinę lietuvių literatūrą
(For a Soviet Lithuanian Literature) (Vilnius, 1947). This is to some
extent recognized now by current literary histories. See, for example, Jonas
Lenkutis, A. Dimitrieva, Istoriya Litovskoj literaturi (Vilnius, 1977), p.
p. 488 ff., passim.

19. Genrikas Zimanas, a Lithuanian Jew and an old communist
revolutionary, was among the principal cultural czars in Lithuania, known
for his rather uncompromising hard line ideology.

health of Balys Sruoga, a former prisoner of a German concentration camp, and driving him prematurely to his grave.

From August 15, 1945, to June 1, 1946, over sixty percent of the chairmen and vice-chairmen of city and district Executive Committees were replaced. In 1946, 2,414 employees of the state administration were fired, and Russian colonists were appointed to their posts. As of April 1, 1945, 6,116 "specialists" with primary and incomplete secondary education were sent to Lithuania. Cattle-cars were routed to Russia packed with "politically suspect and foreign elements," including the citizens of Marijampolė who had stoned the German occupiers and were now singing the Lithuanian National Anthem in tears. They passed by the "specialists" travelling to Lithuania in comfortable trains.

The Fourth Plenum of the CPL removed the Second Party Secretary V. Niunka, replacing him with A. M. Isachenko. The post of the Third Secretary was filled by a merchant from the Ukraine who called himself Kazimieras Liaudis; Mamaev and Sokolov became assistants to the Chairman of the Lithuanian Council of Ministers.

Because Lithuanians did not wish to enroll in the Party and Suslov also prevented them from joining (of the 638 Lithuanian communists who survived the German occupation, only forty-six were readmitted, while fifty-seven new members were newly registered; it is not clear how many were Lithuanians), Russians were soon in charge of these Lithuanian ministries: Communications and Post—Kharitonov (later, for twenty years —Bielianin); Municipal Economy—Astafaev; the State Bank—Biriukov (after the latter's embezzlements—Edinovits); Energy —Bosaev; Railroads—Kozukovskii; Fuel—Yevdokimov; Cellulose and Paper Industry—Filipionok; Light Industry—Teriosin; Fisheries—Zasypkin; Local Industry—Skodin; Industrial Cooperatives—Kalugin; Timber Industry—Ponomarev; Agricultural Cooperatives—Mamaev.

Russified Lithuanians who never did learn to speak Lithuanian, such as Bartašiūnas, Augustinaitis, V. Banaitis, Penkauskas, Vladas Martinaitis, Mikutis, Žemaitis and others began to supervise a number of sectors of the economy and other departments.

Even the zealous Guzevičius was appointed only as Chairman of the Committee for Cultural Educational Affairs. Suslov remained dissatisfied even with these results. He ordered the convening of the Fifth Plenum. The speeches that Suslov delivered are also absent from his selected works. During the Fifth Plenum of the Central Committee of the CPL, which met on April 10, 1945, Suslov declared: "We are obligated not to lessen but to intensify the work of purging the personnel of the Soviet economy from hostile and foreign elements, treating this not as a short-term campaign, but systematically and with determination—that is our first task."

On April 4-6, 1946, the Ninth Plenum was in session, and once more demands were voiced that the NKVD and the security police intensify the struggle with the Lithuanian-German nationalists.

It is difficult to conceive the whole magnitude of the crimes committed in Lithuania. An underground publication dedicated to Victory Day [20] asserts that of the 540,000 inhabitants of Lithuania killed between 1940-1950, roughly half died after May 9, 1945. More than ten percent of all Lithuanians were deported to Siberia. Mikhail Suslov was the initiator of all these killings and deportations.

Mikhail Muravyov, the suppressor of Lithuania's Insurrection of 1863, hung, killed, jailed, or deported to Siberia around ten thousand Lithuanians. For his merits the czar conferred upon him the title of "Graf." The Lithuanian nation "baptized" him The Hangman. The number of Suslov's victims in Lithuania is tenfold. The new Russian czar bestowed on him the title of Hero of Socialist Labor, the Order of Lenin, and several other orders. For a long time now the Lithuanian nation has considered him The Second Hangman.

A widely disseminated rumor has it that after the Fourth Plenum Suslov told a narrow group of like-minded individuals: "Lithuania will be without Lithuanians." In 1946 he left Lithuania convinced that his dreams will come true. But the Lithuanian nation was still alive. [21] In July 1960 he personally travelled to Lithuania to become convinced of this. On the day of his arrival a new riot by the people of Kaunas occurred in the Sports Hall during the USSR boxing championships. [22]

---

20. Reference to May 9, the date of German surrender.

21. Probably a reference to mass demonstrations in Lithuania during the Hungarian events. See Doc. No. 16.

22. Two available eyewitness accounts appear to confirm the events described here. See **Posev**, January, 1974; **Tėviškės Žiburiai**, February 9, 1978.

During the demonstration the police killed ten youths and wounded another dozen or so. The car cavalcade transporting Suslov's party was halted by the funeral procession at whose head were borne the caskets of the dead. Angered by the insolence of the people of Kaunas, The Second Hangman commandeered an airplane and flew off (although it is known that he can barely stand plane rides), refusing to attend an official reception at an officers' club and to see the Song Festival. The Second Hangman returned to Lithuania two more times. Both times all traffic at the Vilnius railroad station was halted and all passengers evicted. None of Russia's czars was as well guarded as this one.

Hitler's associate Hess has now been in jail thirty-five years, but Stalin's lackey M. Suslov freely travels the world and is received with respect. In their sleep retired Western diplomats frequently rub their hands in their pillows, hands that once greeted Hitler, Ribbentrop, Goering, and other Nazis. Contemporary Western diplomats do not find a need to clean their hands after greeting Suslov. But let them know that the hands of M. Suslov, who pretends to be a decent man, are far more bloody than those of Hess, that the blood of the Lithuanian and other nations has not yet dried.

SOURCES

1. LKP CK Partinis archyvas, f. 1774, Lietuvos komunistų partijos (bolševikų) Centro komiteto IV plenumas, Vilnius, 1945.

2. *Kovoje prieš hitlerinę okupaciją, Lietuvos KP(b) atsišaukimai Didžiojo Tėvynės karo metu.* Vilnius, 1948.

3. Bulavas, J., *Vokiškųjų fašistų okupacinis Lietuvos valdymas (1941-1944),* Vilnius, 1969.

4. Dobrovolskis, J., *Lietuviai kariai Didžiojo Tėvynės karo frontuose,* Vilnius, 1967.

5. *Tiesa* and *Tarybų Lietuva,* 1945.

6. *Viestnik Leningraskogo universiteta, No.* 2, 1966.

7. *Vnutrennije voisk SSSR,* Moscow, 1975.

8. *Pogranicnyje voiska,* Moscow, 1975.

16. UNREST IN VILNIUS AND KAUNAS DURING THE HUNGARIAN REVOLT

The students of our school began to organize, two days in advance, a joint demonstration at the cemetery of Rasos.[1] They had been speaking almost publicly of their intention. The night was cold, but pleasant and fair, so almost all of us arrived on time at the cemetery. There we found already gathered crowds of people with lighted candles in their hands. Most amazing was the fact that the entire student bodies of the University and the Institute of Vilnius were present.[2] While standing over the graves of the fallen Lithuanian soldiers, the students started to sing the following songs: "Beautiful is my Fatherland, Country of Sufferings," "Holy, Almighty," and others.

We approached the tomb of Dr. Basanavičius, the Lithuanian national patriarch.[3] The tomb was flooded by candle light. In the Chapel of Our Lady of Vilnius[4] there have never been so many candles as here on the tomb of Basanavičius. Whoever approached the tomb lit a candle; they later melted into a mass of wax which covered the tomb. The echo of our songs could be heard kilometers away from the cemetery.

No. 16. The demonstrations in Vilnius are described in a student's letter, first published in **Lituanus**, No. 1/2, 1962, p. 64. The Kaunas events are described by Elena Juciūtė in her memoirs **Pėdos mirties zonoje** (New York, 1974), pp. 393-395. The author was exiled to Siberia in 1949 for involvement in the partisan movement. She was released in 1956 and witnessed the events described. In 1966 Juciūtė was granted permission to emigrate to the United States.

1. Rasos is an old historical cemetery of Vilnius (founded in 1769), where many Lithuanian notables are interred. It is considered a national shrine, frequently referred to in expression of national sentiment.

2. Reference to the State University of Vilnius and the Pedagogical Institute of Vilnius.

3. Dr. Jonas Basanavičius (1851-1927), a prominent figure in the Lithuanian national renaissance of the second half of the nineteenth century, founder of the first Lithuanian-language newspaper **Aušra** (The Dawn) (1883-1886), an organizer of the first mass political meeting—the Vilnius Assembly of 1905—which set the course for Lithuania's independence. The current dissident **Aušra** considers itself a continuation of Basanavičius' **Aušra**.

4. The Chapel of Our Lady of Vilnius is the principal religious shrine of Lithuania, intimately connected with the major events of Lithuanian history. The portrait of the Virgin has been considered miraculous for over three centuries.

Our national anthem was sung several times. Although previously no one dared to even mention the national anthem,
it now sounded over the city and gave the impression
that Vilnius was free again. When the university students
brought their wreath, tied with black ribbon, and deposited
it upon the tomb of Basanavičius, the crowds began to sing
the national anthem even louder. Thus they sang late into the
night, until more people arrived. The huge crowds started moving toward the center of the city. But here they were met by
police who were sitting in armored cars, waiting for them. The
police demanded that the streets be cleared. Disregarding the orders, the crowds broke through the ranks of police and went
shouting along the streets.

●

I return to the beginning of November—the Feast of
All Souls in 1956. As we know, the second day of November
is All Souls Day. There is a long-standing Lithuanian tradition
to pray for the departed on that day. In the churches each
priest says three Masses. There are Masses in the cemeteries,
where the people decorate the graves with flowers and wreaths
the evening before and burn candles at the graves of their dear
ones. Those who do not have close friends or relatives light
candles on uncared—for graves.

In Kaunas at the cemetery on Trakai Street and Vytautas
Prospect, in which was located the grave of the unknown soldier
with its large monument, there were Masses every year until
the bolsheviks banned them.

Nevertheless, the people gathered in the cemetery on the
eve and in the evening of All Souls decorated the graves, burned
candles, and prayed silently.

It was interesting to see All Souls Day devotions after many
years. At dusk several of us went to the cemetery. I was surprised to see a large crowd of people. Even more amazing were
the many uniformed policemen. Side by side in rows they had
surrounded the cemetery on the outside. Inside there were
many of them on the main paths. There must have been
many chekists dressed in civilian clothes.

The mass of people swayed; it was difficult to cross. The tall monument of the unknown soldier was surrounded by burning candles. Children watched over the candles; they climbed over, lighted, and replaced candles that were almost burned down. A whole swarm of these children fluttered around and upon the monument.

Around them stood a large crowd of people—silent, engrossed in thought, many without doubt praying. I probably did not err much in believing that many of them prayed for fighting Hungary. In Hungary at that time a revolution against the bolsheviks was going on. The Hungarian nation, repressed by the Moscow bolsheviks, decided to get rid of the oppression.

Even though news reached us with difficulty through the "iron curtain," nevertheless, we knew about the Hungarian revolution and sympathized with it. Both the communists and the non-communists here were concerned. The former feared that the revolutionaries would win and the latter that they would lose. Only God above knows how many prayers were said that evening for fighting Hungary.

I prayed and thought about the Hungarian women I had met in Siberia. Where are they now? Probably, all of them returned home, but perhaps they had not yet returned, since they needed some kind of special commission. There were quite a few of them in the camps. One must suspect that there were probably even more men.

We left the cemetery at 9 o'clock and went home.

The next morning we heard that we also had a "revolt." A demonstration had begun at the cemetery. A crowd of people, carrying the national flag, marched down Freedom Boulevard, (at that time called Stalin's Prospect) all the way to the Central Post Office. Here they were attacked by a large band of policemen, many were arrested, others ran away. The revolutionaries had cried: "Long live the Hungarian heroes!" According to reports, they demanded freedom and independence for Lithuania.

I later heard that some of these revolutionaries were sentenced to three years in prison, not under Article 58, but for hooliganism. To those familiar with bolsheviks this seemed to be a very light penalty for "revolution," so the more serious people thought that the "revolution" was fabricated by the chekists to incite those who had returned from Siberian exile. However, the "Siberians" had learned their lesson; they were too smart to fall into the trap from which they had just escaped. The scenario failed: only young delinquents were captured, the students of the Soviet schools, and not those whom they wanted; thus, the court was relatively lenient. The press did not write about this incident; it did not harangue "the enemies of the people," the remnants of capitalism, as it usually did.

The Hungarian revolt was crushed by Russian tanks. Our nation grieved with the Hungarian nation. The communists did not rejoice; they knew that they lost much politically, receiving the infamy of a hangman. It would have been better for them if there had been no such revolts.

The people were particularly disappointed with the Western states, which speak so many beautiful words about human rights, the right of national self-determination, freedom, humanitarianism, but in this case were unwilling to support with a firm word a small nation, heroically fighting for its freedom. None of us had expected such turpitude from the free world; we had a better opinion of them and for this reason the disappointment was devastating.

In school no one talked about the events in Hungary since one had to pretend ignorance; it was dangerous to show one's thoughts, one's sympathies since "the eyes and ears of the king" are particularly vigilant at such times, even without words understanding what one breathes of.

17. MEMORANDUM ON INDUSTRIALIZATION AND THE ENVIRONMENT

Grave concern is increasing on the part of Soviet Lithuanian society, especially on the part of many workers in the fields of science and culture, over the fate of the Nemunas river delta, the Courish Bay, of the sea resorts and, on the whole, of the entire landscape of Lithuania's seacoast. Particular concern is aroused by the plans to build, on the right bank of Nemunas across from Jurbarkas, an oil-refining combinate, as well as a chemical combinate near Darbėnai. These industries, by polluting the waters, destroy the priceless resources of our country.

The anxiety is not without foundation. Here are some striking examples from the not so distant past.

As a result of our ignorance, carelessness and ruthlessness, the Nevėžis river, once abounding in fish, is now polluted to such a degree that all its aquatic life has perished. Extinction threatens the aquatic life of the lower course of the Dangė river, even the mouth of the Nemunas river in the waters of Klaipėda. The lakes of the Telšiai and Šiauliai raions, as well as the Mūša river, have also been fouled.

The project of constructing the superphosphate combinate at Kėdainiai, in the forests of the Nevėžis valley, was completed. The subsequent sad results show the grave errors of the project. Gone already is the Juodkiškiai forest; the pastures nearby are fouled, and cattle breeding is greatly endangered by the operations of this combinate.

No. 17. First published in **The Baltic Review**, January 1967 (No. 33), pp. 23-31. The memorandum, dated March 22, 1966, was addressed to A. Snieckus, the First Secretary of the Communist Party of Lithuania, and M. Šumauskas, Chairman of the Council of Ministers of the Lithuanian SSR. It was signed by 21 prominent writers, artists, professors, and journalists. The original document was not available, hence the signatories could not be determined. The version published here has been abbreviated, omitting several technical arguments. The memorandum was precipitated by the decision of Soviet planner to construct a large-scale oil refinery at Jurbarkas. Although the Lithuanian intelligentsia objected to it for environmental reasons, it is clear in the polemic that followed that the refinery was also considered undesirable for Lithuania on economic and political grounds. After intense lobbying the refinery was shifted to Mažeikiai, where damage to the environment would be less critical. See the introductory study for details.

The Elektrėnai power station, which does not use natural gas as a fuel anymore, uses about 300 tons of sulphur residual oil (mazut) every 24 hours. The project did not take into account the grave consequences of such air pollution...

The central power station of Vilnius, by increasing the city's air pollution, destroyed the Vingis park, which now can never be saved and restored to the state that existed before.

A fate similar to that of the Vingis park threatens the forests of Valakumpiai-Sapieginė if air-polluting industries are going to be concentrated in the areas between Žirmūnai Street and Verkiai highway, or if the Antakalnis power station will not use natural gas for fuel.

Notwithstanding its good points, the Kaunas hydrotechnical dam across the Nemunas at Kaunas is an example of how things should not be done. The essence of its big and totally irreparable failure lies in the fact that the entire sector of the reservoir, from Darsūniškis to Birštonas (even 3 km upwards), is swamped by silt, which settles every spring. Today Birštonas is famous no longer for its beaches, but for its mud flats along the Nemunas.

The worst thing is that the shortcomings of gigantic projects become apparent only after they are completed. The cause of these shortcomings is that the projects are presented in a one-sided manner and that groups active in conservation comprising various experts are slow in presenting thought-out suggestions covering the economic aspects of conservation and landscape configuration...

The more striking examples mentioned here of harm done to nature and of the destroyed or severely damaged balance of nature and its cyclical processes led to the conclusion that the construction of gigantic industrial plants in Western Lithuania, which pollute and contaminate the surrounding land, can also irreparably damage the landscape and destroy the Nemunas delta and bay and the resort areas of the republic. The consequences would irreparably damage the life and well-being of the republic.

For these reasons we feel the necessity of pointing out the following arguments and thoughts:

The growth of industry of the Lithuanian SSR is one of the very important links in raising the well-being of the people. However, nature's laws determine the conditions for the industrialization and urbanization of territories. There are different kinds of obstacles to surmount in the semi-desert regions, in the steppes, forest belt, tundra, and mountains. Lithuania is part of the coastal forest belt. Therefore, Lithuania's industry should observe the laws of this natural belt.

Lithuania is being industrialized under a drastically different environment of the forest belt. This is a specific characteristic of our republic. If, for example, Latvia's territory is 72 per cent covered by flora, Estonia by 79 per cent, and Belorussia by 69 per cent, then Lithuania is covered by less than 50 per cent perennial flora. In the Moscow region, 70 per cent of the territory is covered by natural flora, of which 39 per cent is forest. The Gorki region is covered by 65 per cent and 45 per cent, respectively. In the Buriat ASSR industry is developing in an area which is 100 per cent herbaceous (of which 70 percent is forest). Finland is 71 per cent forest and Sweden is 57 per cent forest, where industry is developing. Although in Germany only 25 per cent of the territory is forest land, 40 per cent of the agrarian land is herbaceous.

The facts given show the complicated, different environments in which we are developing industry. We must, first of all, think of what to build, and afterwards coordinate this in such a manner that the sought-after welfare would not bring with it irreparable evils.

The complexity of the situation is due not only to the density of the population and the damage to our watersheds because of the scarcity of perennial flora, and the scarcity of forests and woodland areas in the republic, but also because there are no farsighted plans for draining the land, for the future of the republic's seacoast, for the fact that this territory is suitable for resorts, vacationing, and tourism.

One must observe that Lithuania's seacoast is part of the complex vacation-resort zone which includes Poland, Kaliningrad oblast, and Latvia. The rapid industrialization of the Baltic coast and the river valleys whose waters empty into the sea creates a real and grave danger by polluting and defiling the recreation land and by poisoning and contaminating the depths and shallows of the sea zone.

Similar thoughts arise as to the future of the Nemunas and of the Courish Lagoon, if the preliminary plans for oil refining are executed in Jurbarkas. The defenders and plan-

ners of the construction of the facility, having the best
intentions (which, unfortunately, are often based on narrow professional considerations to construct a refinery, without
considering possible consequences), maintain without any basis,
that the oil refining combinate will not pollute the waters.
Water conservation always depends on the cost of construction.
The more expensive the project, the more certain is the conservation of water resources. This year, when the planners are
involved in a race to win prizes for saving money in construction, there is a great danger that temporary economic gain
will be bought at the price of the loss of resources in the
future. The N. Gorki oil refining combinate, which cracks various gasolines, mazuts, oils, bitumes, kerosine, Diesel fuel, petro-
chemicals, and gases from crude oil, is considered an example of
not polluting water. On the other hand, a similar plant in
Moscow emits 2,000 kg. of oil and its products as waste
into water. The N. Gorki plant, using the newest technology,
emits... 33,000 kg. a year into the water!

It is maintained that by following the example of the N.
Gorki plant, the Jurbarkas refinery, which will produce 12 million tons a year, will release into the water 135,000 kg. of by-
products of oil a year. *Is this a small amount?* In addition,
each plant refining oil has a proportion of waste oil that is
irreparably lost. The Jurbarkas combinate would lose about
230,000 tons of oil a year. In other words, this amount of oil
would disappear somewhere in the vicinity of the plant. There
is no doubt that a large part of this oil, after cracking, would
be scattered as waste products over the Lithuanian atmosphere
by the westerly winds. The forest of Tauragė would perish,
the waste waters would carry oil into the Nemunas, the Courish
Bay, and the sea and would pollute these waters. How this pollution will be distributed we do not have sufficient data to explain, but it is certain that these amounts will exceed 135,000
kilograms.

The statement that the oil combinate would not be injurious to the fishing industry of the Nemunas delta and bay
does not hold up to criticism. From the point of view of the
fishing industry, even the smallest contamination of this basin
is not permissible; it is hard to overvalue the economic importance of the fishing industry of the basin.

The statement that the oil refinery would not pollute the
coastal resort beaches of the Baltic zone is not true because

the refuse of the oil industry contaminates the soil as well as the sand of coastal areas and kills vegetation. Any sort of oil refuse in the Courish Lagoon is not to be permitted, for it would pollute the Nemunas delta cities, the port of Klaipėda, and ships.

For the sake of the landscape conservation of the Baltic Sea, for the sake of good neighbor relations with the Scandinavian countries, the Great Industrial State—the Soviet Union — should in part concentrate the oil industry and the refining of said oil products for export to the West of the northern hemisphere, in the ice-free port of Murmansk, in this faraway district where there are no conditions for the development of resorts, where the population is sparse and the White Sea wastes near...

The assertion that the refuse of the oil industry would not be harmful to migratory water birds which pass through the Nemunas delta and the Courish Lagoon also raises serious doubts. The grand migratory route of the White and Baltic Sea shores is usually passed by the birds heading to Southwestern Europe and Africa. The birds stop at the Nemunas delta for rest and food. The invasion of oil into this region is especially dangerous. Oil, its products and wastes, as well as mazut form thin layers on the surface. A cubic centimeter of oil product can cover an area of hundreds of square meters. Birds, not seeing the danger, rest on such waters, soil their feathers and perish. In 1953 an unknown ship near the North Sea coast spilled about 500 tons of oil and killed about 10,000 goosanders, *podiceps ruficollis pall,* and various sea ducks. This, of course, was an exceptional case, but every liter of oil and mazut in the water is dangerous. Such occurrences in the Courish Lagoon have already taken place this year.

In addition, we cannot forget that the Nemunas delta and bay shore is not only a stopping station for migratory birds, but is also a special nesting area for water birds. *The Nemunas delta and Courish Bay coastline of reeds with Krokai meadows undoubtedly can and should become a natural reservation not only of Union, but also of European or world significance.*

The world's naturalists are concerned with preserving the most important water basins, swamps, and other watery places of Europe and North Africa from essential change and destruction. With this view in mind, the Nemunas delta and bay are very important. The preservation of such places is organized by the International Union for the Conservation of Nature and Natural Resources and by other international organizations of naturalists. The Soviet Union is a member of all of these international organizations and is a supporter of their activities. Therefore, the pollution of the Nemunas delta by industrial wastes does not coincide with the Soviet Union's supreme goal and tasks in the fields of science and culture.

The conclusion suggests itself that the construction of an oil refinery in the republic would be without purpose. Undoubtedly, Jurbarkas and other growing Lithuanian cities should be industrialized so that they could grow as future cities. But this could be accomplished without an oil refinery. In Lithuania, in our opinion, industry which neither pollutes air nor water should be built. A refinery should only be built, in the worst instance, if it is not possible to do without it, and then only at another site.

It seems that the preliminary plans to build a chemical combinate near the port of Šventoji, on the Latvian border, would be no less dangerous to the Baltic coast. The capacity of this combinate to contaminate water would be especially great. The waste waters of the combinate will be led through pipes to the sea and will be released during the cold weather to a depth of 20 meters. This may sound fine. The pollution will not take place during the vacation season. Our seawater moves in a northerly direction, which means that we will dump all of this chemical filth onto Latvia's fine resort coast, which is part of the general Baltic coastal complex. This complex at present is of great importance, but in the future will be of gigantic importance to an All-Union resort base. Our entire seacoast, having in mind the growing resorts and expanding internal and external tourism, is the guesthouse of the republic. We think that the time has come to declare Neringa a national park, a wonderful tourist attraction, which would abide by the strict regime of a national park. Much has been written in the press about the beauty of our future beach resorts. Let us not contradict ourselves by planning industries which will pollute with petroleum wastes our guesthouse. In spite of all the assurances of the planners, as life has shown, these polluting wastes will be unavoidable! A depth of 20 meters can be found very close to shore. The race for economy in construction offers little hope that the piped wastes will go out far enough from the shore. The sewers should be emptied not at an accidental depth of 20 meters, which would be cheap, but should be piped to a distant and deep part of the sea. However, come what may, this facility is a poisonous knife, which is being thrust into the healthy body of nature; its detrimental effects will be felt not only in undercurrents, but also against the current. When the northwesterly winds pick up, they will carry the polluted water to the port of Šventoji and to the beaches of Palanga and possibly further...

This paper has touched upon our seashore resort areas, the Nemunas delta and Courish Lagoon conservation problems, which are very delicate and complicated and cannot be analyzed in detail here. We only want to evaluate the attempts to industrialize the seacoast of Lithuania in the light of the ideas of conservation and to offer a basis for our plea that these matters be thought on once more before final and fatal decisions are made.

In offering these thoughts we rest upon the experience of conservation, the development of some industrial branches, and the direction of landscape in Soviet Lithuania.

We would consider our aim accomplished if these thoughts would aid the detailed consideration of the questions touched upon and the finding of a balanced and most rational solution.

18. THE TRIAL OF SIMAS KUDIRKA

The court proceedings took place on May 17-20, 1971, in a hall of the Supreme Court of the Lithuanian SSR, in the city of Vilnius.

The chairman of the court was Misiūnas; prosecutor, Petrauskas; and defense attorney, Gauronskis. When the chairman read the name of the defense attorney, Kudirka stated that he declines counsel.

Chairman: "Why do you refuse defense?"

Kudirka: "If Gauronskis is an honest man and defends me according to his conscience, then it can only do him harm. But if he is dishonest and plays the role of a second prosecutor, as often happens in political trials in Lithuania, then I think that my case is already complex enough and one prosecutor is enough."

To the question of the chairman whether he considers himself guilty, Kudirka answered: "I do not consider myself guilty since I did not betray my motherland, Lithuania. I do not consider Russia, called the Soviet Union, my motherland."

In explaining why he attempted to defect to the West, Kudirka spoke for more than four hours.

The defendant responded that he grew up in a very poor family; was familiar with social injustice (he was born in 1929). In 1940, when the Red Army occupied Lithuania and introduced Soviet rule, social injustice was increased because national injustice was added to it. He recalled that in June 1941 people were sent to Siberia whom he considered the most conscientious Lithuanians, including the majority of the

---

No. 18. AS No. 679. Translated from the Russian. A slightly edited English language version was also published by Anatol Shub in the **Washington Post**, August 7, 1971, and in other major newspapers. On November 27, 1970, Simas Kudirka, a Lithuanian sailor on the Soviet ship "Sovetskaya Litva," attempted to jump to freedom while his ship was moored alongside the US Coast Guard Cutter "Vigilant" in US territorial waters off Gay Head, Martha's Vinyard, Mass. A Soviet-American meeting on fishing rights in the North Atlantic area was in progress. The US Coast Guard rejected Kudirka's request for political asylum and forcibly returned him to Soviet custody. Kudirka was taken to Vilnius, tried for treason (article 62 of the Lithuanian Penal Code), convicted, and sentenced to ten years' hard labor in a strict regime camp and confiscation of property. It was subsequently determined that Simas Kudirka was entitled to US citizenship (his mother was a

nation's teachers, whom propaganda branded as bourgeois. In 1941 one occupation was replaced by another. In 1944, before the return of the Red Army, rumors began that the Soviet government had changed. However, in the fall of the same year he realized that if any changes had occurred, they were changes for the worse. He again saw how innocent people were deported to Siberia and saw mass murder. Many of his comrades joined the partisans. Almost all of them died. He didn't have the courage to follow their example. He tried to continue his studies in Vilnius (he finished eight grades), but he was not accepted. He decided to become a sailor.

Chairman: "For what purpose did you choose the sea?"

Kudirka: "My grandfather was a sailor. I have been drawn to far-away countries, I had the wish to see the world, and, besides, I thought that at sea I would forget the tragedy of my nation. I wanted to flee from the strange scene: not a week went by in Griškabūdis and other towns that mangled bodies of Lithuanian partisans were not piled up in the market-place."[1] He wanted to escape the famine that reigned on the collective farms, the disenfranchisement of the collective farmers, the arbitrariness of government-appointed chairmen of the collective farms—all this was reminiscent of the serfdom that existed in Lithuania a hundred years ago. "Unfortunately, I found this kind of injustice and national discrimination even in the fleet. In the press I read about the great Lithuanian

---

natural-born American). After lengthy and difficult efforts on the part of the United States, Simas Kudirka was released after serving almost four years of his sentence. He arrived in the United States in 1975. The denial of political asylum caused an uproar in the United States. A serious effort to reconstruct the events is that of A. Rukšėnas in **Day of Shame** (New York, 1973). For the record of US Congressional investigation, see US Congress, House of Representatives, Committee on Foreign Affairs, Subcommittee on State Department Organization and Foreign Operations, **Hearings on Attempted Defection by Lithuanian Seaman Simas Kudirka** (91st Cong., 2nd Session, Washington, 1970). For a consideration of the legal aspects of the case, see the following studies: Col. Clyde R. Mann, USMC, "Asylum Denied: The Vigilant Incident," and Louis F. E. Goldie, "Legal Aspects of the Refusal of Asylum by US Coast Guard on 23 Navember, 1970, **Naval War College Review,** Vol. 23, No. 9 (May, 1971).

1. Griškabūdis — a small town in the Šakiai district, southwestern Lithuania, where Kudirka lived. Reference to the Soviet practice of dumping killed partisans in town squares as a psychological deterrent and an investigatory technique.

fleet, but in reality there is no Lithuanian fleet: it is Lithuanian only inasmuch as the ordinary sailors are Lithuanians. Lithuanians command this fleet only in exceptional cases; the majority of the commanders don't even know Lithuanian. The top leadership of the so-called Lithuanian fleet lives in Moscow and does not trust us Lithuanians. Permission to sail abroad and go ashore is not generally granted to Lithuanians. The moral atmosphere became especially heavy when Zabiela was appointed a deputy of the captain for political affairs. He was a typical hypocrite and crook. He especially disliked me; he would never issue a permit for shore leave I reject completely the testimony of witnesses that my behavior was a result of family problems. I love my wife; she is faithful to me."

Chairman: "You are insisting that you wanted to find liberty in the United States, which, in your opinion, does not exist in the Soviet Union. How do you explain the fact that they betrayed you?"

Kudirka: "The ordinary Americans received me very well. Seeing that I was cold, they gave me warm clothing, while the Russian sailors afterwards beat me until I was unconscious. They crippled my knee when I lay in prison for several months. I don't consider turning me back as a great tragedy. By the decisions of the Teheran, Yalta, and Potsdam conferences whole nations found themselves in slavery. In the eyes of the American military administration, I, as a Lithuanian, was the legal property of Brezhnev, Stalin's successor, and should have been returned to him."

On May 18, during the cross-examination of the witnesses, sailors acknowledged that they had beaten Kudirka.

The chairman asked the second witness, who knew Kudirka well, why he had sought to flee the Soviet Union. When the witness answered that Kudirka was driven to it, the chairman immediately stopped him from continuing.

To the question of Zabiela, "Would you have defected if you knew that in the USA you would not find work, and if you did, it would have been cleaning toilets?" Kudirka replied, "The job is not important. There is no dishonorable work, and if I cleaned toilets, it would have been with a clear conscience, which is not the way you carry out your work. Your party membership card is only a ration card."

On May 19 prosecutor Petrauskas made the final accusatory statement, in which he expressed his indignation with Kudirka's treachery. He regretted that this case brought great shame to Soviet Lithuania. He demanded as punishement 15 years in a strict regime labor camp as well as the confiscation of all personal belongings. Kudirka spoke in his own defense. He cited Herzen, Marx, and Lenin to explain the difference between socialist theory and practice in Lithuania. In his view, socialism never existed in Lithuania, but rather, a parody of socialism.

Kudirka: "From the standpoint of international law, I am not a criminal. My decision to go abroad does not contradict the United Nations Declaration of Human Rights or even the Soviet Constitution. Therefore, I consider myself completely innocent. However, I know very well that my fate has already been decided by the security organs."

Kudirka described how Senior Lieutenant Urbonas, Director of the Investigatory Section Colonel Kismen, Chairman of the KGB Major General Petkevičius, and many other secret police officials, some of whom had come especially from Moscow, had tried to reeducate him. They had suggested that he condemn bourgeois nationalism in Lithuania and abroad, which had ideologically prepared his treachery, hinting that he would be tried according to Article 82 of the Penal Code of the Lithuanian SSR (the crossing of a border). But Kudirka stated that he was relinquishing his own personal freedom for the sake of his real motherland Lithuania. Six months in solitary confinement had given him sufficient time for deep reflection.

Kudirka: "I remember that when I studied in Vilnius, instead of the two prisons which were there under the Germans, there were seven under Soviet rule, in which there were about 20,000 prisoners. They were overfilled until 1955. Already in 1950, when trainloads of youths from Lithuania came to the concentration camps, the question was being asked: are there any more Lithuanians left in Lithuania? The death of Stalin saved my people from physical extermination. However, the essence of the policy remained the same. Now we are destined to die a much slower death — assimilation. However, we don't want to die. For years our 'brothers in the woods' fought, believing that in the West our struggle was known and supported, even if only morally. Those who died in battle or in the concentration camps believed it as well. Even the state security officials admit that 50,000 Lithuanian partisans died. The Atlantic Charter, which promised the enslaved nations freedom, was an empty promise, costing my people 50,000 dead and 400,000 deported, of whom 150,000 found their graves in the soil of Siberia.[2] We Lithuanians today are living with a belief that has a very strong foundation. We will be saved from the party-ordained assimilation by a stubborn determination not to succumb. World history so far has not recorded another partisan movement that had lasted so long and exacted so many sacrifices. The bravest and most resolute patriots of Lithuania were physically annihilated. But a new young generation has grown up, which intends to go the way of their fathers. When I refused to fulfill the wish of the state security organs, they threatened me with the death sentence. I believe that this promise will be fulfilled. I am a devout Catholic. Therefore, if the Supreme Court sentences me to death, I would request it to invite a priest to give me the last rites of the Catholic Church."

At this point the chairman interrupted Kudirka and said: "I don't understand what you are talking about."

Kudirka: "I ask the Supreme Court not to persecute my mother, my wife and my children. I ask you not to harm them."

Chairman: "Your own conduct brings hardship to your family."

Kudirka: "Not mine, but yours. I hoped to help my family more from America than with the slave wages I receive here. Besides, I hoped to bring them abroad."

The chairman read from a newspaper: "In the US a committee has been created for aiding the Kudirka family." From another newspaper: "The US intends to help the family of Kudirka, although many American families whose breadwinners have died in Vietnam are left to the mercy of fate."

Kudirka remarked: "Evidently, this committee is in the hands of those who are on the side of peace."

Before sentencing on May 20, Kudirka said: "I have nothing to add to what I have already said, only one wish, more

---

2. These figures are very rough estimates, most likely on the high side. See the introductory study for more specific data.

specifically, a request both to the Supreme Court and the government of the Soviet Union: I ask that you grant my motherland, Lithuania, independence."

Chairman: "How do you picture an independent Lithuania?"

Kudirka: "An independent Lithuania, in my opinion, has a sovereign government and is not occupied by any army. The government has a national administration, its own legal system, and a free democratic system of elections. The laws of other countries are not binding on this government, as the laws of Russia are here today. An independent Lithuania wouldn't be dominated by the Russian language as it is today. I would like there to be no more trials such as mine in Lithuania."

Chairman: "Are you perhaps saying that the present court was not democratic and was illegal?"

Kudirka: "Of course, inasmuch as it takes place behind carefully screened windows and closed doors with Russians standing guard. In a democratic trial anyone who wished would be permitted to attend. If I betrayed my homeland, why are you afraid to show the public a traitor? Let the public itself judge me. Unfortunately, the courtroom is empty. Besides my wife and a few chekists (security police), I see no one. There are also a few guards, but they don't know the Lithuanian language and don't know what we are arguing about."

After a short consultation, the chairman pronounced the sentence: "Ten years labor in a strict regime camp with confiscation of personal property."

When he heard the sentence, Kudirka couldn't conceal his pleasure. He had thought he would be shot.

Soon after the trial state security employees took from his apartment a set of "Kaunas" furniture, a rug, and a radio set, amounting in value to some 700 rubles.

Remarks: Kudirka did not know that he had been living under the menace of interment in a psychiatric hospital. However, his relatives and acquaintances refused to yield to the threats of the chekists (security police) and sign statements that he was psychologically abnormal. Doctors of the city of Vilnius, headed by the chief psychiatrist Gutman, also resisted chekist pressure. They pronounced Simas Kudirka completely healthy.

19. SELF-IMMOLATIONS AND DEMONSTRATIONS

EVENTS IN LITHUANIA

On May 14, in one of the squares of Kaunas, Romas Kalanta (born 1953), who had finished secondary education and was the son of a college lecturer, died by self-immolation, under the banner "Freedom for Lithuania." Three of his friends surrounded the burning youth and would not allow anyone to approach him. They were arrested and charged with "premeditated murder with aggravating circumstances" (equivalent of article 102 in the Russian Penal Code). Their names are so far unknown to the *Chronicle*.

R. Kalanta died in a hospital a few hours later. His funeral was scheduled for May 18. A few hours before the appointed time his body was secretly taken from the morgue and buried. People who had arrived for the funeral went to the place of his self-immolation. A very large crowd gathered. The police set about dispersing it. The assembly offered resistance. Rumor has it that one policeman died. After this troops were called in, and they dispersed the crowd. The "disorders" continued on May 19 also. Many people were arrested. Some were given ten to fifteen days' imprisonment for "petty hooliganism." Criminal proceedings were instituted against several people.

A Kaunas newspaper printed a photocopy of a letter from the parents of Kalanta: "A great misfortune has befallen our family—the suicide of our son. Everyone will understand the grief of his parents. But some irresponsible elements, taking advantage of our misfortune, are talking of the persecution of relatives, and trying to disturb law and order in the town.

No. 19. From **A Chronicle of Current Events** (Moscow), July 5, 1972 (No. 26). The self-immolation of Romas Kalanta is beyond dispute. It was confirmed by the Soviet press (i.e., **Kauno Tiesa**, May 21 and 22, 1972; **Tiesa**, October 5, 1972) and widely reported throughout the world (e.g., **The Times**, London, May 22, 1972; **New York Times**, May 22, 1972. et al.). The self-immolation of the other individuals mentioned has not been cinfirmed. Kalanta set himself on fire at a significant site—in a park before a theater where in July of 1940 a puppet parliament under Moscow's control asked for the incorporation of Lithuania into the USSR. The act of self-immolation and the accompanying demonstrations were political in nature.

Others, simply out of curiosity, are following their example, thereby causing us even greater pain. No one has the human right to behave thus. The greatest comfort to our family would be to be left in peace."[1] This letter was reprinted in newspapers in Vilnius in the Lithuanian and Russian languages.

The Chairman of Kaunas City Soviet Executive Committee appeared on Kaunas television with "interpretations." In particular, he said: "The investigatory organs have enquired into and elucidated the circumstances of this suicide. A forensic-medical commission was created. The doctors who participated in its work were: J. Andriuškevičienė, Reader in the Faculty of Medicine at Vilnius University; V. Berneris, Head Physician of Kaunas Psychoneurological Hospital; J. Gutmanas, Chief Psychiatrist of th eLithuanian Ministry of Health; J. Šiurkus, Professor at Kaunas Medical Institute; and other specialists in the field. Having carried out a forensic-psychiatric examination and studied the documents, letters and sketches of the deceased at its disposal, and also taking into account the evidence of parents, teachers, and friends, the commission came to the conclusion that Romas Kalanta was mentally ill and had committed suicide while in a morbid frame of mind. Certain irresponsible persons, a group of juveniles, not understanding and incorrectly appraising the above-mentioned fact, and devoid of any sense of responsibility, tried to disturb law and order in the city... We appeal to school directors, teachers, parents, and young people and call upon them to assist in safeguarding the peace in this city."[2]

In one issue of the paper *Kauno Tiesa* letters were published "condemning the acts of hooliganism."

On May 22 the same paper printed an article, "Who Are They, These Disturbers of the Peace?" The article says: "On May 18 and 19 a small band of hooligans caused a disturbance of law and order. In order to inform our readers who these hooligans are, the editors addressed themselves to the city procuracy. There we discovered that the majority are persons with previous records of conviction on more than one occasion for hooliganism and other criminal offenses. They are long-haired,

---

1. Photocopy of the letter in **Kauno Tiesa**, May 21, 1972. The regime tried to dismiss the unrest as the result of an act by a mentally deranged youth and behavior of juvenile delinquents.

2. Text of the speech in **Kauno Tiesa**, May 21, 1972.

degenerate, perverted hooligans, of unsightly appearance. Here are the character-references we have received on some of them." The article continues with a description of five of those arrested in the square. One of them, Henrikas Pociūnas, a school dropout, has had criminal proceedings instituted against him for "breach of the peace, insurbordination, and use of violence against members of the police force."[3]

— — —

On May 28, during a fair in the market place of the town of Varėna, Stonis (a sanitary technician born in 1949) and three of his friends hoisted the national flag. Stonis' friends were seized immediately by the police, but he himself managed to get away. The next day in the same square he set fire to himself. He died on June 10 in a military hospital. The funeral took place under police and KGB supervision. For the duration of the funeral road-blocks were set up on all roads into Varėna.

— — —

On June, 3, on a Kaunas street (the square in which Kalanta died by self-immolation is under guard) a worker, Andriuškevičius (born 1912), set himself alight for the same reasons. He died the next day in a military hospital. He was buried secretly by the police in an unknown locality.

On June 10, in a Kapsukas street, a worker Zaličkauskas (born 1910) tried to burn himself to death, but was seized. He is now in a military hospital.

— — —

The International Handball Championships for the Baltic Cup were held in the Vilnius Palace of Sport from June 11 to 18.

---

3. Later on, **Tiesa** (October 5, 1972) gave an account of a trial of eight youths involved in the demonstrations. None of them was mentioned in the initial charges of hooliganism. Article 100 of the Lithuanian SSR Penal Code (dealing with the organization of and participation in violations of public order) was applied to the following persons: Vytautas Kaladė, born in 1947, stage hand at the Kaunas Theater; Antanas Kačinskas, born in 1948, a student at Kaunas technical school; Rimantas Baužys, born in 1954, occupation not given; Kazys Grinkevičius, 24 years old, a packer at a Kaunas factory; Vytautas Zmuida, 23 years old, construction worker; Jonas Prapuolenaitis, born in 1951, a student in a technical school; Juozas Macijauskas, born in 1949, a student in a technical school; Virginija Urbonevičiūtė, an appretice in a printing plant, a minor at the time of the demonstrations. All were convicted and sentenced from a year to three years. The official account presents the youths as juvenile delinquents.

Lithuanian students and schoolchildren responded noisily to each encounter: whenever a foreign team came near the Soviet goal, they shouted "Hurrah"; but when luck was on the Soviet side, they whistled. Amongst the spectators there were many policemen and KGB men in disguise. They seized the shouting spectators and drove them away. Those who did not stand up when the Soviet anthem was played were treated likewise. The total number of detainees was about 150. Many of them were released after fifteen days' detention: a few dozen are under investigation. Most of the students detained were not allowed to sit for their state examinations, while the schoolchildren were not given their school-leaving certificates. During the final days of the championship there were many empty seats in the Palace of Sport because tickets were not being sold but distributed free in factories to people on lists approved by party committees, and then mainly in those factories with a majority of Russian workers.[4]

4. Nationalistic demonstrations during sports events, especially involving Russian teams, are rather frequent occurrences reported in the dissident press and through private channels.

20. DEMONSTRATIONS AND RIOTS IN KAUNAS

The funeral of Romas Kalanta was supposed to take place on Thursday, at 4:00 p. m.[1] Already on Monday the atmosphere in the city seemed to be charged with electricity. People were filling the city park, clustering at the site of the hero's death, some were tossing flowers surreptitiously, while the bolder ones went right to the spot to place them. The latter were immediately photographed by officials in civilian clothes. A sizeable pile of flowers had accumulated by evening, but next morning they had disappeared.

Kalanta's body was laid out in a house on Paneriai Street, in the suburb of Vilijampolė. It was very difficult to get a glimpse of his body. The line to his door stretched around the entire block. It was not permitted to place flowers at the casket, except by the relatives. There were rumors that a youth demonstration would take place during the funeral.

On Thursday, at 2:00 p.m., I went to the city park, placed my flowers next to the others, and suddenly heard the people in the park express loud indignation. They were saying that they would not be able to participate in Kalanta's funeral because militiamen had taken the casket with his remains to an unspecified cemetery. Around 2:30 p.m. a great commotion arose among the people in the city park—someone announced that a protest demonstration by young people was approaching from Vilijampolė. And so it was, close ranks of young people soon appeared, their arms closely linked. There were several thousand of them. They were chanting as they marched: "Freedom for Lithuania," "Freedom for Romas' father," "Liars." The office of the Communist Party's Executive Committee is situated across the street from the city park. The crowd veered towards it. Chanting, "Freedom for Romas' father," they raised their fists.

A man came out of the Executive Committee building and urged the crowd to disperse. His speech was interrupted by the screams of a woman as she was being pulled by militia-

No. 20. From an account of an eyewitness visiting the West. The story was first published in the Lithuanian daily in Chicago, Draugas, August 2, 1972.

1. Thursday, May 18, 1972.

men into a car and they twisted her arms behind her back. Someone threw a stone at the government official. Then the militiamen charged the crowd, swinging their whips. The crowd turned to the city park. There, at the site of Kalanta's death, a tall youth climbed on a bench and began delivering a speech. He said that Lithuania was enslaved, that young people must fight their oppressors, etc. His eyes were burning, his words were fiery, his voice strong and inspiring. I, a man of quite a few years, began to tremble with excitement; as I listened to him, my eyes flooded with tears. I realized that Lithuania had not perished yet. Our children, strong and bold, loved their fatherland and were ready to sacrifice themselves for it. The first youth was followed by a second young speaker, then a third. They were constantly being photographed from the sides.

Suddenly there was a stir in the crowd. Militiamen appeared and started beating the demonstrators with truncheons. The youths did not flee but turned around and started chasing the militiamen. On the Freedom Boulevard they grouped themselves in orderly ranks and, chanting the same slogans, marched toward the militia headquarters. At the Garrison Church they were blocked by a large detachment of militia. Then they stopped. One of the youths deftly clambered upon a church column and hoisted the Lithuanian tricolor, our dear flag of independence. "Lithuania, our fatherland, land of heroes," echoed in the air.[2] But the crowd could not complete the Lithuanian anthem. The militiamen suddenly surrounded the youths, started hunting the demonstration leaders, and apprehended most of them right then and there. The crowd, accompanied by truncheon-swinging militiamen, returned to the city park, but was chased away from there by truncheons again.

On Friday the park was jammed with people since the early morning. The militia refrained from beating them, but insisted on keeping them moving. The crowd kept moving in a dense circle. At 4:00 p.m. militiamen began to move the people away from the park. When the people gathered in the street, the militia put the truncheon to work again. They were swinging at everybody, including those who did not participate in the demonstration but were merely sitting on the benches in the center strip of the Freedom Boulevard. They were well

---

2. The first line of the national anthem. The national tricolor — yellow, green, and red.

equipped for that beating since, as it turned out later, they had accumulated truncheons from all of Lithuania, while the factory of "Inkaras" had received a sudden order to manufacture 1000 truncheons. The Freedom Boulevard then became filled with trucks carrying soldiers. They were armed with automatic weapons and tear-gas grenades. They also wore gas masks which turned out to be very useful since the youths were already armed with stones and did not spare them on their enemies. The wailing of ambulance sirens was then heard. Hundreds of people were injured that day by the militiamen, who had driven themselves to a bestial frenzy, and by the security soldiers. The dead body of a youth lay on Mickevičius Street until midnight. At the end of the Freedom Boulevard a 12-year-old was lying on the ground, blood trickling from his mouth. An elderly woman, hit on the head by a militiaman, was carried into a store and lost consciousness. Some people asked the militiamen to allow them to call an ambulance. The answer was: "Let her croak!"

The militiamen were especially irked by the long-haired youths. I saw them grab a young woman by her long hair and pull her to the ground. They kicked the young men as they jammed them into the vans and kept carting them away. Finally, the Freedom Boulevard was completely cleared of people, and not even the residents were allowed to go back home. People started massing in the side streets. They were hunted down there and jammed into the vans parked on Freedom Boulevard. The militiamen kicked them and then beat the arrested people in the vans behind closed doors. The air was filled with terrible screaming.

A few fires flared up in the evening. The court building, the bank, the Philharmonic Hall, and several other buildings were set on fire. A militia motorcycle burned on Daukantas Street, shop windows were shattered by stones. A dead militiaman, a knife in his chest, lay on Mayakovski's Street. A large number of injured militiamen were in the hospitals. But even more wounded people hid in their homes, afraid to admit that they were injured.

On Saturday and Sunday people were still gathering in the streets, but militiamen would promptly arrive and herd them into the vans. There were mass arrests. After a brief interrogation the arrestees would be taken to the Vilnius prison. Those who seemed to be less culpable would be herded into the yard of the militia headquarters, roughed up with truncheons, and then allowed to go home. Youths would be shaved bald. Even some girls were shorn.

The grave of Romas Kalanta is in the cemetery of Romainiai, at a most remote spot, next to shrubbery and a ravine. There is talk that militiamen had held a long watch in that shrubbery.

21. THE SITUATION OF LITHUANIANS IN BELORUSSIA

Vilnius, 1972

LITHUANIAN-INHABITED LOCALITIES IN THE BELORUSSIAN REPUBLIC

The treaty concluded between Lithuania and the Soviet Union on July 12, 1920, set up the Eastern and Southern boundaries of the Lithuanian state. They approximately corresponded to the ethnographic boundaries of Lithuania. In the same year, 1920, Poland occupied Vilnius and about one third of the Eastern and Southern Lithuanian lands. With the collapse of Poland in 1939, the Soviet Union returned to Lithuania (the city of) Vilnius and a small portion of that territory that had been occupied by Poland and that had to be allocated to Lithuania according to the treaty of July 12, 1920. The remaining portion of the Vilnius territory was attached to the Belorussian SSR.[1]

With the introduction of the Soviet system in Lithuania in 1940, the delegates of Belorussia at the Supreme Soviet of the

---

No. 21. From a **samizdat** document, AS No. 1849. The document is a 51-page manuscript; about one third of it is omitted here. The document is being serialized in the underground journal **Aušra**, No. 5 (February 16, 1977) and No. 6 (May 12, 1977). According to the population census of 1970, almost 160,000 Lithuanians lived in the Soviet Union outside the Lithuanian republic. The major Lithuanian communities are found in Latvia (40,000), Kaliningrad Oblast of the RSFSR (formerly East Prussia) (24,000), Belorussia (8,000), and Siberia (ca. 40,000) (P. Adlys: "Lithuanians in the Other Union Republics", **Mokslas ir Gyvenimas**, No. 2, 1972, p. 49). The number of Lithuanians in Belorussia is probably vastly underreported. Still, it is clear that the number has declined precipituously from the 50,000 at the end of World War II as a result of assimilative policies. None of the Lithuanian communities outside Lithuania enjoy national cultural rights (such as schools teaching in Lithuanian and Lithuanian-language publications, organizations, etc.). On the other hand, the Russian communities in various republics are served by Russian institutions. The long-term consequence of such cultural discrimination is the assimilation of the ethnic minority communities, which happen to be situated outside their nominal republics. That appears to have been the fate of the Lithuanian community in Belorussia.

1. Texts of treaties cited in Kaslas, **op. cit.**, Nos. 3, 49, 50.

USSR in Moscow, on August 3, 1940, offered to return six raions to Soviet Lithuania: Švenčionys, Vydžiai, Adutiškis, Astravas, Varanavas, and Rodūnė. The USSR Supreme Soviet accepted the offer. The original pledge of the Belorussian delegates stated that in the above-mentioned raions Lithuanians form the majority of the population.

It was only at the end of 1940 that the first steps were taken to put the proposal of the delegates of Belorussia into practice. By June 1941 the raions of Druskininkai, Švenčionys and Ignalina as well as Dieveniškės were joined to the Lithuanian SSR. The other raions might have been added in the same year, but the war broke out, and the Germans occupied Lithuania, including the Vilnius territory. Following the end of World War II the raions of Vidžiai-Apsas, Astravas, Rodūnė, and Varanavas were not joined to the Lithuanian SSR. Thus, some 50,000 Lithuanians remained in the Belorussian republic.[2]

In the present Breslauja raion nearly 30 hamlets inhabited by Lithuanians are clustered around the Apsas village: Dvarčionys, Misos, Salakundžiai, Ignotiškė, Zabarninkai, Kupčeliai, Paberžė, Potkūniškė, Kumpiniai, Bielūsiškė, Ademeniškė, Černiškės, Taukiniai, Bykauskai, Ažugirė (Zaliesė), Naujasalė, Juodelėnai, Damašiai, Medinkos, Rimašiai, Žirneliškė, Usonys, Ratkūnai, Reževas, Bužionys, Marijampolė and others. Still in the czarist era a Lithuanian school was functioning in the house of Adolfas Gotautas, in the village of Dvarčionys. Before the war, during the Polish occupation, Lithuanian schools were functioning in Zabarninkai and elsewhere. During the German occupation a Lithuanian high school was open in Vydžiai whose environs have now become polonized and belorussianized, but Lithuanian villages still survive (Bagdžiūnai, Ožkaragiai, and others). Prior to World War II some 13,000 Lithuanians lived in the district of Breslauja.

In the Gervėčiai "island" of the Astravas raion there are nearly 20 Lithuanian villages: Rimdžiūnai, Girios, Pelegrinda, Knistuškės, Gudininkai, Celiūnai, Galčiūnai, Gervėčiai, Miciūnai, Mockai, Viciūnai, Gibirda, Petrikai, Milcėjai, Gaigalai, Užupiai, Kerplėšyna, and others. Before the war, during the Polish occupation, Lithuanian schools were functioning in eleven villages: Miciūnai, Galčiūnai, Petrikai, Mockai, Rimdžiūnai,

---

2. The figure is probably a rough estimate, based on the statements by the Belorussian deputies in 1940.

Girios, and elsewhere. All in all, some 11,000 Lithuanians were estimated to be living in the area of Gervėčiai.

About 20 Lithuanian villages are in the former Rodūnė (now Varanavas) raion: Pelesa, Dubiniai, Smilginiai, Vigonys, Klaišiai, Kargaudai, Piliūnai, Pavalakė, Paditvys, Leliūšiai, Senieji and Naujieji Druskininkai, Varliai, Mažeikiai, Kurkiai, Miežonys, Saltaniškis, Kalviai, and others. Some 10,000 Lithuanians were estimated to be living in the entire Rodūnė raion during the Polish occupation. Lithuanian schools were functioning in eleven villages: Pelesa, Sen. Druskininkai, Kargaudai, Piliūnai, Pavalakė, Paditvys, and elsewhere. When Lithuanian church services were abolished in Rodūnė, Lithuanians built a church for themselves in Pelesa. At present the Lithuanians of the former Rodūnė raion form the "island" of Pelesa, which belongs to the Varanavas raion.

Another Lithuanian "island," called Ramaškonys village, is to be found in the Varanavas raion. In addition to Ramaškonys, over a dozen Lithuanian villages belong to that "island": Baziliai, Dainava, Stanišiai, Tusamonys, Bieliūnai, Cesliukiškė, Armoniškės, Lašėkai, Parabiškės, Valatkiškės, Stilgūnai, Naujasodžiai, Dainevėlė, Biliai, Kauleliškiai, and others. During the Polish occupation Lithuanian schools were functioning in Ramaškonys, Stilgūnai, Lazariškės, Cesliukiškė, Tumasonys, Biliai, Liubartai, Balcininkėliai, and other villages. A total of ca. 8,000 Lithuanians was estimated to be living in the Ramaškonys "island" (the former townships of Varanavas and Sėdliškės).

The Lithuanian "island" of Plikiai, now in the Varanavas raion, exists in the former township of Žirmūnai. It consists of the Lithuanian villages: Pasaliai, Babrėnai, Bežemiai, Davronys, Jaskūnai, Dervėgiai, and others. Lithuanian schools were functioning in Plikiai and Sklodonys during the Polish occupation.

In the "island" of Lazdūnai (raion of Jūrotiškis), over ten Lithuanian villages existed before World War II: Grudenionys, Salos, Valdzikai, Pasaliai, Babrėnai, Bežemiai, Davronys, Jaskūnai, Dervėgiai, and others. Some 2,900 Lithuanians lived in them.

In 1971 our tourists discovered a Lithuanian-speaking village of Poškiškė some 30 kilometers east of Dieveniškės.

Before the war and for a while after it, there were Lithuanian residents around Pastoviai (quite recently, ten years ago, Lithuanian students from Pastoviai were attending Adutiškis high school). According to Polish statistical data, 51 Lithuanians resided in the vicinity of Pastoviai, and 89—around Medelas. Some 7,800 Lithuanians were estimated to be living in the "border areas" during the period of Polish occupation. By "border areas" we mean the former districts of Molodechno, Vileika, and Pastoviai.

Prior to World War II some Lithuanians lived in the Bielica township. (Polish statistics dating from 1921 indicate that 518 Lithuanians were living in the Bielica township.)

The Lithuanian "island" most distant from present Lithuania is in Zietela, 240 kilometers south of Vilnius.

It must be noted that during the Polish occupation Lithuanian clubs-reading rooms were functioning in those Lithuanian villages where there were no Lithuanian schools (that is, where the communities were not able to establish them, or where they were closed by the government). In addition to the clubs-reading rooms, there were kindergartens. Lithuanian amateur cultural activities were allowed, folk dance and drama circles and choirs were active. Chapters of the *Rytas* (Morning) and *Šv. Kazimieras* (St. Casimir) organizations developed a far-flung activity.

The Lithuanian villages of the Breslauja and Varanavas raions do not actually form "islands " because they naturally border the Lithuanian SSR. The genuine "islands" are formed only by the Lithuanians of Gervečiai, Lazdūnai, and Zietela. Others "islands" should be termed environs (Lithuanians of the environs) of Apsas-Vydžiai, Pelesa, Ramaškonys.

All the above-mentioned areas were not joined to the Lithuanian SSR following the end of the war. Why haven't they been joined, although agreement to that effect was made in 1940? They were not attached because Lithuania is a small nation and, following the war, there was no need to take Lithuania into account. A similar fate struck East Prussia, which was divided after the war. The larger portion of East Prussia was given to Poland (because there are 30 million Poles and one must take them into account), while the smaller portion, inhabited by Lithuanians since ancient times, was assigned not to Lithuania, but to the Russian Federation and named the Kaliningrad oblast. All Lithuanian place names in the Kaliningrad area have been abolished. The name of Tilžė (Tilsit) has disappeared (it has been named Sovyetsk). It was in Tilžė that Lithuanian books and newspapers were published during the (czarist) Lithuanian press ban, and it was there that Dr. Vydūnas,[3] writer, philosopher, and fighter for Lithuanian culture lived until 1944. The river of Šventainė that flows past Tolminkiemis, where Donelaitis[4] lived and worked, has been renamed Ruskaya, and Tolminkiemis itself has been renamed Shistye Prudy.

The Lithuanian localities of Belorussia have not been joined to the Lithuanian SSR because the plans are to melt them and to transform Lithuanians who live there first into Belorussians and then into Russians. That this is really so became evident from the actions of the local (Belorussian) authorities, initiated in 1944 after the expulsion of the Germans.

1. Lithuanian schools were not allowed to function. Instead of the Lithuanian schools that were active during the Polish occupation, Russian schools were opened.

2. The Lithuanian intelligentsia (teachers and others) were given to understand that they have nothing to do here and that they must leave the Belorussian SSR. They were denied jobs, and those who did not want to leave were intimidated and terrorized in various ways (there were instances when armed persons threatened at night to do away with them if they did not leave the area). No attention was paid to the fact that some of the local Lithuanian intelligentsia had performed important services to the Soviet Government (some were former underground communists who participated in the war against the Germans).

3. The Lithuanian kolkhozes have been dismantled and Lithuanians living in a single location have been dispersed among several kolkhozes to establish a non-Lithuanian major-

---

3. Vydūnas-Vilius Storasta (1868-1953), o noted philosopher, poet, dramatist, cultural leader, the spiritual leader of Lithuania Minor.

4. Kristijonas Donelaitis (1714-1780), the classical Lithuanian poet, whose realistic portrayal of Lithuanian peasants in Lithuania Minor in his poem Metai (The Seasons) made him an international literary figure. Metai is the first major literary work in the Lithuanian language, which has been translated into the major languages of the world. English translation by Nadas Rastenis: Kristijonas Donelaitis, The Seasons, (Los Angeles, 1967). See also Lituanus, Spring 1964, devoted entirely to Donelaitis and his work.

ity. Lithuanians have been removed from managerial posts on the kolkhozes, e.g., Z. Lukoševičius, manager of the kolkhoz of Dubiniai village, in spite of the fact that under his leadership the kolkhoz was one of the leading ones in the raion.

4. Lithuanians have been removed from their posts in the executive and party organs.

5. Lithuanian priests were not allowed to perform their duties in the Lithuanian parishes of the Belorussian SSR. Most Catholic churches were shut down. Most Russian Orthodox churches meanwhile were left functioning or were newly opened.

6. All Lithuanian cultural establishments and bodies that were allowed during the Polish occupation (kindergartens, reading rooms, clubs, amateur theaters) were liquidated.

HOW LITHUANIANS ARE DENATIONALIZED IN THE BELORUSSIAN REPUBLIC

> *Neither schools nor press*
> *they allow us...*
> (Paraphrasing A. Baranauskas)[5]

Article 121 of the Constitution of the Soviet Union declares that "citizens of the USSR have the right to education. This right is secured by teaching in schools in the native language." The above right, guaranteed by the Constitution, is denied to the Lithuanians of the Belorussian SSR, who are the target of a russianization effort using all available means. In Belorussia Lithuanians are exposed to national discrimination. That this is really so can be seen from the facts presented below.

Children whose native language is Lithuanian are taught all the subjects in Russian starting with the first grade (7 years of age). While in school they are forbidden to converse in Lithu-

---

5. Antanas Baranauskas (1835-1902), a bishop and a noted man of letters. The paraphrase is from his poem "Journey to Petersburg" (1859), which was directed at the cultural suppression of the czarist regime. Needless to say, this anti-Russian poem has not been published by the Soviet regime.

anian. Children who do not know Russian find it very difficult to study in the Russian language. Hence the slow scholas-
tic advancement, and Lithuanian children from Russian
schools encounter difficulties in trying to enroll in special and
higher schools, especially if they want to continue their education in Lithuania.

Schools also serve to russianize the families. In the raions
of Breslauja and Varanavas one may encounter families in
which parents converse between themselves in Lithuanian and
in Belorussian with their children. When asked why they do
so, they respond, "so that the child would have it easier in
school." The Belorussian language is little different from
Russian. If a child knows Belorussian, it is easier for him to
understand the subjects taught in Russian in the school.

Lithuanians do not want to entrust their children to Russian schools and so send them to study in Lithuania. Separating children from their families and sending them to Lithuania
far away is not an easy moral and material decision for Lithuanian parents living in Belorussia, so much the more so, as
there is fear and reluctance in Lithuania about accepting them
(apparently Moscow takes a dim view of such doings). So
the parents must plead, make repeated trips, and often return
home having gained nothing, empty-handed and with tears in
their eyes. The Belorussian government took advantage of this
situation and established boarding schools in areas most densely
inhabited by Lithuanians—in Apsas, Gervečiai, and Rodūnė.
Meanwhile, there are no such boarding schools in the more
distant purely Belorussian raions. An effort is made to create
the best possible material conditions for the students in the
above-mentioned boarding schools: they receive full support
(food and clothing), and the boarding school fees are low, so
that even poor parents' children can study there.

One typical example of russianization: In the village of
Paditvis (area of Rodūnė) there was an eight-year Russian
school. Two to three Lithuanian-language lessons were taught
in it each week as a separate subject. In 1970 the school was
liquidated. No eight-year school was left in the vicinity of Paditvis, and the nearest school was seven kilometers away. The
parents' complaints drew the reply of the authorities that now
they could send their children to the Rodūnė boarding school.

The local Belorussian authorities persecute the parents

who send their children to study in Lithuania: they withhold fodder from the cattle; they take away land. Each kolkhoz farmer receives 30 ares of land for his personal use. The manager of the kolkhoz "Victory" in the Breslauja raion, Levchenko, appropriated part of the land (from 7 to 10 ares) thus used from all those who sent their children to study in Lithuania. Citizen Ct. had 20 ares taken away from him (for two children). Citizen R., who had a construction job near his home, was transferred to a brick factory 7 kilometers away and told: "After you'll have travelled 7 kilometers each day, you'll know where you must send your children to school!"

Russianization is furthered not only through the schools. Lithuanian first and last names are russianized. In documents Jonas is registered as Ivan, Jurgis—as Igor, etc. Lithuanian names of places are changed by Russian ones. For example, Juodelėnai in the Breslauja raion has been named Edolovichi, while the village Piliakalnis near Rodūnė has recently been renamed Gorodichsho.

In Belorussian localities inhabited by Lithuanians one never sees Lithuanian books, newspapers, or magazines in the stands. Lithuanian newspapers are never to be seen in reading rooms. School libraries do not accept Lithuanian books. Various obstacles are put in the way of Lithuanians in Belorussia who want to subscribe to Lithuanian periodicals. Whenever a citizen of the Lithuanian SSR wants to enter a subscription for his acquaintances who live in Belorussia, he must travel to the Belorussian SSR and go through the whole procedure of subscription in a local post office. If one enters the subscription in Lithuania, there is the risk that the addressee might never get it. But even if one journeys to Belorussia, one is allowed to enter subscriptions to no more than two persons. To order more means to become suspect: you will be asked where you got the money. Instructions have been issued to detain such persons and to hand them over to the security organs. The fear of the Lithuanian press is most acute and its persecution is most severe in the areas of Ramaškonys and Apsas, where Lithuanian consciousness is weak and where the young generation is beginning to converse in Belorussian. There is the apprehension that the press might revive Lithuanian culture.

Amateur cultural activities (folk dance, theater groups, choirs) are very important for the survival of national life.

Any such amateur cultural activities are prohibited for Lithuanians in Belorussia. The fate of teacher Antanas Šironas is an example of the extent to which Lithuanian cultural activities are being liquidated. Šironas worked for five years (until 1959) in the schools of the Gervėčiai area. The people of Gervėčiai still remember him today with kind words for his ability to work with the young as well as for his sincere devotion to the spreading of education and culture among the people. Šironas organized a broad program of amateur cultural activities in the villages of the Gervėčiai area. The cultural soirees he organized had a varied program: plays, folk songs, dances, etc. Šironas' activity attracted many young people. They not only took part in plays, danced and sang in their villages, but also took their performances to the raion festivals and won prizes. The local authorities did not like Šironas' activity. All his sincere labors and his devotion to the raising of the people's educational and cultural levels only earned him incessant hate and mockery on the part of the authorities. Hoodlums especially engaged for the occasion pelted his performers with rotten apples during the festival in the town of Astravas. Šironas was subjected to all kinds of intimidation (anonymous letters and similar tricks), was terrorized, and finally dismissed from his teaching post. But the security organs could not forgive Šironas his "nationalist" activity even after he had lost his job. His persecution and blackmail continued until he broke down.

Lithuanians in the Belorussian SSR are not only forbidden to organize amateur cultural activities; visits of cultural groups from Lithuania are also prohibited. Until 1972, despite all kinds of obstructions, artistic collectives of university and high school students would still sometimes visit the Lithuanians of the Belorussian SSR with various programs (songs, dances, music, etc.). Lithuanians would meet them with great enthusiasm. Since 1972 such visits have been severely curtailed. Any visit with a cultural group from the Lithuanian SSR to the Belorussian SSR requires a twofold permit: from the Lithuanian and from the Belorussian party organs. As practice has shown, such permits are not being issued.

Complex ethnographic expeditions are organized in Lithuania. Their activities have resulted in publications about Dieveniškės, Merkynė, Kernavė, etc." There were plans to organize a similar expedition to Gervėčiai. After much exertion and a joint Lithuanian-Belorussian group was formed, a permit was finally obtained through Minsk to collect data in the village of Gervéčiai. A good amount of work was done here in the summer of 1970: songs and tales were collected and folk customs and the Gervéčiai dialect were described, etc. In 1971 there were plans to organize such an expedition to the Pelesa area. But this time a permit was not issued. It was not Minsk that denied the permit but (a more clever stroke) the Vilnius Central Committee. It is doubtful whether a publication about Gervéčiai will ever come out. The Rector of the Vilnius Pedagogic Institute, Uogintas, zealously contributed to the liquidation of the activity of the ethnographers.[7]

All the above-mentioned measures are directed toward the liquidation of the Lithuanian element in those localities of the Belorussian SSR which for centuries have been inhabited by Lithuanians. There are no Lithuanian schools in Belorussia, while Russian and Polish schools are plentiful in Lithuania.[8] Russian schools are being opened everywhere (including the villages), as long as there are a few Russian children there. The Vilnius territory is saturated with Russian and Polish schools even in those places where Lithuanian schools existed during the Polish occupation (e.g., in Kalesnikai, raion of Eišiškės). Some 30 kilometers south of Vilnius there is the Lithuanian village of Marijampolė. A Lithuanian school was opened here soon after World War II. A new building was erected, but a couple of years ago Russian classes were established parallel with the Lithuanian ones.

The denationalization of Lithuanians is zealously practiced by Poles who have managed to curry favor with the Russian government. They occupy responsible positions and, under the cover of loyalty, act to the disadvantage of Lithuanians. It is

6. Reference to a series of ethnographic monographs sponsored by the Society for the Preservation of Monuments and Ethnography: Dieveniškės (Vilnius, 1968); Merkynė (Vilnius, 1970); Kernavė (Vilnius, 1972). So far the materials on Gervéčiai have not been published.

7. Vytautas Uogintas (1918-), party worker, graduate of party schools, heads the Vilnius Pedagogic Institute since 1960. His role in this affair has not been elucidated in the available samizdat materials.

8. In 1975-1976, among the day students in general education schools, 3 per cent were receiving instructions in Polish, 12 per cent in Russian, and 85 per cent in Lithuanian. Lietuvos TSR CSV, Lietuvos TSR ekonomika ir kultūra 1975 metais (Vilnius, 1976,), p. 261.

thanks to them that Lithuanians are registered as Poles (in their passports during the census-taking of 1959 and 1970). Especially notorious in this respect is the director of the passport and military office of the Pelesa area, Sawicki. He registers the less conscious Lithuanians as Poles. Even Belorussian-speaking people who know no Polish are registered by him as Poles.

Polish priests use the Church to continue the Polish policies of the prewar period. Church services are in Polish only, although the inhabitants are Belorussians or Lithuanians, with the exception of the church of Gervėčiai where the services are in Lithuanian too.

The Soviet Constitution and propaganda guarantees for all the citizens of the Soviet Union the right to promote their national culture and the right to study in their native language. These are the results of the Soviet national policy in the postwar years (since 1944) in respect to the Lithuanian minority in the Belorussian SSR.

If steps are not taken quickly, soon the Lazdūnai island will vanish. Only old men speak Lithuanian there now. There are also younger people from Lazdūnai who speak Lithuanian, but forced by circumstances, they have settled in Lithuania. Russian schools and the entire atmosphere unfavorable to Lithuanians have resulted in the fact that the young and the children do not speak Lithuanian.

Most of the children and the young people in the Ramaškoniai "island" of Varanavas raion also cannot speak Lithuanian anymore, although their parents converse in Lithuanian among themselves. But here the situation is not hopeless. The inhabitants of that "island" read the Lithuanian press and send their children to study in Lithuania.

The "islands" of Gervėčiai and Pelesa in which both the old and the young speak Lithuanian are still holding out strongly for the time being.

Why is denationalization so rapid these days among the Lithuanians of the Belorussian republic?

1. There are no Lithuanian schools. The schools are Russian, not Belorussian. According to information we have, only two Belorussian schools are operating in the Lithuanian-inhabited localities in Belorussia: one in the Varanavas, another in the Breslauja raion.

2. The activity of the Roman Catholic Church has been completely paralyzed. The churches have been closed, only a few continue functioning and are serviced by old priests (not younger than 60-70 years). When a priest dies, a new one is not admitted and in most cases the church is shut down.

In the postwar period the only Lithuanian priest in Belorussia (Pelesa) Vienažindis, was arrested. The stone church of Pelesa, built by Lithuanians, was closed in 1950, its towers were demolished, and it was transformed into a warehouse. The inhabitants of Pelesa addressed themselves to the local and central government organs concerning the opening of the church. A complaint was drafted to K. Voroshilov, Chairman of the Presidium of the USSR Supreme Soviet. The Commissioner for Religious Affairs in Minsk declared outright that there was no Lithuanian priest in Pelesa now and that there never would be one in the future. The curia of Vilnius had sent a priest, but the local authorities ordered him to leave promptly. They made it unmistakably clear that no Lithuanian priest would ever be admitted to Belorussia to perform his duties there.

3. There are no Lithuanian intelligentsia left in Belorussia, they were liquidated. Not a single Lithuanian agronomist, physician, or teacher is working in his native area. The chief officials in all public offices and kolkhozes are non-Lithuanian, mostly newcomers moved into the area for the purposes of russianization. At present it is impossible for a member of the Lithuanian intelligentsia to get a job in Belorussia. And even if he were to obtain a job, he would not be able to engage in any Lithuanian activity. That is why the young Lithuanians from Belorussia who complete their studies in Lithuania remain in Lithuania to work there.

4. No Lithuanian cultural establishments and organizations are allowed to function. All amateur Lithuanian cultural activity is prohibited.

5. Since cultural events are few or non-existent, and since the normal ways of entertainment and leisure activity are prohibited, the people turn to alcohol for gaiety and relaxation. Alcoholism is very widespread and no one is fighting it. The stores may run out of food or other products, but intoxicating drink is always available. Since state brandy is expensive,

the citizens make their own moonshine, too. Heavy drinking goes on on Sundays and on days of the week; any occasion is proper for getting drunk (name days, paydays, etc.).

6. The Lithuanians in Belorussia are materially dependent and spiritually crippled. Without knowledge of the Russian language, they are barred from jobs and are unable to put their personal affairs in order. All public life is Russian. The Lithuanian language in Belorussia has become declassé, it becomes not only unnecessary but remains a burden which not everyone is able to bear. All the factors that foster and sustain national life cannot reach the Lithuanian in Belorussia. His national consciousness is being extinguished because it is being destroyed by an entire, specially created environment.

This document does not cover all the facts nor does it list all the means whereby the Lithuanians of the Belorussian SSR are being denationalized. To add to the spiritual annihilation of the Lithuanians in Belorussia and to mock them even more grossly, while the national discrimination—both in the ways listed here and those yet to be described—is continuing, public speeches and writings hail the friendship of nations that has become embodied in our land. In practice that friendship of nations amounts to the fact that the big fish (the "brotherly" nation) is allowed to swallow the small fish (a small nation).

To what do they amount, these 50,000 Lithuanians whose fate is at stake? But then their total number is rather small, too. The areas inhabited by Lithuanians are slowly melting away in our own time, before our very eyes. Gone are the Lithuanians of Prussia beyond the Nemunas — in the area of Tilžė (Tilsit), Ragainė, and others, as well as in the Klaipėda area. It was not the German terror that completed their annihilation; they disappeared after the Red Army's march through these lands: some retreated to the West; others were deported to Siberia, where most of them perished. (The present-day Kaliningrad area had some 1.5 million inhabitants in 1939. According to the data of Dr. Vydūnas, 450,000 of them were of Lithuanian origin and 200,000 knew Lithuanian). The destiny of the 50,000 Lithuanians living in the Belorussian SSR is inextricably interwoven with the destiny of the entire Lithuanian nation living in a small area of the Nemunas river basin. With the Lithuanians of Prussia having recently melted away, and now with such a determined effort under way to assimilate the Lithuanians of Belorussia, the thought arises whether a melting process is not planned for us all.

THE STRUGGLE OF THE LITHUANIANS IN BELORUSSIA FOR THEIR RIGHTS

During the postwar years Lithuanians in the Belorussian SSR used all kinds of means to fight for their rights: they sent one delegation after another, wrote statements to various institutions and persons, and, lacking Lithuanian schools in their own country, they have sent and continue to send their children to study in Lithuania.

Of the many statements written and sent by Lithuanians of the Belorussian SSR, we shall mention only some:

1. A statement with 400 signatures in 1945 to the Ministry of Education in Minsk.

2. In 1955—a statement to the Soviet of Nationalities of the USSR.

3. In 1955—to the Central Committee of the Communist Party of the Soviet Union.

4. In 1958—to the Ministry of Education, signed by the inhabitants of the villages in the environs of Minsk and Pelesa.

5. In 1960—to Nikita S. Khrushchev, a statement with 1200 signatures of the inhabitants of Lithuanian villages in the Gervėčiai district.

6. In April 1961—to N. S. Khrushchev, a statement bearing 250 signatures of the inhabitants of Lithuanian villages of the Rodūnė region.

7. In May 1961—to N. S. Khrushchev, a statement with 2100 signatures of the inhabitants of the same region.

8. In 1963—to L. I. Brezhnev, a statement with 810 signatures of the inhabitants of Lithuanian villages in the raions of Varanavas and Smurgainiai.

In addition, statements were addressed to comrades M. Gedvilas, J. Paleckis, and A. Sniečkus.[9]

---

9. Lithuanian party and government leaders: A. Sniečkus—First Secretary of the Central Committee Communist Party of Lithuania; J. Paleckis—at that time Chairman of the Presidium, Supreme Soviet of the Lithuanian SSR; M. Gedvilas — Chairman of the Council of Ministers (until 1956) and Minister of Education.

All the statements were primarily concerned with the opening of Lithuanian schools. Other questions raised in the statements dealt mainly with cultural matters.

The statements sent to the central organs (in Moscow and Belorussia) were returned, as a rule, to the local authorities for solution. The latter not only refused to do anything to change the intolerable conditions, but even made efforts to identify and to punish those who had initiated the statements: they were usually threatened with deportation "where the white bears live," given harder and worse-paid work, etc. The only actual gain achieved by these statements was 2-3 hours of Lithuanian instruction per week since 1960, beginning with the third grade, in some Lithuanian village schools of Gervečiai and Pelesa.

Following are the texts of statements addressed to comrades Khrushchev and Brezhnev. The statements are abbreviated in the interest of space and also because some of the questions are repeated in both statements.

To: Comrade N. S. Khrushchev, First Secretary of the Central Committee of the Communist Party of the Soviet Union.

From: Inhabitants of Lithuanian villages in the Rodūnė raion, Gardinas area, Belorussian SSR.

Statement

... In the second half of September 1939, following the liberation of Western Belorussia by the Red Army, Lithuanians in that territory breathed more freely. Soviet power was created in the Rodūnė raion. Progressive people rejoiced. And why should they not rejoice when they saw, as part of the flowering of socialist culture, Lithuanian Soviet schools functioning freely in Pelesa, Dubiniai, Pavalskė, and elsewhere. The working people of the Rodūnė raion elected their deputies to the People's Soviet of Western Belorussia: Nikrovich, a Belorussian; Karol, a Pole; and Sinkevičius and Šimelionis, both Lithuanians. The people entrusted their fate to them. The secretaries of the Party raion committee were Isachenko, a Ukrainian, and Konstelson, a Jew, while Pinsonenko, a Belorussian, served as chairman of the executive committee. Šimelionis, a Lithuanian, served as managing secretary of the raion executive committee, in which comrades Jonis, Sinkevičius, and others occupied important posts. A number of Lithuanians—Adamonis, Dūda, Žukauskas, and others—were secretaries of district committees. Another Lithuanian, Vaitkūnas, was chairman of the executive committee of the town of Rodūnė. Many Lithuanians occupied important positions in the local economic organs. The first kolkhoz of the raion was established in the Lithuanian village of Dubičiai.

The German occupation interrupted creative activity. The Lithuanians of Rodūnė joined the entire Soviet people in the fight against the German forces of occupation. Comrades Adamonis, Sinkevičius, Žukauskas, Kemenčius, Neviera, Jonis, and others perished in the unequal struggle.

... Following the destruction of Hitlerite Germany, a bright, new life began in Belorussia. However, the Polish nationalists, now having changed their colors and having "become" Soviet patriots, but without having relinquished their sinister goals, began to destroy the most precious treasure of the Soviet system—the friendship of nations. Having infiltrated the Soviet apparatus, they started fomenting national hatred among the inhabitants of the Rodūnė area. This is why, owing to the activity of these Polish nationalists and to the political myopia of the local Soviet and party organs, Lithuanian rights were painfully violated during the postwar period. Of the 14 Lithuanian primary schools, which functioned even during the time of Polish rule, not a single one remains in the Rodūnė raion. Children from Lithuanian villages must go to school, yet in the first grade they are taught to read and write not in their native tongue, but in a language they do not understand. It becomes quite obvious why the students are making such slow progress and why so many children are left behind to repeat the course. Very few children of Lithuanian kolkhoz peasants graduate from high school. That is why some of the more energetic Lithuanians have begun sending their children to study in Soviet Lithuania... At the present time not a single physician, agronomist, teacher, or zootechnician from the Rodūnė area works in his native locality. In the first postwar years intolerable working conditions drove all Lithuanian teachers and other educated people from their raion to Soviet Lithuania.

... Not a single Lithuanian book or newspaper is to be found in the clubs and reading rooms of the Rodūnė raion.

Subscriptions and orders of Lithuanian press from the Lithuanian SSR are being impeded in all ways possible.

... In 1949, the inhabitants of the Dubiniai village established a kolkhoz and called it by the name of Marytė Melnikaitė, heroine of the Soviet Union.[10] The manager of the kolkhoz was a local Lithuanian, Lukoševičius. The kolkhoz acquired a leading position and the people were happy, but not for long. The kolkhoz was soon reorganized and the Lithuanian chairman was dismissed from his post. He was replaced by an individual who had not the slightest idea of the local conditions. The kolkhoz was renamed "Malenkov." Two other Lithuanian kolkhoz chairmen — Remeška and Šiška — were fired. Lithuanians are not wanted in the local Soviets and none are left in them.

... During the general census in 1959 Lithuanians were denied their nationality. For example, Miss Viktorija Stračinskaitė and Stasė Stračinskienė were registered as Poles, although they had begged, with tears in their eyes, for an accurate recording of their nationality.

Post office directors tolerate abuses concerning the Lithuanian press. It is very difficult to subscribe to Lithuanian newspapers—they do not come at all, or only sporadically. In 1958 many inhabitants of this area had entered subscriptions to Lithuanian newspapers, but they either failed to receive any of them or received non-Lithuanian newspapers instead.

During the summer vacation Lithuanian students of the Rodūnė raion had invited tourist-students from Kaunas. A group of student nature explorers arrived at the Pavalkė village. The kolkhoz peasants met them joyfully and had a common dancing and singing session after work. Once the kolkhoz chairman, Kovalchuk, found out about it early in the morning, he hurried to upbraid the kolkhoz peasants who were hosts to the students from Kaunas, and, pounding the table with his fist and screaming, he threatened them with loss of work and other penalties.

... Therefore, we beg you to correct the wrongs that are being inflicted on us and to make it possible for us to take

---

10. Marija Melnikaitė (1923-1943), a Lithuanian girl, one of the few Lithuanians given the title of "Hero of the Soviet Union." She was parachuted into German-occupied territory as a Soviet partisan. Immediately she was caught and executed by German forces.

advantage of the positive accomplishments of the Soviet system. We know that national deviations are alien to our Party and state government, and therefore we beg emphatically that these questions be solved in a positive manner:

1. The review of the possibility of putting into effect the decision of the USSR Supreme Soviet, dated August 3, 1940, "On the transfer to the Lithuanian SSR of part of some raions of the Belorussian SSR where the Lithuanians are in the majority."

2. The opening of Lithuanian primary, seven-year, and high schools in a whole series of villages inhabited by Lithuanian nationals.

3. Making an end to the obstruction of, and creating the conditions for, the participation of inhabitants of Lithuanian nationality in the cultural-political life of their raion in their own native language:

> a. to supply local libraries with fiction and political literature as well as with newspapers and magazines in the Lithuanian language, and to stop interfering with those who read it;
>
> b. to cease the obstruction of Lithuanian amateur art and cultural activities;
>
> c. to stop putting obstacles in the collaboration of our villages with the social organizations and state bodies of the Lithuanian SSR.

4. Giving assistance in order to liquidate the backwardness of local kolkhozes. Meanwhile we, the kolkhoz workers, will do our utmost to create a flourishing socialist economy and culture in our native villages.

Please do not refuse to satisfy our request.

April 3, 1961   (255 signatures)

— — — —

Following the mailing of this statement, a six-person commission arrived in the area on July 25, 1961. The commission checked the facts, interviewed the local inhabitants, agreed that their demands were just, and promised that Lithuanian schools would be opened on September 1, 1961, that the question of libraries and clubs-reading rooms would be solved, and that the inhabitants would be assisted in collaborating with the Lithuanian SSR. The commission refused, however, to attach our villages to the Lithuanian SSR because, according to them, the number of signatures was too small.

Thereupon, in August 1961, a second analogous statement, bearing 2100 signatures, was sent to N. S Khrushchev.

While collection of signatures for these statements was still under way, some raion officials and militiamen were trying to intimidate the local population and to prevent them from signing under the statements. About a month after the departure of the commission, security agents and militiamen of the Gardinas area arrived and kept intimidating the people by telling them that they would be deported "where the white bears live" as punishment for writing and sending these statements, and that their requests would not be granted.

Seeing that the promises made by the commission were not being fulfilled, the people decided to demand once more that the local authorities translate those promises into reality. The Party Secretary of the Rodūnė raion was asked why Lithuanian schools are not being opened. The Lithuanian representatives who came to see him were told that Lithuanian schools would not be opened and that the visitors should stop wasting their time. A telephone inquiry was made to the People's Education Department of the Gardinas (Grodno) area. In his reply, the department chief stated that he was not considering any action concerning this request since he had not received any instructions from above.

Following the change of the political situation in the Soviet Union, a petition was sent to Comrade L. I. Brezhnev:

To: Comrade L. I. Brezhnev, First Secretary of the Central
      Committee of the Communist Party of the Soviet
      Union.
From: Inhabitants of the raions of Varanavas and Smurgainiai,
      Gardinas (Grodno) area, Belorussian SSR

Statement

(This was a joint statement of the inhabitants of the Lithuanian villages of the Gervečiai and Rodūnė-Pelesa area. The opening portion of the statement enumerates villages inhabited by Lithuanians.)

... At the end of the German occupation we were waiting for the opening of the Lithuanian schools, but our hopes and expectations were not fulfilled. Instead, Russian schools were opened in the Lithuanian villages in the fall of 1944 and continue operating to this very day. During the period of the Stalin cult we repeatedly petitioned the local and republican BSSR organs, asking for the opening of Lithuanian schools. Some institutions answered our petitions with promises, while others branded us as nationalists and even threatened us with deportation to Siberia.

Following Stalin's death we renewed our demands for Lithuanian schools. Our requests were granted only in part: two to three weekly lessons of the Lithuanian language were introduced as subjects in a few schools from the third grade up. But the children of most of the Lithuanian villages lack even this possibility to learn their native tongue.

... The discrimination against us, Lithuanians, by the local Belorussian authorities is manifesting itself not only in education but in other fields as well. Here are several facts.

The ordering of Lithuanian publications from the Lithuanian SSR is being obstructed. Local employees of the BSSR postal system willfully replace Lithuanian newspapers by Belorussian or Russian ones.

In 1958 we addressed ourselves to the Ministry of Culture of the Lithuanian SSR, asking them to send us books. But the local authorities refused to accept the books and returned them. This happened in Gervečiai.

Lithuanian newspapers and political literature are nowhere to be found in clubs and reading rooms.

In 1959 students of the Salomėja Neris high school in Vilnius came to the Gervečiai high school as goodwill visitors. As their gift they brought 250 Soviet Lithuanian books. The director of the Gervečiai high school, Pashkovski, refused to accept the gift. After prolonged entreaties he accepted the books, but a month later they disappeared from the school library.

The kolkhoz chairman, Rul, was very hostile toward Lithuanians. It was at his initiative that the monument of Vytautas, Grand Duke of Lithuania, erected in 1930 in the village of Dubiniai, was destroyed in the fall of 1963. This destruction upset the local inhabitants very much.

During the general census taking in 1959 we noticed that the census takers did not complete the questionnaires in ink. Whenever a citizen declared that he was a Lithuanian, the census taker used a plain pencil to enter his nationality, but when a Pole or a Belorussian was involved, the entry was made in ink. When the census takers were asked why they were acting in this manner, they replied that they had received such instructions from the raion officials. In the raion of Varanavas civil servants tried in various ways to persuade Lithuanians not to register as Lithuanians. Following the census of 1959 local officials showed us the census data in the newspapers where one could see black on white that no Lithuanians existed in the Belorussian SSR.

... We have repeatedly addressed ourselves to the raion, republic and central organs, demanding that our legitimate requests be granted. But our requests were rejected.

The aforementioned permits the following conclusions to be drawn:

1. That Lithuanians in Belorussia are not citizens with equal rights;

2. Lithuanians in the Belorussian SSR are denied the opportunity to avail themselves of the right guaranteed in the Constitution to study in their native tongue;

3. The local officials of the Belorussian SSR not only refuse to help, but frequently obstruct our cultural exchanges with the inhabitants of the Lithuanian SSR;

4. The local officials not only withhold their assistance, but frequently prevent the Lithuanians in Belorussia from obtaining newspapers and books published in the Lithuanian SSR;

5. The local organs of the BSSR bar Lithuanians not only from the leading posts, but also from secondary positions in the kolkhozes, village Soviets, and other offices;

6. In 1959 the general census was conducted by crudely violating the rights of the Lithuanians. Lithuanians were deprived of the opportunity to determine their nationality freely: against their will, Lithuanians were registered as Belorussians or Poles.

On the basis of the above information, we ask you most emphatically to resolve these questions:

1. To open the Lithuanian primary, eight-year, and high schools in the localities where Lithuanians form the majority;

2. To remove obstacles for cultural-educational work in the Lithuanian language among the population;

3. To provide us with the opportunity to read books, magazines, and newspapers in our native language;

4. To supply libraries and club-reading rooms with Lithuanian literature published in the Lithuanian SSR;

5. To instruct the local authorities of the BSSR that they treat Lithuanians as citizens with equal rights;

6. To ensure a free mutual collaboration between the Lithuanians in the Belorussian SSR and the population of the Lithuanian SSR;

7. We beg you to protect us from the threats and reprisals of the local officials who are liable to turn against us for having submitted this statement because the officials have reacted in this manner in the past whenever such statements were submitted.

Eighteen years have passed now since we have started submitting statements, demanding our rights..

May this be the last statement and may it bring satisfactory results. We hope to be favored with the attention of the highest organ of the Soviet government.

November 1963.   (810 signatures)

We do not know how the local officials reacted to this statement. There may have been no threats and reprisals, but there were also no positive results. Lithuanians in the Belorussian republic failed to gain the attention of Comrade Brezhnev.

EPILOGUE: THE SITUATION OF BELORUSSIA'S LITHUANIANS IN 1978[11]

During the past five years the situation of Lithuanians in the Belorussian SSR not only did not improve, but, on the contrary, notably deteriorated. Persecution is not ceasing.

Unfortunately, the process of assimilation among the Lithuanians in the Belorussian SSR is continuing. In some villages of Lazdūnai, Ramaškonys, and even areas of Apsas the parents speak Lithuanian while the children already do not know the Lithuanian language. The same is true in nationally mixed families. But even in families where both parents are Lithuanians, the children frequently do not know the Lithuanian language... The parents, asked why they do not converse with their children in Lithuanian, explain that they want to make it easier for the children to study at school. Today in the Lithuanian-inhabited areas of the Belorussian SSR there are now not only Russian, but also Belorussian primary and secondary schools. The number of Russian schools is notably greater. The complete middle schools in Apsas, Rodūnė, Gervėčiai, and Varnavas are Russian. The higher schools of the Belorussian SSR are also Russian. Thus the child gradually shifts from the Belorussian to the Russian language. The older Lithuanian inhabitants are dying out; the youth does not know Lithuanian. Those who study in Lithuania usually remain there. In this manner the Lithuanian language is disappearing in Lithuanian lands. So far the island of Gervėčiai and the environs of Pelesa are persevering. Here parents and children do speak Lithuanian.

---

11. A follow-up report "On the Situation of Lithuanians in the Belorussian Republic," covering the period between 1972 and 1978, appeared in Vilnius in 1978. The samizdat report consists of 46 typewritten pages. It provides details on the situation of Lithuanians in their localities and copies of petitions for national rights to various governmental and party officials, including General Secretary L. Brezhnev. In general, the report is pessimistic about the survival of the Lithuanian minority in Belorussia, finding the conditions for national life worse than five years ago. Nevertheless, it calls for continued aid to the some 30,000 Lithuanians in Belorussia (as claimed by the report), who demand and deserve national rights. The struggle for national rights in Belorussia is seen as part of the overall effort for survival of the Lithuanian nation. The excerpts here are from the introductory part of the report.

The process of assimilation is speeded up by the entire Russian environment. Officials, such as collective farm chairmen, party and administrative representatives, are mostly not local inhabitants. In order to transact business with them, one must know Russian. They do not like Lithuanians. Often one hears the complaint from local Lithuanians that "The officials do not like us." Not only do they dislike Lithuanians, but also everything that is Lithuanian, what is indigenous to the land and precious to the Lithuanian. They not only dislike, but also, given the chance, destroy the monuments of Lithuanian culture.

The persecution of religion and the liquidation of churches is another important factor contributing to the moral decline and assimilation of Lithuanians. After World War II most of the churches in areas inhabited by Lithuanians (Apsas, Vydžiai, Pelesa, Varanavas, Lazdūnai) were closed. Among the open churches in Rodūnė and Gervėčiai, only in the latter Lithuanian services are held.

The current strengthening of persecution of Lithuanian life in Belorussia indicates an aim to destroy it finally and to transform the Lithuanians there into Russians.

A large part of Lithuania's society is indiferrent to the fate of Lithuanians in Belorussia. Such people think that the question of Belorussia's Lithuanians is insignificant, that allegedly there are few Lithuanians there and, therefore, there is no need to worry; they can be "written-off". And many did "write them off." They say that it is necessary to survive here in Lithuania, to entrench here, and that resources should not be wasted on Belorussia's Lithuanians because they are lost; history cannot be turned back.

Those who think this way do not see and do not want to understand that the fate of Lithuanians in the Belorussian SSR is inextricably connected to the fate of the entire Lithuanian nation. The history of the Lithuanian people is written here in Belorussia. They do not see the danger of Slavic encirclement and the penetration of Russians into the Baltic space, which is done under Moscow's direction, according to plan, to take "small pieces." Such people do not see that Russian nationalism is determined to devour not only Belorussia's Lithuanians, but also the entire Eastern Lithuania and, later, Lithuania as well. The assimilation of Belorussia's Lithuanians is only one phase of russification of Lithuania.

22. AN OPEN PROTEST AGAINST CENSORSHIP

To: Ministry of Culture of the Lithuanian SSR
    State Drama Theater of Kaunas
    Lithuanian Theater Association
    Editors of *Literatūra ir Menas*

After years of work in the theater the necessity has matured to expound my accumulated thoughts concerning the principles of activity of the director as an artist and as a citizen.

Spiritual values are the only repayment the creative individual makes to society for the right to live in it. It would appear that conditions for creation are favorable here. But what does experience show? A number of productions staged by me, such as "Warsaw Melody," "Tango," "The Mammoth Hunt," "Moliere," "Holy Lake," and "House of Threat" received lively attention from the public.[1] "The Duel," "The Bolsheviks," and "Mother's Field" received diplomas and awards.[2] The theater is successfully implementing fiscal policy. Such success could satisfy a director. Yet, what is hidden in the background? Years of struggle for the right to stage a mature play, unending disputes with cowardly bureaucrats to prove the importance of a production to society, the needless expenditure of energy in self-defense from demagogic attempts to perceive the intent of playwrights in the yet unstaged plays, the deformation of the texture of the work through categorical insistence on elimination of even essential elements, and finally, the limitation of exploitation of productions or even their complete prohibi-

---

No. 22. AS No. 1383. See also the open letter of Jonas Jurašas to the world theatrical community, AS No. 2149, December, 1974. As a consequence of this protest, which was widely disseminated in the West, Jurašas lost his position as Senior Director of the Kaunas State Theater. In 1976 he was allowed to leave his homeland. Presently he resides in the US.

1. "The Warsaw Melody" is by Leonid Zorin; "Tango" by Slavomir Mrozek; "Moliere" by Mikhail Bulgakov. "The Hunt of the Mammoths" and "Holy Lake" are by the Lithuanian playwright Kazys Saja, and the "House of Threat" also by the Lithuanian dramatist J. Glinskis. The Lithuanian plays are written in a modern vein and can be interpreted as critical evaluations of Soviet life.

2. "The Duel" is by M. Baidzhiyev; "The Bolsheviks" by M. Shatrov; "Mother's Field" by Ch. Aitmatov.

tion, ignoring the opinion of the audience of the theater-going public at large.

Out of the twelve productions staged during five years, I could consider only three as more or less revealing my world view. However, even these were seen by the spectator in a damaged version, with a loss of a substantial artistic impact. The final scene of "Tango" was taken out; "The Mammoth Hunt" was abbreviated. Both productions were later prohibited. And so many spectators did not see them. Especially important scenes of "The House of Threat" were cut out; the composition and final scene were changed.

Compromise was the only way I could preserve for the audience my impaired stage productions. Compromises... They are convenient for occasional adherents who seek a quiet bay in artistic circles.

Is spiritual comfort not a betrayal of artistic conscience? Does betrayal remain unpunished?

On the road of compromises the artist is unaware of how his spiritual resources are evaporating, how he is approaching degeneration.

That road is not for me.

I cannot accept truths imposed from outside. In actualizing alien "truths," the artist becomes a stranger to himself. In isolating himself from his own micro-world, the creator loses his ties with the contemporary planet.

Through my creative work in the theater I want to express the spirit of the times, the complexity of the human condition, its contradictions. The theater is my life and my passion, the meaning of my existence. The theater is a tie, connecting me with people. The theater is one of the most significant means in developing the motherland, it is a barometer, indicating its greatness and uniqueness. A sensitive and purposeful theater, with all the diversity of styles and genres—from tragedy to vaudeville—can change the world view of the people in a few years. An impaired theater, with "elevators" instead of wings, can prostitute the entire nation.

The theater is a school for tears and laughter, an open forum in which the people can condemn an anachronistic and deceitful morality and with a living example reveal the eternal principles of the heart and feelings.

A nation which does not contribute to the creation of a theater is either dead or in a stupor. However, if the theater, through laughter and tears, does not touch the pulse of society and its history—the drama of its people, the true colors of its landscape, if it does not express the national spirit, then it has no right to call itself a theater. It must be called a gambling casino or a place where "time is annihilated" shamelessly (F. Garcia Lorca).

I have devoted all my powers to make the theater the carrier of truth, goodness, and beauty. I sought to realize these ideals also in my last staging of the play "Barbora Radvilaitė". After great theatrical efforts a spectacle was born, which could have been significant in the life of our theater.[3] However, it is not clear when the public will see it. Can it be that the fate of the earlier productions awaits "Barbora Radvilaitė"?

The viewer is the only judge of my artistic work. Freely evolving criteria should not be replaced by opinions formed in the stuffy, hermetically sealed offices (of bureaucrats).

So far I have sought, without receiving permission, to stage J. Anouilh's "Antigone," R. Hochhuth's "The Deputy," T. Rudzevich's "My Little Daughters," Marat's "Sade," L. Zorin's "Dion," and other plays. It was proposed to me to "select" works from plan lists, which do not correspond at all to my sense of the world.

Today the voices of unstaged and impaired works cause me pain. The so-called success of individual productions revolts me. Compromises, tactical cunning, senseless pacing down the bureaucratic corridors, the degradation of human dignity, gloomy prospects—all this forces me to resolve:

— After long deliberations I have decided to refuse to change anything in completed productions;

— I refuse to buy the hope of producing mature works for the price of occasional productions;

— I recognize only those criteria for evaluation of cre-

---

3. "Barbora Radvilaitė" is a historical drama by the leading modern playwright of contemporary Lithuania, Juozas Grušas. The play deals with the life of Barbora Radzivill (ca. 1520-1551), Queen of Poland and Grand Duchess of Lithuania. A descendant of a noted line of Lithuanian nobility, Barbora was a controversial figure in Polish-Lithuanian relations. The staging of the play by Jurašas involved nationalistic undertones and the intervention of Soviet censors.

ative works which are born in the sharp conflict of opinions;
— I create according to the command of my conscience
as an artist and a citizen.

Jonas Jurašas

Senior Director of

Kaunas, August 16, 1972.   The Kaunas State Theater

23. AN APPEAL FOR THE PRESERVATION OF NATIONAL TREASURES

With great exuberance, Lithuanians in the entire world are preparing to meet the 100th anniversary of the birth of M. K. Čiurlionis, the genius of their nation, the great artist and at the same time one of the brightest minds of mankind. Recently a news item appeared in the press of Lithuania: the East German publisher "Verlag der Kunst" is preparing to publish a monograph on M. K. Čiurlionis, only in the German language, however. Besides, only a fourth of the illustrations will be in color.[1] Soon it will be a year since the formation of a committee in Lithuania to prepare for the jubilee. However, so far nothing is yet known that finally the Lithuanian nation will appropriately honor her own Čiurlionis.

Where is the competition to design a monument for the truly deserving genius artist? Where are at least the promises that finally a monograph on the work of M. K. Čiurlionis will be published in the *Lithuanian language* with quality color reproductions of all the works of M. K. Čiurlionis? After all, the great artist painted on inferior paper with paints of short duration and his paintings are rapidly deteriorating. If, on the occasion of the centennial, quality reproductions are not produced, the paintings may not survive until the next anniversary... Is it sufficient to be satisfied with uncertain possibilities for

---

No. 23. AS No. 1386, first published in the Chicago Lithuanian daily **Draugas**, September 16, 1972, Part II. M. K. Čiurlionis (1875-1911) is the most renowned Lithuanian painter. He is among the few Lithuanian artists who has been widely recognized beyond the borders of his native land as a pioneer of modern art. This letter by an anonymous group of Vilnius intelligentsia, which reached the West in mid-1972, is an obvious effort to prod the Soviet authorities to properly commemorate the centennial of his birth. A special concern was raised with the conservation of his paintings, which are deteriorating. For a brief introduction to Čiurlionis, see the special issue of **Lituanus**, No. 2, 1961; also J. Pivoriūnas, "A Lithuanian Individualist: The Art of M. K. Čiurlionis," **Lituanus**, No. 1, 1966.

1. A German language monograph has been published: Gytis Vaitkūnas, **Mikalojus Konstantinas Čiurlionis** (Dresden, VEB Verlag der Kunst, 1975), 278 pages, 201 plates.

restoration? Finally, what if some natural disaster or war occurred? There is only one Čiurlionis!

The newspapers of Lithuania (*Tiesa, Literatūra ir menas, Gimtasis kraštas,* and others), as well as public agencies (the Ministry of Culture and others) often receive letters from citizens, asking what is being done to preserve and to honor the work of M. K. Čiurlionis. The results of "internal pressure" so far are meager...

In the turmoil of history we became accustomed to being cautious, skeptical, angry. It is said that we are slow, stubborn northerners. It is said that we are culturally behind the world. However, one wonders whose fault it is that we are incapable of demonstrating to the world what we can: whether our Lithuanian backwardness must be tied to the pillar of shame or only to various circumstantial obstacles? It is strange, but many Lithuanians have more hope of seeing a monument to Gediminas, Kudirka, Basanavičius, Baranauskas, Maironis, and Čiurlionis somewhere in Chicago, rather than in Lithuania, in the central (or peripheral) squares of Vilnius.

Yes, we are telling the truth: after many years we would like to visit good old Chicago, which has become a mother to many Lithuanians, and to see there what a Lithuanian can do, to see how he loves his native land—so small and pure as a tear drop on the face of God...

No, we are not traitors, enemies of the nation. We want Gediminas in Vilnius, Maironis in Kaunas, Basanavičius in Anykščiai. However, experience has shown that when our brothers, living under foreign skies, take initiative, a movement arises also among the thick-skulled bureaucrats.

We must remember and we do remember: many noted people lived in Lithuania, who dearly loved the Motherland and who gave her everything. We want to honor them, regardless of the conditions and difficulties—economic or other. Only a man who honors the past is a man. Only a man who loves his native land is a man. Only a man who has faith in his people, in his nation, seeking a brighter tomorrow for her is a man.

The future is impossible without culture, without spiritual life, without that which is more valuable than money, government, and all circumstances. We believe in our nation, her vitality, which was confirmed by history. We believe in the higher ideals, goodness, and beauty—finally, in God himself. We also believe this, that Lithuanians in the entire world will do everything in order to safeguard and appropriately honor the cultural heritage of this small but creative and dear nation of ours, that everything will be done—in Lithuania and elsewhere—to demonstrate to the world through Lithuanian perseverence and diligence the spiritual strength and beauty of our nation.

We must remember and we do remember that Lithuania has ancient cultural traditions, only that they were suffocated for centuries by many covetous neighbors... During the brief two-decade rebirth, a giant leap forward was made (though we do not deny the shortcomings of the past). On the other hand, the contemporary cultural achievements of Lithuania should not be denied either. Nevertheless...

We hope that perhaps folios of color reproductions of M. K. Čiurlionis' paintings, published in world-renowned houses, will also reach us in Lithuania. Perhaps some day we will not have to worry that the colors of some paintings have not yet been preserved for the ages.

Čiurlionis is alive and will live forever because his spirit is in us, in the nation of Čiurlionis. We shall never permit the eternal flame of art to flicker out.[2]

---

2. In 1977 an album with quality color reproductions of Čiurlionis' printings was finally published. The printing was done by OPF Univas of Paris. The album, simply entitled **Konstantinas Mikalojus Čiurlionis**, was prepared for publication by a group of art experts headed by Valerija Čiurlionytė-Karužienė. The introduction was written by Lionginas Šepetys, the Minister of Culture at the time.

24. INTERROGATIONS AND ARRESTS OF ETHNOGRAPHERS

Vilnius. In 1973 the following Lithuanians were under investigation by the security authorities of Vilnius: (1) Birutė Andrašiūnaitė, an engineer, on March 28; (2) Marija Božytė, senior in Lithuanian studies at the Vilnius University, on March 28; (3) Birutė Burauskaitė, an engineer, on April 2; (4) Kazimieras Eigminas, a graduate of Vilnius University, a specialist in Lithuanian language, on April 6; (5) Elena Eimaitytė, a graduate in German language, on March 27; (6) Rėda Jakučionytė, an engineer, on March 28; (7) Zenonas Jakučionis, a graduate of the conservatory; (8) Veronika Janulevičiūtė, a member of the Ethnographic Ensemble of the Youth Theater, on March 28; (9) Virginija Jasiukaitytė-Asmontienė, a student in Lithuanian studies; (10) Alfonsas Juška, a biophysics specialist, on March 27-28; (11) Donata Kanevičiūtė, a mathematician, on April 3; (12) Danas Kaukėnas, a reporter of the *Vakarinės Naujienos* (Evening News), on April 4; (13) Kęstutis Labanauskas, a worker in the Institute for the Restoration of Monuments, on March 28; (14) Rimas Matulis, a graduate in the English language, on March 28; (15) Kazimieras Misius, an engineer, on March 27; (16) Egidijus Norvaišas, a graduate student in physics, on March 27; (17) Algimantas Petrauskas, an engineer, on March 28; (18) Teresė Povilaitytė, a graduate in Lithuanian language, on March 28; (19) Alfonsas Ramonas, a specialist in physics-mathematics, on March 27; (20) Albinas Simokaitis, an instructor; (21) Edma Stankevičius, a student in journalism; (22) Jonas Trinkūnas, a graduate student in history-philosophy, on March 28; (23) Zita Vanagaitė, an architect, on April 3.

The secret police interrogated these individuals about their excursions to the Urals and Siberia: Why did they associate with Lithuanian deportees, why did they visit the camps? The

No. 24. From **Chronicle**, No. 6 (May, 1973). This is a report of the initial campaign against the popular amateur ethnographic clubs which evidently were involved in activities defined by the authorities as "nationalistic." The clubs were ordered to redirect their attention to ethnography of the Soviet period. The underground **Aušra**, No. 5 (February 16, 1977), has reported that harassment, interrogations, and searches of amateur ethnographers again were carried out in September and November of 1976.

secret police made the accusation that during the excursions attempts were allegedly made to establish ties with the nationalistic strata of Armenians, Georgians, and other nationalities.

The interrogators reproached them for showing an interest in and calling attention to the destruction of ancient cultural monuments as well as for burning candles on castle-hills while on an outing to the Sambia region of East Prussia.[1]

The secret police was interested in the activities of the Folk Song Club of the Trade Unions Hall in Vilnius and of the Vilnius University Student Club Romuva (which was disbanded two years ago). Questions were asked about the Rasa festival in Kernavė and about the archeological expedition to the Šventoji river.[2]

The interrogated were scolded for their interest in the past and its idealization because nationalistic moods are spread thereby.

They were asked: Why are only Lithuanian songs sung? Why are partisan songs sung? Why is material about the partisan struggles being collected? In the meetings with the Latvians, why are nationalistic moods being propagated? Why are contacts with Lithuanians in Belorussia being maintained, books sent to them, newspapers subscribed, their children encouraged to attend Lithuanian schools in Lithuania?[3]

The secret police inquired why so many youths are attracted to ethnographic activities.

R. Matulis was ordered to sign that he will not participate in and will not organize any meetings without the sanction of official organs.

Kaunas.[4] Following the trial of Šarūnas Žukauskas and his friends,[5] the security resolved to do away with remaining more active amateur ethnographers and other individuals.

---

1. Reference to some pseudo-religious ceremony, probably an imitation of some ancient Lithuanian pagan rite.

2. Rasa festival involves the customs and rites of St. John's eve. Kernavė is the site of an ancient Lithuanian political center, possibly the first capital of the Lithuanian state. The celebration of St. John's at Kernavė probably involved nationalistic overtones.

3. See Doc. No. 21 for details on the situation of Lithuanians in the Belorussian republic.

4. This section is from the **Chronicle,** No. 11 (1974).

5. See Doc. No. 25.

Jucevičius, a postgraduate student who worked in the faculty of chemical technology, was expelled from the Polytechnical Institute; student Albinas Jonkus—from the faculty of sanitary technology; fifth-year student Levija Mozerytė and the assistant of the department of surgical stomatology, Remigijus Morkūnas—from the Institute of Medicine.

Nijolė Muraškaitė, sixth-year student of the Institute of Medicine, received her penalty in the form of a severe reprimand for "behavior" incompatible with the ethics of a Soviet physician. During the examination of her case in the Rector's office, religious belief and church attendance were listed as incriminating charges against her. Similar severe reprimands were directed against sixth-year students Virginijus Skabinskas and Kazimieras Preikša.

The following individuals were subjected to criticism in their places of work: Jūratė Eitniravičiūtė (Industrial Planning), Eligijus Morkūnas (Ethnographic Museum), Margarita Sakalauskienė (Executive Secretary of the Kaunas Ethnographic Association), Audronė Pieseckaitė (Čiurlionis Art Museum), Vilius Semaška (Radio plant), Lukas Mackevičius (Endocrinal preparations plant), Regimantas Kurklietis (same place).

Margarita Sakalauskienė was dismissed from work, while the remaining ones were called repeatedly to the security committee, where an effort was made to persuade them to sign pledges that they would stop participating in anti-Soviet activity. These individuals were discussed in their working places on the basis of information received from the party committee.

Incensed about the above-mentioned reprisals, the amateur ethnographers collected the society's membership cards and relinquished them to the city Soviet of Kaunas, stating that they were leaving the society.

The following amateur ethnographers were repeatedly called to the Vilnius security committee and were being compelled to sign under the official warnings: Alfonsas Juška, Birutė Barauskaitė, Jonas Trinkūnas, Rimas Batulis, Kazys Misius.

The latter was also accused of having sent abroad photographs of Lithuanian crosses. According to the interrogators, it was permitted to collect the photographs of crosses, but their dissemination was forbidden.

25. THE TRIAL OF FIVE NATIONALISTS

AN ARBITRARY TRIAL IN VILNIUS

The article "In Whose Voice," published in *Tiesa* of March 17, 1974, described the trial of five individuals in Vilnius. The article failed to provide the dates of the trial and the sentences meted out to the defendants; only their criminal offenses were mentioned—they allegedly stole typewriters, folk art objects, and ecclesiastical vessels. The article indicated that the case was a political one.[1]

On March 27, 1973, the security organs carried out a well-planned action against the amateur ethnographers in Lithuania and Latvia, comparable in its extent and impact to the analogous drive against the publishers and distributors of the *Chronicle of the Catholic Church in Lithuania.*[2] Over 100 amateur ethnographers were sent at 8 a.m. to the Security Committee's premises in Kaunas, Vilnius, and Riga. House searches were conducted, arrests were made. The most active amateur ethnographers—R. Matulis from Vilnius, J. Eitmanavičiūtė from Kaunas, and others were compelled to sign pledges that "in the future they would not engage themselves in amateur ethnography." The youngest among the amateur ethnographers were being forced to collaborate with the security organs and were subjected to blackmail. The amateur ethnographers were interrogated by Kontrimas, Radzevičius, Aleinikovas, Rimkus, Žilevičius, Sujuta, and others...

Articles began appearing in the press, expressly demanding the renunciation of the exploration of the "feudal epoch" and

---

No. 25. From **Chronicle**, No. 10 (1974). The arrests of the four individuals tried occurred at the end of March, 1973, according to the **Chronicle**, No. 6 (May, 1973). The trial a year later was extensively reported in Soviet press **(Tiesa)**, an indication of the importance ascribed to the case by Soviet authorities. The publicity of the trial was very likely intended as a deterrent.

1. The article in **Tiesa** presented the defendants as criminals, omitting to mention that they were tried under Article 68 of the Penal Code, in effect for political reasons.

2. The extensive campaign to silence religious dissent is reported in the **Chronicle**, beginning with issue No. 10. The campaign culminated in Case 345, involving the trials and convictions of several Catholic activists. Dissident reports of these trials are published here in Doc. No. 64 and 65.

imperatively emphasizing that ethnography is first and foremost the history of factories and enterprises, with impressive fragments from the biographies of personal pensioners thrown in for variety's sake.[3] This indicates that the campaign was one of the links of the neo-Stalinist "cultural revolution," which had already manifested itself in other spheres of culture. Almost all the editors of magazines dealing with cultural issues as well as heads of the cultural offices and associations were replaced by new ones—gray functionaries, such as V. Radaitis, editor of *Literatūra ir Menas* (Literature and Art) and L. Inis, editor of *Nemunas* (Nemunas River), or undisguised reactionaries, such as Uogintas, the present Chairman of the Lithuanian Ethnographic Society.[4] The "Vaga" publishing house is under pressure concerning the further publication of the "Library of Lithuanian Language and Literature."[5] The censorship, performed by *Glavlit*, has been sharpened; translations from foreign languages have been curbed. The editorial boards of *Kultūros barai* (The Fields of Culture) and especially of *Problemos* (Problems) were attacked from dogmatic positions in the pages of the journal *Komunistas*.[6] A (planned) ethnographic expedition to the Belorussian SSR, etc., was cancelled.[7]

The arrestees—Žukauskas, Sakalauskas, Rudaitis and Po-

---

3. For one such critique of ethnographic activity, see the article by J. Kuolelis, head of the Party's Agitation and Propaganda Department, in **Komunistas**, March, 1973 (No. 3).

4. The appointment of ideologically hard-line functionaries and intensification of ideological work were the consequence of the May, 1972, demonstrations in Kaunas following the Kalanta self-immolation (see Doc. No. 20).

5. "Library of Lithuanian Language and Literature" ("Lituanistinė Biblioteka") is a series of classical national works, especially important in the national renaissance of the nineteenth century The series survived the ideological campaign.

6. The philosophical journal **Problemos** was attacked in **Komunistas,** August, 1973 (No. 8), pp. 69-75, for various ideological—philosophical shortcomings. The outcome of it was the "strengthening" of the editorial board. See the announcement of editorial changes in **Komunistas,** January, 1974 (No. 1), p. 96. For a critical evaluation of **Nemunas** and other publications addressed to the youth, see **Komunistas,** February, 1974 (No. 2), pp. 79-86.

7. See Doc. No. 21 for reference to the aborted expedition to Lithuanian-inhabited areas of Belorussia.

vilonis—were kept in prison for almost a whole year, mostly in solitary cells, where "night blends with day, because lights burn incessantly in the cells..." (a prisoner's testimony). When V. Povilonis, for instance, went down with a malfunctioning liver because of malnutrition, he was placed in a hospital, while Žukauskas was thrown into a lock-up for having addressed the jailer in German; such incidents shed light on the state of the prisoners. As for the methods of interrogation, they are characterized by this episode: V. Povilonis was being persuaded that Sakalauskas was employed by the security. Unsettled, V. Povilonis, in his own words, rattled off "all sorts of nonsense" about Sakalauskas. The deceit came to light only when the two men met in prison.

At a later date, on October 23, 1973, another person was added to the case: Aloyzas Mackevičius from Mažeikiai, former candidate to the CPSU membership.

The case was tried by the Supreme Court of the Lithuanian SSR in Vilnius from February 18 to March 5, 1974, judge Ignotas presiding, assessors Kavaliauskaitė and Tamulionis participating. The prosecutor was Deputy Chief Prosecutor Bakučionis. The counsels for the defense were lawyers Kudaba, Gorvainis, Gavronskis, Vaičekauskas and Matijošaitienė. Attendance at the courtroom was limited to the closest relatives, soldiers, security agents, and court employees. Over 90 witnesses were questioned in the court.

All the defendants, except Mackevičius, were charged with anti-Soviet activity according to article 68 of the LSSR Penal Code. How did this activity manifest itself?

1. By establishment of an underground organization seeking to inform society about the criminal activity of the Soviet government toward the Lithuanian nation. Members were sworn in and dues were collected.

2. Distribution of proclamations on the occasion of February 16th.[8]

3. Preparatory work for the underground publication *Naujasis Varpas* (The New Bell).[9]

---

8. The Lithuanian independence day, proclaimed on February 16, 1918.

9. **Naujasis Varpas** (The New Bell) apparently never came out. Its name suggests an ideological and political affinity to the second Lithu-

4. Possession and dissemination of underground literature.

5. Giving financial support to the family of Simas Kudirka.[10]

S. Žukauskas was charged with having created the underground organization; he allegedly swore in new members, duplicated (two copies) the 15th volume (Lithuania) of *Lietuvių Enciklopedija* (Lithuanian Encyclopedia),[11] wrote the text of the proclamation, assisted Sakalauskas in stealing four typewriters, tried to draw Mackevičius into the underground organization and helped him to steal folk art sculptures, and acquired an Era copying machine.

A. Sakalauskas was charged by the court for belonging to the underground organization and hiding anti-Soviet literature. The following titles were discovered at his home during a search: *Mein Kampf* by Hitler, *A Question of Madness* by the Medvedevs, two issues of the *Chronicle of the Catholic Church in Lithuania, Lietuvių archyvas* (Lithuanian Archives), *TSRS užsienio politika 1939-1940* (Foreign Policy of the USSR 1939-1940), *Lietuvos istorija* (History of Lithuania) by A. Šapoka, etc.[12] Sakalauskas allegedly wanted to send a collection of his poems to the West and organized the theft of four typewriters. In 1957 he was sentenced to two years of prison for his attempt to escape abroad in a kayak across the Baltic sea.

Doctor I. Rudaitis was charged with having supported the

---

anian language newspaper **Varpas** (pub. in 1889), a national—liberal magazine which contributed immensely to the development of political consciousness and differentiation among the masses. A **samizdat** publication **Varpas** did appear sometime in 1976, four issues of which have reached the West by mid-1977.

10. The Simas Kudirka case is reported in Doc. No. 18.

11. The 15th volume of **Lietuvių enciklopedija,** published in the United States, is devoted entirely to "Lithuania" — its history, culture, society, and geography. It remains one of the most objective works on the Lithuanian civilization, very highly regarded in Lithuania.

12. Among the works mentioned, two deserve a special notice. **Lietuvių archyvas** is a five-volume compilation of documents and testimony on the first Soviet occupation of Lithuania, 1940-1941. Although it was published during the war under German occupation and to some extent reflects this circumstance, the series contains important documentation for the period, highly embarrassing to the Soviet regime. The work is thus vigorously controlled by the authorities. **Lietuvos istorija** by A. Šapoka, first published in 1936, remains the principal non-Marxist history of Lithuania.

underground organization, having helped to multiply and disseminate the anti-Soviet literature and proclamations, and having amassed the funds for the support of the organization
by speculating with currency. The search at Rudaitis' place
netted the materials for the underground publication which
was being prepared at that time and which he was to edit.

V. Povilonis allegedly belonged to the underground organization, distributed proclamations on the occasion of February 16th, stored anti-Soviet literature at his home, helped to
disseminate it, had a hand in the preparation of the underground publication *Naujasis Varpas*.

A. Mackevičius was charged with not only failing to inform the security about the activity of the underground organization, although he knew about it, but also with involvement
in its activity. At the instigation of Žukauskas, he allegedly
stole folk art objects, robbed the church of Tirkšliai, and delivered the stolen items to Žukauskas. It was not by accident that
A. Mackevičius was joined to the political case with a criminal
hue. Since Žukauskas was acquainted with A. Mackevičius, an
effort was made to incriminate him with thefts—don't you see
what his "moral features" are! The court had no proof what-
soever in addition to the contradictory testimony elicited from
Mackevičius by force. This fact was emphasized by Žukauskas' lawyer Kudaba.

On this occasion the Soviet court wanted to show itself
as an incorruptible defender of the wooden carvings of the
Sorrowing Christ and a protector of church property, which
severely punishes wrongdoers. Will the court also punish those
who organized and carried out the destruction of the Hill of
Crosses, the shrines of Vilniaus Kalvarija, desecrated many
churches,[13] etc. — these criminals are *known!*

Žukauskas confessed having headed the organization
whose purpose was the study and collection of literature. He
wanted to act only within the norms of Soviet legality, he said.
Yet he thought that it was necessary to correct the mistakes
committed by the government. "An enormous wrong has surely
been inflicted on our nation—360,000 Lithuanians have been
deported," Žukauskas related. He confessed having distributed
literature which, in his opinion, was not anti-Soviet, e.g., "The

---

13. Reference to popular national-religious shrines which were
desecrated or destroyed by the Soviet regime.

Trial of S. Kudirka."[14] He denied having committed criminal offenses—he had not stolen folk art objects. As for the typewriters, Žukauskas said, he was convinced that they had been written off and that nobody had incurred a loss.

A. Sakalauskas confessed having participated in the organization's activity and having paid membership dues. "We formed a group for self-education," the defendant stated.

When Sakalauskas' wife was asked about her husband's views, she said: "Normal, as of all decent people. My husband has been working all his life. If only everybody worked that much—it would be quite a contribution to the construction of Communism. He taught the young, gave much of his time to their education. Yet my husband cannot put up with the shortcomings of our life that still exist."

"What shortcomings?" the judge asked.

"I'll start with living conditions... After much trouble and difficulty we got an apartment, but it's all bare..."

"And what should have been there?"

"It would seem that, if an apartment has radiators, they should give out warmth; if there were faucets—water should run from them. But my husband had to put all those things in order with his own hands, sacrificing the time allotted for scientific work...," Mrs. Sakalauskas said. The judge interrupted her and started questioning her about listening to foreign broadcasts.

I. Rudaitis said he had never heard of any underground organization and had never supported it financially. Foreign currency had come to his possession accidentally. As regards the publication in preparation, he also had never heard of it. He read all kinds of books because an educated man must be acquainted with "anti-literature" too.

A. Mackevičius confessed having stolen folk art objects and having robbed the church of Tirkšliai. He had done all those things, he said, to get money because he likes to dress well. He asserted that Žukauskas participated with him in the robberies. Later on, Mackevičius said, he had robbed the church alone, wanting to prove to Žukauskas that he could act independently.

In the courtroom Žukauskas addressed Mackevičius in the following words: "You, Alius, should be responsible for your-

14. Apparently this is the report of the trial, published here as Doc. No. 18.

self and should leave to me what I have done. I'm not going to take responsibility for your crimes."

L. Mackevičius characterized his brother as follows: "Alius is like a Frenchman—when everybody sings, he joins in the song, when everybody falls silent, he shuts up too."

V. Povilonis did not admit having belonged to an underground organization and asserted that he did not distribute any books, but merely kept some at home. He knew nothing about the underground publication and his only link with Žukauskas was ethnography.

Prosecutor Bakučionis called Žukauskas the founder of the organization and asked the court to sentence the defendant to seven years' loss of freedom (the top penalty, according to article 68). In the case of Sakalauskas, the prosecutor's recommendation was five years' loss of freedom. Having then charged Povilonis and Rudaitis, the prosecutor went all out to defend Mackevičius, calling him a wronged person, a victim seduced by Žukauskas and similar individuals.

Defense lawyers can say precious little in political trials; about the only thing they can do is to point out some merits of the defendants. Lawyer Kudaba defended Žukauskas from criminal offenses; lawyer Gorvainis emphasized Sakalauskas' contributions to society; lawyer Gavronskis mentioned that Rudaitis was a good physician and a former antifascist; lawyer Vaičekauskas called Mackevičius "a lost sheep" who may improve completely. Lawyer Matijošaitienė spoke of Povilonis' contributions to the Komsomol and his poor health. Some lawyers tried to place the responsibility on Žukauskas.

All (four) defendants asked the court for acquittal, while Mackevičius asked for mercy.

The court atmosphere was very oppressive—relatives laden with sorrow and resigned lawyers sat in the courtroom. The defendants were not allowed to face the hall! Whenever anyone tried to take notes, a militiaman would turn up and take the notes away. The leaflet issued on the occasion of February 16th was not read in the course of the trial; it was merely mentioned that the leaflet starts with the word "Lithuanian" and ends with the words "Kaunas chapter." The contents of the leaflet should have been analyzed in court! During the trial there was talk of an underground publication in the organizing stage, but the court also failed to reveal the contents of that publication. Nothing concrete was said about the underground organization. Thus, the most important items that resulted in the application of Art. 68 of the LSSR Penal Code were left untouched by the court. This was the procedure of a trial, the purpose of which was the blackening and paralyzing of the ethnographers' movement in Lithuania.

The final statement of Žukauskas lasted about an hour. He said that he was not an enemy of the socialist system, but in his opinion the Soviet government was not a government of the people since it was imported by way of occupation. The "revolution" of 1918 in Lithuania, he said, did not emerge from the masses, but was prepared in Moscow and imported from there to Lithuania by the Red Army together with Kapsukas and Angarietis.[15] Their government was dominated by Poles, Russians, and Jews who had nothing in common with the Lithuanian people, who thirsted for independence. Lithuanians organized an army of volunteers to drive out the new occupying power—the Bolsheviks—from Lithuania. Žukauskas went on to mention the Ribbentrop-Molotov Pact of 1939, sealing the division of the Baltic States. Thus the Soviet power in Lithuania in 1940 was also brought by the Red Army. The so-called revolutions or revolutionary situations in Lithuania are nothing but a loathsome lie. Arrests and deportations were carried out in 1940, and the postwar years were even more terrible: terror, "dekulakizations," "the green lads," "the stribs," mass deportations that have claimed some 300,000 victims.[16] And what about arrests, prisons, camps, various repressions, executions of innocents by shooting, "Stalin's cult"! The deportations to Siberia were not motivated by class, but

---

15. Vincas Mickevičius-Kapsukas (1880-1935) and Zigmas Aleksa-Angarietis (1881-1940) were founders of Lithuanian Communism, both led the Soviet intervention in Lithuania in 1918-1919 to establish a Soviet regime. After the failure of the intervention, Kapsukas and Angarietis worked in the Komintern headquarters in Moscow. Kapsukas died of natural causes, while Angarietis was executed by Stalin, possibly for nationalist deviation. For the history of the Lithuanian Communist Party and the Soviet intervention see Thomas Remeikis, **Communist Party of Lithuania: A Historical and Political Study**, doctoral dissertation, University of Illinois, 1963.

16. "The green lads" designates the national partisans, while "the stribs" is the popular form of the Russian word "istrebiteli" — destroyers, the name given to Soviet activist groups organized to fight the national guerillas.

by national reasons. There are still people now who are denied the right to return to their motherland. This is terribly harmful to Lithuania. Russian chauvinism is manifesting itself to this very day, a policy of denationalization is being carried out. Russians in Lithuania are granted much better living conditions than the Lithuanians. The increase of Russian nationals in Lithuania is explained by the labor shortage, but meanwhile Lithuanians are recruited for (work in) Kazakhstan and other areas of the Soviet Union. This is how colonization is conducted. The Russian empire remains a prison of nations. All the peoples of the world are fighting for freedom, all the progressive forces are supporting them. In what way are we, Lithuanians, worse than others?!

Žukauskas does not consider his activity a crime against the people and the nation and does not ask for a milder sentence, but merely requests that he be released. He addresses himself to the court:

"This is not a court, but a reprisal... Why is it closed? Is the court really afraid that infuriated people might tear it to pieces? You are afraid, you 'who have gathered here for a morsel of gold, for a tasty dish' (V. Kudirka).[17]... Although you are Lithuanians by name, folk wisdom maintains not without reason that your own dog bites more painfully..."

Žukauskas concluded his speech with the words of Mykolaitis-Putinas:[18] "The enemy oppresses us with iron hands, yet liberty remains the dearest word!"

The verdict of the court was made public on March 5, 1974:

Š. Žukauskas, born in 1950, fourth-year student at the Kaunas Institute of Medicine, member of the Komsomol, well versed in the English, French, and German languages, sentenced to six years in a strict regime camp, his property confiscated.

A. Sakalauskas, born in 1938, German language instructor at the Kaunas Polytechnic Institute—five years in a strict regime camp.

---

17. Vincas Kudirka (1858-1899), founder and editor of *Varpas* (see note No. 9 above), an incisive satirist of Russian rule in Lithuania, a principal figure of the Lithuanian national revival.

18. Vincas Mykolaitis-Putinas (1893-1967), one of the most outstanding Lithuanian poets. His latest works evidently included subtle anti-Soviet verses.

V. Povilonis, born in 1947, engineer-technologist—two years in a strict regime camp.

I. Rudaitis, born in 1911, physician—three years in a strict regime camp, property confiscated.

A. Mackevičius, born in 1949, student at Kaunas Trade Institute—two years in a regular regime camp.

Place where the sentence will be served—Solikamsk (Perm region), except for Mackevičius, who will serve his sentence at Proveniškės.[19]

Žukauskas will be kept in the security prison until the fall.

---

19. Proveniškės is a prison in Lithuania.

26. PROGRAM OF THE LITHUANIAN NATIONAL PEOPLE'S FRONT

We, the members of the National People's Front (the Association of Free Democratic Youth of Lithuania, the Lithuanian Catholic Association, and other groups)[1] and all those who support the national movement, being persecuted for our political, national, and religious beliefs in the Lithuanian SSR and throughout the Soviet Union, appeal from the Lithuanian underground to world public opinion and request all free states of the world to defend the Lithuanian, Latvian, and Estonian nations from the destructive imperialism of the Soviets.

The USSR, having officially proclaimed itself the "defender of liberty" for all nations, is no more than the extension of the traditions of imperial czarist Russia. Under cover of "progressive Marxist theory," it has, in real life, repeatedly offended against the freedom of nations and humanism.

Here are the facts.[2] First of all, in 1939, the so-called socialist state, the Soviet Union, together with fascist Germany, divided and destroyed Poland and the Baltic States. The Poland of "the lords," as Soviet diplomats liked to call it, barbarically occupied by the Hitlerites, was named the *oblast gosudarstven-*

No. 26. AS No. 2217, first published in the Canadian Lithuanian weekly Tėviškės Žiburiai, July 1, 1975. The authenticity of the NPF has been questioned by emigré and some dissident sources, perhaps because of its unusually radical interpretation of international relations. The Catholic samizdat (Chronicle and Aušra) has been silent about the NPF, nor has it denounced the NPF as a creation of the KGB. There are indirect contrary indications. Its existence is confirmed by an eyewitness testimony of dissent in the 1960s, published in Tėviškės Žiburiai, July 31, 1975. In addition, several other publications of the NPF have been received in the West, which quite consistently follow the program set in this document. Two such items are published in this anthology: Doc. No. 34 and 36. The nature of the NPF and is program is discussed in some detail in the introductory study.

1. The NPF considers itself an umbrella organization of various resistance groups. The groups mentioned as associated with the NPF have not been confirmed as existing in the available samizdat literature. Most likely, if they exist at all, they are small conspiratorial groups representing diverse ideological viewpoints.

2. See Doc. No. 8 and its notes for documentation of Soviet aggression against Lithuania.

nych interesov Germanii (the sphere of German state interests). The "decent feelings" of the All-Union Communist Party (b) and of the government regarding the Polish people, and internationalism, the hobby-horse beloved by Stalin's propagandists, were donated to Ribbentrop. The annexation of the Baltic States in 1940 became an "internal matter" of the Soviet Union. Lithuania, Latvia, and Estonia, according to the Marxist argument of Molotov, were Russian provinces temporarily torn from their metropole.

How did the Nazis differ from the Stalinists? The answer to that question can best be given by the nations of the Baltic and of Eastern Europe, which have experienced first-hand the meaning of the "dictatorship of the proletariat." Well-versed on this point, too, are all the non-Russian nations of the Soviet Union which one way or another have become part of "Moscow's Marxist Garden of Eden."

And what of the Russian nation? The "great" and "honorable" nation, the propagator of national liberation slogans—is it free? No. According to Lenin, a nation enslaving or oppressing other nations cannot be free. The claims of Moscow chauvinists about the leadership mission of the Great Russians in the quest for world revolution on all continents is a bluff.

The formerly independent Baltic States, unjustly occupied by the Red Army and later incorporated into the orbit of the Soviet Union with the aid of rigged elections in order to mislead naive politicians, have never accepted and never shall accept their deprived status. Old fascist claims about the nonviability of small states should not be part of the "progressive" contemporary policy of Moscow. Contemporary history shows colonialism coming to an end. All the nations of Africa have become decolonized. Small nations of Africa, which had never enjoyed statehood, have created national states. Is it not time for Lithuania, with its long history, beautiful past, and tradition of statehood, to be free? Should not the Soviet empire's prison of nations be abolished so that all non-Russian nations might create their own states?

Soviet expansionism, more modern and refined than the czarist version, has expanded the borders of the USSR at the expense of Lithuania, Latvia, Estonia, Finland, Poland, Hungary, and Czechoslovakia; annexed the Caucasus to Russia,

seized Moldavia from Romania, colonized central Asia and Siberia—and threatens all Europe, now divided and in disagreement.

The whole misfortune is that the former imperialist states
of Western Europe, now having lost their colonies, are not
able to resist communist international expansionism. Full democracy and the capitalist system of rule, preoccupied with
financial competition, apoliticism, lack of ideals, and with its
own internal problems, is forced to appease Moscow. Not only
Western Europe, but even the USA, one of the strongest super-
states of the world, ruled by a financial oligarchy, can barely
defend itself against the interference of Moscow in all the internal affairs of America, to say nothing of any real aid   to
the captive nations. The monopolistic capitalism of America,
potential competitor of Soviet Communism, is concerned not
with the problem of liberating nations, but rather with increasing its profits and with economic expansion in the Arabian and
South American countries, poor and underdeveloped, where
great social reforms are needed—because ignoring them can
lead to the establishment of a communist regime in those underdeveloped countries.

The Executive Committee of the National People's Front,
in an illegal conference in June 1974, after analyzing the history
of our nation's tragedy and the political and moral situation
today in the enslaved land of our fathers, has arrived at the
conclusion that the great powers of the Western world, ideologically weak as they are, have appeased and continue to
appease the dictators in Moscow. The countries of Eastern
Europe (Poland, Hungary, Czechoslovakia, et al.), having re-
volted against the Soviet order in those countries, were crushed
because neither Western Europe nor the USA supplied any
military aid. Propaganda promises have not helped nor will
they help the enslaved Baltic States to free themselves of Soviet
slavery, or help its satellites, which cause Moscow more and
more concern these days.

The National People's Front, the ideological nucleus of
resistance for the entire subjugated land of our fathers, raising
anew the question of self-liberation in the light of our disappointment with the Western world, places foremost our internal
strength, which in solidarity with the entire Baltic area, the
Ukrainian and Caucasian nation, along with the progressive

Russian minds, can by a long and difficult struggle attain national political freedom—separating ourselves from ethnographic Russia and creating free and independent states. The NPF believes that in this new stage of struggle our basic task is to utilize to the maximum all legal and illegal means of warfare.

The NPF claims that the Soviet Constitution, as applied in the territory of the Lithuanian SSR, has become practically a fiction since the workers and the intelligentsia of Lithuania have been deprived of their basic civil rights. Patriotic feelings for one's own nation are forbidden and condemned; only the chauvinism of the Great Russians goes unpunished. So-called local nationalism is punished by exile and imprisonment.

From 1954 until 1964, that is, during the Soviet post-Stalin "renaissance," after the liquidation of Beria, chief of the MGB, after the deposing of Malenkov for his liberalism, after Khrushchev's criticism of the personality cult of Stalin, the political persecution of people throughout the Soviet Union significantly declined, but it did not end. Echoes of revolts in the countries of Eastern Europe reached the youth of the Baltic States, the Ukraine, the Caucasus, and even of Russia, and led to student demonstrations in Vilnius, Kaunas, Tartu, Riga, Leningrad, Moscow, Kiev, and Tbilisi. Peaceful demonstrations by youth against despotism and that apparatus for discouraging free thought, the KGB (already by that time under the control of the central Council of Ministers), forced the government to turn its attention to its citizens who had been the oppressed and disenfranchised slaves of Stalin for the thirty years of his reign.

However, the KGB agents are still alert—they changed their tactics, and acting on instructions, continue to destroy those who dare disagree with their policy throughout the empire they control. In that time hundreds of young Lithuanians, members of the Communist Youth or not, were arrested by the KGB of the Lithuanian SSR and turned over to the so-called People's Court. There, behind closed doors, guarded by Russian soldiers of the Ministry of Internal Affairs (MVD), often without defenders or attorneys, they received "suitable" sentences and were sent into the depths of the Soviet Union: the forced labor camps of Vorkuta, Mordavia. Known intellectuals who spoke out against the dogmas of Marx, the religion of the dictators in the Kremlin, sometimes found themselves in psychiatric hospitals, where KGB "physician-experts" certified them abnormal.

Regardless of all repressions by the KGB within the territory of the Lithuanian SSR, the youth of our oppressed land, its intelligentsia, and its conscientious workers, dismayed with Moscow's anti-Lithuanian policies, became doubtful of the Marx-Engels-Lenin "talmud of freedom and progress" borne on Soviet bayonets, and joined in the activities of the National People's Front. It can be said the NPF, established during 1955 in Vilnius, is still alive today. In its struggle for the reestablishment of an independent Lithuania, the NPF, as an organization of the progressive forces in Lithuania, stands in the front ranks of battle.

The NPF, in solidarity with our brother nations, the Latvians and the Estonians, stands in favor of a federation of Baltic States in the Europe of the future.

In this secret national conference, minimal and maximal strategies for the struggle were discussed and submitted to the entire freedom movement in Lithuania.

We, representatives of the National People's Front, representing the entire movement for struggle and freedom in the country, decided to proclaim to the entire world in Lithuanian, Polish, Russian, German, English, and French the following program for the liberation of Lithuania:

MINIMAL PROGRAM

1. The National People's Front, expressing the efforts of the Lithuanian nation for freedom, and basing itself on the Declaration of Human Rights, which the government of the Soviet Union also signed, demands that all forms of colonialism be abolished, including those in the USSR. The Lithuanian nation has the right of self-determination and secession from Russia. On the basis of Lenin's statement, officially quoted in the Constitution of the Soviet Union (regarding the right of self-determination of nations), we will struggle tirelessly to implement that right in our colonized country.

2. We demand of that puppet of Moscow, the government of the Lithuanian SSR (which was never chosen on the basis of free elections by the Lithuanian nation), the implementation of freedoms of religion, press, demonstrations, na-

tional organizations and parties, including the NPF, the Association of Free Democratic Youth of Lithuania, the Lithuanian Catholic Association, etc.

3. To allow the emigration of those who disagree with the Soviet regime in the Lithuanian SSR. To abolish the draconian law allowing the persecution of the families of those who have fled to the free states. To grant Lithuanian emigrés the opportunity of visiting their relatives anywhere in Lithuania without time limits. To process entry documents and visas in Vilnius, the capital of Lithuania, and not in Moscow.[3]

4. We demand amnesty for all political prisoners sentenced by the courts of the Lithuanian SSR and confined in the concentration camps of the Soviet Union and in the political isolation unit of Vladimir. To return from Siberia all exiles, give them work, lodgings, and all civil rights.

5. To introduce Lithuanian as the primary language in all agencies of the republic, including the State Security Committee and the Ministry of Internal Affairs.

6. To require the central government in Moscow to grant the Lithuanian Ministry of Foreign Affairs the right to maintain contact with foreign countries.

MAXIMAL PROGRAM

1. We demand a mission of the United Nations in Vilnius, the capital of the Lithuanian SSR, and free democratic elections in which all citizens of the Lithuanian SSR would participate, with the exception of soldiers of Soviet garrisons.

2. The provisional people's government thus elected should conduct a plebiscite regarding the secession of the Lithuanian SSR from the USSR. Only citizens of Lithuanian nationality should participate in the plebiscite.

3. After the implementation of the secession, the new government of the republic establishes ties with neighboring

---

3. Western tourists are allowed five days in Vilnius, with one-day side trips to Kaunas and the resort town of Druskininkai. Lithuania is thus the most severely limited republic to tourist access. The policy may be part of the effort to restrict contact with emigrés and other Western tourists, who have been blamed for some of the nationalistic outbursts in the 1970's. (Private communication.)

states and sets its own foreign policy.

4. The NPF suggests the determination of the ethnographic borders of Lithuania, taking as a basis the Polish-Lithuanian peace treaty signed in Suvalkai in 1920, and the Soviet Russian - Lithuanian Republic peace treaty signed by V. I. Lenin.[4]

5. To establish a federation of the Baltic States.

6. To proceed with the creation of a union of Baltic and Scandinavian countries in the future free family of the United States of Europe.

DEMANDS

The National People's Front of Lithuania, basing itself in its program of struggle on humanistic principles, proclaims the theses of peace, democracy, freedom, equality, and self-determination of nations, and demands:

1. To condemn the imperialists of the Soviet Union— the enslavers of the Baltic nations and other nations.

2. To abrogate the Warsaw Pact, an instrument of Soviet policy for dominating the countries of Eastern Europe.

3. To withdraw the Soviet army from the Baltic States, Poland, Czechoslovakia, Hungary, and other territories subject to them, allowing those states to set their own foreign policy.

4. To terminate US military and economic expansionism in Europe, a factor contrary to the idea of unity of all Europe.

5. To liquidate the North Atlantic Treaty Organization (NATO).

6. To establish a United States of Europe from Lisbon to the Urals.

7. To unite both parts of Germany into one democratic state, correcting the past mistakes of the imperialistic policies of the USSR and the USA.

---

4. Lenin did not sign the treaty, although as head of state he had to assent to it. If the boundaries determined by the treaties cited were accepted, parts of contemporary Belorussia and Poland would become Lithuanian territory. Only a small portion of these areas could be claimed on ethnographic grounds, but the entire area is Lithuanian on historical grounds.

8. To end the policies of the Soviet Union and of the United States of America which lead to division among nations and states.

9. To restore peace, freedom, and unity to Vietnam and Korea.

10. To confer national freedoms and the right of political self-determination on all nations of the Soviet Union, national republics annexed by force to Russia or the USSR.

11. To restore the Baltic States as independent entities in a union of Baltic States.

12. To give the Ukrainian and Belorussian nations the right of establishing their own states in friendly association with the Russian and other Slavic nations.

13. To allow the Moldavian nation to determine for itself whether it wishes to be independent or to form the state of Romania-Moldavia.

14. Not to interfere with the restoration of the states of the Caucasus, with their ancient culture: Armenia, Georgia, and Azerbaijan, which seek national independence.

15. To allow the Karelians the right to determine for themselves and to join their brothers, the Finns, in a Finno-Ugaritic state.

16. To grant the Islamic republics of Central Asia: Uzbek, Kazakh, Turkmen, Tadzhik, and Kirghiz the right of self-determination and the opportunity to establish sovereign states in a federation of Central Asian nations.

17. To restore the federation of Siberian nations, with the prerogative of remaining within the structure of a new democratic Russian state, or of choosing its own path of development.

18. To abolish colonialism in all its forms.

Long live freedom, social equality, religious and racial tolerance.

The National People's Front

Vilnius, June 9-14, 1974.

27. A STATEMENT OF POLITICAL PRISONERS ON THE NATIONALITY POLICY

To: The Soviet of Nationalities of the Supreme Soviet of the USSR (Copy to the United Nations)
From: Baltic, Ukrainian, and Caucasian prisoners in Mordovian concentration camps.

A STATEMENT

The Constitution of the USSR guarantees the sovereignty of the national union republics and provides for several basic regulations guaranteeing their sovereignty.

According to the regulations of the Constitution, the supreme power and the local government fully and indivisibly belong to the Soviets of representatives of the working people —democratic, elected, and public organs—while the Supreme Soviet of the USSR theoretically adheres to the principle that equals do not subject equals to their power. Contrary to the Constitution, the CP of the Soviet Union has become a sovereign government. The Communist Party of the Soviet Union, having abused the regulations of the Constitution about the right to exercise an influence on all the governmental organs through its party units within them, has forcibly created a situation which goes far beyond an internal influence on the course of the state's policy, and actually amounts to the transfer of governmental power from the elected democratic institution to the purely political organs, in concrete terms—to the Central Committee of the Communist Party of the USSR.

The organizational structure of the Communist Party of the Soviet Union, which provides for strict subordination of the communist organs of the union republics (which locally practice the same usurpation of power from the elected organs) to the Center, makes the state sovereignty of those republics null and void. Moreover, in a situation where the Communist Party of the Soviet Union and its Central Committee are identical with the communist organization of the Russian Soviet Socialist Republic and simultaneously act as

No. 27. AS No. 1724, undated, probably 1974. Translated from the Russian.

the supreme institution vis-à-vis the Central Committees of the other union republics, the latter are in practice down-graded to the level of obkoms (regional committees) of the Communist Party of the Russian Soviet Socialist Republic.

In its party documents the Communist Party of the Soviet Union proclaims as its goal the creation of a new Soviet nation and the raising of a new man. In advertising the pseudonational assertion that the fusion of nations is a natural and inevitable process, the communists assert that they are merely regulating that process.

With the monopoly of power in its hands, the Central Committee of the Communist Party transforms its own goals into a state policy and uses the entire weight of the state machinery for carrying it out, while branding any disagreement with it or resistance against it a crime against the state.

As regards the individual, the policy of raising a new Soviet man is carried out through the widespread and all-encompassing system of persuasion, spying, compulsion, directed toward a total standardization of thinking and world views. Guided by their utilitarian goal of strengthening the monolithic character of the government as well as their own power, the communists are imbuing their materialistic ideology, their social ideology, and blind obedience to the party's authority with a boundless intolerance, while pretending to be the only holder of a "genuine truth" and elevating to an enormous degree their own party above the entire remaining nation.

In the sphere of international relations, the communist policy is geared toward the fusion of the non-Russian nationalities with the Russian nation. The creation of the new Soviet nation which they advertise turns out to be in practice nothing but the old policy of russification. It is true that this policy is now carried out less crudely and cruelly than in the prewar and the first postwar years, when masses of non-Russian population, and even entire nations, were forcibly deported to remote regions of the RSFSR, where, dispersed among the Russian inhabitants and torn away from their national soil, they were assimilated and have quantitatively supplemented the Russian nation. The empty regions resulting from the forcible deportation of the inhabitants were settled with Russian colonists who alone in the Soviet Union have the right to cultural autonomy beyond their administrative boundaries (Russian schools, publishing houses, theaters, etc. in the territories of all union republics) and are therefore not inclined to assimilate themselves with the local population but, on the contrary, exert a powerful russifying influence on them. The intensified economic buildup in the border national areas today is connected with the sending of a multinational labor force to these areas. Faced with the choice between the local and the Russian language, as a result of the russification of the industry and its management, this labor force chooses the Russian language, thus sizeably augmenting the Russian-speaking population of the national republic and becoming a new and powerful factor of russification of these areas. The russification of industry, higher educational establishments, and technical schools often compels the native inhabitants to give priority to the Russian language.

The same situation can be observed in the key industrial plants (the so-called All-Union dependence plants) which, although situated on the territories of the national union and autonomous republics, are not under their control.

The Russian language has illegally become the state language in the territories of national union and autonomous republics, acquiring a privileged status as a result.

Having arbitrarily appointed itself a mediator in the cultural, spiritual, and economic relations between the nationalities of the Soviet Union and in their relations with the rest of the world, the Russian language is enjoying the privileges of a spiritual banker, amassing values it has not created, and simultaneously as a filter which allows only those things to pass into international life that are in accordance with Russia's interests.

Through the system of state schools the young generation is compelled to glorify Russia and all things Russian in all kinds of ways. The history of the USSR taught in schools is factually nothing else but the history of the Russian empire —the key historical role in it is accorded to Russia and to the Russian nation, while other nations figure only in the light of Russia's state interests. In the unusually condensed courses of the histories of the union republics, only recently allowed to be taught in the schools of the national union republics, the facts of history are also distorted and one-sided. The Russian conquest of the neighboring states and nations as well as their incorporation into the structure of the Russian empire is always presented as a source of great happiness to them. The struggle for freedom of the non-Russian nations against the Russian empire is either passed over in complete silence or depicted as reactionary conservative movement. Today, too, any movement promoting national self-determ nation is branded bourgeois nationalism and cruelly persecuted by state punitive organs.

It is typical that in the Soviet places of detention where political opponents are imprisoned, one finds no Russian nationals who had fought for the separation of Russia from the USSR, while individuals of many other nationalities which organized movements for their separation from Russia are amply represented there.

Convinced that the most favorable soil for man's spiritual growth is an indivisible nation, developing universally, an equal among equals, we protest against the communist attempts to replace the national foundations of society with purely social ones. This cannot be justified either by economic achievements, or by the interests of state security, because only the nation's indivisibility, its native tongue, and traditions guarantee the continuity and progress of spiritual culture—that highest striving of man. The conscious effort by the communists to destroy these natural institutions and to replace them with abstract, fabricated constructions bodes tragic results.

Vitally interested not only in the physical survival and in the economic well-being of our nations, we demand a strict adherence to the regulations of our Constitution, guaranteeing a future for our nations, namely:

1. Obligatory status of state languages for the national tongues in the national and autonomous republics.

2. Granting and embodying the right of cultural autonomy to all national minorities outside their administrative borders, or the cancellation of the exclusive privilege to that right, which is now enjoyed by the Russians.

3. Broadening of the sovereign rights of the union republics to enjoy direct relations with the rest of the world in cultural, political, and economic areas.

4. Formation of military units of the republics, as provided in para. 18 of the Constitution of the USSR.

5. Transfer to the full control of the union and autonomous republics of all the industrial plants in their territories, as well as of the exploitation of natural resources existing in the national territories. Organization of inter-republic relations on the basis of equality.

6. Restoration of full power to the constitutional organs, i.e., to the Soviets of the representatives of the working people. State separation of governmental power from the party influence, establishment of control over the activity of the Communist Party of the USSR.

7. The policy of the governments of the union and autonomous republics must be in genuine accord with their national interests. To defend their national interests, citizens of each nationality must have the opportunity to use the right granted them by para. 125 of the Constitution of the USSR.

8. The failure to observe the norms and the regulations of the Constitution, guaranteeing sovereignty and equality to the nationalities, as well as the policy of the ruling party endangering the very existence of our nations, gives us the moral justification to make use of the right granted by the Constitution (para. 17 of the Constitution of the USSR) to conduct propaganda in favor of our republics leaving the USSR. Our activity, according to the above-mentioned regulations of the Constitution, should not be punishable.

From the Baltic Area:
    Juris Ziemelis
    Jonas Šilinskas
    Antanas Astrauskas
    Astra Gunar

From the Caucasus:
    Ovik Vasilyan
    Mogamed Tagayev
    Gevrog Ekimian
    Valmer Velikian

From the Ukraine:
    Vladimir Bezuglyi
    Apolonii Berniychuk
    Vladimir Glyva
    Ivan Ilchuk
    Levko Lukyanenko
    Dimitrii Pilinyak
    Ivan Pokrovskyi
    Oleksei Stepaniuk
    Andrei Turik

28. PROTESTS AND DEATH OF MINDAUGAS TOMONIS

To: Director of the Institute for the Conservation of Monuments

From: M. Tomonis, senior scientific worker at the chemical laboratory of the ICM

EXPLANATORY STATEMENT

On April of this year I did not go on a tour of duty to inspect the monument to the Red Army—the liberator of Lithuania—in Kryžkalnis for reasons not within the jurisdiction of the Institute for the Conservation of Monuments: I do not recognize the present status of Lithuania. I am profoundly convinced that for the sake of progress every conscientious citizen must seek with his entire life to rectify the errors committed by anyone on the personal level and those on the level of the entire state. Without condemnation and full consciousness of the errors of the past, it is impossible to build a future.

Among the most important errors committed in the period of the personality cult and still completely or partially unrectified, I count the following:

1. Mass deportation of innocent citizens; and

No. 28. The first statement is from **Chronicle**, No. 10 (1974); the second statement is from **Chronicle**, No. 20 (December 8, 1975); and the appeal is from **Chronicle,** No. 21 (January 25, 1976). Mindaugas Tomonis was a promising poet, a number of his poems were published in Soviet press and in the Lithuanian press abroad. His confrontation with the regime led to a confinement in a psychiatric hospital. **Chronicle, No. 12** (1974), has reported that Tomonis "received such large injections of insulin that they resulted in a shock: he would lose consciousness, then, after the injection of glucose, he would begin to recover again and would start flinging himself about, and would therefore be tied to his bed for several hours." In addition, powerful tranquilizers with disorienting side effects were administered, according to dissident reports (see below). The dissidents have charged that the KGB is responsible for his death; if he was not actually killed, then he was led to his tragic end through psychiatric mistreatment. The KGB reacted to the charges through Tomonis' father, who obviously was "inspired" to write an open letter to several Lithuanian newspapers in the West, explaining his son's death as a simple suicide (text of the letter in **Akiračiai**, January, 1977). The dissidents reaffirmed their charges in **Aušra**, No. 6 (May 12, 1977).

2. The incorporation of the Baltic States into the present federation on the area of the former Russian empire at a time when the quest of nations for full-fledged cultural statehood was unusually intensified.

I consider it impossible to contribute to the immortalization of events that have done away with Lithuania's statehood and have generated so much injustice. I will agree to honor the joint struggle with the neighboring nations against German Fascism, by restoring and conserving the monuments erected for that purpose, only when the following will be fully guaranteed:

1. That memorial monuments, indicating a civilized attitude, respect for man, and the decency of our society, be erected in the most important sites where masses of innocent citizens had perished because of the "personality cult."

2. That the freedom of self-determination, guaranteed (formally so far) in the Constitution, be legitimated by means of an additional law providing a mechanism for its realization, i.e., a national referendum to be held periodically in each republic. The Baltic republics, as well as others, should their inhabitants so desire, must regain a genuine and complete statehood, the same cultural-economic independence enjoyed by the rest of the socialist nations.

3. That the threat of the appearance of a new era of personality cult be abolished. This can be achieved by the introduction of a multi-party system, i. e., by permitting the establishment of the Social Democratic, Christian Democratic, and other parties with appropriate press organs, by conducting truly democratic elections, thereby reducing the influence of the party which has violated the interests of the people. These measures would strengthen the democratic nature and effectiveness of state rule within the framework of socialism.

The global process of progress demands the continuous democratization of the community of socialist nations and rapid advance in all spheres of life. The realization of the ideal of a universal socialist-communist society will be impossible, unless the states that have created this system will enjoy a great authority and will become known in the entire world for their respect of human rights, tolerance of different opinions, careful regard for them, magnanimity, and justice.

April 5, 1974   *Mindaugas Tomonis*

M. TOMONIS — A VICTIM OF THE SECURITY POLICE

*"Tomonis, Mindaugas (b. Aug. 28, 1940 in Vilnius) —
technologist in chemical engineering, candidate of technical sciences (1968). In 1962 graduated from the Polytechnical Institute of Kaunas, until 1963 worked as an
engineer in the Daugeliai (raion of Šiauliai) combinate of
construction materials. 1966-1969 a scientific contributor
to the Construction and Architecture Institute; from 1969,
chief of the chemical laboratories of the Institute for the
Preservation of Monuments. He has published scientific
articles on the hardening of cement and reenforced concrete."*

(The Little Lithuanian Soviet Encyclopedia,

Vol. 3, p. 560)

The *Chronicle* wrote about M. Tomonis' refusal to restore
the monument to the Soviet Army in Kryžkalnis and his commitment to the psychiatric hospital in N. Vilna. After three
months of forced treatment, Tomonis returned in weakened
health. The opportunity to participate in the creative work of
the institute was taken away from him.

On June 25, 1975, M. Tomonis wrote a letter to the
Central Committee, Communist Party of the Soviet Union.[1]
In this long letter one can feel the unrealistic faith in the
good will of the Party leaders by this young scientist, reared
during the period of Soviet rule.

At the beginning of the letter the author notes that lies,
which are upheld by the government officials themselves, have
universally spread through the country. The Soviet authorities
do not have the right to demand that the citizens behave
morally and conscientiously since there is so much compromising evidence in their own actions. The blood of the in-
nocently murdered millions is on their conscience. Cynical
lies keep on flowing. Although it seems to the communists
that under socialism lies become "holy," nevertheless, they
cannot be excused. The time has come to carry out a "humanitarian revolution," which, according to Tomonis, could be carried out by the 25th Party Congress.

In the seven points of this "revolution," M. Tomonis pre-

---

1. The complete text of Tomonis' letter is not available.

sents its principal purposes and methods. He suggests the abolition of the errors of the period of the "cult of personality" and
"subjectivism" (Khrushchev's), the honoring of the graves of
the victims of Stalinism, the nonhindrance of the spread of
truth in the arts, the press, and general life. M. Tomonis writes:

"To condemn the unjust aspects of the foreign policies
of Stalin—such as the liquidation of the three Baltic States
—Lithuania, Latvia, and Estonia. That the incorporation of
the Baltic States was not a historical necessity, but a mistake
is shown by the example of socialist Mongolia.[2] As you well know
the Baltic republics are dissatisfied with the ever-increasing
"melting" of the local inhabitants into the mass of immigrants,
who are called social imperialistic colonizers. Moreover, these
nations wish (as is totally natural) to have a complete state
and cultural life, as do the other neighboring socialistic states,
as do the nations of the insignificant and backward countries
in Africa and Asia. We, Lithuanians, for many years having
had a common history with Poland, do not want to live worse
culturally than the neighboring Poles or the Negroes...

The Baltic republics must regain (in accordance with the
referendum as formulated in the Constitution) their sovereignty, for which in the course of history many of their best sons
perished. Only a non-human or one who thinks of a large state
—imperialistically—can fail to understand this. The return of
sovereignty to these states would strengthen the forces of the
socialist camp, would raise its authority."

In speaking of religion, Tomonis advocates the elimination of discrimination against believers.

"The Christian faith is based on the same scientific-philo-
sophical basis as are the others. Since this faith and the art
which has been created and is being created in its spirit fulfill the spiritual and cultural needs of believers, it is essential
to abolish all restrictions that impede Christians and other believers from living meaningfully, from feeling themselves fully
legal members of the community; not only from working with
others, but from having equal rights. Free religious education,

---

2. This is an allusion to the expectations of a number of Lithuanian
communists and leftist intelligentsia in 1940 that Stalin would not
incorporate Lithuania into the USSR but would merely transform it
into a satellite on the model of Mongolia.

religious-cultural publications must be permitted; the doors to disputation in lecture rooms and radio and television programs must be opened wide..."

"Attention must be directed to the fact that there are no antagonistic contradictions between socialism and religion. On the contrary, religion assists socialism—it raises the morality of the believers, ennobles them, lifts their spirits, urges them to work well, to conscientiously serve high ideals. Religion and socialism, as systems of morality, are not antagonistic. Both of them seek spiritual freedom and deep humanity."

In the political sphere, M. Tomonis advocates the abolition of the existing restrictions of civil rights, the ending of the persecutions of dissidents whose numbers are ever-increasing. M. Tomonis proposes: "The abolition of the abnormal anti-democratic one-party system. I, for example, as a conscientious 20th-century Christian, will not participate in elections until there will be opportunities to vote for advocates of cultural, spiritual, Christian interests."

"Remembering that until now only the highest ruling apparatus of the Party really had all the initiative in the ruling of the state, I officially declare that I, as many of my fellow countrymen, do not recognize the socialistic status of the Lithuanian SSR, I demand a referendum to change the governing status of Lithuania: to establish separate states or a Baltic federation with an independent internal system of all the Baltic republics outside the borders of the USSR."

At the end of the letter M. Tomonis condemns the communists who oppose progress. He blames them for the fact that dissatisfaction among the people is increasing and that no prospects of improving the condition of the country are seen. Such communists, according to Tomonis, "are the real counter-revolutionaries."

In conclusion he proposes the rejection of the cult of the Communist Party of the Soviet Union and hopes that among the members of the Central Committee humanity will triumph.

"Only this is worth fighting for. First with oneself, with one's inertia, indecision... The only entrance through tomorrow's doors is a clear conscience, real justice, sincere love of people."

After sending this letter, M. Tomonis was again forcibly

placed in a psychiatric hospital. Two days later (June 29) his mother died. Only after great efforts was the son allowed to leave for a few hours to pay his last respects to her. On July 25 M. Tomonis was released from the hospital on the condition that during the next three weeks he take moditen injections.[3]

Having lost the possibilities of working creatively, isolated in his place of work, M. Tomonis suffered a deep depression, which was increased by the actions of his immediate relatives. Since Mindaugas' father had participated in the activities of the Lithuanian Activist Front (LAF)[4] in 1941, the KGB used this fact for blackmail. Security agents tried to convince Mindaugas through his immediate relatives and acquaintances. The news spread among the people of Vilnius that the KGB was taking steps to destroy M. Tomonis—to force him to end his own life.

On November 5, 1975, M. Tomonis was found on the Vilnius-Pavilnys railroad line, killed under the wheels of a train.

— — — —

TO THE INTELLECTUALS OF WESTERN EUROPE AND THE SOVIET UNION:

H. Boell, G. Grass, L. Kolakowsky, E. Ionesco, A. Sinyavsky, A. Solzhenitsyn, and A. Sakharov.

The Lithuanian nation has again suffered a painful misfortune: on November 5 of this year the talented poet and scientist Mindaugas Tomonis was killed under a train. Once again the mysterious hand of the KGB destroyed a creative 35-year-old man of noble spirit.

Last year M. Tomonis, chief of the chemical laboratories of the Institute for the Preservation of Monuments, a candidate of the technical sciences, in an open declaration expressed a strong protest against the oppression of the Lithuanian nation and demanded basic rights for it. Because of this brave protest,

---

3. Moditen B is a powerful tranquilizer with many serious side effects which can disorient a person.

4. The Lithuanian Activist Front organized and led the revolt against the Soviet regime in June of 1941. For history, see Algirdas M. Budreckis, **The Lithuanian National Revolt of 1941** (Boston, 1968).

M. Tomonis was confined to psychiatric hospital No. 5 in Vilnius on Vasara St., and was held there for four months.

On June 25 of this year M. Tomonis addressed the Central Committee of the Lithuanian Communist Party with a letter warning them of the danger of neo-Stalinism and protesting against the suppression of Lithuanian culture. On June 27 he was once again forcibly confined in the psychiatric hospital. Being unable to endure this misfortune of her son, his mother died of a heart attack on June 29.

A month later M. Tomonis was released from the hospital, but recently, i.e., before November 5, he was again summoned to the hospital, but did not go.

M. Tomonis lived the entire period after his second return from the psychiatric hospital ignored and persecuted in many ways.

His family, two children and a wife, is left without a provider, the nation lost an idealistic patriot, a talented poet, and a scientist. Several scores of lines of courageous words of truth cost M. Tomonis his life.

Similar things have happened to other Lithuanians.

On November 5, 1969, exhausted by the continuous struggles for the right to be a conscientious artist and Lithuanian, the talented graphic artist Arūnas Tarabilda died from an insult.[5] This artist, also 35 years old, was interrogated while he was alive and afterwards was placed as a recruit into a tank division where, it is thought, he was exposed to excess radiation. In this way his meaningful stanzas of creation destined for Lithuania were cut short.

In the fall of 1970 the talented scholar, professor of Lithuanian language at the University of Vilnius, Dr. J. Kazlauskas died under mysterious circumstances. He was a 40-year-old progressive and active scholar, who had incurred the displeasure of the authorities by his brave theories of Baltic studies.[6]

---

5. Arūnas Tarabilda (1934-1969) was a talented graphic artist. No further details are available on the circumstances of his death.

6. Jonas Kazlauskas (1930-1970), a doctor of philological sciences, editor of the internationally respected linguistic journal **Baltistica**, was found drowned in the Neris river in Vilnius. The exact circumstances of his death remain a puzzle. There was a confrontation with the authorities prior to his death. Moscow rejected an invitation to Prof. Kazlauskas to lecture at the Pennsylvania State University. There is also

Other similar facts could also be given.

Today in Lithuania the lips of the most talented and creative persons who have not broken off ties with their nation are locked. Silence is the price of existence. But those who decide to speak out in an effort to achieve happier days for their nation expect considerable harassment, and their lives end quite unexpectedly.

Under conditions of oppression and conformism it is exceptionally difficult for a nation to raise and bring to maturity noble tendencies, creative and energetic personalities. Therefore, their loss is tantamount to national extinction. In the present circumstances physical genocide is no longer possible. In its place a refined, deceitful, and consistent destruction of the Lithuanian nation's creative persons is used. This is shown by the events of the last few years; this is confirmed by the fate of M. Tomonis. The Lithuanian nation, which for centuries had its own government and created its unique culture and considerable spiritual treasures, cannot be left to the vagaries of the historical process. She wants to go with the progress of life, she wants to make use of the same rights and freedoms that other countries possess.

Honored friends of Lithuania! Your talented works, full of humanism, are also well known in Lithuania. Your ideas received warm approval in the hearts of many Lithuanians. Your names are mentioned with respect and love.

We ask you to issue a protest against the wrongs done to of Lithuania, for brighter days, for basic human rights.

We ask you to help us in our holy struggle for the freedom us, against the repression of the intelligentsia and its cunning destruction, against the tragic fate of M. Tomonis and other intellectuals.

---

a possibility that his linguistic theories may have produced official criticism. Apparently Kazlauskas was asked to write an article for **Encyclopedia Britannica**. Samuel McCracken, in reviewing **Britannica** (**Commentary**, February, 1976, p. 67), wrote: "Some of the flavor of Mr. Preece's operation is conveyed in a recent article by him in the Britannica's house organ, in which he jocularly reveals that shortly after a world-famous authority on linguistics had agreed to write for the encyclopedia, his chained body was fished out of an East European river." This fits the circumstances of the Kazlauskas death quite well. The pattern of confrontation with the regime, followed by a mysterious death, is thus again repeated in the Kazlauskas case.

29. A REQUEST FOR EMIGRATION BY TOMAS VENCLOVA

TO THE CENTRAL COMMITTEE OF THE COMMUNIST PARTY OF LITHUANIA

This letter should not be a great surprise to you. I am a writer, translator, a scholar of literature. In all these fields, I have worked considerably. I think that I have served my fatherland and nation well and have earned the bread that I have eaten during my life. Nevertheless, I have achieved considerably less than I was able, but that was not my fault.

My father Antanas Venclova was a convinced communist. I honored him and still honor him as a person. Among other things, he taught me to be faithful to my principles. But in my youth, observing life and participating in it, I formulated a system of values different from my father's, which later experience only strengthened. This was no secret to my father or to anyone else.

Communist ideology is foreign to me and, in my opinion, to a great extent incorrect. Its absolute domination brought our land many misfortunes. Barriers on information and re-

No. 29. Text in **Chronicle**, No. 20 (December 6, 1975). Tomas Venclova (b. 1937) is among the most promising poets and literary scholars of contemporary Lithuania. Well versed in Western culture and literature, he has produced a volume of poetry **Kalbos ženklas** (The Sign of Language, Vilnius, 1972), which is within the intellectual classical tradition of the West. Because his work did not exactly fit within the framework of socialist realism, the opportunities for further creative activity became severely limited. The request for an exit was a shock to the republic establishment and the nationally oriented intelligentsia. Emigration of a prominent intellectual, son of an old revered communist intellectual and writer Antanas Venclova (1906-1971), who could be considered as the elder statesman of Soviet letters, represented not only a devastating rejection of the system, but was also viewed as a national loss (see, for example, the remarks of the Lenin Prize laureate Eduardas Mieželaitis in **Literatūra ir Menas**, January 17, 1976). At the beginning of 1977 Tomas Venclova was allowed to leave the country with a five-year visa. However, by a decree of the Presidium of the Supreme Soviet of the USSR of June 14, 1977, Tomas Venclova was denied Soviet citizenship for "acts smearing the name of Soviet citizen". Photostatic copy of the notification of this decision by the Soviet consulate in San Francisco in **Draugas**, September 8, 1977. Presently Venclova resides in the US.

pressions aimed at those who think otherwise force society into stagnation and the country into a backwardness that is perilous not only to its culture. In the long run, this can also become dangerous to the state that tries to strengthen itself by such methods. I cannot change any part of this. I could not change this even if I had as much power as you have now. But, nevertheless, I can and am even obliged to openly express my opinion about this. That is already something.

I formulated these views a long time ago and independently. For a number of years now, I have not written or spoken any word that would contradict them. I look at communist ideology seriously and for this reason I do not agree to repeat its formulas in a mechanical or deceitful manner. By not repeating them, I can only bring upon myself discrimination, of which I have already experienced a good amount.

In my land the opportunities of broader and public literary, scientific, and cultural activities are barred to me. Every humanist—and not only one in the Soviet Union—must often prove his loyalty to the ruling ideology so that he can work. That is not difficult for kowtowers and careerists. That is not difficult for people who sincerely believe in the justice of Marxism (although to some of them it perhaps seems to be an irritating and demeaning procedure). That was impossible for me.

Unfortunately, I do not know how to write "for the drawer." I seek contact with an audience and will seek it by all available means. I would not be able, nor would I want, to work except in a literary or cultural field. However, my possibilities for cultural work grow narrower every year and my whole existence in this land becomes purposeless and doubtful.

Everything that I write here also applies to my wife who is also a cultural worker (a theater director).

Please permit me, on the basis of the Universal Declaration of Human Rights, to emigrate with my family. The example of my friend Jonas Jurašas and other friends show me that this is not impossible. Since my wife is a Jew, we could travel to Israel. This decision is final. I also ask that the members of my family who hold views other than mine and remain in Lithuania not be discriminated against.

Tomas Venclova

May 11, 1975

30. A PAMPHLET ON THE CONSEQUENCES OF SOVIET RULE

THOUGHTS ON THE OCCASION OF THE VICTORY CELEBRATION

Thirty years have passed since the flames of the war died out. One should, therefore, rejoice, but the *Lithuanian has something to mourn.* The land of the Nemunas is like a pea on the road, persecuted by both East and West. The former announced the "thousand-year reich," but now there is talk of an eternal one. The brown "liberators" planned to transfer "the unsuitable Lithuanians" to the Urals, the reds tried even more — to scatter Lithuanians through all of Siberia. It is difficult to discover in our nation a family in which some close relative did not "voluntarily" travel to look at the white bears... the families of the 1941 deportees were torn apart—the men separated. The exploiters of the twentieth-century slaves selected from the deportees those capable of working and used them, giving them 400 grams of bread a day; 200 grams sufficed for the others... Babies die not only in Africa, where droughts are spreading, but also in the land of communistic humanism where a certain category of people became slaves. The Lithuanian deportee heard the words "They brought you here to die!" That was not an empty phrase. The children born of Lithuanian mothers scattered their bones from the Urals to Magadan, from the cold Archangel, Vorkuta, and Norilsk to the hot zones of Kazakhstan.

There was a plan to create a *Lithuania without Lithuanians,* who were to meet the same fate as the Kalmuks, Tatars, and other small nations—they were to be transferred and melted in the kettle "of the brotherly nations." Fortunately, the death of Stalin halted this "historical happening" and brought some relief—the coarse method of physical genocide was abandoned and replaced with moral genocide.

Lithuania resurrected itself from the rubble of the war, but not as it was foreseen in the July 12, 1920, treaty

---

No. 30. From **Chronicle**, No. 17 (July 4. 1975). Editorial note indicates that this is text of a **samizdat** pamphlet, "which reflects the thinking and feelings of many Lithuanians."

in Moscow. Soviet Russia does not honor its treaties. 20,000 sq. km. were torn away from Lithuania and given to Belorussia and Poland. 40,000 Lithuanians, who had Lithuanian schools during the Polish occupation, are now dead to the Lithuanian nation—whoever tried to fight for the right to teach Lithuanian felt the heavy hand of Minsk.[1]

In the whirlwind of the last war Lithuania lost about 540,000 people. The greater half died after May 9, 1945... Even according to the offical statistical information, despite the flood of colonizers, today there are 40,000 fewer inhabitants in Lithuania than at the time of the 1897 census.[2]

There is rejoicing in freedom, but who will count the deported dead, the formerly imprisoned, the still imprisoned, the oppressed?

There is rejoicing in our new communities and new homes, but we do not mention the ruined farms, which were left without masters, the destroyed and disappearing architectural monuments, the crumbling churches, forbidden to be repaired, the pipes of the precious organs which were carried away by children, and the demolished statues.

There is boasting about the industrialization of the country (for that reason importing the needed labor force from the "fraternal republics") but silence about the harming of nature. Gas is sold to foreign countries at speculator's prices while Lithuania's power plants have to be run by petroleum dregs which pollute the environment.

There is talk about the thousands of liters of milk, but we are drowning in a river of millions of liters of alcohol by which our nation's physical and moral health is being sapped. There is trumpeting about the cultural and educational growth, but the expenses of education, health insurance, and social welfare are derived from the profit coming from the

---

1. See Doc. No. 21 for details of these charges.

2. Soviet calculations put wartime and immediate postwar population losses at approximately 850,000. See A. Stanaitis, P. Adlys, **Lietuvos TSR gyventojai** (Vilnius, 1973), p. 13. The last statement is dubious, for in 1897 within the present-day territory of Lithuania there were ca. 2,800,000 inhabitants, o number which was reached in early 1960s. The population of Lithuania in 1975 was estimated at 3,290,000. See Stanaitis and Adlys, **op. cit.**, p. 12; **Lietuvos TSR ekonomika ir kultūra 1974 metais** (Vilnius, 1975), p. 29.

sale of alcohol. From every citizen the government collects more than 150 rubles a year for alcohol. It is forbidden to establish temperance societies, just as it was not allowed by the czarist government, which closed the organized societies of Valančius' time.[3]

Second-rate party literature, translated and worthless publications, published in large quantities and detrimental to the youth, dominate the book trade; e.g., "Zuikių pasakos" (The Bunny Tales) had 50,000 copies printed. Lithuanian literature (Baranauskas, Valančius, Pietaris) is not published in its entirety and in very small quantities (5,000 copies), of which a considerable portion is sent abroad for propaganda purposes; as a result, the ordinary people, because of the large number of teachers and students, cannot obtain these publications.[4] Original studies of Lithuanian history are not published.[5]

Russian schools are established in Lithuania irrespective of the number of Russian inhabitants in the area, but 170,000 Lithuanians, living in Siberia, Kazakhstan, Belorussia, and the Kaliningrad oblast do not have a single Lithuanian school. When several years ago the last Lithuanian high school in America was closed, our press made considerable noise, but no one shouts that tens of thousands of Lithuanians in various

---

3. For the role of Bishop Motiejus Valančius (1801-1875), see Doc. No. 32. The temperance societies, sponsored by the bishop as a means of dealing with the problem of alcoholism, were suppressed by czarist authorities because they obviously interfered with the interests of state liquor monopoly. The problem of alcohol consumption in Lithuania is suggested by statistics, published by Aušra, No. 3 (June 15, 1976): in 1974 156.3 rubles per capita were spent on alcohol, consumption was 9.7 liters per person, which is about four times more than in 1940.

4. This charge can be substantiated. For example, in the case of Vincas Pietaris (1850-1902), his historical novel "Algimantas" is omitted from a collection of his works because of its romantic nationalism. See Vincas Pietaris, Rinktiniai raštai (Vilnius, 1973). Similarly anti-czarist and anti-Russian works of Valančius have been excluded from a collection of his works: Motiejus Valančius, Raštai (Vilnius, 1972, 2 vols.)

5. This is an exaggeration. However, original studies of Lithuanian history, especially for the pre-Soviet period, are relatively rare; the bulk of historical studies concentrate on the Soviet period, the revolutionary movement and events.

places are living without even elementary Lithuanian schools.[6]
In the prewar period considerably smaller Lithuanian ethnic
communities in the region of Vilnius or in Latvia had their
own schools, there were junior highs (in Gervėčiai) and high
schools (in Vilnius, Švenčionys, Riga). In some places, e. g.,
Komi ASSR, the Lithuanians tried to organize sports clubs,
but the security police immediately suppressed them. The Soviet
press is concerned that Lithuanians in America become denationalized, but how many Lithuanian families are there today
whose children can barely say a Lithuanian word, are unfamiliar with Lithuanian letters! In Lithuania itself the Russian
language plays an increasingly important role in the school
curriculum, at the same time leaving a smaller place for
the Lithuanian language, literature, and history. That is a sad
prognosis for the denationalization of our nation.

We dare to even talk about Lithuanian sovereignty when
85 per cent of the industrial plants belong to Moscow and
only local industrial concerns are left under the direction of
the republic. The Lithuanian Ministry of Foreign Affairs confines itself to supplying propagandistic literature to Lithuanians abroad. The military commissariats are engaged only
in the selection of recruits, who are scattered through the depths
of the Union, since the "16th Lithuanian division," which
was created for propaganda purposes during the war and
disbanded after the war, no longer exists.[7] The "sovereign"
state does not even have the right to keep its political prisoners
in its territory.

Pirčiupis is a part of every tourist route, but only few
know that this tragedy was provoked by Sniečkus, Zimanas,
and Šumauskas according to Moscow's directives.[8] Do many

6. Reference to St. Anthony's High School in Kennebunkport, Maine,
run by the Lithuanian Franciscans, which had to close in 1969 for
lack of students and support.

7. The 16th Lithuanian division of the Red Army was formed in
early 1942 as part of Stalin's effort to harness nationalism for defense
of the Soviet state. The division eventually was part of the Red Army,
which pushed the Germans out of Lithuania. It was disbanded immediately after the war. J. Dobrovolskas, **Lietuviai kariai Didžiojo Tėvynės karo frontuose** (Vilnius, 1967).

8. Pirčiupis is a small village in the raion of Varėna where on
June 3, 1944, the German military authorities executed most of the
inhabitants as a retaliation for a Soviet partisan attack, killing several

know how many Pirčiupiai there are in Lithuania? Only a few years ago Moscow allowed the remembrance of Ablinga.[9] There are many Pirčiupiai where the guilty are not Germans! Rainiai, Pravieniškės, Musteika (Marcinkoniai district, Varėna raion) where on June 24, 1944, all the fourteen men who were in the village at that time were assembled and shot.[10] That is not mentioned, just as every day details remain unmentioned if they do not correspond to the party line. They do not dare to tell the truth about a derailed train or a crumbling bridge, or even allow the publication of condolences in newspapers. In similar cases abroad there are general days of mourning. When an effort is made to tell the truth, when the attention is directed to abnormalities and deficiencies, that is called slander. For example, the Chronicle of the Catholic Church in Lithuania is called a collection of slanderous statements.

In other socialistic countries the number of priests increased after the war, new seminaries and churches were built (Poland at this time has over 18,000 priests; that is 4,000 more than before the war) but we are losing priests—in place of the two or three priests who die, one new priest is allowed, whose preparation is carried out under abnormal conditions since the suitability of teachers and students is determined by the security people and the party...

Religious teachers who practice their faith are dismissed from work. The people do not have prayer books: they are not permitted to be printed officially and those produced secretly are confiscated (near the churches and during searches). Among juveniles and youths crime is increasing, the number

German soldiers. There exists a strong suspicion that the incident was deliberately provoked by communist partisans, led by such revolutionaries as Sniečkus, Zimanas, and Šumauskas, to precipitate German retaliation. Soviet version of the event: S. Sinkevičius, Pirčiupiai (Vilnius, 1974); and Pirčiupių tragedijos kaltininkai (Dokumentų rinkinys) (Vilnius, 1975).

9. Albinga is a small village in the Klaipėda raion, where at the beginning of World War II Nazi execution of 42 villagers occurred. A memorial was put up only in 1960. The reasons for this delay are not known.

10. Reference is to places where the Soviets committed atrocities while retreating from Lithuania at the start of World War II. K. Palėkis, Genocide (Germany, 1948).

of illegitimate children is growing, venereal diseases are spreading, abortions are numerous, divorces are increasing—the moral balance is sad, indeed. An interest in our land's past is considered a crime, ethnographers are closely watched—the Lithuanian is being spiritually smothered.

There is shouting about the abundance of the harvests, but not only a liberated but also an occupied soil yields this harvest. If today there is no shortage of bread and other goods—the merit belongs not to the "liberators," but to that part of our nation which preserved the high moral qualities: diligence, honesty, determination. The Lithuanian had these traits even when he lived without "the liberators." It is hard to believe that the new generation, reared "in modern ways," will be more diligent and honest. Bad signs are already visible.

In evaluating the past everything that was good, the vestiges of which are still in use today, is not mentioned, if not slandered. Unfortunately, these healthy foundations are shaken by the new winds, the sense of national uniqueness and moral strength is burning out, there is an accelerating trend toward uniformity without unique content. Moscow's pincers are striving to strangle the Lithuanian spirit, to smother the Lithuanian mind... Will we surrender? Will we permit the East wind to bury our little land? Will our fate really be like that of the Prussians?[11]

---

11. The Prussians were a Lithuanian tribe which inhabited the territory known as East Prussia. The Prussians became extinct as a result of German colonization and assimilation.

31. AN EDITORIAL FROM THE UNDERGROUND JOURNAL "AUŠRA"

THE FIRST RAYS OF "AUŠRA"

Famous Vaidevutis
Would the days of Gediminas
Resurrect. But where is Vaidevutis?
Maironis

Almost a hundred years later *Aušra* appears anew. It is as if the history of Lithuania is repeating itself—the czarist occupation changed into a Soviet one. The danger to the existence of the Lithuanian nation arises anew. Especially in peril are the spiritual values: religion, morality, language, literature, and all Lithuanian culture. The enemies of our nation and its children who do not look to the future are preparing the destruction of the nation. This is being done through deceit, lies, and deception. Consciously and deceitfully Lithuania is being spiritually weakened and physically destroyed. Part of the nation does not notice this disaster and is not concerned with the impending danger. Sometimes through ignorance and sometimes for a bite of bread they become accomplices with suppressors of our nation.

Today there is an effort to remain silent about the heroic Lithuanian past. Thus, it is not suprising that in our schools so little room is given to the history of ancient Lithuania, that so little historical literature is published, and even this is unmercifully mutilated by the censors, and that the prewar Lithuanian history textbooks are conscientiously being de-

---

No. 31. **Aušra** (The Dawn), No. 1/41 (October, 1975). **Aušra** (1883-1886) was the first Lithuanian language newspaper. It was not directly a political press, but sought to awaken the Lithuanian self-consciousness, especially through romantic accounts of the past. Although short-lived (only 40 issues were published), it was a major milestone in the cultural and political awakening of the Lithuanian nation. The underground **Aušra** proposes to continue the work of its predecessor, numbering its first issue 1/41. The author of the motto and the concluding poem Jonas Mačiulis-Maironis (1862-1932) can be considered as the poet of national rebirth. His romantic nationalistic verse was an important influence not only on the political consciousness of the new Lithuania, but also a lasting influence in the development of modern Lithuanian literature.

stroyed. By distorting the historical facts, an attempt is made to blacken Lithuania's past.

Not only the past of the nation, but also the dark sides of the present are not mentioned. There is talk about the growing cities, boasting about the resorts and growing industries, but silence about the spreading crime, labor camps, and horrible diseases.

Few concern themselves in a suitable manner with Lithuania's future, especially its spiritual cultural values. The attention and efforts of the nation are directed only at the raising of material culture—to industries, plants, and sports, while the fields of spiritual culture are abandoned. A nation that is spoiled and sated with material goods and excessive drinking is not difficult to denationalize and destroy.

We must raise our nation from its spiritual slumber. In the words of Maironis, we need a new Vaidevutis... The newly resurrected *Aušra* is attempting to accomplish this task.

The program of *Aušra* remains the same as it was a hundred years ago:

— to show Lithuanians their past
— to correctly evaluate the present and
— to assist in the conception of the future of Lithuania.

Aušra does not have any political purposes—to raise revolutions or to return the capitalistic system. Its task, even in the most difficult times, is to awaken the spirit of the Lithuanian, to nurture national solidarity, the morality of the nation, to foster general progress. The Lithuanian nation will survive if it will be culturally superior to its oppressors. That is why ancient history should repeat itself: the Romans conquered the Greeks, but Greek culture conquered the Romans.

Aušra will not advocate national hatred. It considers as its friends peaceful and good-willed people of all nations who wish Lithuania well and want to share with it cultural values.

Aušra believes that it will be supported by all those who sincerely love Lithuania regardless of their convictions, party affiliation, or status. Today many important officials do not cease loving their Motherland and as much as possible are concerned with its welfare.

Aušra does not claim that it will deal with all the problems of Lithuania. It welcomes the *Chronicle of the Catholic*

Church in Lithuania, which is already in its fourth year, and will joyfully greet other new publications.

We believe that the ideas propagated in *Aušra* will spread among the youth. After becoming familiar with Lithuania's past, we would like them to love their native land even more.

It is nice to toil, to suffer for the Motherland.
The work for one's native land is blessed.
Happy the one who at the rise of Dawn
Will with his brothers as a giant toil.

Shoulder to shoulder, men, who are able,
Let us begin working for our beloved land,
Let's resurrect our Lithuania.

Only let's begin working more quickly,
Only let's love more ardently!
Only, men, let's move the world!

To work—to work, everyone whose chest is burning,
The first furrow of an abandoned field is
The most difficult, but how full of dreams.

Maironis

The publishers of *Aušra*

32. ON THE STRATEGY FOR NATIONAL SURVIVAL

THE IMPORTANCE OF BISHOP M. VALANČIUS TODAY

A hundred years have passed since the death of Bishop Valančius, but his character and his activities are still very relevant. The struggles of the past and the victories achieved ought to help us understand the present, where the strength of our nation lies. We must learn from the past so that we do not lose the contemporary battles.

The times of Bishop Valančius and our own times have many similarities, but there are also differences. A hundred years ago there was an attempt to make Lithuania Orthodox, then Russian. Today the goal is to make it atheistic, and then gradually to russianize it. Marxist theorists clearly state that after achieving Communism, nations will disappear and there will be one language. Marxist teachers feel uncomfortable in our country when they are asked which language this will be?

In these times the greatest obstacle to the denationalization of Lithuanians is the Catholic faith and national solidarity. Accordingly, the most important efforts of Lithuania's enemies are directed at these two fronts.

In the struggle against the Catholic Church, the methods of the czarist authorities of Valančius' time are almost blindly copied.[1] An effort is made to force into clerical positions people obedient to the authorities, who, like Bishop Žilinskas [2]

No. 32. From **Aušra**, No. 1 (October, 1975). This is a concluding part of a long study by an unknown author, commemorating the centennial of Valančius' death. Bishop Motiejus Valančius of Samogitia (1801-1875) was a unique personality in Lithuanian history. Ideologically conservative, nevertheless he was an ardent defender of Catholicism and national values from assault by the czarist regime.. His tactic, however was not an outright confrontation with the oppressors (he opposed the revolt of 1863, for example), but a realistic policy of advancing religion, enlightenment, and moral development of the people within the framework of the czarist administration. Though not intended, his work in effect contributed to the foundation on which a program for national liberation could be based. For an interpretation of his role, see the introductory essay by Vincas Trumpa in Kun. Antanas Alekna, **Žemaičių Vyskupas Motiejus Valančius** (Čikaga, 1975), pp. IX-XXX.

1. See various documents on religious persecution in Part III.

and others, would obediently carry out the orders of the Soviet authorities.

Entrance to the theological seminary is impeded so that with the shortage of priests the faith of the people would be more rapidly destroyed.

There is interference in the appointment of priests so that incompetent priests or those whose standing is compromised would work in the more active parishes, while priests with influence and high moral standing would be forced to remain without work.

Churches are being closed, the building of crosses is forbidden, as is the building of new churches, and those that are constructed are taken away, as in Klaipėda.

Monasteries and Catholic schools are closed, the Catholic press is banned; priests are forbidden to make collections; travel to parish festivals is being limited; and in places even the giving of sermons is restricted.

Priests are forbidden to teach catechism to children and this was not done even by the czar!

Through the so-called parish committees, the government tries to break into the inner life of the Church in order to control the activities of the priest.

And how much pressure and humiliation must be endured by students and intellectuals who wish to remain faithful to their consciences! In the pages of the *Chronicle of the Catholic Church in Lithuania* we find many facts testifying to the violence, deceit, and coercion, with the help of which efforts are being made today to separate Lithuanians from the faith.

Under cover of the slogan that religion is the opium of the people, a systematic war is being waged against the Catholic Church, the largest obstacle to the spiritual oppression and denationalization of the Lithuanians.

Lithuania is being made atheistic through the press, radio, television, lectures, and the schools. One of the methods in the fight against the Church is the destruction of the priests' authority in the eyes of the people, so that in this way the influence of the priest among the people would be undermined. For this purpose the basest lies are used, accusing the priests of murder, and so on.

---

2. Bishop V. Žilinskas of Vilnius (1803-1863) maintained a collaborative attitude in respect to the czarist court.

It is more difficult to protect our nation's spiritual treasures now than at the time of Valančius, since at that time there were no means of communication, such as radio, television, films, comfortable travel, and so on.

In czarist times the persecutors of Catholicism and the Lithuanian culture were the police, Orthodox clergy, and foreign teachers. At the present time, in exchange for money, comfortable position, and good living conditions, this work is carried out by the Lithuanian intelligentsia, especially the teachers. They forget that by opposing religion they are destroying morality and are preparing the doom of their nation.

Today there are incomparably many more of those for whom Maironis wrote these verses:

And you, who only carry the name of a Lithuanian,
But would smother the spirit of the young Motherland,
May the distant future commemorate you
As the degenerate of our days!

Without any doubt, a great deal of the responsibility for the atheism of our nation must rest especially with the priests of the larger cities, whose indolence and sometimes even offensive living make many intellectuals and students disinterested in religious as well as national problems.

The fact that today many Lithuanians are involved in the work of making Lithuania atheistic and denationalized can partly be explained by the lack of knowledge and the uncritical belief in the propaganda of the enemy. They do not notice that the proffered materialism is a new belief, which is not substantiated by the latest scientific data.

The worst thing today is that the denial of religion to youth undermines their morality. It is then revolting to be concerned with spiritual and moral problems. The completely skeptical youths become representatives of the new bourgeoisie, which is concerned only with easy and loose living.

As long as the Lithuanian's spiritual world, religion, world view, and morality, urging the love of the Motherland, is different from the materialistic world view, it will not be compatible with the denationalized, atheistic, morally depraved mass of the oppressors.

That is why today every conscious Lithuanian, during this difficult period for Lithuania, ought to learn from Valančius. Instead of destroying, he ought to uphold Lithuanian religiosity as a source of national strength. Everyone has a duty to raise the national consciousness, to study the national history, and understand its lessons. The duty of every Lithuanian is to surpass the oppressors in spiritual culture: morality, science, art, literature. These are the means to preserve our nation's spiritual values and to acquire more autonomy and freedom.

Today the graduates of the middle and higher schools are becoming more and more aware as Lithuanians, and increasingly they are interested in Lithuanian history and ethnography; Šapoka's *History of Lithuania* is read day and night.[3] However, the majority are still unable to appreciate the significance of faith and morality in the life of the nation.

An interest in the spiritual values and the quest for freedom and the right to think and create independently has begun in the Soviet Union and is also finding an increasingly wider response in our country. Hopefully, these efforts will grow into a powerful religious-moral and national movement of rebirth, which will have a decisive influence on the future of Lithuania.

P. Rimgaudas

---

3. **Lietuvos istorija** (Kaunas, 1936), edited by A. Šapoka, remains the authoritative (though somewhat dated) non-Soviet history of Lithuania.

33. AN APPEAL OF ANTANAS TERLECKAS

TO THE CHAIRMAN OF THE COMMITTEE FOR STATE SECURITY OF THE USSR J. V. ANDROPOV

On December 23, 1974, five chekists and two Komsomol activists came with Christmas greetings. Their holiday "gift" was a search order. It was a kind of anniversary since the first search was carried out at my parents' home (in the village of Krivasalis, raion of Ignalina) thirty years ago.

Between 1944 and 1947 I was searched many times without a warrant from the prosecutor. In 1949-55 the chekists were too busy to waste time with searches. Usually they would invite one to the Military Commissariat and from there would transfer him to the MGB.

After the 20th Party Congress I was searched more frequently with the formal sanction of the prosecutor. Sometimes my apartment was also secretly searched. For example, on October 16, 1964, the chekists came to my mother-in-law, Uršulė Keraitienė, who was at home, and took her away to "discuss" the affairs of her son-in-law, who according to them rarely goes to church, but in his fight against the Soviet government is cooperating with the Russians and even the Jews. Other chekists investigated my books and notes at the same time.

Why has the KGB been terrorizing me for over 30 years?

My parents had had only 3 ha. of land, and they frequently hired themselves out as laborers to the landowners. In 1940 the Soviet government gave them 3 ha. of land, and in 1944 — 7 ha.[1] My mother's brother in 1940 - 1941 often tried to convince my father that Stalin alone saved our family

---

No. 33. Lithuanian text in **Chronicle**, No. 21 (January 25, 1976). Russian text: AS No. 2431.

1. After the Soviet Union occupied Lithuania in June of 1940 and set up a Soviet regime, a land reform was carried out, giving additional land to many landless peasants and small landholders. On the return of the Soviet regime to Lithuania after World War II, an even more radical land reform, obviously designed to impoverish the peasantry and prepare the way for collectivization of agriculture, was implemented. See Pranas Zundė, "Lithuanian Economy: Introduction of the Soviet Pattern," in V. Stanley Vardys, ed., **Lithuania Under the Soviets** (New York, 1965) p. 141 ff.

from poverty. However, he, along with his wife and small children, were deported to Siberia in June 1941. On the way he was separated from his family and died in the labor camps several months later. His wife also died of starvation. The night of the 14th and the 15th of June will remain in my memory forever. My parents went to say farewell to the deportees to Siberia. As I waited for them, I was only a lad of 13, but I became mature overnight. That night an indestructible hatred of Stalin was born in my soul...[2] As a student I listened to lectures about Stalin's selfless love of my little Lithuanian nation; I detested those who affirmed that lie.

In June 1941 the Germans replaced the Russians. They shot people simply because they were born Jews. Hating Fascism and terror with all my heart, I rejoiced at the opportunity to help Russian prisoners of war. But, to my amazement, in 1942 in Švenčionys, the Russian-speaking guards did not let me near them. Only in the winter, when the relatively kinder older German soldiers became guards, was I able to bring the prisoners my last piece of bread. My parents more than once sheltered escaped Russian soldiers and helped them. But on its return in the spring of 1945 the Soviet army "repaid" my father by arresting him. In truth, he was only beaten.

On July 27, 1945, I was arrested "for participation in the underground organization 'Geležinis Vilkas' (The Iron Wolf)," about which I knew nothing.[3] When the NKVD soldiers transferred us six "wolves" to the sergeant of the Švenčionėliai KPZ,[4] the soldiers were harassed for not shooting us on the spot since "all Lithuanians are fascists and bandits." These "bandits" were between 13 and 16 years old at that time. No one in my family or even in the whole village served the occupants. Only one youth came to the German army induction center, and he soon ran away. No one joined the Red Army

---

2. Reference to the mass deportation of about 35,000 "enemies of the people" during June of 1941.

3. "Geležinis Vilkas" was an extreme right-wing nationalist underground group during the first half of the 1930s. It evolved into the pro-Nazi Lithuanian Nationalist Party, which had no significant influence in Lithuania and was shunned even by the Nazi German authorities in Lithuania during the war. Terleckas certainly must have been too young to be associated with this group.

4. KPZ are initials for local NKVD control posts, manned by the military units of the NKVD.

either. The youths of the Krivasalis village became partisans (whom you call bandits). I did not follow their example, since I was afraid of weapons and blood and believed that I could endure the terror of that time without participating in any of it. However, the KGB organs did not allow me to remain an observer on the sidelines.

My first arrest in 1945 lasted only two months, but it taught me quite a lot about the methods of the Soviet organs and their agents. Lieutenants Mikolaichik and Pavlov, and sergeant Kisenkov worked out on me and my friends with their gunstocks, clubs, and other "weapons." They even staged our execution, ordering us to dig our graves... Nevertheless, I did not leave the prison with a feeling of hatred for my tormentors, I quickly forgot everything, forgave everything. But the security organs did not forget anything. They probably saw that during the two months they were unsuccessful in making me an "understanding Lithuanian" and began to spy on me. They frequently searched me, even on trips, in buses and trains.

In the fall of 1946 I arrived in Vilnius to study and rented a room with a friend at the technical school. We were different characters. B.'s father and brother had been sentenced in 1945, and another brother, a leader of a partisan band, died in March 1945 in the forests of Labanoriai in a battle between 400-500 Lithuanian partisans and the NKVD military units. V.'s friends—Juozas Bulka and Adolfas Kurila —were not my friends. But nevertheless, on May 19, 1949, I was taken to the MGB and accused of maintaining relations with them. It seemed that Kurila had been arrested and Bulka was enlisted as a spy and sent to one of the partisan groups. V., with whom Bulka and Kurila were friends, was not even called to the MGB. Why? Was it because in 1945 V. hid from arrest in connection with our case, and I was given the opportunity to become acquainted with Soviet prisons, and, in the eyes of the MGB, I was considered more dangerous than he?

In April 1950 I was again taken to the KGB. Since in June 1949 I joined the Komsomols, the chekists proposed that I was to reveal that Bulka, as an agent, had turned traitor to the security organs. They also put me in charge of monitoring student opinion and reporting to them by telephone. I never called them, but for a while I was left in peace.

On April 24, 1952, my friend A. was arrested on charges

of having planned the assassination of the Chairman of the Presidium of the Lithuanian SSR Supreme Soviet J. Paleckis.[5] Captain Danilchev (now a lieutenant-colonel in the MVD) appealed to me as a Komsomol member and a son of poor parents to help unmask A., a son of the bourgeoisie. When I refused, the captain, in the name of the organs of state security, threatened to take revenge on me for the rest of my life. In the fall of the same year, at the instigation of the chief of the cadres section of the Vilnius State University, Mrs. Monokhina, I was expelled from the Komsomols. They threatened to expel me from the university, too, and draft me into the army. I was saved by my social origin and, more importantly, by the death of Stalin. The chekist Bulygin (now a lawyer) threatened to "jail me," but Stalin's death prevented him from doing so.

After graduating from the university in 1954, I began to work at the Lithuanian republic office of the USSR State Bank. There were no other Lithuanians in the agency. The Russians, who had worked here ten years or more (some of them worked in Lithuania in 1940-1941), did not know a word of Lithuanian and knew almost nothing about Lithuania. I could not convince them that the Lithuanian language was not a German dialect, that the Lithuanians did not cooperate with the Germans during World War II, that Lithuania was the only German-occupied country where the Germans were unable to organize SS legions (this was the reason why all the Lithuanian institutions of higher learning and some secondary schools were closed).[6] They used to ask me in what language I spoke with my daughter and to what school I intended to send her. I had to explain that the self-consciousness of Lithuanians was higher than that of the nomads of the Soviet North. What expressions marked the faces of my listeners when

---

5. No further corroborative evidence on the assassination plot of Paleckis, a rather moderate communist, is available.

6. Unlike in most of the occupied territories, German occupational authority in Lithuania permitted the functioning of scientific and higher educational institutions. The boycott of the SS legion and refusal to register for labor service by students finally brought German repressions. On March 16-17, 1943, 46 prominent political and cultural leaders were arrested and sent to concentration camps and almost all the institutions of higher education were closed. See A. Rukša, "Lietuvos universitetų istorija," in Pranas Čepėnas, ed., Lietuvos universitetas 1579-1803-1922 (Chicago, 1972), pp. 239-40.

I laid before them the facts about a time in history when
such Slavic cities as Kiev, Kursk, Minsk, Smolensk were ruled
by Lithuanians and that the present-day Odessa was founded
by Vytautas, the Grand Duke of Lithuania!⁷ Rumors began to
circulate that I was a nationalist. Complaints were sent to the
KGB. The bureaucrats convinced the chief of the office Kny-
va to remove me, and in the fall of 1955 I was transferred to
the Dzerzhinski section, with lower pay. But "the thaw" after
Stalin's death still continued and the manager returned me to
the post of assistant head of the city office and permitted me
to take up postgraduate studies.

One of the consequences of Stalin's death was the organization of Lithuanian schools in the ethnographically Lithuanian
lands joined to the Belorussian SSR.⁸ I joined in this movement which was headed by the academicians Balčikonis⁹ and
Ivanauskas.¹⁰ With student groups I travelled to the Belorussian SSR, visited the Lithuanian regions, and brought them
Soviet Lithuanian newspapers and books. At the same time
Lithuanian schools were being established in the Lithuanian
lands which were under Polish control, I corresponded with
the teachers in those schools and sent them Soviet Lithuanian
books. I did not think that my actions were contrary to the
Soviet Constitution. But the KGB was of a different opinion.
They placed their agent Titlius, an employee of the "Vaiz-
das" printing firm, among the ranks of the activists for Lithuanian schools in the BSSR. He suggested V. Laugalis organize
an underground organization "Liaudies frontas" [People's
Front] and repeatedly demanded that there be an economist in
the leadership. At the time of the Hungarian events Laugalis
invited me to one of the meetings of his associates. Only one
friend of Laugalis, J. Semėnas, whom I saw for the first time,
came. We parted without deciding anything. Several months
later Laugalis approached me with the request to get a type

---

7. Vytautas the Great (1350-1430) presided over a Lithuanian
empire which stretched from the Baltic to the Black Sea. In 1397 he established forts on the Black Sea at the site of present-day Odessa.

8. Details in Doc. No. 21.

9. Juozas Balčikonis (1885-1969) was a prominent specialist of the
Lithuanian language, compiler and editor of a comprehensive dictionary
of the Lithuanian language.

10. Tadas Ivanauskas (1882-1970) was one of the best known naturalists in Lithuania.

font from Titlius. I refused. That is how my "underground" activities ended. "The Hungarian spirit" soon evaporated. The Lithuanian "conspirator" also became quiet.[11] Laugalis left to teach in the raion, but a year after our first and last meeting the KGB decided to arrest us.

The search during Christmas eve of 1957 did not produce the expected results. I was interrogated nonstop for 48 hours. The interrogation was conducted utilizing the advances made in the field of conditioned responses by the academician Pavlov.[12] When that was of no avail, strong narcotics were used. Captain Kolgov (now a lieutenant-colonel) convinced me to drink a bottle of lemonade... After that for a whole week I became wary of not only my own fate but also of the fate of those dear to me. At the dictation of the captain I wrote "a sincere confession."

Living conditions in the KGB prison were still bearable. All efforts were directed to augmenting moral torments. As if by accident, they placed me in cell 27 from whose window each morning I could see my pregnant wife walking our four-year-old daughter to the nursery past the trolleybus stop. I was not allowed to shave for a month and then they brought my parents to see me so that my appearance would torture them and the tears of my parents would torture me. Seeing that I was able to endure isolation, they transferred the Jesuit Father Aleksandras Markaitis to my cell. This was already his third time here, his health had been broken, and he was tormented by the fear that he would once again be taken to the Deputy Chairman of the Lithuanian KGB Martavičius where he would again be brutally beaten as he had been in 1949. In the quiet spring evenings somewhere nearby a tape recording of my children's voices was played.

In addition to participation in the "National Front",[13] I was also charged with trying to destroy the principles of Marx-

---

11. See Doc. No. 16 for description of demonstrations during the Hungarian revolt.

12. Reference to the famous Russian physiologist Ivan Pavlov and his experiments with dogs on the conditioned response.

13. It is not clear whether "National Front" is the same organization as "People's Front" mentioned earlier. No further data is available on these clandestine organizations. It is possible that these groups may refer to the "Lithuanian National People's Front," which claims to have been founded in 1955. See Doc. No. 26.

ist philosophy and of distributing the statement and testament of the Deputy of the Lithuanian SSR Supreme Soviet and the classic of Lithuanian literature A. Vienuolis. In the December 1, 1955, session Vienuolis condemned the polonization of the Vilnius region, and in the 1957 session A. Vienuolis was not allowed to defend our Siberian deportees. However, both these addresses of Vienuolis and his Testament, in which he asked to have a cross on his grave, were disseminated in the Lithuanian "samizdat." [14]

Even the inquest did not dare to introduce such "criminal" materials into the case. But they played their role in determining the sentence. During the trial recesses Prosecutor of the Republic V. Galinaitis was constantly running to the judge's chambers and talked for long periods of time in private with the judge. We saw photocopies of the previously mentioned "materials" in the hands of the prosecutor.

My relations with the Lithuanians of Belorussia and Poland were also not forgotten. [15] Although, according to the interrogator Pilelis, they did not violate the letter of the Penal Code, they characterized me as a Lithuanian nationalist. The anti-Soviet agitation that I supposedly carried out during the philosophy seminar could not be proved and I was sentenced to "only" four years. I was convicted not of accomplished acts, but of what I might have done if the vigilant chekists had not prevented me.

Seven other Vilnius intellectuals, with whom I was not acquainted, were also tried in the same case. One of them was accused of distributing copies of the selected letters of the Lithuanian literature classic Vaižgantas [16] who had died in 1933, and of the poem "Vivos plango" by V. Mykolaitis-Putinas, [17] which was written in 1943 and attacked the Hitler terror in

---

14. Antanas Žukauskas-Vienuolis (1882-1957), a highly regarded novelist and short story writer, who occasionally displayed leftist realist tendencies in his writings, wrote a doctrinally acceptable novel **Puodžiūnkiemis** (Vilnius, 1952) as a means of extricating his son from Stalinist repression. The text of his speeches and the "testament" so far have not been available in the West.

15. See Doc. No. 21.

16. Juozas Tumas-Vaižgantas (1869-1933), a noted writer and publicist of national orientation, a popular priest and political personality of independent Lithuania. It is not clear whether the letters mentioned are from prewar publications or a new **samizdat** collection.

Lithuania. The court "established" that the poem was written in 1947 and was therefore anti-Soviet...

After the trial, Captain Khlopov (now a lieutenant-colonel) tried to convince me that the "harsh climate and hard physical work would cleanse your nationalistically polluted brain." And how they cleansed! At one of the Ozerlag [18] construction sites I experienced the taste of this bitter bread.

After returning to my homeland, the cowardly bureaucrats considered my brains not yet sufficiently cleaned to even allow me to take a position as an economist with a salary of 100 rubles. I finally succeeded in getting a job as a controller.

Many of my friends remained in the labor camps. I corresponded with some of them regularly. The KGB did not like this. Surveillance was intensified. They even attempted to enlist a close relative of mine to spy on me. I wrote about my misfortunes to J. Skeivelis at the labor camp. The invitations to come to the KGB for "discussions" became more frequent. Lieutenant-Colonel Dushanski (now retired), the head of the section for international counterintelligence, Lieutenant-Colonel Kardonovski, the chekist Karpuchin with unclear duties and rank, Captain Česnavičius (now a lieutenant-colonel) — all of them said that I should be ashamed of my nationalism. I, however, asked them why Russians, Arabs, and Africans are proud of their nationalism, and Lithuanians should be ashamed? Why is the love of Russia here considered to be Soviet patriotism, but the love of Lithuania—bourgeois nationalism? High officials of the Cheka offered me a choice: either to write a newspaper article condemning the social system of the former independent Lithuania or to once again sit in the defendant's bench.

I did not write the article and the case was transferred to the social court of the "Puntukas" factory. [19] The head

---

17. Vincas Mykolaitis-Putinas (1893-1967) was perhaps the most outstanding poet of modern Lithuania, writing symbolic-philosophical verse. There is no conclusive evidence when his poem "Vivos plango" was written or against which tyranny it was directed; nevertheless, it is generally viewed as the poet's denunciation of Soviet tyranny.

18. Ozerlag — apparently a special labor camp.

19. Social court here probably refers to a type of semi-formal ostracism by one's peers, practiced in Soviet state on minor dissenters or the so-called antisocial elements of society.

of the laboratory B. Grabauskas assumed the task of reeducating me. In a coarse manner he tried to modify my convictions, forced me to become a member of the people's militia,[20] the trade union, and ordered me to participate in the holiday demonstrations. In case of disobedience Grabauskas applied economic sanctions: I was paid 30 per cent less than my co-workers who barely had a secondary education. With a family of six, I lived in a 23-sq. meter apartment without conveniences. My wife was constantly promised a raise and a two-room apartment, but when the time came someone called her supervisor and all hopes of improving our conditions dissipated.

In the fall of 1967 Captain Česnavičius stopped me near the KGB building and imposed "a conversation." He accused me of disseminating Alexander Solzhenitsyn's anti-Soviet letter to the USSR writers' convention.[21] He asserted that (the letter) was a falsification by foreign spies, which Alexander [Solzhenitsyn] himself would unmask.

At that time I was taking correspondence courses in history at the Vilnius University. Three times I had publicly defended the history of my nation. On May 23, 1968, during discussions on literature at the "Sigma" club, I accused the playwright Dalia Urnevičiūtė and other writers of disregarding historical truth. Captain Česnavičius, the chekist Karpuchin, and others once again tried to fabricate a "case" against me, however, even "the mistreated" refused to testify falsely.

For a while I attended lectures in the history of Lithuania and Russian literature as a full-time student. In a short time Prorector of Vilnius State University Bronius Sudavičius forbade me to attend these courses. In the beginning of 1969 he even called a special meeting of the instructors of the Lithuanian history department, demanding that they take measures that I do not receive a history diploma. This task was undertaken by the head of the department Stasys Lazutka,

---

20. People's militia—"draugovininkai" in Lithuanian, "druzhiniki" in Russian—a type of popular vigilante force, officially sanctioned by the authorities, for maintenance of public peace and order on local level.

21. Reference to Solzhenitsyn's letter of May 16, 1967, to the Fourth Congress of Soviet Writers, in which he denounced censorship. English text of the letter in Leopold Labedz, ed., Solzhenitsyn: A Documentary Record (London, 1970), pp. 64-9.

who had offered his assistance as advisor of my diploma work. Although I knew about Lazutka's work in the Central Committee (where he was head of a section) and in the post of the Prorector of Vilnius State University, he nevertheless succeeded in convincing me by his supposed liberalism.[22] I wrote the diploma work, "Lithuania Under Russian Rule, 1795-1915," and presented it to my advisor.

On the morning of April 25,[23] three booted security officials came to my house, among them Captain Česnavičius. They took the old prewar journals, books on Lithuanian history, and notes from journals and newspapers. Several days later Major Kazys (now a lieutenant-colonel), returning the first draft of my diploma work, warned me that if I valued my freedom, I should not show my work to anyone, for it is full of hatred for Russia... Prison for a lack of love in my heart for czarist Russia? But why should I love it? Was it because, with the aid of diplomatic and military forces, it destroyed the Lithuanian-Polish state and in 1795 brought slavery to my nation? Or, perhaps, because it took my father into the army to protect its imperialistic interests and returned him home an invalid?

At that time the KGB continued its efforts to create "a case." A certain Juozas Bernotas appeared. He invited me and V. Petkus[24] to help him fight against the Soviet authorities and tried to shame us for our inactivity, and so on. He suggested that we form a committee to defend Ginzburg and Galanskov.[25] This experienced provocateur left empty-handed.

22. Stasys Lazutka (b. 1923) is a Russian-born historian and party bureaucrat. He has specialized in 19th century history, particularly the Revolt of 1863. In 1951-54 he was in charge of the Science and Culture Department of the Central Committee of the Lithuanian CP. He served as Prorector of Vilnius University in 1959-1963. He is obviously a political historian.

23. Probably in 1969.

24. Viktoras Petkus, one of the more active dissidents, a member of the Lithuanian Group to Monitor the Implementation of Helsinki Agreements. **Chronicle**, No. 21 (January 25, 1976) indicated that he was one of the more active observers at the trial of S. Kovalev in Vilnius in December of 1975. Petkus was tried and convicted in July of 1978. Report of the trial in Doc. No. 47.

25. Alexander Ginzburg and Yury Galanskov were among the first Moscow dissident intellectuals tried for samizdat. Ginzburg produced the **White Book**—a record of the Sinyavsky-Daniel trial, and Galanskov

On January 14, 1972, returning home late in the evening I found Captain Trakimas (now a major). He took me to listen to the long and angry monologue of Colonel Česnavičius. That night in Moscow during a search at Peter Yakir's[26] Simas Kudirka's speech[26] at his trial was found, and in Vilnius at Stasys Jakas', the typewriter on which this speech was typed.[27] The KGB decided that this was my handiwork, and again the invitations, interrogations began...

Jakas was reproached how he, a communist, and his friend, the Komsomol member Vaclovas Sevrukas,[28] were "caught on the fishing pole of the nationalists." They asked him to help unmask the nationalists, and they promised him freedom for statements against me.

---

published an almanac **Phoenix 1966**. They were tried and convicted for long terms in prison in January of 1968. Galanskov died in prison in 1972. Their story has been reported in **A Chronicle of Current Events,** beginning with its first issue in February of 1969. Amnesty International is publishing English translations of this journal. See also Peter Reddaway, ed., **Uncensored Russia** (New York, 1972), which contains the contents of the first ten issues of the Moscow **Chronicle.**

26. P. I. Yakir (b. 1923), a member of the Initiative Group for the Defense of Human Rights in the USSR, was arrested on June 21, 1972, and tried for a number of anti-Soviet activities—the possession, compositions, and dissemination of various document, including **A Chronicle of Current Events.** His trial was part of Case 24, designed to silence dissent. Apparently for cooperation with the prosecution and testimony on dissident activities, and repentence, Yakir was sentenced to 3 years' imprisonment and 3 years' exile. Subsequently the sentence was further reduced. Report of the trial and subsequent events in **A Chronicle of Current Events,** December 31, 1973 (No. 30).

27. Stasys Jakas (b. 1941) was an active participant in the production and distribution of **samizdat** materials in Lithuania. He was arrested and tried together with many others in connection with Case 24 (the Yakir and other related trials). He was convicted to 2 years in a strict regime camp on November 30, 1972, by the Supreme Court of the Lithuanian SSR, under Article 199-1 of the Lithuanian Penal Code (the dissemination of slanderous fabrications, degrading the Soviet state and social system). Among the "slanderous" materials possessed by Jakas: **A Chronicle of Current Events, Lietuvių archyvas** (documentary materials on Soviet occupation of Lithuania in 1940-41), Avtorkhanov's **Technology of Power,** and others. Report of Jakas' trial in **A Chronicle of Current Events,** December 31, 1972 (No. 28). See Doc. No. 18 for the text of Kudirka's defense speech and account of his trial.

28. Vaclovas Sevrukas was also tried in connection with Case 24 in Vilnius in January of 1972, under Article 68 of the Lithuanian Penal

Not obtaining any evidence against me, they could not bring me to trial, but Lieutenant-Colonel Baltinas prophetically noted that I was swaying on the edge of a precipice and that one way or another I would end up in prison.

On May 24, 1973, the police stopped two shippers from the cafe supply service where I was temporarily acting as a supervisor. L. Geic and F. Svirski admitted that in a quarter of a year they took out products without documents worth 210 rubles. At the police station the shipper persuaded the counter employees and waiters that in nine months I had appropriated huge sums of money, with which I financed the nationalist underground. In return for this evidence against me, those caught red-handed were released and I was arrested.[29]

Everyone in the city police office was maliciously jubilant. The Senior Lieutenant Gedmantas of OBCHS[30] admitted that he had been following me for several years and that he had been assigned to the task of fabricating a bribery case (against me) "Then," he said, "15 years would have been assured me, but now I will still have to work."

The interrogations did not begin with an explanation of the circumstances of the case, but with "discussions" on secondary topics. Major Liashchenko, in whose character it was easy to recognize KGB training, considered me as already condemned and was surprisingly frank. When the conversation turned to national questions, I did not deny that small nations were doomed to assimilation. But this would happen only after many centuries, and in my opinion there was no need to speed this process by artificial means. The major as-

---

Code (anti-Soviet agitation and propaganda). A psychiatric commission at the Serbsky Institute judged him to be a mental case. He was confined to a hospital from which he was discharged in July of 1972. In the fall of 1974 Sevrukas was allowed to emigrate, presently resides in the US. His case is reported in **A Chronicle of Current Events**, Nos. 24-30. Sevrukas himself has written an account on the Vilnius' offshoot of Case 24 in **Keleivis** (Boston), September 30 and October 7, 14, 21, 28, 1975.

29. Details of Terleckas' trial for the alleged pilfering of state property are also reported in **Chronicle**, No. 9 (1974). This account supplements Terleckas' contention that the trial was a fabrication of the KGB to harass and punish him.

30. OBCHS are initials for a department of the Ministry of Internal Affairs for the struggle against the pilfering of public property.

serted that the natural assimilation process is "agonizing" and thus all methods speeding the merger of nations are justifiable. Condemning my viewpoint, he ended the "conversation" with these words: "You did not see how we crushed the Hungarian counterrevolution. If you, Lithuanians, had seen it, you would not raise your heads. Lithuania! Like a flea, we will (the major made an expressive move with the nail of his large finger on the table) your Lithuania—and there is none!"

After the search of my apartment Major Liashchenko left, carrying only my set of old Lithuanian magazines. As my family later related, he was especially angered by the map (published in people's Poland) hanging in my room, where Lithuania was depicted with its 16th century boundaries. For how can one show such a map to school children!

In the preliminary interrogation cell (KPZ) there always appears someone with a similar fate, someone able to contact the outside world and supposedly to help you. In the very difficult first days of imprisonment, these people try to affect one with tales about the impending punishment, about the senselessness of opposing the government, about the possibility of release by becoming an obedient collaborator. As a rule, these people try to find out what the interrogators failed to get. In my cell there "accidentally" appeared the assistant director of supplies of one of the Vilnius factories J. Žemaitis, whose childhood friend was none other than the KGB Lieutenant-Colonel Dushanski.

Since I did not listen to this "supplier," after a few days the gates of the Lukiškės prison closed behind me. In an eight-square-meter cell there were six of us: murderers, robbers, pickpockets, and some mentally retarded persons. An indescribable stench came from the smoke of home-grown tobacco and from the toilet. The soup contained dried potatoes and salted tomatoes (9 rubles a month for food). After a few days I was transferred to another similar cell. The purpose— that rumors could be spread that the new arrival was a "stukach" (a security informer). And those are killed up here. In addition, the security major Streltsov, entering the cell, greeted me as an old acquaintance, even though I was seeing him for the first time. But for being connected with the "tattler" (the epithet for the security officer), one could also be killed.

Rumors of a demoralizing nature are rampant. The baggage thief Gorelov asserts that he read in *Izvestia* about the death of academician A. Sakharov... However, the thief next to me, Lionia, remembers that he had seen the same Gorelov in a Vilnius railway station wearing the uniform of a police officer.

A new interrogator appears, Lieutenant Vasiliauskas, who is ardently striving to "create" an important criminal case. However, there is no evidence, except for the statements of the two shippers. I asked prosecutor Topol for permission to see my lawyer. This was refused, for I am of age and not blind and will be able to meet with my lawyer only after the completion of the inquest. I then refused to give a deposition. An order was issued to send me to the psychiatric committee for a mental evaluation and at the same time was transferred to a cell with the scoundrel Boris Bershtein who had been sentenced for 15 years. The latter, pretending to be a lawyer, tried to convince me that I would perish in the vaults of the mental hospital. Although on June 12 a commission declared me to be sane, on September 4 I was thrown into cell 379 of the mental hospital prison.

It is impossible to express in words the atmosphere and the tortures of its prisoners. The indescribable unfortunates —Anicetas Skarulis, Vaclovas Strupinskas, Jonas Liubartas, Petras Ivanauskas. One is singing, another is praying, the third is looking for food scraps in the toilet.. All of them are crying from the painful aminozene injections with which they are treated three times a day. Valius Šaltis, who is only pretending to be sick, is also "treated" with aminozene.[31] The fate of his family is sad: the Germans shot his communist father. They tied his oldest son to a tree next to the murdered father, and he went insane during the night. The mother married a second time and Valius is her 19-year-old son.

The informers in the cells and the listeners in the corridors had been telling the administration for a long time that Šaltis was only pretending to be insane. Moreover, it is no secret that the authorities can observe everything from the closed-circuit television unit. So why torture him with aminozene.

Once in a while Dr. Strimaitienė visits the cell. But in her

---

31. The nature of the drug referred to has not been determined. Probably he has in mind some kind of tranquilizer.

eyes one can see nothing but a burning hatred for her patients. It was without reason that one who was committed here
for the distribution of a leaflet in Panevėžys told me that the
psychiatrists of this hospital are themselves seriously ill—but
they are not treated with aminozene.

As a rule one is not called for interrogations from the
mental hospital. But interrogator Vasiliauskas, in an effort to
increase the pressure, considered it necessary to invite me
and to tell me that my wife, after an operation, is in a hopeless state, that the children are left alone, that I am considered
to be a schizophrenic and, in addition, new evidence in my
case had been found. At the same time the interrogator spread
rumors in Vilnius that I was in a mental hospital. He tried
to convince my wife that a cruel punishment was awaiting
me and that it would be better for me if she confirms my
mental illness. My wife answered this with two protests.

On October 8 Dr. Senionienė called for me. Before beginning the conversation she gave me some kind of a pill. She was
interested only in my political convictions and argued questions that would only be heard from a KGB worker. As I
left, she asserted that I will have "to be a guest" in this hospital
until the spring. However, four days later I was called to a
commission which, it seems, was convened only to sign the
previously prepared decision that I was sane.

Although I was not given any drugs injurious to my
health and was treated extremely politely in the evaluation
section, I am convinced that the majority of the employees
of this hospital receive wages not only from the organs for
protection of health. The hands of the physicians would not
tremble fulfilling ignominious orders "from above." If my wife
had not protested, I would have been released from here in
ruined health, as happened to the candidate in the technical
sciences Mindaugas Tomonis.[32]

From the cells of the hospital one is usually transferred
to the interrogation wing of the prison. For three days I was
also placed in a solitary confinement room with broken
windows. Afterwards I was thrown into cell 149, where a
chronic mental hospital patient, the murderer Stasys Jonaitis,
and another one feigning insanity were confined. Here condi-

---

32. The Tomonis case is reported in Doc. No. 28.

tions were more unbearable than in the mental hospital cell. Only after my persistent protests was I transferred to cell 173, where the majority of the prisoners were relatively healthy. But whenever I looked at the piece of glass which served as a mirror, a totally sick-looking man peered at me...

The interrogation continued, but they began to send me to the city police department for the interrogations, and sometimes returned me from there in an ordinary automobile. They probably wanted to give me the opportunity to look at Vilnius in the fall and to compare a free life with my existence in the dirty Lukiškės hole...

Once in a while they allowed me to see my brothers. Since my wife was seriously ill, the news and meetings were never happy. The pressure during the interrogations was also intensified. Interrogator Vasiliauskas, not finding any guilt in my case, would distort the statements of witnesses even during the confrontations with my accusers. At the trial, the defense lawyer demanded my acquittal since my guilt was not proved. Nevertheless, I was sentenced to one year. They could not extract any more. One must admit that our present-day court is not the same as in 1958. Now it is necessary to have at least formal proof of guilt. And a year among us is still not considered a punishment. Moreover, after sitting in prison for seven months, one cannot expect to be found not guilty. Such things simply do not occur in our country.

The remaining five months were filled with greater dangers. Despite my requests to be in isolation, I was transferred to a general cell. Here among the criminals it was difficult to protect one's dignity. They would take away things, beat up the weaker. Eighteen would gang up on one. They also forced me to participate in the beatings. After I refused, they threatened that in the event the one being beaten died, they would testify that I was the instigator of the beating.

On January 18, 1974, I was placed among 750 criminals in the Vilnius strict regime camp in the former church of the Heart of Jesus (of the Sisters of the Visitation) and in the convent attached to this church. Here the vigilant eye of the KGB was also felt. That eye was the security officer Major Ivanov. The camp was full of provocateurs, who offered their assistance in every way, tried to draw you into their snares. On my last night at this labor camp, the warehouse where I worked was robbed. The provocateurs spread rumors that this was done by my friends. Interrogations began. Fortunately, no witnesses appeared.

After returning to my family I hoped that I would have suffered enough for my political and nationalistic views so that the KGB would finally leave me in peace. But my hopes were in vain. Several days later police Captain Deneikin and afterwards Lieutenant Ganatauskas summoned me. They behaved very crudely. The latter, for example, declared that he had the right to summon me every month for five years for "reeducation," that I would not think of stealing, say, even the fire hose from the theatre, where I then worked as a fireman.

On December 2, 1974, I came to a trial which was said to be "open." The defendant was my acquaintance Petras Plumpa and his friends. I was admitted, but on the next day I was ordered to leave the court room.[33]

During the visit of the American ballet troupe "City Center Joffrey Ballet," the KGB ordered that I not be allowed to come to my place of work.[34] I then came as a spectator. Immediately the fire security chief Mykolas Sližys appeared and did not allow me to even go to the employee's refreshment room to drink a glass of beer. Three of them, led by the KGB chief officer for the theatrical establishments of Vilnius, Lieutenant V. Gulbinas, accompanied me even to the men's room.

After the departure of the Americans, the mentioned citizen Sližys, the chief of the cadre section Lupščienė, and former theater director Laurušas talked to me. These theater workers explained to me that the Opera and Ballet Theater was an ideological institution, a cradle of Lithuanian culture, special security item No. 1, whose security was assigned to the KGB and the latter demanded my dismissal from here since I "saw and heard many things." According to the director, if a person who graduated from two university departments works in such a place for 65 rubles a month, he is either sick or he has other reasons... He suggested that I submit a "voluntary" request to

---

33. Petras Plumpa and four others were tried in December of 1974 for the production and dissemination of the **Chronicle**. The trial is reported in detail in **Chronicle**, No. 13 (December, 1974); excerpts from the proceedings in Doc. No. 63.

34. The American ballet troupe performed in Vilnius in December of 1974.

be released from the job. I appealed to the prosecutor with a request to protect me from discrimination. I was then transferred for nine months to be on guard in the closed automatic fire alarm facility so that I could not influence people who truly thought in a Soviet way...

On December 23, 1974, I was stopped on the road by chekists who drove back to my apartment and ransacked everything looking for issues of the *Chronicle of the Catholic Church in Lithuania.*[35] Major Kalakauskas was very surprised that I, in his opinion a Russian hater, read Russian books. Was I not afraid of becoming russified? I told the chekist that even my grandchildren will not be russified. As for my hatred, today I am not the only one angered that an official, having worked in Lithuania for 30 years or longer, rudely interrupts: "Speak Russian!" or "I do not understand your language!"

This is one of many facts. In 1972 I ordered bottled gas. It was not delivered even after several requests. The reason —I made the order in Lithuanian. I expressed my anger not in the *Chronicle of the Catholic Church in Lithuania,* but sent it to the organ of the Central Committee of the Communist Party *Tiesa.* Although my statement was not published, the gas supply agency began to accept orders in the native language. However, after my arrest they took revenge on my family: they would take a long time to fill an order or would deliver bottles of gas which were only partially filled.

At the present time they once again do not accept orders in Lithuanian. I will have to strive anew for what is guaranteed in the Constitution. I do not like all your laws, but being a Soviet citizen I honor them. But I demand that my rights also be honored.

My children also receive the attention of the KGB. Major Krasnikov, during a search, asked my wife's mother whether her son-in-law was not hindering her grandchildren from becoming Soviet men. I was reminded of them more than once during the interrogations. At school they receive "special" attention; e. g., on May 14, 1974, the counselor of my son Gintautas invited my wife and informed her of the concern of the school officials that our 15-year old son "on such a

---

35. Reference to a campaign of the KGB to silence the Catholic **Chronicle** and the related Case 345.

day" (it was the anniversary of Romas Kalanta's self-immolation[36]) disappeared somewhere for a whole hour... But I doubt
that all this "concern" affects my children more than life
itself. And life differs a lot from what they are taught in the
schools. Searches, arrests, and KGB summons affect my children
more than Soviet or anti-Soviet propaganda. They were
searched before being born! (In 1957 my wife was eight months
pregnant during a search and a few days later she gave birth
to our son Ramūnas). Later their book cases and clothes were
searched. Ever since in 1972 the KGB car GAZ-69 carried me
away, the three-year-old Ramūnas is afraid of cars of that
model. After returning from the courtroom he told his grandmother that when he grows up, he will blow up all prisons.
And no one incited him.

One comes to the conclusion that all of the KGB efforts
to "reeducate" me are intended solely to frighten me, to
break me physically and mentally and turn me into an obedient
robot. Many chekists have told me this to my face without
any scruples and not just once. Even in 1958 Captain Janke-
vičius (now a retired lieutenant-colonel) said: "It is necessary
to scare you that you become frightened. Otherwise you will
begin to shoot at us from behind corners. If your knees do not
tremble in fear when you pass the KGB building, then they
will shake after you return from Siberia." On February 15,
1972, Captain Markevičius (now a major) boasted that the
court sent to the other world all those he has interrogated. At
that time Major Kazys ran into the office and bulrted: "Terleckas? Aren't you in prison yet? I won't be able to fall
asleep knowing that you are still treading on our Soviet soil!"
Lieutenant-Colonel Baltimas totally openly also expressed: "We
will never have a peaceful life." A short while ago during
the funeral of Mindaugas Tomonis I carried his coffin and
quietly participated until the end of the ceremony. A chekist
named Vladas, through a 16-year old schoolboy, sent me a
warning whose meaning was: "And we will also get rid of
you." Does the KGB really believe that they will be able to
frighten me so much that I would be afraid to go to the
funeral of a friend?

Even the summons are designed "for the purpose of
frightening one." For example, in 1972 I was led down long

---

36. Doc. No. 20.

corridors, and everywhere on the doors there blazed red plaques: "Interrogation in process." I knew after the May demonstrations in Kaunas and the June unrest in the Vilnius Sports Palace that there was no shortage of KGB "guests".[37] But could all of them have been interrogated at the same time?

Since there are many Russians and Jews among my friends, the chekists try to frighten them too, that they are on friendly terms with people whose hands are stained with blood. God grant that the hands of our opponents would be so clean. In connection with this, I would like to mention a man already imprisoned for over 25 years in the labor camps. Jonas Abukauskas commanded a partisan band in 1948 and received orders to shoot a "defender of the people."[38] The wife and young children begged him to spare their husband and father. Jonas did not follow his order. A little while later he surrendered to the authorities. He was arrested and sentenced to be shot. He spent almost a year in death row. His wife married another, he never saw his daughter, but Jonas never regretted that he had so often been merciful to his enemies. In one of the barracks of a labor camp, where only Latvians and Lithuanians were being held, an escape was planned. When the attempt failed, Jonas Abukauskas and three others took complete responsibility on themselves. Their terms were accordingly extended. If Jonas endures the 28 years in prison, in my opinion he will be my dearest guest.

KGB agents in closed lectures at various institutions do not mention me with a good word. Acquaintances, having heard this, intimidate me. It is said that it is now my turn. But I am calm. First, because I believe in the worth of any sacrifice. I think that not a single drop of blood is shed in vain. Second, because the KGB, even though it is afraid of my convictions, does not believe that I would attempt any concrete actions. Otherwise their surveillance would be more professional. Now it is being done too openly. I am followed even by chekists whose faces I know, e.g., the theater manager P. Vaivada. It seemed that no one in Moscow would be interested in us. However, on the day of departure—March 3, 1975—at

---

37. Reference to Kalanta's self-immolation and the following demonstrations. See Doc. No. 19 and 20.

38. The "istrebiteli," who were organized to fight the nationalist partisans after the war.

the Belorussian station [39] "our" Vilnius agent, who often watched V. Petkus' apartment, appeared.

Although the KGB could find no means to fire me from the theater, the discrimination continued. In February [40] a meeting of Lithuanian cultural workers took place in this theater. I was dismissed from my guard duties. On October 6 I spent only four hours at work, but I was ordered to leave work and come the next day, and again the next day I was asked to leave. Don't they trust me? Don't they want me to see that during the holidays soldiers run around with mine detector and examine even the desks in the offices? Although 7 of the 22 firemen at the theater had spent time in the labor camps, on November 7 on duty was the 15 year-termer Albinas Žiedūnas, a former chorusmaster of Lithuanian ensembles. Even more, when in May of this year two television sets disappeared (not in my place of guarding), police captain Bertanavičius interrogated only me.

After a search in 1974 the KGB asked me whether I wanted to change my political views. Obviously not! After enduring so much for 30 years, I do not have the strength to fall in love with your government. It seems that not much is demanded of me: from time to time to praise the government and during the holiday demonstrations to march by the tribunal with a poster and a red flag in my hands. But I have been cured of even such cheap obedience. I do not know how to love my enemies. And that the chekists are my enemies, was declared directly by Lieutenant-Colonel Baltinas. When I asked him how I should address him, the verbatim answer was: "Only not 'comrade'. You are our enemy." But what kind of hostility is this if it is not expressed in actions? No court has proved any of my anti-Soviet activities. I never fought against the Soviet government and did not instigate others. I can be loyal and remain so even if it is your government in Lithuania. I remain silent. I remained quiet for five years voluntarily. So what does the KGB want from me with its frequent searches, interrogations, and threats?

Citizen General, they most probably try to convince you that from the tens of thousands of Lithuanians who were in

---

39. The Belorussian station is the railway station in Moscow.

40. Apparently in 1975.

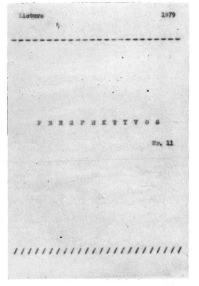

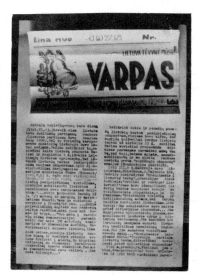

Title pages of *samizdat* journals dealing with national problems, politics, and culture.

On November 27, 1970, Simas Kudirka (top), a Lithuanian sailor, sought freedom by jumping his Soviet ship but was returned to it by the US Coast Guard. His patriotic defense speech during the trial in Vilnius marked the resurgence of overt nationalism in the 1970s. For details, see Doc. No. 18. According to the dissidents, Mindaugas Tomonis (bottom) was a victim of foul play by the KGB for his dissident activities. For details, see Doc. No. 28.

The self-immolation of Romas Kalanta in May of 1972 sparked two days of nationalistic demonstrations and violence in the streets of Kaunas. The self-immolation was carried out as a protest against the Soviet occupation of Lithuania, in front of the theatre where, on July 21, 1940, a puppet diet asked for Lithuania's incorporation into the USSR. For details, see Doc. No. 20.

The close ties between Moscow and Vilnius human rights activists were demonstrated during the trial of Sergei Kovalev (top, right) in Vilnius in December of 1975. The trial was observed by Academician A. Sakharov. He is shown here (top, left), while he was in Vilnius, with the Lithuanian dissident Antanas Terleckas and a group of friends.

Scenes from the trial of dissident Romas Ragaišis in 1978 and 1979.

Viktoras Petkus, the leading dissident personality in the 1970's, the founding member and spokesman for the Lithuanian Helsinki Group, was tried in July of 1978 and sentenced to ten years of incarceration. For details, see Doc. No. 47.

Original members of the Lithuanian Helsinki Group: (top) Ona Lukauskaitė - Poškienė and Rev. Karolis Garuckas (d. in 1979); (bottom) Eitan Finkelstein and Tomas Venclova (emigrated in 1977).

Antanas Terleckas (top left), under arrest since October of 1979, a prominent leader of the national movement; for details, see Doc. No. 33. Balys Gajauskas (top, right), a former partisan and a member of the Lithuanian Helsinki Group, was given a ten-year sentence in April of 1978; for details, see Doc. No. 46.

The Lithuanian Helsinki Group was reconstituted in 1979 with the addition of three new members (bottom, l. to r.): Bronius Laurinavičius, Mečislovas Jurevičius, and Dr. Algis Statkevičius.

your labor camps almost all of them "have quieted down."
Only a very small handful of the "mentally ill" continue their
losing struggle against the Soviet authorities. One has only
to destroy this handful and then there will be the same peace
and quiet in Lithuania as in Belorussia. Do not believe this.
During the demonstrations in Kaunas in the streets there were
no former inmates of the labor camps.

They probably also conceal from you such incidents as the
unrests in June 1972 at the Vilnius Sports Palace when, during
the International Handball Games, high schoolers and students
were enthusiastic for the successes of the Swedish, German
and other teams, for all of them except the Soviet. On the
following day the tickets had to be distributed in those factories
and establishments where the Lithuanians comprised only 10-
20 per cent of all the workers. Is this not worth pondering?
One might also consider why the parallel Russian and Lithuanian classes disappeared from the Vilnius schools? Nationalists could not have been able to do this. I am convinced
that one cannot blame the Lithuanian communists. So who
is guilty then?

Senior-Lieutenant Daugalas has stated that it is dangerous
for one with my political views to live in Lithuania. What
is to be done? I do not want to emigrate. The danger of a
conscious Lithuanian assimilating is smaller in Lithuania than
in the West. I do not regard the Lithuanian nation or language
to be superior to others. But it would be a great misfortune
for me if I would have to talk with my grandchildren in a
foreign language.

Our reality is very distant from my ideal. But I believe
in progress. And this progress, it seems to me, does not require my assistance. That is why I remain aloof from all the
"Chronicles" even though the KGB has more than once harassed me about them. In my opinion, the *Chronicle of the
Catholic Church in Lithuania* is only a danger to you as an
indicator of the existence of the Lithuanian underground. But
with the aid of the Vatican you will certainly succeed in suppressing it.

I believe that gradually everything will turn out well.
Although the Lithuanian KGB Captain Markevičius longs for
the days of Stalin, although he regrets that today he cannot
without interrogations and a trial send me and "those like

me" beyond the Arctic Circle to foment the polar bears—those times will not return.

I ask you to order the Lithuanian KGB to leave me in peace. [41]

With respect,
Antanas Terleckas

Vilnius, November 23, 1975

---

41. Since the writing of this appeal to the KGB, Terleckas continued to be active in dissident circles. He was one of the Lithuanian activists, who, together with Academician Sakharov, closely followed the trial of S. Kovalev in Vilnius in December of 1975. In August of 1977 news reached the West that Terleckas, together with his friend V. Petkus (see note 24 above), were arrested. Terleckas was arrested on October 30, 1979, apparently for signing a petition denouncing the Nazi-Soviet pact of 1939 on the occasion of its fortieth anniversary. Text of the statement in Doc. No. 74.

34. POLITICAL BULLETIN OF THE NATIONAL PEOPLE'S FRONT

PROCLAMATION ON THE FEBRUARY HOLIDAY OF NATIONAL REBIRTH

May light and truth
Accompany our steps...

Fellow Lithuanians:

The National People's Front, which has issued its Manifesto,[1] a program of Liberty and Peace for the entire decade to come, and has then disseminated it in the Lithuanian SSR and subsequently abroad, leading under its flag all groups, associations and organizations of the National Movement, salutes all compatriots on the occasion of February 16, our National Holiday, a common symbol of all of us of the Beacon of Rebirth after a long czarist Russian slavery. This date has lost none of its immediacy, and today more than ever before February Sixteenth must inspire us for new advances of freedom on the difficult road toward our political independence which we shall attain if, one and all, we will rally to its defense.

On this occasion the NPF addresses itself to all honest Lithuanians, all patriots, all religious believers and nonbelievers, pupils, students, young men and women, members of the Young Communist League of the Lithuanian SSR, factory, *kolkhoz* and *sovkhoz* workers, the labor intelligentsia and soldiers, and invites them to join in the official commemoration of the National Holiday, to honor all freedom fighters without any distinction, who have perished in the fight for Lithuania's freedom and independence against all enemies, no matter with what colors they disguise their aggressive, expansionist nature.

The National People's Front, standing firm in its patriotic and internationalist positions, sternly declares to its govern-

---

No. 34. The text of this "Political Bulletin of the NFL (No. 21)" was received by the Supreme Committee for the Liberation of Lithuania and disseminated through its **Elta** releases. The text published here is from the Chicago Lithuanian daily **Draugas**, February 20, 1976. The motto of the proclamation is taken from the National Anthem.

1. See Doc. No. 26.

ment, not elected by the Lithuanian people on the basis of free elections, that all and any efforts to force us to be silent are in vain. We demand that V. Lenin's Theses on Freedom and the Self-determination of Nations[2] be embodied in practice. Jointly with our allies—the Lithuanian Free Democratic Youth Association (a substitute for the Young Communist League), the Lithuanian Catholic Association, and other nationalist, socialist groups,[3] we demand:

1. The right to self-determination, a plebiscite;

2. A free foreign policy, a Lithuanian representative at the United Nations.

Young Lithuanians, join our march because the spirit of the time as well as the love and respect for our common Motherland—Lithuania—demand this. Multiply and disseminate this holiday proclamation everywhere. Be circumspect because the KGB is watching you; avoid provocateurs, foreign spies, and agents. By disseminating this leaflet you will perform a service for Motherland, Liberty, and Peace.

Long Live February Sixteenth—the National Holiday of all Lithuanians!

Long Live the Union of Lithuania's Patriots!

Long Live a Free, Independent People's Lithuania!

Vilnius, December 25, 1975

NPF

---

2. Apparently a reference to Lenin's theses on "The Socialist Revolution and the Right of Nations to Self-Determination" (1916), in which Lenin among other things stated: "The right of nations to self-determination implies exclusively the right to independence in the political sense, the right to free political separation from the oppressor nation. Specifically, this demand for political democracy implies complete freedom to agitate for secession and for a referendum on secession by the seceding nation." See Lenin, **Collected Works** (Moscow, 1964), vol. 22, p. 146.

3. See Doc. No. 26, notes, for an explanation of the organizations mentioned.

35. AN ARTICLE ON LINGUISTIC ASSIMILATION

NEW METHODS OF RUSSIFICATION IN THE SCHOOLS

Russian imperialism has firmly subjected the schools to its service. What the Red Army began with bayonets and tanks, what the security organs maintain by means of their courts and jails is to be completed and consolidated by the schools. The task of the schools is to perpetuate Russian domination in all the enslaved countries, to instill in the younger generation the state ideology—which has become a religious surrogate—and gradually to russify it. The eternal annexation of various peoples into the Russian empire must culminate in their organic assimilation. In pursuit of this goal, the schools openly and directly attack and undermine any other ideologies, callously intrude into the students' consciences, and advance atheism by the most devious means. At present the state "religion" is much more prejudiced and intolerant than any other religion in the past. The principle that the ruler determines his subjects' religion reigns supreme in the Soviet Russian empire.

Russification policies are carried out quietly and under disguise. Such terms as internationalism, international friendship, Soviet patriotism, the Soviet people, are often cited to conceal russification. Nevertheless, the accomplishments, superiority, and selflessness of the great Russian people are constantly emphasized. Cautious attempts are made to suppress national culture; obscure, deemphasize and slander a nation's past; and to emphasize artificially Russian cultural influences. In other words, one strives to quench imperceptibly national consciousness and love of country, gradually insinuating the Russian mentality and consciousness. Similar methods are im-

No. 35. From Aušra, No. 2 (February 16, 1976), slightly abbreviated. The same issue of Aušra contains another article on the threat of linguistic assimilation—"The Spirit of the Muravyov Era." It is a polemic with a number of reports, delivered to the 1975 Tashkent conference on the improvement of teaching of the Russian language. These articles are a response to the recent campaign to increase the use of Russian in all spheres of life.

plemented in the field of language; bilingualism is firmly and methodically promoted. Up till now the native language has not been openly attacked, as had been done under the czarist rule. But the Russian language is now much more openly imposed. Traffic signs, advertisements, and inscriptions must be in two languages and even of equal size. Some agencies' papers are written only in Russian. The number of hours of Russian radio and television broadcasting is by no means proportional to the number of Russian-speaking inhabitants of the republic. In the bookstores and libraries Russian books indisputably preponderate, even though the mass of buyers and readers is Lithuanian. But a particularly important role is assigned to Russian in educational planning and programs. It is through the schools that the Russian language must root itself deeply.

At this time one more step is being taken toward the realization of virtual bilingualism. To encourage the use of Russian in everyday life, opportunities for practicing Russian are expanded during extracurricular activities. An interesting article relating to this matter appeared in the December 10, 1975, issue of *Tarybinis Mokytojas* (The Soviet Teacher). L. Kojelienė, inspector for School Administration of the Lithuanian SSR Ministry of Education, flatly states the following in her article "Olympics": "It is essential to extensively involve students in extracurricular activities in the Russian-language environment." Extracurricular activities must not only improve knowledge of Russian as a school subject, but must also awaken "an interest in the Russian language, a love of Russian books." Most importantly, they ought to accustom students to the use of Russian in everyday life. The procedures and methods L. Kojelienė recommends in her article leave no doubt what one aims at. "During exercises, an instructor of Russian language and literature can go far beyond the limits of his program," thereby opening them up to "great and inexhaustible possibilities." He may employ means of large-scale participation, organizing literary presentations, debates, lectures, or he may "create an environment congenial to literature—setting up bulletin boards, exhibits of individual writers and their works, displays." Clearly, such an "environment congenial to literature" will be nothing but a Russian environment within a Lithuanian school.

In connection with these large-scale, group and individual, occasional and continuous forms of extracurricular work with

Russian, one should employ "dialogues,... studies of short story structure; grammatical, vocabulary, and literary games, class outings; discussion about slides... the posting of articles on bulletin boards." Such occasional methods are suggested, as "Russian-language days and weeks, Russian book festivals, literature mornings, etc."

One is reminded of other methods besides the setting up of exhibits and displays, compiling of albums, lectures, receptions with writers or translators, corresponding with literary museums. These may be "Russian-language almanacs and school newspapers that print the students' best work, essays, reviews of films, and presentations, material pertaining to literary debates." As we see, the trajectory is high, the target chosen is distant. Children in schools are accustomed not only to converse in Russian, but also to write, to create. Russian is introduced into the creative sphere, thus making it the means of expressing the inner world. Reading and other such contests not only encourage certain creative talents, but also evaluate them right in the school. Ethnology dealing with the past of one's own people is persecuted and interfered with. At the same time, a "literary ethnology" is practiced which deals with such questions as these: "Russian writers in our republic"—not Daukantas, Valančius, Kudirka, or Putinas, but... Russian writers![1] "Great importance is attached to school outings to places of literary interest." Pray tell—which places? Probably they are not within boundaries of our republic, for "much valuable material is brought back from such outings—material which could be utilized not only for extracurricular activities, but also for class work." Since this is for Russian-language classes, the material must be sought in a Russian environment. But, "one should especially cultivate students' art activities associated with Russian, including the upper, middle, and even beginning classes." That is very clearly put. How else could the children become better accustomed to speaking Rus-

---

1. Reference to Simonas Daukantas (1793-1864), one of the earliest national historians and an important figure in national rebirth; Bishop Motiejus Valančius of Samogitia (1801-1875), a noted spiritual and national leader in the early struggles against russification policies; Vincas Kudirka (1858-1899), founder of the second Lithuanian-language newspaper Varpas, a giant figure in the Lithuanian national renaissance; Vincas Mykolaitis-Putinas (1893-1967), one of the greatest Lithuanian writers of the twentieth century.

sian, if not by singing Russian songs and memorizing entire pages of plays...

These and other methodical prescriptions are not mere suggestions about how to use extracurricular activities to increase interest in a given subject. Work in this field is to be examined in an organized manner. It is already known that "this school year there will be in our republic a Russian language and literature olympiad... the winner will have the right to participate in the concluding Russian language festival. Over the course of it, students will participate in literary and musical compositions... contests, writing articles for the festival's bulletin board, composing short stories on assigned themes... They will be awarded prizes." These are carrot-and-stick policies. The carrot encourages the children to cherish the Russian language; the stick warns the schools and teachers not to take Russian lightly. "The olympiad represents a review that demonstrates how well the students have mastered Russian..." Further, such olympiads "in future will occur every two to three years."

In the school curriculum Lithuania's history is distorted and caricatured; the students' knowledge of the Lithuanian language and literature is insufficient, their mastery weak. At the same time the preoccupation with Russian is intensified. It is not enough that Russian is introduced too early—at a time when the children have not consolidated their mastery of the native language. Now they are required to supplementally pursue this language, using it to discuss, sing, compose short stories, write articles, prepare almanacs, put on plays. Where will such a stress on Russian lead to if not to bilingualism? And from here, one advances to total domination of Russian. We observe this in the autonomous republics, where the local languages are practically barred from public life and used only for propaganda purposes, when one language must demonstrate the equality of all the nationalities. "The assimilation of a foreign language and the further advance towards bilingualism sometimes lead to supplanting of the native language." [2] So writes

---

2. A. Panda, "The Influence of Bilingualism on Certain Features of Folk Culture," **Sovetskaya etnografiya**, No. 2, (March-April, 1972); I. S. Gurvich, "Modern Trends in Ethnic Processes in the USSR," **Sovetskaya etnografiya**, No. 4 (July-August, 1972); the reference to the No. 5, 1974, issue of the journal appears to be erroneous.

M. N. Gubuglo in his article, "The Consequences of Social-Ethnic Bilingualism" *Sovietskaya etnografiya*, No. 2, 1972) The same article (p. 33) states that "The assimilation of a second language is the crucial point in the supplanting of a language. And the last stage of linguistic assimilation, the final supplanting of a language, is directly tied to an individual's indifference to his ethnic group's stability—the group from which he disengaged himself, having lost one of its principal characteristics." (p. 36). Indifference to an "ethnic group," or, more correctly stated, to one's people, is inevitable once the language is lost. This fact is not denied even by Soviet ethnographers. Relying on concrete data relating to the assimilation of Karelians, the article's author comes to the conclusion that "the spread of bilingualism, the continued expansion of the Russian language's sphere... promotes the process of cultural internationalism. The substitution of the native language... is directly tied to the Karelians' diminishing recognition of their spiritual and material cultural elements." (p. 35). These are facts, wrapped in scientific terminology, which speak about the terrible process of the destruction of all the nationalities, especially the smaller nationalities. "Studies of language pattern developments in Karelian villages demonstrated that, along with a horizontal expansion of bilingualism, there occurs an expansion of it in depth. The Russian language slowly becomes the means of communication within the people. According to the 1970 all-Union census, more than 96 per cent of Soviet Karelians speak Russian or consider it their native language." (*Sovietskaya etnografiya*, No. 5, 1974, p. 28).

From the national language to bilingualism; from bilingualism to one of two languages! This represents something of a detour from the primitive, though straight, czarist path of an open prohibition of the language and printing. The Russian imperial Soviet regime makes this detour for propaganda purposes, yet the goal remains the same. "The insinuation of Russian or the expansion of bilingualism is an important integrating factor, contributing to a further strengthening of the Soviet people's monolithicism." (*Sovietskaya etnografiya*, No. 4, 1972, p. 30). This "Soviet people's monolithicism" is a pot —a Russian pot—which melts all of its subject nationalities so that the "brotherly" Russian nation could become even bigger. The most enlightened and progressive Russian people see this and condemn it (A. Solzhenitsyn, A. Sakharov and others).

Unfortunately, our own intellectuals do not want to see and understand this—obediently carrying out every whim of the subjugator.

Today the schools are required to be the gravediggers of the national consciousness. During the czarist period the Lithuanian schools slipped out from the government's hands and were concealed in the huts of the peasants and at the spinning wheels of mothers.[3] They preserved the Lithuanian language, faith, and nationality.

Vytautas D.

---

3. Reference to the illegal and widespread national schools, usually conducted in peasant households, which to a significant extent counteracted czarist assimilationist policies and provided the foundations of national rebirth in the second half of the nineteenth century).

36. DECLARATION OF THE NATIONAL PEOPLE'S FRONT

In the name of Lithuania
May unity flourish

Citizens: Patriots of Lithuania, Forward to a Free People's Lithuania

Commemorating the 36th anniversary of the tragedy of the Baltic States, we, the Association of Lithuanian Patriots, the Lithuanian Catholic Association, and the Association of Free Democratic Youth of Lithuania,[1] appeal to the world, protesting to the USSR government in Moscow against the persecution of the Lithuanian, Latvian, and Estonian people. The renowned postulates of peace, freedom, cooperation of peoples, and democracy of the 1975 Helsinki Conference are being ignored. Once again we must remind everyone that in 1940 the USSR committed a brutal act of aggression against the independence of Lithuania, Latvia, and Estonia—even though it officially represents itself as an upholder of the principles of freedom and peace. Molotov and Ribbentropp, the contemporary politicians and ringleaders of the USSR and Fascist Germany, decided to liquidate the Baltic States. They wiped these countries off the map of Europe. In June of 1940, three small, sovereign and neutral states were annexed by the Red Army. Moscow's propagandistic assertion that Lithuania "voluntarily joined the framework of the USSR" is a foul lie. The Lithuanian people do not and never have believed this. It cannot be hushed up that the great Western European states and America quietly sanctioned the annexation of the Baltic States. The propaganda of Western countries about their alleged nonrecognition of the

No. 36. Translation from a text published by the Lithuanian newspaper in Canada, **Nepriklausoma Lietuva**, August 25, 1976. The date of this declaration is uncertain, probably May or June 1976. The motto is from the National Anthem.

1. For comments on the mentioned underground organizations, see Doc. No. 26, notes. This declaration introduces a new partner of the NFL—the Association of Lithuanian Patriots (Lietuvos Patriotų Sąjunga). This is the first, and so far the only, reference to such an organization in the **samizdat** press. There is no corroborating evidence that such an organization in fact exists.

Baltic States as parts of the USSR are empty phrases.[2] For a long time naive patriots of Lithuania believed their words; now we will not be deceived. We fully perceive the imperialistic goals of these countries (political, military, economic). Neither the USSR nor the US defended, are defending, or will defend our national interests. They are concerned about other matters —such as dividing up the world into their spheres of influence. All great imperialistic states are, have been, and will be the enemies of small countries. We should not delude ourselves with illusions about receiving our freedom from others. Do not forget, however, that time is working in our favor. Time has forced the world's plunderers to release the colonialized peoples. Nearly all the former African colonies have already created states, taking one step forward—to statehood. (The USSR supported them in this struggle.) What about our issue? The USSR has taken the opposite view. We were forced to take two steps backward, losing our independence and statehood. We have a right to restore it. Not only do we have that right, but an obligation as well. That is our sacred duty and obligation. On the basis of the principles of international law, justice, and humanism, V. Lenin's doctrines about a people's right to freedom, self-determination, and secession from the metropolis, today we make the following demands:

1. The Moscow government must cease interfering in the internal affairs of the Baltic States, relinquishing for all time all pretensions to the territory of Lithuania, Latvia, and Estonia, which we do not consider to be parts of the USSR.

2. Because the aggression of the USSR against its neighbors is condemned by international law, we have a legal and moral right to repudiate the status of a so-called Soviet socialist republic, which has been forced upon us. We annul all in-

----

2. Obviously, this charge is exaggerated. The NFL's definition of international politics resembles to some extent the Chinese point of view. It views the United States, along with the USSR, as one of the hegemonial powers seeking the delineation of spheres of influence, not as a state vitally concerned with the liberation of Eastern Europe from Soviet control. In a way, the NFL believes that something like the so-called Sonnenfeld doctrine defines the real East-West relations. Elaboration of this viewpoint is found in the Program of the NFL published in Doc. No. 26. The official State Department summary of Helmut Sonnenfeld's briefing of American ambassadors in a meeting in London in December of 1975 was published in the New York Times, April 6, 1976.

stitutions of the USSR forced upon us, whose basis is anti-national.

3. In the people's name we demand from the government of the USSR new, free, democratic elections and a plebiscite for all Lithuanian citizens of the Lithuanian SSR. We are for a secession from the framework of the USSR (this is guaranteed by the USSR Constitution) and the status of a People's Republic in a bloc of socialist states. We are for an end to the recruitment of youth of the LSSR into the Soviet Army and its consignment to the interior of the USSR. We have a constitutional right to serve in our territory, in our national units. We are for the return of all prisoners and exiles to our own country, for the central Moscow government has no juridical right to hold the arrested outside the republic's borders.

4. We demand the right to have national youth organizations and parties, which are presently forbidden and whose activities find expression in illegal forms. The All-Union Lenin Communist Youth League does not satisfy us. This organization is foreign and imposed on us from above. It has nothing in common with the spirit and aspirations of the Lithuanian people. It is no secret that more than half of Lithuanian Komsomols directly or indirectly support the ideas that the Association of Free Democratic Youth of Lithuania promulgates (at present still illegal). The Association's ideals are known to all: freedom, equality, brotherhood, national unity, and the restoration of a national sovereign state. The Communist Party of Lithuania, a branch of the Communist Party of the USSR, is a territorial unit and non-national. Since a territorial unit is incapable of any substantial independent achievements and especially because the Lithuanian Communist Party did not and does not defend national interests, it did not and does not enjoy the confidence of the entire nation. An exception to this is the minority of Jewish-Lithuanian collaborators, who actively participated in the physical and spiritual destruction of the Lithuanian people during the period of the Personality Cult.

5. Once again, we inform the free world of the persecution of Lithuanian intellectuals and new arrests and persecutions of young patriots and repressions and restrictions on the clergy of the Catholic Church in Lithuania. Persecutions are aimed at that segment of the clergy which does not side with

the Church hierarchy—the hierarchy, which pays homage to
the cult of the Soviet administration and sometimes proclaims
the presence of freedom of worship in the USSR.

6. We demand the return of those Lithuanian ethnic territories that were joined to the Belorussian SSR.[3] There Lithuanians have no means to develop their national culture. It is
time to liquidate the so-called Kaliningrad region, a colony of
the RSFSR, which has nothing in common with ethnic Russia.[4] East Prussia — populated by the Prussians, a Lithuanian
tribe, and conquered by a Western order of knights—belongs
to the Prussians. The former inhabitants (Prussians and Germans) were unjustly expelled from their native land by foreign
powers, the trio of victors over the German Reich: the USSR,
the US, and England. We demand the restoration of Lithuania
Minor (Prussia) with full political, economic, and cultural
autonomy within the jurisdiction of a future Lithuanian state.

7. We demand the abrogation of RSFSR laws in effect
within the territory of the Lithuanian SSR, which hinder the
maintenance of cultural ties with other countries. There must
be no limitations for the tourists of Western countries who are
relatives of local citizens. The draconian laws of the USSR
that discriminate against Lithuanians as a nation, denying
them their own representatives abroad, must be annulled immediately. There must be no limitations for individuals wishing to emigrate to rejoin their families. Unrestricted tourism
and reemigration of Lithuanians without any preconditions,
without any reprisals for their so-called anti-Soviet past, be-

---

3. The fate of the Lithuanian population left within the boundaries
of the Belorussian SSR is presented in great detail in a samizdat
document, "About the Situation of Lithuanians in the Belorussian Republic," excerpts of which appear in Doc. No. 21.

4. The Potsdam Conference, "pending the final determination of
territorial questions at the peace settlement," placed the city of Koenigsberg
and the adjacent area, formerly known as East Prussia, under Soviet
control. There remains some question as to the permanence of this
territorial disposition. See Jonas Stikliorius, "Lithuania Minor in International Treaties," in Martin Brakas, ed., Lithuania Minor ("Studia Lituanica
III") (New York, 1976), pp. 9-65. Presently, the area known as Kaliningrad Oblast of the RSFSR is populated mostly by Russian colonist and
military elements. There is indirect evidence that Moscow wanted to
merge the oblast with adjacent Lithuania, but this was allegedly resisted
by the Lithuanian communist leaders.

cause the laws of the RSFSR cannot apply to citizens of Lithuania.

8. We proclaim June 15-18 National Days of Mourning.[5] In protest against the USSR invasion of the Baltic States, we propose that the national flag bound with a black band be raised throughout the republic.

9. July 21, now designated as the founding holiday of the Lithuanian SSR, is to be boycotted.[6] We call it the day of national betrayal, refusing to participate in the demonstration organized by the puppet regime of the Lithuanian SSR and the parade of the USSR Army's garrison in Vilnius. Throughout the republic we proclaim a silent demonstration—our protest against the state administration of the LSSR, which was never elected on the basis of free elections by the Lithuanian people.

10. We warn the "ochranka" of the USSR (the KGB) against any kind of reprisals against the youth of the Lithuanian SSR, to which we will respond with a mass protest. The accusation of the KGB that we are nationalists are unfounded and do not stand up to critical examination. We, the Younger Generation of Lithuania, born and matured in a socialist society, support a free and independent People's Lithuania, and not a restoration of moribund capitalism. We are for amity among all nations, socialism, democracy, and peace. Cognizant of our people's historical mission, as well as every other people's, we cannot as patriots remain by the wayside when our fate is being determined and was determined by a foreign state. We are able to represent ourselves, without any caretakers and intermediaries. The obfuscations of Moscow and its puppet government of the LSSR about our unfavorable geographic situation and the smallness of our population are frivolous fables. Every nation, large or small, no matter what its geographic position, can follow a path of its own choosing. We have such a path and will follow it—the path of national unity toward national freedom and political independence.

Long live the unity of all the Lithuanian nation.

Long live the amity of the Estonian, Latvian and Lithu-

---

5. Dates of the occupation of Lithuania, Latvia, and Estonia by the Red Army in 1940.

6. On July 21, 1940, the puppet "People's Diet" proclaimed Soviet rule in Lithuania and adopted a declaration on the accession of Lithuania to the Soviet Union.

anian nations and their successful common struggle for the restoration of independent Baltic States.

Long live humanism and peace.

Long live the great and immortal principles of freedom, which are worthy of struggle.

Patriots, do not forget that in this struggle for freedom we are not alone. The Ukrainian, Georgian, and Armenian patriots, Slovaks, Czechs, Hungarians, Poles, and others are with us.

Long live tolerance and cooperation with intellectuals and patriots of the Russian nation, who have been able to root out from their hearts the weeds of great nation chauvinism, which flourished throughout history.

N.P.F.

Vilnius, 1976

37. THE CASE FOR INDEPENDENCE

Dispossession of independence is a painful loss to the Lithuanian people. If the Lithuanian nation wants to live, it cannot leave its fate in foreign hands, which are intent on lulling the Lithuanian nation to sleep and suppressing its life. The Lithuanian nation must regain its freedom and independence!

A nation's existence, freedom, and further development is best assured through its own independent state. But could Lithuania recover its independence? Skeptics point to the following:

1. The Soviet Union will never, of its own good will, agree to permit the restoration of an independent Lithuanian state. No one will force it to since the Soviet Union is great and the most powerful state in the world.

2. Lithuania is too small and, for economic reasons, would be unable to sustain herself as a sovereign and independent state. Present-day industrial production requires such a high level of technology, so much capital, and is such a large-scale activity, that a small state would not be able to accomplish it all on its own power.

3. The economy of Lithuania is presently a component part of the Soviet Union's economy; it is very closely bound up with the latter and dependent on it. Severing ties with the Soviet Union's economy is already practically impossible.

What can be said in answer to these arguments?

1. Although Article 17 of the Constitution of the Soviet Union states that the right of free secession from the Soviet Union remains with the Soviet republic, it is difficult to believe that the Soviet Union will, of its own free will permit the restoration of an independent state of Lithuania. This will not occur as long as the Soviet Union is ruled by a Communist Party that has aggressive imperialist goals. This has been openly acknowledged by Prof. Kirsanov, a Communist Party lecturer from Moscow. Speaking in 1941 to Lithuanian writers, artists,

No. 37. From Aušra, No. 4 (October 20, 1976). This is a conclusion of Part II and most of Part III of the article "The Loss of Independence—a Painful Misfortune of the Lithuanian Nation." The first part of the article examines the achievements and progress of independent Lithuania. The second part surveys what the Lithuanian nation has lost culturally, economically, and politically during the Soviet period.

and musicians in Kaunas, he asserted: "Peter the Great was the first monarch who understood Russia's mission—to take over the Baltic lands and to approach the Atlantic Ocean. Perhaps some call the Soviet Union imperialistic even today? Yes, we are the avant-garde of the proletariat and, in the same sense, imperialists. Thanks to fate or its spirit, the peoples of the Soviet Union, through the revolution and Communism, are marching to save the world. The Baltic countries were occupied by force because they were not mature enough for Bolshevism. But we bolsheviks need not be concerned—and we are not concerned—with the means—as long as there is one foot of the world, one human being, who does not stand in the shadow of the red flag. The Baltic countries' early, and therefore glorious, annexation to the Soviets is not some sort of accident, but a consequential result of communist-bolshevik policies and national liberation... Cast off your dreams of liberation, you undiscerning! The Soviet Union will advance throughout the world—even through ruins, through fire! (Liudas Dovydėnas, "Mano kelias į Liaudies seimą," *Lietuvių Archyvas*, 1942, Vol. III, p. 47.)

Foreign Commissar of the USSR V. M. Molotov spoke in a similar vein to the Foreign Minister of the People's Government of Lithuania Prof. V. Krėvė-Mickevičius. On June 30, 1940, he stated: "If the Russian czars, beginning with Ivan the Terrible, sought to break through to the Baltic Sea, it wasn't because of personal whims, but because the course of the development of the Russian state and nation demanded it. It would be unforgivable if the government of the Soviet Union did not take advantage of an opportunity that might not occur another time. The leadership of the Soviet Union has decided to join the Baltic states into the family of the Soviet Republics." (Prof. V. Krėvė-Mickevičius, "Bolševikų invazija ir Liaudies vyriausybė," *Lietuvių Archyvas*, 1942, Vol. III. p. 11).

The Soviet Union seized Lithuania by force and will not easily relinquish her. But it is incorrect to think that the Soviet Union's power is unshakable. History does not know a state that did not succumb to the demands of the advancing ages and did not crumble. The proud Roman Empire, which held world power, fell. The mighty British Empire, which had many conquered countries in all the continents and in all the oceans' islands of the world, disintegrated. Almost all of the large number of nations it ruled are now free. If the less developed African peoples are completing their liberation from the former imperialist states, then the day of liberation for the subjugated peoples of the Soviet Union will come.

Nations, which defend their sacred rights, preserve their determination to prevail advancing centuries, regain their freedom. The Spanish suffered seven hundred years of Arab suppression but did not slacken in the struggle, and recovered their freedom. The Irish endured for four hundred years, fighting English repression, and today Ireland is independent. And the Lithuanian nation, if it will not be lulled to sleep, will retain its resolve to triumph and to regain freedom, will restore its independence despite a lengthy struggle for it.

Steponas Kairys, the well-known activist of the Lithuanian nation, signer of the Lithuanian Declaration of Independence of February 16, 1918, long-term Chairman of the Lithuanian Social Democratic Party, wrote in his work *Tau, Lietuva* (For You, Lithuania): "I am firmly convinced that the present global rivalry between the East and West will be won not by Communism, but by the Free World, which more and more inclines toward democracy and socialism. It will prevail because Communism—having become barbarism, having trampled in the mud the most beautiful ideals of humanity—has nothing with which to attract people on its own merits. Humanity will decide the victory." (St. Kairys, *Tau, Lietuva*, Boston, Mass., 1964, p. 98.)

The Soviet Union is governed by the Communist Party, which bases its rule not on the will of the people, but on the force of arms, lies, and deceit. The elections that are carried out do not constitute the expression of the population's will; they are a farce of voting by which the Communist Party only ridicules and expresses its contempt for the wishes of the people.

But such is the dialectic of society's development, that a force of liberation rises against subjugation, and that repression gives birth to a freedom movement. The movement for freedom is also rising in the Soviet Union. The dissident movement, the *samizdat Chronicle of Current Events* the *Chronicle of the Catholic Church in Lithuania* the sacrifice of Kalanta's life, the resolute and aggressive voices of Sakharov and Solzhenitsyn are heard not only in the Soviet Union, but also make a deep impression in the Western nations—these are clear signs of a freedom movement. A freedom movement that expresses itself so resolutely cannot be stopped by anyone.

A fortunate man is a free man. When a thirst for freedom arises in a nation which has deep roots, nothing will succeed in holding it back. Even when the nation loses its leaders, new branches will sprout from the roots; other leaders will emerge, and the struggle will continue until victory is attained.

2. Economic causes cannot interfere with the restoration of independence. In the present conditions of the world's economic development, not only small but large states as well are compelled to join supranational economic associations, such as the European Economic Community and COMECON. An independent Lithuania will be able to join a similar association, but without coercion and withoug losing its sovereignty, like the Western states, which did not forfeit their sovereignty in the European Market.

3. Lithuania's industry is currently being expanded not so much in consideration of Lithuania's interests as in the interests of the Soviet Union. With the creation of an independent state, it will be necessary to reorder Lithuania's industry and reduce its dependence on the economy of the Soviet Union. Certainly, it can continue maintaining close ties if this will not infringe on Lithuania's sovereignty. Beyond that, economic bonds with other countries will help fill the gap, which will ensue when the economic ties with the Soviet Union will be reduced.

The Lithuanian nation, in its striving to restore independence, must prepare for a long and difficult struggle. The enemy has great power and also is infinitely deceitful, cruel, and hypocritical. He proclaims enslavement to be liberation, religious persecution—the defense of faith and freedom of conscience, the championing of national rights—bourgeois nationalism, and the advocates of subjugation and repression—true patriots and the best sons of the Lithuanian nation. The enemy is clever, he has developed tested methods of maintaining repression, which he skillfully utilizes. Fighters for liberty of the nation must be prepared to bear and endure not only physical, but also moral blows.

One needs caution and skill for the struggle, but, most of all, stamina and an unshakable conviction that freedom will

be won. Addressing Lithuania's youth, the engineer, Stepas Kairys, wrote: "Believe in yourselves and do not be misled into
thinking your enemies are invincibly powerful. That is not so.
The Soviet Union—supported by violence and lies—is full of
internal contradictions and—in the face of an enemy's attack
—will crumble faster than the 'invincible' empire of the czars.
Therefore, youth, believe firmly in our victory, that Lithuania will be free!" (*Ibid.*, p. 10)

The Lithuanian nation has deep roots and an unextin-
guished determination for freedom. The prophecy will be fulfilled: the good Lord will come to the Lithuanian nation
and its morning of freedom shall dawn.

Sigitas Tautgina

38. ON THE THREAT OF NUCLEAR ANNIHILATION

Concealing themselves behind titles of peace and Communism, the socialist imperialist aggressors have turned our entire country into a missile field. Lithuania has been transformed into a forward base for nuclear weapons on the Soviet Union's Western front so that, shielded by a peaceful population, they could launch the death-bearing rockets, slay people inoffensive to us and, hiding behind the brotherly grave of the three Baltic nations, escape a retaliatory nuclear strike.

Lithuanians, a horrible death hovers overhead. You are doomed to die for Moscow! At this moment your life, the life of your childrens, brothers, and sisters has become inescapably bound to your resoluteness and integrity. Only a scoundrel, for whom a personal career and profit are more precious than the lives of millions of people, can ignore such a peril.

The day has come to join the battle, shoulder to shoulder with the Latvian and Estonian brothers, for our lives and those of our kin.

The Lithuanian National Revolutionary Council, the Human Rights Committee, the Lithuanian chapter of Amnesty International, the Lithuanian Freedom Fighters Movement, and the Free Lithuanian Communist Party have formed, for the purpose of peace and liberty, a united Lithuanian Revolutionary Liberation Front.[1] It expresses its solidarity with the liberation movements of all peoples and the universal aspirations for peace and seeks to save our country's inhabitants from a terrible death. The LRLF appeals with an SOS for help to the states of the entire world. We believe that they will make the right decision and support us in the peaceful struggle for the right to live.

No. 38. From the underground bulletin **Varpas** (The Bell), No. 3. The date is uncertain, probably in 1976. The publication is an organ of the Lithuanian Revolutionary Liberation Front. See the introductory study for analysis of this underground organization.

1. The constituent organizations of the LRLF are most likely fictitious, intended for effect. Certainly no Amnesty International chapter in Lithuania has emerged so far. Even if the chapter did exist, it would be inconsistent with the legal approach of Amnesty International to join a revolutionary front.

Lithuanian, this is not a struggle for territories or government, nor is it a party strife. Whoever you may be: a believer or an atheist, a member of some party or an independent—your are a Lithuanian. It is time to forget all the injuries and misunderstandings, even those bespattered with blood. Take a position without delay in the honorable struggle in the Lithuanian Revolutionary Liberation Front. The time will come when Lithuania's fate will be decided by the UN—your life will be at issue. Remember, your voice in that arbitration will be decisive. To make it more powerful, gather people around you. Explain to them the frightful situation, which the present-day Kremlin rulers conceal from millions of people. They are bending over backwards, enunciating through the radio and the press peace policies and business contracts. Brezhnev is decorated, while Soviet-made tanks, airplanes, and military advisors are simultaneously sent to Africa. Even before the conclusion of one conference (military force reductions, disarmament, nuclear arms limitation questions), new consultations and conferences are organized. They pledge to pursue the world's aspirations for universal peace and national liberation in conformity with the Declaration of Human Rights. Yet in reality they hide behind that sacred document and, totally rejecting it, try innocent people for their thoughts and convictions.

Lithuanian, as you fight for the liquidation of the missile fields in Lithuania and also for the protection of your life, so too you can help the cause of world peace. Do not believe in that peace for which one is still negotiating thirty years after the war. Do not expect to survive if agreement is reached not to test nuclear weapons in the Arctic and Antarctic, the Pacific Ocean, and other seas. Do not believe in any sweet lie about peace and the beautiful future which the present Moscow rulers promise. That is a snug cradle to put you to sleep, to lull the working people.

In the struggle for life, liberty, and peace there is one path: your active participation in the movement of all humanity for human rights.

Lithuanian, your duty is to take the first step in this struggle. Actively and uncompromisingly demand that the Soviet administration of Lithuania publish in the press and in thousands of pamphlets, regardless of Moscow's edicts, the

Universal Declaration of Human Rights which was signed and ratified by the government of the Soviet Union, but which to the present is concealed from the masses and unknown to the public. Today the entire mankind struggles for peace on the basis of the Universal Declaration of Human Rights. In other states nearly every person is familiar with it, but in the Soviet Union only one in a thousand knows what is written in it.

Lithuanian, this is your first battle in the Lithuanian Revolutionary Liberation Front, the struggle for your total victory!

Down with the Death-Breathing Weapons in the Baltic!
Remove the Grim Reaper of Nuclear War from Lithuania!
Peace and Freedom for the Baltic!

May the love for Lithuania
Burn within our hearts
In the name of Lithuania
May unity flourish![2]

The Lithuanian Revolutionary
Liberation Front

---

2. These are the concluding lines of the National Anthem.

39. AN APPEAL OF THE LITHUANIAN REVOLUTIONARY LIBERATION FRONT

A fourth decade is passing since the tempest of war subsided along the Baltic shores. In that time many states of Europe and the entire world, without rights during the war's storms, are now leading, in one way or another, a sovereign existence. Several dozen new states have established themselves in the world. Numerous peoples, who for centuries were under colonial subjugation, have regained freedom and independence. They are recognized by the UN as juridically fully entitled to manage their cultural, economic, and political life. In consequence of the political machinations, which Hitlerite Germany and the Stalinist Soviet Union started 35 years ago, the tiny Baltic states of Estonia, Latvia, and Lithuania are to this day held in a hopeless situation; they cannot determine their own fate.

During the postwar years the Moscow rulers attempted to break the national spirit of the Lithuanian people. They shipped hundreds of thousands of families in sealed boxcars to Siberia. Those who tried to flee or resist they called "bandits" and shot without any trial; the military courts "Moskovskoe OS"[1] were peculiar in that people were tried by them in absentia. Tens of thousands of the nation's best youth, convicted under Article 58, were transported for punishment to camps and prisons.[2] In our tiny Lithuania, which on January 1, 1941, consisted of 249 counties in 25 districts, the Moscow rulers deployed 250 chekist army garrisons in order to execute their despicable plans. Over 30,000 young tillers of the soil, militarily unprepared, fell in this unequal struggle.

The years passed. The Moscow rulers, unable to conceal their crimes from the free world and evading the working people's wrathful vengeance, put the blame for all the villainy on Stalin, Beria, and other party members. But these repulsive theatrics did not essentially change the situation: instead of

---

No. 39. From the underground bulletin **Varpas**, No. 4, probably 1976.

1. "Moskovskoe osoboe soveschanie"—a special session, in this case a special tribunal for dealing with political cases.

2. Article 58 of the RSFSR Penal Code, dealing with political crimes.

the garrisons of executioners, there appeared missile encampments. For this reason the specter of death today, as never before, has spread its wings over the land of tiny Lithuania. It is no secret for the entire world and especially for those of us living here that Lithuania's territory constitutes for Moscow's strategists the Soviet Union's western outpost. In the course of arms competition among the states, in the event of an armed conflict, the people of the Baltic area are doomed.

We do not know our tomorrow, whether we are fated to live and create a bright future in peace, or whether we shall perish meaninglessly in a nuclear war.

Therefore, considering that on July 12, 1920, Soviet Russia signed a peace agreement with Lithuania and recognized it *de jure* as an independent state;

Considering that the other states of the world also recognized Lithuania's independence, of which not one has to the present withdrawn its recognition [3] (discounting the outburst by the former Prime Minister of Australia Whitlam, which the new government of Australia honorably rectified before the world[4]);

Considering that the people of the Lithuanian republic are dissatisfied with their material well-being because the present economy of Lithuania is dependent on the economic policies of the Soviet Union, which are geared to armaments;

Considering that the puppet administration at the Lithuanian republic, compelled to submit to Moscow, is without authority to decide the country's internal and external affairs;

Considering that the Lithuanian nation needs completely free political, religious, and cultural expression, which is currently inhibited by various repressions;

Considering that the whole world knows the Soviet Union occupied (Lithuania);

---

3. Although recognition of the Soviet annexation of Lithuania has not been extended by several states, including the United States, most states now recognize de jure or de facto the Soviet control over Lithuania.

4. The Labor Government headed by Prime Minister E. G. Whitlam recognized the Soviet Union's effective control over the Baltic States on August 3, 1974. The successor government, headed by Prime Minister Malcolm Fraser, rescinded the recognition in April of 1976. Edgar Dunsdorf, **The Baltic Dilemma: The Case of the De Jure Recognition of Incorporation of the Baltic States into the Soviet Union by Australia** (New York, 1975).

Therefore, we, the Lithuanian National Revolutionary Council, Amnesty International of Political Prisoners, the Lithuanian Freedom Fighters Movement,[5] loyally adhering to the aspirations of all the peoples of the world for liberation and universal peace, working in the Lithuanian underground, form a united *Revolutionary Liberation Front* for the struggle against the death sentence imposed on our country by foreigners—to perish in the fire of a nuclear explosion.

The LRLF fights for peace and liberty, embracing the Declaration of Human Rights as the program for our activity. In struggling for our goal and hoping to avoid bloodshed for us, as well as for those who oppose this aim, the LRLF proclaims to the world that it expects humaneness from the leaders of the Communist Party of the Soviet Union and political prudence from the state leaders of the Soviet Union not to oppose the settlement for the Baltic area by other states for peaceful life by accepting the expounded demands in this SOS Appeal, pertaining to the government of the Soviet Union:

1. To withdraw the armed forces of the USSR from the Lithuanian territory.

2. The government of the Soviet Union itself must proceed by restoring the Independence of Lithuania, by correcting the mistakes committed by czarist and stalinist Russia.

3. With the withdrawal of the armed forces of the USSR, UN military control is introduced until the Lithuanian people will have determined independently, by means of free elections, the country's form of government, which in no way would violate the norms established by the Declaration of Human Rights, and which would guarantee Lithuania's existence in peace—as a model of peace in the world.

Therefore, on basis of the Declaration of Human Rights and the accords signed in Helsinki, the LRLF, being in the underground, undertakes the entire responsibility for the on-going liberation struggle. Championing the sacred aim of the Lithuanian Motherland for Peace and Liberty, the LRLF appeals to the center of world Catholicism, the Vatican, Christ's vicar Pope Paul VI, the United Nations, the UN General Assembly, and directly to all states.

---

5. The existence of these constituent organizations has not been corroborated. See note 1, Doc. No. 38.

The LRLF appeals to the leaders of all states, to all political parties, organizations, and their heads. It appeals to the Estonians, Latvians, Lithuanians, who, because of possible repressions, left the native land, who fought for its freedom and are still fighting today.

Oh world, all the people of good will, do not allow the burial of three nations in the Baltic area to take place! These nations have lived here for centuries; they burn with a desire to live freely, but in the present situation are condemned to perish. The Lithuanian people are appealing with an SOS for your aid.

We ask the world to support our SOS appeal and help realize it.

The Lithuanian Revolutionary Liberation Front

40. AIMS OF THE SECULAR CURRENT OF NATIONAL DISSENT

OUR TASKS

The occupation of Lithuania has a religious, national, political, and economic character. The occupant extracts a tangible gain through the exploitation of the Lithuanian economy. According to the economists, the profit earned from Lithuanian agriculture and industry amounts to billions of rubles. The Kremlin throws out crumbs for Lithuania's health care and education. The largest part of the income plundered in Lithuania is utilized to finance the instruments of war and to maintain the apparatus of suppression (the KGB, the MVD, the Central Committee). Millions of rubles of profit in Lithuania are squandered away on anti-Lithuanian propaganda. Daily tons of poisonous bolshevik lies are expelled into the atmosphere with the aim of extracting the roots of national world view from the Lithuanian consciousness, of inducing atrophy of the capability for independent thinking, of dulling the sense of hunger for liberty. Only because of the wondrous vitality of our nation and the aid of Providence, we have not suffocated yet; we have preserved a healthy national consciousness, even though in the past few years the Kremlin has especially intensified the policy of national genocide.

Moscow sends abroad billions of rubles, earned by the sweat of Lithuanians, to disorient the emigrants, to divide and infect them with spy mania, to divert their activities in the direction desired by Moscow. Only the intervention of the security (the KGB) can explain the calcification of propaganda of our emigrés that evokes a deep sorrow and concern in every thinking Lithuanian. Therefore, our aim is to fight bolshevik disinformation wherever it is manifested.

There are people who think that it is sufficient for a Lithuanian to have deep religious convictions, that a deeply

---

No. 40. Translated from Aušrelė (The Little Dawn), February 16, 1978. Aušrelė, possibly a one-time publication, obviously issued by Catholic dissidents (the name implies its connection with the samizdat journal Aušra), is actually an anthology of articles published in Laisvės Šauklys (The Herald of Freedom), a samizdat journal issued by non-Catholic nationalist intelligentsia. Not a single issue of Laisvės Šauklys was available for examination. Its first issue appeared in May of 1976. The journal apparently was silenced by the KGB in 1977 after eight issues. The article translated here is most likely a statement of purposes, published in the first issue of Laisvės Šauklys.

convinced Christian will naturally become a conscientious Lithuanian. Others affirm that primacy should be given to stimulation of national conscientiousness. According to the latter, even a nationally conscientious atheist will never fight the Church. We are endeavoring to unite these two viewpoints.

The youth, brought up in the rationalistic and atheistic school, is very little interested in religious literature. Besides, during 36 years not a single religious book for the wider public appeared in the underground. The youth is more interested in secular literature. The youth needs religious literature as well. However, first of all it is necessary to neutralize those evil seeds in the consciousness of youth, to liquidate the spirit of distrust of the clergy, acquired in the school.

Cosmopolitanism, propagated by the occupant and, unfortunately, even by some of the clergy, is especially dangerous to Lithuania. Thanks to them, "Religiously motivated voices, devaluing national loyalty, are penetrating into our midst." (Juozas Girnius, *Idealas ir laikas*, 1966, p. 52).[1] Nationally oriented intelligentsia is reproaching the Lithuanian clergy for their national indifference. The clergy is reproaching the intelligentsia for ignoring the meaning of the Catholic Church. All this creates a danger to national unity.

In view of this danger, our newspaper will fight the manifestations of cosmopolitanism and will strenghten the unity of the clergy and the laity.[2]

We shall be guided by the Second Vatican Council "Decree on the Ministry of the Laity," in which the laymen are considered full members of the Church and clergy are obligated "...with Christ in mind and paternal love to deliberate the projects, suggestions, desires submitted by laymen, to recognize reverently that true freedom which belongs to everyone in this world."

We shall be guided by the criteria that "truth is the highest authority and therefore everyone is free to evaluate everything critically."

The Publishers

---

1. The work cited here is by an emigré philosopher, published in Chicago, Ill.

2. See Doc. No. 48 for the response of Catholic dissidents to the editorial of Laisvės Šauklys, which is critical of the tactics and policy orientation of Catholic dissent.

41. FORMATION OF THE LITHUANIAN GROUP TO MONITOR HELSINKI ACCORDS

We, Tomas Venclova, Father Karolis Garuckas, Ona Lukauskaitė-Poškienė, Viktoras Petkus, Eitan Finkelstein, announce the formation of a Lithuanian Group to Promote Implementation of the Helsinki Agreements in the USSR. The aim of the Group is to promote the observation and fulfillment of the humanitarian articles of the Final Act of the Conference on Security and Cooperation in Europe. The Group intends to concentrate on those articles which relate to human rights and basic freedoms, including freedom of thought, conscience, religion and belief, and also contacts between people (the reunification of families, meetings with relatives, residence in other countries, etc.).

We are prepared to accept statements from individuals, groups, and organizations on matters relating to violations of the (humanitarian) articles of the Final Act on the territory of Lithuania, relating to Lithuania or specifically to Lithuanian problems.

We hope that the participant states of the Helsinki Conference will consider that the contemporary status of Lithuania was established as a result of the entrance of Soviet troops onto her territory on June 15, 1940, and will pay special attention to the observance of humanitarian rights in Lithuania.

Vilnius
November 25, 1976

> Tomas Venclova, 28-60 Požėlos, Vilnius.
> Father Karolis Garuckas, Priest of the village of
> Ceikiniai, Ignalina raion
> Ona Lukauskaitė-Poškienė, 32-37 Kleinerio, Šiauliai.
> Viktoras Petkus, 16-4 Garelio, Vilnius.
> Eitan Finkelstein, 21 Liepos, 10-10, Vilnius.

No. 41. English text of the announcement from Commission on Security and Cooperation in Europe, **Reports of the Helsinki-Accord Monitors in the Soviet Union** (Washington, D.C., February 24, 1977). This compilation of reports and the companion Volume 2, dated June 3, 1977, and Volume 3, dated November 7, 1978, contain all the documents of the Lithuanian group in English translation. The formation of the Lithuanian group was announced in Moscow, in the apartment of Juri Orlov, on December 1, 1976. Until the Belgrade review conference the group produced two general memoranda (on national and religious conditions, which are repeated here as Doc. Nos. 45 and 71) and 12 numbered documents on particular cases of violations of human rights.

42. AN APPEAL TO THE LEADERS OF EUROCOMMUNISM

To the leaders of the Italian, French, and Spanish Communist Parties, Enrico Berlinguer, Georges Marchais, Santiago Carillo.

In the second half of October, 1976, a new wave of searches, arrests, and interrogations swept through Lithuania. The KGB reminded Lithuania and, at the same time, the whole world, that the Helsinki Declaration is a typical maneuver to deceive public opinion.

In the late evening of October 19, two residents of Vilnius were locked up in the underground cells of the security police: the defenders of human rights Jonas Matulionis and Vladas Lapienis.

Who are thse people?

J. Matulionis is 45 years old and has completed Lithuanian studies at Vilnius University. He subsequently studied at the Conservatory of Music, from which he was expelled for his solo singing in one of the churches in Vilnius. He worked at the Republic Library and afterwards as Director of the Art Gallery. Several years ago he was forced to res:gn from his position because of his attempts to reprint texts of the gospels. Recently he had been employed in a Vilnius store as a commercial artist.

V. Lapienis is an economist, a graduate of the Faculty of Economics, Vilnius State University. At present he is retired. Not long ago the Vatican radio familiarized its listeners with the gist of his letter to Secretary General of the Central Committee, CPSU, L. Brezhnev.[1]

Both of these individuals demanded those rights for the faithful of Lithuania that are indisputably recognized in democratic countries by people of all conceivable persuasions.

During the search it was learned that several issues of the *Chronicle of the Catholic Church in Lithuania* and A. Solzhenitsyn's *Gulag Archipelago* were confiscated. It is this

---

No. 42. From **Aušra**, No. 5 (February 16, 1977).

1. Reference to the letter to Brezhnev, dated April 23, 1976; Lithuanian text in **Chronicle**, No. 23 (June 13, 1976). The letter requests intervention to prevent infringements of his constitutional rights, the rights of Catholics.

literature that constitutes the basic incriminating material. The Lithuanian public is astonished at the unfounded nature of such accusations.

We know that in recent months the Italian publisher Matriona has brought out ten issues of the *Chronicle* in the Italian language.[2] Thus, any Italian who buys this publication and keeps it in his house—assuming he were living in the territory of the USSR—would become a state criminal; he would be liable to long years of imprisonment or isolation in a psychiatric hospital. The same could be said of the readers of the *Gulag Archipelago* in the West. All these individuals, who keep the *Gulag Archipelago* in any language on their shelves, are criminals in the eyes of the USSR prosecutors. Fortunately, these people are presently out of their reach.

What is the *Chronicle of the Catholic Church in Lithuania?*

It is an information bulletin of Lithuania's Catholics, which publicizes objective and verified facts about the persecution of Lithuanian Catholics. Since not only Catholic publications, but all noncommunist publications are prohibited in Lithuania, the *Chronicle* is published underground. Furthermore, it is difficult to obtain in Lithuania the publications of the Western Communist Parties. They are sold a few issues at a time only in the principal newsstands of the larger cities.

As for A. Solzhenitsyn's *Gulag Archipelago*, no one else could so emphatically testify to the veracity of the facts presented in this work as the inhabitants of Lithuania.

On June 15, 1940, none other than Soviet tanks trampled upon Lithuania's national sovereignty, turning her economic and cultural life into perpetual chaos. From that day the real master of Lithuania became Moscow. A few hundred Lithuanian communists, whose greater part consisted of national minorities, were invited to assist in the work of dissolution. In this manner the communist ideology became the "reigning" ideology, although it is doubtful if Lithuania's sparse Communist Party could have come to power in a thousand years by an evolutionary path. But the subjugators were not bashful. From the very first day of occupation they began in the country

---

2. **Cronaca della Chiesa Cattolica in Lituania** (Milan: La Casa di Matriona, 1976), translated by Msgr. Vincas Mincevičius.

arrests, trials, the disregarding of an honorable nation's past, the destruction of its cultural values. During the days of June 14-18, 1941, forty thousand of Lithuania's most enlightened and noble-hearted inhabitants were exiled from Lithuania to Siberia and other uninhabited regions by order of the Kremlin. Transported in sealed livestock cars, without food and water, many died along the way. Not surprisingly, the subsequent fascist occupation was not as oppressive and cruel as this period of Soviet repression.

In 1944 Lithuania again fell under bolshevik slavery. This time, however, Lithuania's youth resolved to die on the field of battle rather than in Siberian labor camps. Thus arose Lithuania's partisan resistance, which, in its heroism and tragedy, is incomparable to many of the recent liberation movements of certain African, Asian, and Latin American peoples. Unfortunately, in their haste to heal wartime wounds, the Western nations were little concerned that the youth of Lithuania was perishing for the freedom of its country, that the denuded corpses of the fallen were being laid out on the streets to be mocked and to spread panic among the people. Even in the smallest towns of Lithuania jails were being set up at that time, while 50,000 Lithuanian freedom fighters and their supporters perished in the armed national resistance.[3] A much greater number of Lithuania's population was imprisoned in the Gulag Archipelago or scattered throughout various exile areas.

It seems to us, therefore, that A. Solzhenitsyn's *Gulag Archipelago* not only accurately, but we would even say dispassionately, recounts what in fact occurred; it is merely a part of the uncountable agonies that millions of Russians, Ukrainians, Poles, Germans, Lithuanians, Latvians, Estonians, Tatars, and people of other nationalities experienced having been caught in one way or another in "the flow of the great sewage system." Lithuanians are exceedingly grateful to A. Solzhenitsyn for what he revealed to the world. If it were possible to obtain the *Gulag Archipelago* freely in Lithuania, this book would be kept in every family as a reminder of an epoch of the nation's suffering.

---

3. **Samizdat** sources are not consistent concerning the number of partisan casualties. 50,000 appears to be somewhat inflated, unless indirect casualties of the partisan war are added here. See the introductory study for consideration of this problem.

This was not the first time that Lithuania has fallen under Russian slavery. It endured the czarist yoke for fully 126 years. The losses experienced throughout this period were, however, negligible compared to the three decades of bolshevik subjugation. We consider the interval from the beginning of the occupation to Stalin's death as a time of physical genocide. Today such an open annihilation of hundreds of thousands of people would seem impossible; M. Suslov's theory of translocating and dispersing the Lithuanian people throughout Russia's empty land is practically unrealizable.[4] Yet, despite the changes of the last two decades, Moscow's design remains the same: to russify the Lithuanian people (and not only the Lithuanian!), to dissolve them in the colorless sea of colonists, to dislocate its language, ethics, to homologize its customs and culture. At present more and more Russians are being brought into Lithuania.[5] And, naturally, the worst elements of the Russian people serve this colonization.

Along with this are closely intertwined general economic patterns. Every year Moscow appropriates 60 per cent of Lithuania's national income, utilizing these funds for the confrontation with the Western world, with which our people are intimately tied by virtue of spiritual, cultural, and ideological similarities. When Lithuanians wish to build an object useful to their country from their modest surplus, they are again compelled to journey to Moscow and there, through bribes and appeals, to plead for favors. On the other hand, unnecessary and even harmful industrial projects are constructed

---

4. M. Suslov was in charge of pacification in Lithuania in 1944-1946. The dissidents have claimed that Suslov openly talked about "Lithuania without Lithuanians." Many details, some from secret party archives, on the activity and role of Suslov in Lithuania are provided in a samizdat pamphlet "Mikhail Suslov—The Second Hangman of Lithuania," which is also reprinted here as Doc. No. 15.

5. According to Soviet population statistics, population increased by 124,000 from January 1, 1971, to January 1, 1975, of which 99,500 was natural increase. This suggests that over 24,000 immigrants settled in Lithuania, or about 8,000 annually. Mechanical population growth constituted about 19 per cent of the total population growth during the period 1971-1975, while only about 12 per cent during the previous decade. Lietuvos TSR ekonomika ir kultūra 1974 metais (Vilnius, 1975), pp. 29, 35; Thomas Remeikis, "Political Developments in Lithuania During the Brezhnev Era", in George W. Simmonds, ed., Nationalism in the USSR and Eastern Europe (Detroit, 1977), p. 171.

here, without consulting the Lithuanians, without taking into account the country's limitations of space and ecology. They do, however, facilitate vigorous russification of the nation. Foreigners are brought in in abundance and established in such plants and factories. Because of the permanent inefficiency and dilapidation in the entire Soviet Union, the inhabitants of Lithuania have to equalize the situation through their labor and products. Year after year all the best food and industrial products are transported to Moscow, Leningrad, and other Russian cities; in their place we receive surrogates.

We do not intend to list all our nation's hardships and misfortunes. We merely want to emphasize: for thirty years we have known only this kind of Communism! We contend that for our people it is unacceptable!

As for the Communist Parties of Western Europe, we have had sufficient occasion to note that for long years they have assisted Soviet propaganda in masking the crimes of the USSR. It now appears they are—though cautiously—attempting to side with the persecuted. If that is true, if the Western communists truly respect elementary human rights, if they declare themselves for national independence of all peoples, we await their open voice for Lithuania and other enslaved nations.

For the present, we have one request: put in a word for our country's new victims, Jonas Matulionis and Vladas Lapienis, for whom prolonged imprisonment could be calamitous. The state of health of these individuals is critical.[6]

If the Western Communist Parties are truly concerned with moral purity, if they want to atone for their old mistakes, which were committed by endorsing the genocidal policy of the USSR, they must now say clearly and unequivocally: "We do not support the nationality policy of the USSR as it is administered, the suppression of the cultures of small nationalities, their spiritual genocide."

We want to believe that the communists of the Western nations will find the time and opportunity to familiarize themselves more thoroughly with our painful problems and will extend to us a helping hand to save our most noble-hearted people.

The Lithuanians

---

6. See Doc. No. 72 about the disposition of the case against Lapienis and Matulionis.

43. FORMATION OF A BALTIC COMMITTEE FOR NATIONAL EMANCIPATION

The Committee of the National Movement of Estonia-Latvia-Lithuania has decided:

1. To elect three chairmen for a term of four and a half years from the Committees of the National Movement in Estonia, Latvia, and Lithuania.

If at the end of their terms the opportunity does not exist to reelect them, then they are delegated to carry on their functions until the time when there will be an opportunity to reelect them.

2. If the Supreme Committee of the National Movement of Estonia-Latvia-Lithuania cannot function or if its members are persecuted, then under any circumstances this work will be done by the already formed subcommittee.[1] In such a case all the public functions of the Supreme Committee of the National Movement of Estonia-Latvia-Lithuania devolve upon these three organizations: the Estonian World Council, the World Federation of Free Latvians, and the Supreme Committee for the Liberation of Lithuania (Tomas Venclova must be made its member).[2]

3. To elect as honorary members of the Supreme Committee of the National Movement of Estonia-Latvia-Lithuania:

No. 43. From Aušra, No. 8 (October, 1977). The program of the committee has not been announced, but presumably it dealt with national rights and national emancipation. Apparently the committee fell victim of KGB action, which was carried out in a coordinated manner beginning with August 23, 1977, three days after the announcement of the committee, in Vilnius, Riga, and Tallin. See the reports of searches and interrogations in the **Chronicle**, No. 30 (November 1, 1977). The formation of the committee constituted part of the evidence against Viktoras Petkus, the principal leader of the organization. For details about Petkus' trial, see Doc. No. 47.

1. There is no evidence that such a subcommittee ever came into being.

2. These are the major political organizations of the Estonian, Latvian, and Lithuanian emigrés. As far as is known, these organizations never received formal instructions to carry on the activities of the committee, a task which is impossible anyway. Emigré organizations are not in a position to direct national liberation from abroad. Tomas Venclova, the founding member of the Lithuanian Helsinki Group, has been permitted to leave Lithuania. He was stripped of Soviet citizenship while abroad. Presently he resides in the United States. Venclova's request for emigration is published here as Doc. No. 29.

Edgars Anderson (USA), Jurgis Baltrušaitis (France), Petr Grigerenko (USSR), Andre Kung (Sweden), Czeslow Milosz (USA), Ernest Jopik (England), Arnold Lusis (USA), Yuri Orlov (USSR), Ulaf Palme (Sweden), Andrei Sakharov (USSR).

4. The Supreme Committee of the National Movement of Estonia-Latvia-Lithuania will regularly publish its document collection "EsLaLi" or other publications in Estonian, Latvian, Lithuanian, and English.[3]

The Committee of the National Movement of Estonia
The Committee of the National Movement of Latvia
The Committee of the National Movement of Lithuania

Vilnius, August 20, 1977

---

3. It is evident from Aušra, No. 10 (March, 1978) that the committee did prepare a number of statements, addressed to Kurt Waldheim, the Government of Great Britain, Jimmy Carter, the Government of the Federal Republic of Germany, the Government of Israel, and Leonid Brezhnev. These documents were seized by the KGB apparently before they culd be sent out. The contents of these documents are not known.

44. NATIONALIST DEMONSTRATION IN VILNIUS AFTER SOCCER GAMES

October 12, 1977, The *Evening News* informed its readers about "the recent" inappropriate behavior of the soccer fans at the Vilnius Žalgiris Stadium and in the city streets after the game. It complained that "after the game ended, some of the spectators did not disperse but demonstrably gathered and marched in a crowd through the city streets, shouting, blocking traffic," that "some soccer 'fans' threw firecrackers onto the track, and the lights of rockets occasionally flared up in the stands," and that "the disorder was caused by individuals, seeking cheap thrills and often drunk." Later it became evident that "the hooligan actions of the culprits at the Vilnius Žalgiris Stadium and in the streets" were the work of "mostly youths and teenagers" and that "the People's Court sentenced to ten days of arrest for hooligan activity worker V. Kiznys, a worker at the Radio measurement plant J. Safronov, the third year student at the Vilnius Institute of Construction Engineering R. Augustinavičius, while the Polytechnical High School student A. Karčinskas was assessed a thirty ruble fine." The paper suggested that "stricter control be instituted so that inebriated citizens, their pockets filled with bottles of alcohol, would not get into the stands."

One thing is quite clear to the readers of the newspaper, namely that there is no shortage of hooligans anywhere today, including the stadium. Nonetheless, it is not totally clear how those four "hooligans" organized a large crowd that, shouting something, managed to fill the city streets in a way that even automobile traffic was halted.

No. 44. Excerpted from a lengthy article in **Aušra**, No. 9 (January, 1978). The **Evening News** cited in the article refers to the evening newspaper of Vilnius. The name "Žalgiris" of the stadium and the soccer team is a Lithuanian translation of Gruenwald or Tannenberg, a place where the Lithuanian and Polish forces achieved a decisive victory against the Teutonic Knights in 1410. Thus "Žalgiris" carries strong nationalist connotations. The riots following the soccer games were widely reported in the Western press, which was alerted about the incidents by the Soviet dissident Alexander Podrabinek. See, for example, one such report in **The Washington Post**, October 31, 1977. The Soviet press could not ignore the publicity and attempted to ridicule Western reports in a lengthy article in the weekly **Literatūra ir Menas**, February 11, 1978.

In fact it happened thus. In the early morning of October 7, 1977, the flags of the USSR and the Lithuanian SSR were placed on all the houses of Vilnius by watchmen and cleaning women. When one of them was asked what he was proclaiming by these flags, he answered, "We don't know what the order means." It seems that on that day the Kremlin had approved the new Constitution of the USSR and in the evening at the Vilnius Žalgiris Stadium "Žalgiris" of Vilnius was playing against Vitebsk's "Dvina" for the second level soccer championship. "Žalgiris" won 3-0. The twenty thousand seat stadium was filled to capacity. The victory by the Lithuanian soccer team caused such enthusiasm among the spectators that it carried over into a sporadic outburst of national feeling.

Many police and security agents were in the stadium. However, they seemed helpless to quiet the impassioned spectators. The crowd surged out of the stadium, organized itself spontaneously, and headed for the Green Bridge. Here it encountered a human barrier. A large group of police officials of various ranks firmly joined their hands and tried to stop the crowd so that it would not reach the streets of the central city. However, the barrier was easily broken and the police were scattered in the onrush of the crowd. The crowd continued on Lenin Prospect carrying one of the flags torn down on Melnikaitė Street. The streets were filled with shouts of "Russians, get out of Lithuania," "Freedom for Lithuania." At Vienuolis Street a group of policemen jumped in and took away the Soviet flag that was borne by an eleventh grader from Kaunas. It later became clear that the security men were very angry that those carrying the flag were laughing all the time, that is, they were degrading the flag. Of course, the huge crowd also obstructed traffic and shoved back the trolley buses which impeded their march. The procession marched on singing Lithuanian songs. Verses of the Lithuanian national anthem were also heard. At the Vilnius Security Headquarters and the Lenin Square (a monument to Lenin stands in the middle of the park), the crowd was met by a strong, more adequately organized group of police, security men, and MVD officers. The crowd was split up and shoved onto secondary streets. It seems the principal battle between the demonstrators and the armed state officials occurred at the foot of the Tauras Hill. Many individuals were arrested. They were dragged into automobiles and driven to an assembly point at Kalnai Park. Here they were severely beaten, some were released apparently in an effort not to over-crowd the prisons with hundreds of arrested youths and so as not to publicize the events too much; others were taken away. Altogether so many were arrested that there would not have been enough room in the jails. After the dispersal of the crowd, the emergency room of the First Soviet Hospital, located on the other side of Lenin Square, was filled with injured people. Quite a few security men had black eyes.

The hard-earned victory by the authorities over the popular masses greatly annoyed the upper levels of the government. Several high security officials were punished for poor preparation "for the soccer matches." But, nevertheless, they had been preparing because at 5 p.m. of the same day the 21st of July Street (by the side of the security building) was filled with empty cars, about which it was not known what they had brought, nor for what they were waiting.

Two days later on October 10 a match between "Žalgiris" and "Iskra" of Smolensk commenced at 7 p.m. at the same stadium. "Žalgiris" won again, 2-1. And again a sense of pride in their team filled the crowd of many thousands; the Lithuanians can at least defeat the Russians in soccer.

This time government officials were better prepared. Several hundred policemen and an equal number of their auxiliaries were stationed in the stadium itself. Nevertheless, after this match a spontaneous crowd once again marched toward the center of the city, shouting completely un-Soviet slogans that are rarely heard in public. This time troops from the MVD division quartered at Suvorov Street reenforced the police and security forces. After storming across the bridge once again the crowd turned down Bridge Street and entered Cathedral Square, where it encountered four rows of variously attired keepers of the peace. In aggressive thrusts the policemen and the MVD troops began to break up the leading sections of the crowd into small groups, surrounding and attending the demonstrators. Everything was done to make sure that the crowd would not break through to Lenin Prospect. Headquarters for the repressors were established at the Literary Cafe, situated at the beginning of Lenin Prospect. The struggle was intense. Part of those arrested were dealt with promptly. Security agents in civilian dress were particularly active in this respect. They would force far behind their backs the arms of youths already separated from the crowd, while others seized them by their hair and smashed their heads against the sides of cars, severely injuring and bloodying their faces. During the fight police cars were also smashed and some were overturned.

Despite the efforts of police, security officials, and the army, the crowd broke through onto the Lenin Prospect and even reached Cherniakhovski Square and the Vilnius Hotel. While the harassed crowd defended itself on Lenin Prospect, many windows, including those of the headquarters of the Central Committee of the Lithuanian Communist Party, the show windows of the store "Svajonė" and others, were broken by rocks and bricks. At Cherniakhovski Square the crowd was dispersed. Many of the participants were arrested. All the broken windows, except for the "Svajonė" show windows, were replaced during that same night. Throughout the conflict shouts of "Go away, Russians," "Freedom for Lithuania," "Freedom for political prisoners" rang through the streets. Countless times the demonstrators who shouted these slogans climbed on the backs of their friends but covered their faces with scarves so that the security agents would not recognize them. The bravest fighters in the crowd were those who had been beaten up on the evening of the proclamation of the Constitution of the USSR. The high school students, considered to be the window-breakers, were immediately punished at their schools. The chiefs of institutions, whose employees had participated in these demonstrations, were also punished, as were the Communist Party members whose children had been arrested by the police or security agents.

During those two days many people were arrested. Forty-four percent were detained for a longer time; a significant number of Russians was in this latter group. This fact particularly annoyed the security men, most probably because it made it difficult to press political charges against the others, i.e., the Lithuanians.

Several days after the second soccer match the chiefs and party secretaries of institutions and plants were called to the offices of the regional committees of the Communist Party.

The interrogations continue. A considerable number of university students are threatened with expulsion and subsequent induction into the army.

45. LITHUANIAN HELSINKI MONITORS ON THE SITUATION IN LITHUANIA

To: The Belgrade Conference of the Thirty-Five Signatories of the 1975 Helsinki Act

From: The Lithuanian Public Group to Support the Implementation of the Helsinki Agreements

A STATEMENT

ON THE PRESENT SITUATION IN LITHUANIA

The present *status quo* in Lithuania is the result of an ultimatum, submitted at 11:00 p.m. on June 14, 1940, in Moscow by Molotov, the Chairman of the Council of the People's Commissars of the Soviet Union and Commissar of Foreign Affairs, to Urbšys, the Lithuanian Minister of Foreign Affairs.[1] The army of the Soviet Union, on these grounds, crossed the frontier of Lithuania already on the following day, June 15, at 2:00 p.m. and occupied the main Lithuanian cities.

Molotov's deputy, Dekanozov, was dispatched to Lithuania and tried to standardize the country's life in accordance with the Soviet pattern. The results were terrible: not only were all the political parties outlawed, the private press liquidated, social organizations suppressed, but, beyond that, over forty thousand people were imprisoned or deported to Siberia, nobody being spared, neither infants, nor elderly people.

It is no wonder, then, that at the outbreak of the German-Soviet war the four largest Lithuanian political parties tried to restore Lithuanian state sovereignty, but the Nazis swiftly paralyzed their efforts.[2]

No. 45. This document is translated from the Lithuanian text in Aušra, No. 8 (October, 1977).

1. For the documentation of Soviet aggression against Lithuania and the illegal process of annexation, see the sources cited in note No. 2 of Doc. No. 8.

2. For details on the efforts to reestablish independence at the beginning of the German-Soviet war, see the article by Zenonas Ivinskis, "Lithuania During the War: Resistance Against the Soviet and Nazi Occupations," in V. Stanley Vardys (ed.), **Lithuania under the Soviets** (New York, 1965), Ch. 4; also Algirdas Martin Budreckis, **The Lithuanian National Revolt of 1941** (Boston, 1968).

When in 1944 the Red Army once more entered Lithuania, as early as on November 11th, a special bureau, attached to the Central Committee of the Communist Party (Bolshevik) was formed in Moscow under the leadership of Suslov.[3] The following year alone more than four thousand employees were purged from various agencies in Lithuania. By April 1947, 1350 more people were discharged because, in April 1945, 6116 officials, who could not speak Lithuanian, were sent to Lithuania. According to KGB Colonel Mikhailov, stationed in Vilnius, fifty thousand Lithuanians perished with weapons in their hands, three times as many were sent to prisons and camps, where the casualties were as high as in the forests, and how many had to be deported to Siberia!

After Stalin's death some of the deportees were allowed to return, and some of the political prisoners were released from camps. But, alas, to this very day, many are not allowed to return to Lithuania, their motherland, and are kept in exile without trial and indefinitely. We publish at least some of their names:

Stepas Bubulas, Kostas Buknys, Antanas Deksnys, Alfonsas Gaidys, Algirdas Gasiūnas, Robertas Indreika. Antanas Jankauskas, Jonas Karalius, Leonas Lebeda, Kostas Lekšas, Juozas Mikailionis, Aleksas Mosteika, Petras Paltarokas, Povilas Pečiulaitis, Vytautas Petrušaitis, Albinas Rašytinis, Vincas Saliokas, Vytautas Slapšinskas, Jonas Sarkūnas, Benius Trakimas, Valdas Vaitiekūnas, et al.

The situation of the Lithuanian language is difficult. Five times as many Russians are living in Lithuania today than prior to World War II, especially in Vilnius and Klaipėda. Therefore, in some offices it is impossible to make oneself understood in Lithuanian, for instance, in the Vilnius railway station, in some post offices, on the street with the policemen on duty, etc. In Latvia, where on the eve of the war there were eighteen Lithuanian schools, they have all been closed. Many lands, recognized as part of Lithuania by the peace treaty between Lithuania and the Soviet Union, signed on July 12, 1920, today are under the Belorussian administration. Lithuanians are autochthonous in those lands.They have no Lithu-

---

3. The postwar situation and Suslov's role in Lithuania is described in some detail in Doc. No. 15.

anian schools, while in Apsas and Vydžiai the churches have been closed; the church of Pelesa, built by Lithuanians after World War I, has been transformed into a warehouse, its towers have been razed, while Rector Vienažindis was imprisoned in 1950. Consequently, Lithuanians in Belorussia have no schools, no churches, and Lithuanian priests are not allowed to take up residence there.[4]

The census data indicate that the number of Russians and of Poles in Lithuania is about equal, but various advertisements, slogans, posters, booklets, etc. in Vilnius are in two languages —Lithuanian and Russian—only. There is a Russian drama theatre in Vilnius, Russian-language classes are set up in Lithuania's higher education establishments, while the Polish language is allowed only in the Vilnius Pedagogical Institute.

The smaller national minorities are faring even worse. During the war the Jews suffered more than any other inhabitants in Lithuania. Prior to World War II they had 122 primary schools, three grammar schools, and 14 high schools. At present the Jews do not have a single school, or a press of their own, although, according to the 1970 census data, there were 16,000 of them in Vilnius alone and 4,000 in Kaunas. Twenty-four thousand declared themselves as Belorussians in Vilnius, but they do not have their own school and the Belorussian religious services were also abolished in churches in the postwar years. When private schools were forbidden after the war, the Karaites suffered a special loss, because the *Kenese* (Karaite place of worship) of Trakai had a parochial school attached to it; the Tatars also suffered a wrong with the closing of their mosques and schools.

The Lithuanians in Latvia are given the explanation that if they want to study in Lithuanian, they must go to Lithuania, but the Russians are not told that their children should go to Russia to learn Russian. The Ministry of Education has specified that the curriculum of the senior class in Lithuanian high schools contain only four weekly hours of the Lithuanian language but five hours of the Russian language. The same Ministry manages to demand and obtain a fluency in Russian from all Lithuanian graduates, but the same Ministry is helpless to make the same Russian graduates learn at

---

4. See the lengthy **samizdat** document on the situation of Lithuanians in the Belorussian republic in Doc. No. 21.

least a little Lithuanian. The publishing houses have even
gone further: in some Lithuanian books Russian texts are now
being printed without a Lithuanian translation. Various administrative officials and the press have begun talking about the
bilingualism of Lithuanians—the Lithuanians are alleged to
like Lenin's language. But what is to be done if in Lithuania itself it is impossible to communicate in Lithuanian?

In schools the history of Lithuania and of the world are
taught in a special manner—it is not a history of states, or
nations, or kings, or dukes, but the history of economic relationships and of the so-called "class struggle," elucidated by the
party line. Therefore, not a single textbook of Lithuanian or
world history, or any publication on the subject published
prior to 1940, is allowed into the schools. Not only those, but
all books published prior to the above-mentioned events have
been removed from all school libraries and most of them have
been destroyed. The exception has been made only in favor
of some institutions of higher learning and scientific institutions, where such publications have been placed in the so-
called special funds, which are accessible only with special
permission. It is especially strange that even certain books by
individuals who have occupied various important posts after
the events of June 1940, published prior to those events, have
also ended up in the special fund, e.g., the book *SSSR—mūsų
akimis* (USSR Through Our Eyes) by Justas Paleckis who, for
three decades, has been officially the country's top administrative
official.[5] Even such classics of Lithuanian literature as *Algimantas* by Vincas Pietaris [6] and others have ended up among
the forbidden books. The history of Lithuanian literature has
been arranged in such a way that several writers who had retreated to the USSR during the war years are being recognized
as great Lithuanian classics, while there is silence about the
mass of Lithuanian writers who had fled to the West, or some
of them are mentioned only after their death. The writers who
have returned from the camps or from Siberia also have a
difficult time.

---

5. Justas Paleckis, long-time Chairman of the Presidium of the
Lithuanian SSR Supreme Soviet, was a leftist journalist. In 1933 he traveled in the Soviet Union and published an account of his journey.

6. The novel **Algimantas** is written in a nationalistic and romantic
vein. Because of some of its anti-Russian passages, the novel has not been
published in the selected works of Pietaris—**Rinktiniai raštai** (Vilnius,
1973), nor has it been published separately.

To this very day KGB agents keep seizing prewar books or periodicals whenever they are engaged in a house-search. Where are they deposited? Only the KGB could answer this question.

The Soviet press explains the matter as follows: "It was necessary to reevaluate the cultural heritage of the Lithuanian nation from the Marxist-Leninist point of view: by taking over its democratic and socialist tendencies, to critize the bourgeois-nationalist conceptions, especially in the areas of history, literature, and other social sciences. It was also necessary to broadly propagate scientific atheism a helper in the struggle against the religious views disseminated by the church." (Algirdas Rakūnas, *Klasių kova Lietuvoje 1940-1951 metais*— The Class Struggle in Lithuania, 1940-1951, Vilnius, 1976, p. 178).

The propagation of so-called scientific atheism continues today and the means to propagate it have not improved.[7] Let the official press speak for itself:

"When we were healing the war-inflicted wounds, developing education, culture, improving health care, there was an unusual space shortage in our republic. Therefore, it was completely natural for the local government organs to use the nationalized spacious rectory buildings for these vitally important matters. (Article by J. Aničas, in *Už socializmo sukūrimą Lietuvoje*—For the Creation of Socialism in Lithuania, Vilnius, 1969, p. 306). We would like to add that not only rectories, but also parish halls, their libraries, and even the buildings housing church servants were used for that purpose. Many libraries were destroyed in this manner, e.g., the Marian library in Marijampolė (now Kapsukas), which contained over 50,000 books. One might add that the old archives of the dioceses were seized by force for the same purposes.

The Soviet press continues as follows: "The use of selected former cult buildings mostly for culture, education, and health care, in the process of improving the social servicing of the population, was a very humane affair and the substantial majority of the working people gave its support to it." (*Ibid.*, p. 306). May we express our doubts if the "substantial majority of the working people" did approve, for instance, the

---

7. A more detailed brief on the legal status of religion in Lithuania will be found in the group's communication to the Belgrade Conference, which is published here as Doc. No. 71.

transformation of the St. Casimir Church in Vilnius, built
in 1604, into a warehouse for alcoholic beverages for an entire
decade. And is not the period of the "healing of the wounds"
and of "postwar humanism" lasting a bit too long? Perhaps
it is time to begin to return to the communities of religious
believers at least their surviving possessions? After all, three-
quarters of the churches in Vilnius, including the Cathedral-
Basilica itself, remain closed. Much is being written and talked
about the care for the architectural and artistic monuments.
The Church of the Sisters of the Visitation in Vilnius (built in
1729) also bears the inscription that it is an architectural monument, but that did not prevent the destruction of its interior in
1965 and its transformation into a prison. That status also did
not prevent the removal of the bells on September 8, 1966,
from the All Saints Church (built in 1620, also in Vilnius)
after it had been closed. A two-story chapel in Antakalnis,
Vilnius, erected 300 years ago, was destroyed in the same year,
although it was in nobody's way—even today the site remains
empty and the trees that used to surround the chapel are still
there. And only a couple of years ago the popularly venerated
Hill of Crosses near Šiauliai was devasted again. This sad
list could be continued endlessly. May we also add that all
Catholic monasteries in Lithuania remain closed, while of the
former four theological seminaries only one is allowed to continue; and even that seminary could take in only five new
seminarians three years ago, while the average mortality of
priests *per annum* is four time as large. The Jews and Tatars
of Lithuania, meanwhile, have been left without any clergy.

The Constitution of the USSR guarantees to the atheists
the right to antireligious propaganda, yet the believers are allowed only the performance of their cult rituals, and not religious propaganda. How, then, is the equality of all citizens
to be understood? Because the freedom to perform the cult
rituals so far remains limited to the paper of the Constitution—
the believers are not allowed to celebrate even their major holidays, which is part of the concept of performance of religious
cult rituals. Religious believers continue being fired from work for
celebrating their holidays; when children stay away from school
on such holidays, their parents are summoned to appear and
receive a scolding. Television and radio are permeated with
atheism, and meanwhile both these organizations are maintained with the money of the believers also. The believers of

all religious denominations in Lithuania do not have their own press. And if that were not enough, not only the laity but also the clergy are forbidden to teach prayers to the children, although for the latter it is their direct duty and an inseparable component of the very concept of the cult. The priests who dared to do that have been incarcerated, imprisoned in camps, or otherwise punished.

There is one more painful wound. Our entire older generation in Lithuania remembers how, before the war, one could freely purchase in Lithuania such Soviet Russian dailies as *Izvestiya* or *Pravda*, while at the *Mokslas* bookstore in Kaunas (under the patronage of the USSR Embassy), and later in a similar bookstore in Vilnius, one could purchase the writings of Marx, Engels, Lenin, and Stalin in Russian. We do not even dare to dream that we shall live to see the day when the central dailies of Paris, London, and New York would be freely sold here. But we do not forget for an instant that a considerable portion of our nation, especially its intellectuals, has emigrated or retreated to the West. There they have created a sizeable press, a prolific literature, and have published a huge Lithuanian encyclopedia. And all the efforts to have the above-mentioned press reach us, too, have been in vain. And whenever a few samples of those publications reach our libraries, they are kept there behind nine locks, or again are available only with a special permit. Meanwhile, the communist literature published in Lithuania reaches the West without any obstruction. Our officials regard us as small children and strictly determine what we are to read, and what we aren't.

In our statement we have touched only upon a portion of the instances where the agreement signed on August 1, 1975, in Helsinki has been violated. We could also submit materials on how the reunion of families and a series of other questions are being evaded. The purpose of this memorandum is to draw the attention of the states-signatories of the Helsinki agreements to the fact that no agreement in the world is possible if it is observed only by a single party who has signed it.

Rev. Karolis Garuckas
Eitan Finkelstein
Ona Lukauskaitė-Poškienė
Viktoras Petkus
Tomas Venclova

Vilnius, July 17, 1977

46. DECISION OF THE COURT IN THE CASE OF BALYS GAJAUSKAS

Copy

DECISION

Criminal Case No. 87

(1978)

On behalf of the Lithuanian SSR, in the City of Vilnius, on April 14, 1978:

The Collegium for Penal Cases of the Supreme Court of the Lithuanian SSR, consisting of the presiding member S. Raziūnas, lay assessors A. Burokaitė and F. Stanionis, secretary G. Jablonskaitė, including Prosecutor J. Bakučionis and defense attorney G. Gavronskis, in a court session has examined the criminal case in which Gajauskas, Balys, son of Jonas, born on February 24, 1926, in the village of Vygreliai, raion of Vilkaviškis in the Lithuanian SSR, a USSR citizen, a Lithuanian, not a party member, having a middle education, single, penalized on September 18, 1948, according to RSFSR Penal Code Article 58-1 "a", Articles 58-8, 58-10 (part 1) and 58-11, in force in the territory of the Lithuanian SSR, with loss of freedom for 25 years, and released on May 3, 1973, after serving his sentence, worked as an electrician for the board of Electrical Assembly No. 5 in Kaunas, lived at 3-8 Spynų Street, Kaunas, was accused of the infractions defined in Article 68 Part 2 of the Penal Code of the Lithuanian SSR and has determined the following:

B. Gajauskas, previously having served a term for especially dangerous offenses against the state, during the years 1974-1977 spread anti-Soviet agitation and propaganda, seeking to

No. 46. Translated from the Lithuanian text of the court decision, published in **Aušra**, No. 11 (May, 1978). Balys Gajauskas is among the prominent personalities of Lithuanian dissent in the 1970s. He was arrested on April 20, 1977, and tried one year later for "anti-Soviet agitation and propaganda" (Article 68 of the Penal Code). In 1948 he was sentenced to 25 years for participation in the postwar partisan movement, specifically for an alleged killing of some Soviet official (see **Aušra**, No. 11, for a brief account of this). The court decision suggests the scope of Gajauskas' activity as well as his contacts with Moscow dissidents.

undermine and weaken the Soviet government. For dissemination purposes he obtained and kept anti-Soviet literature, slandering the Soviet state and social system. With the help of people of similar viewpoints, he duplicated and distributed this literature. For dissemination purposes he translated into Lithuanian Vol. I of A. Solzhenitsyn's *Gulag Archipelago*. He committed this offense in the following circumstances:

I. THE KEEPING OF ANTI-SOVIET LITERATURE FOR THE PURPOSE OF DISSEMINATION AND ITS DISSEMINATION

In 1974 B. Gajauskas, for the purpose of dissemination, obtained and maintained the books *Bolshevism* (in Polish), Solzhenitsyn's *Gulag Archipelago*, Vol. 1 (in Russian), and *God Today* (in Lithuanian), as well as 2 copies of the tenth issue of *Chronicle of the Defense of Rights in the USSR* (in Russian), and the publication *God and Motherland*, No. 1 and 2. He gave this anti-Soviet literature to L. Stavskis to read, while he himself translated the volume of *Gulag Archipelago* into Lithuanian for dissemination.[1]

Defendant B. Gajauskas did not plead guilty. He explained that he did not know where he obtained the book *Bolshevism* and that it had been in his home for some time. He received Vol. 1 of the *Gulag Archipelago* in 1974 from S. Kudirka.[2] He did not possess the brochures *Chronicle of the Defense of Rights in the USSR* and *God and Motherland* at all. He received Vol. 1 of *Gulag Archipelago* already translated into Lithuanian from S. Kudirka. He had made a handwritten copy of this translation and had destroyed the original that he was given.

The guilt of B. Gajauskas for possessing anti-Soviet literature for dissemination purposes, as well as its dissemination, is confirmed through the following evidence:

---

1. Among the anti-Soviet publications cited here, **Bolshevism** was published in Lublin, Poland, in 1938 by a group of clergy. It supposedly slandered the Soviet system. **God Today (Dievas šiandien)** is a theological essay by Jonas Gutauskas, published in Chicago in 1973. **God and Motherland (Dievas ir Tėvynė)** is a Catholic **samizdat** journal devoted mainly to the refutation of atheistic propaganda of the regime.

2. Simas Kudirka—a Lithuanian seaman who unsuccessfully tried to defect to the US. His case is presented in Doc. No. 18.

Witness L. Stavskis stated that B. Gajauskas had given him the book *Bolshevism* to read and, having read it, he returned it to him. Later, in 1976, he was given a portion of Vol. 1 of *Gulag Archipelago* to read and take care of, as well as the brochures *Chronicle of the Defense of Rights in the USSR* and *God and Motherland*, which he found and removed. During the trial he recognized and pointed out this literature, specifying that he had received it from B. Gajauskas and had read it.

During the December 23, 1974, search the book *Bolshevism* and a portion of Vol. 1 (pp. 193-272) of *Gulag Archipelago* (2 t. 95-105 1)[3] were removed from B. Gajauskas.

During the February 7, 1977, search of L. Stavskis' home, a portion of Vol. 1 (pp. 1-192) of *Gulag Archipelafo*, No. 1 and 2 of the brochure *God and Motherland*, as well as two copies of *Chronicle of the Defense of Rights in the USSR* (2t. 165-174 1.) were removed.

During the preliminary inquiry B. Gajauskas showed that he himself had translated vol. 1 of *Gulag Archipelago* (1t. 163, 140-143 1.). L. Stavskis testified that B. Gajauskas had given him Vol. 1 of this book and later divided it in half and taken back a portion of it. Experts determined that the segment of *Gulag Archipelago* taken from B. Gajauskas, along with the segment taken from L. Stavskis comprise one copy of the book (3t. 34-39 1.). Handwriting experts determined that the handwritten manuscript of the translation of this book into Lithuanian was written by B. Gajauskas (3t. 111-128 1.), which corresponds to the admission of B. Gajauskas during the preliminary inquiry that he himself had done the translating (1t. 25-26, 44-46 1.).

This testimony negates his explanation that he supposedly received the translation from S. Kudirka and made a copy.

In addition to this, translations in B. Gajauskas' handwriting have been found in several notebooks and on separate sheets of loose-leaf paper, which also indicate that they are, in fact, translations and not copies (7t. 22, 23, 21 packages).

The translation itself while possessing the book, as well as the translation in several carbon copies, attest to the use of the translation for dissemination purposes.

---

3. Reference to volumes of evidence compiled by the prosecution, here meaning Vol. 2, pp. 95-105.

There is, likewise, no basis for disbelieving L. Stavskis' testimony to the effect that B. Gajauskas gave him the book *Bolshevism* to read and safeguard and the brochures *God and Motherland* and *Chronicle of the Defense of Rights in the USSR*, which B. Gajauskas denies.

In the book *Bolshevism* the work of the Soviets of Deputies of Working People, the internal policies of Soviet government, and the spheres of life of Soviet society are slandered and maligned. In the book *God Today* it is slanderously asserted that Communism is a coercive system, which has brought about slavery, starvation, animalistic behavior, etc. In the brochure *Chronicle of the Defense of Rights in the USSR* are found slanderous articles regarding violations of civil rights, persecutions in the Soviet Union, as well as repressions. In the publication *God and Motherland*, the Soviet state and social system, the policy of the Party regarding the religious believers are slandered, and (the people) are urged to concentrate themselves for the fight against the Soviet rule in Lithuania. Therefore, the possession of this literature for dissemination purposes, its duplication and dissemination, is anti-Soviet agitation and propaganda, which seeks to undermine and weaken the Soviet government.

II. THE POSSESSION AND DUPLICATION FOR DISSEMINATION PURPOSES OF DOCUMENTS OF THE LITHUANIAN NATIONALIST BANDS

In addition to the literature mentioned in the first section of this decision, B. Gajauskas, in 1974, acquired anti-Soviet documents of armed nationalist bands that were active in the republic during the postwar years.[4] These include the constitutions, instructions, rules, and protocols of the so-called Movement of the Freedom Struggle of Lithuania (MFSL), Lithuanian Freedom Army (LFA), and the "Vanagai" (Hawks) organization, as well as the publications of these organizations —*The Bulletin of the MFSL, The Bell of Freedom, The Partisan, The Word of Freedom* (in Russian), the memorandum of the resistance movement of Lithuania to the United Nations Organization (in English), the memorandum of the United

---

4. For details about the activities of the postwar resistance organizations mentioned here, see the Introduction and Doc. Nos. 1 through 15.

Democratic Resistance Movement of Lithuania to the UNO and to the councils of ministers of some of the larger nations (in English) [5]; and a number of other works similar in nature.

In seeking to protect these documents from possible searches, in the fall of 1976 he brought them to the apartment of L. Stavskis, seeking to duplicate them and use them for dissemination. That same fall he came to L. Stavskis and, with the help of an unidentified person, photographed them with his Zenit-3M camera. He made photocopies of a portion of these documents, which were given by his mother A. Kilčiauskienė to O. Grigauskienė for safekeeping and were found in the latter's possession during a search.

In addition, for the same purpose B. Gajauskas made copies of the above-mentioned memorandum, the order of the "Hawk" organization, a poem, and another document, which does not have a title, all of which were found and removed.

During the trial B. Gajauskas did not acknowledge guilt. He explained that he did not keep and did not have documents of armed nationalist bands. He photographed them at L. Stavskis' apartment while learning how to take pictures and made a few photocopies of each. He allegedly received four documents from L. Stavskis, and, having made copies for his own curiosity, he destroyed them.

Even though B. Gajauskas did not acknowledge guilt, his guilt regarding the possession of the described documents and their duplication for the purpose of dissemination is confirmed through the following evidence:

Witness L. Stavskis testified that B. Gajauskas brought the documents of armed nationalist bands to his home in the fall of 1976 and after a while returned with an unknown person, photographed them all day long, and developed the film. He took a portion of the film and left the rest with him. Later he also took a portion of the documents.

On February 7, 1977, a Zenit-3M camera, a photo enlarger, and other photo equipment were removed from B. Gajauskas (lt. 156-158 l.). That same day the negatives of seven rolls of film with 200 frames and 322 pages of documents of bourgeois nationalist bands (lt 165-174 l.) were removed from the home of L. Stavskis. Criminological investigation determined

---

5. Text of this memorandum is published here as Doc. No. 8.

that the negatives of band documents were photographed with the Zenit-3 M camera taken from B. Gajauskas.

Prints were made from the negatives taken. It became evident that they contained the images of band documents found at L. Stavskis' apartment. This confirmed the testimony of L. Stavskis that B. Gajauskas photographed the documents he had brought to his home with his Zenit-3M camera. Fingerprint analysis determined that on some of the documents taken from L. Stavskis, fingerprints of B. Gajauskas were found (3t., 5-15 1.). This confirmed that he had the documents.

It is evident from the search protocol that on February 12, 1977, various handwritten works and transcripts, as well as several photocopies of documents of the nationalist bands were found at, and removed from the possession of O. Grigauskienė (2t., 191-194 1). Witness O. Grigauskienė testified that they were brought to her for safekeeping by the defendant's mother A. Kilčiauskienė. The latter testified that they were not found during the search, that they belong to B. Gajauskas, and that she took them to A. Grigauskienė so they would not be found. Therefore, the possession of documents of bourgeois nationalist bands and the production of several photocopies of each, which were found at O. Grigauskienė's home, testifies about the intent to disseminate this literature. B. Gajauskas' explanation that he did not keep the mentioned documents for dissemination purposes is negated by the aforementioned evidence.

The documents of armed nationalist bands are anti-Soviet literature, they are full of slanderous fabrications about the Soviet government in Lithuania, and they give instruction on the ways and means of the struggle to destroy it. Therefore, the possession of such literature and its duplication for dissemination purposes without a doubt testifies about the resumption of activities of the above-mentioned bands, adapting them to the contemporary situation in order to weaken and undercut the Soviet government. This activity is nothing but anti-Soviet agitation and propaganda.

In the accusation it is affirmed that B. Gajauskas enabled others to disseminate the band documents because his mother A. Kilčiauskienė gave part of them to O. Grigauskienė. This accusation is retracted because A. Kilčiauskienė did this without the knowledge of B. Gajauskas and, still further, she herself had no such purpose.

III. THE COMPILATION OF LISTS OF CONVICTED
PERSONS FOR THE PURPOSE OF ANTI-SOVIET
PROPAGANDA

Upon returning from his place of imprisonment, B. Gajauskas collected data about Lithuanians convicted for especially dangerous offenses against the state. Through two men who
shared similar viewpoints, Kovalev and A. Ginzburg, he publicized the compiled list in the illegally published *Chronicle
of Current Events*, as well as in reactionary newspapers printed
abroad, such as *Dirva, Europos Lietuvis* and *Mūsų Lietuva*,
seeking to undermine and weaken the Soviet government.[6] In
these publications the convicted persons are presented as the
victims of "slavery," as well as participants of "national" and
"resistance" movements.

B. Gajauskas, under trial, did not acknowledge guilt. He
explained that S. Kudirka gave him the list of convicted persons
as he was leaving the USSR. He copied the lists and kept them
for his own interest. He does not know how they ended up
abroad to be presented to the hostile news media.

B. Gajauskas' guilt regarding the compilation of lists of
convicted persons and their use for anti-Soviet agitation purposes is determined through the following evidence:

On December 23, 1974, three handwritten lists of persons
(Lithuanians) convicted for especially dangerous offenses
against the state were removed from B. Gajauskas' possession.
Handwriting experts determined that these lists were written
by B. Gajauskas (3t., 111-128 l.).

The lists of convicted Lithuanians taken from Kovalev
on December 23, 1974, were typewritten in Russian (10t.,
29-37, 42-47 l.).

During a search conducted on January 4, 1977, lists of
convicted persons (Lithuanians), typed on five pages, were
found and removed (2t., 234-243 l). The removed lists are
similar. The lists taken from A. Ginzburg contain additions
and corrections, determined by handwriting experts as having
been made by B. Gajauskas (3t., 173-192, 198-202 l.). This
confirmed that the lists of convicted persons compiled by B.

---

6. One such list, however of an unknown authorship, has been
published in emigré press. See, for example, **Darbininkas** (N.Y.), November 1, 1974.

Gajauskas were given by him to Kovalev and A. Ginzburg and were printed in reactionary publications abroad. B. Gajauskas' contentions that he rewrote them is unfounded. First of all, the three copies of the lists found in his possession are identical, including the corrections and additions. It is unbelievable that he, having the originals, would have made copies of them, and especially in triplicate.

In addition, during the preliminary inquiry B. Gajauskas testified that he himself had made up lists of convicted Lithuanians, having received data about them from various known and unknown individuals. He also explained the meaning of the numbers written next to the names (1t., 33-37 1., 103-106, 171-182 1.). From this evidence it follows without a doubt that S. Kovalev and A. Ginzburg received the lists from B. Gajauskas, since, according to B. Gajauskas, he had not given these lists to anyone, but he and the aforementioned persons, who shared similar viewpoints, were acquaintances.

Illegally collecting the names of the convicted, compiling a list, and then turning over this list to S. Kovalev and A. Ginzburg, he clearly knew that they would be publicized and used for anti-Soviet agitation and propaganda and was seeking the same.

In this manner, given the evidence mentioned and described in sections I, II, and III of this decision, it is undisputably confirmed that B. Gajauskas spread anti-Soviet agitation and propaganda, seeking to undermine and weaken the Soviet government in the USSR. His activities correspond to those covered in Article 68 Part 2 of the Penal Code of the Lithuanian SSR.[7]

---

7. Sometime after the trial Gajauskas wrote a lengthy rebuttal of the court's arguments and sent it to the Prosecutor General of the USSR. Text of this statement has been received in the West. A summary of it by the ELTA Information Service follows:

"On April 20, 1977, I was detained by KGB agents who groundlessly accused me of violating article 68 of the Penal Code. On April 14, 1978, the Supreme Court sentenced me to ten years of loss of freedom and five years of exile, although I was not culpable. The court examined my case without regard to objectivity, partly falsified my depositions as well as those of my witnesses, and consciously presented a mendacious evaluation of the 'anti-Soviet literature', which was found during the search of my apartment."

Gajauskas goes on to list all the "errors" and "falsifications" of the court, focusing especially on the alleged "large amounts of anti-

IV. PENALTIES AND OTHER QUESTIONS

B. Gajauskas drew no conclusions from his trial and sentencing for especially dangerous offenses against the state. The fact that he shows no desire to mend his ways also attests to the importance of isolating him from society for a long period of time. Various other anti-Soviet writings found in his possession, as well as his own written works, further attest to this need and indicate his hatred for the Soviet government, its party, and its administration's policy of peace. Because B. Gajauskas' previous sentencing is not annulled, he is therefore recognized as an especially dangerous recidivist, and he is given a supplementary sentence of exile.

The court, in accordance with Articles 331-333 of the Code of Penal Procedure of the Lithuanian SSR, decided to find Balys Gajauskas, son of Jonas, guilty of having violated Article 68 Part 2 of the Penal Code of the LSSR and to sentence him to ten years in prison and five years in exile.

Soviet literature." Among them was a Polish-language book **Bolshevism**, published in 1938, in Lublin, and the Lithuanian-language book **God Today**, published in Chicago. The court was not able to prove that Gajauskas disseminated those books or gave them to others to read. Neither could it prove that, through his Moscow friends Orlov and Ginzburg, he had transmitted abroad the lists of Lithuanian political prisoners. No proof was found to substantiate this allegation that he had translated into Lithuanian a part of Solzhenitsyn's **Gulag Archipelago**, a manuscript which was found in his place. Finally, no solid proof was presented that Gajauskas had made photocopies of the archives of the postwar Lithuanian anti-Soviet guerillas, with the alleged purpose —in the words of the court—"to adapt the ideology of the bandit gangs to the contemporary conditions and to weaken as well as to destroy the Soviet government."

"Such a verdict of the court compromises the Soviet government," Balys Gajauskas continues. "The leaders of government are right in saying that the Soviet Union is a powerful state that has broken out from the capitalist encirclement and has become a bulwark of the socialist system. And yet the court asserts the contrary; the mere fact that an individual will hold in his hands a book which contains several ideas that cantradict the communist ideology may weaken or disintegrate the Soviet system. To assert that possession and dissemination of literature is anti-Soviet agitation and propaganda parallels the absurd assertion that 'possession of a weapon is tantamount to murder'."

The verdict of the court states that "a large amount of anti-Soviet literature" was discovered at Gajauskas, place. "What does it mean?" Gajauskas asks. "How much was there? A ton? Ten tons? Maybe hundreds of tons?" He cites some examples of alleged "anti-Soviet

On the basis of Article 26 of the Penal Code, he is found to be a particularly dangerous recidivist and is to serve his sentence at a strict regime colony of corrective labor.

The sentence is to commence as of April 20, 1977.

B. Gajauskas is fined 136 rubles, 76 kopecks for court expenses to be paid to the state.

The material evidence in his case is to be safeguarded with his file. The "Zenit-3M" camera, photo enlarger, and other duplicating equipment and material are confiscated.

Personal belongings taken from the convicted are to be returned to him or to his relatives.

This decision cannot be appealed nor protested according to the casation system.

Assessors: A. Burokaitė and F. Stanionis
Verified copy: (Signature) Court member (S. Raziūnas)

---

weapons," such as the seven-year old protocol of the case of Simas Kudirka, a copy of Pečiulaitis' U.S. citizenship papers, the telephone number of the U.S. Consul in Moscow, an inscribed photograph of his friends, Aušra and Jonas Jurašas, who have left for the West, the Encyclical of Pope John XXIII, **History of Lithuania** by Šapoka, personal letters, notes, clippings from Soviet newspapers, his mother's reminiscences recorded when he was serving a 35-year term in the labor camps.

Gajauskas quotes the examining magistrate as saying to him: "You have earned ten percent, maybe one percent, but we will sentence you for the whole hundred percent."

"The Soviet leaders speak of peace today. But the concentration camps represent a not lesser threat to mankind than war; peace will remain impossible as long as we shall continue living in fear and slavery. A peace in concentration camps is a poor alternative to war. No, mankind must fight against concentration camps with the same zeal it fights against war. Only when concentration camps collapse, will the people be able to breathe freely. Otherwise we, nations with highly developed cultures, will enter the third millenium shoulder to shoulder with developed systems of concentration camps."

"My trial in Vilnius," Gajauskas concludes, "is an example of how one purposely destroys a man who reads books. Such a trial belongs to the list of the trials of the Inquisition. It is a farce of a trial. My crime consists of having thought independently and having valued democracy more highly than the communist dogmas. I committed a crime because I wanted to make use of all the fruits of the human, and not only those that are officially allowed, because I wanted to communicate with people of all nationalities. Now, as I and my friends proceed on the road of trials and tribulations, I still have the flame of hope and liberty before my eyes. Here, too, separated as we are for long years from our dear ones and relatives, condemned as we are to a humiliating death, even here we remain faithful to the ideas of democracy and liberty."

47. THE TRIAL OF VIKTORAS PETKUS

On July 11, 1978, the trial proceedings of Viktoras Petkus began in Vilnius. Judge—Ignotas, prosecutor—Bakučionis. V. Petkus is charged in accordance with the LSSR Penal Code Articles 68, Part 2; 70; 122, Part 2; and 241, Part 2.

Thirty witnesses were summoned to the trial proceedings:

1. Karolis Garuckas
2. Ona Lukauskaitė-Poškienė
3. Jonas Volungevičius
4. Romas Ragaišis
5. Jadvyga Petkevičienė
6. Birutė Pašilienė
7. Ina Jaškūnaitė
8. (Mrs.) Jaškūnienė
9. Mart Niklus (an Estonian)
10. Ens Tarto (an Estonian)

No. 47. From **Aušra**, No. 12 (August, 1978). A briefer narrative about the trial proceedings is found in **Chronicle**, No. 34 (August 15, 1978). Also the **Chronicle of Current Events**, No. 50, contains a lengthy account of the proceedings, meshing closely with the described proceedings by the Lithuanian sources. Additional information contained in the **Chronicle** is given in footnotes at appropriate points of the trial proceedings. Petkus himself refused to participate in the proceedings.

In the 1970s Petkus gradually emerged as the leading dissident personality in Lithuania, active in the Catholic and the national-political currents of dissent. Apparently he had close ties with the democratic dissidents in Moscow. He was the founding member and spokesman of the Lithuanian Helsinki Group, an organizer of a circle of youths for the study of Lithuanian history and literature (in which he reputedly excelled), and the initiator of the joint Baltic national committee. These activities resulted in three charges. He was tried for "anti-Soviet agitation and propaganda" (Article 68 of the Penal Code), mainly for his activities in the Lithuanian Helsinki Group; for "organizational activity... also participation in an anti-Soviet organization" (Article 70), in effect for organizing the Committee of the National Movement of Estonia, Latvia, Lithuania; and for an alleged contribution to the delinquency of minors (homosexuality and alcoholism) (Articles 122 and 141). The latter charges of moral degeneracy represent the frequent tactic of the Soviet regime to discredit the dissidents. The account of the trial in **Tiesa**, July 16, 1978, emphasized his alleged moral deficiencies, remaining vague as to the exact nature of his nationalist and human rights activity.

11. Ivars Žukovskis (a Latvian)
12 Juris Ziemelis (a Latvian)
13. Ints Calitis (a Latvian)
14. Dainius Šeputis
15. Lina Šeputienė
16. Regimantas Paulionis
17. Edmundas Paulionis
18. Kazys Paulionis
19. Mindaugas Garbis
20. Jonas Šliauteris
21. Vytas Šliauteris
22. Česlovas Kavaliauskas
23. Ona Poškutė
24. Marija Poškutė
25. Viktor Kalninš (a Latvian, absent)
26. Irina Serdane (a Latvian, absent)
27. Rimantas Čivilis
28. (Mrs.) Čivilienė
29. Marijus Buračas
30. Eitan Finkelstein (refused to be present)

TESTIMONY OF THE WITNESSES

Karolis Garuckas, 70 years old, a priest, a member of the Group to Implement the Helsinki Accords.

"Praised be Jesus Christ! Greetings to you from all those who are unable to get into this hall because of..." Here, the judge cuts off Father Karolis, asking him to sign the warning Articles 189 and 190.[1] Rev. Garuckas refuses to sign them, stating that he himself is a member of the Helsinki Group, that he considers these trial proceedings unlawful and unconstitutional, and refuses to give any evidence. The judge reads the testimony given during the preliminary interrogation, which confirms that Rev. Garuckas himself is a member of the Helsinki Group and that he joined it of his own free will, and that he is convinced that such a group is necessary in the fight for human rights. Here the judge tried to suggest that Rev. Garuckas had not been familiarized with all the documents that he had signed. Garuckas replied that he certainly

---

1. These articles of the Penal Code provide penalties for the refusal to testify or for deliberately false testimony.

was not informed about the provocative documents that security personnel slipped in front of him. He knows well, he continued, that all the documents and statements of the Helsinki Group have been carefully verified, the facts about violations of human rights have always proved true, and that the Helsinki Group is performing a valuable and necessary job. If the court considers this an offense, let it punish Garuckas himself as well. "I would be happy to meet the same fate as Bishop M. Reinys, Father Andriuška, and others. Viktoras Petkus fought for human rights—in an immensely honorable and just way. That Lithuania would have more sons like him."

The judge asked Father Garuckas to be seated. The court's examination was concluded.

— — —

Jonas Volungevičius, 38 years old, former political prisoner.

"Praised be Jesus Christ!" (addressing Petkus) "I know Petkus to be a good Catholic, a just and honorable man, and a patriot of Lithuania, and I consider it a great honor to have made his acquaintance This trial is unjust and illegal, and therefore I categorically refuse to participate in it."

The judge poses a question: "Have you signed a statement regarding Algimantas Žyprė?" [2] "Yes, I have signed a statement concerning Algimantas Žyprė, who has been unjustly committed to the psychiatric barracks in a labor camp. I refuse to answer any further questions of the court."

— — —

Jadvyga Petkevičienė, a medical nurse, living in Šiauliai.

"Praised be Jesus Christ, Viktoras!"

"What do you know about this case?"

"I don't know anything about this case. I know Viktoras to be a decent, honorable person, and this trial to be a confrontation with a member of the Helsinki Group. I refuse to give any sort of evidence."

"However, in the preliminary inquiry you confirmed that you had signed a statement regarding Žyprė?"

---

2. Algirdas Žyprė (b. in 1927) is among the political prisoners confined to a psychiatric facility. His case was the subject of Document No. 12 of the Lithuanian Helsinki Group (Text in **Aušra**, No. 8, October, 1977). For Žyprė's complaint about his situation to the Prosecutor General of the USSR, see **Violations of Human Rights in Soviet Occupied Lithuania: A Report for 1977** (Chicago, 1978), pp. 191-194.

"I confirm that even now. I will not respond to any other questions."

The judge asks the witness to be seated. Petkevičienė begins looking for something in the inside pocket of her jacket. It appears that she might produce a weapon, so the guards jump up and the judge and the prosecutor become uneasy... Petkevičienė produces a half-wilted rose and, amidst the guards' confusion, presents it to Viktoras Petkus, saying, "It's for you, Viktoras, from the youth and the believers of Lithuania. Praise to you, son of Lithuania, who gave your freedom for the rights of your motherland, your nation, and man."

— — —

Birutė Pašilienė, 50 years old, former political prisoner, living in Klaipėda.

"I don't know Viktoras Petkus and have never had anything to do with him; that is why I have nothing to do with this case."

"At the time of a search at your place, a typewriter was removed, as well as a document creating the Supreme Committee of the Estonian, Latvian, and Lithuanian National Movement. All this material had been typed on the typewriter that had been removed from your premises during the search. How could these documents have turned up at your place if you don't know Viktoras Petkus?" [3]

"It was fully established during the interrogation that on August 18 and 19 I was being interrogated at the Vilnius security headquarters and that on August 20 and 21 I was on duty, so that on those dates that the document was dated I was not at home and did not type it. The typewriter found at my place is not mine. Security functionaries have recently seized two typewriters from me, and I have been forced to look for new ones to purchase. I have asked all my acquaintances who could sell them to me. Who brought these I don't know because I was not at home."

"But someone was at home if 'someone' delivered the typewriter?"

---

3. **Aušra**, No. 10 (March, 1978) reported that a number of documents of the Baltic committee, addressed to the governments of Great Britain, the United States, the German Federal Republic, Israel, and to L. Brezhnev, were discovered on the premises of Pašilienė. Apparently these documents were not sent out, for their texts never reached the West and were not published in the **samizdat** press.

"Yes, my 85-year-old mother was at home. She died this past April."

"How can you explain that the documents found at Viktoras Petkus' are similar to those found at your place, even typed on the same typewriter, which has been established by experts?"

"Once again I state that I do not know this honorable man, Petkus, have never received any documents from him, and for the first time saw the document found in my apartment at the time of the search. The interrogator implied that he found it in my desk drawer, however, I myself saw it for the first time in the interrogator's hand, and I was not even apprised of its contents. That is all I can say about the material found in my apartment. All that has nothing to do with Viktoras Petkus. I categorically refuse to answer any other questions."

"Have you signed the document regarding Algimantas Žyprė, who was committed to the psychiatric barracks?"

"Yes, I signed it. I feel I have acted correctly because Žyprė has already been released from the psychiatric barracks. That proves that he was really committed there unjustly."

"How could you sign a document not knowing the person?"

"I have heard a lot about Žyprė over the radio. The whole world is talking about it."

— — —

Ona Lukauskaitė-Poškienė, a member of the Helsinki Group, living in Šiauliai. "Hello, Viktoras." (She bows to him sincerely. V. Petkus responds by rising.)

"Do you know the defendant?"

"Yes, I know Viktoras Petkus because I, like he, am a member of the Helsinki Group. I know Viktoras to be a good, decent, just, and principled person. He is deeply religious, loves his country and his people, has a keen intellect, and has done much in defense of human rights, always being extremely just. I, as a member of the Helsinki Group, have written a protest regarding this trial.[4] Please consider my protest valid and cut short these shameful and illegal trial proceedings without dealy." (Lukauskaitė-Poškienė felt faint and sat down.)

---

4. Text of the protest in **Aušra**, No. 8 (October, 1977). Besides Lukauskaitė-Poškienė, it was signed by about 80 persons, many known participants in the dissident movement.

"But you did not refuse to speak at the time of the interrogation?"

"Yes, but each time I demanded that this penal case be cut short without delay and that Viktoras Petkus be released. I will no longer respond to any questions posed by the court."

The judge allows the witnesses to remain in the courtroom.

— —

Romas Ragaišis, living in Vilnius, former political prisoner.

"Greetings, Viktoras!"

When the judge asks him to sign the warning Articles 189 and 190, he categorically refuses to sign them, explaining that Article 189 legalizes the use of force and he himself is opposed to any use of force, much less would he violate his own conscience. (He states all this in a very forceful voice.) The judge, confused for a while, eyed his counsellors, then stated that even if Romas Ragaišis does not sign them, he will be held punishably accountable for his refusal to give evidence or for giving false evidence.

"What do you know about this case? Do you know Viktoras Petkus?"

"I have known Viktoras Petkus for over 10 years. I'm proud of that. He is an educated, fine, civilized person. He loves literature, especially poetry, is a great lover of his country and a man of great erudition. I am well acquainted with his activities in the public interest and consider him an honorable and decent person. Being a member of the Helsinki Group, he was very necessary and useful to our society. In his activities he has exposed a number of administrative offenses and staunchly defended civil human rights. Viktoras Petkus' arrest is illegal, as are all these trial proceedings, and, therefore, I refuse to participate in this judicial investigation. I will no longer respond to any questions of the court."

The judge consults the prosecutor; he, however, replies that "if the witness refused to answer you, he will not answer me, either."

— — —

Ints Calitis, a Latvian, a former political prisoner. He refused to sign the warning articles.

"I have known Viktoras to be a decent, good, and honest person. I know nothing about the case."

"However, during the preliminary inquiry you confirmed

Viktor Kalninš' evidence when confronted with Viktor Kalninš himself?"

"Yes, during the search at my place material dealing with the National Movement of Estonia, Latvia, and Lithuania was removed, but both at the inquiry and now I state that this material cannot be used against Viktoras Petkus in accordance with Article 68 of the Penal Code; therefore, it is irrelevant to talk about this."

"Did Viktoras Petkus meet with Viktor Kalninš in your apartment, and who organized this meeting?"

Our meeting has nothing to do with Viktoras Petkus' case."

The judge reads evidence given by Calitis during the interrogation, which on confrontation with Viktor Kalninš partially confirms evidence given by Viktor Kalninš against Viktoras Petkus.

"This evidence was obtained from me by extortion, I therefore ask the court to consider it invalid. It is fabricated and incorrect. I refuse to give any more evidence in this trial."

— — —

Juris Ziemelis, a Latvian, a former political prisoner.

"I know Viktoras Petkus to be a decent, good, and honest person. I refuse to participate in this trial because I consider this trial illegal."

"However, in the preliminary inquiry you gave evidence, when confronted with Viktor Kalninš, that Viktoras Petkus had come to Latvia regarding the matter of founding the Supreme Committee of the National Movement of Estonia, Latvia, and Lithuania and that the specific guidelines for the work of the committee were being discussed?"

"The Riga KGB used extortion to obtain this evidence. For this evidence Viktor Kalninš was issued a visa to leave for the US; his evidence was literally purchased by the Latvian KGB, and therefore this evidence cannot be used against Viktoras Petkus as incriminating material according to Articles 68 and 70 of the Penal Code. These trial proceedings are illegal, and I categorically refuse to give evidence during them. As for my evidence given during the preliminary inquiry, please consider it invalid as it was obtained by means of extortion."

— — —

Ivars Žukovskis, a Latvian, a former political prisoner.

"What do you know about the Viktoras Petkus case?"

"I don't know anything."

"When and under what circumstances did you meet Viktoras Petkus?"

"In Riga in 1976."

"What did you talk about during the meeting?"

"About everyday matters."

"What do you know about the Es-La-Li (an abbreviation of Estonia—Latvia—Lithuania; that abbreviation was used in the seized documents) Committee?"

"I don't know anything."

"In 1976 Viktor Kalniņš telephoned you and said that some Lithuanians have arrived at his place and you went to the meeting?"

"I don't remember."

"What was talked about?"

"Questions that interested us, for example, why residents of Lithuania get better services (food provision) than residents of Latvia."

"Who acquainted you with the documents of the Es-La-Li Committee?"

"The Riga KGB, by showing me Kalniņš' evidence."

— — —

Viktor Kalniņš, a Latvian, a former political prisoner, has presently emigrated abroad.[5]

Read in court was his evidence as incriminating evidence against Viktoras Petkus in drawing up the penal case according to the LSSR Penal Code Articles 70 and 68-2. On the basis of Viktor Kalniņš' evidence read in court, it is suggested that Viktoras Petkus came to Latvia in the summer of 1977 to discuss the foundation of the National Baltic Committee. After that there was a meeting about this question in Trakai (Lithuania),

5. Viktor Kalniņš was allowed to emigrate and reached the West just prior to the trial of Petkus. Given the importance of Kalniņš' evidence, it remains a serious question why he was allowed to leave without giving oral testimony. The dissidents have charged Kalniņš with the selling out of Petkus. The **Chronicle** (No. 34) writes: "At the trial, evidence by the Latvian Kalniņš was read regarding the planned formation of the committee for liberation of Estonia, Latvia, and Lithuania. Kalniņš' evidence encumbering V. Petkus' case was obtained as the price for his permission to emigrate to the West. And in fact, even before the trial Kalniņš and his family were already in the West. Yet, on the basis of his own testimony, he should have occupied the defendant's bench along with Petkus. Where's the logic? One member of the organization gets prison, the other—freedom in the West."

and on August 15-17, 1977, Viktoras Petkus had come to Riga, where, under his leadership, the founding documents were drawn up and an appeal was made to the governments of Western countries to recognize this committee as valid and official. (V. Kalninš testified in detail about the founding process of this committee and the future prospects envisioned for the committee.) The court, on the basis of this material, recognizes Viktoras Petkus as an anti-Soviet activist-recidivist.

— — —

Ens Tarto, an Estonian, a former political prisoner.
"What do you know of this case?"
"As in the preliminary inquiry, so also at this trial, I refuse to give evidence and request the court to explain what Viktoras Petkus is charged with."
"For a witness that is not necessary to know."
"In that case I refuse to be a part of these proceedings."
Twice Ens Tarto had been convicted for his political beliefs: 1956 to 1960 and 1962 to 1967—a total of nine years. He answered the questions of the court only in Estonian and spoke only through an interpreter.

— — —

Mart Niklus, an Estonian, a former political prisoner, 34 years old, employed as an instructor at the Tartu city foreign-language program.
To the usual first question of the judge, he responded in Estonian, demanding a qualified interpreter. Silently, Mart Niklus refused the warning form presented for his signature and, not waiting for the questions of the judge, began speaking, "Although this is already the second day of the trial proceedings, it nevertheless is not yet clear to me what Viktoras Petkus is charged with. What..." (The judge cuts him short.)
"Here we present the questions, and your responsibility —only to answer them."
"I don't know your codes, procedures, your methods or habits; in addition, I do not know whether the trial proceedings are open or closed, and I do not know who comprises the court."
"Please hear me out. For refusal to give evidence, we can hold you to punishable accountability."
"Please hear me out as well. I take your statement as a threat to obtain evidence by force, which automatically puts me in a defensive position." The interpreter did not translate

this phrase for the judge, however the slip regarding punishable accountability that had been placed in front of Niklus for his signature was removed.

"In my whole life no one has ever insulted me, slandered me, sneered at me as during the interrogations regarding Viktoras Petkus' case. That is why I have become skeptical and do not trust documents prepared in advance—because they are usually used against me. I ask the court to accept my written statement regarding this question."

Mart Niklus hands in his statement, and the judge agrees to familiarize himself with it. Having read the statement, the judge turns to Mart Niklus: "You speak and write Russian very fluently and, therefore, you can give your evidence in Russian."

"Now I am upset and tired from a long wait and so I cannot give evidence in any other language but my native language. That is why I again request a highly qualified interpreter."

"You are not responding to the questions presented to you and you are restructuring the order of the court. What do you know in this penal case?"

"As I already said, I have no idea about it."

"You have talked about the Es-La-Li Committee and the situation of your nation in Calitis' apartment in Tartu?"

"The question is posed absurdly. Calitis lives in Latvia and has no apartment in Tartu."

"The interpreter will accept responsibility for presenting the question incorrectly."

"Once again I emphasize the necessity of a qualified interpreter during the trial proceedings. I have been at Calitis' apartment in Riga with his family at dinner."

"When was Viktoras Petkus last in Tartu?"

"About a year ago in the summer."

"In August."

"I don't disagree with that."

"And what do you know about the Es-La-Li Supreme Committee?"

"At the preliminary inquiry I was presented with some carbon copies of unsigned documents."

"An expert has established that some of the documents taken from Viktoras Petkus were typed in Russian on your Erika typewriter. What can you say about this?"

"I have not been familiarized with the expert's conclusions, and it is possible to have differing opinions on this question. Since the KGB has been interested in my typewriters for several years, and, in addition, the KGB has constant access to my apartment (a few years ago during a search, the keys to my apartment disappeared), I suspect that these documents are simply forged by the KGB. In addition, the typewriters were seized from me unsoldered, which greatly infringes on the security of confiscated items and creates for the KGB the capability to write on my typewriter, which they enjoy, and later to present this as incriminating evidence against me or Viktoras Petkus I need these typewriters for my professional work as an instructor and, therefore, I ask the court to return them to me.'"

"Certainly. Now please explain how your typewritten autobiography found its way to Viktoras Petkus."

"I typed the autobiography myself. How it got to V. Petkus I don't know. I don't recall."

"On July 25, 1977, during a search, two tickets were found at your place: Tartu-Pilva and Pilva-Moscow. How can you explain this trip to Moscow?"

"You have been incorrectly informed. I turned in these tickets of my own free will. In addition, I have been compensated for the expenses of this trip that never took place. The purpose of the trip—to travel around the country on vacation."

—   —   —

Young witnesses were questioned primarily for the purpose of charging Petkus with immoral behavior. If any of the youths said that on the occasion of Easter or Christmas there was dry wine on the holiday table, in the proceedings this was qualified as "Contributing to the delinquency of minors."

—   —   —

Maryté Poškuté, the tenant of the apartment in which V. Petkus lived for a number of years.

"Do you know Viktoras Petkus?"

"Yes, I know him very well—he is our roomer. God grant that all people would be as decent as our dear Viktoras." (She is given the warning paragraphs to sign.) "I am deeply religious, and so I speak only the truth, so there isn't any need to sign." (She forcefully pushes the paper aside.)

"Do you have two rooms?"

"I used to have one room; that is why it was divided with a plywood partition. I frequently stayed in this side because that was where the heater was."

"Did young people often gather at Viktoras Petkus'?"

"Young people loved Viktoras Petkus very much; his place was always full of them."

"Did they drink often? What time did they leave?"

"Lord, help me; I am deeply religious and won't tell an untruth. Not only did Viktoras never drink, not only did I never see him drunk, but over the number of years that he lived at our place, I have never even found a cork in straightening up his room!"

— — —

Onutė Poškutė, the tenant of the apartment where V. Petkus lived, the sister of Marytė Poškutė.

"Praised be Jesus Christ, dear Viktoras!"

V. Petkus rises and greets his dear "landlady."

She refuses to sign the warning slip, stating that she is a Catholic and always tells the truth.

"Do you know Viktoras Petkus?"

"Yes, I know him well. He is a very decent, very good Catholic, an honest and honorable person. God grant more such sons to our Motherland! Then, neither police nor the *druzhinik* would be necesary. Not only was he himself very honorable, but he taught others to be decent and honorable. He was greatly loved by youth, read much, and loved poetry. Can a bad person love God and poetry?"

"During his meetings with youth, was drinking a frequent occurrence?"

"He lived at our place for over ten years; not once was there such an instance. He is a real patriot of his country. That is why he was concerned with inculcating in them lofty moral principles and lofty convictions."

— — —

Some sort of a soldier from a KGB detachment, a *Rimantas Čivilis*, who apparently had given the court desirable evidence, was brought to the trial. He was not admitted to the witnesses' room but had a privileged place in the courtroom. While the witnesses were being questioned, he was seated apart from them, behind the prosecutor. None of the witnesses knew him.

The soldier's mother, Čivilienė, also apparently gave desirable evidence to the court; she left the courtroom through the employees' entrance.

Since the aforementioned witnesses were questioned separately, their testimony is not accurately known.[6]

—   —   —

During the recess while the witnesses were being questioned, Mart Niklus and Ins Calitis made a request to have the trial proceedings translated into Estonian and Latvian since this case concerns the interests of both Estonia and Latvia. The judge overruled the request without so much as giving a reason. Mart Niklus attempted to cite the Soviet Constitution, but the judge called for police employees to "restore order to the court." Mart Niklus was compelled to withdraw his rightful demand.

Speaking through an interpreter, Mart Niklus requested that his statement be taken in writing. Ch. Lillena (the interpreter) looked to the judge and, seeing no approval, refused to accept the statement from Mart Niklus. This statement was nevertheless submitted to the judge, but with no result.

The questioning concluded only at 11 p.m.; however, both the witnesses and the numerous friends and acquaintances of V. Petkus who had gathered stood in front of the court building for a long time.

On the following two days none of V. Petkus' well-wishers was admitted to the courtroom.

On July 14, the day of the sentencing, many young people arrived from all over Lithuania. Of course, since it was a work day, many who wanted to be a part of this throng of protesters

---

6. Rimantas Čivilis and his mother Čivilienė, probably under duress, gave testimony on the alleged homosexuality of Petkus. The **Chronicle** (No. 34), wrote: "The only witness who would testify against Petkus, a young soldier Čivilis, was escorted into the courtroom by uniformed men. As early as the second day of the trial he was tearfully telling some teenage boys that the first time security agents made him give testimony he was completely drunk and basically did not understand anything, but agreed with everything they told him to confirm, and that later on he wasn't able to deny his testimony. Poor young man! He had never been sexually molested by Petkus, but those who forced him to give false evidence certainly ravished him morally. The youths who came to Petkus' apartment and there together studied Šapoka's **History of Lithuania** and religious books had never seen him in the apartment of Petkus."

weren't able to come. But from those who gathered (there were over 70 people), one could tell how popular and loved Viktoras Petkus was. In the hands of all those who arrived there were flowers— a sign of respect for Viktoras Petkus. That really irritated the KGB employees. And the intense prayers of the believers enraged them. Several times they demanded that there be no praying in front of the court building since it "disturbs the peace."

Each day the confrontation with the sons and daughters who loved their motherland became more difficult: ten take the place of one condemned one. You can't stop the flow of the river!

Viktoras Petkus was one of the fearless fighters for human rights, but he is not the last. In our nation there are sons and daughters who will not be afraid to sacrifice their freedom and well-being for the freedom of their nation and for human rights, for the freedom of religion in Lithuania! They will not be afraid even if the fighters for freedom and justice are punished inhumanly harshly!

Viktoras Petkus' sentence: 3 years in prison, 7 years in a labor camp, and 5 years of exile. THE MOTHERLAND WILL NOT FORGET THE SACRIFICES OF HER SONS AND DAUGHTERS!

48. SECULAR AND RELIGIOUS ORIENTATIONS IN DISSENT

LET US HAVE UNITY, LET US HAVE UNITY!

"In the name of Lithuania"

Rejoicing, we followed the steps of *Laisvės Šauklys* (The Herald of Freedom). We admired the national conscientiousness of authors of many articles, their spiritual strength and courage to call everything by their real names... Wishing to contribute to the dissemination of this newspaper, we have repeatedly reprinted its articles. And in this publication we are repeating them in an anthology: why and how Lithuania is being occupied and denationalized. Since truth, and especially the history of Lithuania, is being scrupulously concealed from the Lithuanians, we are of the opinion that a youth, having read these articles, at least will open his eyes and begin to look around.

However, for months, day and night our wounded hearts suffered after hearing the voice of *Laisvės Šauklys:* "While Awaiting the 'New' *Aušra*" (*Laisvės Šauklys*, No. 8). It is difficult to believe that the editors or the authors of articles of this newspaper might be of the same opinion as those laymen, who wrote the cited address to the clergy. In other words, the editors of *Laisvės Šauklys* are of the opinion that the article

No. 48. The leading article of **Aušrelė** (The Little Dawn), dated February 16, 1978, slightly abbreviated. Most likely this is a non-periodical publication. The name, as well as the content of this article, suggests that it is issued by the publishers or associates of **Aušra**. The article is a response of Catholic dissidents to a number of criticisms by non-clerical, liberal-nationalist dissidents, especially those associated with the non-Catholic **samizdat** journal **Laisvės Šauklys**. The polemic suggests at least an incipient differentiation of the dissident movement into clerical-nationalist and liberal-nationalist currents, a development reminiscent of the ideological differentiation of the national movement at the end of the nineteenth century. Unfortunately, **Aušrelė** does not reprint the article from **Laisvės Šauklys** and we can have a feel about its contents only from brief quotes or the nature of the response. The rest of **Aušrelė** merely reprints without comment a selection of articles from **Laisvės Šauklys**, possibily in response to the charge that the well organized and financed Catholic dissent movement is not aiding the non-Catholic dissidents. Again, unfortunately, not a single issue of **Laisvės Šauklys** had reached the West to provide a more complete record of the ongoing debate.

"While Awaiting the 'New' Aušra" is worthy of attention and discussion. Therefore, we (by the way, also laymen), respecting the editors and encouraged by the noble tasks raised by the editorials of *Laisvės Šauklys,* resolved to respond. It would be an offense to permit the countrymen at home and abroad to be misled by the words of "laymen" because the real political situation in Lithuania is quite different from that shown in the cited article; it is obvious that the laymen who undersigned this article do not represent the entire laity of Lithuania. In expressing our opinion, we request the editors of *Laisvės Šauklys:* do not permit a few laymen to destroy the unity among Lithuanians, prove to them that it is necessary to find a common language in the Motherland, that all hidden stones must be cast into the abyss. (...)

They (the laymen) object to all those who do not have ."political judgment", including, in their words, those "tragic heroes" who issue *Aušra,* the *Chronicle of the Catholic Church in Lithuania, Dievas ir Tėvynė* (God and Country), including as well those whom they call "loyal" and "semi-loyal" clergy.[1] But do those, for whom everybody is lacking, possess a political judgment themselves? (...)

Let us begin with the amazing conclusion of the "laymen": "It is impossible to find a common language among ourselves and the clergy." Let us just reflect! How terrible! If this is so, then Lithuania is condemned to death. It will not be saved by the "tragic heroes", in the words of the authors, nor by "the underground publication" of laymen, which could "teach" the clergy. While the laymen and the clergy are "teaching" each other, the occupant will transform the clergy as well as the laymen into atheists and will denationalize them. After all, the recent past has already shown that such teachers are best "taught" by security committees and are relatively easily forced to become slaves for freedom, to "cease activity", or to renounce their viewpoint. No, Lithuania is the same Motherland for the laymen and the clergy; therefore there is also a common language. Only the national traitors in the enslaved Motherland do not wish to converse in Lithuanian.[2]

---

1. I.e. those, who cooperate with the Soviet regime or are disposed toward an accommodation with it.

2. This should not be taken literally. Obviously, the expression "common language" refers to the presence of a common basis for cooperation or a common viewpoint.

The second conclusion of the "laymen" is also fundamentally wrong: "The clergy lacks political judgment, the past has not taught them anything." How can one ascribe to all the clergy of Lithuania the statements and activity of a handful of clergymen, even though they may be "priests with great authority", who in reality do not possess political judgment? Of course, it is shocking to read the panegyrics of people like Aničas [3] for "loyal" bishops, priests. Certainly, such poverty of spirit, superficial faith, the lack of national conscientiousness and political judgment among such clergy are striking. It is also clear that the atheists will brag about "loyal" clergy for a long time, because even today a whole column of their agents await their turn—at least after their death they will be "honored". However, even the blind can see that only a small part of the clergy is loyal to Communism (often without realizing that one of the principal tasks of Communism is the formation of atheistic world view in the conscience of all without exception).

At the moment the number of such "loyalists" among the laity constitutes a considerably larger percentage. After all, almost all the lay intelligentsia, working in responsible positions, obediently implement the directives of the occupant and diligently poison themselves and their countrymen through words, work, and example; they disseminate lies through radio, the press, television; in the universities they energetically educate the younger generation in the spirit of atheism and "internationalism". Who, if not the Lithuanian laity, coerces the children and youths to join the Pioneer and Komsomol organizations? How many of them are, in the security and party committees, agencies of Soviet government, various associations engaged in promoting communist ideology? Where is their political judgment? Is not their idea of the Motherland, morality, the future and the past expressed by three words: bread and games. Why don't the "laymen" see this? After all, on June 18, 1940, there were only 1800 communists, the majority of whom were not Lithuanians.[4] There was no and cannot be

3. Jonas Aničas, a historian and Soviet propagandist, writing frequently on ideological questions, religion and the Church, and nationalism. Among his works, which classify the clergy into "reactionary" and "progressive," is **The Establishment of Socialism in Lithuania and the Catholic Church** (Vilnius, 1975).

4. While the exact number is problematical, the contention that a majority of the tiny Communist Party of Lithuania at the time of the

any talk about some kind of influence by them in the Lithuanian society. We were amazed and disgusted when during the demonstrations they used to carry a portrait of one of the "fathers" of Communism. And today we ourselves already hang such portraits and hundreds of thousands of layment participate in such demonstrations. Today we ourselves, sometimes risking freedom, are struggling so that a "perfect" Soviet constitution would be in effect and are amazed when someone dares to demand the expulsion from Lithuania the rotten ideas of Lenin and all the occupants.[5] Indeed, we should not be afraid of the truth: the occupants already have turned the majority of lay intelligentsia into loyalists, disoriented the consciousness of even the fighters for freedom of Lithuania and its Church.

Yes, there are such "loyalists". They are created by Communism and especially by the security organs. We do not think there is an issue about this fact. We also believe and it is clear that so far the security organs have made a stronger effort to dehumanize the clergy than the laity. The biography of Rev. A. Ylius obviously shows this: if he had permitted at least once to denounce in his name the postwar partisan struggle, then today the atheist propaganda would refer to him not as a priest-bandit, but as "loyal" to the Soviet system, possibly as a bishop.[6] Therefore we should rejoice that the clergy, compared

---

Soviet occupation consisted of non-Lithuanians is very plausible. For example, half a year after the occupation (January 1, 1941), after intensive recruitment of natives, still only 53 percent of the party membership was Lithuanian. See the statistics in **Mažoji lietuviškoji tarybinė enciklopedija** (Vilnius, 1968), Vol. 2, p. 381.

5. This may be a critique of the tactics of the democratic movement or those who want to reform the system from within, who seek to remedy the abuses of constitutional law through legal means.

6. Rev. Antanas Ylius was a participant in the postwar partisan movement. He was arrested on October 22, 1945, tried in August of 1946, and sentenced to 10 years in prison. Rev. Ylius is among the favorite targets of Soviet propagandists, who have accused him of all kinds of offenses, including terrorism, but which have not been proven. Such is the nature of a short documentary film about him "In the Shadow of a Cross", the exposition in the Museum of Atheism in Vilnius, and numerous articles in the press. Rev. Ylius has protested the distortions of his political past in a statement to the Prosecutor of the Lithuanian SSR (text in **Chronicle**, No. 16). According to the underground journal **Dievas ir Tėvynė**, No. 2 (1976), in 1974 the Prosecutor, as well as the

to the laity, have maintained their integrity reasonably well (and only because their belief in God was and remains deeper, stronger).

It is quite understandable if occasionally an honest clergyman or layman in the Motherland or abroad may err for a time in accepting as truth lies, which are embellished with the most beautiful ideas. There is nothing unusual if Canon Rauda "placed the sign of equality between the 'istrebiteli' and the Lithuanian partisans."[7] In other words, all were engaged in killing. (Such a sign of equivalency, perhaps even more forcefully, was also placed by a majority of the laymen, the intelligentsia). After all, the Canon may not have known that in order to compromise the partisan struggle, security agents infiltrated among the partisans, and sometimes the partisans, incited and deceived by them, murdered truly innocent people.[8] (...) Thus it is not easy all at once to evaluate everything correctly. In our opinion we should help each other to comprehend reality and to search patiently for a common viewpoint. After all, we are not communists to condemn each other for all times for some error of our forefathers or of the past.

---

security organs, have acknowledged the distortions. The same issue of Dievas ir Tėvynė contains a long biographical sketch of Rev. Ylius. Despite the problems with the regime, Rev. Ylius has been permitted to serve as pastor since his release in 1956.

7. Canon Petras Rauda (1894-1974) served two sentences for nationalist activity. The second term of ten years, beginning in 1957, he served in the Mordovian camps with other illustrious prisoners, including Cardinal J. Slipij. whom he knew. It is not known when he might have equated the partisans and their "destroyers". In the course of the partisan war the Soviet authorities put pressure upon the bishops and the clergy to condemn the partisans. Very few expressed a direct disapproval. A general "Do not kill!" appeal was issued by many, but this applied to both warring sides. Canon Rauda may have been one of those echoing such a statement although his nationalist activity seems to contradict this. A brief biography of Canon Rauda is provided in Chronicle, No. 10. For more details on the attitude of the bishops and individual clergy toward the partisan movement, see Aničas, op. cit., esp. Ch. 3.

8. A partisan underground newspaper Laisvės Varpas, on October 1, 1947, reported the formation of special MVD groups to imitate the partisans, to infiltrate the partisan ranks, and to sow confusion and dissension. There is no doubt that many of the innocent victims in the partisan war were in fact killed by such Soviet security units.

It is completely correct to say that contemporary youth can be attracted only by relating Christian ideas to the national ones. It is however also true that even the conscientious Lithuanian patriot (as he is called by the laymen), if he is at the same time an atheist, often also aids in the struggle against the Church. How many Lithuanians are there, who, in propagating their atheistic beliefs, found a common cause with the occupant?! No, every Lithuanian should be a Catholic, although, we agree, he does not have to be a militant proclaimer of the Gospel. It is important that he live according to the teachings of the Gospel. Therefore, the idea of the laymen that the Catholic Church of Lithuania will live as long as the nation is alive (obviously, without Lithuania its Church cannot exist) must be corrected as follows: the nation will be alive as long as the Catholic Church of Lithuania is alive. Is it possible that the "laymen" do not understand what miracles are brought about by faith? No regime can dehumanize a deeply religious person; he will never exchange spiritual values for material advantage for himself and his children. Such a man is free even in slavery. Thus faith is a power which cannot be unseen by any conscientious layman. There is no other such power in the world, which could help Lithuanians in Lithuania to survive as Lithuanians.

We would also like to express doubts concerning some questions of tactics, which were dealt with by the "laymen" in their article. It is not true that *Aušra* is a stepchild of the *Chronicle*. Far from it. Also we should not forget that the name of the *Chronicle* alone often does not permit it to deviate from its subject matter. Therefore, it would be unwise to complain for withholding (the publication) of some article. Besides, after all, all of us often lack direct information; it is imperative to be on guard against provocateurs and the like. Also it is not true that the laymen are very poor, incapable even of acquiring the means of publication. We think that it is clear to many that, for example, the income of some uncommon entrepreneur or an ordinary physician is several times the income of the "richest" clergyman. Why couldn't there be among them even a few "tragic heroes", who would contribute their income to underground publication? .

It is also questionable whether we should isolate ourselves completely and not participate in any festivity abroad. On the contrary, it would be nice, if from every traveler abroad the world public would find out directly the truth about the Soviet Union, about the enslaved Motherland. Besides, we should not forget that such trips often constitute the only connection between us and the free world. There are people in Lithuania who would walk on their knees through the entire outside world, only if they had the opportunity, in order to elicit aid from their countrymen living in freedom, at least convenient means for publication in underground conditions. Regarding Bishop Sladkevičius (of course, we are not judging who is right), we also heard this opinion: it was feasible to utilize the opportunity (to travel abroad) and, perhaps even at the price of life, to show the truth to the Vatican and the world or to attempt to return as a militant leader of the Lithuanian Catholic Church, as a Wyszynski of Lithuania...[9]

It is incomprehensible on what basis the laymen contend that the clergy of Lithuania have an organization in existence for 600 years. It should be said that they had... After all, the Security already has demolished it considerably. First of all, what is the worth of an organization without a leader? And who heads the Catholic Church in Lithuania today? Is it not evident that until the present almost all the leaders of the Lithuanian Catholic Church merely executed the directives of the Security? For this reason only a part (luckily a large part) of the clergy, not in an organized manner but individually, often in the catacombs, proclaim the Gospel according to their best abilities in a manner taught by Christ and His Apostles. Some of the clergy lock themselves in their churches and proclaim the Gospel only to those who themselves come to the church. They are afraid even to consider that it is necessary to sacrifice and to carry the light of Christ to every Lithuanian family. There are also priests who already aid the Security to expel the children, youths from church; who, having honestly performed the duties of a priest, do not dare to acknow-

---

9. Apparently the issue here involves a delegation of Lithuanian clergy to the Eucharistic Congress in Philadelphia in the summer of 1976. Probably the article in **Laisvės Šauklys** criticizes a number of clergy who did agree to travel on the grounds that they were used for propaganda purposes. Bishop Sladkevičius, though in conflict with the regime (see Doc. No. 61), was asked to join the delegation, but the bishop refused. In effect, the Catholic dissidents here are criticizing Bishop Sladkevičius for not utilizing the opportunity to publicize the plight of the Catholic Church.

ledge this openly; who are more concerned about a comfortable home and the material well-being of relatives, about opulent dinners, than about the souls of men. Would this be the case if the Church had an organization? And when the clergy will have an organization (and it surely will have it), without doubt this organization will be the principal power in Lithuania which will lead the nation and its Church to a bright to-morrow.

Finally, should we indict the publishers of the *Chronicle* for suggesting the publication of a new newspaper?.[10] After all, this was an excellent suggestion. What is wrong with still another newspaper? The number of newspapers in Lithuania is not important. It is important that all these newspapers or just one newspaper would unite us and reach at least a significant portion of our countrymen, that they would show to the countrymen the real face of Communism, and that they would help to preserve and for some to regain the faith and national consciousness. In our opinion all publications are necessary, and their articles are excellent merely because they state the truth. Let us not insist that all begin communicating in the same genre. Let us also not forget the conditions under which these articles are prepared: no publication really has an editorial board. Therefore, we should only rejoice for the existence of every publication.

It is hard to believe that in Lithuania there are "underground workers" who do not like the struggle against the Church, against the deep faith of countrymen. They try to show that the atheistic press is lying, that atheism is not a science. It is self-evident that under our conditions it is often impossible to respond to all the reproaches of the atheists in a manner that the scientists and theologians in the free world would respond. However, if they, supplementing and correcting the responses, would point out publicly the errors of specific propagators of atheism, many such publicized defenders of atheism, even if they would not convert, at least would avoid becoming more "famous"—under the cover of a scientist's

---

10. Private communication suggests that the editors of the **Chronicle** refused to publish a number of articles not relevant to their religious orientation. The **Chronicle** has limited itself to the defense of religious freedom on what it considers a strictly legal basis (according to the letter of Soviet law) and only occasionally reports on other matters. The result of such a policy has been a proliferation of underground journals.

title would cease blindly misleading our countrymen. Would this not be of great advantage to the nation? Besides, we already have enough novices who ought to expand their religious knowledge. We even doubt whether a deeply religious layman would say: "Even this *Chronicle* contributes almost nothing to the national and religious consciousness of youth." A. Jakš-tas [11] would exclaim: "What has obscured your mind!" The *Chronicle* does not "contribute almost nothing", but already has contributed much. It is a fact which is impossible to ignore, which already is inscribed in history.

Let us cast the hidden stones of revenge into an abyss. The name of a Lithuanian obligates us. Let us get to know Christ, our Teacher, our King, and live for the Motherland. Let us learn to conquer our pride and we will find the key to unity, the common language of Lithuanians.

Also Laymen

---

11. Aleksandras Dambrauskas (pseud. Adomas Jakštas) (1860-1938), a poet, scientist, and publicist, an important figure of national awakening. He was among the more tolerant clergy, who saw the need of unity among the differing ideological movements in order to achieve national emancipation.

PART THREE

DOCUMENTS ON RELIGIOUS DISSENT

49. FROM A LETTER TO POPE PIUS XII

Holy Father, Shepherd and Leader of all Catholics, we, the Catholics of the Lithuanian Republic, ask for Your Holiness' intercession. Through the word and order of Our Lord Jesus Christ, you are our Leader and Shepherd. We, who are being persecuted, destroyed, terrorized; hungry, naked, drowning in our own blood; left without even the natural rights of men; isolated completely from the rest of the world—we plead for Your help and care. We are now living through the eighth year of this occupation of terror and oppression. At the risk of our lives, we send You this document of our country's sufferings, showing the shame of the twentieth century's atheism-communism, unmasking in the eyes of the world the base lie about freedom of religion in the USSR. While the horrid oppression of the occupant has not yet destroyed and devoured us, we are writing the real truth, the harsh tragedy of our nation. This document represents the testament of the death of our Motherland.

Eighty-five per cent of the Lithuanian nation is Roman Catholic. The influence of religion was, and still is, very strong. Our nation has a very special devotion to the Blessed Virgin Mary and honors her greatly. Pius XI called Lithuania the Land of Mary. There are countless shrines and crosses on the roads and byways of our land. These crosses are symbols of our nation's suffering. Bolshevism knows well that until it destroys the influence of religion, the nation will resist and will be immune. Its heaviest blow, therefore, is aimed at religion. According to the bolshevik leaders, religion is as opposed to Bolshevism as water is to fire. Thus, all religions

No. 49. Complete Lithuanian text in J. Daumantas-Juozas Lukša, **Partizanai** (Chicago, 1962, 2nd ed.), pp. 432-448. According to the Soviet historian of the Church J. Aničas, the letter was written by "a group of reactionary priests"; see his work **Socialinis politinis Katalikų bažnyčios vaidmuo Lietuvoje 1945-1952 metais,** (Vilnius, 1971), pp. 58-59. The identity of the authors has not been revealed. The letter was brought out to the West by the partisan leader Juozas Lukša at the beginning of 1948 and delivered to Pope Pius XII on October 1, 1948, some eight months after the letter reached the West. The Vatican accepted the letter with some reserve, in part because it was first publicized in the international press before reaching the Papacy. There was no formal or, as far as is known, informal response of the Pope to this appeal for help.

and religious traditions were destroyed in the USSR before the war. In 1943, under different circumstances and in order to improve public opinion and sentiment abroad, freedom was officially granted for the practice of religion, especially to the Russian Orthodox Church. The main motive in this was the desire to unite the Orthodox churches of various nations (Bulgaria, Greece, Rumania etc.), to strengthen the Orthodox Church, and then to use it to spread communistic influence in those countries. Allowing religion to exist temporarily, they made certain that religion would only serve to strengthen Communism, the influence of bolshevik imperialism abroad. The newly appointed priests of the Russian Orthodox Church scarcely differ from NKVD espionage agents. Their role and function is to express and enforce the ideas of the State from the pulpit and to turn in suspects. Listening to the sermons of these priests, one cannot find even a trace of Christian teachings. One merely finds hate for other denominations, revenge, lies and bolshevik propaganda. God is Russian in character, similar to Lenin. The Russian Orthodox Church is only an espionage agency cloaked in the robes of religion.

Stalin's constitution grants freedom only for external religious ceremonies, leaving the road open and clear for all antireligious propaganda. The State continuously blares anti-religious propaganda with all the force of the methods and media that it commands. Officially religions can practice only their rites and ceremonies, but propagation of religious doctrine and ideas is completely forbidden and banned. That is why even today the Russian Orthodox Church in the USSR does not have its own press, except for religious calendars, and sermons are virtually nonexistent. There are and cannot be any religious or philosophical books, newspapers, or periodicals. Religious literature imported from abroad is also banned. In such a setting religion cannot live and flourish, exchange new ideas, and the new generation cannot understand and know religion and theology in the light of new findings, research. In both methodology and experience, all the secular sciences will surpass the dated methods of religion and theology. According to the bolshevik rationale, a few years will pass, the older generations will die out, and the youth, seeing religion's backwardness and lack of progress, will naturally turn its back on it. Experience shows that such reasoning is valid because communication and cooperation with science, art, literature, and the press is necessary for progress in any discipline. The same type of religious freedom is being planned for Lithuania. Catholic priests must become espionage agents, must sever all ties with Rome, must aid the State in every way—in other words, they must become tools of the State. Lithuanian Catholics did not agree to this. That is when the reprehensible terrorization and destruction began. This terrorization is furtive and concealed. Officially, everything is all right, but in reality things are different. It is pleasant and reassuring to hear the powerful politicians of Moscow speak. But behind the scenes other directives and orders are given. The harsher an official is toward religion, the more he is valued. No law restricts him. The orders are to put on pressure, victimize, do whatever one wants, only avoid public scandal. The following are examples of this terrorization:

1. THE NATIONAL CHURCH

Great pressure for the formation of a national church, as in the formerly Polish part of Ukraine, already began in 1944.[1] With promises, intrigues at first, and finally terrible censures and deportations, the government tried to force the clergy, especially the more active priests, into spreading propaganda directed against the hierarchy of the Church, seemingly because of its lack of activity, insinuating the idea of closer cooperation between the Church and the state and thus forming a group of activists which would become the nucleus of the national church. At the same time the official press unceasingly denounced the Pope, writing of his alleged frauds, deceptions, and betrayal: Rome is the nest of abnormals, of hangmen. The Pope was and still is the betrayer of the Lithuanian nation. The Pope is the "Number One Enemy" of all nations and of Lithuania, and so forth. The Lithuanian Ro-

---

1. Evidence on the attempt to form a "national church", i.e. separation from Rome, is meager. The main conflict was over the formation of parish committees, which, at least in theory, would have placed church affairs in secular hands. The Lithuanian hierarchy vigorously opposed the policy. See the account of this conflict in Aničas, **op. cit.**, pp. 17-27; and the monograph **Arkivyskupas Mečislovas Reinys** (Chicago, 1977), pp. 198-218, a study of the life of Archbishop Reinys by an anonymous author in Lithuania.

man Catholics listen because they are forced to, but they hear nothing. The government finds no assistants or stool pigeons.

4. SURVEILLANCE OF PRIESTS

Each priest is under constant surveillance by several persons. The neighboring houses report who visits the priest, with whom he meets. Wherever the priest is a more frequent visitor, someone is engaged to find out what is discussed there. Several agents are present at every sermon. Unaware of each other's identity, they must give resumes of these sermons. If there are variations and any trace of mildness and laxity, the spies are punished. Even a person to whom the priest merely speaks on the street is immediately suspect.

5. TAXATION OF PRIESTS

A priest must pay an income tax to the government. Pastors are taxed as much as 100,000 rubles, vicars up to 50,000 rubles per year. A pastor's tax equals the yearly wages of ten government officials of high rank. If the tax is not paid, the individual is sought out by force. It is not possible to pay this tax because the congregation, although willing, is unable to meet such an exorbitant price. Parishioners normally earn only a tenth of the wages necessary to keep them from dying of hunger; they live by selling off their belongings. Inability to pay the tax results in the seizure and sale of the priest's personal and even liturgical articles. Sale of such articles at government prices does not even pay a small part of the tax. The law allows the government to force the priests to pay off the rest through working on road construction and other public works. Fearful of the people's indignation and reprisals, however, the government has not as yet put this law into effect.

10. TAX ON CHURCHES

Every church is taxed up to 50,000 rubles per year. It is a superhuman effort to collect such a sum from a congregation which can barely keep body and soul together as it is. It would be hard on the priest to announce this from the pulpit. This, as everything in the USSR, is a half-secret. If the tax is not paid, the church property is appraised and often seized. The church is even closed. Some churches of other religions have already been closed.

14. SEMINARIES

In 1944 there were three seminaries. Although even to this day all facilities taken over for military use have not yet been vacated, in 1946 two of these seminaries were closed and the seminarians were allowed to move to the seminary in Kaunas. In that same year the government decreed that Lithuania was to have a maximum quota of 150 seminarians—the rest, about 200, were dismissed. There are hundreds of testimonies that the number of seminarians will be reduced to 60. In such a way Lithuania would obtain eight new priests per year, while each year 25-30 priests die, not counting those arrested and deported. There are parishes even now where three or four pastors have been arrested one after another. Often a single priest serves two or three parishes. Old, invalid priests have returned to their priestly duties and sometimes serve two parishes. The seminaries are financed solely through the offerings of the congregation.

18. THE SITUATION OF THE CONGREGATION

A worker or clerk who is known to be Catholic is tormented in every possible way. He never attains a higher position or gets a better job. He is tolerated only because of the shortage of labor. The Lithuanian farmer is especially religious. Working on his plot of land, he is fairly inaccessible to government agents. There were very few rich farmers in Lithuania. Most were poor, working from morning to night to earn their living. But the bolshevik land reform affected even this hardworking farmer. The government accused him of cooperating with the Germans or of something similar and seized his land, even though it often was already seeded. Because of minor offenses, often fabricated, he is called "a kulak." The "kulaks" are protected by no law. Every true Lithuanian is a "kulak," regardless of whether he is a farmer or a laborer or an old invalid. The farmer is patient, enduring much just to be able to work on his own plot of land. No matter how much he is pressured and abused by the government, he can manage to hide one thing or another and can therefore live better than people of other professions. That is why in 1947 the government plans to force all farmers into collective farms, so that each would earn a meager living and would not concern himself with anything else. In this way the farmer would be more easily controllable and malleable and the government would profit even more. In the USSR all belongs to the state; there is no such thing as private property. Everyone—farmer, laborer, or clerk must "steal" from the government if he does not want to die of hunger. Wages are small, enough for only a few days. The people therefore steal whenever they have a chance. Under the circumstances, this is no disgrace.

21. THE RESULTS OF PERSECUTION

The results of this three-year Lithuanian religious-national resistance are grave and terrifying. Oppression, fear, bloodshed, and suffering exist everywhere. More than 100,000 have died from torture or from the cold and hunger in Siberia. New victims are found every day. There is no home in which tears have not been shed. Forty per cent of the priests, that is more than 400, have gone underground or are in Siberia.[2] Only one free bishop remains in all of Lithuania. Two bishops died (Karevičius and Karosas) and four were arrested and imprisoned: Borisevičius, Matulionis, Ramanauskas, and Reinys.[3] The curia is suppressed, the seminary barely functioning, the convents and monasteries destroyed or scattered. No one knows when the police may come. So that no word would leak abroad, everything is done very quietly.

---

2. The precise number of priests exiled is not known. One source has compiled a list of 310 priests who were exiled from Lithuania, about half of whom eventually returned. This would constitute about 25-30 per cent of the priests remaining in Lithuania after the war. See Matas Raišupis, **Dabarties kankiniai** (Chicago, 1972), p. 429.

3. After 1947 only one bishop remained in his post. Kazimieras Paltarokas (1875-1958), Bishop of Panevėžys, was the only bishop to escape repression and to remain in his post until his death. Bishop Pranciškus Karevičius died in 1945 and Bishop Antanas Karosas died in 1947. Vincas Borisevičius (1887-1947), Bishop of Telšiai, was executed by the Soviet regime in January of 1947 for alleged participation in the nationalist underground. Archbishop Teofilis Matulionis (1873-1962), Bishop of Kaišiadorys, was exiled from Lithuania until 1956. He was not permitted to resume his duties upon the return to Lithuania. Pranciškus Ramanauskas (1893-1959), Bishop of Telšiai, was also exiled to

This is how Stalin's Constitution grandly guarantees freedom of religion in practice. Everything is done only for purposes of propaganda abroad. In reality there is no freedom of religion, just as there is no freedom for any individual in the USSR. Even if the government gives some ray of hope, a slight indication of more freedom, this is done only to strengthen Communism and to improve foreign opinion. In practice the harsher strictures are not as terrifying as the daily fear of provocation, the constant spying, and the frightening uncertainty.

Three years have passed since this deadly battle began. We fight and resist in every possible way. If we had not resisted, we would not exist today. Thousands of our youth, men, young women, and even old people are already hiding in the forests. The occupants fear the forests. There alone can we find freedom...

Holy Father, we know that in these troubled times you are burdened by many cares. Yet, because of the suffering that we have endured, we dare to ask You, as our Leader, for intercession and aid. We no longer have neighbors whom we can trust with our own and our nation's future. The occupant surrounds us from all sides. Led by Your Holiness, we, the children of Catholic Lithuania, are the only remaining Catholics in the North—an island surrounded by other denominations. We will not be able to endure such pressure for long. We will all perish. Our faith, our traditions, our customs, even our language will be destroyed. We often think of the invasions of the Turk and Arab hordes during the Middle Ages, when such great Roman leaders as Urban II and Innocent III arose. The hordes from the East today do not fear diplomatic words and fine speeches. We often ask ourselves where the nations of our Western culture have disappeared, where are the millions of Catholics? Are there no more lovers and champions of truth in the world, no more great men? Do they not know how their fellow Catholics are being persecuted? Have the world's Catholics fallen asleep with the

---

Siberia, returned to Lithuania in 1956, but was not permitted to return to his pastoral duties. Mečislovas Reinys (1884-1953), Archbishop of Vilnius, was sent to Vladimir prison, where he died in 1953. The bishops were repressed for a combination of reasons, including alleged involvement in the nationalist underground and the opposition to the establishment of secular controls over the Church.

deceptive slumber of tranquilization and assuagement? Do
they believe that these hordes will stop once they have destroyed us? No. In the USSR two hundred million people of
every national background, such as we, are making weapons
day and night for the conquest of the entire world. Even today
the weapons we have made aid the rebels in Greece and the
strikers throughout the world. Even today this Asiatic con-
queror has enslaved half of the world and is reshaping it to suit
his tastes. The time for the final struggle between East and
West—the time of woe for the hypnotized and the sleeping—
will soon come. Bolshevism is prepared to annihilate the civi-
lizations of the world, its culture and its Christianity. Let us
not be deceived: Bolshevism only awaits a suitable moment.
Let us not mislead ourselves: Bolshevism is stronger than many
think. Atomic power soothes the fears of the West, but Bolshevism will soon have weapons equally potent and powerful.

Holy Father,

1. We ask You to declare a Lithuanian Day for the
world's Catholics, as your revered predecessor Benedict XV did
in 1917.[4] Let the world see the suffering of the Lithuanian
Catholics, their woe and persecutions at the hands of twentieth
century atheism.

2. We beg of Your Holiness a public word of sympathy
and hope to the Lithuanian nation. We endure immense suffering for union with You, Your Holiness. Holy Father, say a
word of comfort as once the first Pope, St. Peter, did in Rome's
Coliseum. Holy Father, we are suffering no less for our Holy
Mother the Roman Catholic Church.

3. We ask you to bring our plea in some manner before
the United Nations. Perhaps the nations of the world will end
our suffering.

4. We ask you to increase the broadcasts of the Lithu-
anian radio hour.[5] Let it give more news of our persecution.
Are we, who are dying for our holy faith, not worthy of this?
Indeed, 100,000 of our nation were tortured to death or await

---

4. Pope Benedict XV (1854-1922) was very active in organizing
aid for war devastated countries. He gave a direct monetary contribution
to Lithuania and declared a "Lithuanian Day" for church collections
throughout the world.

5. A Lithuanian language program of the Vatican radio has been
continuously broadcast from 1940 to the present.

death in Siberia mostly because they refused to give up the faith of their forefathers and their nation, and did not betray their fellow Lithuanians.

Holy Father, we hope and trust that you will hear our plea. We have endured and suffered much, very much, for our faith, for our loyalty to the Apostolic See. That is why we have hope that You will intercede for us and aid us. We are dying, but dying we wish to hear a word of comfort from You and from the world's Catholics—so that our children will no longer have to endure this slavery of their souls. We hope that Your influential and powerful word will shake the leaders of the nations that love freedom and truth from their sleep. Holy Father, our letter is not up to our standards. We are writing it in the underground, by flickering lamp-light, expecting the police at any moment. We are purposely not mentioning the time and the place because we are unwilling to give the police any data. When this letter reaches you, perhaps we will no longer be alive. Many of those who bear this letter will be felled by the shots of the NKVD.

Holy Father, give Your blessing to us who are dying for the freedom of our religion and our nation.

May Jesus Christ, the Lord of the Living and the Dead, reign forever.

The Roman Catholics of the Republic of Lithuania, Vilnius,

Occupied Lithuania, September 20, 1947.

50. A STATEMENT BY REV. VLADAS ŠLEVAS

FROM THE ARCHIVES OF THE CHRONICLE OF THE CATHOLIC CHURCH IN LITHUANIA

On Aug. 7, 1968, the Rev. V. Šlevas sent the following statement to the Chairman of the Council of Ministers of the USSR, Comrade Kosygin:

"The Lithuanian SSR is a country of believers. At present it has about three million residents. About two million believe in God and make use of religious services. Neither the priests nor the faithful, as a rule, oppose the present system of government. (Diplomatic phraseology—Ed.) The Lithuanian people are industrious, honest, zealous, and friendly, as well as disciplined. However, we note that some of the officials of our Republic restrict some of our activities and we feel their performance is somewhat deficient. For this reason I turn to you, Honorable Prime Minister, and request your assistance and support in the name of all priests and believers.

1. There are about 800 churches with priests in the Lithuanian SSR. In a country with six dioceses there is only one seminary, while previously there were three. Only about 30 seminarians are allowed to attend this sole seminary. Only about five or six priests are ordained each year. But what is their impact on six dioceses? Between 25 and 30 priests per year die or leave their posts because of ill health. Parishes which have lost their leaders suffer most. This groundless limitation severely restricts the Catholics' freedom of religion, thus violating the laws of the Soviet Union.

Moreover, certain government officials interfere with the ordination of seminarians who have completed their studies. Spiritual leaders are not allowed to complete this process without official permission. (That is, ordain new priests—Ed.) That is intolerable; it is arbitrary.

2. Electricity is used in the churches of the Lithuanian SSR as in other buildings. It is still unclear to us why the church has to pay such a high fee for its electric power. Col-

No. 50. **Chronicle**, No. 9 (1974). Editorial notes in the text of this document were added by the editors of the **Chronicle**.

lective farmers pay four kopeks per kilowatt for their power. Collective farms pay one kopek per kilowatt for power used in the common endeavors of the farm. The church, which is supported by these very same collective farmers as well as other people, has to pay as much as 25 kopeks per kilowatt. Why this is so, we do not know.

3. Lithuanian believers do not have any prayer books. Some have gotten old; others are worn out. A good new prayer book (*A Liturgical Prayer Book*—Ed.) is now ready for publication. A publication permit has been obtained, but its appearance has been repeatedly delayed on the pretext of a paper shortage.

I believe in your sincerity, your friendliness to our nation and its believers. For this reason we await your cordial assistance. We are convinced that the limitations on candidates for the seminary will be abolished, that payments for electricity will be equalized with those of the collective farmers, at four kopeks per kilowatt; we also sincerely believe a new prayer book will soon be printed and will be freely circulated among the believers in Lithuania.

With my highest esteem, gratitude, and hope,

Rev. V. Šlevas.

A similar statement was sent to the government of the USSR by the Rev. Alfonsas Pridotkas, the pastor of Batakiai.

On Oct. 5, 1968, the chairman of Skaudvilė area informed Father Šlevas that on October 7 he is to call on Rugienis, the Representative of the Council for Religious Affairs.

On October 7, both "criminals," Fathers V. Šlevas and Alfonsas Pridotkas called on Rugienis, who angrily scolded the priests and threatened them.

Soon after the "visit" with Rugienis, both priests were transferred to other parishes.

At that time when the clergy of Lithuania began sending their first statements to the Soviet government, members of the clergy and believers in all of the dioceses of the country agreed with the idea that it is necessary to fight for one's faith. Many regretted that much time had been spent without taking any action.

51. A STATEMENT BY THE CATHOLIC CLERGY OF LITHUANIA

To: The Chairman of the USSR Council of Ministers
Copies to: 1. The Chairman of the Lithuanian SSR Council of Ministers
2. Catholic Church leaders in Lithuania
From: The Priests of the Catholic Church in Lithuania

A STATEMENT

In his article "To the Rural Poor," Lenin, generalizing the tasks of the Social Democratic Party, wrote: "The Social-Democrats further demand that everybody shall have a full and unrestricted right to profess any religion he pleases." (Lenin, *Collected Works*, Moscow, 1961, VI:404)

In criticizing the government of the czar and the means used against those who had different beliefs, Lenin wrote: "Everybody must be perfectly free not only to profess whatever religion he pleases, but also to disseminate or change his religion... that is a matter for each person's conscience and no one has any right to interfere." *(Ibid.)*

The USSR Constitution guarantees to its citizens freedom to practice any religion. The laws of the Soviet Union will defend the rights of the faithful to practice their religious rites. Article 143 of the Penal Code speaks about the penalties for anyone who interferes in the exercise of these rights. But in reality it is not so. The laws which protect the rights of the faithful are violated without consideration. The Catholic Church in Lithuania is condemned to die. The facts speak about this. When in 1940 there were four seminaries for priests in Lithuania and about 1,500 priests, after 1944, there was only one seminary left, in Kaunas. About 400 seminarians flocked to it from all the dioceses. In 1946, in the very middle of the school year, only 150 seminarians were permitted to stay. During the last few years in all the five courses in the seminary the limit is 30 seminarians. If a seminarian leaves or gets sick, no one is allowed to take his place. About 30 priests die in Lithuania every year, but only 5 or 6 are ordained. Already

---

No. 51. AS No. 766. Quotations from Lenin which could be traced are from the English version of the official edition of **Collected Works**.

at this time many priests have to serve in two parishes. There
is a good number of parishes where the pastor is 70 years
old. Even invalids have to serve as pastors, for instance, in
Turmantai.

Young men who want to enter the seminary encounter
many more difficulties than those who intend to go to other
schools of higher education. The candidates are not chosen by
the representatives of the Church, but by the officials of the
government. This is not normal. What would we say if candidates for music would be selected by veterinarians or other
specialists?

In January of 1969 the priests of the diocese of Vilkaviškis
addressed themselves to the Chairman of the USSR Council
of Ministers concerning this abnormal situation in the interdiocesan seminary in Kaunas.[1] During the month of February
of the same year they contacted the still-active bishops and
administrators of the dioceses about this same matter.[2] Because
of these actions, two priests, Rev. S. Tamkevičius and Rev. J.
Zdebskis, lost their work certificates. They had to seek other work;
they cannot perform their priestly duties.

In 1940 there were 12 bishops in Lithuania, today there
are only two left: Bishop Matulaitis-Labukas, born in 1894, and
Bishop J. Pletkus, born in 1895.[3] Two still effective and able
bishops have been exiled to distant parishes: J. Steponavičius
(for 9 years) and V. Sladkevičius (more than 10 years), although according to Articles 62-69 of the Penal Code deportation for a maximum of five years is prescribed, and only
for grave offenses.[4] But what have our shepherds done, to be

---

1. Text of the letter in AS No. 768, dated January 8, 1969.

2. Probably a reference to the letter of the priests of the Diocese of
Vilkaviškis, dated December 31, 1968. Text in AS No. 769.

3. Bishop Matulaitis-Labukas was consecrated in Rome in December
of 1965 when he was in attendance at the Vatican Council meetings.
Presently he acts as the head of the Lithuanian bishops conference.
Bishop Juozas Pletkus of Telšiai was consecrated in February of
1968, died in September of 1975.

4. The cases of bishops Steponavičius and Sladkevičius are presented
in Doc. No. 61 and 67. Articles 62-69 of the Lithuanian SSR Penal Code
deal with "crimes against the state". The two bishops have not been
charged, tried, or convicted for any crime although in fact they have
been exiled from their dioceses, Bishop Steponavičius since 1961 and
Bishop Sladkevičius since 1958.

punished for an indeterminate time without any court action or proved guilt?

From time immemorial Vilnius has been the center of religious life, but today this city is not allowed to have its own bishop, even though other smaller religious communities, the Orthodox, for instance, have their bishop, and others an equivalent religious leader.

According to the Church Canon Law, the capitular vicars are only temporary administrators who are chosen when a bishop dies or leaves office. The Archdiocese of Vilnius and the Diocese of Panevėžys now have been administered by capitular vicars for 9 years, and that of Kaišiadorys for 23 years.

It is not always, even for those who have official authorization, that the bishops and administrators are permitted to visit the parishes and confer the Sacrament of Confirmation according to the canons of the Church. In the Diocese of Panevėžys this sacrament has been conferred only once since 1961. In other dioceses it is permitted to be conferred only in the centers, for instance, in Vilnius or Kaunas but very rarely in the regional cities. Those who want to receive the Sacrament of Confirmation have to travel from distant places, endure all the hardships with their small children. Thus, great pressures and difficulties are created.

The pastoral work of the priests is being hindered in a number of ways: one is not allowed to help the neighboring parishes in religious services nor to invite the necessary number of priests on special occasions of devotion. The faithful who want to confess have to wait for a long time, suffer inconvenience, and lose much of their precious time. On special days of devotion in some churches about 1000 people come for confession. If only three minutes would be given to each penitent, one priest would have to hear confessions for 50 hours, and this is impossible.

Specialists in all fields come together for conferences to perfect themselves and learn from the experience of others. Church Canon Law also requires that the priests should make a three-day retreat at least every three years. Such retreats at this time are forbidden not only at the diocesan centers, but also in the deaneries: even priests of one deanery are not permitted to meet.

Official representatives of the government (the Representative of the Council for Religious Affairs, leaders of raions and districts) give various directives to the priests by word of mouth only. It happens that these orders contradict one another. For instance, a representative of the chairman of the executive committee of Varėna raion forbade the pastor of Valkininkai to accompany a funeral procession to the cemetery, while a representative for religious affairs declared that the priest can accompany a procession to the cemetery, but he cannot do it from the home to the church. On April 15, 1969, the representative for religious affairs in Švenčionėliai, in the presence of government officials and the members of the church committee, told the pastor that when there is a priest in the procession of the deceased, no hymns are allowed, but this can be done without the priests. If a person is buried with religious rites, an orchestral procession is not permitted, collective farms and organizations cannot help materially.

Catholics in Lithuania cannot avail themselves of the freedom of the press for their religious needs. They cannot make use of the radio and television, of movie theaters, schools, lectures. We do not possess even the most elementary religious textbook, prayerbook, or other religious writings. During the Soviet period not even one catechism was printed. Only in 1955 and 1958 was a *Catholic Prayer Book* printed and in 1968 a *Liturgical Prayer Book*. However, both editions had a very limited number of copies so that only a few families could acquire them. Besides, the *Liturgical Prayer Book* was supposed to include a short explanation of the truths of the faith, but the representative for religious affairs would not allow this to be printed. The priests and the churches received only one copy of the *Roman Catholic Ritual* and *Resolutions of the Second Vatican Council* were available only for the priests, one copy each. The faithful do not even have a chance to see these books.[5]

---

5. During the Soviet rule, the following religious books have been published: Katalikų maldaknygė (Catholic Prayer Book) by Rev. Dr. J. Stankevičius, 1957; **Romos katalikų apeigynas Lietuvos vyskupijoms** (Roman Catholic Ritual for the Dioceses of Lithuania), in two parts and a supplement, 1966; **II Vatikano susirinkimo nutarimai, konstitucijos, dekretai, deklaracijos** (Resolutions, Constitutions, Decrees, Declarations of the Second Vatican Council), 1968; **Liturginis maldynas**(Liturgical Prayer Book), 1968; **Naujasis testamentas** (The New Testament), 1972;

Although the USSR Constitution guarantees freedom of conscience, and parents do want and request that their children would be educated in a religious spirit, the priests and the catechists, however, are forbidden to prepare children for their First Communion. The Representative of the Council for Religious Affairs allows the children to be examined only individually. Those who do not follow this unwritten law are severely punished. For instance, the government officials have fined Rev. J. Fabijanskas for catechization; Rev. M. Gylys and Rev. J. Zdebskis were sent to a forced labor camp. In Anykščiai O. Paškevičiūtė prepared children for their first confession. For this she was deported to a forced labor camp, where she suffered exhaustion, sickness, and death. Parents themselves have the right to prepare their children, but they have no means to do so: they are not prepared for this job, have no time or religious books. In like manner, during the czar's reign, workers and serfs could not make use of the right to give their children a higher education.

Children who frequent the church experience much abuse. They are made fun of, wall newspapers write about them. In schools, children are constantly taught that religious parents are backward, have no knowledge, and can give them no directives. Thus, the authority of the parents is destroyed. When children cease to respect their parents, it is difficult to control them both in school and outside. Besides, religiously minded children are not allowed to take an active part in the liturgy, sing in the choir, participate in processions, or serve Mass. Thus, the rights of believing children and parents are severely violated. They are harshly discriminated against, coerced, and forced to compromise others. For instance, on the 26th of December, 1967, the secondary school principal Baranauskas and other teachers in Švenčionėliai kept the II-VI class students for two and a half hours to force them to write letters against the local pastor Rev. Laurinavičius. An ambulance had to be called for one of those youngsters, J. Gaila, because of the threats. Second-grade student K. Jarmalis was sick for a couple of months because of fear. The pastor, who had allowed the chil-

---

Psalmynas (The Book of Psalms), 1973. The number of copies printed, normally indicated in Soviet publications, is not given for any of these publications. All were issued in very limited editions. For example, Chronicle, No. 6 (1973) claims that only 10,000 copies of The New Testament were printed, or approximately 10 copies per parish.

dren to serve Mass and participate in a procession, was removed from Švenčionėliai. The offended parents of those children turned to Moscow. How much time was lost, expenses incurred, health impaired? Just recently Rev. A. Deltuva was fined 50 rubles because he allowed children to serve Mass. According to the law, the convictions of one who believes and one who does not should be equally respected, but practice goes its own way. In many hospitals, for instance, in Vilnius, Utena, Pasvalys, and Anykščiai, even when sick people ask to receive the sacraments, their request is refused. In 1965 a driver, K. Semėnas, and Miss B. Sudeikytė married in a church. By this act they lost their previous grant of a piece of land where they were going to build a house. Notwithstanding the fact that all the material was bought for the construction, they were told: "Let the priest give you land."

In Pasvalys, Anykščiai, and other places, even taxicabs may not bring the witness of the marrying couple to the church. There is much suffering for the intellectuals, who secretly baptize their children, marry, or attend Mass in church. These facts are brought up at their place of work; often they are reprimanded or even lose their jobs. For instance, in 1965, P. Cicėnaitė, a school teacher in Daugeliškis, was released from her job by the school director because she would not forsake the church. When the school officials told her to leave, she, wishing to have her book "clean," wrote a request to be released from work Often the faithful are released from work or are punished because of their convictions, covering this fact with some other motives.

In 1956 the Pension Act bypassed the servants of the church. Organists and sacristans can only dream about pensions. For instance, P. Pagalskas joined a collective farm when the Soviets came to Lithuania. As all other citizens, he delivered his horse and farming tools to the authorities. He was working in the office of a collective farm as an accountant; on Sundays he played the organ in the church. When he had the misfortune to get sick and became an invalid and could not work in the office, he became a night watchman on a collective farm. When he reached old age (b. in 1889), he applied to the Social Welfare Office of the Ignalina raion. An answer came back from this office that organists do not receive any pension.

Many of the churches are not allowed to ring bells, use

loudspeakers, or any other technical means. Materials are not allotted for the upkeep of the churches. The cities are growing, but since 1945 only two churches have been built in Lithuania (one of which, in Klaipėda, has been turned into a music hall), many older churches are serving as storage places, museums, and so forth.[6]

These and many other painful facts which we have mentioned here show that the priests and the faithful are discriminated against and that they cannot fully use those rights which the USSR Constitution guarantees them.

Consequently, we have dared to address ourselves to you, Mr. Chairman of the USSR Council of Ministers, hoping that you will correct this unnatural situation of the Catholic Church in the Lithuanian SSR and see to it that we, the Lithuanian priests and faithful, will be able to exercise the rights prescribed in the Constitution as all other citizens do.

The priests of the Archdiocese of Vilnius: (40 signatures).

August 1969

---

6. The case of the Klaipėda church which was transformed into a philharmonic hall is reported in **Chronicle**, No. 2 (1972) and No. 4 (1972). The second new church built during the Soviet rule has not been identified. **Chronicle**, No. 18 (August 31, 1975) supplies a list of churches which have been closed or converted to various other functions.

52. THE DEFENSE SPEECH OF REV. ANTANAS ŠEŠKEVIČIUS

Penal Case No. 5817

The Accused Rev. Antanas Šeškevičius, son of Kazimieras, born in 1914

DEFENSE IN COURT

In the raion of Molėtai, on July 27, 1970, the prosecutor has accused me as follows: "Šeškevičius, at the close of the month of June and at the beginning of July 1970, collected the children of Dubingiai parish in the church and there instructed them in the catechism. This is in direct violation of the established statutes and, in particular, against the Penal Code of the Lithuania SSR, Article 143, section 1."

To this I reply:

1. As a priest, I am authorized by the precept of Christ-God: "Go, therefore, and make disciples of all nations and teach them to observe all the commands I gave you." (Matt. 28:19 20).

2. The Church, through Canon 1329, likewise authorizes me: "One of the more serious and personal obligations of the priest is to teach the children their catechism." Therefore, for me it is a clear case of duty in conscience to teach all people all of Christ's revealed truths, which includes catechism for children.

3. The Constitution of the Lithuanian SSR, in its basic statute, Article 96, guarantees: "The freedom for all citizens to fulfill their religious cult."

For the Catholic Church the essence of religious cult resides in the preaching of Christ's teachings, offering the Holy Sacrifice of the Mass, and in the administration of the Sacraments. In a word, the Constitution grants freedom to

---

No. 52. Excerpts from AS No. 882. The trial of Rev. Šeškevičius is described in detail in AS No. 652; see also AS Nos. 653, 654, 655, 656 for other relevant documents. The trial of Rev. Šeškevičius was the first case involving the catechization of children which was widely reported in the West. It can be considered as the beginning of a civil disobedience campaign of dissident priests which led to widely publicized trials of clergy and the emergence of the dissident press—the **Chronicle of the Catholic Church in Lithuania.** Rev. Šeškevičius was convicted and sentenced to prison for one year.

practice these three religious functions. Therefore, the priest, in accordance with his conscience, has the full right to preach Christ's teachings to adults as well as to children, while, at the same time, both adults and children have the full right to develop religious knowledge and receive the Sacraments, as this is essential to the fulfillment of their religious cult. For example, how can a priest permit a child to approach the Sacraments, of which he is desirous, but of which he has no understanding? It is the duty of the priest to instruct this child. According to the Constitution, the priest has the right to prepare children to receive the Sacraments and it is he, and not the parents or others, who is responsible for the administration of the Sacraments as well as teaching the specially prepared truths of faith necessary for the worthy reception of the Sacraments. Certainly, parents and others can and should assist the priest in this regard, but the final word is that of the priest.

Therefore, I, as a priest, according to the Constitution, have the right to fulfill this duty in conscience—to ascertain the religious knowledge of the children and to instruct them in the truths of the faith, which instruction could not and would not have been obtained from other sources. It is for this reason that the faithful support the priest with their contributions—that he might render them service in matters of religion, including the instruction of their children.

4. Even though the Constitution guarantees freedom in the practice of religious cult, nevertheless, for doing this, I am put on trial today; having employed this freedom of cult, I am considered guilty and in jeopardy of imprisonment according to the Penal Code, Article 143, Section 1, which states that there is a separation of Church and State and School and Church.

Since this statute is not clear, therefore, it seems to me, there is need to present the clarification made by the Presidium of the Supreme Soviet of the Lithuanian SSR, especially in regard to this particular section: "To clarify the statute concerning the separation of Church and State, and Church and School, violation of which would draw penalties on the Church according to Article 143 of the Penal Code of the Soviet Socialist Republic of Lithuania, we understand this to mean: 'The systematic implementation, through the process of organization, of inculcating religious teachings in minors' ".

In actuality this clarification is never mentioned in the bill of accusation. Moreover, in no way am I guilty of violating this statute, for:

1. I did not in any way undertake to organize religious instructions; I did not visit among the children; I did not register them; I did not devise a plan or a curriculum, nor did I designate a time for teaching. If, through sermons to the parents, who were preparing their children for the first Sacraments, I mentioned, and, as a priest, I was duty-bound to do so, that those children, who were ready for the first Sacraments, would be examined on a special day before the evening devotions, this does not, in view of the statute, establish the sense of organization, but was simply an announcement for those who were interested, that their children may receive the first Sacraments. If I mentioned a designated time, it meant that I would be available from that time on and not in any sense did it mean all should come together at that hour and leave together at the conclusion. And thus it was that some came at the mentioned time, others at a later time and still others at a later time, or even at another time. In the bill of accusation I am accused in this manner: "Šeškevičius would gather the children of Dubingiai parish in the church." In a word, I am accused of organizing the children. However, there is no indication in the presentation of the case to show how I gathered the children. On the contrary, in the very bill of accusation, a multitude of witnesses have testified that parents and children came to the church, that whoever wanted to came to the church, even the Chairman and the Secretary of the Executive Committee for the Molėtai raion came to the church, as well as Chairman Leisys of Dubingiai, and all found the priest in church, yet no one has testified that they found him teaching the children in the school, or in the city, or in the town. According to the law of the Church, the priest is obliged to give service to whoever comes to the church and requests this of him. He cannot reject them if they come for his service.

The bill of accusation further points out that 17 children were found in the church. On Sundays one would find many more children, and one would hear the priest preaching the very same catechetical matter, but then, could it be said that he collects the children? Should a case be made against him for this?

2. The law states: "The systematic implementation of religious instruction." In no manner did I ever institute systematic instructions. This is done in schools; each day, according to prescript, there is the regular taking of attendance, an ascertainment of progress in knowledge, reports are made and instruction and homework are given according to a syllabus. In no way did I do this; here, all transpired on chance occurrence; there were no reports; no examinations; no systematic instructions; no homework; no syllabus; the children did not even have catechism books.

Therefore, to instruct systematically would be an impossibility. I am further accused of instructing the children on five different occasions. Even these occasions were not on a daily basis, but on happenstance occurrences. At most, the ascertainment of the children's knowledge would last for about a half hour. In this short period of time it is next to impossible to establish a judgement, much less to talk about systematic instructions.

I examined the children's knowledge of the fundamental truths according to the norms laid down by the Diocesan Curia which indicate: "If children do not sufficiently understand, the priest is obliged to make the matter clear." (Archdiocese of Kaunas, Dioceses of Kaišiadorys and Vilkaviškis, Curia Stipulation No. 1874, issued Oct. 11, 1954). And this was my method of procedure. If a priest did not clarify that which parents or children did not understand, then the children would not be able to receive the Sacraments for lack of fundamental and essential knowledge. If, on occasion, several children would present themselves together, this would be a chance occurrence; it could have been that no one would come; some came at one time, others at other times. If more came at one time, I could not dismiss them.

To take each one separately to some other room was next to impossible, as our church is in a residential building with very little privacy. Also, if I had taken each child to some other place, I would have been accused of instructing the children secretly, in a private chamber. All that I did was done in the church and at a rapid pace so as not to detain the parents from their labors. Therefore, for the five examination periods in no manner can I be accused of giving systematic instructions. To prepare children to receive the first Sacraments within a time-period of a few weeks on chance occasions cannot be termed systematic, even though the priest has the right to do so according to the Constitution. If my procedure can be called systematic, what then is non-systematic? One says a few words and the label—systematic—is attached, a school is in progress, and one must stand trial in violation of Article 143.

3. There is another condition to be met for the statute to be violated: "That the instructions are in transgression of the statute's established rules." In other words, the organization of children for religious instruction and the systematic implementation of this is forbidden if there is a violation of the statute's established rules. If there is no violation of rules, then there is no ban. If so, then non-systematic instructions would be permissible. Now just what is the preparation of children for first Holy Communion?

I did not violate any rules, as there are none to violate. Having been away from Lithuania for the past 20 years, I have not been in the practice of preparing children for first Holy Communion. This being the first instance, due to the shortness of time, that I have initiated the examination of their knowledge, I could have made mistakes and I would have been grateful to anyone who would have made this known to me or warned me. No one did so, and then, later, asking some of my confreres about these rules, not one was aware of them and, therefore, could not tell me anything about them. How can anyone violate rules when no one knows of them and which were never promulgated? Even now, while I stand here being judged, I would wish that you, Sirs, the official representatives of the government, make known what these rules are and when they were promulgated, in order that the citizens could uphold them.

Logically, in accordance with the stated clarification, one must conclude that there are several established statutes, for mention is made of "statutes" and not "statute," and, as a consequence, there must be several rules, not just one; for, "rules" are mentioned. They must be rules *(pravila)*, and not instructions. When this case was being established against me, I was read an instruction in the Russian language regarding the institution of the statutes for religious cults, given on March 16, 1961 *(Instrukciy po primeneniy zakonodatelstva o kul-*

tach ot 16 marta 1961 g.), which has no statutory validity in the Republic of Lithuania, as it was not promulgated by the Supreme Soviet. How can citizens uphold these instructions if they are not aware of them? Every Republic has its own Constitution, with specifically affixed articles and its own penal code, and for this reason, all statutes which are to be validly binding must be promulgated by the Presidium of the Supreme Soviet of the Republic of Lithuania, for the 23rd Article of the Constitution states: "The Supreme Soviet of the Lithuanian SSR is the sole law-making organ of the Lithuanian SSR."

Had I known of these rules, I would have taken note of them. But there were no rules. And any instructions or rules which are secluded in the confines of one's pocket or kept in a desk drawer, have no legal binding force, as is evident to anyone.

Therefore, I did not undertake to organize religious instructions, did not systematically instruct the children, and did not violate any promulgated rules regarding the statutes. For these reasons, I am not guilty of violating Article 143, Section 1. This is also evident from the testimony of the witnesses.

5. Art. 143(1), the violation of which I am accused of, is not to be interpreted haphazardly, but in accordance with Lenin's principles. And he, even as far back as 1902-03, stated: "The Social-Democrats further demand that everybody shall have a full and unrestricted right to profess any religion he pleases." Each one has the right not only to profess his chosen faith, but also to propagate that faith (Lenin, *Collected Works,* Moscow, 1961, VI:404). In the light of this, so much the more is the priest permitted to fulfill his duties.

In the decree for the separation of Church and State and School from Church, as published on Jan. 23, 1918, the ninth paragraph states: "The School is separated from the Church. It is forbidden to teach religious truths in all governmental and public schools as well as in private schools where general subjects are taught. Citizens may teach and be taught religion privately."

In accordance with this decree, which was never abrogated, it is forbidden to teach religion in public, governmental, and private schools where general subjects are taught. Therefore, again in accordance with this decree, the preparation of children for First Communion is fully permissible.

This is confirmed by the practice prevalent in other fraternal Socialist Republics which uphold Leninism. For example: in Poland, in Democratic Germany, in Hungary, in Czechoslovakia—everywhere, religion is systematically taught in churches or in buildings attached to churches. No obstacles are placed for the instruction of children in preparation for first Holy Communion, and priests are completely free to teach catechism. They truly embody the principles of Lenin and no one brings them to trial. But, in our own land, where we profess full freedom of conscience and religious liberty, where Lenin's teachings are a basic foundation, priests are accused and brought to trial for fulfilling their duties, and that, not a complete fulfillment, but only an attempt at it.

6. The United Nations accepted the Declaration of Human Rights on December 10, 1948, to which the Soviet Union also subscribed by becoming a cosigner. The 18th Article of the Declaration states: "Everyone has the right of freedom of thought, conscience and religion; this right includes freedom... either alone or in a community with others, in public or private, to manifest his religion or belief in teaching, practice, worship and observance."

Our government, in accepting the Declaration, thus also accepted: "To manifest his religion or belief in teaching," but why is this not put into practice? According to the subscribed Declaration, it is permissible not only to catechize, but to instruct in matters of faith, for every person has the right to learn of his faith. And I am on trial because I tested the religious knowledge of several children and proffered a few words of explanation to those in need.

According to this, not only should there not be a case against me, but there should be a freedom for all to be instructed in their faith outside the limits of the school classroom.

7. In the United Nations meeting in Paris on December 14-15, 1960, the Convention against Discrimination in Education was drafted. It was ratified by the Presidium of the Supreme Soviet of the USSR on July 2, 1962, and received legal status on November 1, 1962. It was promulgated in *Vedemosti Verkhovnovo Soveta SSSR* in No. 44, 1962, and also in *Vyriausybės Žinios*.

Article 1(2) of the Convention states that "the term 'education' refers to all types and levels of education."

Article 5 states: "The States Parties to this Convention agree that: (b) It is essential to respect the liberty of parents and, where applicable, of legal guardians to choose... the religious and moral education of the children in conformity with their own convictions."

In the light of this Convention, how can parents insure for their children a religious and moral training, when the priest is forbidden to employ even a few words of explanation in matters not clear at the time either to the parents or the children? For this the priest is brought to trial by that government which ratified that Convention...

The Convention in itself is not contrary to Article 143, for it forbids, just as Lenin did, the teaching of religion in schools, but it says nothing of forbidding the teaching of religion privately in churches...

Therefore, in accordance with the Constitution, with the principles of Leninism, and with our international commitments, teaching religion privately is permissible. At the same time, in accordance with the establishment of general rights, there can be no practice contrary to the Constitution. If this were so, then the Constitution would give with one hand and contrary practice would take it away with the other, and the Constitution would become only an array of beautiful words...

53. THE CASE OF REV. JUOZAS ZDEBSKIS

Every summer thousands of Lithuanian mothers prepare their children for their first confession and Holy Communion. This is an arduous and very responsible task that demands from both parents and priests a great deal of dedication. Soviet regulations forbid priests to teach children, so that the atheists may more easily sow the seeds of their ideas. Some priests, having experienced the reign of Stalinist terror, do not want conflicts with the government and confine themselves only to the examination of children. Other priests are brave and listen to God rather than man; at the risk of their freedom, they teach children the foundations of faith.

In the large Prienai parish, about 300 children are prepared every year for their First Communion. So it was in 1971. On July 16, the children, together with their mothers, met in the Prienai church for catechism lessons. While Father Zdebskis was teaching and questioning the children, a band of functionaries forced their way into the church. They photographed the children, asked their last names and drew up a statement. A commotion developed in the church. Angered at the behavior of the Soviet officials, the parents of Prienai addressed the Control Commission of the Central Committee of the CPSU...

This statement was signed by 89 parents and was sent to Moscow. Unfortunately, Moscow did not reply to the Catholics of Prienai.

The office of the prosecutor of Prienai began the interrogation of the children, parents, and Father J. Zdebskis. Interrogator A. Pakštys searched Father Zdebskis' apartment.

On August 26 the interrogator telephoned Father J. Zdebskis and asked him to stop by his office "for a while." Here, the priest was arrested.

On August 30 Father Zdebskis was taken to Vilnius. From early morning a crowd of people stood near the militia office, waiting for the time when the priest would be taken away. Security agents photographed the people and wanted to disperse them. "What are you hanging around for? Do you want to see a miracle?" "More than a miracle!" answered the people. At 4 p.m., with crowds of people crying, Father

No. 53. Excerpted from **Chronicle**, No. 1 (1972).

Zdebskis was led into a car and taken away.

On September 3 Father Zdebskis' apartment was again meticulously searched. Someone started rumors that Father Zdebskis was arrested not for teaching children, but because a radio transmitter, etc., were found among his belongings. Since government functionaries spoke this way, it seems that they wanted to compromise the arrested priest even more and to prevent the believers from defending him.

During the latter half of September the faithful of Prienai took another statement to Moscow, a statement that was heard around the world.

— — —

To: The Control Committee of the CPSU
    The Supreme Soviet of the USSR
    The Council of Ministers of the USSR

A STATEMENT OF THE BELIEVERS OF
PRIENAI PARISH

Newspapers and the radio instill in us the belief that the Lithuanian SSR has religious freedom; however, in reality this is not so.

We are not permitted to publish religious books—we have never seen any. We do not even have small catechisms. The last edition was in 1940.

Often we are not able to attend Mass since we are forced to work on Sundays, even though Church law forbids it.

We are short of priests. Every year about 20 priests die, but the seminary is permitted to accept barely 10. Besides that, we know what hardships those who enter the seminary suffer from government officials.

Our priests are arrested for preparing children for their first confession. On August 26, our priest, Father J. Zdebskis, was arrested for teaching the catechism and now his trial is awaited.

All this compromises the Soviet Constitution and laws in our eyes.

Therefore, we ask the government of the Soviet Union: give us true freedom of religion; give our priests the freedom to perform their duties without hindrances and fear; order the release of our priest Juozas Zdebskis.

Prienai, September 12, 1971

— — —

This statement was signed by 2,010 believers. This was a brave protest of the people against religious persecution.

The government did not foresee that the believing people were like a volcano that only temporarily ceased to burn. We cannot foretell the future consequences. One thing is clear: that believing Lithuanians will fight for their rights!

Weeks and months raced by, but the day of Father Zdebskis' trial was delayed and a diligently kept secret. On the eve of November 11 news spread like lightning through Prienai: "The trial of Father Juozas will be tomorrow in Kaunas."

Tomorrow will show the true face of the Soviet government toward the believers.

From early morning people filled the staircase of the courthouse up to the third floor and the yard. Many people had flowers in their hands. Everyone was waiting for the arrival of Father Zdebskis. Militia was scurrying around. As the hour for the trial approached, they started "to put things in order"— they forcibly pushed the people outside. They even drew blood as they were pushing one woman. The Catholics were thrown out and their places in the court room were taken by a large throng of security agents.

In addition to them, in the courtroom were the witnesses —the children and their parents and personnel from various agencies in Prienai. They had to act out a show—an open court in session... to which the security personnel admitted only atheists. Without a doubt, the government did not want to popularize this trial.

The arrests of the faithful began on the staircase. One young man was arrested because he asked the militia why only atheists were allowed to be inside and believers were excluded. The young man was punished with 15 days in the guard house. A priest who accompanied Father Zdebskis' mother was arrested in the court corridor and was taken away for interrogation to the security office.

Outside the court, the crowd continued to grow. The militia began to arrest those people who had flowers in their hands and forcibly shoved them into cars. A great deal of confusion and shouting developed. An order was given to the militia to disperse the crowd, which numbered about 500-600. After roughly dispersing the crowd, they began to arrest lone individuals. A priest who happened to be walking by was arrested and charged with organizing the demonstration. Throughout the day the militia guarded Ožeškienė Street to prevent the people from assembling. "Why are you standing around here like pigs?" This is how the militia functionaries "greeted" the people. People were even chased out of nearby shops. A militia man came into one of the shops shouting, "chase the pietists out of here." Most of those arrested were released in the evening. One was taken to a psychiatric hospital and later was sentenced to 15 days in the guard house.

This day the people demonstrated their solidarity with the priest who was on trial, while the crowd of security agents and militia showed how the Soviet government deals with the rights of believers.

Antiochus, king of the Syrians, in order to keep the Jewish nation in fear, every month killed those who he thought had remained faithful to the laws of God. Many chose to die rather than give up their faith. (1. Mac 1:50-67)

Father Zdebskis' trial had the same purpose—to keep the nation cowed so that no one would dare to demand more freedom.

— — —

A summary of the prosecutor's speech follows:

"Parents and guardians have complete freedom to teach their children religious subjects. There are penalties for obstructing the practice of religion. Vatican II's Declaration on Christian Education states that in addition to the parents, the government also has rights regarding children. Father Zdebskis transgressed the law of separation of Church and State. During July-August 1971 Father Zdebskis organized and systematically carried out the teaching of minors—about 200-300 children; therefore he should be punished according to the law..."

Further, the prosecutor argued that Father Zdebskis actually organized and taught the children. According to the statement of witnesses and the words of the accused Father Zdebskis, the crime is real and fully proved. The teaching of children was also done by Father Zakaryza, but because of contributing circumstances, the prosecutor's office withdrew charges against him. In ending his presentations, the prosecutor asked the court to sentence Zdebskis to one year's loss of freedom to be served in a general regime camp.

Defense attorney Riauba argued that Father Zdebskis did not organize the teaching of children. There is no such documentation in the case. He only made an announcement regarding the concern for religious training of children. There was no compulsion. In the addendum to the Penal Code, the Presidium of the Lithuanian SSR Supreme Soviet indicates how to apply the article on the separation of Church and State, noting the organizing and systematic teaching. Mere teaching is not sufficient. Besides, some children had come only once. Is this systematic teaching?

The defense attorney mentioned Lenin's injunction not to insult the faithful and that the prosecutor did just that by relying on unfounded rumors about Father Zdebskis. In completing his presentation, the defense attorney asked the court not to apply Article 143 of the Penal Code, but to leave it up to the executive committee to fine Father Zdebskis 50 rubles.

After this Father Zdebskis made his final statement. The judge interrupted his speech several times, not permitting him to state his desired thoughts; we therefore present the text of Father Juozas Zdebskis' address:

— — —

I

On August 16, 1971, I was arrested and a criminal case was brought against me for teaching the children this summer religious truths in the church of Prienai. One of the charges states: "About 70 children and 50 parents were found in the church. He is being accused of violating part 1 of Article 143 of the Penal Code of the Lithuanian SSR, which deals with the separation of the Church from the State. The charge was made at the time of arrest."

What was the reason for my behavior? It is necessary to repeat the same motive which I stated in the church when a group of atheists, who entered the church, asked whether I am aware that it is prohibited to teach children. It is fitting to answer with the same words that the first disciples of Jesus used to their supreme court: "Better for us to obey God than men!" (Acts 5:29)...

It would seem that the state would have no other purpose in legislating than to provide for the well-being of the citizens, which is impossible except with freedom of conscience, and with the parents' rights to raise their children. The Constitution of the USSR recognizes the freedom of conscience and the right of parents to their children. The Declaration of Human Rights has been signed and ratified...

The official position in regard to this matter not only in the past but during the present year states the same—there is complete religious freedom in Lithuania.

The freedom of the Catholic Church, as a juridical person, must manifest itself in the permission to function. If one is allowed to live, one is thereby permitted to eat, breathe, and so on. If the priests are officially permitted to exist, then, naturally, this includes the permission to carry out their basic functions, i. e., to sacrifice, to forgive sins in the name of God (to judge), and to teach. It turns out that I am being tried for performing my direct duties...

II

It is necessary to demonstrate in court the psychological circumstances as well, which no doubt had an influence on my activity, for which I am being tried. These circumstances have been brought about by living conditions in which *the atheists themselves or individual institutions did not observe the law on freedom of conscience* according to which I am being tried today.

The word "atheist" as used here is most suitable in this situation, because an atheist, be he a security worker, administrator, or educator, in this case shows himself to be the same —as one who battles against God.

The laws of the USSR deal with the problem of freedom of conscience through the separation of the Church from the State. Regrettably, because of certain atheists, *the Church does not feel separated from the State, but on the contrary—subordinated to the interests of the atheists.* This is often accomplished through *deceit and treachery.*

For the same reasons, the faithful feel discriminated against. *They feel unequal before the law.*

The facts, which are widely known by the public, cannot be unknown to the procuracies. Why are they silent?

We can recall a fact or two which are closely related to our case...

First of all, the believers sense an inequality before the law, which is especially clearly brought out by the fact that the atheists have their own press and schools, while the faithful are denied this.

If priests are being punished for the preparation of children for their first confession, then we would like to ask whether a single case was brought against the atheists for the violation of the interests of the believers, especially according to the supplement of Article 143 of the Penal Code, issued in 1966. After all, there are such instances. For example, a year ago a teacher of the middle school of Vilkaviškis was dismissed from work because she was a believer, and as such having no right to work as an educator, nor anywhere else. Is this not a violation of the freedom of conscience? This is not the only fact in our society.

Also the efforts of the atheists to prevent the public, especially the youth, the pupils, the employees, from participating in the Mass.... There are a number of instances where the teacher did not permit students participating in a funeral to enter the church and even took them out of the church. Is this not a violation of the freedom of conscience? These and similar facts, which are widely known by the public, cannot be unknown to the procuracies. Why are they silent? Should we wonder why the believers do not feel equality before the law?

For the faithful it is especially incomprehensible why the authorities have not responded to a single petition of the faithful concerning the present abnormalities with respect to believing people. After all, it has been announced in the press that the appropriate organ must respond to petitions within a month. The reaction of the believers toward the present case can be an example. This summer, when a group of atheists came to the church where the children were taught the truths of faith and began to photograph stealthily and to ask the children their names, the mothers began to defend their children. An uproar arose in the church. After this event, 89 parents wrote a protest to the Commission of People's Control of the Central Committee of the CPSU. There was no official answer to the letter, although the address of the senders was given.

In view of such and similar facts the question inevitably arises: is the community of believers outside the limits of the law? Is such a situation conducive to a respect for the Constitution? Should we be surprised if the public begins to believe that the constitutional freedom of conscience and that the ratification of the Declaration of Human Rights, etc. were done only for propaganda purposes? Also if they consider as propaganda the 1966 addendum to Article 143 concerning the penalties for violations of the rights of the believers...

Let us look further.

In a number of cases *the behavior of the atheists amounts to obvious deceit and fraud* in regard to matters of conscience...

1. In a country where the Constitution guarantees freedom of conscience, is the freedom of conscience not violated by the deceitful efforts of the atheists to destroy the Church from within, by making it appear as if bishops are at their posts, that instructions are coming from the bishop's chancery, while actually the assignment of priests and many other decisions are dictated by the atheists, who are trying to put the Lithuanian Catholic Church in a situation similar to that of the Russian Orthodox Church?

2. Does not the effort to compromise certain priests and even bishops in the eyes of the faithful and even the Vatican suggest treachery? For example, is it through the effort of the believers that the energetic and healthy bishop Sladkevičius is titled "sedi datus" in Vatican's world register of bishops?

3. Are these facts not suggestive of treachery: there is a seminary, but it is permitted to accept and to ordain only 4 or 5 new priests, while 20-30 priests die annually in Lithuania? This is also shown by efforts to exclude from the seminary students and professors who are especially bright and of high moral character.

4. It is the same with the teaching of children. They are permitted to receive the First Communion; but what does the regulation to examine the children one at a time mean? Such a law is not formally on the books. How can you prepare children one at a time in those parishes where there are several hundred children during the summer? The parents rightful-

ly expect help from us priests in this matter. And what can be done? Permit the children to receive their First Communion unprepared? What man does not know, he cannot love. Is this not a treacherous effort to *quietly take away the children from their parents?* Then the atheists will be able to say: we have freedom of conscience—the people themselves have rejected religion...

However, such freedom of religion is like *having permission to live, but being forbidden to be born...*

Recalling again these facts, some of which I have noted as examples, which are widely known by the general public and cannot be unknown by the prosecutors' offices, I want to ask, why is all this being tolerated, while I am being tried for violation of freedom of conscience? How can a citizen be penalized according to laws which, as we see, in many cases are not obeyed by individual governmental institutions? Does not the fact that such a trial of a priest is conducted constitute a violation of freedom of conscience as would also the effort to take away children from their parents? Perhaps it would be possible to accuse me of violating the freedom of conscience if I had taught the children without the knowledge of the parents.

Has the state forgotten the requirements of its Constitution by tolerating all this?

Finally, the article itself, under which I am being tried, seems to have no clear definition. For example, we can recall a similar case in 1964 when I was sentenced to a year in prison for teaching children. After several months an order came from the authorities to release me and to overturn the conviction. The reason for the acquittal was this: "It was determined that the children were not coerced or compelled." The court was aware of this when it sentenced me to prison. But the court did not even mention coercion of the children. The case involving Article 143 was explained this way: that it is forbidden to organize and teach religious tenets in schools (not in churches). In spite of the fact that I was not charged with this, the court still tried me. How can this be understood? I was later acquitted, then why am I again being tried under the same article? Even now, the court knows well that there was no coercion of the children. This is witnessed to by the appeal of the parents, in this matter, to the USSR government: the children were being taught not in a school, but in a church; they were taught in accord with the wishes of their parents.

Under the same circumstances the law cannot be interpreted one way on one occasion and a different way on another occasion...

III

What is the outcome of all this?...,

The first possibility—to choose the way of so-called *peaceful cooperation with the atheists.* Attempt to serve two masters and cater to the whims of the atheists—the priest should perform his duties and not be dangerous to atheism. He himself should drive the youth from church and not allow them to participate in rites and processions or to serve Mass. In preparing children for their First Communion, he should be satisfied only with the teaching of prayers and require no understanding of the mysteries of the Mass—the center of all Christian life. Priests should not think about what the situation will be in this country after 10-20 years! This means that priests should not perform their rightful obligations, but should decide the conflict with this conscience by considering their dinner menu. They must try to forget that the children will still hear of God—but of a god *who truly does not exist.* (Neither do I believe in such a god as is portrayed in our local press and radio...)

You have shown me thousands of young people behind bars. Not one of them knows of a God whom it is necessary to love, and who loves us. No one has spoken to them of such a God, no one has taught them to find happiness in doing good to everyone, even one's enemies. I know well that if we priests do not speak about such things, then the stones will begin to cry out and God will hold us responsible for their fate!

This is what is meant in our situation by peaceful cooperation with the atheists. This is what believers living abroad cannot understand at all.

The second possibility is to be a priest according to Christ's design, to be determined to fulfill the obligations called for by Christ and Church Law. It means at the same time to accept everything that Providence will permit one to suffer.

As we can see in this situation—to choose windows with bars. In the words of the interrogators, "You did not want roast duck, so now you will eat prison bread."

If the courts do not judge us priests now, then our nation will judge us! And finally will come the hour of judgment by the Almighty. May God help us priests to fear this more than your judgment.

I recall once more those thousands of young people behind bars. In their childhood they did not know how to obey their parents... the land on the banks of the Nemunas is dear to me. I know well that it will not be there if its children will not have the strength to obey their parents. I spoke to them about this. I told them that this is a commandment of God.

If your conscience considers this a crime, then consider me a fanatic and judge me, but at the same time you will judge yourselves!

I ask the court to consider the psychological conditions to which I referred and not to forget that the decision of the court may cause thousands of believers to think that some paragraphs of the Constitution are for propaganda purposes only. Can there be respect for requirements that make one act against one's conscience? Can there be any respect for laws that forbid one to fulfill one's obligations?

I must repeat once more the words of the first apostles, which they said to their court, "Better for us to obey God rather than men."

— — — —

There was a two-hour recess after Rev. J. Zdebskis' address. Returning after a lengthy consultation, the court, in the name of the Lithuanian SSR, announced this judgement:

"Juozas, son of Vincent Zdebskis, born in 1929, is guilty under Article 143 of the Penal Code of the Lithuanian SSR and is sentenced to one year's loss of freedom, which is to be served in a general regime corrective labor colony, the sentence commencing August 26, 1971."

On December 9, 1971, the judicial Council for Criminal Cases of the Supreme Court of the Lithuanian SSR decided that Rev. Zdebskis was found guilty appropriately and that the given punishment is fitting for the crime and his person.

54. THE CASE OF REV. PROSPERAS BUBNYS

During the summer of 1971 the bishop had to come to Raseiniai to administer the Sacrament of Confirmation. The priests of the raion were instructed by the bishop to check on the religious knowledge of those to be confirmed and to issue certificates.

P. Bubnys, pastor of Girkalnis Parish, announced to the believers that parents should bring their children for testing to the church. The parents did so until one day a group of representatives from the Raseiniai raion Executive Committee intruded into the church. Upon finding children waiting for the priest in the church, the representatives started to round them up and dragged them through the village to the firehouse. There, with warnings and threats, they forced them to make written statements to the effect that Father Bubnys had taught them religious tenets. The children were so terrified that they cried and some even got sick.

On October 12, 1971, a People's Court was held in Raseiniai. Only officials and witnesses had the right to participate in the proceedings. The believers stood outside the doors. No one believed that Father Bubnys would be found guilty—the state officials found him examining only one child; the other children were waiting their turns in the church. Only when the court recessed for consultations and the car of the militia arrived at the court, did it become clear to everyone that Father Bubnys would be found guilty. In the name of the Lithuanian SSR, the court found Father P. Bubnys guilty and sentenced him to one year in a strict regime camp. After the decision was read, Father Bubnys was arrested and, while the people were in tears, he was taken to Lukiškis prison.

Father P. Bubnys had written up his defense speech before the trial; we present it here.

DEFENSE SPEECH OF REV. P. BUBNYS

Honored Court,

I have an important civil duty to make a statement on

No. 54. From **Chronicle**, No. 1 (1972).

an important question regarding life: am I guilty because of teaching religion? The question arises—is the avowal of religion (avowal not before trees or stones, but before men) as well as the preaching of religion an evil, forbidden thing of itself? If it is permitted, then do I have a right and obligation to do so?

The community of the United Nations and the country's Constitution rose above the principle of medieval mentality—he who rules determines the religion of the people—and recognized freedom of conscience and freedom of religion. In admitting my guilt for teaching religion, I would admit my transgression against the concept of man and spiritual progress for which mankind has struggled throughout the long ages. I respect the right of parents themselves to decide if their children will be religious or not. They themselves brought their children for testing of their religious knowledge. No one was assigned a certain day for bringing their children in. In trying to save the time of working people, they adjusted to the schedule of the one bus which goes through Girkalnis. I did not deliberately make an effort to ignore the officials and their demands.

In addition to duties to the state, I, as a priest and pastor, also have duties according to my conscience to my religion and the Church. The essential duty of a priest, imposed upon him by Christ Himself, is to preach the Gospel, to teach all nations, and to bestow God's grace through the sacraments. If the Soviet government still has not definitely closed the seminary in which religious matters are learned and studied, then it agrees that this knowledge should be used in teaching the faith. When he is ordained, every priest obligates himself to God Himself and through the bishop's appointment receives the Church's injunction to teach and bless the People of God. Therefore, if he acts according to his conscience, he cannot not preach and teach religion, bearing in mind the words of St. Paul: "Woe to me if I do not preach the Gospel!" (1 Cor 9:16). In the same way, parents have the right to teach their children religion. If they support a priest at their own expense, does the priest have the right to refuse to serve those parents in these matters? How absurd—to have the right and means and yet to forbid their utilization? This would be like allowing a man to hold a hammer in his hand, but forcing him to drive nails with his fist. Such a demand is incomprehensible to a sane person; therefore, it is not surprising that a majority of the people do not understand it at all.

If every moral person must not be hesitant in matters of right and morality, then it is more important that a priest not remain silent, a priest—who through Christ is permitted to recognize God's truth. There is no other name under heaven by which we will be saved except the name of Jesus. (Acts 4:12). The teaching of Christ is the foundation of man's culture and well-being. As sanity is better than insanity, so spiritual culture is more worthy than material culture. Time and place alter the laws of man, and some laws contradict those which preceded them, but Christ's laws are supported by man's nature and will continue as long as man lives. Christ's story did not end with His death on the cross. He is eternally alive and today is a witness to this. He comes, as he promised, not delaying, with great power and might as One who holds all power on heaven and earth. To Him belong all believers and all non-believing persons—as many as there are of them. He is the winnower and He will separate the grain from the chaff.

In view of this, my conscience forces me to fear not for my "guilt" because I taught children the tenets of their faith, but for my negligence in carrying out these important duties; considering the time accounted for by the prosecution, I spent less than ten minutes per child in examining their knowledge of the essentials (for First Communion). How can one then talk about teaching?

My only justification is that I did not have sufficient time before the arrival of the bishop in Raseiniai. I cannot accept either merit before God or guilt before the law.

If today I must publicly state whether I taught religion or not, then I cannot defend myself or repent of it since this would signify going against my conscience or a lack of concern for the Creator's laws regarding man. If the laws of man do not coincide with the Creator's natural laws, then it is not nature which errs, but man's understanding; and because of this, men suffer and will continue to suffer until man reconsiders his errors in falling away from the Creator's plan.

At this solemn hour allotted to me, dust of the earth, I cannot renounce our beloved Jesus who urged that little children not be stopped from coming to Him. I want to say: Praise be to Jesus Christ!

— — —

Three months after the conviction, on December 9, 1971, the Supreme Court confirmed the decision of the People's Court of Raseiniai.

The believers of Girkalnis parish and the neighboring parishes, deeply affected by the injury to the priest, disillusioned by the local government, addressed a statement to the Chairman of the Presidium of the Supreme Soviet of the USSR and the Prosecutor General of the USSR:

A STATEMENT

On October 12, 1971, in Raseiniai (Lithuanian SSR) Rev. Prosperas Bubnys, residing in Girkalnis parish, Raseiniai raion, was sentenced to one year in prison. On December 9 the Lithuanian SSR Supreme Court upheld that decision.

The priest's "crime" was that he conscientiously carried out his duties: he helped parents to prepare their children for their First Communion and Confirmation.

We prefer to believe that an error was made. Our Constitution guarantees freedom of religion and conscience, and Lenin's decree on the separation of Church and State states: "Citizens have the right to learn about religion on their own initiative." Our pastor taught at his own initiative. He did not go into the schools to teach the children. It was just the other way around: the representatives of the executive committee of Raseiniai, accompanied by the school's teachers, actually pushed their way into the church and, finding the children waiting for the pastor (to examine them on their religious knowledge), caused an uproar. The representatives rounded up the terrified children and dragged them through the town to the firehouse; there they locked them up, and by using threats, forced them to write statements accusing their pastor. (Some children even got sick because of the threats.). Threatened, frightened, and crying, the children wrote statements in which they made no distinction at all between the words "to teach" and "to examine." The enemies of the freedom of conscience took advantage of this so they could accuse a priest of systematically teaching children. And if the priest did teach the children not to steal, not to play wild pranks, to respect their parents, and to love their neighbors—is this a crime? From our experience we clearly see that children brought up in the faith grow up to be better individuals, with fewer bad habits. Therefore, we want to rear our children in this manner, but we do not have any published materials from which we can teach our children religious truths. (During the years of socialism in Lithuania, catechisms or other religious guides have not been published at all.) Only one option is left to us: to ask the pastor to help us. It is unfortunate that our pastor has been sentenced to prison for religious service.

The arbitrariness of the atheists and of the government insults and demeans us believers greatly; such things indicate that believers are not equal under the law with unbelievers. Only atheists are permitted to rear their children freely, that is, atheistically; believers lose all their rights and ability to rear their children according to their beliefs. Furthermore, the atheists have more rights to interfere in the rearing of our children than we the parents have. They attempt to force children who are not their own to become atheistic persons; they chase them out of churches, frighten them, and do not permit them to receive First Communion; but the priest, who was asked by the parents "on their own initiative" to teach faith and morals to their children, is sentenced to prison.

We ask you not to permit such arbitrary violations of our parental rights. We ask for the freedom of conscience and equal rights as promised by Lenin and as promulgated by the Soviet Constitution.

We ask that catechisms be published so that we could have something from which to teach our children.

We ask that the priests be allowed to teach children in the church the tenets of our faith—in keeping with Lenin's decree.

We also ask your help for the release of Rev. Bubnys from prison.

P.S. 1,344 believers from Raseiniai raion, of whom 570 are from Girkalnis parish, have signed this statement. We attach 43 pages of signatures to this appeal.

We await a response at this address:

Lithuanian SSR, Raseiniai raion
    Girkalnis
    Blažė Lukinskaitė
    Anelė Kazimerskytė

December 11, 1971

55. A STATEMENT BY THE PRIESTS OF THE ARCHDIOCESE OF VILNIUS

To: The Chairman of the Council of Ministers of the USSR

Copies to: The Chairman of the Lithuanian SSR Council
of Ministers

The Representative of the Council for Religious Affairs of the Lithuanian SSR

The majority of the inhabitants of our republic are believers. They could participate much more actively in the public and political life of our country if they had more favorable conditions. The Constitution, the Penal Code, and the international conventions theoretically guarantee the believers rights equal to those of other citizens. Overseas radio broadcasts, the press, and the revolutionary decrees of Lenin speak about this. But in reality, it is often otherwise.

The number of priests is continually decreasing in Lithuania. This is happening not through the fault of believers but because of the administrative obstacles of the government. The activities of the Kaunas Seminary, the only one in Lithuania, are unusually restricted. The state strictly limits the number of those studying there; many who wish to enter, cannot. Those who wish to enter the seminary are interrogated by various officials and are terrorized at their places of work. Under such conditions, some candidates study theology and become priests outside the bounds of the seminary; the Representative of the Council for Religious Affairs of the USSR Council of Ministers does not permit such candidates to carry out their functions. (Such was the case with Rev. Vytautas Merkys and Rev. Petras Našlėnas). Is this a normal situation? At the same time J. Rimaitis, in his information pamphlet for overseas consumption, *Religion in Lithuania* (Gintaras, Vilnius, 1971), states that, "The Lithuanian government does not lay obstacles to training clergymen." (p. 21).

The Soviet government tells the whole world that "the Church may freely make use of the main means of religious propaganda (*Ibid.*, p. 30). In reality, it is not so: the believers of Lithuania do not have their own press, they cannot use radio and television, and they do not have even the simplest textbook on religious truths. "Every citizen may freely... buy prayer books, the Bible, and other religious literature," writes J. Rimaitis further (p. 24). In fact, the Bible has not been published at all; it is the same with other religious books needed by believers. The prayer books, published in a very small number, have not been available for a long time, while we need more than half a million copies of them.

The Soviet press writes that the canonical activities of the Church are not restricted. However, more than 10 years have passed since Bishop Julijonas Steponavičius and Bishop Vincentas Sladkevičius have been permitted to carry out their rightful duties.[1] And it is the same for priests who have served their sentences (or have had them waived); sometimes they have to wait for years before the Representative of the Council for Religious Affairs will yield and permit them to perform their priestly duties.

Lenin's decree of January 2, 1918, permits chidren to be taught religion privately. Priests and parents, reading the press, understand that Lenin's decree is still operative. In the meantime, more than one priest and layman (Rev. Antanas Šeškevičius, Rev. Juozas Zdebskis, Rev. Prosperas Bubnys, and Ona Paškevičiūtė,[2] have been sentenced to forced labor merely for carrying out their canonical duties—the preparation of children for their First Communion on church premises.

According to the international convention signed by the USSR on November 15, 1961, parents are guaranteed the right to rear their children in religion and morality in keeping with their beliefs[3]; nevertheless in our country the state organs sometimes forbid children (boys and girls alike) to even passively attend religious services even though their parents require it or encourage it. In our country's schools children are forced to fill out various questionnaires, which are incompatible with freedom of conscience, to reveal publicly their religious beliefs; the activities of the Catholic Church are pre-

---

1. See Doc. Nos. 53 and 59.

2. The cases of Rev. Šeškevičius, Rev. Zdebskis, and Rev. Bubnys are reported in Doc. No. 52, 53, 54. No details are available on the case of Ona Paškevičiūtė.

3. Apparently a reference to the UN Convention against Discrimination in Education, adopted on December 14, 1960.

sented to them in a distorted manner, anti-church literature is foisted upon them; they are ridiculed and even punished for church attendance; by means of moral coercion they are forced to join anti-religious groups.

Adult believers also suffer often for their religious beliefs; they are not permitted to obtain higher positions. Those who are suspected of being believers are threatened with loss of jobs and are even actually fired under various other pretexts. For example, take the case of Ona Brilienė, a teacher at the Vilkaviškis middle school. Even after the decision of the Supreme Court of the Lithuanian SSR that she be rehired (since she was fired merely for attending church), she was not permitted to work in that town even as a floor sweeper. On the whole, the conduct of the people's courts in deciding the cases of believers is shocking: the courts (and similar institutions) often base their decisions on some kind of secret (unknown even to the Soviet jurists) instructions and pass sentences for failure to obey them (for example, the cases of Rev. Šeškevičius in Molėtai, Rev. Zdebskis in Kaunas, and Rev. Keina [5] in Varėna). In the Soviet courts children are questioned and forced to be witnesses against their own will, or against the wishes of their parents; and sometimes they are forced to bear witness falsely (for example, in the case of Rev. Keina on December 7, 1971, in Varėna People's Court).

Therefore, we ask for the following:

1. To allow the Kaunas Seminary to function freely and to accept all candidates acceptable to the Church.

2. To put into practice the USSR Constitution's guarantees regarding freedom for the religious press; that is, to publish prayer books, catechisms, hymnals, the Bible, and other religious books which the people need greatly and which they demand.

3. To permit Bishop Julijonas Steponavičius and Bishop Vincentas Sladkevičius to perform their duties as bishops and to permit all priests living in our country (including the Ukrainians) freely and publicly to do their work as priests.

4. To abrogate the explanatory text of Article 143 of the

---

4. The case of Ona Brilienė is reported in detail in **Chronicle,** No. 3 (July 20, 1972).

5. The case of Rev. Keina is reported in **Chronicle,** No. 1 (1972).

Penal Code of the Lithuanian SSR, which is in conflict with the international convention signed on November 15, 1961, and with the Constitution of the USSR. The wording "the organization and systematic inplementation of religious instruction to minors in violation of established legal rules" is often abused by the people's courts of our country.

5. To void all the various secret instructions, unknown to us, which touch upon religious life.

6. To review once more the cases of individuals sentenced for religious reasons and to acquit them.

We ask you to decide the matters presented in this statement in Moscow because previous appeals by believers, which were sent from Moscow to Vilnius, were not handled in a business-like manner, but only brought new disappointments to believers.

Our complaints are substantiated by many painful facts. If it becomes necessary, we are able to provide you with many more such facts.

December 24, 1971

Signatures: Rev. R. Blažys, Rev. B. Budreckis, Rev. A. Merkys, Rev. D. Valiukonis, Rev. C. Taraškevičius, Rev. A. Ulickas, Rev. J. Kardelis, Rev. J. Jakutis, Rev. J. Grigaitis, Rev. K. Žemėnas, Rev. A. Čiuras, Rev. K. Garuckas, Rev. V. Miškinis, Rev. A. Petronis, Rev. A. Simonaitis, Rev. B. Laurinavičius, Rev. M. Žemaitis, Rev. J. Kukta, Rev. K. Vaičionis, Rev. J. Baltušis, Rev. B. Jaura, Rev. Pukėnas, Rev. J. Vaitonis, Rev. A. Dzekan, Rev. D. Akstinas, Rev. L. Ivancik, Rev. J. Karukievic, Rev. P. Jankus, Rev. A. Lakovic, Rev. K. Molis, Rev. P. Velicko, Rev. S. Valiukėnas, Rev. V. Merkys, Rev. V. Zavadskis, Rev. A. Keina, Rev. A. Jasmantas, Rev. N. Jaura, Rev. J. Budrevičius, Rev. S. Tunaitis, Rev. M. Petravičius, Rev. N. Pakalka, Rev. K. Vasiliauskas, Rev. J. Lauriūnas, Rev. A. Andriuškevičius.

We ask that your reply be sent to these addresses:

1. Rev. B. Laurinavičius, Adutiškis Post Office, Švenčionys raion, Lithuanian SSR.

2. Rev. K. Pukėnas, Nemenčinė Post Office, Vilnius raion, Lithuanian SSR.

3. Rev. P. Blažys, Tilžė Post Office, Zarasai raion, Lithuanian SSR.

56. AN APPEAL OF 17,000 TO THE UNITED NATIONS

To: Mr. Kurt Waldheim
Secretary General of the United Nations

AN APPEAL OF THE LITHUANIAN CATHOLICS

Taking into consideration that Lithuania is not represented in the United Nations Organization, we, the Catholics of Lithuania, must address ourselves to you, Mr. Secretary General, through appropriate channels.

Our appeal was precipitated by the fact that religious believers in our republic cannot enjoy the rights set out in Article 18 of the Universal Declaration of Human Rights. On these grounds our clergy, groups of believers, and individual Catholics have repeatedly addressed themselves to the highest state organs of the Soviet Union, demanding that the violations of the rights of the believers be stopped. Several petitions by believers were transmitted to the Soviet government, including:

A statement of the Catholics of Prienai, signed by 2,000 persons, sent in September of 1971.

A statement of the believers of the parish of the Santaika, raion of Alytus, bearing 1,190 signatures, sent in October of 1971.

A statement of 1,344 parishioners of the parish of Girkalnis, raion of Raseiniai, sent in December of 1971.

No. 56. Text in **Chronicle**, No. 2 (1972). According to the note preceding the text of the memorandum, the petition was initiated after the trials of Rev. Zdebskis and Rev. Bubnys (see Doc. No. 53, 54). The 17,000 signatures were collected in two months. The organizers of the petition decided to send it to Secretary General of the CPSU Brezhnev by way of UN Secretary General Kurt Waldheim because, according to the dissidents, the previous communications to Soviet leaders were intercepted by the KGB and republic authorities. Texts of the particular communications mentioned in the petition will be found in Doc. No. 53 (Statement of the Catholics of Prienai), Doc. No. 54 (Statement of the Girkalnis parish), and **Chronicle**, No. 1 (1972) (Statement of the Santaika parish). The petition reached the UN around Easter of 1972. Although Mr. Waldheim refused to comment on the document (see **New York Times**, July 23, 1972), it can be assumed that it was transmitted to Moscow.

All these statements were transmitted to various of the highest offices of the USSR, but not a single one of them has sent an official reply, although state agencies are obliged to respond to citizens' statements in the course of a month. The unofficial reply (to those statements) manifested itself by increased repressions toward the believers.

The Catholics of all of Lithuania, in addressing a memorandum to the Secretary General of the Communist Party of the Soviet Union, Mr. Brezhnev, were determined to remind the Soviet leadership of their disenfranchised condition, but the organs of Soviet militia and KGB have suppressed the mass collection of signatures by means of threats, arrests, and iron handcuffs.

Such actions by the authorities have prompted the belief that the present memorandum, signed by 17,000 believers, will not achieve its goal if it is sent by the same means as previous collective declarations. Therefore we, the Catholics of Lithuania, are addressing ourselves to you, Honorable Secretary General, and are asking that you relay the said memorandum, signatures included, to the Secretary General of the Communist Party, Mr. Brezhnev.

Respectfully yours,

Representatives of Lithuania's Catholics

February 1972

— — —

To: Secretary General of the Central Committee, Communist Party of the Soviet Union, L. Brezhnev,

Moscow—The Kremlin

MEMORANDUM
OF THE ROMAN CATHOLICS OF LITHUANIA

After World War II nations have risen from the ruins and desire a permanent peace. A genuine peace is grounded in justice and respect for human rights. We, the Catholics of Lithuania, painfully deplore the violations of the believers' freedom of conscience and the persecution of the Church that persist in our nation to this very day.

It is now more than ten years that bishops J. Steponavičius and V. Sladkevičius have been subjected to the hardships of exile, without a proper court verdict and without a set term, although they have not committed any crimes.

In November of this year two priests, J. Zdebskis and P. Bubnys, were sentenced to one year of prison for having instructed youngsters in the foundations of the Catholic faith at the request of their parents and in fulfillment of their own priestly duties. These priests helped the youngsters to prepare themselves for their First Communion not in school but in the church and used no compulsion; only those received instruction who wanted it.

Meanwhile, the believing children of believing parents were forced to speak, write and act against their consciences, yet those who coerce them are neither reprimanded nor tried.

The priests are no longer able to provide proper service to us believers because they are too few. There are many cases where one priest serves two and sometimes even three parishes. Even aged and invalid priests are compelled to work. This is so because the priests' seminary is administered not as much by the bishop as by a state representative. The state authorities have limited the enrollment in the seminary to merely ten theological students annually.

The appointment of priests to specific parishes is also directed by a state official.

Although the Penal Code of the Lithuanian SSR provides for punishment of those who persecute believers, in practice such penalties are never enforced. In 1970 the education department of Vilkaviškis dismissed the teacher Mrs. O. Brilienė from her job because she is a believer. Meanwhile, the authorities in Vilkaviškis refuse to employ her even as a street sweeper. No one punishes such officials, although because of their arbitrariness, the members of the intelligentsia are afraid to practice their faith publicly.

State officials do not allow the believers to restore churches that have burned down, as for example in Sangruda, Batakiai, and Gaurė. It is only with the greatest difficulty that permission is given to furnish a little chapel in a residential building, but one is never allowed to transfer it to a churchyard.

We could point out many more cases of discrimination which have embittered our life and have sown disillusion-

ment with the Soviet Constitution and laws. We therefore
ask the Soviet government to grant us the freedom of conscience which has been guaranteed by the Constitution of the
USSR but which has not been put into practice heretofore.
What we want is not pretty words in the press and on the
radio but serious governmental efforts that would help us
Catholics feel like citizens of the Soviet Union with equal
rights.

December 1971

Addition to the Memorandum

Seventeen thousand and fifty-four signatures are enclosed
with the memorandum. It must be noted that the memorandum was signed by only an insignificant portion of religious
believers in Lithuania since the organs of the militia and of
the KGB have used all kinds of means to interrupt the collection of signatures. Several persons active in the collection of
signatures were arrested in Kapsukas, Šakiai, Išlaužas, Kapčiamiestis.

If the state organs will continue giving the same kind
of treatment to the complaints of the believers, we will feel
compelled to turn to international institutions: to the Pope
in Rome, the Head of our Church, or to the United Nations
Organization, an authoritative institution that protects human
rights.

In addition, we should like to inform you that this memorandum is the result of a national calamity: social ills,
such as crimes committed by minors, alcoholism, and suicides,
have increased tenfold during the period of Soviet power in
Lithuania. Divorces and the destruction of unborn babies have
also reached a dangerous level. The farther we move away
from the Christian past, the more the terrible consequences of
compulsory atheistic education come to light, the wider the
spread of an inhuman way of life, in the absence of God and
religion.

We address ourselves to you as the highest authority of
the Party with a request for the most serious and responsible
consideration of the facts presented by us and for the adop-
tion of an appropriate decision.

Representatives of Lithuanian Catholics

February 1972

57. REACTION TO THE UN APPEAL

The foreign press, radio, and television publicized this memorandum widely. World opinion supported the 17,000 Catholics who dared to demand their rights publicly. Pope Paul VI in his Easter address remembered the "Silent Church."

How did the Soviet state organs react to this?

In their opinion this memorandum slanders Soviet reality; therefore, the KGB organs are searching intensely for the initiators of the memorandum. Alas, so far they have exposed only a few signature collectors. The state organs suspect that the memorandum was organized by "anti-Soviet" priests.

On April 11, 1972, J. Rugienis, the Representative of the Council for Religious Affairs, called the bishops (who are functioning) and the administrators of the dioceses of Lithuania to the office of the Kaunas Archdiocesan Curia and together with Orlov, Moscow's representative, forced them to sign the so-called "pastoral letter to the believers" in which both the signers and signature collectors of the memorandum are slandered as follows:

> "3. Furthermore, in some parishes there have recently appeared irresponsible individuals. Near the churches or even within the churches, or sometimes by visiting homes, they, in the name of the priests and the faithful, gather signatures on sheets with texts or even without any text, requesting that the pastor be transferred, that a church not be closed, that a certain priest be appointed, that the pastor or assistant pastor not be removed, and so forth. These signature collectors later change or add a text, attaching it to the collected signatures. That is a fraud. We are very surprised that there are such believers who sign things without knowing what they are signing and without thinking about the possible results. We must remember that the irresponsible signing of documents affects relations between the Church and the State and gives rise to misunder-

No. 57. **Chronicle,** No. 2 (1972). The complete text of the pastoral letter has not been published in **Chronicle,** but is available in AS No. 1109. The dissidents prepared a lengthy point by point refutation of the pastoral letter. Text of this refutation, dated May of 1972, has not been published in the **Chronicle** possibly because of its strong critique of the bishops and administrators of dioceses for subservience to the Soviet regime. The text of the refutation is available in AS No. 1381.

standings. These kinds of things can bring no good to the Church..."

An order was issued that this letter be read on Sunday, April 30, 1972, in place of all sermons scheduled for that day.

It was immediately clear to all priests that this letter was written on instructions from the state since the bishops did not know about the signature collection from reliable sources and, most important, the attitude of the "pastoral letter" toward the collection of signatures clearly was not proper. Discussions on what to do took place among the priests—to read the letter or not?

Many priests received the following advice:

Reverend Father,

Times of trial have come upon the priests and the Catholic Church in Lithuania. On April 30 all priests are authorized to read the letter compromising the bishops, the priests, and the believers.

1. On April 11 Rugienis and the state representative from Moscow forced the ordinaries to write this deplorable letter.

2. This letter is slanderous. Seventeen thousand believers did not sign empty sheets, but signed under a text which is known to the whole world.

3. This letter wounds and compromises the fine daughters and sons of the Lithuanian Catholic Church who dared to sign the memorandum.

4. This letter irrevocably compromises the ordinaries themselves.

5. Priests are bound to obedience of the bishop only in CIC matters. No one can oblige a priest to read a slanderous thing.

6. Conscientious priests will not read this letter even if they have to suffer for it.

Priests, we appeal to your priestly conscience: being messengers of Him who called Himself the Truth, do not bow to lies and force and do not betray your Nation and the Church for a bite of food.

On the appointed Sunday special individuals from the raions were sent to the churches; they were to keep track of which priests read the letter and which did not read it. The "pastoral letter" of April 11th was used by the atheists for their own propaganda purposes. For example, prior to April 30th, at a meeting of parents of the middle school in Aukštoji Panemunė, state representatives reprimanded the parents because some people had been signing various papers often without knowing why. To increase the veracity of their words they read supporting thoughts from the bishops' letter: "If you don't believe us, here's what your bishops say."

Very few priests read the entire letter; some did so because they did not know what else to do in this situation, others did so to indulge the civil state. Some priests read only the part dealing with church matters, omitting the falsehoods, and others gave sermons as usual on that Sunday.

After April 30th the KGB organs attempted to obtain more specific information about the reading of the letter; they even used priests loyal to them for this work.

58. "THE TRUE STATE OF THE CATHOLIC CHURCH IN LITHUANIA"

On August 12, 1972, the newspaper *Sovietskaya Litva* published an article by J. Rimaitis, entitled, "Churchmen Accommodate." The article states that in the war against religion, administrative attacks can do irreparable harm by hurting the feelings of believers in all kinds of ways. "Unfair methods in the war against religion not only fail to destroy the basis of the spread of religion, but on the contrary, lead to a strengthening of religious fanaticism, to secret forms of ceremony and cult; they cause mistrust and discontent among believers, and goad them on." [1]

Rimaitis repeats the old principle of the atheists, calling for uncompromising war against religion. This principle allows for a detente, when a sharp reaction arises among believers, to allow the believers to calm down, and for striking anew when better methods are found.

Reaction from Lithuanian priests and faithful against the restriction of religious freedom began in the summer of 1968 and reached a climax at the beginning of 1972.[2] With the arrest of the priests Juozas Zdebskis and Prosperas Bubnys, written protests poured in from the faithful, spelling out the persecution of believers. The Soviet government ignored these protests of the people and failed to react, just as it had done with the protests of priests from 1968 to 1971.

The first serious conflict with government officials occurred on Ožeškienė Street the day of Rev. J. Zdebskis' trial in Kaunas. It was only by force that the militia dispersed the crowd gathered at the courthouse to honor the priest on trial.

Especially great annoyance was caused the government by the news that signatures were being collected on a memo-

---

No. 58. **Chronicle,** No. 4 (1972).

1. The article by Rimaitis can be considered a criticism of Justas Rugienis, the Representative of the Council for Religious Affairs. A former KGB worker, Rugienis was extremely disliked for his crude manners and tactics in dealing with the clergy and believers. He was released from his position in February of 1973, according to the **Chronicle,** No. 6 (May, 1973). Rugienis was a convenient scapegoat for the religious unrest.

2. This is a summary of events described in Doc. Nos. 50-57.

randum to the Soviet government. Government functionaries expected to ignore this petition in silence also. However, the memorandum of the Catholics caused one unexpected development after another. The document, signed by seventeen thousand believers and sent to the Secretary General of the Central Committee through United Nations Secretary General Kurt Waldheim, immediately became known to the whole world. Public opinion favored the bold action of the believers and condemned the restriction of human rights in the Soviet Union.

The Soviet government decided to remedy the steadily deteriorating situation. In April it forced the administrator of the Archdiocese of Vilnius, Monsignor Č. Krivaitis, to declare, for foreign consumption, that there is freedom of religion in Lithuania. The faithful in Lithuania learned of this interview with ELTA only from foreign radio broadcasts. Rumor has it that Msgr. Krivaitis' statements to the press were not exactly as reported.[3]

On April 11 all officially functioning bishops and administrators of dioceses were invited to the chancery of the Archdiocese of Kaunas. Under pressure from representatives of the government, they signed a so-called pastoral letter. With this, the government tried to compromise the organizers of the memorandum and the faithful who had signed it.

Even though, on April 30, some priests read the pastoral letter from the pulpit in modified or abbreviated form, or in its entirety, nevertheless the expected results did not occur. Some listeners did not grasp what was being condemned in the letter, while others were scandalized and offended at the government's attempt to use spiritual leaders in the service of atheism. News of this shameful act of coercion soon appeared in the press abroad.

Security agents looking for the organizers of the memorandum and for the channels by which accurate information about the Catholic Church in Lithuania is reaching the free

---

3. ELTA is the Lithuanian news agency, a subsidiary of TASS. The interview here referred apparently was released by TASS. See the report of the interview by James Yuenger, **Chicago Tribune**, April 9, 1972. The interview with Msgr. Krivaitis was part of an effort to counteract the appeal to the UN. Although Msgr. Krivaitis did not directly refer to the UN appeal, he attempted to refute some of its charges.

world, were overtaken by the tragic events of May. On the
14th of that month, in the city park of Kaunas, young Romas
Kalanta immolated himself in protest against the persecution
of freedom in Lithuania. Everyone excitedly discussed this tragic protest against national injustice, coercion, and against the
Soviet government's arbitrary policy towards ethnic groups.
The prevented burial of Kalanta turned into a spontaneous demonstration demanding national and religious freedom. The
army and militia dealt roughly with the demonstrators, but
government officials were disturbed, as it became obvious that
freedom is not the desire of priests alone, but of "their own,"
i.e., of the youth reared under Communism since childhood.
Most of those arrested were Komsomols, born and reared during
the Soviet era.[4]

In the summer of 1972 some relaxation of tension was
evident. Children preparing for their First Communion were
harassed in only a few places: N. Radviliškis and Šunskai. A few priests were given administrative sentences for not
turning children away from the altar. The Representative of
the Council for Religious Affairs, J. Rugienis, hardly persecuted
the clergy at all.

Without a doubt, this was a calculated step by the atheists
to restore calm in Lithuania, to repair their image, damaged
in the eyes of the world, and, if possible, to convince everyone,
including the Vatican itself, that the unrest was caused by
the tactlessness of one official or another. Now, however, all
is taken care of. Allegedly, the life of the faithful goes its normal
way.

How do the faithful and priests of Lithuania itself evaluate
the present situation of the Catholic Church in Lithuania?
All of them are quite concerned that *the Soviet government
is trying increasingly to throttle the Catholic Church in Lithuania with the hands of the clergy and the faithful themselves.*
How is this done?

I. CHURCH LEADERS ARE USED TO SERVE THE
INTERESTS OF THE ATHEISTS

The Soviet government, wishing to hide its treatment of
the Catholic Church in Lithuania from the world, and nurtur-

---

4. See Doc. Nos. 19, 20 for the Kalanta events.

ing hopes of deceiving the Vatican to get concessions from it, has more than once forced some Lithuanian bishops and administrators of dioceses to disseminate false information abroad. Examples are the interview of Bishop J. Labukas with *L'Humanité;* the interview of Monsignor Krivaitis, Chancellor of the Archdiocese of Vilnius, with the editor of *Vilnis,* Jokubka, and his 1972 interview with ELTA; Bishop Pletkus' radio broadcasts to Lithuanians abroad, etc. In these interviews it has been stated that the condition of the Catholic Church in Lithuania is normal, and that the faithful are not persecuted by the government. It is unclear whether the above-mentioned persons really spoke thus since it has been known on a number of occasions that reports of interviews have been intentionally distorted.

In view of the fact that the priests and faithful of Lithuania have no way to inform the world about the true state of the Church, a most pitiful situation has developed over the years. When the Vatican conferred the title of Monsignor on certain priests "loyal" to the Soviet system, thus to all appearances approving their behavior; when it nominated as bishops the hand-picked candidates of the government, remaining silent about the painful situation of the faithful in Lithuania, voices were heard to say, "The Vatican is deceived! The Chekists have infiltrated the Roman Curia! We have been betrayed!"

At such a difficult time the only recourse left to the Catholics of Lithuania is to trust in Divine Providence and to seek ways by which the true message might reach the Vatican and the rest of the world, that the most deadly thing for the Catholic Church in Lithuania is not persecution, but the noose being tied by some of our own people.

In an effort to undermine the influence of the priests on the faithful, the government has more than once forced bishops to curtail priests' faculties. In 1968, His Excellency, Bishop Labukas, under pressure from Rugienis, for several months forbade the Rev. S. Tamkevičius to preach. In July

---

5. The Soviet regime has attempted to blunt the charges of religious discrimination and persecution by supplying periodically willing clergy for interviews with foreign communist press. A number of such interviews in the Lithuanian communist press abroad, particularly in the newspapers **Vilnis** (Chicago) and **Laisvė** (Brooklyn), have been published.

1970, the bishop limited the faculties in the Diocese of Vilkaviškis and of the Archdiocese of Kaunas from the pastor of Alksninė, Canon Bronius Antanaitis, former chancellor of the Diocese of Panevėžys, exiled in 1960 to the Diocese of Vilkaviškis. A circular letter of March 30, 1971, limited the faculties of priests to hear confessions and to preach. Priests from an outside diocese may not preach or hear confessions without permission from the local chancery. The restriction evoked protests from priests. In time of persecution the faculties of priests should be expanded, not curtailed. The bishops had to make these restrictions on priests in their own name, while the chief perpetrator, the Representative of the Council for Religious Affairs, Rugienis, remained in the shadows.

Bishops can appoint only certain priests to parishes; Rugienis often directs which priests to transfer, the bishop has only to sign the appointments. It is not by accident that the most zealous priests are scattered in small, out-of-the-way parishes, while lax, or physically incapacitated men, or those who have compromised themselves in the eyes of the faithful often occupy the most important ecclesiastical posts.

Rugienis himself suggests to the bishops which priests favored the regime and which ones out of grace should be appointed to which parish. Without Rugienis' approval, the bishop may not transfer any priest, even in case of necessity. For example, in September of 1972, Bishop Labukas, under pressure from Rugienis, forced the pastor of Juodaičiai, Father Pesliakas, under threat of suspension, to take over the duties of assistant in the parish of Viduklė. If a zealous priest raises the spiritual level of a parish, if he gets to know the people and the situation, Rugienis takes steps to have him transferred and lets the bishop appoint a lax or disedifying priest, so that everything might fall apart once more.

Rugienis forbids the bishops to mention that he (Rugienis) controls the appointments of many priests. Thus, priests know absolutely nothing about their appointments in advance. They are pushed around like billiard balls, according to the shots Rugienis calls. If the people ask why a priest is being transferred, Rugienis refers them to the bishop, who lets them understand that he is powerless to do a thing.

Priests, seeing the bishops so pressured by government officials, sometimes try appealing to Canon Law, saying: "This transfer is uncanonical; please do not transfer me to a small parish." Under direct or indirect pressure, Bishop Labukas, on November 19, 1970, obtained from the Holy See a dispensation from canons regulating the assignment of priests. This dispensation, in the opinion of the priests, subjected the bishop to Rugienis' manipulations still more. Before the bishop could always object to Rugienis, "I cannot transfer a good pastor to a small parish because canon law does not allow me to do so." Now, however, the representative of the government can reply to the bishop's objections, "You have the Pope's dispensation, so transfer this priest from this parish."

The bishops were forced to cover up Rugienis' calculated interference in clergy appointments in a circular letter dated March 30, 1971, in which they write: "The ordinaries, desiring to improve the quality of ministry to the spiritual needs of the faithful, have decided to change the procedure of assigning priests to parishes. It has been decided in the future to assign young, zealous, and suitable priests as pastors where there is much work, and to send older priests, unable to cope, to smaller parishes, where it will be easier for them to serve as pastors." Reading the letter, one would think that ordinaries in Lithuania act with complete freedom, assigning priests as they see fit. However, the practice has been, and remains, quite the contrary. Immediately after publication of the circular letter, the young and energetic Father P. Dumbliauskas was transferred from Garliava to the little parish of Šunskai, while the pastor of Šunskai, Father I. Pilypaitis, born in 1903, was assigned to the parish of Aleksotas, in the Archdiocese of Kaunas.

Bishops are also forced to interfere with the struggle of priests and laity for freedom of belief in Lithuania. In December 1970 the assistant pastor of Kėdainiai, Rev. A. Jakubauskas, was threatened with suspension if he ventured beyond the parish bounds of Kėdainiai and Apytalaukė. At that time the priest was preparing to collect signatures on a petition that bishops not be put to the task of destroying the Church. In a "pastoral letter" of April 11, 1972, those collecting signatures and those signing the petition for religious freedom in Lithuania were chided.

Bishops are likewise forced to keep in check congregations of religious sisters working underground, lest they "step out of line" and draw the attention of the government. It is no wonder, then, that some of the latter have contented themselves with prayer, and have not done their full share for the religious life of the people, even though meanwhile the raging storm of atheism has been destroying the life of the Church.

In September and October of 1970 the priests of Lithuania, in an attempt to prevent the subjugation of the Catholic Church's leadership to the ends of the regime, addressed to the bishops and administrators of dioceses an appeal in which they spelled out the kinds of appeasement which are intoleraable. The appeal was signed by 59 priests of the Diocese of Vilkaviškis and 50 from the Archdiocese of Vilnius.[6]

II. CO-OPTING PRIESTS FOR ATHEISTIC WORK

Priests are forbidden to teach children the truths of the faith; they are allowed only to test them. Since parents most often do not know how to prepare children well for First Communion, many priests, especially in large parishes, admit them to communion with little or no preparation.

For example, in the parish of Aušros Vartai in Vilnius, for a time children made their First Communion without even learning their prayers properly. They would come in droves from Belorussia, where there are no priests. Their parents do not know how to prepare them since the printing of catechisms or other religious literature is forbidden. Since the priests refuse to teach the children, *the faithful conclude that if the priest is afraid of the authorities, then the parents have even more to fear.*

And so people begin to excuse their children lightly when the latter miss their religious obligations on the slightest pretext: "The teacher will scold the child, will write a bad recommendation so the child will not be accepted for higher studies," etc.

---

6. The letter here referred has not been published in the **Chronicle**, again possibly for its rather fundamental critique of the role of the Lithuanian hierarchy. Text of the letter is available in AS No. 692. The priests charged the hierarchy with complacency in providing leadership, neglect of the only seminary and failure to increase the number of seminarians, the lack of consultation with the priests on the appointments of clergy and the subservience to the regime in this matter.

The government requires pastors not to allow youngsters to serve at the altar or to participate in processions. Priests who disobey are punished. Priests are especially pressured on this point at the present time. Some, resolved to bear any harship, do not forbid children to participate in religious ceremonies. Others, seeking to appease the government, or valuing a good assignment, or complacent in their tranquility, "don't want any unpleasantness with the authorities," and keep children from taking part in processions or serving at Mass. So, in place of youngsters at the altar, one frequently sees old men.

Without a doubt, in this regard an extremely negative effect resulted from the letter written under pressure on May 31, 1961, by Dr. J. Stankevičius, administrator of the Diocese of Kaunas and of the Diocese of Vilkaviškis: "According to the directive of the Representative for Religious Cult Rugienis, young men and women who have attained eighteen years of age may participate publicly in liturgical services. Younger children may not serve Mass, may not sing in the choir, may not carry banners or scatter flowers in procession. Children are to take part in liturgical-religious events only in the company of their parents." After this letter some priests began to excuse themselves more easily, although lately in many parishes children have begun to participate in religious services. Since children in many places take part in services, it is very difficult for Rugienis to fight it.

Security organs try to co-opt priests to serve as their agents. To draw them into this sinister work of ruining the Church, security officials cajole and threaten the clergy, promising in exchange to let them work in a good parish, to be made deans, to advance even higher, to study in Rome, travel in the United States, at times they offer them a monthly wage outright. Security agents blackmail morally weak priests, "If you don't sign up to cooperate, all your transgressions will be dragged out into the open." The security agents have been successful in enlisting one or the other problem priest, forcing him to carry out assignments for the Soviet government. Such co-opted priests never work seriously for the police; rather, feeling an internal conflict, they finally succumb psychologically, have an emotional breakdown, or take to drink. Such priests try to justify their actions, claiming that they are not wrecking the Church, but merely seeking "dialogue" with the Soviet government. *The Vatican, it seems, does not understand what such "dialogue" means. It is a complete betrayal of the Church's cause.* This is borne out by the experience of priests since the war. Foreigners often consider priests working for the security apparatus as able to adapt to conditions under persecution. This shows utter ignorance of the situation in our country.

Bishops are forced by the government to assign more active priests "on probation" to timid pastors, or to those working as security agents. The security people frighten such pastors with responsibility for all their assistants' "intemperate actions." They order them to see that they do not deliver "anti-Soviet" sermons, do not travel too much, etc. For example, the pastor of Prienai, Rev. Berteška was ordered to inform security agents every time his assistant, Rev. Zdebskis, left the parish. These days many of the more zealous priests suffer more from their own than from government functionaries. In this manner the government polarizes the clergy, pits priest against chancery, and chancery against priest. Priests working for security organs call their conscientious colleagues hot-heads, extremists, revolutionaries banging their heads against the wall. They consider themselves, on the contrary, as wise, and able to calmly "keep up the good work," even though meantime their church is left with just a few old folk.

Security organs try to involve co-opted priests in Soviet propaganda. For example, in the publication by J. Rimaitis, *Religion in Lithuania,* published in English and Italian strictly for readers abroad, and also in J. Aničas' book, *The Socio-Political Role of the Catholic Church in Lithuania 1945-1952,* we find mendacious statements by some priests, concealing the persecution of the faithful throughout the postwar era.[7] Undoubtedly, the government at times succeeds in forcing even a priest who does not sign up to make such statements about "freedom" of religion in Lithuania.

---

7. Rimaitis' work was published in 1971. Aničas' work referred here is a Lithuanian language study **Socialinis politinis katalikų bažnyčios vaidmuo Lietuvoje 1945-1952 metais** (Vilnius, 1971). A somewhat revised and updated English language version of this work also has been published under the title **The Establishment of Socialism in Lithuania and the Catholic Church** (Vilnius, 1975). It is an obvious effort to counteract the unfavorable foreign opinion in respect to Soviet treatment of religious organizations.

The special task of co-opted priests is to "straighten out" the thinking of tourists from abroad, and especially of priests. They describe the situation of the Church falsely, as if religion were not harassed, as if all who wished to could pray, as though the seminary provided enough priests for parish work, and as if some priests were just hot-heads. If it weren't for them, the bishops could obtain more privileges from the government, etc.

In an effort to prove how good the Soviet government is to priests, visitors from abroad might be shown the villa of Monsignor Krivaitis on the Neris River or the home of Rev. S. Lydis, pastor of Immaculate Conception parish in Vilnius, etc. The foreigner cannot get to some out-of-the way hole and see how priests sometimes lack the bare necessities of life. For example, the pastor of Valkabūdis, Rev. A. Lukošaitis, spent the summer of 1972 in a tent pitched in the church-yard because the government would not let him purchase a house, even though a building confiscated from the parish stands practically empty.

To know the real truth, to fell the well-masked treachery of the Soviet officials, their hypocrisy and deceit, one must spend a longer time in Lithuania. So it is not surprising that even the Vatican was deceived for a long time. From the view-point of us who live in Lithuania, decisions unfavorable to the Catholic Church in Lithuania have been made. Even now the priests and faithful of Lithuania are disturbed that the Holy See, while defending victims of discrimination all over the world, barely recalls the "Church of Silence and Suffering," does not bring up and does not condemn covert or overt perse-cution of the faithful in the Soviet Union.

In Lithuania no one believes that a dialogue with the Soviet government is possible. It is needed by the atheistic government only so that, having gained our confidence, they might more easily wreck the Church from within. In Lithu-ania it is plain to all that the Church will not be destroyed if priests are imprisoned, if school children are forced to speak and to act against their own convictions, if there is no press, no officially published prayer book or catechism. However, the Catholic Church in Lithuania will lose the people if it loses credibility by pandering to the Soviet regime. This is what hap-pened to the Orthodox Church in Russia.

According to the program of the Communist Party, all educated professionals: teachers, physicians, agronomists, and others, must be "enlightened" in their thinking and prepared

III. ENLISTING THE FAITHFUL TO ATHEISTIC ENDS

to "enlighten" others. In the hospital at Švenčionys, an order from the medical director remained posted for a whole year, directing that every physician, including those who were known believers, be prepared at all times to give one lecture on a medical subject, and one on some anti-religious theme. More than once teachers known as believers have been assigned to lead atheistic groups in school. Believers at work are assigned to atheistic committees in factories and offices. Thus it is believed they can be forced to speak and act against their inner convictions. Not wishing to lose their position, or at the least to put up with unpleasantness, the educated sometimes give in and become auxiliaries of the atheists. It is impossible even to approximate how many teachers, terrorized by the atheists, have spoken against their faith, how many students they have recruited for atheist groups as such. It is no accident that one often hears in Lithuania that teachers have contributed most toward making the nation godless, and by the same token, to its denationalization.

Terrorized by the atheists, uninformed Catholic parents often undermine religion. When a child is in doubt whether or not to join the Komsomols, believing parents often advise him or her to join, fearing that otherwise the child might be harassed.

The atheists even try to harness believing school children to their atheistic ends. Pupils have more than once been required to speak against their beliefs, to sketch anti-religious caricatures, or to deride a friend for the practice of religion. Children, usually picking up the attitude of subservience from their elders, hide their religion from their classmates. Soviet education encourages such behavior, calling it "a positive effect of the collective."

Compare the facts described above with atheist propaganda:

"Neither the Soviet state nor its governmental agencies interfere in the Church's internal affairs." (J. Aničas, J. Rimaitis), *Tarybiniai įstatymai apie religinius kultus ir sąžinės laisvė*, Vilnius, 1970, p. 21.)

"The Party fights for complete freedom of conscience and regards with respect every sincere conviction in the area of faith." (A. Balsys, *Kur susikerta ietys*, Vilnius, 1972, p. 58.)

59. ON DISCRIMINATION AGAINST BELIEVERS

To: The Presidium of the Supreme Soviet of the USSR

Copy to: The Representative of the Council for Religious Affairs, K. Tumėnas

A COMPLAINT OF THE BELIEVERS OF LITHUANIA

The decree of the Presidium of the USSR Supreme Soviet, dated April 12, 1968, "On the Procedure for Consideration of Citizens' Proposals, Statements, and Complaints," states: "Under the contemporary conditions of development of Soviet society complaints are normally a way of reacting to instances of violation of the rights of citizens and their interests, safeguarded by law... The complaints also indicate that there are serious shortcomings in the work of many organs of the state and society."

V. Kuroedov, Chairman of the Council for Religious Affairs, writes:[1]

"It is necessary to react with great sensitivity to the complaints of believers that their rights are being violated. All complaints must be considered and resolved in strict conformity to the decree of the Presidium of the USSR Supreme Soviet, dated April 12, 1968." *(Religion and Law,* 1970, p. 24).

In the beginning of March 1973 we, the believers of Lithuania, decided to address ourselves to the agencies of Soviet government in Lithuania, requesting the end of discrimination against religious students, not to force them to speak and act against their beliefs, to teach history objectively in the schools, and not to restrict the publication of essential religious literature. To make the Soviet government aware of the

No. 59. **Chronicle,** No. 6 (1973). The initiators and organizers of this complaint and the two petitions allegedly signed by over 30,000 believers are not revealed in the **Chronicle,** as is normally the case, nor is the reaction of the Soviet authorities.

1. Vladimir A. Kuroedov is the Chairman of the Council for Religious Affairs of the USSR since 1961. He is associated with the rather devastating campaign against religion and its institutions promoted by Khrushchev. See Donald A. Lowrie, William C. Fletcher, "Khrushchev's Religious Policy 1959-1964," in Marshall, op. cit., ch. 7. The statement of Kuroedov cited here is from his **Religiia i zakon** (Moscow, 1970).

opinion of Lithuanian believers, signatures were collected for
the complaints and addressed to the Ministry of Education of
the Lithuanian SSR and to the Representative of the Council
for Religious Affairs K. Tumėnas. If one is to believe the Soviet
press, then all those who make the governing organs aware
of present ills and demand their elimination strengthen socialist
legality, participate in the control of the state, and are moral
individuals, deserving respect. (Cf. *Švyturys*, 1973, No. 6,
pp. 8-10).[2]

But as soon as the security officials found out about
the petition, the "witch hund" began: innocent people were
subjected to searches, inquisitions, and threats of imprisonment.
This is how the security officials of Vilnius, Kaunas, Panevėžys,
Lazdijai, Ignalina, and elsewhere behaved. K. Tumėnas, the
Representative of the Council for Religious Affairs, ordered the
Lithuanian bishops and administrators, through the deans and
priests, to impede the collection of the signatures by the people.
The security officials succeeded in confiscating a part of the
petition.

Despite this "reaction with great sensitivity to the complaints of believers," 14,284 believers signed the statement addressed to the Ministry of Education of the Lithuanian SSR,
while 16,498 believers signed the statement addressed to the
Representative of the Council for Religious Affairs.

Since the officials of state security considered the appeal
of the believers to the Soviet government a political crime and
are terrorizing the circulators of the petition, we are refraining
from sending the original copies of statements, with all the
signatures, to the aforementioned agencies. This will be done
only when the believers will become convinced of the good
will of the Soviet government and when the officials of state
security will cease interfering in the religious affairs of the
believers.

The Presidium of the USSR Supreme Soviet has requested
expression of opinions concerning the fundamental principles
of laws on education, submitted by the Council of Ministers
of the USSR in April of this year. The proposal completely

---

2. *Švyturys* is an illustrated bi-weekly magazine of mass appeal.
The issue referred here contains an article on the treatment of citizens'
complaints, including the criticism of improper reaction of the Soviet
authorities.

ignores the rights of religious parents and children. It is contrary to Article V of the Paris "Convention against Discrimination in Education," adopted on December 14-15, 1960, which demands that the parents be assured religious and moral upbringing of children in harmony with their beliefs.[3] Our statement to the Ministry of Education of the Lithuanian SSR sufficiently informs the Soviet government about the kind of teaching and upbringing of children of religious parents that is desired in Lithuania.

Enclosures: Text of the Statement to the Ministry of
            Education of the Lithuanian SSR

            Text of the Statement to the Representative of
            the Council for Religious Affairs K. Tumėnas

May 14, 1973

— — —

To: The Ministry of Education of the Lithuanian SSR

A STATEMENT BY THE STUDENTS AND PARENTS OF LITHUANIA

We, students and parents, comprehending well the purposes and obligations of the school to the younger generation, are often disappointed because the students are not offered that which they really need.

The textbook on *Social Science* notes: "Patriotism is among the best of innate manifestations of man. It manifests itself as love of the land where we were born and grew up, as love of its history." But how can the students know the past of Lithuania, when the *History of the Lithuanian SSR* by J. Jurginis is brief—barely 100 pages—and one-sided, while the *History of the Lithuanian SSR* by A. Gaigalaitė (148 pages) relates only

---

3. The proposed Fundamental Principles of Legislation on Education of the USSR and Union Republics was published in Lithuania in **Tiesa**, April 5, 1973. The objections are probably to the various provisions of the proposed legislation, calling for "communist upbringing", "secular education without the influence of religion", and similar expressions, which may conflict with the right of parents to determine the world view of their children.

to the revolutionary movement and the postwar years? At the same time the *History of the USSR* consists of four parts—with a total of 650 pages.[4] For this reason the student knows a lot about Pugachev, Peter I, and others, but they know practically nothing about the great past of Lithuania.

The greatest evil is the forcible atheistic indoctrination of the students. It is said that religion in the Soviet Union is a private matter, that the Constitution of the USSR guarantees everyone freedom of conscience, yet practice indicates the contrary.

Religious students are repeatedly ridiculed, rebuked for religious practices; their caricatures "decorate" school wall newspapers. Religious medals and crucifixes are taken away from the students. At times teachers even take the students out of church; for example, from funeral services.

Religious students are forced to speak and write against their beliefs, to draw anti-religious cartoons. Those who refuse to be hypocritical find their grades lowered to failing.

The teachers force religious students to join atheistic organizations and clubs and, for this reason, many are encouraged to be hypocritical.

A number of teachers use their class time for atheistic propaganda. Atheism is proclaimed in the school and beyond its confines even through trickery, for example, by showing "miracles," by cruelly ridiculing and deliberately distorting the Catholic faith.

The grade for conduct is lowered to barely passing solely for church attendance.[5] The beliefs of religious students are

---

4. Of the textbooks mentioned here, only the Lithuanian history texts were available for examination. J. Jurginis, V. Merkys, **Lietuvos TSR istorija** (Kaunas, 1972) is a general history, 109 pages, for the seventh to ninth year of school. It tends to emphasize the revolutionary movements and economic factors in history and presents a rather biased view of Lithuanian-Russian relations. A. Gaigalaitė, R. Žepkaitė, **Lietuvos TSR istorija** (Kaunas, 1969) is a text for the tenth-eleventh years of school. It is a history of Lithuania since 1917, mostly devoted to the Soviet period.

5. Each student in primary and secondary school is evaluated for "conduct" on a scale of 5. The grade for conduct can be lowered from the normal 5 virtually for any behavior considered as deviant, from participation in religious life to hooliganism. A conduct grade of 3 seriously affects the student's future life chances.

noted in the character reference, thereby making it more difficult for them to enter schools of higher education.

Students are often required to respond to questionnaires dealing with religious convictions. We cannot understand why the conscience is forcibly violated. Some students, unwilling to air their convictions, hypocritically answer the questionnaires. Who benefits from this?

We have mentioned only certain cases of violation of the conscience of students, but even this forces the conclusion that the Soviet school is most interested not in teaching or upbringing, but rather in developing atheists. Such "upbringing" destroys the authority of the school and irreversibly harms the students.

We are tired of compulsory atheism and this evokes a reaction: the rejection of ideas advocated by force. How can this be reconciled with the Constitution of the USSR, which proclaims the freedom of conscience?

Therefore, we request the Ministry of Education to put an end to such harmful practices and request that no one hinder the students from enjoying the freedom of conscience.

March 1973

14,284 Signatures

N.B. About 25 per cent of the signers are students.

— — —

To: The Representative of the Council for Religious Affairs
    K. Tumėnas

A STATEMENT OF THE BELIEVERS OF LITHUANIA

In the March 1, 1973 edition of *Gimtasis Kraštas* we read a statement of Bishop R. Krikščiūnas:

"The Catholics of Lithuania publish books that are needed.

---

6. **Gimtasis Kraštas** is the organ of the Lithuanian branch of the "Rodina Society," a propaganda institution for relations with compatriots abroad. Although the newspaper is directed at the diaspora, it is also available on the newsstands in Lithuania.

Recently we published *The Ritual of Roman Catholics for the Dioceses of Lithuania, The Prayer Book, The Resolutions of the Second Vatican Council,* and other books. The odor of printer's ink is still present on the very significant publication *The New Testament.*"[7]

We believers wanted to buy *The New Testament.* Regrettably, the local priests explained to us that they received only a few copies of *The New Testament*—approximately one copy for 300 believers...

If Lithuanian Catholics publish their own religious books, why is it that in the postwar years the most important book of all, namely the catechism, has not been published? Why were only 10,000 copies of the Bible published? Why did we not see *The Resolutions of the Second Vatican Council,* could we not get *The Prayer Book,* even though every Catholic is supposed to have it? It is not enough that we are unable to secure the Bible for ourselves, we now hear that someone is sending thousands of copies to Lithuanians abroad? Is it possible we will have to ask our relatives abroad to send us the Bible, which was published in Lithuania?

Since it is clear to us that religious books are published in very limited quantities and not by Catholics, but at the request of the bishops and you, the Representative, by the Soviet government, we are therefore requesting the reprinting of the Bible and the *Prayer Book* in sufficient quantities so that every Catholic family could have at least one copy of each. In addition, we are asking for a permit to publish an extensive catechism. If we are not granted these requests, it will be difficult to believe in any statement about the publication of the most needed Catholic books in Soviet Lithuania.

March of 1973

16,498 Signatures

---

7. See note 5, Doc. No. 51, for bibliographical information on these religious publications.

60. "THE CARES OF THE CATHOLIC CHURCH IN LITHUANIA"

The goals of the atheists in regard to the Church remain unchanged—they want to destroy it at any price.

In Stalin's times they wanted to destroy the Church physically.[1] The year 1946 marked the beginning of the arrests of bishops and priests. Bishop Borisevičius was executed by shooting in 1947. Archbishop M. Reinys died in the prison of Vladimir in 1953, while serving a 25-year sentence. In 1956 Bishop P. Ramanauskas and Archbishop T. Matulionis returned to Lithuania after years in a labor camp, their health broken, but they were not allowed to perform their duties and both died shortly afterwards.

In 1956-57 hundreds of priests returning from labor camps join the apostolic work. The atheistic government begins to realize that reprisals will not break the Lithuanian Catholic Church. Those who had perished in the camps were considered martyrs and some of them, as T. B. Andruška, S.J., even inspired prayers for his canonization.

The "gallant" chekists of Nikita Khrushchev again arrested many priests in 1957-58: Canon P. Rauda, Canon S. Kiškis, T. A. Markaitis, S.J., Rev. A. Mocius, Rev. J. Balčiūnas, Rev. A. Jurgaitis, Rev. A. Bunkus, Rev. A. Švarinskas, T. F. Adomaitis, MIC (who had been active in Siberia among German Catholics) and Rev. P. Jakulevičius. All of them, except Rev. Jurgaitis and Rev. Bunkus, were sent to prison for the second time, while for T. Markaitis, S.J., it was the third time.

This time, too, violence brought no results—those arrested did their apostolic work in the camps, and upon their return to Lithuania again joined the pastoral activity.

The atheist government is making a special effort to destroy the Roman Catholic Church from the inside—with the clergy's and the believers' own hands. The Representative of the Council for Religious Affairs has eased into the more important posts such priests who either enter into compromises with the atheists or are inactive. Pastoral work in the cities

---

No. 60. Lead article of **Chronicle**, No. 10 (1974).

1. A popular account of Stalinist repression of bishops and priests, including some of those mentioned here, is found in Matas Raišupis, **Dabarties kankiniai** (Chicago, 1972).

has suffered the greatest damage. Moreover, the atheists have been successful in their efforts to have the Vatican promote, on the basis of unobjective information, certain clergymen who have not merited it. "Why does the Holy See value such priests and set them as examples for others?"—the Lithuanian priests were wondering. Not a single priest, save perhaps Canon K. Žitkus, was given recognition for good pastoral work. Those who misled the Vatican wanted to disarm the zealous priests psychologically and to compromise the Roman Curia.

A habit that inflicts great damage on the Church has taken root in the curiae of Lithuanian bishoprics—the habit of concealing everything from the priests and believers. Ominous rumors, having penetrated the curtain of silence of the curiae, insist that the atheists are determined to proceed with the final liquidation of two Lithuanian bishops who are the pride of the believers—H.E. Bishop J. Steponavičius and H.E. Bishop V. Sladkevičius. The atheists want to inflict that blow on the Lithuanian Church with the Vatican's own hands—by appointing new candidates, selected by the atheists themselves, to the posts of the exiled bishops. The following individuals are being mentioned as candidates for bishops' posts: Msgr. B. Barauskas, Msgr. Č. Krivaitis, Canon Andriukonis, Rev. Dr. V. Butkus, Rev. B. Baliukonis, Rev. Vaičius, and others.[2] The Lithuanian believers are certain that the atheists are not motivated by their love for the Church in wanting to see as bishops candidates who lack the confidence of the community of the believers and among the clergy. The wishes of the Lithuanian believers are expressed in the words of Rev. St. Yla: "The bishop we want to see is not a mannikin clad in episcopal garments, but a human being, a father and a teacher."[3] The

---

2. At the time Msgr. Barauskas was Chancellor of the Diocese of Telšiai; Msgr. Krivaitis—the Apostolic Administrator of the Archdiocese of Vilnius (in place of the exiled Bishop Steponavičius); Rev. Dr. Butkus —the Rector of the Interdiocesan Seminary in Kaunas, Rev. Baliukonis— the Chancellor of the Diocese of Vilkaviškis; Rev Vaičius—Administrator of the Diocese of Telšiai. The position of Canon Andriukonis could not be determined. The dissident priests are particularly anxious to block the consecration of Rev. Butkus and Msgr. Krivaitis for what they consider moral shortcomings (never specifically stated) and the alleged subservience to the Soviet authorities.

3. Rev. Stasys Yla is an emigré priest, a popular publicist and scholar, presently residing in the US.

truth of this statement is attested by the flood of greetings by priests and believers sent to H. E. Bishop Sladkevičius on the occasion of his 15th anniversary of exile (April 17, 1974). There cannot be any doubt that the sacrifice and the example of the bishops in banishment have not contributed less to the Catholic Church of Lithuania than the bishops now in office. An almost irreparable harm would be inflicted on the prestige of the Lithuanian Catholic Church and of the Vatican if the bishops venerated by the Catholics and the priests were to be pushed aside.

WHAT LITHUANIA NEEDS AT PRESENT IS NOT NEW BISHOPS BUT PRIESTS

The atheist government has reserved for the bishops the right to consecrate four to eight priests a year and to bury dead priests. Even the conferring of the Sacrament of Confirmation and the appointment of priests to parishes is strictly regulated by the atheist government. Moreover, the atheists want to arrange Lithuania's church life in such a manner that the priests would be subordinated to the church committees, and not to the bishops. In a situation of this kind the existing bishops are quite sufficient for Lithuania and new ones are not desirable. If the atheist government wants to show its good will, let it allow the banished bishops to perform their pastoral duties.

The Catholics and priests of Lithuania feel a great need to pray that as much as possible objective information about the situation of the Roman Catholic Church of Lithuania reaches the Holy See, and then the Holy Father will arrange its affairs in the best possible manner.

In their striving to destroy the faith, the atheists want to become absolute rulers of the people's spiritual world, unhampered in the pursuit of their goals by the people's belief in God and religious morality. Atheist Marxism seeks to have all people think, speak, and act only in accordance with the Communist Party's program. In fighting against religion in Lithuania, the atheists are trying to break down the spirit of the Lithuanian nation, to take away the spiritual values, to enslave the Lithuanian population, and to denationalize the religious masses. Once the Lithuanians become atheists, begin forming ethnically mixed families, stop treasuring their own

Christian culture, conditions will be created for their sub-
mersion in a monolithic mass of people, to use Lenin's language.

The people are, alas, totally disillusioned with Marxist
Communism. Our students and the intelligentsia study Marxism
only under compulsion. The atheist government, whether it
wants to or not, is compelled to employ all the ideological and
administrative means in order to retain the people's spiritual
world in their hands.

Atheism in Lithuania has become a quasi-official religion;
at its service are the press, radio, television, and it is disseminated by all possible means. Not only teachers and educators, but all members of the intelligentsia are forced to promote
atheism. At a time when book stores are jammed with atheist
literature, the Catholics almost completely lack their own publications, and what they do possess is confiscated by the security.
The Siberian prison awaits the contemporary book smugglers,
as it once did in the czarist times. Things were easier at the
time of press ban, because the czar did not have as many spies
as well as traitors coming from the nation itself.[4]

The atheist government does not have enough confidence
in propagandistic means and resorts to well-organized administrative measures. The Council for Religious Affairs, attached to the USSR Council of Ministers, supervises—in official
parlance—the execution of laws concerning religious cults. In
reality, this body combats religion in the entire Soviet Union
by using administrative means. Councils for coordinating atheist
activity are active in the centers of the republic; their branches,
the raion atheist councils, are headed by deputy chairmen
of (raion) executive committees. These deputies enjoy an almost limitless license to terrorize priests within the raion limits
and to restrict their freedom of action. Usually such restrictions are conveyed verbally, while the deputy fidgets with a
secret instruction taken from a safe—the atheists do not want
to leave their shameful documents behind for Lithuania's
history.

---

4. Reference to a ban on Lithuanian press in the Latin alphabet
following the 1863 revolt against the czarist rule. It was one of the
measures of russification instituted by the czarist regime. The ban was
to a great extent circumvented by massive smuggling of books into
Lithuania, mostly from East Prussia. The ban was lifted in 1904.

Each district has an active atheist council whose task is to organize atheist activity, to spy on the priests' work and on the believers, etc.

The religious situation in Lithuania is closely followed by the Committee for State Security since each more distinct manifestation of religiosity among us is considered a threat to Soviet power. The present situation of the Catholic Church is a source of great anxiety both for the Communist Party's Central Committee and for the Committee for State Security —the faithful are attending churches in large numbers, are receiving sacraments, and even dare to defend their rights.

Moscow demands that in combatting the Church the atheists use the means tested in Russia after the October Revolution. But the desired results are more difficult to attain in Lithuania because the center of the Catholics is not in Moscow, but in Rome.

The atheists have become convinced that the most convenient way of destroying the Church is from the inside, through the parish committees and through the Church hierarchy that is currying favor with the atheist government.

According to the Soviet Constitution, the Church has been separated from the state, yet the state is interfering in Church affairs, large and small, through the office of the Representative of the Council for Religious Affairs, as well as through church committees.[5] There is an effort to pack the latter with the maximum number of individuals who are favorable or even completely loyal to the atheists. The Church leaders immediately saw through that ruse of the atheists which threatened to paralyze pastoral work. Presently the atheists are trying to introduce into Lithuania an arrangement that exists in Russia, the Ukraine, Belorussia, and elsewhere—the church committees must be the real masters of the parishes, while the priests are merely hired hands. The church committee must take care

---

5. The church committees were supposed to serve as instruments of secular control and were vigorously opposed by the hierarchy. The committees were finally accepted by the end of the 1940s, but functioned in a manner permitting ecclesiastical control of church affairs. The current concern of the dissidents stems from the Soviet efforts to strengthen the role of church committees, at the same time imposing a stronger control over the committees themselves by local secular authorities. See the introductory study for an evaluation of the role of church committees.

of the parish's financial affairs, perform the necessary repairs; the believers who want to bury the dead baptize infants, or to get married, must turn to the church committee. In this manner an attempt is made to dissuade the people from practicing religion. Since the church committee hires priests, the episcopal functions become meaningless or, even worse, the bishop remains a mere stage prop to conceal from the world the atheistic violence backstage.

Currently Lithuanian priests are being compelled, without the bishop's knowledge, to accept the new contracts with the church committees from the raion executive committees.[6] The contracts are formulated in a one-sided manner and are exceedingly vague, especially in regard to the closing of the church. Point four of the contract states: "This contract may be cancelled... c) in case of a decision made according to the established procedure to close the house of prayer (the cult building), the use of which was permitted by this contract." The believers cannot be in agreement with any arrangement that entails the closing of a church.

In order to prevent resistance, contracts are made surreptitiously, not simultaneously, and even by using deceit. It is deplorable that even the priests themselves—and therefore what can one expect of the faithful?—have been acting in some cases without forethought and in a flighty manner. The priests who clearly see through the atheist ambitions are waging resistance against signing vaguely formulated contracts and disagree with the relinquishing of ecclesiastical jurisdiction to church committee members intimidated by the atheists. The present contracts are the first step toward the final strangulation of the bishops' and priests' freedom of action.

Thank God, the bishops have so far disagreed with the non-ecclesiastical arrangement which the authorities are trying to sell. There are indications, however, that new efforts will be undertaken presently to transform the church committees in Lithuania into all-powerful masters of the parishes. Tarasov,

---

6. **Chronicle,** No. 11 (1974), provides a copy of instructions to local executive committees concerning the conclusion of new contracts with the church committees and the renewal of church committee membership. The instruction suggests that "loyal people" be included in the committees and that those who were convicted, exiled, or are generally "reactionary" be removed from the committees.

Title pages of Catholic *samizdat* journals.

A sample of the more than 17,000 signatures of Catholics on a petition to the UN. For details, see Doc. No. 56.

At issue: production of religious literature. Catholic activists who have been sentenced to various terms for production of religious literature, including the *Chronicle of the Catholic Church in Lithuania*. (Top, clockwise) Nijolė Sadūnaitė, Ona Pranckūnaitė, Vladas Lapienis, Petras Plumpa. For details, see Doc. Nos. 63, 65, 72.

At issue: the right of the Church to survive as an institution. Members of the Catholic Committee for the the Defense of the Rights of Believers (top, l. to r.): Revs. J. Zdebskiṣ, S. Tamkevičius, V. Velavičius, J. Kauneckas, A. Svarinskas. A rare public outing of the seminarians (bottom), who, the dissidents charge, are under intense pressure from the KGB.

At issue: the appointment and reinstatement of exiled bishops. The two exiled bishops V. Sladkevičius and J. Steponavičius (top), officiating at the funeral of Rev. K. Garuckas in April of 1979. Cardinal L. Lekai of Hungary (bottom, second from left) in the Cathedral of Panevėžys, while he was on a mission for the Vatican, October, 1979.

At issue: catechization of children and performance of religious rites. The trial of Rev. J. Zdebskis (top, left) in 1971 for catechization of children was among the events leading to Catholic dissent; for details, see Doc. No. 53. The First Communion procession in Marijampolė, summer of 1978, symbolizes limited gains for Catholic rights. Among the numerous limitations on performance of religious rites was the prohibition of funeral services in church, as occurred in Lazdijai in 1965 (bottom).

At issue: desecration of shrines and churches. The Hill of Crosses (bottom, left), a national/religious shrine which has been frequently desecrated by the regime. A public march to the Hill of Crosses (top), commemorating the Tenth Anniversary of the Friends of the Eucharist in 1979. The church of Žalioji parish (Vilkaviškis raion) has been transformed into a mill, so the faithful hold services outside in the cemetery.

Public dissent led to a growth of confidence among the believers and to massive demonstrations of faith. Symbolic of Catholic assertiveness are the marches to the shrine in Šiluva: the 1977 march (top) and the 1979 march of about a thousand Friends of the Eucharist, led by the newly ordained priest, the Rev. Kąstytis Krikščiūnaitis (bottom).

Representative of the Council for Religious Affairs, has made a statement to that effect.[7]

The activity of the church committees according to the atheist plan is in total contradiction to the ecclesiastical order, where authority is derived not from the people, but from Christ himself. It is therefore not surprising that ever since the revolution, the leaders of the Church have rejected the idea of such committees. That struggle has claimed victims: Bishop Ceplak, Msgr. Butkevičius, Bishop T. Matulionis, and others.[8] Only following the mass closing of churches and arrests of priests, as well as after several priests of the city of Vilnius had betrayed the Church in making concessions, did the bishops lift the injunction against the formation of church committees.[9] Yet heretofore these committees, with some small exceptions, have not directly interfered with pastoral work.

The atheists, who have absorbed the practices of the czars, want to use the hierarchy of the Roman Catholic Church

7. **Chronicle,** No. 8 (1973), mentions Tarasov as an official of the Council for Religious Affairs of the USSR. He has visited Lithuania in July of 1973 in connection with the request of the believers of Klaipėda to return their church, which was transformed into a philharmonic hall. The same issue of the **Chronicle** publishes a complaint of believers addressed to him. Apparently Tarasov is Moscow's deputy for religious affairs in Lithuania. No further details are available on Tarasov's statement concerning the role of church committees.

8. Bishop J. Ceplak (1857-1926), a Polish prelate, served in the Soviet Union. In 1923 he was tried and condemned to death (sentence commuted to 10 years in prison after international pressure) apparently for opposing secular control over church affairs and property. Msgr. Butkevičius was tried together with Bishop Ceplak; no further information is available on him. The Lithuanian Bishop Teofilis Matulionis (1873-1962) also served in Russia. From 1910 he was a pastor of the Church of the Sacred Heart of Jesus in St. Petersburg. In 1923 he was tried and convicted to three years in prison for refusing to sign over to the state the church and its property. In 1929 he was secretly consecrated bishop, spent most of his time in Soviet prisons and labor camps. In 1933 he was permitted to return to Lithuanian under the agreement for exchange of prisoners between the Soviet Union and Lithuania. In 1943 he became the Bishop of Kaišiadorys. After the war Bishop Matulionis was exiled from Lithuania. He returned home again in 1956, but was not permitted to assume his post at the Diocese of Kaišiadorys.

9. Reference to a number of priests in Vilnius who agreed to form church committees before the episcopate gave its sanction in the second half of 1948. See **Arkivyskupas Mečislovas Reinys,** p. 216.

in the struggle against that Church. They want to ease into
leading posts concession-prone bishops or priests, who would
carry out decrees harmful to the Church, spread erroneous information to the believers of the world about the so-called
freedom of the Church, proclaim to the priests the regulations
of the atheist government. restricting pastoral work, e.g., catechization of children, the ban against canonical visitation of
parishes, etc. When the clergymen who are noted for their
concessions to the government are about to visit Rome, they
are instructed in Moscow on what to speak there, what to
pass over in silence, with whom to socialize, and whom to avoid.
On their return, they are obligated to favor the appropriate organs with a "general confession."

At present, there is a great deal of talk among Lithuanian
priests that the Vatican might nominate new bishops whose
candidacies would be put forward not by Lithuania's believers,
but via clergymen who are currying favor with the government. If these new bishops, inclined to make concessions to the
government, were to be appointed, the atheists would achieve
the following goals:

1. The Holy Father's authority, heretofore very strong
among Lithuania's believers and priests, would be destroyed.
The Lithuanian priests have demonstrated their fidelity to
the Apostolic See even under the most difficult conditions. The
efforts of the atheists to create in Lithuania a national Catholic Church, refusing to recognize the Pope's jurisdiction, were
doomed to failure. One of the priests, sentenced to a 25-year
term, was offered freedom, St. John's Church in Vilnius, and a
bribe of 100,000 rubles for assisting in the above.[10] The Church
of Silence will never be able to comprehend a diplomacy that
would create conditions for the triumph of the atheists and
(would indicate) that not even the Vatican supported the priests

---

10. Specific documentation of the efforts to form a national church,
separated from Rome, is not available. One effort to develop a schism
between the Pope and the Lithuanian clergy was a petition, circulated
by the Representative for the Cult in 1949-1950. It involved the condemnation of the Pope as a war-monger. It was a reaction to the Pope's decree of
July 13, 1949, excommunicating Catholics for collaboration with the
communists. According to dissident sources, there were very few signers
and the project was abandoned. Text of the petition in **Chronicle,**
No. 15 (1975).

and the believers fighting and suffering for the faith. The atheist government may promise much and sign the most beautiful treaties in return for diplomatic concessions, but those treaties will remain as dead as the "Declaration of Human Rights" signed by the atheist government. The priests and believers in Lithuania are of the opinion that the life of Bishop B. Borisevičius might have been saved if the bishops and Catholics of the world had reacted properly at the right time. The same can be also said about the massive arrests of priests.

2. The honorable Lithuanian bishops, such as Archbishop J. Matulevičius, Archbishop M. Reinys, Archbishop T. Matulionis, and others have raised the archepiscopal authority in the community of believers to a high plateau. If the Holy See were to nominate unsuitable candidates to bishop's posts, episcopal authority would be destroyed and simultaneously grave harm would be inflicted on the Lithuanian Church.

3. *The Chronicle of the Catholic Church in Lithuania* mentions only a small portion of the facts—it is unable to collect more because of the persecution—attesting to the atheistic persecution and the woes of the believers. The believers in Lithuania expect support from their spiritual leaders. Meanwhile, the clergymen picked by the government proclaim that in our country the Church is not being persecuted. How great would be the disappointment of the Lithuanian believers if the Vatican were to increase the number of such clergymen.

4. The appointment of new bishops capable of entering into compromises with the government would be a moral blow to the exiled bishops H. E. Bishop J. Steponavičius and H. E. Bishop V. Sladkevičius, who are respected by the nation. Their sacrifice would be thus devalued, their loyalty to the Holy Father and to the Church would be in a sense condemned, and the possibility of their return to their duties would be ultimately destroyed.

5. At a time when the atheist government uses all possible means to coerce Church leaders, forcing them to issue decrees harmful to pastoral work, the Lithuanian priests would find it easier to orient themselves if such decrees were signed not by the bishop but merely by the administrator of a diocese.

Therefore the priests and believers of Lithuania do beg the Holy Father and the Roman Curia to see to it that:

a. No new bishops who curry favor with the atheists should be appointed.

b. In appointing bishops, the exiled bishops or priests authorized by them should be consulted. This can be put into practice, provided the candidacies of new bishops are announced in the Vatican not later than one half year prior to their nomination.

c. No diplomatic concessions should be granted to the atheists on the basis of trust in their good will. Concessions from the atheists are impossible by way of negotiation—the Catholics of Lithuania will have as much freedom as they will gain through struggles. The truth of the above is attested by more than one contemporary victory gained by fighting. The Catholics of Lithuania will be strong enough to gain anything only when they receive the broad support of world public opinion and of the leading figures in the hierarchy of the Catholic Church.

The Catholics of Lithuania are grateful to the organizers of the Vatican broadcasts, the press of the Lithuanians abroad as well as of Catholics and non-Catholics in the whole world which publicizes the offenses of the atheists in Lithuania, as well as to those who pray and act to help Lithuanian Catholics achieve more religious freedom. It is deplorable that the "Voice of America" pays no attention to this matter. Therefore, it is not surprising that fewer and fewer people are listening to its broadcasts. Lithuanians who are suffering for their faith are not easily interested in economic crises or political wheelings and dealings.

The society of Lithuanian believers, painfully experiencing the rage of security organs and witnessing the best sons of the Nation and the Church ending up in prison one after another, are astounded that the Catholics of the world have failed to defend those arrested. The atheist government seeks to ensure that, with the world silent, it can deal with them more easily.

61. THE CASE OF BISHOP V. SLADKEVIČIUS

To: The Representative of the Council for Religious Affairs of the Lithuanian SSR

A STATEMENT

We, the undersigned priests of the Diocese of Kaišiadorys, ask that the Kaišiadorys Bishop Vincentas Sladkevičius, now living in the raion of Biržai in Nemunėlio Radviliškis, be allowed to fulfill his duties as bishop of the Diocese of Kaišiadorys.

July 30, 1974

The Sender: Canon Jonas Dzekunskas living in the raion of Kaišiadorys in Žiežmariai.

45 priests of the diocese of Kaišiadorys signed this declaration:

T. Akstinas, A. Alkovikas, A. Anusevičius, A. Arminas, A. Černa, Z. Červokas, J. Čiurlionis, J. Danyla, Canon J. Dzekunskas, P. Genevičius, P. Gerbutavičius, J. Gylys, Z. Gustainis, Canon J. Jonys, A. Jurgilas, J. Kaušyla, I. Kavaliauskas, J. Kazlauskas, Canon St. Kiškis, B. Klimas, E. Kraujalis, P. Leskauskas, J. Matulaitis, J. Masalkas, K. Miknevičius, A. Milašius, H. Misiūnas, Z. Navickas, Z. Neciunskas, M. Petkevičius, Canon J. Pilka, V. Pinkevičius, L. Puzonas, S. Smolinskis, Z. Stančiauskas, St. Stankevičius, R. Šalčiūnas, P. Žiugžda, J. Tomkus, P. Valadka, P. Venckus, Č. Zazeckas, J. Zubrus, J. Žvinys, K. Žilys.

A similar declaration was sent to the Council for Religious Affairs in Moscow.

On August 5, 1974, the Representative of the Council for Religious Affairs, K. Tumėnas, invited the present pastor of Daugai, Canon Jonas Pilka.

"Why are you not satisfied with the present Kaišiadorys administrator?" asked the Representative. "Here is a statement that you signed. We know that you do not occupy the last place among the initiators of the statement."

"This statement is not directed against the administrator," Canon Pilka explained. "We have Bishop V. Sladkevičius, whom the government officials do not permit to fulfill his duties. Therefore, we the priests of the Diocese of Kaišiadorys are asking that the bishop be permitted to fulfill his duties, since, when an administrator rules a diocese, the situation is not normal."

"Yes," agreed K. Tumėnas, "the situation is really abnormal, but with such statements you are doing a great disservice to the administrator of the Diocese of Kaišiadorys."

K. Tumėnas further explained that V. Sladkevičius was consecrated without the permission of the authorities and therefore cannot fulfill the duties of the bishop of Kaišiadorys.

"Did Bishop Sladkevičius request that the priests ask the government for permission to fulfill his duties?" asked the Representative.

"No, he did not ask this."

"Perhaps he does not want to fulfill the duties of a bishop and you, without discussing it with him, are making such efforts."

"If a bishop accepted the bishop's consecration, by the same token he wants to fulfill the duties of a bishop."

"When did you decide to write such a statement?"

"During the funeral of Canon Povilas Bakšys."

"Why are there no arguments in this statement about why you want Bishop V. Sladkevičius to fulfill his duties as bishop?"

"What kind of arguments do you need?" retorted Canon Pilka.

"He is the bishop of Kaišiadorys and we priests are requesting that he be allowed to fulfill his duties."

"The Vatican made a mistake," explained K. Tumėnas, "and should repair it."

"Bishop J. Steponavičius was consecrated with the approval of the authorities, but he was not allowed to fulfill his duties..."

"He did not obey Soviet laws."

The Representative asked who organized the statement, who wrote the text, gathered signatures, and so on. Canon Pilka refused to be an informer.

62. A DEBATE ON THE TACTICS IN THE STRUGGLE FOR RELIGIOUS FREEDOM

On March 19, 1972, the first issue of the *Chronicle of the Catholic Church in Lithuania* tentatively made its appearance, with no way of estimating how much interest it would meet with at home or abroad. The atheistic government accused it of wrong-doing and tried to stifle it by massive searches and arrests. But the government was unsuccessful. State security officials, realizing that they would hardly be able to destroy the *Chronicle of the Catholic Church in Lithuania* by such tactics, resorted to "more subtle" means: attempting to compromise it and its publishers. The priests and faithful of Lithuania know how the security agents force some priests to speak against the *Chronicle*. Not long ago it became known that government officials even went to Bishop Matulaitis-Labukas, demanding that he condemn the *Chronicle* in a public letter. The bishop refused on the basis that such an action would only compromise the ordinaries of Lithuania in the eyes of the faithful, as had happened when they condemned the Memorandum of the 17,000.[1]

In the beginning of September, Bishop Labukas and other ordinaries of the Catholic Church in Lithuania received an anonymous communication, signed in the name of "a group of priests of the Diocese of Vilkaviškis." The letter condemned "reactionary" priests of the Diocese of Vilkaviškis and demanded that Bishop Labukas, on his visit to the Vatican, denounce from there those who "try to turn back the wheel of history."

The priests of Lithuania believe that Bishop Labukas could be coerced by security organs to take this anonymous communication to the Vatican as evidence of what "zealous" priests think about the present situation of the Catholic Church in Lithuania.

Since the anonymous statement is the subject of wide discussion among priests and laity, the *Chronicle of the Catho-*

No. 62. **Chronicle,** No. 12 (1974). The **Chronicle** has presented three responses to the anonymous letter attacking the dissident priests. The response of the priests of Vilkaviškis and Vilnius is presented here. The response of the priests of Panevėžys appeared in **Chronicle,** No. 14 (1975), which is omitted here because it covers essentially the same ground as the two responses presented here.

1. See Doc. No. 48.

lic Church in Lithuania would like to acquaint its readers not only with the anonymous statement, but also with two replies which priests of the dioceses of Vilkaviškis and of Vilnius wrote. Their names are well known to the *Chronicle*.

THE ANONYMOUS STATEMENT

To: His Excellency Bishop Juozas Matulaitis-Labukas,
Apostolic Administrator of the Archdiocese of Kaunas
and of the Diocese of Vilkaviškis.

Copies to: His Excellency, Bishop Juozapas Pletkus; His Excellency, Bishop Romualdas Krikščiūnas; His Excellency, Bishop Liudvikas Povilonis; Monsignor Česlovas Krivaitis, and Canon Juozapas Andrikonis.

The only begotten Son of God was sent by his Father to earth, so that redeeming the entire human race by his Incarnation, he might renew it and unite it. And before offering himself on the cross, he prayed to the Father for the faithful, "that all may be one" (Jn. 17:21). He gave his disciples a new commandment of love for one another, so that the believers might grow together into one Body. If this is true of the faithful, how much more is it true of priests, the builders of that Body of Christ.

Today, that unity among priests is especially lacking. Your Excellency knows well the attitudes of the priests in the dioceses you govern. You are well enough aware especially of the actions of some reactionary priests of the Diocese of Vilkaviškis, which, contrary to the will of Christ, tear down his Church rather than build it up. They slander and smear in the eyes of the faithful many zealous workers in the vineyard of Christ, not excluding even the ordinaries themselves, who, according to the idea of the Second Vatican Ecumenical Council and of recent popes, are zealously working in the present circumstances of life, which, it is true, do not tend to spoil any one. It is no secret that the conditions of our religious life and work are not easy, but within their confines it is possible to work successfully for the good of the Church and salvation of souls.

In the decrees of Vatican II much is said about the relationships of priests among themselves, about their duty to create the Body of Christ. "This requires, especially in our times, many new forms of adaptation." (Decree on Ministry and Life of the Priest).

Thanks to energetic priests who understand the spirit of the times, the churches of Kauno Naujamiestis, Pajevoniai, Šakiai, and others have been resurrected from the ruins. In many places temporary houses of worship have been erected, as in Kapčiamiestis, Bartininkai, Pilviškiai, and elsewhere, and many churches have recently been restored to all their splendor. It can be said without hesitation that today the churches of our diocese are being restored, decorated, and beautified on a much wider scale than in prewar years. And who did all this? Was it those who consider themselves and are even called by Vatican Radio "noble Lithuanians"? No! It was mostly those who are considered by the reactionary priests to be tools of the atheists for the purpose of wrecking the Catholic faith and the Church in Lithuania.

A strange paradox! The atheists' tools are restoring and decorating churches when they should be wrecking and ignoring them, while the so-called "priest patriots," "fighters for the freedom of the Church and religion" try in every way to turn back the wheel of history, thirsting only for vain publicity on foreign radio and in their press, and to become uncrowned martyrs, in order to satisfy their boundless self-love and thirst for praise.

Everyone knows the old adage, "Divide and conquer." It would not be so frustrating if this division were caused by the atheists, but how can we justify our own disagreement? Is this not pouring water on another's millwheel?

Your Excellency knows well that local government organs in some raions are beginning to rescind permission to restore churches; they refuse to assign the necessary materials, and in some places they are beginning to restrict the attendance of priests at religious observances, etc. Is this not a just reaction of the Soviet government against chauvinistic propaganda carried on by some reactionary priests? Why do the bishops of our curia and the administrators of dioceses not react to this? Is such an attitude good for the Church?

The seminary administration complains that candidates are lacking for the first-year class, that this year there was a more careful screening.[2] Could the problem here have been

---

2. One of the complaints in respect to the seminary charges is that the state interferes in the recruitment and selection of candidates for priest-

caused by the so-called secret seminary, for which reactionary priests try to recruit their own candidates? Finally, Your Excellency knows well how much these priests, secretly ordained by someone, are worth and how useful they are. A priest carries out the duties of his calling fully and is useful to the Church only when he is working in the church, and not burrowing about beneath its foundations.

Your Excellency, we know well your many years of experience in chancery work, and we are no less acquainted with your practical views on life and on contemporary trends in society; we know that you are able to call a spade a spade, but we would also want you to remain objective in evaluating the present situation which has arisen in the Diocese of Vilkaviškis.

Pope John XXIII expressed the thought that we should not look for that which divides us, but for that which is common to us all and unites us. We should like Your Excellency to look into the future through the eyes of this great pope of our times, and as much as you can, to put an end to these divisions having nothing in common with the spirit of Christ, and to the unfounded slander of those "who have worked a full day in the scorching heat" (Mt. 20;12). We would wish that your pastoral words would help make a reality those words in the prayer of Jesus: "That all may be one" (Jn. 17:21).

Before long, Your Excellency will be visiting the Vatican. We should like to hear from you while you are there, as our shepherd, the truth about our diocese and its priests, since, if you keep silent, the *Chronicle of the Catholic Church in Lithuania* will speak for you, and it represents neither the Catholic Church of Lithuania, nor our diocese.

A Group of Priests of the
Diocese of Vilkaviškis

September 1, 1974

---

hood. See, for example, the article "The Activity of the KGB Organs in the Seminary," **Chronicle**, No. 3 (1972).

3. References in the **Chronicle** as well as private communications do indicate an underground activity of priests and members of religious orders, including a secret seminary training program. Details are neither available nor would they deserve publicity for obvious reasons.

A RESPONSE TO THE LETTER OF SEPTEMBER 1, 1974, TO THE BISHOPS AND DIOCESAN ADMINISTRATORS OF LITHUANIA BY "A GROUP OF PRIESTS OF THE DIOCESE OF VILKAVIŠKIS"

These days there is being circulated in the Diocese of Kaišiadorys an anonymous letter addressed to Bishop Matulaitis-Labukas in the name of a group of priests of the Diocese of Vilkaviškis. Copies were sent to Bishops B. Pletkus, L. Povilonis, R. Krikščiūnas, Monsignor Č. Krivaitis, and Canon J. Andrikonis.

The political content of the letter is disguised by quotations from Sacred Scripture, mixed with contemporary atheistic terminology: "reactionary priests," "turning back the wheel of history," "the just reaction of the Soviet government," "underground priests." The letter was most likely inspired, and perhaps even written, by the atheists.

The question arises: Why do they, who claim to defend the Church, not dare to sign it? For such a letter they would receive only praise from the atheistic government! The priests of the Diocese of Vilkaviškis have more than once written to Bishop Labukas on matters vital to the Church, and they had the nerve to sign, even though they expected, as a result, punishment from the atheistic government. And so it came to pass. Father Vaclovas Degutis was removed as Dean of Lazdijai and from his pastorate, and sent to the boondocks, while his associate Father Gvidonas Dovidaitis to this day is despised by the government.

The authors of the anonymous document are pained by the lack of unity among priests, but they do not make it clear why they seek unity among priests—to build up the Church or to destroy it? Or perhaps the authors are concerned because in the not-too-distant past the priests of Lithuania did not condemn the activities of Pope Pius XII in a united fashion, and there were only a few priests who "adapted to the conditions of the times."[4]

Who are these "reactionary priests" of the Diocese of Vilkaviškis? From the contents of the letter it is apparent

---

4. Reference to the petition, circulated by Soviet authorities in Lithuania, condemning Pope Pius XII for his decree of July 13, 1949, excommunicating Catholics for collaboration with the communists. Text of the petition in **Chronicle**, No. 15 (1975).

that there are not many of them, they do not rebuild churches, they slander zealous priests, and seek publicity in the foreign press to become uncrowned martyrs.

The anonymous group, if they had the least bit of conscience and civic courage, would present the facts: Who, when, and how did the "reactionaries slander zealous priests?" We are convinced that fathers Antanas Šeškevičius, Prosperas Bubnys, and Juozas Zdebskis showed up in the pages of the foreign press because they did their duty zealously and taught children the catechism without heeding the prohibitions of the government.[5] The authors of the letter should also know the names of other priests who have been repressed.

The authors of the anonymous letter, wishing to mislead world opinion, distracting it from the persecution of the Church, speak about current church renovation in Lithuania.

As a matter of fact, the priests of Lithuania, having trod the path to Golgotha in their homeland and in Siberia, and who have remained faithful to the Church, pay great heed to church renovation, since all other fields of endeavor—work in school, the press, catechization, etc.—are restricted or completely forbidden. Between 1955 and 1957 the government had assigned small quantities of building materials for church repairs. Later, church renovation depended completely upon the shrewdness of the pastor. The atheistic government not only failed to help, but in every conceivable way interfered—not giving permission to repair in some places, and elsewhere even closing churches; for example, in Klaipėda, Kaunas, Žagarė, Pašilė, and elsewhere.

Priests working in the Diocese of Vilkaviškis have never heard that zealous renovators and rebuilders of churches in Šakiai, Pajevonys, or elsewhere were called tools of the atheists. This is a product of the anonymous authors' fancy.

Can the priest who believes, knowing the present circumstances, accuse zealously laboring priests of the wish "to turn back the wheel of history?" That is atheistic talk. The authors of the anonymous communication, knowing the old principle, "Divide et impera," should draw the appropriate conclusions.

Unfortunately, in the letter the problem of the seminary is treated superficially. Some candidates, for example, Father Juozas Čepėnas, the assistant pastor of Raseiniai, waited ten

---

5. See Doc. No. 52, 53, 54.

years to be accepted. Vytautas Merkys, a seminarian in the fourth year of theology, was expelled from the seminary with the assistance of militia officials. At that time the authors of the anonymous document kept silent. The term "reactionary priests" was less often used than it is today. Who then, at that time, was responsible for putting the seminary under such pressure? One must not forget that after the "reactionary priests" began to fight for the rights of the seminary, the government allowed twice the number of candidates to enroll.[6]

The communication mentions a secret seminary. Until now only security agents mentioned it during interrogations. We are convinced that a hungry man has the right to bread. If the official seminary, forced into a strict government mold, does not satisfy the needs of the faithful—16 priests have died this year, while only eight students finished the seminary—then priests must be prepared underground. There is only one thing to fear: that history might blame the priests of Lithuania for being too late. When the atheists abolish all restriction on the official seminary, the underground seminaries will lose their reason for existence. Today the Catholic Church in Lithuania desperately needs priests, and this problem should be the concern of all: bishops, priests, and the faithful.

The authors of the anonymous letter are annoyed by the idea of underground priests. Did they go underground of their own free will? Until 1944 there were no underground priests in Lithuania. Where and when did the underground priests "burrow under the foundations of the Church"? Can the way these priests come to the assistance of the diminishing numbers of priests be characterized as burrowing under the foundations of the Church? How, then, are we to understand the decree of the Second Vatican Council on the Lay Apostolate, if the pastoral work of repressed priests is considered as wrecking the Church? We are deeply convinced that the underground priests are examples of faith, courage, and self-sacrifice for many.

We would like to remind the "zealous defenders of unity among priests" of the recent past of the Ukrainian Greek-

---

6. In 1968 only 6 candidates for the seminary were allowed by the Soviet regime. See the statistics provided in **Chronicle**, No. 6 (May, 1973). In 1974 about 13 candidates were permitted to apply, but only 10 were finally enrolled; see **Chronicle**, No. 12 (1974).

Catholic Church. In 1946 a group of priests in Lvov called a notorious "synod," which decided to join the Greek-Catholic Church of Ukraine to the Russian Orthodox Church. According to Canon Law, only bishops can call a synod. In this "synod" of Lvov, the bishops took no part nor did they ratify its decisions. Precisely because of this "synod," 5 million Ukrainian Catholics have not one officially operating church, while all the bishops and hundreds of priests have gone underground and a large portion of them have become uncrowned martyrs.[7]

It appears that the anonymous group could lightheartedly, if the atheists so wished, characterize as "underground" burrowing under the foundations of the Church, all the apostles and other Christians of the early ages.

In the letter it is said that "reactionary priests" slander and even instruct the bishops, while the anonymous individuals themselves demand that Bishop Labukas be "specific," that he speak over the Vatican Radio, and they accuse the chanceries of not reacting to "the chauvinistic policy of reactionary priests." The difference between the one and the other is simply that the one group, when writing petitions concerning the most serious problems of the Church add their signatures, while the other, seeking some vague unity, remains anonymous.

The anonymous group is very dissatisfied that the *Chronicle of the Catholic Church in Lithuania* is broadcast over the Vatican Radio. It must be rememberd that the facts will always speak; when they cease, the *Chronicle of the Catholic Church in Lithuania*, having become unnecessary, will fall silent.

In the letter mentioned above, the atheists in Lithuania tried to deal the Church a blow at the hands of the clergy themselves, to misinform world public opinion and the Apostolic See, to compromise the priests in the eyes of the faithful and psychologically to disarm the young clergy and seminarians.

It remains only to cite the words of St. Peter: "Be sober, be watchful. Your adversary the devil prowls around like a roaring lion, seeking someone to devour. Oppose him with your strong faith."

The Priests of Vilkaviškis

September 25, 1974

---

7. For a brief history of the fate of the Ukrainian Catholics see Paul Mailloux, S.J., "Catholics in the Soviet Union," in Marshall, op. cit., ch. 17.

To: His Excellency Bishop J. Matulaitis-Labukas
Copies to: All bishops and administrators of dioceses in Lithuania.

Your Excellency:

Not long ago you received an anonymous letter from a "group" of priests of the Diocese of Vilkaviškis. The author or authors did not dare to sign, even though there is no danger threatening them as a result of that letter, either from church or civil authorities. The allegations made and the questions raised in that letter are posed in a not altogether true light; therefore, justice would require one to examine the other side of the question—*audiatur et altera pars.*

The anonymous letter speaks of some priests' activities "tearing down the Church rather than building it up," and it speaks about their slanderous activities. It is regrettable that this allegation is not supported by facts: What activities "tear down the Church," and by what calumnies are the confreres and bishops being besmirched? As for the latter allegation, one must note that public acts are always publicly evaluated, but not every evaluation is of itself a calumny.

The letter rejoices over restored and renovated and generally well-kept churches and states that all this is due completely to those priests who are considered the atheists' tools. This is something of an overstatement. Were churches not also renovated by those whom the anonymous letter calls "reactionary"? The repairing of masonry or wooden churches does not constitute all of a priest's work: Much more important than this construction of lifeless church buildings is the building up of "the living Church": catechism, sermons, and work with people in general. Unfortunately, some forget this latter element.

The anonymous letter speaks of priests who "are trying to turn back the wheel of history, desiring only vain publicity... to satisfy their boundless self-love and thirst for praise." We do not know what the author has in mind here—by what actions they seek to publicize themselves and to satisfy their thirst for praise. Perhaps by catechizing children? But that is the command of Christ: "Go, therefore, and make disciples of all the nations." (Mt 28:19). "Let the children come to me." (Mt 19:14) That is also the law of the Church: Paragraph 1329 of the Code of Canon Law considers the teaching of religion to children one of the most serious of a priest's duties.

Can a priest's conscience be clear if he does not fulfill this duty? Who can excuse him from this duty? The civil government? But it is "better to obey God than man." (Acts 5:29) Can we call those who wish to be faithful to the commandments of Christ and the Church and who heed the voice of their priestly conscience vain seekers of praise? It is sad and painful indeed that there are priests who abandon this duty: They do not work with youth, sometimes they even allow children to receive the sacraments without checking their understanding of religious truths. Is that perhaps the "fulfillment of priestly duties?"

Did the apostles, on whose feast-days we wear the red chasuble, to signify the blood of martyrdom, "thirst for vain praise, or seek to satisfy a boundless love of self"? Did those who said, "Judge for yourselves whether it is right in God's sight for us to obey you rather than God" (Acts 4:19), wish to "turn back the wheel of history"? They wished only to be faithful to Christ—all else was unimportant to them. We wonder whether it is honorable to impute all sorts of unworthy motives to those priests who, for teaching catechism to children, are fined or sent to prison?

The anonymous letter writes that the actions of some priests are opposed to the will of Christ. They do not build up the Church of Christ, but tear it down. It is too bad that they do not specify what kind of actions. Would it be catechizing?

The anonymous communication mentions that the organs of civil government have lately become stricter with the Church. It would be interesting to know when they were less strict, unless it was during the war. After all, the goals of the atheists have not changed.

According to the anonymous letter, the seminary administration is complaining about a lack of candidates, saying that this year there has been a more careful screening of applicants. Is it reactionary priests who are to blame for this, as the anonymous letter states? How can there not be a shortage of applicants, if for a quarter of a century the entrance of applicants into the seminary has been restricted! It would be interesting to know when the civil government did not carry out a "careful screening of applicants."

The anonymous statement touts "a secret seminary."

At the present time this is just talk. But even if it were true, what would be wrong with it? To be concerned about vocations is everyone's duty. Why do the ordinaries speak in one of their letters about "Good Shepherd Sunday"? Why did Christ say, "The harvest is good but laborers are scarce" (Mt 9:37)? Finally, there would be no talk about a "secret seminary" if the civil government allowed all those who wish to enroll in the seminary.

The anonymous letter speaks sarcastically about "priests secretly ordained by someone." Who is that "someone"? The bishops? A disrespectful reference to the bishops casts aspersions on priestly honor and betrays an unchurchmanlike spirit: this is the speech of a deserter, not of a soldier...

Stones are cast at "underground" priests. Would there be any, if the civil government did not interfere with their work? Do these priests not fulfill their duties better, do they not show more idealism and self-sacrifice than many who work officially and publicly? Is not meanness of spirit betrayed by such a negative attitude toward confreres who, unafraid of danger, having spent their energies and health in a forty-eight-hour work week, find the energy in themselves to give their limited leisure time to pastoral work? How many of us working officially show such idealism, dedication, and love of souls as these "worker priests"?

Finally, in the history of the Church such a practice is not a first. When priests were not allowed to work freely in England, they used to study on the continent and then travel in secret to the British Isles, where imprisonment and death awaited them. Priests have similarly operated in Mexico, China, and elsewhere during times of religious persecution.

The anonymous author cites the ecumenical decree of Vatican II on the work of the priest in conformity with the changed conditions of the time. It is not known how the author of the letter explains this directive. Perhaps the "new forms of pastoral work" should be understood to involve the refusal to catechize the children, to have them serve at Mass, and to participate in processions?

The anonymous author maintains that the priest "is useful to the Church only when he is working in the church itself." It would be interesting to know when the work of the priest in performing "verbal functions" and administering sacraments are not useful to the Church? History provides numerous examples of the work of the priest performed not in the church, but in barns, forests, camp barracks—recording this in golden letters. It would be interesting to know how the anonymous author would substantiate his claim that such priests, having given all their strength, health, and time to the Church, "are burrowing under the foundations of the Church"? Is this not a slander?

The anonymous author mentions the *Chronicle of the Catholic Church in Lithuania,* which allegedly represents neither the Catholic Church in Lithuania, nor the Diocese of Vilkaviškis. The question should be put differently: are the facts mentioned in the *Chronicle* true or not? No one has recorded the ban on Lithuanian press, the massacre of Kražiai.[8] Only the fact that it really happened is important.

The *Chronicle* would not have appeared if the rough attack on the believers, especially the children, had not occurred. Can a mother be silent if her child is being mistreated? Can the priest watch quietly as the atheists, declaring the freedom of religion, in reality break their own word and with cruel acts of violence, which have been only partially recorded in the *Chronicle,* mock the believers who supposedly have equal rights?

The anonymous author appeals for unity. But for what kind of unity? For agreement with the canons of the Church or with the instructions of the atheists? A similar question once arose for the older generation of priests: to agree with Bishop Valančius, who wholeheartedly worked for souls and for the people and suffered from the czarist regime; or to agree with Bishop V. Žilinskas, the favorite of the czarina, who was concerned not with the Church, but with hunting and feasting; or to agree with the administrator of Seinai, Monsignor Antanavičius, who used to read the decrees of the czar from the pulpit?[9] For purpose of illustration we can recall the French

---

8. The massacre of Kražiai refers to the 1893 attack by some 300 Cossacks on the believers in the church of Kražiai (in the district of Raseiniai), who were trying to prevent the closing of the church. The attack resulted in 9 officially recorded deaths and some 50 seriously injured.

9. For the historical role of Bishop Valančius see Doc. No. 32 and notes. Bishop V. Žilinskas (Zylinski) of Vilnius (1803-1863) maintained a close relationship with the czarist court and has been accused of

Bishop Pierre Cauchon, an English appointee and a careerist, who, with the assistance of clergy like himself and without regard to the canons of the Church, while other members of the capitula were in English prisons, condemned Joan of Arc. All this was done in the name of the Church... Unfortunately, history viewed this differently—Joan was crowned, while Cauchon, who was acting not in the name of the Church and not with the Church, was thrown into the trash heap of history.

Once Christ reproached the chief apostle Peter, even calling him Satan, because he considered not God but the thoughts of men (Mt. 16:23). Why such an angry reproach? Because Peter did not want Christ to suffer. The rock can turn into a stone of indignation if it does not want to understand that it is necessary to "take up the cross" (Mt. 16:24). God can be betrayed in the Church itself if the "wide road" is taken (Mt. 7:13)—the road of comfort and peace. Peter can become a Satan if, seeking to evade Golgotha, he defends not souls, but his own comfortable life. Later, Peter corrected his error, recalling the words of his Teacher: "Whoever would save his life will lose it" (Mt. 16:25). He died because he disobeyed Nero, but by dying, he saved the most precious possession of man—his conscience.

Your Excellency, let us all discuss these questions with our conscience, with a sense of responsibility to the Church, God, and history. May the Spirit of Truth and Love, the Spirit of Courage and Strength lead us all! May the grace of the Lord protect us all!

For reasons known to all, the authors of this letter, the priests of the Archdiocese of Vilnius, because they are in a weaker position than the anonymous author of the letter of September 1, 1974, do not affix their signatures.

Glory be to Jesus Christ!

September 22, 1974

---

collaboration with the czarist regime to the detriment of the Church. Similarly, Msgr. J. Antanavičius (1853-1916), administrator of the Diocese of Seinai (now in Poland), is known for his open condemnation of the revolutionary activity of 1905.

63. THE TRIAL OF CATHOLIC ACTIVISTS

The trial of Case No. 345 began on December 2, 1974, in the Supreme Court at Vilnius. Only security interrogators and their invited correspondents were allowed to take notes.

DECEMBER 2 — THE FIRST DAY OF THE TRIAL

The following notice was tacked to the door of Hall No. 101 of the Supreme Court (Vilnius, Lentpiūviai Street 24): "The case against P. Petronis, P. Plumpa, J. Stašaitis, V. Jaugelis, and A. Patriubavičius is being heard in this hall."

Only close relatives—children, brothers, and the like—were admitted to the hall after stating their names and relationship to the accused. Plainclothes security officers guarded the door.

The defendants were brought to the hall from security isolation prior to the admittance of relatives, correspondents, and other security-invited observers. On entering and leaving,

---

No. 63. Excerpts from **Chronicle**, No. 13 (1974), which is entirely devoted to a detailed report of the trial of Catholic activists involved in the production and dissemination of religious literature. The charges included production and dissemination of the **Chronicle**, reproduction of religious books, the production of some 20,000 copies of prayer books, and the assembly of the Soviet copying machine "Era." The defendants in the case were all laymen, with middle education (except one with primary education), ranging in age from 26 to 63. The trial was one of a series of trials emanating from Case 345, which began with massive searches and interrogations in November of 1973 as an effort to break the Catholic dissent. The security campaign against the dissidents has been detailed in **Chronicle** beginning with No. 8 (1973). One of the principals involved in the case — Nijolė Sadūnaitė — was tried separately (see Doc. No. 65). Two other trials are reported in **Chronicle**, No. 13 (1974) and No. 16 (1975). Also related was the trial of Sergei Kovalev, a biologist and former researcher at Moscow University, a member of the Soviet chapter of Amnesty International. He was tied in Vilnius in December of 1975 under Article 70 of the RSFSR Penal Code for "anti-Soviet" activity, including the alleged utilization and dissemination of the Lithuanian **Chronicle**. Kovalev was given the sentence of seven years in a strict regime camp, to be followed by exile of three years. The Kovalev case has been widely reported in world press and is not presented here. The court proceedings and events during the trial in Vilnius are presented in detail in **Chronicle**, No. 21 (January 25, 1976). **The Case of Kovalev** (New York: Khronica Press, 1976) is a Russian-language record of the trial.

they were guarded by six or seven soldiers. When the defendants were brought in singly, they were led by two soldiers and preceded by a third. When they were brought in in pairs, one soldier walked them. The accused were not allowed to look around the courtroom. They were seated several meters apart in this order: Stašaitis, Plumpa, Jaugelis, Patriubavičius, and Petronis. Four armed guards stood nearby, preventing the defendants from looking back into the courtroom. The chairs of the first two rows, three or four meters behind the defendants, were pushed together and occupied by four soldiers. Further back, two rows were similarly occupied by four more soldiers and an officer.

DECEMBER 16—THE NINTH DAY OF THE TRIAL
THE SPEECH OF PROSECUTOR BAKUČIONIS

The prosecutor began speaking of the October Revolution and its immeasurable worth, of the infallible leadership of the Party and the Soviet government, and of the tremendous progress made in all areas.

"We are obliged to be proud," spoke the prosecutor, "that we live under a socialist system and can build the dream of all people—Communism."

Further, the prosecutor explained that there exist two camps in the world, and that the capitalist camp has used the Church in its battle.

The prosecutor did not forget to emphasize that we have full freedom of conscience and beliefs. The world's most humane Constitution, continued the prosecutor, guarantees the right of citizens to the profession of any kind of faith. This right is protected by the laws of the Penal Code. However, there are people who wish to harm the Soviet system. They feel the provisions of the Constitution are not adequately carried out.

The *Chronicle*, stated the prosecutor, is a means to disorient the people, to turn the public against the Soviet school system and its character-building function. In the *Chronicle*, facts are misrepresented and slanderously and prejudicially imbue people with anti-Soviet, nationalistic opinions. "It is clear to us on whose water wheel the water is being poured," continued the prosecutor, "and who is benefitting from the favors of these calumniators."

Here the prosecutor named several witnesses who, in his opinion, had proved the libelous nature of the *Chronicle*.

"It is not enough that the *Chronicle* publishes fantasies about church life, but it also includes events unrelated to faith."

"Of course," spoke the prosecutor, "some facts show that individual party and government officials, misunderstanding their goals in atheistic activity, have made some mistakes. But this is not typical; this cannot be attributed to the entire system, as is done in the *Chronicle*. If an event occurs, it cannot be reported prejudicially or exaggerated. If such a publication fell into the hands of a person unfamiliar with what is going on, it could turn him against our system."

The defendants Petronis and Plumpa, working together, duplicated the *Chronicle*. They both have substantial life experience, having completed the "school of hard knocks." Petronis, at age seventeen, traversed Europe to reach Rome, is educated, has literary talent. Plumpa learned about life during his imprisonment, having seen both the good and the bad.

The prosecutor charged Plumpa with assembling an "Era" for Petronis and duplicating anti-Soviet literature in Semaška-Semaškevičius' apartment. Besides that, Plumpa had falsified his documents. "Therefore, for Plumpa, one who has served time for political activity and who organized and duplicated a libelous publication, the *Chronicle*, in accordance with Article 68 of the LSSR Penal Code, I recommend 5 years' loss of freedom, the sentence to be served in strict regime camps," recommended the prosecutor, "and 3 more years' loss of freedom, sentence to be served in strict regime camps; for falsification of documents in accordance with Article 212 of the Penal Code. In all, 8 years' loss of freedom."

According to the prosecutor, Plumpa failed to respond during interrogation and spoke objectively only after familiarizing himself with the case against him.

The prosecutor charged Petronis with organizing the duplication of anti-Soviet literature. He duplicated the 6th and 7th issues of the *Chronicle*, *Žvilgsnis į gyvenimą* (A Look at Life), arranged the duplication of *Dievas šiandien* (God Today) and other books. Besides that, Petronis collected material for the *Chronicle* and participated in its publication. According to the prosecutor, this was proved by the notes found in Petronis' possession, which were very similar in contents to the *Chronicle*. According to Articles 68 and 70 of the LSSR Penal Code, the prosecutor recommended for Petronis 5 years' loss of freedom, sentence to be served in strict regime camps.

The prosecutor charged Jaugelis with duplicating and circulating the 6th issue of the *Chronicle*, with collecting signatures for the Memorandum[1] and spreading lies about the Soviet system. In accordance with Article 199-1 of the LSSR Penal Code, he recommended for Jaugelis a 3-year sentence, to be served in general regime camps.

Stašaitis was charged by the prosecutor with the duplication of the 6th issue of the *Chronicle* and with the intention of duplicating the book *Ieškau Tavo veido* (I Seek Your Face). However, Stašaitis should receive a lighter sentence because of his frankness during interrogation and admission of guilt. In accordance with Article 199-1 of the Penal Code, the prosecutor recommended imprisonment for a year and a half in a general regime camp (Penal Code Article 246).

DECEMBER 17—THE TENTH DAY OF THE TRIAL
CLOSING STATEMENTS OF THE DEFENDANTS

Petronis spoke very quietly and with difficulty. He was obviously physically broken. He reminded the court that it had been "an entire year since they had seen more than a patch of sky... and look at Jaugelis—he looks like a man already in his coffin..."

Petronis affirmed again that he had not acted in an anti-Soviet manner. In his opinion, he had erred in duplicating the *Chronicle* because he had hurt his own work. "However, in what publications are polemics with atheists possible?" asked Petronis. "How are we to defend ourselves from attacks against all that is central to our faith? The *Chronicle* is a shield against atheistic attacks and blows." Furthermore, he had duplicated the *Chronicle* not on his own initiative, but at the request of someone named Josephine, who had asked him to keep her "Era" and duplicate the literature she brought.

Petronis stated that the letters he had written to various

---

1. Doc. No. 56.

agencies, informing them of present-day injustices, did not constitute anti-Soviet activity but reflected a desire to rectify these injustices.

The prosecutor had named Petronis as a reporter for the *Chronicle*. "But I began collecting information over twenty years ago. The *Chronicle* did not even exist then," Petronis noted pointedly.

Petronis regretted that he was charged with the systematic dissemination of known falsehoods, libelous to the Soviet system, because such dissemination had certainly not taken place.

The defendant reminded the court that his primary goal in life was apostolic—to bring good to others. "I was the poorest of proletarians," spoke Petronis, "and so Articles 68 and 70 are completely misapplied to my work."

Petronis also described his poor health and asked that his sentence be reduced—that he at least be allowed to serve his time in general regime camps where he could practice his profession and be of service to people. The long year of interrogation had been punishment enough. He explained that before he died he wanted to bid farewell to his birthplace, live freely, and prepare for eternity.

Stašaitis spoke at length, beginning with his youth, about the formation of his world view, about his dreams of doing good. "Sometimes our good intentions bring only pain to others," he spoke.

In the defendant's opinion, the *Chronicle* adds nothing of value to people's religious life. It contains subjective, exaggerated facts. Now efforts should be directed not to the *Chronicle* but to living according to Christ's words: "Render to God what is God's and to Caesar what is Caesar's."

While in security isolation, Stašaitis began to understand that what was necessary now was not an exaggerated battle but an appeal, which was more appropriate to Christians and which would aid them in coming closer to atheists. During his long detention he came to understand his errors; regarding his punishment, he would be satisfied if the court complied with his lawyer's recommendations.

He ended his statement with a poem written during his imprisonment.

Plumpa asked how much longer his sentence which he

had served after his first conviction, would drag on? Ten, fifteen years, or for a lifetime? "Is not the sentence I received and served enough punishment?" asked Plumpa. "Or perhaps the words spoken to me by the Vilnius police, that I had ruined my whole life, should be considered as true? Perhaps during interrogation they were justified in asking why did you marry? Why did you have children?"

"How could I have harmed any ideological activity by my employment in Vilnius in the 3rd sanitary district where I carried buckets of clay and was assigned to the most dangerous jobs?" asked the defendant.

The prosecutor mentioned that Plumpa had not gone to the countryside to work and had not earned the public's trust.

"What better way to earn public trust than by working the meanest of jobs?" asked Plumpa.

Responding to the prosecutor's charge that he, Plumpa, had written the introduction to Medvedev's book, *A Question of Madness*, the defendant pointed out that this was illogical. In 1972 the defendants Žukauskas and Sakalauskas were accused of duplicating this book with that same introduction, whereas Plumpa is being charged for this action in 1973.[2]

Plumpa described how, during interrogation, he was called a bandit and counter-revolutionary, even though that had not been proved to this day.

"According to the paragraphs with which I am charged, it would seem that I agitated, libeled the Soviet system, and organized. Permit me to ask: "Where? When? Why? Where is the proof? Where are the witnesses?" asked Plumpa.

Security personnel let slip that his parental rights would be terminated and that the state would raise his children as atheists, said Plumpa.

Completing his statement, Plumpa requested that his family not be persecuted.

Jaugelis' closing statement charged the Soviet government and atheists with the persecution of Catholics.

"Who are we in the eyes of the atheists?" asked Jaugelis. "Fanatics, ignoramuses, out of step with life. The peasants have a saying: if a man is told a hundred times that he is a dog,

---

2. The trial of Žukauskas and Sakalauskas is presented in Doc. No. 25.

then after the hundred first time he will bark. Probably that is why the majority of the faithful cannot even imagine the possibility of a religious press, of sending their children to religious schools, of electing their representatives to government."

"Who will speak for us; who will aid us, if all government positions are filled by atheists, and we, the believers, are left at the very bottom of the proletarian class?"

In Jaugelis' words, only those "whose brains have been dried out from fear" can claim that there is freedom of religion in Lithuania and that believers are not persecuted.

Jaugelis spoke about how people were afraid to act according to the dictates of truth and conscience, but rather obeyed the orders of government officials. However, "we are not a herd of four-legged animals, with whom you can do as you please."

"How do you understand the word 'freedom'?" asked Jaugelis. "Perhaps as the closing of churches and their conversion into warehouses and concert halls? Perhaps as the imprisonment of priests for catechetizing children? Or perhaps as the turning of children against their believing parents? Why are our birthrights ignored?"

"Lies, cheating, coercion, and injustices are perpetrated on innocent people everywhere," continued Jaugelis.

"All this is happening in a country where freedom, equality, brotherhood, truth, and other noble-sounding words are loudly proclaimed."

"However, today there are numerous people who are concerned only with truth, freedom, and the well-being of others. How many such people have died on the tundras of Soviet Russia, having suffered hunger, illness, torture? They died enslaved, as martyrs, but they were not vanquished. To this day, some of the most noble hearts, the brightest minds are decaying in prisons. How many of them are being 'treated' in psychiatric hospitals?"

"And here we stand before the highest tribunal. Here should be the fairest people. And what do we see? Betrayal, lies, and coercion. The thought occurs that perhaps some are born to be slaves and others to enslave."

"Millions of martyrs died or suffered for Christ, for the truth that he preached. Let not the atheists think that there are none today who are unafraid to suffer for the truth, for their faith and matters of the Church."

Jaugelis expressed the desire of all the believers that they be considered equal with atheists, that parents be allowed to raise their children according to their own beliefs, and that churches not be closed.

Jaugelis ended with a poem about Lithuania, "The Martyr," which we reproduce:

> Lithuania, our homeland, our birthplace.
> How many times have foreign feet trampled you?
> How many times have you been washed in blood, yet
> You never lacked noble hearts who would shed tears for
> you?
> They did not fear suffering and death for your sake.
> Even now such hearts will be found.

DECEMBER 23—THE ELEVENTH DAY OF THE TRIAL

The following sentences were issued:

1. To *P. Petronis*, in accordance with Article 68, part 1, and Article 70 of the Penal Code, four years' loss of freedom; sentence to be served in strict regime colonies.

2. To *P. Plumpa*, in accordance with Article 68, part 2, and Article 70 of the Penal Code, seven years' loss of freedom, and in accordance with Article 212, part 2, of the Penal Code, three years' loss of freedom. Consolidating the two sentences, in accordance with Article 42 of the Penal Code, eight years' loss of freedom; sentence to be served in strict regime camps.

3. To *J. Stašaitis*, in accordance with Article 199-1 of the Penal Code, one year's loss of freedom and release.

4. To *V. Jaugelis*, in accordance with Article 199-1 of the Penal Code, two years' loss of freedom; sentence to be served in general regime colonies.

5. To *A. Patriubavičius*, in accordance with Article 246, part 2, of the Penal Code, one year and one month's loss of freedom and release.

64. A PROTEST AGAINST ARBITRARY TRIALS AND CONVICTIONS

To: The Secretary General of the Central Committee, CPSU

The Presidium of the Supreme Soviet of the USSR

The Prosecutor General of the USSR

The Presidium of the Supreme Soviet of the Lithuanian SSR

The Prosecutor of the Lithuanian SSR

The Curiae of the dioceses of Vilnius, Kaunas, Panevėžys, Telšiai, and Kaišiadorys

From: The undersigned priests of the Lithuanian SSR, Archdiocese of Vilnius.

A STATEMENT

The Catholics of Lithuania, lacking religious literature, are suffering severely. It is true that during the Soviet period, the following books were published: Canon J. Stankevičius' *Prayer Book, Liturgical Prayer Book, The Resolutions of the Second Vatican Council, The Ritual, The New Testament, The Book of Psalms.* They did not satisfy the needs of the faithful since they were published in such small numbers as to be useful only to the atheists for foreign propaganda to say "we have freedom of religion." For example, the parish of Ceikiniai, having 3,000 parishioners, received only ten copies of *The New Testament.*

During this famine of religious literature, there appeared people who, knowing that Article 135 of the Constitution of the Soviet Union and Article 97 of the Constitution of the Lithuanian SSR guarantees the freedom of religion and of the press, and also knowing that the civil government of the Lithuanian SSR, in contradiction to these laws, does not permit Lithuanian Catholics to print religious books, decided to secretly print and distribute prayer books. Some of them were arrested in 1973. In December 1974 the Supreme Court of the Lithuanian SSR sentenced P. Petronis to the loss of freedom for four years in a strict regime corrective labor colony, P. Plumpa to the loss of freedom for eight years in a strict regime cor-

No. 64. **Chronicle**, No. 17 (July 4, 1975).

rective labor colony; J. Stašaitis to the loss of freedom for one year and V. Jaugelis, to the loss of freedom for two years in a general regime corrective labor colony.

Tiesa (Dec. 23, 1973 and Dec. 29, 1974), writing about these people, did not specifically tell the general public what publications they were printing and distributing. It wrote: "they illegally printed and distributed publications spreading imaginary inflammatory rumors, slandering the Soviet state and the social system."

Tiesa is silent about what the names of these publications were. Only the administrator of the Vilnius Archdiocese Msgr. Č. Krivaitis, at a press conference in America[1] on February 25, 1975, revealed that these people, after a long investigation, were punished for the *Chronicle of the Catholic Church in Lithuania*. Msgr. Č. Krivaitis does not mention the printing of prayer books since, according to him, "The Catholic Church in Soviet Lithuania is functioning normally" (*Gimtasis kraštas,* Nov. 8, 1973).

The Soviet press often brings to the public's attention, criticizes and condemns, for the good of the people, various deficiencies and crimes. However, no one mentions the crimes against the faithful although they are sometimes so great that they even conflict with the Soviet Constitution and the Declaration of Human Rights. All of the Soviet press should write about them, but they remain silent. That is why the *Chronicle* fulfills this task.

The *Chronicle* does not write anything against the Soviet system, it only raises the facts, whose truth no one can deny, about crimes against the faithful. Are the declarations of the faithful of the Ceikiniai, Adutiškis, Mielagėnai, Ignalina, and other parishes made to the officials of the civilian government of a slanderous nature? No! No one can prove that. When there will be no persecution of the faithful, then there will be no more declarations and complaints of the faithful, and thus the *Chronicle* will not exist. Under the present conditions, the *Chronicle* is the cry for help of the suffering children of the Catholic Church in Lithuania.

We do not consider the decision of the Lithuanian SSR

---

1. Msgr. Krivaitis was in the US in February of 1975 as a guest of the National Council of Churches.

Supreme Court just and ask that it be abolished because:

1. If our principal law—the Constitution of the Lithuanian SSR guarantees freedom of conscience, religious cults,
and press; if on December 10, 1948, the General Assembly
of the United Nations accepted the Universal Declaration of
Human Rights, which was signed by the Soviet Union; then
the faithful ought to have the means and opportunities
to know their faith and profess it publicly. Otherwise, what
is a right worth if there are no possibilities of using it? To
teach the faith, catechisms, prayer books, and religious literature, which the Soviet Lithuanian civilian government does
not permit to be printed, are necessary. In this way the decision
conflicts with the Lithuanian SSR Constitution and the Universal Declaration of Human Rights.

The Lithuanian SSR Supreme Court accused P. Petronis
and J. Stašaitis of the production and distribution of prayer
books; in the trial, most of the witnesses talked only about
their printing, binding, and distribution. However, the LSSR
Supreme Court in its conclusions mentioned only the multiplication and distribution of the *Chronicle* and other anti-Soviet
materials. Therefore, the LSSR Supreme Court, in sentencing
P. Petronis and J. Stašaitis, who produced and distributed prayer
books, behaved improperly. Religious literature is an essential
matter for the faithful. Even though the courts will judge and
punish the believers with the harshest penalties, they will continue to produce religious literature as much as they are able
for as long as the government will not permit it to be printed
officially.

2. The LSSR Supreme Court accused P. Plumpa and V.
Jaugelis of the multiplication and distribution of the *Chronicle,*
and in March 1975 sentenced J. Gražys to loss of freedom
for three years for binding of the *Chronicle.* N. Sadūnaitė, arrested in 1974, is still being interrogated and is awaiting trial.[2]

We consider illegal the sentencing of some and the imprisonment of others, since in the activities of the above-mentioned persons *there was no crime.* The Universal Declaration
of Human Rights (article 19) states that "Everyone has the
right... to seek, receive and impart information and ideas
through any media..." Therefore, in multiplying and distrib-

---

2. The Sadūnaitė trial is reported in Doc. No. 65; the Gražys trial
is reported in **Chronicle**, No. 16 (1975).

uting the *Chronicle*, they were not guilty of any crime. The LSSR Penal Code cannot contradict the Constitution and the Universal Declaration of Human Rights.

In addition, the *Chronicle* is not a publication of slander, but of true facts. That the faithful of Lithuania are living in a period of religious oppression cannot be disproved by the interviews given to foreign newspapers and radio by Lithuanian bishops, diocesan administrators, or priests. For example, the administrator of the Vilnius Archdiocese, Msgr. Č. Krivaitis, as reported in *Tiesa* (Feb. 20, 1975), in a New York press conference in 1975 declared: "In Soviet Lithuania the believers have all the conditions to practice religion. Neither they nor their children are persecuted for their belief. We, the clergy, have all the necessary conditions for our work."

If that were the truth, if we had all the conditions for work, why then do eight priests serve two parishes each in the Vilnius Archdiocese and Rev. Alfonsas Merkys even serves three—Turmantas, Tilžė, and Smalva. Why, in the diocese of Vilnius, are parishes served by priests of such ages: P. Bekiš (77 years old); the pastor of the Holy Spirit parish in Vilnius, L. Chomski (90); the pastor of Baltoji Vokė parish, L. Ivančik (79); pastor in Korviai, L. Laucevič (80); pastor in Rudininkai, A. Liachovič (80); pastor in Mickūnai, S. Malachovski (77); pastor in Eitmoniškiai, and V. Novicki (78); the pastor of Parudaminis. These priests, except for Rev. P. Bekiš, do not have assistants.

The examples given show how great a shortage of priests exists in Lithuania. But at the same time, many candidates, desiring to become priests, cannot enter the theological seminary since the security agencies do not permit them.

In 1974 in Lithuania 22 priests died and only eight were ordained. Ten new clerics were admitted. Therefore, the condition of the faithful cannot be considered normal. The Church is restricted.

3. The case and trial of the above-mentioned "criminals" is the most vivid proof of the lack of rights of the faithful. The articles of the code do not exist even for the Lithuanian security organs in their battle with the faithful. The LSSR Code of the Penal Process (article 106) states that only in cases of very grave complexity can the term of confinement during the investigation of the case be extended by the Prosecutor General

to nine months after the day of the arrest. The confinement of P. Petronis and P. Plumpa during the investigation of their case lasted 12.5 months (Nov. 19, 1973, to Dec. 2, 1974); of J. Gražys—11 months (April 24, 1974, to March 24, 1975). Having all this before our eyes, we ask that the decision of the LSSR Supreme Court on the previously mentioned persons be repealed, that the convicted and interrogated be released, and that the faithful of Lithuania be guaranteed the right to use the freedoms that the Soviet Constitution and Universal Declaration of Human Rights guarantee.

Lithuanian SSR, April 28, 1975

Rev. Karolis Garuckas, Ignalina raion, Ceikiniai

Rev. Alfonsas Merkys, Zarasai raion, Smalva

Rev. Bronislavas Laurinavičius, Švenčionys raion, Adutiškis

Rev. Kazimieras Pukėnas, Vilnius raion, Nemenčinė

Rev. Stasys Valiukėnas, Vilnius, 7-3 Kretinga St.

Rev. Pranas Šviontek, Vilnius, 20 Nugalėtojai St.

65. THE TRIAL OF NIJOLĖ SADŪNAITĖ

Nijolė Sadūnaitė was arrested on August 27, 1974. During a search of her house, No. 11 of the *Chronicle of the Catholic Church in Lithuania*, which was being copied by typewriter, was discovered.

During the preparatory interrogation, N. Sadūnaitė refused to reveal anything, and therefore the interrogators threatened to put her into a psychiatric hospital. For two months she was not allowed to receive any food from the outside.

At the end of January 1975, N. Sadūnaitė wrote a complaint to the prosecutor, protesting the willful actions of the interrogators and their threats to place her in a psychiatric hospital.

In March 1975 the interrogators inquired of the Vilnius psychiatric hospital on Vasara street as well as of the Naujoji Vilnia psycho-neurological hospital to find out whether N. Sadūnaitė was ever treated there. They received a negative answer.

In April 1975 the case of N. Sadūnaitė was separated from case No. 345 and was given an individual case No. 416.

On June 16, 1975, the Supreme Court of the LSSR started trying N. Sadūnaitė's case. The trial session began at 10:00 a.m. The presiding judge was Kudriashev, and the state prosecutor was Bakučionis.

The following witnesses were invited to the trial: Jonas Sadūnas (brother of Nijolė), Vladas Sadūnas (cousin), Regina Sadūnienė (wife of Vladas), Povilaitis (director of a middle school), Kusleika, and Bronė Kibickaitė.

At the beginning of the trial the witnesses were segregated in a separate room. As soon as they had made their statements, they were removed from the courtroom in order to prevent them from hearing the trial in action.

No. 65. **Chronicle**, No. 17 (July 4, 1975). Nijolė Sadūnaitė was born in 1938. Her father was an instructor in the Agricultural Academy. Sadūnaitė grew up as a very religious girl, became involved in the care of an ill and old priest (Canon P. Rauda, who had served a number of years in labor camps). She was tried for participating in the production of Catholic **samizdat** and other dissident activities. She was convicted to a strict regime camp for three years. The testimony of witnesses and other details of the trial are omitted here.

The only persons present in the courtroom were six soldiers and five security agents (Pilelis, Jankauskas, Platinskas, and others). The only person allowed by the presiding judge to remain in the courtroom was Jonas (Sadūnas), the brother of Nijolė. Outsiders were not allowed to enter the courtroom. Security men would inform them that the trial was closed.

Nijolė Sadūnaitė refused to answer the questions of the court.

"Since not I, but you are the criminals who are violating the most elementary human rights, guaranteed by laws, by the Constitution, and by the Universal Declaration of Human Rights, and since you are defending lies, coercion, and violence because, after having slandered and sentenced innocent people, you torture them in prisons and camps, therefore I shall not answer any questions of the court, just as I have not done so during the interrogation, thus expressing my protest against this trial," the defendant declared.

"My eyes were opened by the trial of the Rev. A. Šeškevičius in 1970.[1] He was sentenced for fulfilling his sacerdotal duties; and I was threatened by Lieutenant Gudas, an agent of the security, with a similar case as that against the Rev. Šeškevičius and with prison for having hired a lawyer for him. Kolgov, a former security agent, threatened to punish my brother and my relatives if I refused to stop taking care of 'Rev. Šeškevičius' defense. It appears that hiring a lawyer to defend a priest is a 'great crime.' Since, according to you, I am an especially dangerous offender against the state, I am refusing a lawyer, for I do not want to provoke your terror against those who would hire him for me. This is one side of the coin, while the other one is simply that truth does not need any defense because it is omnipotent and invincible! Only perfidy and lies, being powerless against the truth, require weapons, soldiers, and prisons in order to prolong their villainous dominion, but only for a brief while at that. The saying is true that a prejudiced government digs its grave with its own hands. I am right and I agree not only to sacrifice my freedom for the sake of justice, but I would be glad to give my life as well. There is no greater happiness than suffering for the sake of truth and for the good of the people. Therefore I need no defense attorney. I will speak myself in his place."

---

1. See Doc. No. 52.

THE DEFENSE SPEECH

"I want to tell you that I love one and all like my brothers and sisters and, if need be, I would not hesitate to lay down my life for each of them. There is no need for this today, but I must tell the bitter truth to your face. It is said that only those who love have the right to censure and to scold. I take advantage of this right in addressing myself to you. Every time people are being tried for the *Chronicle of the Catholic Church in Lithuania* the words of Putinas are most relevant[2]:

> *And in tribunals, the assassins*
> *Condemn the just with proud audacity.*
> *Altars collapse beneath your boots,*
> *Your laws disintegrate the truth,*
> *Both sin and virtue fall apart...*

You know very well that the supporters of the *Chronicle of the Catholic Church in Lithuania* love their fellow human beings, and this is the only reason why they are fighting for their liberty and dignity, for their right to enjoy the freedom of conscience, which has been guaranteed by the Constitution and by the Declaration of Human Rights to all citizens irrespective of their convictions. They are fighting so that all those things remain not merely beautiful words on paper, not only mendacious propaganda, as until now, but to see the embodiment of them in reality. Are not the words of the Constitution and of the laws powerless since they are not applied in everyday life, while the discrimination of religious believers has been made lawful and reigns supreme? The *Chronicle of the Catholic Church in Lithuania*, like a mirror, shows the crimes of the atheists against the believers. Since wickedness does not admire its own ugliness, it is horrified by its own image in the mirror. It is for that reason that you hate all of those who tear away from you the veil of lies and hypocrisy. But that does not deprive the mirror of its value! A thief steals money, but you rob the people by depriving them of what is most precious to them—their fidelity to their beliefs and the pos-

---

2. Vincas Mykolaitis-Putinas (1893-1967) was the leading poet of Lithuania. Some of his philosophical-symbolic verse could be interpreted as anti-Soviet.

sibility of transmitting this treasure to their children, to the young generations. Does not the Convention against Discrimination in Education, accepted on December 14-15, 1960, demand in its fifth article that parents be guaranteed the right to give their children a religious and moral education in accordance with their own convictions? Meanwhile, the protocol of interrogation contains the following entry by teacher Rinkauskienė, who was questioned in connection with my case: Since there is only one Soviet school, there is no need then to confuse the children and to teach them hypocrisy. And who is teaching hypocrisy to the children? The teachers of her kind, or the parents who have been guaranteed the right to have the children educated according to their convictions? Only when the children for whom the school had destroyed parental authority go astray, the accusation, for some strange reason, is directed against the parents, and not the children.

Miss Keturkaitė, teacher at the 10th middle school in Klaipėda, writes, the following in her protocol of interrogation: "Since I am a history teacher, I have the occasion to explicate questions of religion to my students. In explaining the emergence of Christianity and, simultaneously, the myth of the appearance of Christ..." How can teacher Keturkaitė explain the questions of religion when she is incompetent to do so and when she is even an illiterate in historical questions, since she is still clinging to the obsolete atheist myth that Christ was, allegedly, a legend. Such illiterates "educate" and "teach" the young generation; by taking advantage of their pedagogical authority, they are inculcating lies into the students' minds.

The interrogators, Lieutenant-Colonel Petruškevičius and the chief of the section of the Department of Investigation, Kazys, threatened me many times by saying that they would have me put in a psychiatric hospital for refusing to answer their questions, although I had explained previously that I kept my silence in protest against this case. When I got tired of their threats, I wrote statements of protest to the Prosecutor of the Republic, the chief of the Security Committee, and to the chief of the Department of Investigation, whom I asked that my statement be attached to my case file. The statement was not attached. All that happened was that the Deputy Prosecutor of the Republic, Bakučionis, whose office is right here, replied in writing that they had the complete right to have a psychiatric examination conducted but, in the opinion of the interrogators, there were still no grounds for it. But my statement did not deal with that at all; it protested against the willful actions of the interrogators, whose aim was to intimidate the person under investigation and to force her to gamble with her conscience. The statement said, and I quote: 'Does the interrogator have the right to threaten the defendant with psychiatric hospitalization or a psychiatric examination when the defendant holds on to her views and does not gamble with conscience and her beliefs? During the interrogation, Lieutenant-Colonel Petruškevičius threatened me many times with shutting me up in a psychiatric hospital where things would be much worse than in a prison. And the only reason for the threats was my refusal to answer his questions. As soon as the deputy chief of the Department of Investigation, Kazys, saw me for the first time, he "diagnosed" me extremely authoritatively as a schizophrenic, an individual with a schizophrenic mentality, and promised that I would have to undergo an examination by the psychiatric commission, whose member he was. When I refused to answer the questions of the chief of the section of the Department of Investigation, Major Rimkus, he repeatedly threatened me with psychiatric examination. Is the entire Soviet system of justice based on fear alone? If I am mentally ill, then what I need is treatment and not to be threatened with my illness. Is it the person's fault if he is ill? But the interrogators themselves do not believe it since it is already five months now that they keep threatening me with a psychiatric hospital in an effort to break my will. Such behavior of the examining magistrates violates human dignity, and I protest against this behavior of theirs toward me.'

In attempting to force testimony, the interrogators have violated article 187 of the LSSR Penal Code, which states:

Any attempt on the part of the person who is conducting the inquest and the preparatory investigation to force testimony during the interrogation by using threats and other illegal actions is punishable by a loss of freedom up to three years. The same activity involving the use of violence or the mockery of the individual under interrogation is punishable by a loss of freedom from three to eight years.

After I had submitted my statement, the chief of the Department of Investigation, Rimkus, reproached me for complaining and said ironically: 'You must really be abnormal, reacting as you do... You have no idea of all the juridical fine points...'

Yes, I know neither the juridical fine points nor the gross points, because I have not studied the subject. Only now I know that the Soviet interrogators find it utterly normal to lie not only to the defendant, but also to complete outsiders. But isn't that spiritual hooliganism, which should be punished because spiritual traumas are more difficult to heal than physical ones?

You are not at all interested in redressing the crimes—on the contrary, you tolerate and promote them. This is proven by the fact that the witnesses who were questioned in connection with my case, those witnesses who demonstrated the veracity of the facts published in the *Chronicle of the Catholic Church in Lithuania*, were first of all asked about who might have transmitted this information to the publishers of the *Chronicle of the Catholic Church in Lithuania*—to whom did they tell this or that, who had seen or heard something, or anything to that effect. The word of truth—this is what you fear! The interrogators did not question or even invite those who, guided by hatred against those who think differently, fired St. Jasiūnaitė, teacher at the Kulautuva middle school, whose only crime was wearing a little cross. Having been subjected to all kinds of mockery, she was refused for a long time even the most menial kitchen helper's job.[3] The interrogators did not summon Markevičius, Chairman of the Executive Committee of the Panevėžys Council of Working People's Deputies, and Indriūnas, chief of the Department of Finance, who fired the secretary-typist Marytė Medišauskaitė, a nine-year veteran in her position, for attending church.[4] Yet you proclaim everywhere that religion is a private matter of the citizens and that all people have equal rights, regardless of their convictions. How beautiful is your

---

3. The case of Miss S. Jasiūnaitė goes back to 1956. It is reported in **Chronicle**, No. 10 (1974).

4. Miss Marytė Medauskaitė (or Medišauskaitė) was dismissed from work on the suspicion that she was a nun. The case is reported in **Chronicle**, No. 10 (1974).

propaganda and how ugly is the living reality! The interrogators failed to react to the crime of Kuprys, director of the Akmenė school, and of the members of the Department of Education, when they fired a teacher for stepping into a ladies' room in the small park where Romas Kalanta had immolated himself, during her excursion to the city of Kaunas with her students.[5] What a crime! A teacher is no longer suited to educate the children?! How ridiculous — the ghost of Romas Kalanta keeps haunting you to this very day. But what is the teacher's fault?

The interrogators failed to warn a single chief physician when they, misusing their position, refused to allow dying patients to avail themselves of the services of a priest, although both the patients and their relatives had asked for it. Even criminals are granted their last request. Yet you dare to mock man's most sacred convictions at the most difficult moment of his life, at the hour of his death and, like robbers, you subject thousands of believers to a most painful moral robbery. That is your communist morality and ethics!

In the pages of *Kauno tiesa* (Kaunas Truth), Augus, a lecturer at the University of Vilnius, slandered Pope Paul VI, the late Bishop Bučys, the Rev. Laberge, and the Rev. Račiūnas in the crudest manner possible.[6] When was that disgusting slander ever revoked? It was not revoked because lies and slander are your daily bread!

Frightened by the ideas of Mindaugas Tomonis, engineer of monument restoration and a doctoral candidate in technology, you shut him up in the psychiatric hospital on Vasara

5. The case is reported in **Chronicle**, No. 10 (1974). The name of the teacher is not given. Apparently the case involved the visitation and student inquiry about the place where Romas Kalanta immolated himself in national protest in May of 1972. See Doc. Nos. 19, 20.

6. The case goes back to 1945. Bishop Pranciškus Bučys (1872-1961), superior of the Marian fathers, resided at that time in Rome. Allegedly encouraged by the Secretary of State of the Vatican (the present Pope Paul VI), Bishop Bučys assigned the Rev. P. Račiūnas to engage in intelligence activities about the Red Army. Allegedly, the information was to be transmitted to Rev. Laberge in Moscow. Rev. Račiūnas spent some 16 years in Soviet camps. The slander refers to an article of Augus of March 1, 1974, accusing Rev. Račiūnas of spying. The charges are refuted in an open letter by Rev. Račiūnas. Text of the letter in **Chronicle**, No. 10 (1974).

Street, for the purpose of "curing" him of his own convictions!

Who gave the atheists the right to give orders to the rectors and tell them which priests they are allowed to invite to the religious retreats and festivals and which they may not? Does not the historic decree "About the Separation of the Church from the State and of the School from the Church" assert that the state does not interfere in the internal activity of religious bodies? In Lithuania, the Church is not separate from the state, but enslaved by it. Governmental organs interfere in internal affairs and in the realm of canon law in the most crude and impermissible ways, ordering priests around as they please, and punishing them in disregard of the laws.

These and hundreds of other facts testify that the atheist goal of transforming everyone into their spiritual slaves justifies all means—slander, lies, terror!

And are you rejoicing in your victory? Over what does the triumph of your victory rise? Above moral ruins, above millions of murdered unborn infants, above the rape of human worth, above petty creatures transformed into crooks, infected with fear and with the poison of life's baser passions. All of that is the fruit of your endeavors. Jesus Christ was right when He said: 'By their fruits shall you know them.' Your crimes are pushing you more and more rapidly into the refuse heap of history.

Thank God, not all the people have broken down. We do not have quantitative support in society, but quality is on our side. Besides prisons and camps, we must condemn all actions that bring injuries and humiliations in their wake, that sow inequality and oppression. To struggle for the embodiment of human rights is the sacred duty of everyone! I rejoice in having been granted the honor of suffering for a while on behalf of the *Chronicle of the Catholic Church in Lithuania* of whose rightness and necessity I am convinced. I will remain faithful to this until my last breath. Therefore, go on issuing your laws as much as you please, but keep them to yourselves. One must distinguish what has been written by man from what God has commanded. The payment to Caesar is only the small amount left over after one has paid God his due. The most important thing in life is the liberation of one's heart and mind from fear, because concessions to evil are a mighty crime."

N. SADŪNAITĖ'S FINAL STATEMENT IN COURT

"This day is the happiest one in my life," the defendant spoke. "I am being tried for the *Chronicle of the Catholic Church in Lithuania,* which fights against physical and spiritual tyranny over man. This means that I am being tried for truth and for the love of my fellow human beings! What can be more important in life than love of humanity, of man's freedom and dignity? Love of one's fellow human beings is the greatest love of all, and the struggle for human rights is the most beautiful song of love. May it resound in everybody's heart, may it never grow still! I have been granted an enviable lot, an honorable destiny—not only to struggle for human rights and for justice, but to be sentenced and condemned as well. My punishment shall be my triumph! The only thing I regret is that I had but little time to work on behalf of my fellow human beings. It is with joy that I shall take my road to slavery, and I agree to die so that others might live. Today I stand next to eternal Truth—Jesus Christ—and I recall His fourth blessing: 'Blessed are those who thirst for righteousness, because they shall be nourished!' How can I fail to rejoice, when God Almighty has guaranteed that light should conquer darkness, and truth should triumph over base lies and deceit! I agree not only to stay in prison but also to die in order to accelerate the coming of that day. As for you, I want to remind you of the words of the poet Lermontov: 'And yet there is, there is a just court of God!' God grant that the verdict of this court be favorable to us all. I shall pray to God the Merciful all the days of my life that He grant this to you. I would like to finish with some stanzas that were born in prison:

> The harder the road you have to tread,
> The more intense the life you lead.
> With the resolve of justice we must burn,
> To conquer Evil against all odds.

> Are the brief earthly days to be spent in repose?
> No, they were given us to fight for many hearts.
> Only he who shall give to the struggle his all
> Will be sure that he is on the righteous road.

And no greater happiness can be felt
Than in the resolve to die for man.
Then a bright feast will pervade your soul,
Beyond all prisons and glacial camps.

Let us then love one another, and we shall be happy. Unhappy are only those who do not love. Yesterday you were astonished at my good spirits during such a difficult moment of my life. This proves that love for my fellow human beings burns in my heart because all burdens become light only when one is filled with love! We must condemn evil with all severity, but we must love man even when he errs. And this can be learned only in the school of Jesus Christ, who is the only Truth, Way, and Life to all. May Your Kingdom come then to the souls of us all, kind Jesus.

From these court chambers I would like to ask you to release from prisons, camps, and psychiatric hospitals all men who fight for human rights and for justice. This way you would prove your good will and would handsomely contribute to the increase of harmony and goodness in this life. And the beautiful slogan, 'man is brother to man,' would become reality."

66. AN OPEN LETTER TO THE ARCHBISHOP OF BERLIN

To His Eminence Alfred Cardinal Bengsch, Archbishop of Berlin

Eminence,

Your visit to our Motherland on August 22-26 of this year was an unexpected, but very pleasant surprise for all the faithful. We not only saw Your smiling face and heard warm words about our faith, but the hope that more objective information about the condition of the Catholic Church in Lithuania would reach the Holy See and the wide world was reborn in us.

As much as the radio jammers permitted, last year we conscientiously followed the statements of Cardinals Wyszynski, Slipij, and Yourself at the Bishops' Synod in Rome. We understood that You have a generous heart and the Christian courage to support those persecuted for God and the Church and that you want to and are capable of understanding our misfortune and worries.

Until the very last hour, the exact date of Your arrival was kept from the priests and faithful. The bishops living in exile— J. Steponavičius and V. Sladkevičius—were not even informed. In the basilica of Kaunas your visit was announced only the evening before, and the priests in the provinces did not know anything. Priests loyal to the government were assigned the task of arranging your visit and it seems that they did not disappoint the government. All those who could have talked at great length about the true condition of the Church were not allowed to meet you. They did not show you the desecrated churches, but drove you to Pirčiupis (for the sake of objectivity, it should be remembered that in Lithuania there are graves not only of Nazi victims, but also of Soviet—in Pravieniškės, in the woods of Rainiai, and elsewhere[1]). In Panevėžys the

No. 66. **Chronicle,** No. 19 (October 15, 1975). Cardinal Bengsch was on an obvious mission for the Vatican to investigate conditions of the Church, including issues raised by the dissidents. See the previous documents for details on the religious situation summarized here.

1. See note 8, Doc. No. 30 on Pirčiupis. Soviet atrocities in 1940-1941 are described in K. Pelėkis, **Genocide** (Germany, 1948).

singing of hymns was not allowed so that too great an impression would not be made and the displeasure of the government would not be incurred. In Kaunas, it was not permitted to hang the portrait of the Holy Father at the doors of the basilica or to greet You away from the doors. Despite the efforts of the government and its trustees, thousands of the faithful came to honor You and bear witness to their loyalty to the Church and the Holy See.

In the name of the priests and faithful of Lithuania we apologize to You for the discourtesies made during your visit (the case of Pirčiupis) and that we could not greet You in the way that we would have wanted. Since we could not personally talk to You about the woes of the Catholic Church in Lithuania, we want to do this in the pages of *The Chronicle of the Catholic Church in Lithuania*.

— — —

After the Red Army crossed the borders of Lithuania, the persecutions of the Catholic Church were immediately begun. On July 2 (1940), diplomatic relations with the Holy See were severed and the Concordat was annulled; all the Catholic organizations were closed. Catholic schools were nationalized; the publishing of Catholic newspapers and books was forbidden. The monasteries were ravaged, and of the three seminaries for priests, only one (in Kaunas) remained, and its buildings were taken away during the 1940-1941 school year. Soviet government officials told Bishop V. Brizgys that they should not beguile the young people, and that within five years even the bishops themselves will be asking the government for employment.[2]

On June 14, 1941, the massive deportation of Lithuanians to Siberia was begun. In a brief time, about 35,000 persons were shipped out in cattle cars: husbands were separated from their families—many of the deported found death in the Gulag Archipelago.

---

2. For details, see Vysk. Vincentas Brizgys, **Katalikų bažnyčia Lietuvoje 1940-1944 metais** (Chicago, 1977), pp. 9-117.

The retreating Red Army murdered many of the faithful; its hand did not pass over the priests, e.g., in Lankeliškiai the priests Dabrikla, Peliekas, and Balsys were murdered; in Pusna, V. Balčius; in Merkinė, A. Juknevičius.

On July 7, 1946, the Bishop of Vilnius, Mečislovas Reinys, who died in Vladimir prison on December 8, 1953, was arrested. In the fall of the same year, the Bishop of Telšiai Borisevičius lost his freedom and was shot in 1947. On December 18, 1946, the Bishop of Kaišiadorys Teofilis Matulionis and his vicar-general Juozapas Labukas were arrested; somewhat later, the Coadjutor Bishop of Telšiai, Pranciškus Ramanauskas. Only the Bishop of Panevėžys Kazimieras Paltarokas remained free.

Again, Lithuanians were deported to Siberia many times, and others were sentenced to very long punishments—up to 25 years; most of them were later rehabilitated.

On August 13, 1946, by order of the Representative for Religious Cults, Gailevičius, the number of clerics in the sole remaining Kaunas seminary was reduced from 300 to 150; later this number was reduced to 25 seminarians. At the present time the Soviet government, influenced by world public opinion, has once again raised the number of clerics to 50.

After the death of the administrator of the Kaunas Archdiocese, Msgr. St. Jakubauskas, Canon J. Stankevičius was elected in his place. After the arrests of the administrator of the Vilkaviškis Diocese, Canon Vizgirda, and of the administrator of the Kaišiadorys diocese, Msgr. Br. Sužiedėlis, by the will of the Soviet government, Stankevičius became the administrator of these two dioceses.

In 1950 Representative for Religious Cults Pušinis mentioned that a special labor camp would be created for the priests —an artel of fishermen in which about 200 of the most zealous priests would work. Pušinis prophesized that after two years, only "teeth and nails" would remain of the Church in Lithuania. In fact, many of the churches were closed and several hundred priests traveled to the Gulag Archipelago.

In 1949-1950 Moscow's institution of religious cults, headed by Polianski, forced the priests of Lithuania to sign a declaration condemning Pope Pius XII; however this action failed, since barely 19 of the 1,000 priests signed.

Already in 1946, the Soviet government began to found parish committees, which were to be the sole masters of the parishes. The priests would only be the servants of the cult. Even now, the Soviet pass for priest has the notation "servant of the cult." Due to the resistance of the priests, the Soviet government has until now failed to fully implement the idea of parish committees, but it has not abandoned the idea. The government wishes the priests in Lithuania to be totally dependent on the parish committees, blindly fulfilling the commands of the Soviet officials. For example, in Belorussia the members of the church committee are being required not to allow children into the church, to make reports to the government about individuals who made use of religious services, and so on.

— — —

After Stalin's death many faithful, many priests, and two bishops—T. Matulionis and Pr. Ramanauskas—returned to their homeland from the camps. Fear ebbed somewhat and pastoral work increased. The government permitted the consecration of two new bishops, Julijonas Steponavičius and Petras Maželis. To the untrained eye it might have seemed that an attempt was made to at least partially compensate the Church for the wrongs it had suffered, but in reality the plans of the Soviet government had not changed, only its tactics. So that the crass persecutions would not raise a spirit of martyrs, the faith in Lithuania was being destroyed by very deceitful means, even using the clergy in this work.

In order to intimidate the weak-willed priests, the more active priests were once again arrested and sent to the camps of Mordovia. In 1957, Bishop Vincentas Sladkevičius, who had been consecrated without government permission, was exiled to N. Radviliškis, and in 1958 Bishop Julijonas Steponavičius was exiled to Žagarė simply because he was conscientiously fulfilling his pastoral duties. In 1957 Bishop T. Matulionis wanted to take over the administration of the Kaišiadorys diocese from Canon J. Stankevičius, but the government refused permission and exiled him to Šeduva in the Diocese of Panevėžys. Gradually relatively inactive priests and those most subservient ("loyal") to the Soviet government were appointed as administrators of the dioceses and, with few exceptions, as deans and pastors of the large parishes.

In the elections of the diocesan administrators, even deceit was sometimes practiced. For example, during the elections for the administrator of the Kaišiadorys Diocese, it was announced to the capitula that Bishops T. Matulionis and V. Sladkevičius desired the election of Canon P. Bakšys as administrator. In fact, these bishops had directed that they not elect Canon P. Bakšys administrator.

The Representative of the Council for Religious Affairs, the former security chief of Kėdainiai Rugienis, crassly terrorized the diocesan administrators and priests. Various officials of the State Security Committee and Council for Religious Affairs would spend many hours with Canon J. Stankevičius and compel him to make unlawful concessions. As a consequence, the Kaunas curia sent out one newsletter after another to the priests, stating that the Council for Religious Affairs does not permit Christmas visitations of parishioners by priests, the preparation of children for First Communion or for serving during Mass, and that it is forbidden to bless crosses built by the faithful, and so on.

A style of subservience to the government was created in the pastoral field. The diocesan administrators began to consider worthy those priests who knew how "to live with the authorities," that is, priests who blindly obeyed government officials, regarded their priestly duties lightly, and kowtowed to the church and civil authorities.

At the present time the authorities are fighting against the Catholic Church in Lithuania by methods tried in Russia and are seeking to join them to the interests of the Soviet government. Here are the most important methods of this struggle:

Persons willing to comply with the directives of the atheistic government are appointed to high Church positions. For example, the rector of the seminary, Rev. Dr. V. Butkus, abandoning his direct duties for political-propagandistic purposes, frequently travels to communist-organized conferences of peace supporters.

The administrator of the Vilnius Archdiocese Msgr. Č. Krivaitis, while travelling in the United States, did not speak

the truth about the present condition of the Church in Lithuania, that is, he carried out the directives of the Council for
Religious Affairs.

Priests are appointed to the parishes in such a manner that
the needs of the faithful would be served as poorly as possible.
For example, in the large Alytus parish, in the Diocese of Vilkaviškis, after the death of the pastor the bishop was unable to
find a candidate acceptable to the government. Finally, the
very sickly Rev. Kavoliūnas was appointed pastor.

Through the Representative of the Council for Religious
Affairs, the State Security Committee directs the appointments
of priests to the parishes.

— — —

The Holy See and the world are being misinformed about
the true condition of the Church in Lithuania, even by figures
high in the hierarchy of the Church in Lithuania, who are
thus even more compromised in the eyes of the priests and the
faithful. This has happened with Msgr. Č. Krivaitis, Msgr.
Barauskas, and others.

The Holy See can be misinformed even by the circulars
of the bishops. In 1973 Bishop J. Labukas issued a circular
that young and devoted priests will be appointed to large
parishes and the old priests to the small. In Lithuania everyone knows that bishops cannot independently appoint priests.
Immediately after the issuing of the circular, the young
and devoted pastor of Garliava Father P. Dumbliauskas, because of demands of the government, was appointed to the
small parish of Šunskiai, and in his place an old priest not
known for his pastoral work was appointed.

— — —

For propaganda purposes certain priests are allowed to
travel abroad. Even in this, the Holy Year, the excursion of
priests to Rome was organized not by the leaders of the Church,
but by the Council for Religious Affairs, which, aided by officials of the State Security, selected the candidates and, with
the invitations, ordered them to fill out the necessary forms.
This was clearly shown by the Representative of the Council
for Religious Affairs K. Tumėnas. When the pastor of Kreke-
nava Msgr. Dulksnys asserted that he did not want to travel

to Rome, K. Tumėnas told the Bishop of Panevėžys R. Krikščiūnas that "If he does not go, he will be relieved of his
duties as pastor."

Every time the clergy travel to Rome from Lithuania,
they receive very detailed instructions from the government
and on their return give a report in writing. The late Canon
J. Stankevičius vividly attested to this in his diary, "The Crossroads of My Life": "We traveled to the Vatican. The principal directive was this: the whole matter here must be accomplished in such a way that it would benefit the Soviet
Union and harm the Catholic Church... Every time, in a direct or indirect manner, we had to prove how we had aided
the Soviet Union and harmed the Catholic Church... The true
benefit to the Soviet Union was seen and appraised by the
degree to which we had hurt the Catholic Church."[3]

The priests of this year's excursion assert that they did
not have to give an accounting to the government, but some
of them tried to convince Lithuanians living abroad that the
Chronicle does not present the whole truth, that even morally
correct priests are harmed because of its publication, and so on.

The Soviet government, in an attempt to demonstrate to
the world its "freedom of the press," published for the Catholics *The Resolutions of the Second Vatican Council, The Ritual,
The New Testament,* and *The Book of Psalms;* a large part of
these books were sent abroad for propaganda purposes. Even catechisms are not published for Catholics; for printing them and
prayer books by private means, the faithful are imprisoned, e.g.,
Povilas Petronis, Jonas Stašaitis, and others.

Church heads are forced to speak out against priests and
laymen who actively fight for Church matters. In 1972, on demand of the government, the administrators of the Lithuanian dioceses issued a circular condemning the memorandum of the 17,000 Catholics, which revealed to the world
the truth about the actual condition of the Catholic Church
in Lithuania and its organizers.

---

3. Canon J. Stankevičius (1903-1974) served as administrator of the
Archdiocese of Kaunas and Dioceses of Kaišiadorys and Vilkaviškis
in the period 1947-1965. His diary, consisting of 196 typrewritten pages,
is mentioned also in **Vyskupas Mečislovas Reinys, op. cit.,** p. 205. So
far, the diary is not available in the West.

Because of the persecution of the faith, part of the pastoral work is done under catacomb conditions, and the Soviet government, not being able to control it, rightfully fears it. The more the activities of the official Church are restricted, the more will the secret pastoral work be intensified. Government-inspired priests try to portray the underground pastoral work as harmful and destroying the unity of the Church and normal Church-state relations. In truth, if the Catholic Church in Lithuania would not adapt to catacomb conditions now, it would face the fate of the Orthodox Church in Russia—it is almost smothered.

The Soviet government is concerned that the Holy See approve the tactics of the priests most subservient to the government. The priests of Lithuania are convinced that only a misinformed Holy See could appoint as monsignors almost all of those subservient to the government—Rev. P. Bakšys, Canon Barauskas, Canon Č. Krivaitis, and others. By this action the priests dedicated and wholeheartedly devoted to the Church were psychologically disarmed.

The press, radio, television, and especially the brochures prepared for distribution abroad, e.g., J. Rimaitis' *Religion in Lithuania,* discuss at great length the freedom of conscience in Lithuania, respect for the rights of the faithful, and so on, but today, only collective farmers and workers can quietly exercise their religious rights. Professionals are often warned by their supervisors in private conversations that they must not go to church, for otherwise they will have problems at work; this forces them to hide their convictions and fulfill their religious duties in secret.

The foreigners who come to Lithuania do not see police officers standing at the church doors and interfering since this would hurt Soviet propaganda. On Sundays and especially on holy days thousands of official and unofficial agents, masquerading as faithful, observe the praying people, listen to the sermons, observe the processions. Afterwards the Party and State Security give the leaders of institutions directives on which workers still need "education."

— — —

Destroying the Church from the inside, the Soviet government does not refrain from the most inhuman methods of warfare. Priests are slandered, accused of crimes that never occurred. Professionals, especially teachers, who openly practice their faith, are dismissed from their jobs, e.g., the teachers O. Brilienė, A. Kezytė, and others. Believing middle-school students are forced to enroll in the atheistic Pioneer and Komsomol organizations, to speak against the faith, and so on.

The seminary is so restricted that every year ten parishes in Lithuania are left without priests, since about 20 priests die in a year, but the authorities allow only 10 to 12 youths to enter the seminary. They keep healthy and talented students from entering the seminary, and the most suitable priests from being professors and leaders at the seminary. The living conditions of the seminarians appall everyone—they are even forced to pray in a cellar chapel where there is a lack of air, though it would be easy if the government permitted it for them to use the chapel of the cathedral. The harsh living conditions ruin the health of many seminarians.

In the near future the fate of Belorussia and the Ukraine awaits us. In the Ukraine, the 5 million Eastern Rite Catholics do not have a single legitimate church, not a single legitimate bishop or priest. In Belorussia, a small handful of invalid and old priests are left. Tens of thousands of German, Polish, and other nationality Catholics in Karaganda and other places in the Soviet Union do not have the right to build even temporary houses of worship.

The tourists who visited Rome assert that the officials of the Holy See advise us not to enter into conflicts with the Soviet government. We do not know if indeed this is the opinion of the Holy See, but adhering to such a principle we would have to abandon essential pastoral work, e.g., teaching catechism to children, and would be in constant conflict with our consciences if we remained "servants of the cult." This is what the Soviet government is striving for.

— — —

We are sincerely convinced that our living conditions are difficult to comprehend for people in the Western world. Only by living in our land for a long time, especially being in the interrogation rooms and prisons, can one discover the whole deceit of the atheistic government.

We believe that the Holy See, through its diplomatic activities, sincerely wants to help the persecuted Church, but because of the lack of specific information, they in some cases assist the atheists. Therefore, we dare to warn: Do not believe the promises of the Soviet government since they will not be kept. Do not believe those who officially come from the Soviet Union—they are all more or less required to complete the assignments of the Party and the State Security.

We pray to God that our enemies will not break into the leadership of the Church and accomplish its ruin from within. We do not want to believe that the atheists have grounds for rejoicing that they have loyal persons in the leadership of the Church.

The current persecution of the Church is protected by a veil of lies and deceit, and that is why they especially brutally crush those who try to part this curtain of lies, bringing to public view the persecution of the believers. Petras Plumpa, Virgilijus Jaugelis, Juozas Gražys, Nijolė Sadūnaitė, and others were harshly punished because of the *Chronicle* on charges of slandering the Soviet government. When, in October of this year, five Spanish terrorists were executed, a wave of protest swept the world, but when people are tortured for truth, freedom, convictions, and religious matters, the voices of protest are so weak and timid. This is precisely what the government of the Soviet Union is trying to achieve—to smother the Catholics of Lithuania in the quiet of the night. Those who want to help us today and all those in the Soviet Union who love truth and freedom should raise in public the facts of the persecution by all available means and tear down the veil of lies that forcibly enshrouds the truth.

We, the publishers of the *Chronicle* ask you, Your Eminence—in the name of many priests, faithful, and sufferers for the faith—to convey to the Church, the world, and people of good will our cry for help. Especially, do not let those be forgotten who, following the example of P. Plumpa, B. Jaugelis, P. Petronis, J. Gražys, N. Sadūnaitė and others, chose the way of the cross in the solitary dungeons of Gulag Archipelago for the laws of God, the Church, and the future of their countrymen.

The publishers of the *Chronicle of the Catholic Church in Lithuania*

67. A STATEMENT BY BISHOP JULIJONAS STEPONAVIČIUS

To: The Chairman of the Lithuanian SSR Council of Ministers, J. Maniušis.

Copies to the Bishops of Lithuania: J. Labukas in Kaunas, J. Pletkus in Telšiai, L. Povilonis in Kaunas, R. Krikščiūnas in Panevėžys, V. Sladkevičius in Nemunėlio Radviliškis, Canon J. Andrikonis in Vieviai, and the Curia of the Vilnius Archdiocese.

From: Bishop Julijonas Steponavičius, residing in Žagarė, in the raion of Joniškis.

A STATEMENT

This is already the fifteenth year since I have been dismissed from my direct duties and forced to settle in the place assigned by the administrative authorities, in the town of Žagarė in the raion of Joniškis. When I was removed from my post, I was not accused of anything. I still do· not know why, for what action, and for how long I shall be exiled from my diocese. It is true that the Representative for Religious Cults at the time, J. Rugienis, told me that I was being removed by the decision of the Lithuanian SSR Council of Ministers. But my request to become acquainted with this decision, to receive a copy of it or even merely to be allowed to read it, was denied by the Representative. Wishing to remove me as quickly as possible, he employed force, using the assistance of the administrative agents, who forced me to leave Vilnius and the borders of the Vilnius diocese. That is why it is still not clear to me whether the dismissal from my duties was carried out by a decision of the Lithuanian Council of Ministers or by the will of the Representative for Religious Cults.

While serving in my post, I conscientiously tried to fulfill the duties of a bishop-pastor, caring for the spiritual welfare of the priests and faithful. I do not feel that I had violated any Soviet laws. I have not done or spoken any evil anywhere or at any time against the Soviet Union and the Soviet system.

At the suggestion of the Soviet authorities I have traveled to Hungary and after returning from there made an announcement over the radio. Having received an invitation, I participated in the Peace Conference. I tried to calm down the priests and faithful when government officials annoyed them by their administrative interference in Church life. I had to defend my juridical rights when the Representative for Religious Cults tried to narrow them by administrative interference. Here are examples of administrative interference:

1. When, in January 1958, I began to fulfill my duties as the Apostolic Administrator of the Vilnius Archdiocese with the rights of a resident bishop, the Representative for Religious Cults declared that I should announce to the priests that they may neither teach children in preparation for their First Confession and Holy Communion nor examine them as a group, but can only examine them individually. After I explained that on a visit to Moscow Bishop K. Paltarokas discussed and came to an agreement with the Council of Religious Cults that priests may prepare children for their First Confession and Holy Communion in small groups and, after his return home, announced this agreement in a newsletter, the Representative called this agreement a fantasy of Bishop K. Paltarokas. After I declared that I cannot announce a regulation forbidding the priests to prepare children for First Confession and Holy Communion and allowing them to examine the children only individually, since the regulation is contrary to my conscience as a bishop, the Canons of Church Law, and the decisions of the Archdiocesan Synod, the Representative told me that priests as well as the bishop not fulfilling this regulation will encounter unpleasantries. And in fact cases were filed against priests not obeying the Representative's regulation on teaching catechism to children, and the bishop was constantly upbraided.

2. The appointment and transfer of priests belong to the administrator of the diocese. The Representative for Religious Cults issues to priests assigned to another parish a servant-of-the-cult registration form, which is necessary for a priest to register in his new place of work. Utilizing the right of granting the registration form, the Representative began to interfere in the appointment of priests. The appointment of every priest must be approved by the Representative. Moreover, the Representative began to repress certain priests by taking away their registration forms and demanding that the administrator

of the diocese appoint another priest to the position of the repressed, and leave the repressed priest without a parish without priestly duties. Most often priests were repressed for having engaged in purely church work, e.g., for holding retreats for priests and faithful. I defended the injured priests. I did not agree to release them without priestly duties, I transferred them to another parish, and would not appoint another priest to their positions until the Representative issued a registration form to the repressed priest appointed to another parish. Defending the abused priests, I had to hear frequent threats from the Representative that the diocese might be left without a bishop.

It seems that I was correct in defending repressed priests since today the agency of the Representative does not take away priests' registration and does not demand that the diocesan administrators leave these priests without priestly duties.

3. According to the Canons of Church Law and the decrees of the Holy See, the true masters of the theological seminary are the ordinaries of the dioceses. Hence the ordinaries of the dioceses of Lithuania have the right to freely appoint the leadership and teachers of the Interdiocesan Theological Seminary in Kaunas and accept and expel students. Meanwhile, without any legal basis, the Representative has taken over these rights. The final selection of candidates to the priesthood is made not by the church authorities, but by the Representative and other officials who examine the suitability not only of youths wishing to enter the seminary but also of those studying in the seminary, and weed them out at their own discretion.

In 1958 the Interdiocesan Theological Seminary in Kaunas endured one of these very painful "weedings out" when, in accordance with the command of the Representative, the rector was dismissed, certain teachers were relieved of their duties, and many students were expelled, among them the cleric of the Vilnius Archiodiocese, Vytautas Merkys. The Representative accused him of being anti-Soviet. Rev. Vyt. Merkys, expelled from the Seminary, entered the Academy of Agriculture, where he was an exemplary student; later he achieved fame as a diligent and conscientious worker and for several years already has been fulfilling priestly duties in the city of Chmelnick in the Ukraine as an exemplary priest and good, loyal Soviet citizen. When I attempted to defend Rev. Vyt. Merkys while he was being mistreated, the Representative attacked me, saying that I was defending an anti-Soviet cleric and threatened to exile me.

4. The areas of purely religious, spiritual life were not forgotten. In 1960 the Representative for Religious Cults told me that it is forbidden for children to participate in religious services—for boys to serve during Mass, for girls to participate in processions; to make retreats for the believers; to invite, without the approval of the authorities, priests to assist during parish feasts; for priests to visit their parishioners, to make collections at Christmas time; for priests in larger groups to hold group retreats. The Representative demanded that I announce all these prohibitions to the priests in writing and remind them that those not complying with these restrictions will be punished. He, however, acquainted me with these prohibitions only verbally.

After listening to these illegal and inconsistent demands, I declared that I cannot announce them to the priests since as a bishop of the Catholic Church:

a. I am required to raise the religious and spiritual life of the believers and priests and not hinder and destroy it. The Canons of Church Law and the regulations of the Archdiocesan Synod demand that priests attend retreats and hold them for the faithful.

b. I must urge all my parishioners, regardless of age, to participate in religious services and ardently use the methods of redemption—prayer and the sacraments.

c. I do not know of any Soviet law forbidding children to go to church and participate in liturgical services. If state laws do not forbid children to receive the sacraments of Baptism, Penance, Holy Eucharist, and Confirmation, then on what basis is it demanded that they be forbidden to participate in liturgical services which are less significant than the reception of the sacraments?

Finally, the USSR Constitution as well as the commitments signed by the Soviet authorities recognize the freedom of conscience and of participation in religious cults to all citizens, regardless of age.

After refusing to carry out these demands, I was soon dismissed.

The facts presented in this declaration show that excuses were constantly sought to dismiss me. In refusing to carry out the various illegal demands of the Representative for Religious Cults and in defending my own rights as well as those of my parishioners, I was often threatened with dismissal from my duties. I was called stubborn, impossible to talk to, and disloyal by the Representative. But can the defense of the rights of the faithful, priests, and myself be considered a crime and disloyalty to the Soviet system?

In answer to my last statement, written in 1972 to the Chairman of the Council of Ministers of the USSR, the Representative for Religious Cults, J. Rugienis, who was assigned the task of replying, said that as of now I may not fulfill my direct duties. It is interesting to see how long the "as of now" will last. For according to the 28th Article of the Lithuanian SSR Penal Code, exile is assigned from one to five years. But now I have been living my fifteenth year in exile, and that is not because of any crime I have committed, but because of the mistakes and arbitrary wishes of the Representative for Religious Cults and certain security organs.

I ask the Chairman of the Council of Ministers to give his attention to the injustice done to me and the abnormal situation of the Vilnius Archdiocese. The capital of the Lithuanian SSR, Vilnius, does not have a Catholic bishop; the Vilnius Archdiocese has been ruled by a temporary administrator-priest for fifteen years; while the Orthodox, who are a minority confession in our republic, have a permanent bishop in Vilnius.

When the Church, celebrating the Holy Year, urges all to make peace, when the results of the discussions on Security and Cooperation in Europe grant the possibilities of achieving mutual trust and of implementing full religious freedom, it would be nice if misunderstandings would be banished and peace and trust would be established under our skies.

I trust that the case of my exile will be reviewed and I will be allowed to fulfill my duties as bishop-pastor of the Vilnius Archdiocese.

Žagarė, September 15, 1975

Bishop Julijonas Steponavičius,
Apostolic Administrator of
the Vilnius Archdiocese

68. LECTURES BY THE REPRESENTATIVE OF THE COUNCIL FOR RELIGIOUS AFFAIRS

This year, the Representative of the Council for Religious Affairs, Kazimieras Tumėnas, began to "enlighten and educate" the bishops, the administrators of dioceses and deans. In February he gave a lecture at the diocesan chancery of Telšiai; on February 18, at the chancery of the Archdiocese of Kaunas; on March 18, at the chancery of the Diocese of Kaišiadorys; and on April 17, at the chancery of Panevėžys.

In his lectures, Tumėnas attacked the *Chronicle of the Catholic Church in Lithuania*.

Tumėnas explained that relations between state and Church are improving. There are problems and difficulties, but these can be resolved.

Long experience shows that the Soviet government will maintain good relations with the Church only when the latter capitulates. At the present time, vital problems of the Church are going unresolved; e.g., the publication of catechisms, the question of the seminary, etc.; only new ways of destroying the Church are being sought.

The way Tumėnas sees it, villages are shrinking and consideration should be given to the consolidation of parishes. However, he did not say that with urban expansion, consideration should also be given to the construction of new churches; for example, in the suburbs of Vilnius, Kaunas, Klaipėda, Šiauliai, Panevėžys, Alytus, and other cities. In the development of Lazdynai in Vilnius there are 40,000 people, and there is no church.

Tumėnas admitted that at times officials act badly, tactlessly. Why, then, are they not punished? They can terrorize believers, destroy wayside crosses, establish quotas for the seminary, exile bishops, and teachers can spy on churches with impunity and dragoon children who are religious believers into godless organizations.

The Representative of the Council for Religious Affairs said that the Vatican Radio has taken a bad line. One can agree that the Vatican Radio could learn from Moscow Radio how to turn out propaganda. The broadcasts of the Vatican

Radio at the present time are a great moral support to the Catholics of Lithuania and even to non-Catholics. Thousands of people listen.

The representative for cult emphasized that a catechism would not be published. He stated that while there could be more relaxation, there would be none because then the *Chronicle* would claim, "We obtained it by our own efforts."

What is the *Chronicle* guilty of? Isn't it true that, up to the time of its birth, two bishops were exiled, the seminary saw quotas established, believers were persecuted, etc.?

The believers of Lithuania do not expect favors. They require not favors, but justice—at least the observance of Soviet law.

Tumėnas promised to grant in the near future permission to freely print 80,000 copies of a prayer book and to see about the problem of the production of religious articles.

Using the money of the faithful, the atheists are publishing books and pamphlets on a massive scale, while believers are not even allowed to reprint a catechism. It is not clear to Catholics during which five-year plan the re-opening of shops for the production and sale of religious goods will be allowed.

The representative for cult explained: "It is important that anti-Soviet elements not enter the seminary. It is too bad when young men come in with the wrong ideas. When they finish the seminary, they get involved not in the priesthood, but in the publication of the *Chronicles*. It is necessary to improve the quality of seminarians..."

The Catholics of Lithuania ask Tumėnas, the KGB, and all the others not to interfere in the affairs of the seminary because the Church needs not security personnel in cassocks, but dedicated shepherds.

On September 15, 1975, Bishop Julijonas Steponavičius wrote a petition to the Chairman of the Council of Ministers of the Lithuanian SSR, requesting to be restored to his duties as Apostolic Administrator of the Archdiocese of Vilnius.[1] On November 24, 1975, a similar petition was sent to the Chairman of the Lithuanian Council of Ministers by the priests of the Archdiocese of Vilnius.[2] Moreover, on October 4, 1975, the

1. Text of Bishop Steponavičius' statement in Doc. No. 67.

priests of the Archdiocese of Vilnius wrote an open letter to the Central Committee of the Communist Party in Lithuania concerning the falsehood of an article by instructor J. Aničas, a doctoral candidate in history, in which he tries to prove that in Lithuania there is complete freedom of conscience.[3]

These communications, submitted in writing, were answered verbally by the Representative of the Council for Religious Affairs K. Tumėnas and his associate.

The Representative summoned Bishop Steponavičius to his office in Vilnius. He gave him a vague reply, promising to confer further with Moscow. He affirmed that the answer to the question depended on negotiations between Moscow and the Vatican.

Representative of the Council for Religious Affairs Tumėnas replied to the above-mentioned petitions of the priests, but not to all the priests of the Archdiocese of Vilnius at once.

In the spring of 1976, the deans of the aforementioned archdioceses were summoned to the chancery of the Archdiocese of Vilnius. Here, Representative Tumėnas spoke mainly about the *Chronicle of the Catholic Church in Lithuania*. He threatened to uncover it and to punish its producers severely.

The Representative was angry because the *Chronicle of the Catholic Church in Lithuania* writes of such matters as the preservation of the ecology of Lithuania and about nationalism. These things concern them too.

If Bishop Steponavičius wants to return to his duties, the Representative continued, he will have to do certain things; e.g., forbid the *Chronicle,* with which the bishop himself allegedly cooperates.

Good priests are also the concern of the Representative, he said, and, therefore, if anyone has any candidates for the seminary, he should inform either the Representative or Krivaitis (the Rev. Česlovas Krivaitis, Administrator of the Archdiocese of Vilnius[4]). The two of them would have to pass on the candidates together.

---

2. Apparently a reference to a petition of priests dated September 25, 1975; text in **Chronicle**, No. 21 (January 25, 1976).

3. Text of this letter in **Chronicle**, No. 22 (April 18, 1976). J. Aničas is the principal regime historian of religion and religious institutions, propagandist of the atheist viewpoint.

4. Monsignor Krivaitis apparently enjoys the confidence of the Soviet authorities and evidently will be consulted by the regime on candidates

Moreover, Representative Tumėnas summoned the priests of the following raions:

On March 15, Šalčininkai; March 17, Švenčionys; March 24, Ignalina; March 27, the raion of Vilnius, with the exception of the city of Vilnius; April 2, Trakai; April 7, Varėna.

In some raions Representative Tumėnas spoke; in others, his associate Ruslanas. Both said clearly that the petition of the priests for the return of Bishop Steponavičius to the See of Apostolic Administrator of Vilnius would not be honored because the bishop had not mended his ways. The main indication of his recalcitrance, added the Representative, was the bishop's appeal to the civil government, which even reached abroad.

In Švenčionys Tumėnas' associate repeated several times that Bishop Steponavičius is unacceptable to the Soviet government. When the priests asked for an explanation of what the bishop was guilty of, the speaker replied, "I cannot tell you." The priests insisted. The speaker, losing his poise, blurted, "The bishop, in administering the diocese, paid attention only to Canon Law. He paid no heed at all to the laws of the state. The Soviet government cannot allow the Church to be, as it were, a state within the state."

There can be no talk of the return of Bishop Steponavičius. "We need bishops who will pay attention not only to Canon Law..." As an example of a good shepherd, he offered Bishop Romualdas Krikščiūnas.[5]

In Šalčininkai, the Representative's associate said, "It does not appear that the bishop's attitude has changed since he wrote his protest to the government in the tone of a prosecutor, blaming only the government for everything. He cannot be allowed to return to his duties because there would be much unpleasantness in the future. It will be better if in Vilnius there is no bishop at all."

---

to the seminary. The dissident priests on numerous occasions have shown distrust of the Monsignor.

5. Bishop Romualdas Krikščiūnas of the Diocese of Panevėžys, born in 1930, was consecrated in 1969. He graduated from the Kaunas seminary in 1954, was permitted to study in Rome, where he received the degree of Doctor of Church Law. He is a shepherd brought up during the Soviet period, apparently gets along with the secular authorities. For this reason, some dissident priests have expressed doubts about his loyalties.

In Trakai he affirmed that the bishop's return depended on him, the Vatican, and the government. "The bishop must be broad-minded."

In Varėna, to spite the priests, Representative Tumėnas said, "If you want the bishop to return, go to the pope. We don't appoint bishops; the pope does."

At Ignalina the Representative said: "We have invited you here to reply to your two petitions. In one of them you request the return of Bishop Steponavičius to Vilnius."

"Regarding Steponavičius, he has either not established contact with the Soviet government, or he has not fulfilled certain requirements of the law... Apparently he felt that he had to have a serious disagreement with the government of the republic, and not just with Rugienis, as you wrote in your petition." The Representative alleged that Steponavičius wrote the government a letter "that wound up where it should and where it should not."

"It was explained to him that at the present time it is impossible for him to return to Vilnius. I have met with him, and I think that we will meet again several times. I have been working at this position since just recently; we will see how he behaves. I want to see, and he should see—his future depends on him. If he is seriously considering returning, he must change his attitude."

"Your communication regarding the Aničas articles constitutes an attack on laws now in effect and on the state... Aničas wrote his articles as a private individual—a correspondent of the Academy of Science, and not as an official."

(Now he is director of a section of the Central Committee of the Communist Party of Lithuania, his articles would thus assume a different value.)

"Hence you should send your response to his article directly to him. There are some doubtful statements in his articles. I would differ with him on some of his writings."

A voice was heard from the audience: "If he wrote articles in the newspapers and spoke on television, let him now publicly retract. Even though we are 'private individuals' no one lets us write columns in the newspapers or speak on television..."

Representative: "... In our country it is forbidden to establish any kind of schools, organize illegal groups, clubs—even church-affiliated. Citizens can study religion privately. The children may be taught at home by parents, older brothers and sisters, or others..."

Voice from the audience: "How can parents or anyone else teach children religion if we are not allowed to print any religious publications, even the catechism?"

The Representative returned to the question of Bishop Steponavičius: "It is more difficult now for Bishop Steponavičius to return to Vilnius to work. About the question of his serving as bishop elsewhere, we will see. The question is not unresolvable."

Voice from the audience: "And why can't Bishop Steponavičius do his work? For what offenses has he been punished by banishment from Vilnius?"

The Representative: "He has not been punished, but merely relieved of his duties."

(Laughter in the audience): "Is removal from duties then not a punishment? Perhaps it's a reward."

The Representative: "The government decided that it would not allow Steponavičius to work in Vilnius because he has been disloyal to the Soviet government."

Voices from the audience: "Specifically, what has he been guilty of?"

The Representative: "I do not know. The Representative at that time was Rugienis.[6] Ask him. He will explain. He will explain." (He repeated that in anger.)

The Representative responded to the last part of the open letter of the priests from the Archdiocese of Vilnius, in which they ask the government to abrogate all laws and regulations against freedom of conscience:

"I must say that among us there is not a single regulation contrary to freedom of conscience. There is none. Religious freedom is something else entirely. The Constitution guarantees freedom of conscience and other freedoms named in the Constitution. As for religious freedom—there is no such thing

---

6. Justas Rugienis, born in 1909, is one of the old Lithuanian revolutionaries, member of the Communist Party since 1930. Due to his revolutionary activity, he completed his higher education (a law degree) only in 1955. He served as the overseer of religious institutions from 1957 to 1973, when he was replaced by a younger, better-educated, and more diplomatic man—Kazimieras Tumėnas.

among us. Religious activity assumes a state character and is regulated by state laws."

"If it seems to you that somewhere there is in reality denial of the freedom of conscience, you have the right to ascertain this and to report it to us. I do not know of any local government regulations that deny freedom of conscience—I have never heard of any. Even the raion government cannot promulgate such regulations."

Voice from the audience: "In my parish we had the following incident: One man, a believer, comes to church on Sundays, and since he knows how to play the organ, he plays for us during services. For this the supervisor told him in no uncertain terms: 'Choose between the Church and your job with us. If you want to play in church, you cannot work here.'"

The Representative: "That is not right. In such a case, let me know. I will intervene."

Voice from the audience: "It happens that something allowed by the government in one raion is considered a criminal offense in another, and we ourselves do not know how to act if there is no official direction from above."

The Representative: "Read the *Government News*. There you will find in the near future the laws for religious associations.[7] In putting them together, the documents of the Russian Soviet Federated Socialist Republic were used as a guideline, with modifications to suit the needs of our country... As for the traditional Christmas visitation of parishioners, it is forbidden. Nor does that ruling contradict the principle of freedom of conscience. Basically, such visitations were tied in with collecting dues, and every kind of dues collection is forbidden."

Voice from the audience: "And what if the home visitation is done without any collection of dues? What if we merely visit parishioners to become acquainted with them? Even the *raion* tax department demands that we tell them how many believers we serve. How can we tell the number in the parish if we are forbidden to visit them?"

----

7. A decree of the Presidium of the Supreme Soviet of the Lithuanian SSR of July 28, 1976, No. IX-748, "Status of Religious Societies," has been supplied by the Lithuanian Public Group to Promote the Implementation of the Helsinki Agreements. A copy of the text has been filed with the Commission on Security and Cooperation in Europe, Washington, D.C. The decree is essentially a copy of the RSFSR law.

The Representative: "Visiting the families of believers is not forbidden. You can visit them not necessarily in winter, around Christmas. You can visit them in the summer or in the fall. That is not forbidden."

Voice from the audience: "Believers out in the country are more apt to be free from work during the winter."

The Representative: "No escort is allowed. Besides, some people may not want the priest to visit them."

Voice from the audience: "But what if the faithful themselves invite the priest—even in writing? For example, in the village òf Didžiasalis in the parish of Ceikiniai."

The Representative: "If you begin to go from house to house, you will be in violation of the rules... The public blessing of homes with all the trimmings is forbidden. Blessing from within—nothing special—you will be doing nothing very wrong... You are allowed to bless a new home."

Voice from the audience: "You accuse Bishop Steponavičius of last year giving the *Chronicle of the Catholic Church in Lithuania* a copy of his petition to the Soviet government. But this has not been proved. What is the evidence that he did it himself?"

The Representative: "I do not know. Perhaps you were the one?"

Father Garuckas: "Or perhaps it was you. If we do not know for sure, then we have no right to accuse anyone. Someone else could have given the information to the *Chronicle* —it was no secret."

The Representative, after a few moments, reacted with annoyance.

Father Valiukonis: "What can be done so that any young man really wishing to do so might be able freely to enroll in the seminary?"

The Representative: "If we decide that any candidate upon completion of his seminary course is going to engage in anti-Soviet activity, we will not allow such a person to enter the seminary."

Voice from the audience: "All the current candidates are products of Soviet schools—some of them even of institutions of higher learning. Many have worked in various Soviet agencies or industries. They have performed well and have been awarded medals. How can you decide that they are going to engage in anti-Soviet activity? For example, the teacher Antanas Klikūnas of Telšiai was not accepted."

The Representative: "... If you have candidates for the seminary, let me and Krivaitis know. We will be able to help them. By the way, it seems (he added with a little sarcasm) that you lack candidates from Lithuania. As far as I know, you have a Ukrainian studying..."

Voice from the audience: "You know that Krivaitis is of no use to us."

The Representative: "Well, it seems to me that up to now no one has complained about Krivaitis."

Father Valiukonis: "What about the number of seminarians? Is it still going to be limited by the government?"

The Representative: "That question is being decided by the Ordinaries."

Fr. Valiukonis: "I wonder, if we asked the Ordinaries, whether they would concur with your statement..."

The Representative: "You can ask them."

Voice from the audience: "It would be very good if the Representative would put in writing everything that he is saying today. It would then be clearer to us all."

The Representative: "The very reason that we have invited you all to one place is so that no written report would be necessary."

69. A LETTER TO THE VATICAN

To the Beloved Shepherds of the Roman Catholic Church and Friends of Lithuania

His Eminence Cardinal Antonio Samore

His Eminence Cardinal Josef Slipij

Our nation on its way to Golgotha—in the Gulag Archipelago, Siberia, and in exile in the Western world—has met many remarkable personages. Some of them have extended a hand of physical and moral assistance, while others by their personal example and heroic suffering strengthened our nation's resolve to struggle for God and for the most elementary human rights. To those noble spirits we are grateful, and we pray the Most High to grant them every kind of blessing.

Among those good friends of ours are you, honorable shepherds. Today, as we continue our life-and-death struggle for victory, oppressed as we are with difficulties, we wish to open our hearts to you. We trust you will hear and understand us.

To our misfortune, all who travel from here to Rome and back undergo briefings in Moscow and are required to render a written account of themselves. Objective information, therefore, is possible only from the deep underground. Even this reaches the West belatedly through the *Chronicle of the Catholic Church* or through individual tourists.

The atheists, supported by government propaganda and by the State Security Committee, are disseminating the idea worldwide that in Lithuania there is no religious discrimination, and that the Soviet Union does not even know the meaning of the term "political prisoner." To this propaganda machine are bound even certain clergy.

Last year the Soviet Union sent to the USA a delegation of clergy of various religions, among them the administrator

No. 69. **Chronicle**, No. 23 (June 13, 1976). Cardinal Samore, an influential official in the Vatican, served in the Vatican legation in Lithuania in the prewar years and is considered an ardent friend of Lithuania. Cardinal Slipij, leader of the Ukrainian Catholics, served many years in Soviet prisons. He was in the same prison cell with the Lithuanian priest Račiūnas (see note below). This letter of the editors of the **Chronicle** is an obvious effort to short-circuit an accommodation with the Soviet regime which might be unacceptable to the dissidents.

of the Archdiocese of Vilnius, Monsignor Česlovas Krivaitis.[1] The delegation failed in its purpose, because the Ukrainians and the Lithuanians demonstrated and showed the world the truth concerning the disguised persecution of the Church in Ukraine and Lithuania. However, the atheists attained this much: they compromised in the eyes of the faithful a high-ranking clergyman.

The Catholic public thought that on this matter Bishop Juozas Labukas, Chairman of the Lithuanian College of Bishops, would have something authoritative to say, and that he would force the compromised clergyman to resign his post.

However, on his return Monsignor Krivaitis was met in Vilnius by Bishop Romualdas Krikščiūnas, pastors from Vilnius, and the Representative of the Council for Religious Affairs, K. Tumėnas. During the festive dinner at his suburban villa, Monsignor Krivaitis told Tumėnas, "Minister you gave me a very difficult assignment."

"But you carried it out honorably," the Representative for the cult encouraged the Monsignor.

With the failure of one trick, the atheists seized upon another. Via Vatican Radio we learned that from August 1 to 8 the 41st International Eucharistic Congress would be taking place. Immediately the rumor spread that a delegation from Lithuania would be bound for the USA, headed by several bishops. Now we know approximately the make-up of this delegation: Bishop Liudas Povilonis, Bishop Romualdas Krikščiūnas, Bishop Vincentas Sladkevičius, Canon Juozas Meidus, the Rev. Dr. Viktoras Butkus, Canon Čėsna, the Rev. Pranas Račiūnas MIC, the Rev. Jonas Juodelis, and the Rev. Vytautas Sidaras.[2]

---

1. Msgr. Krivaitis visited the United States in February of 1975 with a "Delegation of Representatives of Christian Churches in the USSR" as a guest of the National Council of Churches.

2. The Lithuanian delegation to the Eucharistic Congress in Philadelphia arrived on July 28, 1976, consisting of nine clergy. Included in the delegation were Bishop Liudvikas Povilonis, Bishop Romualdas Krikščiūnas, the Rector of the Interdiocesan Seminary in Kaunas Rev. Viktoras Butkus, and a number of pastors and diocesan administrators. Bishop Sladkevičius refused to go, but two pastors, Rev. Pranas Račiūnas and Rev. Jonas Juodelis, who had spent time in Soviet prisons, did participate.

After Easter Bishop Labukas visited the exiled Bishop Sladkevičius and indicated that the Representative of the Council for Religious Affairs K. Tumėnas had assigned him the task of organizing the delegation. It must be recalled that the same Tumėnas had organized the delegation to Rome for the Holy Year.

One other circumstance must be noted. During the fifteen years of Bishop Sladkevičius' exile, Bishop Labukas had not visited the exiled bishop; and now, at the order of Tumėnas, he did not let eighty years of heavy burdens nor poor eyesight deter him.

The Catholic public has begun to be restless not only regarding the delegation being organized by atheists, but especially concerning the honored exile, Bishop Sladkevičius. It is thought that the plan is to compromise the former long-term prisoners Rev. Pranas Račiūnas and Rev. Jonas Juodelis in the eyes of believing political prisoners. Undoubtedly, this delegation, by its passive attendance, is supposed to demonstrate to the West the freedom of religion in the Soviet Union and in Lithuania.

Bishop Sladkevičius rejected this offer and staunchly refused to go to America. He demanded that reparation first be made—that after fifteen years in exile he be allowed to assume the See of Kaišiadorys. At the present time Bishop Sladkevičius lives under inhuman circumstances, discriminated against by both spiritual and civil authorities. The diocesan chancery of Panevėžys urged by the government, at the death of pastor of N. Radviliškis, Bronius Šukys, forced Bishop Sladkevičius to assume the duties of pastor in a small village parish, and to be overwhelmed by the routine of small repairs.

At the end of April Bishop Labukas invited Bishop Sladkevičius to come to the Kaunas chancery. Bishop Sladkevičius went to see Bishop Labukas and once more stated that under the circumstances he would not be able to travel to the USA. Then Bishop Labukas said that in that case Bishop Sladkevičius could remain in exile for life, adding, "I told them that the 'Red Guards' would attack you." (Very often officials, diocesan staff, and some seminary professors call the most zealous priests by this Chinese name. This title was given to zealous priests by officials of the State Security Committee).

The attempt was made to pressure Bishop Sladkevičius into joining the delegation being organized by Tumėnas for several reasons. First of all, they wanted to compromise an honorable bishop in the eyes of the faithful. The atheists do not like martyrs. They prefer deserters and compromisers. Bishop Sladkevičius himself thought that he might not be allowed to return, and that he would be then placed permanently in a different exile.

At the beginning of this year (1975) the Representative of the Council for Religious Affairs K. Tumėnas gave lectures in all diocesan chanceries throughout Lithuania regarding the economic condition of the country and Church affairs.[3] The conclusions arrived at by Tumėnas went something like this:

The deans must see that the priests keep quiet, that they do not write protests. In that case might it be possible to come to an agreement with the Vatican regarding the appointment of new bishops. He promised he would allow the publishing of a limited number of prayer books. He staunchly refused to allow the publication of catechisms. Hence, the attitude of the civil authorities towards the Church has not changed.

Not long ago, Cardinal Alfred Bengsch visited Lithuania.[4] It is rumored that Bishop Labukas has been invited for a return visit to Berlin.[5] On that journey he will be accompanied by the Rev. Dr. Butkus, who has the complete confidence of the civil authorities. Priests and faithful believe that through Bishop Labukas, the Soviet government will offer the Apostolic See a compromise: to allow Bishop Sladkevičius to return to the diocesan See of Kaišiadorys, while the See of the Archdiocese of Vilnius would go to the Rev. Dr. Butkus. Bishop Steponavičius would remain in exile for good. If this plan goes through, it would be the most painful tragedy of our religious life.

The rector of the seminary, the Rev. Dr. Viktoras Butkus, is an active participant in the communist movement of peace supporters. He travels abroad freely, spending at least a third of the academic hear not in the seminary, whose spirtitual life and morale are unenviable, causing concern among all. Because of the limits imposed by the government, there is no

3 See Doc. No. 68.

4. See Doc. No. 66.

5. There are indications that Bishop Labukas, the Chairman of the College of Bishops of Lithuania, made a return visit to Cardinal Bengsch in Berlin sometime in August or September of 1976. No details of this visit are available.

quantity; and because of the negligence of the seminary administration, there is no quality. The rector of the seminary leaves much to be desired in his personal life. Several years ago, Rev. Sigitas Tamkevičius wrote to Bishop Labukas calling attention to certain facts in the rector's personal life. Nevertheless, there is a rule among us, that he who is protected by the civil government goes unscathed by the Code of Canon Law.

If Rev. Butkus were to become a bishop, this would be a great misfortune for the Catholic Church and a great comfort to the atheists working to wreck the Church from within.

Honorable Shepherds, faithful friends of our nation, we ask you to place this complaint of our nation at the feet of the Holy Father.

The Editors of the *Chronicle of the Catholic Church in Lithuania*

Good Shepherd Sunday, May 9, 1976.

70. "A FRESH BREEZE OR A NEW DECEIT?"

To a casual observer it might appear that fresh breezes have begun to blow in the Catholic Church of Lithuania. In January, 1977, a representative of the Council for Religious Affairs, P. Makurtsev, warned Party activists in Lithuania to treat priests more politely, and leaving for Moscow, he spoke of the easing of government policy with regard to the Church.

Before Easter the authorities of the city of Šiauliai allowed the ringing of the bells of the Church of Saints Peter and Paul, after twenty years.

At the end of January, 1977, the principal Mass on the occasion of the jubilee of the Servant of God, Bishop Jurgis Matulevičius, was celebrated by the exiled Bishop of Kaišiadorys, Vincentas Sladkevičius. A few years ago, on the occasion of the anniversary, even registered priests celebrated Mass in the sacristy at Marijampolė.

Priests in many places teach children catechism openly, with the government content to levy fines. No one speaks of trials such as those of Father Šeškevičius, Father Zdebskis, or Father Bubnis, nor does anyone believe that they could take place at this time.

What is the significance of all this?

Perhaps the Soviet government is demonstrating good will and beginning to live up to what is written in the Constitution of the USSR and in the laws ascribed to in international agrements: the Universal Declaration of Human Rights, the Helsinki Final Act and elswhere—things talked about for nineteen years, but never effected.

Perhaps it means the repeal of "untimely methods," which evoked a reaction from believers?

Perhaps it is a small victory for all those struggling for human rights in Lithuania, in the Soviet Union, and throughout the world, since the Soviet government with its ruthless administrative measures has compromised itself rather badly throughout the world and damaged the progress of its foreign policy?

Or perhaps this is a routine trick of the Soviet government

No. 70. Editorial of **Chronicle**, No. 27 (April 28, 1977).

prior to the conference of European nations at Belgrade, where it will be assessed how the Helsinki Accords are being carried out?

The near future will provide accurate answers to these questions. However, even now it is quite clear that the Soviet government is not acting in good faith. The diminution of the persecution of the Church is merely a tactical maneuver by the Communist Party. If foreign governments to whom the USSR is bound by economic ties, for instance that of Jimmy Carter in the US, fight for the implementation of human rights, if the mass media of the world publicize how in the Soviet Union international agreements regarding human rights are shattered, then this temporary maneuver of the Communist Party in easing the persecution of the faithful could last for a very long time.

The lack of good faith is demonstrated by many facts in the Soviet Union. For more than thirty years the atheist government has been persecuting priests and faithful, basing its actions on secret instructions, which it kept from public view. On July 28, 1976, the Presidium of the Supreme Soviet of the Lithuanian SSR made those instructions the law of the land, drastically curtailing the rights of believers.[1] We can take no comfort in the fact that the aforementioned decree of the Presidium of the Supreme Soviet is so far still only on paper because any day it can be implemented with all strictness.

On January 19, 1977, Deputy Chairman of the Council for Religious Affairs P. Makurtsev instructed Party activists how to improve atheistic propaganda and how to strengthen the monitoring of laws concerning religious cults.

The Soviet government occasionally allows the reprinting of prayer books which the Catholics need, knowing that if they are not allowed to be printed in the open, they will be printed underground.

Catholic have been allowed to publish one or two religious books which hardly reached the masses of the faithful, either because of limited editions, or because they were intended for

---

1. The Decree on Religious Societies of the Presidium of the Supreme Soviet of the Lithuanian SSR is essentially a copy of the decree of the Presidium of the RSFSR Supreme Soviet of June 23, 1975. English translation of the Russian decree in **Radio Liberty Research,** No. 155-76 (March 31, 1976). Text of the Lithuanian decree (in Russian) in **Arkhiv samizdata,** No. 2841.

priests; e.g., *The Ritual, The Decrees of the Second Vatican Council,* etc.[2]

The government also allowed the Catholics of Lithuania to receive the Holy Father's gift of Latin brevaries and Missals. The Soviet government knows that these books will not improve the religious knowledge of the faithful since the Latin texts make impossible the implementation of liturgical reform and also make impossible the full participation of the faithful in the Sacrifice of the Mass. This car-load of religious publications sent from the Vatican certainly served the purposes of atheistic propaganda.

The Catholics of Lithuania are not allowed to publish the kind of religious literature which would acquaint the faithful with the basic truths of their religion, e.g., for thirty years after the war the leadership of the Catholic Church in Lithuania was unable to obtain permission from the Soviet government to publish a catechism. The catechism appears exceedingly dangerous to the Soviet government because it would be read by children and young adults, who must not learn anything about their faith.

The Soviet government has increased the number of those allowed to enter the seminary, but at the same time it has stepped up efforts to cripple the seminarians spiritually. These efforts to recruit seminarians as spies and traitors show clearly enough the "good will" of the Soviet government. "Be a priest, but help the atheists to destroy the Church," they say. One has to wonder and thank Divine Providence that in spite of these massive efforts by the KGB the seminary still produces many goods priests, of whom the faithful can only be proud.[3]

Some day the priests of Lithuania will write their memoirs concerning the price they paid to resist the efforts of the KGB and not become grave-diggers of their nation and their Church.

Easing the persecution of the Church did not hurt the atheistic government much. In the first place, many priests and faithful, having experienced the heavy hand of persecution, have been disoriented in the present situation, and are not struggling to regain lost positions: to catechize children openly,

---

2. Only five or six religious books have been published since World War II. For details, see note No. 5, Doc. No. 59.

3. This is among the most frequent concerns of the dissident priests. See, for example, the alarm about alleged KGB interference in the seminary, published as an editorial in **Chronicle**, No. 26 (March 19, 1977).

to ring church bells, to make pastoral home visitations, to recruit young people for active participation in religious services, etc. To this day there are in Lithuania priests who are afraid to let boys serve Mass, or to participate in processions, e.g., at St. Anthony's Church in Kaunas, in the churches of Šiauliai, etc. To this day some priests report to the raion administration when there are to be religious festivals, or even retreats, and request permission of the administration of the raion for a few priests to come in.

Other priests fail to make use of pastoral resources which the raion administration does not even forbid. For example in Kaunas, at the Church of the Resurrection, on Sunday evenings they do not even preach, even though large numbers of the faithful come to services. There are pastors who on the occasion of a funeral will not preach themselves, nor will they allow the assistant to preach. Diocesan chanceries take little interest in such matters and fail to warn the transgressors.

Most of the faithful, especially the educated, are overcome with fear of practicing their religion openly, of rearing their children Catholic and of refusing to submit to lies or pressure.

There is no doubt that the "good will" of the Soviet government would dissipate in a moment if priests and faithful took firm steps to revitalize religious life. Those parishes, where youngsters begin actively to go to church, begin to expereince various difficulties.

In the present situation of the Catholic Church in Lithuania we urge all priests and faithful to shake off their fear and to struggle for the right to believe and to live in freedom.

We ask the governments of all nations to follow the example of US President Jimmy Carter in constantly reminding the government of the Soviet Union to respect the rights of its citizens.

We especially ask our brethren abroad and all friends of Lithuania in the free world to bring up at the Belgrade Conference and on other occasions the question of the infringement of human rights in Lithuania, making use of the material in the *Chronicle of the Catholic Church in Lithuania.*

Truth, freedom, and humanism must triumph.

The Editors of the
Chronicle of the Catholic Church in Lithuania

71. A STATEMENT OF THE LITHUANIAN HELSINKI GROUP ON RELIGIOUS CONDITIONS

To: Belgrade Commission to Monitor the Implementation of International Agreements, signed in Helsinki in 1975.

A STATEMENT

ON THE SITUATION OF THE ROMAN CATHOLIC CHURCH AND OF OTHER BELIEVERS IN LITHUANIA

In the Soviet Union the struggle against religion is a programmatic demand of the Communist Party. The "freedom of conscience" is understood here in a unique way. In his pamphlet *Tarybiniai įstatymai apie religinius kultus (Soviet Laws on Religious Cults)* (Vilnius, 1963), A. Veshchikov describes freedom of conscience as follows: "We understand freedom of conscience as the ultimate liberation of all men from religious superstition." (p. 10) The same idea is also expressed by J. Aničas and J. Rimaitis in their brochure *Tarybiniai įstatymai apie religinius kultus ir sąžinės laisvė* (Soviet Laws on Religious Cults and Freedom of Conscience) (Vilnius, 1970):

"A genuine freedom of conscience is possible only when... all available scientific, cultural and ideological means are used to help man liberate himself from the influence of anti-scientific religious world-view. As long as the believers have not shed religious superstition, freedom of conscience is impossible." (p. 54)

Such and understanding and interpretation of freedom of conscience is self-contradictory: wherever there is compulsion, strictures and struggle, there freedom cannot exist. Simultaneously, this interpretation also contradicts international obligations which have been assumed: The Universal Declaration of Human Rights, The Helsinki Final Act, The International Covenant on Economic, Social, and Cultural Rights, and The International Covenant on Civil and Political Rights.

As a member of the United Nations Organization, the Soviet Union has assumed the obligation to honor and respect human rights and fundamental freedoms, but it has not changed

---

No. 71. From **Chronicle**, No. 29 (August, 26, 1977).

its stand toward religion within its own state. Not only did the old laws remain valid, but on July 28, 1976, already after the Helsinki Accords, the Presidium of the Supreme Soviet of Lithuania confirmed the Decree on Religious Societies, 53 articles in all, a fact on which we have reported in our Document No. 2, 1976. Once more we draw attention to the fact that these regulations are based exclusively on various Soviet decrees and regulations, created prior to the Helsinki Accords and discriminating against the believers, e.g., anti-religious propaganda is allowed, but religious propaganda is outlawed, only the performance of religious cults is permitted, etc.

Article 26 of the International Covenant on Civil and Political Rights states:

"All persons are equal before the law and are entitled without any discrimination to equal protection of the law. In this respect the law shall prohibit any discrimination and guarantee to all persons equal and effective protection against discrimination on any ground such as race, color, sex, language, religion, political or other opinion, national or social origin, property, birth or other status."

The international agreements on basic human rights and freedoms state that they have the precedence over the internal laws of states. Since the Soviet Union recognizes the principle, it should amend Article 124 of the USSR Constitution and Article 96 of the Constitution of the Lithuanian SSR, which state: "The church has been separated from the state and the state from the church. The freedom of performance of religious cults and the freedom of anti-religious propaganda are granted to all citizens."

THE CHURCH IS SEPARATED FROM THE STATE

The term "separate" is not used by the state organs in a single meaning. When it is applied to the Church, it is understood in the sense that the Church has no right to intervene in the state's internal affairs—that is, the Church cannot indicate which persons should be elected to the country's Supreme Soviet or its Presidium, who should be chairmen of the raion executive committees, professors or lecturers at the universities, etc. But when the term "separate" is applied to the state, it has an entirely opposite meaning: the organs of the Soviet government decide which bishops are not allowed to perform

their duties (Bishops Steponavičius, Sladkevičius), which young
people cannot enroll in the Theological Seminary—and go on
harassing them (M. Petravičius, A. Čiūras, et. al.)—they even
instruct which priests may be invited to religious festivals, and
which one not (A. Kleina, K. Garuckas, V. Černiauskas, etc.).
The state authorities have told the Rev. Bronius Laurinavičius that "without our knowledge" a priest cannot even hammer
a nail into a church wall. The atheists themselves acknowledge
that the term "separate" is not used with a single meaning.
J. Aničas and J. Rimaitis write:

"In the literature that discusses the question of the separation of church and state, the two are sometimes presented as
parties of equal significance. e.g., 'The state organs do not interfere in the activity of the church; church in its turn does
not mingle in the affairs of the state.' This interpretation is
doubtlessly incorrect. The sovereignty of the Soviet state gives
it the right to regulate various areas of social life. The church,
in spite of its specific character, cannot be an exception."

If one thinks logically, the separation of the Church from
the state should mean that it is entirely free, independent
from the state, and runs its own affairs. But, according to the
customary situation and according to various laws and regulations issued by the civilian administration, it would appear that
the Church has not been separated from the state but is merely
strictly controlled by the state administration. When the Soviet
press writes about the state-Church relations, it frequently asserts
that the Soviet state and its government organs do not interfere with the internal affairs of the Church, i.e., with its canonical and dogmatic activity, but actual experience shows something entirely different: the state disregards the canons of the
church law and determines what is permitted to the Church,
and what is not. This is acknowledged by the atheists themselves.
A. Veshchikov writes:

"Soviet laws forbid the centers of the clergy to issue any
regulations and rules to the faithful. *The clergy is also forbidden
to guide or even to base itself on previous religious laws*" (p. 20).

THE SCHOOL IS SEPARATED FROM THE CHURCH

Article 13 of the International Covenant on Economic,
Social and Cultural Rights states:

"The States Parties to the present Covenant undertake to have respect for the liberty of parents and, when applicable, legal guardians, to choose for their children schools other than those established by the public authorities which conform to such minimum educational standards as may be laid down or approved by the State and to ensure the religious and moral education of their children in conformity with their own convictions."

The same principle is repeated in Article 18 of the International Covenant on Civil and Political Rights and is emphasized by the Universal Declaration of Human Rights: "Parents have the right of priority in determining how their children should be educated." (Article 26)

Article 56 of the Fundamentals of People's Education in the USSR and its Union Republics admits theoretically:

"If regulations established by an international treaty or an international agreement of which the USSR is a party differ from those promulgated by the educational laws of the USSR and its Union republics, then the regulations of the international treaty or of the international agreement are applied."

But the practice is different.

In the Soviet Union, where the school has been separated from the Church, the entire educational apparatus is in the hands of the state and *there are no other schools* except those of the state. The goals and the tasks of those schools is determined by the fundamentals of the legislation on people's education of the USSR and its Union republics, which demand "secular education without religion" (Article 12), "permeation of teaching and education with the spirit of Marxist-Leninist ideas, socialist internationalism, Soviet patriotism, and communist views" (Articles 19, 31, 36, 41), and state that "Parents and persons who represent them must educate children in the spirit of high communist morality" (Article 57), "education in the family must be organically harmonized with the educational activity of schools, pre-schools, and extracurricular institutions, and social organizations." (Article 57)

The practical application of the above-mentioned articles of the fundamentals of the legislation on the people's education is described by P. Mišutis, Deputy Chairman of the Council for the Coordination of the Republic's Atheistic Propaganda, in his book *Improvement of Ideological Activity* (Vilnius, 1974):

"The Fifth Plenary Meeting of the Central Committee of the Lithuanian Communist Party (1963) has emphasized that the scientific-atheistic propaganda is a general party matter." (p. 197).

"The differentiation of atheistic activity has recently improved... Atheistic education in schools is also being identified. The main load of the formation of the materialistic worldview is transferred to the classroom process, but without relinquishing the atheistic circles and clubs whose activity in some schools even goes beyond the school limits. It is very important to improve the atheistic education of parents who are still believers, which is exactly what the collectives of many schools are trying to do."

"There are important tasks in the education of young and of the university students... The department of atheism and of history of philology, established in the Vilnius V. Kapsukas State University, is accomplishing a lot in this respect and is playing an increasing role in the coordination and organization of the scientific atheistic activity of university students in the entire republic... Therefore it is very important to improve work with them, as with the young in general. Those youths who are still religious believers must be taken away from the influence of the church." (p. 202)

Such are the goals of all the schools. Perhaps, then, the children of the believers and the religious young can be taught religion privately?

Lenin's decree of January 23, 1918, "On the Separation of the Church from the State and of the School from the Church" allows for private religious instruction (Article 9), while Article 43 of the Penal Code of the Lithuanian SSR forbids it. The violation of this (43rd) Article is described as follows:

"Organization and systematic performance of religious instruction for minors, in violation of the rules established by law. The violation of the rules established by law refers to religious instruction of minors in any form (e.g., organizing religious organizations and any kind of schools, circles, groups; holding regular meetings of children on questions of religious instruction; religious instruction performed by parents not only with their own children but also with children of other believers). The exception here is religious instruction performed by the parents themselves." (Commentary to the *LSSR Penal Code*, Vilnius, 1974, p. 226).

The same idea is expressed in Articles 17 and 18 of the Decree on Religious Societies. Thus, Lenin's decrees do not harmonize with the contemporary state laws.

THE FREEDOM OF RELIGIOUS PRACTICE

The Universal Declaration of Human Rights states in its Article 18:

"Everyone has the right to freedom of thought, conscience and religion; this right includes freedom to change his religion or belief, and freedom, either alone or in community with others and in public or private, to manifest his religion or belief in teaching, practice, worship, and observance."

The freedom to perform religious cults is assured by the USSR and LSSR constitutions, yet the believers in Lithuania do not have it. A. Veshchikov openly acknowledges that religious associations "have strictly limited functions, according to Soviet law." (p. 31) J. Aničas and J. Rimaitis repeat the same: "Religious communities are formed for the performance of cults only." (p. 38)

The term "freedom to perform religious cults" encompasses *not only the holding of religious services or the participation in them, but everything that is closely linked to the cult ritual.* To perform the cult rituals of the Catholic Church one needs priests, liturgical vessels, hymnals, sheet music, rosaries, organs, and similar things.

The Catholics of Lithuania receive as many new priests as it is allowed by the civilian administration, which determines how many will study at the Theological Seminary. The bishops and administrators of Lithuania cannot offer the Sacrament of Confirmation without the permission of the organs of the atheist government: the activity of priests is limited to the residence of the members of the parish which they service and to the church of the parish where the priest works (Article 19 of the Decree on Religious Societies); solemn processions to the cemetery on All Souls' Day—the priests are punished for that, e.g., the Revs. Alfonsas Svarinskas, Jonas Survila, and others; in many places servicing of patiens in hospitals with the Last Sacrament is being obstructed, and priests are forbidden to visit the faithful although they ask for it (the Rev. K. Garuckas and others).

After the Second Vatican Council the faithful of almost the entire world perform the cult ritual in their native language, but the Lithuanians still do it in Latin because it is impossible to print missals and other books necessary for the performance of the cult in the Lithuanian language. As for the manufacturing of religious vessels and organs, Lithuanians can only dream about it. According to the regulations governing religious communities, the parishes, existing in Lithuania, are not considered judicial entities and do not have the corresponding rights; by the same token, they cannot have their own regulations, cannot be subjects of property, law, and obligations, cannot conclude contracts, inherit in accordance with a last will and testament, and act as participating parties in courts and arbitration proceedings. Article 22 of the above-mentioned regulations states:

"The property indispensable for the performance of the cult, both that which has been transferred, according to contracts, for the use of the believers who form a religious community, and that which has been acquired or donated to them for cult purposes, belongs to the state." Even the "insurance compensation for a burnt (damaged) house of prayer is transferred to the appropriate executive committee of the Council of Working People's Deputies, which has the authority over these buildings" (Article 29).

Most Lithuanian Catholics, especially members of the intelligentsia, *cannot* participate in the cult rituals because they are dismissed from work for that, e.g., teachers, etc.

During the years of Stalin's rule, Lithuanians, deported to distant areas of Russia, used to make rosary beads from bread, stringing them on a thread, and pray. Today we see in many hands not those bread rosaries, but crude rosaries made in the underground, prayer books and hymnals copied by hand. Quite a few have gone to prison for secretly printing prayer books, e.g. P. Petronis, J. Gražys, et al. The apartments of the believers are adorned by photographed pictures of no esthetic value, or metal images of the Crucified, forged or cast secretly.

Can all that be called freedom to perform religious cult?

THE FREEDOM OF ANTI-RELIGIOUS PROPAGANDA

The freedom of anti-religious propaganda means that each Soviet citizen has the right to freely express his atheistic convictions and proclaim them orally and through the press. This right is assured by the Article 124 of the USSR Constitution and Article 96 of the Constitution of the Lithuanian SSR. The freedom of anti-religious propaganda in the Soviet Union means a struggle against religion and is like an unshakable law. It is one of the programmatic points of the Communist Party. A. Veshchikov writes:

"The materials of the XII Congress of the Communist Party of the Soviet Union provide leading instructions on how atheistic activity should be further developed. The Congress made a profound analysis of the question of the overcoming of religious survivals." (p. 29)

The Constitution *does not grant* the freedom of religious propaganda to their citizens who are religious believers, thus making them unequal vis-a-vis the atheists in the eyes of the law, and discriminating against them. As a result of this, Catholics in Soviet Lithuania *do not have* any religious newspaper or magazine, Catholic books, or even a catechism, while at the same time bookstores are inundated with atheistic books. Newspapers and magazines are brimming over with the atheistic articles, trying to "dethrone" the Catholic Church, but the Catholics cannot reply to them because they do not have their own press. Therefore, the Catholics of Lithuania cannot take advantage of those rights and freedoms that are enshrined in the international agreements and that the Soviet Union has obligated itself to honor and to put into practice.

Therefore, we are addressing ourselves to the Belgrade Conference, whose task is to monitor the observance of the main agreements on human rights and freedoms, signed in Helsinki in 1975, and are asking to help us to see that the international accords which have been assumed should not remain on paper only but would be concretely applied, and that:

1. the term "freedom of conscience" be understood and interpreted in the same manner as it is understood by the people of the entire world;

2. the people should have the right not only to anti-religious, but also to religious propaganda;

3. the (religious) believers be granted the rights of meeting, press and expression;

4. those articles of the fundamentals of legislation on education that restrict the freedom of religion and conscience be abolished;

5. all those who have contributed to the universal respect and observation of human rights and fundamental freedoms (N. Sadūnaitė, P. Plumpa, P. Petronis, S. Žukauskas, J. Gražys, and others) he released from prisons and camps.

The Lithuanian Public Group to Support the Helsinki Agreements:

Rev. Karolis Gureckas
Eitan Finkelstein
Ona Lukauskaitė-Poškienė
Viktoras Petkus
Tomas Venclova

Lithuanian SSR, Vilnius
April 10, 1977

72. THE TRIAL OF VLADAS LAPIENIS AND ONA PRANCKŪNAITĖ

(AN EXCERPT FROM THE DOCUMENTS OF THE SUPREME COURT OF THE LITHUANIAN SSR)

Chairman of the Court—S. Raziūnas, People's Assessors— V. Burokevičienė and B. Kilius, Secretary—O. Jablonskaitė, Prosecutor— J. Bakučionis.

The Accused: 1. Vladas Lapienis, son of Antanas, born on June 6, 1906, charged according to Article 68, Part 1 of the Lithuanian SSR Penal Code; 2. Ona Pranckūnaitė, daughter of Jonas, born on January 2, 1935, charged according to Article 199-1 of the Lithuanian SSR Penal Code.[1]

THE COURT HAS ESTABLISHED THAT:

In the Lithuanian SSR, during the period between 1972 and 1976, 25 issues of the *Chronicle of the Catholic Church in Lithuania* have been published illegally, these issues were reproduced and disseminated. The collected materials of the *Chronicle* have been tendentially selected and are clearly slanderous. With the aid of these material the internal policy of the USSR in respect to the Catholic Church in Lithuania is presented in a distorted manner and an effort is made to suggest an alleged suppression of the freedom of conscience and the persecution of believers and, thereby, to dispose (the people) against the Soviet government.

The collections of the *Chronicle* have been transmitted to anti-Soviet centers of bourgeois emigration abroad, which have used the slanderous materials in their disruptive activities against the USSR, reprinting them with commentaries in *Darbininkas*, *Draugas*, and other reactionary newspapers published in the USA as well as broadcasting them through the anti-Soviet programs of radio stations (Vatican and others).

No. 72. The excerpt from court documents is taken from **Chronicle**, No. 32 (March 26, 1978). The description of the trial appeared in **Chronicle**, No. 29 (August 26, 1977). This trial represents the continuation of Case 345, involving KGB campaign to silence the **Chronicle**. The campaign began on November 14, 1973, and resulted in several trials. These trials are reported here in Doc. No. 63, 65.

1. Article 68 of the Penal Code deals with "Anti-Soviet agitation and propaganda," Article 199-1 with "Deliberate dissemination of slanderous fabrications degrading the Soviet state and social order."

THE CRIMINAL ACTIVITY OF VLADAS LAPIENIS

Vladas Lapienis, during the period 1974-1976, seeking to weaken the Soviet government, spreading slanderous fabrications degrading the Soviet state and social order, wrote statements to republic and all-union state and party organs of the same content, which he disseminated and published in the illegal publication *Chronicle*. Nos. 9, 11, 15, and 23. Later this material was placed in the reactionary papers published abroad.

In the Spring of 1976 V. Lapienis supplied a typewriter for A. Ruzgienė and gave her Part I of A. Solzhenitsyn's *Gulag Archipelago* for reproduction. On this typewriter six copies were typed, of which one was given to Kiurka (the Pastor of Utena) and five to Lapienis, who disseminated them.

On October 19, 1976, Lapienis brought along to K. J. Matulionis *Chronicle* No. 24 and twelve unbound copies of it, which, in preparation for dissemination, together with K. J. Matulionis he checked and corrected the typing errors. The dissemination was not accomplished because they were detained on the spot.

For purposes of agitation and propaganda V. Lapienis kept literature of slanderous anti-Soviet content: the periodicals *Chronicle* (12 copies), *Aušra, Chronicle of Current Events* (in the Russian language); books and pamphlets published abroad: *Gulag Archipelago, Simas, Cultural Repressions in Lithuania, Problems of Lithuanian Character, Divergence and Convergence, Contemporary Social Economic Systems and Their Perspectives;*[2] also articles: "Answer to V. Trumpa," "An Open Letter to Leonid Plyushch", and also an article on one of the leaders of the CPSU (Mikhail Suslov—the Second Muravyov the Hangman", ed.).[3]

---

2. Besides Solzhenitsyn's work, only two can be definitely identified: **Simas** is a Lithuanian language account of the attempted defection of Simas Kudirka, written by the emigré writer Jurgis Gliauda and published by Viltis in Cleveland, Ohio in 1971. Kudirka's case is presented here as Doc. No. 18. **Problems of Lithuanian Character** is most likely an essay by the emigré philosopher Juozas Girnius, published in 1947.

3. "An Answer to V. Trumpa" probably refers to a response of Tomas Venclova to the suggestion of emigré historian Vincas Trumpa that Venclova should reconsider his decision to seek emigration. Text of Venclova's request for emigration in Doc. No. 29. The article on Suslov's role in Lithuania is published here as Doc. No. 15.

Lapienis did not acknowledge guilt. He explained that he did not seek to weaken the Soviet government by slanderous fabrications. In the statements he raised issues, seeking to defend the interests of the Church and the believers, but he did not place them in the *Chronicle* and does not know who transmitted the statements to the editors of this publication.

It was established that V. Lapienis collected anti-Soviet literature, prepared materials for the *Chronicle*, reproduced and disseminated it and other hostile literature. The aims of his activities are indicated also by the articles found in his possession: "Advice on how to behave under interrogation."

THE CRIMINAL ACTIVITY OF ONA PRANCKŪNAITĖ

O. Pranckūnaitė systematically reproduced literature containing evident slanderous fabrications, degrading the Soviet order.

O. Pranckūnaitė acknowledged guilt. She explained that in the Spring of 1975 she became acquainted with one man from whom she received two typewriters and for whom she reproduced the illegal publication *Chronicle*, Nos. 13, 14, 15, 17, 19, 20 (5-6 copies each) and No. 20 (about 10-12 copies). She also reproduced for this man *Problems of Lithuanian Character*.

A large supply of typing and carbon paper was found at O. Pranckūnaitė's (apartment), and in the bathroom of her apartment an assembled electrographic copying apparatus, which also indicates that she systematically reproduced illegal and anti-Soviet literature.

The following witnesses were called in the trial of V. Lapienis, O. Pranckūnaitė. and J. Matulionis: K. Sinkūnas, N. Kunaitis, J. Paškauskas, S. Peckevičius, A. Ruzgienė, E. Lapienienė, B. Aleksis, and J. Sutas.

— — —

During July 20-25, 1977, the Supreme Court of the Soviet Republic of Lithuania tried the criminal case of Vladas Lapienis, Jonas Kastytis Matulionis, and Ona Pranckūnaitė. So dilligently was the date of the trial kept secret that many of the defendants' friends did not even know about it. However, others did know about the trial, but did not dare to come to the courtroom. When security officials saw that very few spectators were present, all were allowed in. Those whose presence was less desired were prevented from entering the courtroom by trickery. E.g., Vladas Lapienis' wife was put on the list of witnesses and therefore not permitted to attend the trial. The trial took place on July 20, 22, and 25. V. Lapienis had refused the services of an attorney. Many circumstances of the trial are not known to the *Chronicle.*

Ruzgienė, Aleksis, and Lapienis' wife were summoned as witnesses. Ruzgienė admitted that V. Lapienis gave her a typewriter, which she used to type five copies of *Gulag Archipelago,* and then gave all the copies to Lapienis.

Aleksis, a former colonel in the army of independent Lithuania, talked about the *Chronicle;* he testified that on reading the first issues he had thought the *Chronicle* to be merely an unnecessary harassment of the government, but he now believes that Lapienis deserves praise if following the dictates of his conscience, he contributes to its publication.

Jonas Kastytis Matulionis, tired and worn out from extensive interrogations, said that he regrets his participation in the *Chronicle...*

Ona Pranckūnaitė spoke in a low voice and only briefly. Spectators in the courtroom could only hear her complaining about her deteriorating health.

Before V. Lapienis' closing statement the court declared a recess and permitted spectators to return to the courtroom only after V. Lapienis finished speaking. The *Chronicle* was able, however, to get the text of his closing statement.[4]

— — —

On July 25 the decision of the court was announced. The decision was read so quickly and silently that even V. Lapienis, who had been standing near by, had to declare that he did not hear and comprehend everything. People at the other end of the courtroom did not hear anything.

V. Lapienis was sentenced to three years in a strict regime camp and to two years of exile. Jonas Kastytis Matulionis—two years on probation. Ona Pranckūnaitė—two years in a regular camp. Typewriters and office supplies belonging to V. Lapienis were confiscated.

---

4. Lapienis' defense speech is omitted here. It makes the same essential points as those convicted in earlier trials of religious activists.

73. ON VATICAN'S OSTPOLITIK AND THE CATACOMB CHURCH

Seeing the wish of our fellow countrymen abroad and friends of the Catholic Church in Lithuania to help us, and knowing how the atheists of the Soviet Union are trying to mislead world public opinion, we are determined at least in brief outline to inform our fellow countrymen, the faithful of the entire world and people of good will, what are the current matters concerning Lithuania and the Catholic Church here which require speedy and forceful decisions, and what the thinking of our clergy and laity is.

Regardless of the greatest risks, we are trying to do everything to see that the Faith survives in our land.

— — — — —

The atheists of the Soviet Union are hatching fresh plans to destroy the Catholic Church in the Soviet Union. It is said that while making certain concessions to the Holy See, they want the headquarters of the Catholic Church in the Soviet Union to be established in Moscow. In charge would be a clergyman who has capitulated to the government, with the rank of Cardinal. Under his jurisdiction would be all the Catholic dioceses in the Soviet Union: those of Lithuania, the Ukraine, Belorussia, and the rest. Thus the first step toward schism would be set up. Even now some Orthodox clergy are heard to say, "Since the Catholic Church acknowledges the Patriarch of Moscow as a legitimate member of the ecclesiastical hierarchy, the time is approaching for the Catholics of the Soviet Union to renounce the Holy Father of Rome." They say that the Patriarch of Moscow would be able to lead them.

We find it difficult to understand the recent so-called *Ostpolitik*. In our opinion, it has greatly hurt the Church in Eastern Europe. We hear such arguments:

> "The Soviet Union is a powerful country, whose physical power today we cannot overcome. It is necessary to seek diplomatic avenues to dialogue with that power, with the aim of defending the faithful who are there from complete annihilation."

No. 73. From **Chronicle**, No. 28 (June 29, 1977). This is a an excerpt from a lengthy report on the situation of the Catholic faith in the entire Soviet Union.

In our opinion, it is not diplomatic efforts which keep them from atrocities, but the necessity of reckoning with the might of powerful states, world and national public opinion, and fear of a new Nuremberg trial.

Representatives of the Soviet Union eagerly seek diplomatic ties with the Apostolic See in order that, having obtained concessions from the Catholic Church, they might even more subtly persecute the Church, especially at the hands of Church leaders who have capitulated to them. Bishops accommodating themselves to the atheists often interfere by their directives, or verbally or in writing, often forbidding persecuted ministers the celebration of Holy Mass in private homes, the hearing of confessions outside one's own diocese, in private apartments, and especially the confessions of women religious.

The Catholics of Eastern Europe are impressed by a bold defense of the Faith. If the Catholics of Lithuania can be defended by non-Catholics and even persons of atheistic persuasion, like Academician Andrei Sakharov or Sergei Kovalev, at the risk of their freedom, then all the more do we expect a word of intercession from our brethren, the Catholic bishops, and faithful of other lands. Thank God, we are lately hearing their voices raised in our defense.

One gets the impression that Catholics, unwilling to spoil relations with the atheists of Moscow, have chosen the tactic of silence. One bishop of Lithuania, upon his return from Rome, asserted that the Holy Father, in an audience, advised the faithful of the Soviet Union: "Pray and wait quietly and patiently."

We are accustomed to being deceived, and we do not believe that the Holy Father would so have advised us. We have the Gospel, the decrees of the Second Vatican Council concerning the missions and the apostolate; we hear the words of our Holy Father, Pope Paul VI, over the radio, speaking of the duty to evangelize the world of today, without regard even for one's life. How can we be quiet and wait, when the atheists and other enemies of the Church are not quiet and do not wait? Can we calmly watch and wait when hundreds of thousands of youths, students, and intellectuals are longing for the Gospel, disenchanted with atheism and with the moral rot stemming from it? If we do so, we are all guilty. The Apostle Paul cried, "Woe to me, if I did not proclaim the Gospel!" An example to us in this regard could be the various sects in the Soviet Union. They are supported spiritually and materially by their brethren abroad. Among their members they have developed an apostolic spirit which fears neither suffering nor death. They are provided with the latest literature, they have created a disciplined organization with leaders at various levels: the small group, the village, city, community, region, republic, etc.

For long years the Catholic Church in the Soviet Union was, as it were, moribund, showing no signs of greater apostolic effort. Now the situation has changed significantly. We need not soporific slogans, but words of encouragement, suitable leeway for action, and the requisite authorization, without which we do not feel we have the right to send anyone forth in the name of the Church, or to urge anyone on to apostolic work demanding heroism. Our strength lies in our unity with the Holy Father, and a bold, well-organized defense of the Church.

We can rejoice that in this regard the Catholic Church has made significant progress. Thanks to those efforts, the facts regarding the persecution of the Faith in the Soviet Union have forced even the Communist Parties abroad to condemn the persecution of believers being waged by the Soviet Union.

— — —

In spite of long, determined and bitter persecution by the atheists, the Catholic Faith in Lithuania is alive. We can boast to the Holy Father that we have had very few priests among us renounce their priesthood, there is no dearth of vocations to the priesthood or religious life, Eucharistic life is flourishing, and the sacrament of penance is appreciated. You have plenty of data showing how courageously the clergy and faithful of Lithuania are defending their Faith.

In our country the soul of the apostolate is alive, thirsting to spread the Catholic Faith throughout a vast land which has been subjected to atheism. The Catholic Church is working effectively in catacomb fashion: An underground press is flourishing, catechization is going on on a broad scale, in spite of all kinds of sacrifices, and religious communities exist. There is no lack of responsible officials or even members of the Communist Party who, albeit secretly, hold the Faith. On their death-bed they ask to be buried with the Catholic liturgy. We have several bishop-martyrs: Archbishop Teofilius Matulionis, Mečislovas Reinys, Vincentas Borisevičius, and Povilas

Ramanauskas.[1] For their loyalty to the Church Bishops Juli-
jus Steponavičius and Vincentas Sladkevičius have been exiled
from their dioceses.[2] About six hundred Lithuanian priests have
been in prison without ceasing there to spread the teachings
of Christ.

However, the atheists in Lithuania do not cease by any
means disrupting the life of the Catholic Church.

1. The first means of undermining the Catholic Church
in Lithuania consist of the energetic and relentless efforts of
the atheists to introduce into the hierarchy of the Catholic
Church in Lithuania individuals who would agree to carry
out their directives: a) to spread abroad lies about so-called
freedom of religion in Lithuania—it is on this condition that
the banished bishops have been promised that they would be
allowed to return to their duties; b) to help mislead the Vatican
and to help place in episcopal sees candidates acceptable to
the atheists; c) to thwart pastoral efforts by ignoring the decrees of the Holy Father; d) to promote bad priests, assigning
them to responsible positions; and to persecute zealous priests,
assigning them to the hinterlands; e) to neglect religious education, etc.

The atheists have partly succeeded in carrying out their
plans, but not entirely. The newly appointed bishops presently
concern themselves with pastoral efforts as much as possible.
Those who on account of age are unable to function, and
to resist the demands of the atheists, would be acting honorably
if they resigned.

2. The atheists interfere with candidates wishing to enter
the seminary, they try to recruit those who enter, and they
try to see that the level of education and training in the seminary
is at a low level. The bishops are not able freely to appoint the
administration of the seminary, nor its faculty. They are powerless to remove from their positions individuals obviously unfit
for such duties. The seminarians lack theological manuals. The
seminary library is very poor and is not being replenished with

---

1. These bishops were victims of Soviet postwar repression. For details, see note No. 3, Doc. No. 49.

2. The two exiled bishops constitute the major bone of contention
between the dissidents and the Soviet regime. Their cases are presented in
Doc. Nos. 61 and 67.

books of a purely religious nature published abroad. It is no wonder that the level of education and of spiritual training at the seminary in Kaunas is quite low. Often young priests revive spiritually once they begin their priestly ministry.

3. One of the greatest means of wrecking Catholicism in Lithuania is the well-organized compulsory atheistic education of the children, without regard either to the Declaration of Human Rights, or to the Final Act of the Helsinki Conference. Even now, priests are fined for teaching children catechism. Teachers in Lithuania are pressured in various ways by the Ministry of Education to educate children in atheism. A segment of opportunistic teachers performs this task zealously. According to the statistic of the atheists in Lithuania, 70 per cent of the children entering school are religious believers; only 30 per cent finish middle school with their faith intact. Their faith is further undermined in institutions of higher learning. All university students are required to complete a course in so-called "scientific" atheism.

Since youth are forbidden to go to church, and there is a great dearth of religious literature, a great part of the young people are not so much atheists, as religious illiterates. The fruit of atheism is a moral degeneracy among the young which has caused even the atheists concern.

4. One of the things most detrimental to the Faith and morals of the Lithuanian people, and demeaning, is the mass recruitment of people by all means possible to become informers for the KGB by bribery, blackmail, the threat of being discharged from work, the most attractive promises of furthering one's career, and of going on to higher education. Those who do not agree to become informers are threatened with all sorts of punishment. Those who agree to become informers are often pardoned for criminal offenses. All are subject to recruitment, beginning with elementary school children, and ending with bishops.

It must be admitted that such pressure, extending over the years, has produced results. Hence Lithuanians today do not trust one another, fear to speak out, and are constantly afraid of being betrayed.

Especially subject to such recruitment are seminarians. Those who do not agree to become agents of the KGB are threatened that they will not be accepted for the seminary, or that they will not be ordained. Seminarians are placed under particular pressure during vacation. Sometimes they are required to agree to defect publicly from the priesthood after a few years as priests.

5. On July 28, 1976, a new law was promulgated in Lithuania, by which it is planned to restrict the work of the Church even more.[3] One section of the new law allows for priest to perform his ministrations only in the church for which he has been registered. According to that regulation, priests are forbidden from helping neighboring priests to hear confessions when the latter are overwhelmed with work during feastdays or funerals.

The same law forbids the teaching of religion. The teaching of religion is allowed only in the seminary. All who teach children prayers or catechism must now expect new persecution—now based on the law.

The same law forbids clergy from carrying out pastoral visits during the Christmas season even though Canon Law requires this. The same law directs that the question of establishing new parishes be decided not by the faithful, but by the members of the Executive Committee of the raion.

The Catholic Church in Lithuania is operating on two levels: overtly and covertly. Forced to operate entirely in catacomb fashion are all religious communities of men and women; young men secretly preparing for ordination to the priesthood, almost all students and various officials who are afraid to be seen in church or to receive the sacraments, in order not to suffer for it.

A significant number of priests operating with official approval are forced also to operate in catacomb style: preparing children for First Communion or Confirmation, visiting patients in hospitals where the priest is not admitted by the medical staff, and witnessing the marriages of officials.

The Catholic Church is operating in exclusively catacomb fashion or semi-catacom fashion in broad areas of Russia. It is able to operate because it ignores the restrictions of the atheists. Such activity is quite difficult since it is bitterly persecuted by the atheists. However, it is difficult to squelch when properly

3. Decree on Religious Societies, Russian language text in **Arkhiv samizdata**, No. 2841; English translation in **Lituanus**, Spring, 1979, pp. 61-72.

organized. The Church operating overtly can be destroyed in a moment by the atheists by closing churches and arresting bishops and priests.

However, it is very difficult to subdue the Church of the Catacombs, since they are unable to keep track of its activities. The Church operating in catacomb conditions does not interfere with the local Church operating overtly, it does not try to discipline or to split it, but tries as much as possible to complement its work. As much as possible, it upholds the authority of the ruler of the diocese, tries to win the conditions necessary for freer operation, defends the rulers of dioceses from government persecution and pressure, and blocks misleading statements emanating from them.

As for the relationship of the Church of the Catacombs with the atheistic government, the government is quite unhappy about the activity of the Church of the Catacombs because it is unable to control it. While the Church operating in the open has certain privileges, the Church of the Catacombs is persecuted. Therefore priests and religious operating clandestinely are termed agents of the Vatican or foreign spies.

Those making these accusations know themselves that it is not so. Even the Catholic Church operating in catacomb conditions is not about to plan an uprising, nor to fight the Soviet system by force. It does not forbid Catholics to serve in the Soviet army, to participate in social action, or to work in state offices or factories. Many Catholics are exemplary, trustworthy workers. Even the sisters, who have been driven underground, are appreciated as conscientious medical personnel, who conscientiously nurse Party members and security agents. The Church operating in catacomb conditions does not seek to disrupt good relations between the Apostolic See and the Soviet Union. It wants only to proclaim the doctrine of Christ to all people without hindrance.

A great pastoral error was committed when the bishops, priests, and people of Lithuania were not prepared in time juridically or pastorally for pastoral work in catacomb conditions. The more freedom of religion increases, the less will become the significance of the Church of the Catacombs. The greater the persecution, the more deeply the Church will be forced to burrow into the catacombs and the more will its significance grow.

In recent times, relations between the Apostolic See and the Soviet Union have improved. The representatives of this country regularly visit the Holy Father. Cardinals visit Moscow and Leningrad. No one denies that it is necessary to use all diplomatic channels, seeking contacts even with an atheistic government, working for world peace, justice, and racial equality. The atheists eagerly seek better relations with the Apostolic See. However, by that diplomatic activity they wish to obtain concessions by which they would be able to hurt the Church more.

As a rule, they do not honor their promises or their agreements. The pronouncements of the new bishops of Hungary or Czechoslovakia give us no joy. The atheists threaten that if their demands are not met, if the activities of zealous Catholics are not restricted, a new bloody persecution of the faithful could break out, such as took place from 1917 to 1923, and from 1930 to 1938. We do not feel threatened by bloody persecution so much as by the slow, silent strangulation throttling the Church with its own hands.

THE DEMAND FOR FREEDOM AND INDEPENDENCE

74. A PETITION OF BALTIC CITIZENS FOR RESTORATION OF INDEPENDENT STATES

To:

The Government of the U.S.S.R.
The Government of the Federal Republic of Germany
The Government of the German Democratic Republic
The Governments of all nations which have signed the Atlantic Charter

Mr. Kurt Waldheim, Scretary-General of the UN

In Soviet jurisprudence the term *National Sovereignty* refers to a nation with all its rights, with political freedom, with a real possibility to determine fully its own destiny, and primarily the potential for self-determination, including the ability to form its own independent state. National sovereignty is characterized by political, territorial, cultural, and linguistic independence—manifesting itself in a state with full sovereign rights in all social aspects, with a guarantee of their full realization.

National sovereignty cannot be bestowed nor taken away; it can only be damaged or restored.

In 1919 Lenin acknowledged the *de facto* existence of Estonia, Latvia, and Lithuania, which had recently seceded from Imperial Russia. In 1920 Soviet Russia concluded peace treaties with these nations, extending to the Baltic States *de jure* recognition as well. In the name of the Soviet government, Lenin renounced in perpetuity all sovereign rights to Estonia, Latvia, and Lithuania, but nineteen years later Stalin and Hitler infringed on the sovereignty of these nations. August 23rd of this year marked the 40th anniversary of the signing of the Molotov-Ribbentrop pact, implementation of which meant the end of Estonian, Latvian, and Lithuanian independence.

On the 23rd of August, 1939, Germany and Soviet Russia signed a non-aggression treaty, including a secret protocol on the division of Eastern Europe into so-called spheres of influence. The aim of the secret Molotov and Ribbentrop talks was to

---

No. 74. Translated from a Russian text of the petition, which reached the West in the fall of 1979. The petition was widely reported in Western press. See the August 24, 1979, dispatches from Moscow by Reuter, Agence France-Presse, UPI. Most of the signers of the petition are Lithuanians.

decide the fate of Finland, Estonia, Latvia, Lithuania, Poland, Bessarabia, and Northern Bukovina. Finland, Estonia, and Latvia were to go to the Soviet Union, and Lithuania to Germany.

On September 28, 1939, the Soviet Union and Germany signed a treaty of friendship and demarcation. The pact amended the secret protocol of August 23, so that now Lithuania as well was to go to the Soviet Union, with the exception of the left shore of the Šešupė river, which in case of necessity would be occupied by the German armies.

Between the 15th and 17th of June, 1940, on orders of the government of the U.S.S.R., the Red Army effected this case of necessity by occupying the territories of Lithuania, Latvia, and Estonia, including that part of Lithuania which was to have gone to Germany.

On January 10, 1941, the German ambassador to the Soviet Union, Dr. Von Schulenburg, on the one hand, and Chairman Molotov of the Council of People's Commissars of the U.S.S.R. on the other, signed a new secret protocol in which the object of negotiation was the aforementioned district in Lithuania. The German government renounced in favor of the Soviet Union its claims to the territory west of the Šešupė river in return for monetary compensation in the sum of 7.5 million dollars in gold or 31.5 million reichsmarks.

The Molotov-Ribbentrop pact turned out to be the conspiracy of the two greatest tyrants in history, Stalin and Hitler, against peace and humanity, which laid the basis for the Second World War. We consider the 23rd of August a day of infamy.

On August 14, 1941, President Franklin D. Roosevelt of the U.S.A. and Prime Minister Winston Churchill of Great Britain signed the so-called Atlantic Charter, consisting of six points. Point 2 proclaimed that the U.S.A. and England "desire to see no territorial changes that do not accord with the freely expressed wishes of the people concerned." Point 3 recognizes "the right of all peoples to choose the form of government under which they will live; and they wish to see sovereign rights and self-government restored to those who have been forcibly deprived of them." The Soviet Union signed this Charter on the 24th of September, 1941.

In the declaration by the U.S.S.R., it was stated that in foreign affairs"... the Soviet Union will follow the principle of national self-determination... the U.S.S.R. favors the right of each nation to national independence, territorial integrity, and the right to decide its own social system and that form of government which the people would judge to be necessary for their country's economic and cultural development."

It would be well to recall that according to international law it is impossible for a nation to practice self-determination if its land is occupied by a foreign army. This is also emphasized in Lenin's Decree on Peace, which states that if a nation "has not had the opportunity for free elections, without the presence of foreign forces or the influence of an occupying power, the joining of their territory to another country is annexation; namely, it has been taken over by force."

The results of the well-known Munich pact of September 29, 1938, were abrogated by the very fact of Germany's defeat in the war. The government of the Federal German Republic, under pressure from public opinion in Czechoslovakia, admitted the Munich pact to be invalid from the very moment of its signing.

However, the Molotov-Ribbentrop pact seems juridically to be still in effect. We consider that the silence of the world on this matter supports aggressors—past, prsent, and future.

We request:

— that the Soviet Union publish the full text of the Molotov-Ribbentrop pact, including the secret protocols. We wish to recall that Lenin's Decree on Peace declared that the Soviet government renounces secret diplomacy. We also ask for declarations that the Molotov-Ribbentrop pact was invalid from the moment of its signing:

— that the Federal Republic of Germany and the German Democratic Republic declare the Molotov-Ribbentrop pact null and void from the moment of its signing, and we ask them to assist the Soviet government to nullify the consequences of that pact: namely, to withdraw foreign troops from the Baltic States. In order to accomplish this, it would be fitting to create an appriopriate commission, to be made up of the represreprsenta-tives of the Moscow, Bonn, and East Berlin governments, to nullify the results of the Molotov-Ribbentrop pact.

We ask the governments signatories of the Atlantic Charter, on the basis of their moral responsibility, to denounce the Molotov-Ribbentrop pact and its consequences. We would like to call attention to the fact that an action is not an internal affair when it essentially endangers peace and security, trampling accepted international norms. The principle of self-determination of peoples and nations recognizes any method in the struggle against colonialism, which is an international crime. That is why it is just that people around the world support wars of liberation. Furthermore in accordance with the Declaration on Principles of International Law, every state is obliged to work for and support the realization of the principles of equality and national self-determination.

We remind the Secretary-General of the United Nations that this international organization is the successor of the League of Nations, of which Latvia, Estonia, and Lithuania were full and active members until the Molotov-Ribbentrop pact come into effect. Consequently, upon you rests the juridical responsibility for the fate of the Baltic States.

We request:

— that in the General Assembly of the UN, the consequences of the nullification of the Molotov-Ribbentrop pact be taken up. We wish to mention that the principle of self-determination is confirmed in present international law; for instance, such significant documents as the United Nations Charter (paragraphs 1, 13, 55, 76), and the Declaration on the Granting of Independence to Colonial Countries and Peoples, which was adopted in the General Assembly on December 14, 1960; the resolution of December 20, 1965, of the General Assembly, recognizing the rights of colonial areas to independence; the International Convention on the Elimination of All Forms of Racial Discrimination, passed by the 50th Session the General Assembly on December 21, 1965; the International Covenants on Human Rights, passed by the 21st Session of the General Assembly, December 16, 1966; and the Declaration of Principles of International Law, passed during the 25th Jubilee Assembly, October 24, 1970. These and other United Nations international instruments affirm the rights of peoples to equality and self-determination.

This means:

— The right of all nations to determine their own destiny; that is, under conditions of complete freedom to choose internal and external political status without external interference, and to realize, in accord with their own wishes, their political, economic, social, and cultural development;

— The right of each nation to decide on the disposition of its own resources;

— The obligation of each state to foster the principles of equality and self-determination, as presented by the United Nations Charter;

— That equality and self-determination have been proclaimed as the main principles in international law in the final documents of the Conference on European Security and Cooperation.

You know, Mr. Secretary-General, that the above-mentioned international documents, which are binding, are being transgressed by some members of the United Nations. We request that the next session of the General Assembly take up the matter of Latvia, Estonia, and Lithuania, since the peoples of these nations have been deprived of their rights, and the opportunity to determine their own destiny.

August 23, 1979.

Romas Andrijauskas, Stasė Andrijauskienė, Alfonsas Andriukaitis, Edmundas Bartuška, Vytautas Bastys, Vytautas Bogušis, (Rev.) Vladas Bobinas, Romas Vitkevičius, Jonas Volungevičius, Jonas Dambrauskas, Jonas Eišvidas, Rimas Žukauskas, Ivars Žukovskis, Alfredas Zeideks, Juris Ziemelis, Liutauras Kazakevičius, Leonas Laurinskas, Rimas Mažukna, (Rev.) Mocius, Mart Niklus, (Rev.) Napoleonas Narkūnas, Sigitas Paulavičius, Angelė Paškauskienė, Kęstutis Povilaitis, Jadvyga Petkevičienė, Jonas Petkevičius, Jonas Protusevičius, Sigitas Randis, Endel Ratas, Henrikas Sambore, Julius Sasnauskas, Leonora Sasnauskaitė, Algis Statkevičius, Kęstutis Subačius, Enn Tarto, Antanas Terleckas, Erik Udam, Ints Calitis, Petras Cidzikas, Arvydas Čekanavičius, Vladas Šakalys, Jonas Šerkšnas, Zigmas Širvinskas, Mečislovas Jurevičius, (Rev.) Virgilijus Jaugelis.

A STATEMENT OF RUSSIAN DEMOCRATS

The Baltic Republics of Lithuania, Estonia, and Latvia have been annexed into the Soviet Union in disregard of the wishes of the people of these lands, essentially as a result of the occupation of the Baltic States by the Soviet Army.

Since we support the principles of equal rights and self-determination of all nations, and respect the right of each nation to determine its own destiny, we recognize that in the present historical conditions, the question of self-determination for Lithuania, Latvia, and Estonia must be decided by referendum, and that this should be held under conditions in which the people could freely express their wishes and intentions.

We suport the Lithuanian, Estonian, and Latvian representatives' call to consider the injustices done to these nations, and their rights to determine freely their own destiny.

Malva Landa
Viktor Nekipelov
Andrei Sakharov
Tatiana Velikanova
Arina Ginzburg

APPENDICES

A NOTE ON SOURCES

Various published reference works, studies, and articles used in this study are cited in the footnotes as appropriate and together they constitute a rather extensive bibliography on Lithuanian opposition to Soviet rule. The focus here is on the original sources used in this work, which are largely unpublished or in *samizdat* form and which are in need of description and evaluation.

THE PARTISAN WAR

Original sources on the partisan movement which are available in the West are spotty and widely scattered among private papers of individuals who were involved in the resistance movement abroad. A number of partisan couriers sent to the West between 1946 and 1952 brought out some direct evidence and reports about the partisan struggle. Perhaps two or three dozen substantive reports written by resistance leaders in Lithuania and the direct personal testimony of partisan couriers are available. Copies of about a thousand pages of letters, reports, and memoranda pertaining to the partisan movement have been obtained from various private collections and constitute the principal source on the subject. Particularly valuable have been the papers of Mr. Bronys Raila, collected during his association with various resistance organizations and political leaders abroad, primarily with what eventually became the Lietuvos Rezistencinė Santarvė (Resistance Union of Lithuania). A fairly complete archive of this organization is in the possession of Mrs. Marija Žymantienė, the wife of the late Prof. Stasys Žymantas, a principal figure in the emigré efforts to maintain liaison with the partisan movement. The papers of Prof. Žymantas were only partially available to the author. In addition, a very valuable collection of materials is in the possession of Col. Antanas Šova, who headed the liaison efforts with the partisans for the Supreme Committee for Liberation of Lithuania, a coalition of political parties and resistance groups abroad. His papers are particularly valuable for the history of the last years of armed resistance and the role of the CIA and emigré political groups in the resistance movement in Lithuania. Copies of important documents were also obtained from Karolis Drunga, Algirdas Vokietaitis, and Bronius Kviklys.

Among the published materials, mention should be made of the memoirs of one of the partisan leaders, Juozas Lukša, written in the West. The story is a rather romanticized version of the partisan movement up to 1947, when Lukša arrived in the West. Nevertheless, it is useful for some of the factual data contained in it and for the light it throws on the motivations of the partisans. The book, entitled *Partizanai už Geležinės Uždangos* (Partisans Behind the Iron Curtain) (Chicago, 1950), was published under the J. Daumantas pseudonym. The second edition, entitled *Partizanai* (Chicago, 1962), contains a number of documents brought out by Lukša.

The partisans had a very prolific underground press; some newspapers were even type-set. A good sampling of partisan publications during 1946 and 1947 is available in the West. The following periodicals were utilized for this study:

Aukštaičių Kova	— No. 1(15) (April 16, 1947)
Aukuras	— No. 4 (April 18, 1947)
Kova	— March 22, 1947
Kovos Keliu	— No. 9 (July 10, 1946)
Laisvės Rytas	— No. 3 (February 14, 1947) — No. 5 (March 15, 1947)
Laisvės Varpas	— No. 3(5) (February 25, 1946) — No. 113 (March 20, 1947) — No. 122 (October 1, 1947) — No. 123 (October 15, 1947) — No. 124 (November 1, 1947) — No. 126 (November 27, 1947)
Laisvės Žvalgas	— No. 23(4) (November 20, 1946) — No. 5(50) (February 20, 1947) — No. 6(51) (March 20, 1947) — No. 7(52) (March 31, 1947)
Mylėk Tėvynę	— No. 4(9) (May 20, 1947)
Partizanas	— No. 6(20) (July 20, 1951)
Už Tėvų Žemę	— No. 17(29) (November 1, 1946) — No. 18(30) (November 20, 1946)

The archives of the KGB, of course, contain the most extensive collection of materials, though probably still far from everything. There is still a good deal of documentary evidence hidden by the partisans and some of it may still reach the West. For example, in a recent trial Balys Gajauskas was accused of photo-copying documents of the Movement of the Freedom Struggle of Lithuania, the last central organization of armed opposition (see Doc. No. 46 for details). Whatever materials are available to Soviet authorities have not been generously shared with the public. But, in an effort to discredit the partisans as "bandits", "spies" of foreign governments, and simple war criminals, the Soviet government has published a series of booklets under the general title "Faktai kaltina" (Facts Accuse), which principally contain excerpts from secret police interrogations of captured partisans and testimonies of witnesses. These "documentaries" were put together by the Editorial Board for the Publication of Archival Documents of the Institute of History, Academy of Sciences of the Lithuanian SSR. The testimonials in these booklets are extremely tendential and selective, ideologically biased, and probably tainted by the coercive interrogation methods of Stalinist police. Still, they are a valuable source for factual information about the partisan movement, its organization, and policies. The following booklets in the series "Faktai kaltina" deal particularly with the guerilla war:

Žudikai bažnyčios prieglobsty ("Faktai kaltina", 2) (Vilnius, 1963.

Archyviniai dokumentai apie nacionalistų antiliaudinę veiklą ("Faktai kaltina", 3) (Vilnius, 1961).

Hitlerininkų penktoji kolona Lietuvoje ("Faktai kaltina", 4) (Vilnius, 1961).

Archyviniai dokumentai apie nacionalistų antiliaudinę veiklą ("Faktai kaltina", 5) (Vilnius, 1962).

Buržuazinių nacionalistų gaujų siautėjimas Dzūkijoje ("Faktai kaltina", 6) (Vilnius, 1964).

Hitleriniai parašiutininkai ("Faktai kaltina", 8) (Vilnius, 1966).

Kruvinos žudikų pėdos ("Faktai kaltina", 9) (Vilnius, 1968).

Kraują sugėrė Dzūkijos smėlis, ed. by. A. Vabalas (Vilnius, 1960).

The following are secondary Soviet works on the partisan movement, which deserve attention for the wealth of factual data contained in them. The first one is a Soviet story about the two Lithuanian partisan groups parachuted into Lithuania in 1950 and 1951 by the CIA. The second work gives the Soviet version of the partisan underground and particularly emigré political groups abroad involved in the resistance movement. And the third one is a description of what the title claims as "class war" in Lithuania.

M. Chienas, K. Smigelskis, E. Uldukis, Vanagai iš anapus (Vilnius, 1960).

J. Jakaitis, Išdavystės keliu (Vilnius, 1976).

A. Rakūnas, Klasių kova Lietuvoje 1940-1951 metais (Vilnius, 1976).

INSTITUTIONAL NATIONALISM

Because institutional nationalism involves a very subtle manipulation of the established order to advance national interests, in effect a "bourgeois nationalist" deviation, the activity is not easily documentable and must be largely inferred from indirect and fragmentary evidence. What has been called the "Kremlinological" approach—the putting together of discrete pieces into a comprehensible picture—is in order here. There are three principal sources of information for such an analysis. First, a good deal of information is available in the official press. Statistics, party and ideological criticisms, purges, esoteric discussions of policy, polemics, even literary works provide some of the pieces for the puzzle. Second, the official press can be supplemented and evaluated through private interviews with Soviet officials and the intelligentsia, in Lithuania and abroad. Although this is obviously not a systematic survey research, it is nevertheless very rewarding for the information and insight that such interviews provide. Opportunities for such interviews have increased tremendously since the 1960s. Regrettably, the listing of such interviews held by the author, a normal and necessary procedure in scholarly works, is obviously inappropriate in this case. Third, the dissident intelligentsia, especially those who have managed to emigrate, have provided participant testimony on the politics and attitudes of the leading elites in the republic. The writings of such former and present dissidents of Lithuania as Tomas Venclova, Jonas Jurašas, Aušra Jurašienė, A. Štromas, Eitan Finkelstein, T. Ženklys, and others were valuable resources for this study.

OPPOSITION IN THE 1970s

The stream of underground materials reaching the West from Lithuania beginning with 1970 has steadily risen during the decade. Most of the *samizdat* output from Lithuania is deposited in *Arkhiv Samizdata*, a collection of *samizdat* materials from the Soviet Union, maintained by Radio Liberty in Munich. Copies of *samizdat* materials are shared with selected depository libraries. The archive has been issuing a multi-volume collection of its holdings under the title *Sobranie Dokumentov Samizdata*, which is available in selected depository and subsribing libraries. Volume 17 of this publication is entirely devoted to Lithuanian *samizdat*, including most of the materials appearing by the end of 1975. The reader should consult the *Register of Documents* issued by the archives for specific Lithuanian holdings.

Lithuanian *samizdat* is mainly in the form of periodical journals. Relatively few individual manuscripts of books or papers have reached the West. Of the reported issues of various journals, about 75% are available in the West. These available periodical materials alone comprise about 4,000 pages and provide the bulk of evidence for this study and anthology. The following issues of various periodicals were utilized for this study:

Alma Mater	— No. 1 (January—March, 1979)
	— No. 3 (July—September, 1979)
Aušra	— No. 1 (October, 1975) — No. 16 (May, 1979)
Aušrelė	— February 16, 1978
Dievas ir Tėvynė	— No. 1 (1976) — No. 7 (1978)
LKB Kronika	— No. 1 (March, 1972) — No. 39 (July 22, 1979)
Perspektyvos	— No. 2 (1978); No. 9 (1979)
	No. 11 (1979)
Rūpintojėlis	— No. 6 (October, 1978)
Tiesos Kelias	— No. 1 (January, 1977)
Varpas	— No. 1 (1975) — No. 4 (1976)

Among the individual *samizdat* works available in the West, the following deserve a special mention for their relevance to this study:

Papers of the National People's Front, six items.

Documents of the Catholic Committee for the Defense of the Rights of Believers, Doc. No. 1 (November 13, 1978) — Doc. No. 23 (September 23, 1979), with addenda.

Apie lietuvių padėtį Baltarusijos respublikoje (On the Situation of Lithuanians in the Belorussian Republic), a two-part report: first part covers the period up to 1972, 50 pp.; the second part is an update, 1972-1978, 46 pp.

Bažnyčia ir "LKB Kronika" (The Church and the Chronicle of the Catholic Church in Lithuania), 1977, a polemic of non-dissident priests against the Chronicle.

Arkivyskupas Mečislovas Reinys, a *samizdat* monograph on the life of the Archbishop, published in Chicago, 1977.

NAME INDEX